Buddhist Path, Buddhist Teachings

Buddhist Path, Buddhist Teachings: Studies in Memory of L.S. Cousins

edited by

Naomi Appleton and Peter Harvey

equinox

SHEFFIELD UK BRISTOL CT

Published by Equinox Publishing Ltd.

UK: Office 415, The Workstation, 15 Paternoster Row, Sheffield, S1 2BX
USA: ISD, 70 Enterprise Drive, Bristol, CT 06010

www.equinoxpub.com

Chapter 1 is an updated version of a chapter first published in Volume 32.1 of the Buddhist Studies Review.

Chapters 2-16 first published in Volume 35.1-2 of the Buddhist Studies Review.

First published in book form 2019

British Library Cataloguing-in-Publication Data

A catalogue record for this book is available from the British Library.

ISBN-13: 978 1 78179 637 5 (hardback)
ISBN-13: 978 1 78179 892 8 (paperback)
ISBN-13: 978 1 78179 638 2 (ePDF)

Library of Congress Cataloging-in-Publication Data
Names: Appleton, Naomi, 1982- editor.
Title: Buddhist path, Buddhist teachings: studies in memory of L.S. Cousins / edited by Naomi Appleton and Peter Harvey.
Description: Bristol : Equinox Publishing Ltd., 2019. | Includes bibliographical references and index.
Identifiers: LCCN 2018032327 (print) | LCCN 2018049195 (ebook) | ISBN 9781781796382 (ePDF) | ISBN 9781781796375 (hb)
Subjects: LCSH: Buddhism.
Classification: LCC BQ4034 (ebook) | LCC BQ4034 .B83 2019 (print) | DDC 294.3--dc23
LC record available at https://lccn.loc.gov/2018032327

Edited and typeset by Queenston Publishing, Hamilton, Canada

Contents

Preface 1

Naomi Appleton and Peter Harvey

1. Lance Cousins: An Obituary, Appreciation and Bibliography 3

Peter Harvey

MEDITATION AND THE BUDDHIST PATH

2. The Four *Jhānas* and their Qualities in the Pali Tradition 19

Peter Harvey

3. Paths of Monastic Practice from India to Sri Lanka: Responses to L.S. Cousins' Work on Scholars and Meditators 45

Bradley S. Clough

4. 'I'm Not Getting Anywhere with my Meditation ...': Effort, Contentment and Goal-directedness in the Process of Mind-training 63

Amaro Bhikkhu

COMPARATIVE MYSTICISM

5. John of the Cross, the Dark Night of the Soul, and the *Jhānas* and the *Arūpa* States: A Critical Comparative Study 83

Elizabeth J Harris

6. Emptiness and Unknowing: An Essay in Comparative Mysticism 99

Rupert Gethin

INTERPRETING BUDDHIST TEACHINGS

7. Ambiguity and Ambivalence in Buddhist Treatment of the Dead 117

Richard Gombrich

8. The *Alagaddūpama Sutta* as a Scriptural Source for Understanding the Distinctive Philosophical Standpoint of Early Buddhism 131

P. D. Premasiri

9. An *Ekottarika-āgama* Discourse Without Parallels: From Perception of Impermanence to the Pure Land 145

Anālayo

Abhidhamma

10. Equal-headed (*samasīsin*): An Abhidharma Innovation and Commentarial Developments 157
Tse-fu Kuan

11. Calligraphic Magic: Abhidhamma Inscriptions from Sukhodaya 183
Peter Skilling

12. The Relation of the *Saccasaṅkhepaṭīkā* Called *Sāratthasālinī* to the *Vinayavinicchayaṭīkā* Called *Vinayasāratthasandīpanī* 211
Petra Kieffer-Pülz

Schools and Scriptures

13. The Formation of Canons in the Early Indian *Nikāyas* or Schools in the Light of the New Gāndhārī Manuscript Finds 249
Mark Allon

14. Theriya Networks and the Circulation of the Pali Canon in South Asia: The Vibhajjavādins Reconsidered 269
Alexander Wynne

Literature

15. Yasodharā in *Jātakas* 287
Sarah Shaw

16. *Jātaka* Stories and *Paccekabuddhas* in Early Buddhism 305
Naomi Appleton

Index 319

Preface

Naomi Appleton and Peter Harvey

This volume presents sixteen papers in tribute to the late L. S. Cousins (1942–2015). All the authors have been influenced by Lance's teachings and publications in a variety of ways, and we share a profound sense of gratitude for the opportunities we had to converse with Lance and benefit from his wisdom and generosity.

The volume opens with a personal account of the debt that the field owes to Lance, written by Peter Harvey. The papers are then presented under six headings, each relating to a key aspect of Lance's work.

The three papers in the 'Meditation and the Buddhist Path' section (Harvey, Clough, Amaro) address a key theme of Lance's personal and academic interest, namely the practice of meditation, particularly *jhāna* meditation, and its role in paths to awakening. The two papers on 'Comparative Mysticism' (Harris, Gethin) complement these by placing Buddhist meditation in a wider, comparative context. Three papers under the heading 'Interpreting Buddhist Teachings' (Gombrich, Premasiri, Anālayo) address other key teachings in early Buddhism, reflecting some of the broader interests of Lance, in making sense of early Buddhist teachings. Papers on Abhidhamma follow (Kuan, Skilling, Kieffer-Pülz), paying tribute to Lance's important contributions in this field by offering explorations of Abhidhamma terms, inscriptions and commentarial texts. Another key area in which Lance advanced our understanding is in the development of the various early schools of Buddhism, hence the inclusion of two contributions in a section 'Schools and Scriptures' (Allon, Wynne). While Lance's work was primarily focused on meditation, history, and systematic thought, in the later years of his life he was persuaded to read *jātaka*s with Shaw and Appleton at his house, hence their closing contributions in the 'Literature' section

As well as being an appropriate tribute to a respected teacher and colleague, we hope that this volume will advance Buddhist Studies scholarship by drawing together important contributions that all speak to core questions in the field, such as the nature of the path, the role of meditation, the formation of early Buddhist schools, scriptures and teachings, and the characteristics and contributions of Pāli texts.

Naomi Appleton is Senior Lecturer in Asian Religions at the University of Edinburgh.

Peter Harvey is Emeritus Professor of Buddhist Studies at the University of Sunderland.

— 1 —

Lance Cousins: An Obituary, Appreciation and Bibliography

PETER HARVEY

Lance Cousins, a great scholar of early Buddhism, died in Oxford early on Saturday March 14, 2015, of a heart attack. He was aged 72 and is survived by his ex-wife, two children, and a brother and sister. Many in the field of Buddhist Studies and Buddhist practice are in his debt.

Lance was born on April 7, 1942 in Hitchin, Hertfordshire. After Letchworth Grammar and Hertford (now Richard Hale) Grammar schools, in 1961 he attended St John's College, Cambridge, reading History and then Oriental Studies. In the Upper Sixth Form at Hertford, he had won the Classics prize and at his request was awarded *A Buddhist Students' Manual*, edited by Christmas Humphreys. In his first term at Cambridge, he took the Higher Certificate Stage of the Dhamma Examination, run by the Young Men's Buddhist Association in Colombo; attaining first prize, he was awarded Sangharakshita's, *A Survey of Buddhism*. At Cambridge, he studied Sanskrit with Sir Harold Bailey and Middle Indian with K. R. Norman. After his MA he started a doctorate with K. R.Norman which involved work on an edition of the *Saṃyutta Nikāya ṭīkā*, which led on to his first publication 'Dhammapāla and the *ṭīkā* literature' (1972).

1970 saw both his election to the Council of the Pali Text Society (this lasting till the mid-1980s) and his appointment as Lecturer in Comparative Religion at the University of Manchester. There he taught Buddhism, Jainism, Hinduism, Pali, Sanskrit, comparative mysticism, and methodological issues in the cross-cultural study of religious experience.

In the early 1990s, by which time he was a Senior Lecturer, he took early retirement in his early 50s, prompted by disillusionment with some of the then current changes in academic life. In 2000, he moved to Oxford and became active at Oxford University until his death. He taught Pali and Middle Indian in the Faculty of Oriental Studies, and Buddhism in the Faculty of Theology. He became a member of the common room (2001–2007, 2009–2015) and supernumerary Fellow (2007–2009) of Wolfson College, and contributed widely to Buddhist and Indological Studies in Oxford, working as a Research Fellow of the Oxford Centre for Buddhist Studies.

In 1995, he guided Peter Harvey and Ian Harris in their founding of the UK Association for Buddhist Studies, and became its first President, 1996–2000. He then re-joined the Council of the Pali Text Society, and was its President 2002–2003. In 2005 he was the Bukkyo Dendo Kyokai Visiting Professor at SOAS, with his lecture series leading to a series of published articles. He was given many awards, including one from the Thai British Buddhist Trust UK for his distinguished contribution to the advancement of Buddhism in the UK, and an honorary PhD in Buddhist Studies from the Mahamakut Buddhist University, Bangkok. He was a frequent visitor to Sri Lanka and Thailand in relation to both scholarship and practice. In 2012, he led a meditation retreat in Sri Lanka, with monks and nuns in attendance, adding to the many he had led in the West.

Lance Cousins was a person of great learning, which he used both with the sharpness of discerning wisdom in challenging fixed ideas and comfortable scholarly orthodoxies, and with a compassionate generosity of spirit in helping other scholars. Naomi Appleton says of him, 'I think I learnt something from every single conversation that we had, even from casual chats over coffee'; and Geoffrey Samuel, 'He was my first real teacher in relation to Buddhist studies and much else, a generous scholar with an original and creative mind'. He was very helpful to young scholars attending the Spalding Symposia on Indian Religions, and very active in e-mail discussion lists on Buddhism, Pali and Indology. I remember an American scholar meeting him in the flesh for the first time at a 1995 conference in Hawai'i, after being impressed by his many his posts on Buddha-L list, and saying, 'ah, so you're Lance Cousins!'

He was a great help to and influence on other scholars of Buddhism, for example:

- Maurice Walshe, in his *Dīgha Nikāya* translation, *Thus Have I Heard: The Long Discourses of the Buddha* (Wisdom, 1987), thanked 'Ven. P. Vipassi and Messrs KR. Norman and L.S. Cousins, whose collective brains I have picked on knotty points'.
- He gave detailed feedback and guidance to myself for the first edition of my *An Introduction to Buddhism: Teachings, History and Practices* (Cambridge University Press, 1990), and his suggestions also led me to write several articles.
- He supervised the doctorate of Rupert Gethin, published as *The Buddhist Path to Awakening* (Brill, 1992), which Steven Collins has described as a 'magisterial study'. In the preface to this work, Gethin describes his supervisor as '*a true paṇḍita who first opened my eyes to many things*'.
- Noa Ronkin, in her *Early Buddhist Metaphysics: The Making of a Philosophical Tradition* (Routledge, 2005), says, 'I am also grateful to Lance Cousins, who elaborated the Abhidhamma intricacies, made shrewd observations and invaluable suggestions, and offered useful references'.
- Sarah Shaw, in her *Buddhist Meditation: An Anthology of Texts from the Pāli Canon* (Routledge, 2007), having thanked Richard Gombrich, goes on to say 'L.S. Cousins has taught me for even longer and I have had many conversations with him about the subject. No amount of footnotes can fully acknowledge my debt to either of them'.
- Tse-Fu Kuan, in his *Mindfulness in Early Buddhism* (Routledge, 2008), says that 'I owe a great deal to Mr L.S. Cousins, who read my [Oxford] thesis carefully, provided constructive criticism and suggestions, and generously directed me to many useful sources'.
- He is also mentioned in the acknowledgements section of such books as Richard Gombrich's *Theravāda Buddhism* (Routledge, 1988 and 2006), Damien Keown's *Buddhism: A Very Short Introduction* (Oxford, 1996), Naomi Appleton's *Jātaka Stories in Theravāda Buddhism* (Ashgate, 2010), Cathy Cantwell's, *Buddhism: The Basics* (Routledge, 2010), and Bradley Clough's, *Early Indian and Theravāda Buddhism* (Cambria, 2012).

Lance wrote as 'L.S. Cousins', the S. being for Selwyn. His book-length publications primarily revolved around work on Pali texts, translations and translators:

1974. *Buddhist Studies in Honour of I.B.Horner*, edited by L .Cousins, A. Kunst and K.R. Norman. Dordrecht: D. Reidel Publishing Co.

1979. Revised reprint with indexes, and list of some variant readings, of the *Aṭṭhasālinī* ed. E. Müller (1897). London, Pali Text Society, pp. 432–510.
1992. Special Issue in honour of K.R. Norman, *Indo-Iranian Journal*, ed. Cousins et al, 35 (2/ 3).
1995. *Mahāniddesa Part III* (index volume). Oxford: Pali Text Society.
1996. *The Dispeller of Delusion (Sammohavinodanī)*, 2 vols, trans. Bhikkhu Ñāṇamoli, extensively revised for publication, with annotations and index, by L.S. Cousins, Nyanaponika Mahāthera and C.M.M. Shaw. Oxford: Pali Text Society.
1999. *Reverse Index to the Mahāniddesa*, with Y. Ousaka and M. Yamazaki, digital edition. http://hirose.sendai-nct.ac.jp/~ousaka/EngH.html

He was also working in the early 2000s with Somadeva Vasudeva, a visiting scholar from Kyoto University, on transliterating a number of *sūtras* of a newly discovered *Dīrgha* Āgama, including a fragment on when the consumption of meat is not appropriate for a monk. At the time of his death, he was preparing for publication: i) a collection of lectures relating to meditation, to be edited by Sarah Shaw as *Buddhist Meditation: Old and New*, and ii) a translation of the *Yamaka* commentary and, with Charles Shaw, of the *Yamaka*. The first third of the latter has now been published: *The Book of Pairs and its Commentary: A translation of the Yamaka and Yamakappakaraṇaṭṭhakathā*, Vol I (2018), tr. C.M.M. Shaw and L.S. Cousins. It includes Lance's translation of the relevant portion of the ancient commentary, the *Pañcappakaraṇa-aṭṭhakathā* and is intended as the first of a planned three-volume translation of the whole *Yamaka* and its commentary.

His publications, though, were primarily in the form of incisive and original articles, the quality of which is reflected in the fact that in *Buddhism: Critical Concepts in Religious Studies*, an eight-volume collection of influential articles on Buddhism, edited by Paul Williams (New York: Routledge, 2005), eight of the 110 entries are by Lance Cousins: three more than any other author. These are: 'Pali Oral Literature', 'The Dating of the Historical Buddha: a review article' (in vol. 1); 'Buddhist *Jhāna*: Its Nature and Attainment according to the Pali sources'; 'The "Five Points" and the Origins of the Buddhist schools'; 'Person and Self' (in vol. 2); '*Sākiyabhikkhu/ Sakyabhikkhu/Śākyabhikṣu*: A Mistaken link to the Mahāyāna?' (in vol. 3); 'The *Paṭṭhāna* and the Development of the Theravādin Abhidhamma', and '*Nibbāna* and Abhidhamma' (in vol. 4).

A list of his publications, other than the above books, is given at the end of this review. Their titles give an indication of the focuses of his scholarship: Pali literature, Buddhist history, especially early Buddhist schools, Abhidhamma and meditation.

He bequeathed his extensive library to the Samatha Trust's Manchester Centre for Buddhist Meditation (https://www.samatha.org/samatha-trust-library), as a reference library for scholars. Details of its holdings are being entered an online catalogue: https://samathalibrary.libib.com/i/lance-cousins-library-reference

Lance was a self-effacing person who shunned publicity and preferred to only be photographed as a member of a group of people. His scholarly contributions and influence can be seen in the list of his publications, but he was also a great practitioner of Dhamma, though he felt that while scholarship and practice should inform each other, they should not inappropriately affect each other. In his time in Cambridge, he was active in the Cambridge University Buddhist Society (founded 1955); in Manchester, he founded and ran the University Buddhist Society, which had speakers from many traditions, and for which he taught samatha meditation. In Cambridge, he was greatly inspired by the meditation teachings of Boonman Poonyathiro, an ex-monk from Thailand who taught a systematic form of samatha meditation through mindfulness of breathing. This led to him and a few others, including Paul Dennison, founding the Samatha Trust (http://www.samatha.org) in 1973, with him as its founding Chairman. This lay organisation is now probably the second largest Theravāda Buddhist group in the UK, with the largest being the Forest Sangha, led by Western monastic pupils of the Thai teacher Achan Chah. The Samatha Trust runs many introductory classes and follow-on groups around the UK, and more recently in Ireland and the USA, a residential meditation centre in Wales (f. 1987), and a non-residential one in Chorlton, Greater Manchester (f. 1977). Much of this comes from the impetus and guidance of Lance, along with the continued visits from Boonman Poonyathiro. Its teachers come from many walks of life, and include other Buddhist scholars such as Rupert Gethin, Sarah Shaw, Valerie Roebuck and myself. Leading scholars in other fields are included, such as Grevel Lindop (poet and one time Professor of Romantic and Early Victorian Studies, University of Manchester), Jas Elsner (Humfrey Payne Senior Research Fellow in Classical Archaeology and Art, University of Oxford).

In his meditation teaching, Lance included one-to-one 'reporting' with a teacher to mindfully reflect on and explore experiences. He encouraged group work to explore aspects of Buddhism neglected in the West, such as Abhidhamma, the 'thirty-two marks of a great man', the *devas*, and the 'universal emperor' (*cakkavatti*). He also had an interest in aspects of astrology, such as birth-charts, in Jewish *kabbalah* and in unconventional mystics such as Gurdjieff and Ouspensky.

The Samatha Trust has set up a tribute page on their website: 'Lance Cousins – A True Paṇḍita': http://www.samatha.org/lance-cousins. On this, Amaro Bhikkhu says of him, 'Lance was a visionary leader and exemplary in his commitment to Dhamma practice.' Other comments include the following.

Some emphasize his qualities as a wise and compassionate guide:

> 'Lance will be known to many as a teacher of great wisdom and skill; many will also have benefited from the generous way in which he shared his deep experience and learning by way of comment and advice.'
>
> 'Over the years Lance has devoted himself, tirelessly, consistently and compassionately to helping whoever he came into contact with find and develop their path.'

'I was young and without direction. He revealed a path to me. For the first part of my journey he was my kind, wise guide. Now I am older it is still a great adventure. Thank you so much Lance.'

'I was at the Manchester Centre at a time in the 80s when Lance approached me and said "you're very unhappy aren't you?" to which I could only say "Yes". He said nothing but placed his hand on the middle of my back. Heat welled in my chest and I felt elated and uplifted somehow. I knew that it was a taste of how I could turn my life around, if I really worked at it, and my faith in the Practice grew stronger.'

Some emphasize the power of his silent presence:

'You spoke so much with silence.'

'Having met Lance at his home, I was most struck by his compassionate presence, his ability to listen and relate and his stillness. A truly great being!'

'It felt healing to be in that straight, open presence of his and also to share the joyful twinkle in his eye.'

Some speak of him as a mischievous magician:

'For me, Lance was a master magician. We had our differences, but when I see him in my mind's eye, I see those eyes that were pure starlight and a smile that was as mischievous as anything I have ever known. He was the gatekeeper and guardian of a universe beyond my imaginings. I am full of gratitude for his immense wisdom, compassion and dedication to the Path. His spirit lives on in so many of us who were touched by his brilliance.'

'At his final Abhidhamma course I was able to witness the magician in motion. Lance had the ability to make the simplest anecdotes ring profoundly true, allowing things that we knew, or maybe half-knew, to become cemented in place.'

Some speak of his knack of challenging people in a way that helped them grow:

'Lance constantly challenged us to be more aware and awake. Thank you!'

'A delightfully argumentative man who greatly enjoyed debate.'

'Lance admonished me 30 years ago. The reverberations are still with me to this day ... Like quiet thunder!'

'He wanted us to be independent, free-thinking and not lose our own birth religious identity. I am filled with gratitude and admiration that one man should be so generous with his time, wisdom, heart and humour. He boldly went where most are not willing to go, risking being controversial yet only acting from compassion. We can only try to follow his example.'

Some speak of his patient, undemanding nature:

'That knowing smile, with compassion and understanding; never reproving.

> Saying just enough to a difficult arrogant student so as not to raise his ire. That how he patiently taught me for 35 years.'
>
> 'Of the many gifts you gave me, perhaps the greatest of all was your gift of equanimity. Your teachings were opportunities to be taken, or missed, never a burden imposed. So I am grateful above all for your willingness simply to offer and let go, asking nothing back;'

Some talk of his great skill as a teacher:

> 'When Lance really got underway at a Dhamma talk or discussion there was nothing quite like it. He was unflinching in the way he acted or spoke to help people. A great man.'
>
> 'His talks in the evenings were rivetingly interesting and to the point. His ability to relate to your practice during reports was very "human", helpful and challenging. I was amazed at his ability to talk, one evening, on a subject given to him by the audience; he did it without preparation and did it without hesitation.'
>
> 'His (lunchtime) lecture on meditation was simple and to the point, and his answers to questions had insight, precision and honesty. I remember leaving with the impression that everybody including myself had left with more awareness.'

For myself, I can say that Lance was an inspiration to both my Dhamma practice and my life as an academic focusing on Buddhist studies. His way of being a scholar of Buddhism inspired me to resolve to seek to take a similar route. His firm, gentle and probing guidance helped keep my philosophical mind earthed and my heart facing in the right direction. Meeting him was typically like meeting a mirror that helped one see oneself and see what needed to be done. His penetrating gaze could see deeply while his compassion gave careful guidance. Prompts and suggestions were given briefly, to be understood as one worked with them. What a debt I owe to this amazing man.

Articles and reviews

All the following are downloadable from https://oxford.academia.edu/LS-Cousins, unless otherwise stated.

Pali literature

1972. 'Dhammapāla and the *Ṭika* Literature', *Religion*, 2, pp. 159–165: a review article (of Lily de Silva's edition of the *ṭīkā* to the *Dīgha Nikāya*), which discusses the relation of the 'Dhammapāla' author of commentaries to the 'Dhammapāla' author of sub-commentaries.

1983. 'Pali Oral Literature', in *Buddhist Studies Ancient and Modern*, ed. Philip Denwood and Alexander Piatigorsky, London, Curzon Press, and Totowa, N.J., Barnes & Noble, pp. 1–11: on the *suttas* as showing techniques of improvisation found in other oral literature.

2013. 'The Early Development of Buddhist Literature and Language in India', *Journal of the Oxford Centre for Buddhist Studies*, 5, pp. 89–135: http://jocbs.org/index.php/jocbs/article/view/57/88

1997. Detailed analytical review article on Bhikkhu Ñāṇamoli and Bhikkhu Bodhi, *The Middle Length Discourses of the Buddha: A New Translation of the Majjhima Nikāya*, reviewed in *Journal of Buddhist Ethics* 4, pp. 260–80: http://blogs.dickinson.edu/buddhistethics/files/2010/04/cous1.pdf

1996. 'The Dating of the Historical Buddha: a review article', *Journal of the Royal Asiatic Society*, 6(1), pp. 57–63: a review of a large conference on this issue.

2003. '*Sākiyabhikkhu/Sakyabhikkhu/Śākyabhikṣu*: a mistaken link to the Mahāyāna?', *Nagoya Studies in Indian Culture and Buddhism: Saṃbhāṣā*, 23, pp. 1–27: a critique of this term as signifying a Mahāyānist.

Early Buddhist schools

1991. 'The "Five Points" and the Origins of the Buddhist Schools' *The Buddhist Forum Volume II*, ed. Tadeusz Skorupski, London, School of Oriental and African Studies, pp. 27–60: on the points attributed to the Mahāsāṃghika Mahādeva, but originating as earlier Abhidhamma discussion points between the Sarvāstivādins and what were later to become the Theravādins: https://www.academia.edu/15728091/The_Buddhist_Forum_II (An earlier and unrevised version is in: *Buddhist Essays : A Miscellany: A Memorial Volume in Honour of Venerable Hammalawa Saddhatissa* ed. P. Sorata, L. Perera and K. Goonesena, London, World Buddhist Foundation, 1992, pp. 79–126.)

1994. 'Person and Self', in *Buddhism into the Year 2000: International Conference Proceedings*, (no named editor), Bangkok and Los Angeles: Dhammakaya Foundation, pp. 15–32: on the central idea of the Pudgalavādin schools.

2001. 'On the Vibhajjavādins: the Mahiṃsāsaka, Dhammaguttaka, Kassapiya and Tambapaṇṇiya branches of the ancient Theriyas', *Buddhist Studies Review*, 18(2), pp. 131–82: on early roots of what became the 'Theravāda': http://ukabs.org.uk/buddhist-studies-review-vols-1-22/

2012. 'The Teachings of the Abhayagiri School', in *How Theravāda is Theravāda? Exploring Buddhist Identities*, ed. Peter Skilling et al, Chiang Mai, Silkworm Books, pp. 67–127: on a Mahāyāna-leaning Sri Lankan fraternity.

2013. 'Tambapaṇṇiya and Tāmraśātiya', *Journal of Buddhist Studies*, 11, pp. 21–46: on the ancient Sri Lankan school. (oxford.academia.edu only has the abstract, but the article is downloadable from: http://archive.is/www.ocbs.org

2017. 'On the Earliest Buddhist Schools', in *Holy Wealth: Accounting for This World and the Next in Religious Belief and Practice: Festschrift for John R. Hinnells*, ed. by Almut Hintze and Alan Williams, 21–48. Wiesbaden: Harrassowitz. (Not at oxford.academia.edu)

Abhidhamma

For Lance Cousins, this is not a dry scholastic literature, but an exploration of subtle relationships and a great aid to practice. Richard Gombrich once described him as the leading authority in the West on *Abhidhamma.*[1]

1983–1984. '*Nibbāna* and Abhidhamma', *Buddhist Studies Review*, 1(2), pp. 95–109: an exploration of *Nibbāna* in the *Nikāyas* and then how the Abhidhamma systems shared in seeing it as an atemporal, non-spatial unconditioned reality that was neither mind, in the usual sense, nor material: http://ukabs.org.uk/buddhist-studies-review-vols-1-22/

1981. 'The Paṭṭhāna and the Development of the Theravādin Abhidhamma', *Journal of the Pali Text Society*, 9, pp. 22–46: on how the outlines of the developed Theravādin theory of the *citta-vīthi*, or the process of perception as a series of specific mind-states, lie in this canonical Abhidhamma text: http://www.palitext.com/JPTS_scans/JPTS_1981_IX.pdf

2003. 'Summary of the *Abhidhammāvatāra*', in *Encyclopedia of Indian Philosophies, Vol. IX Buddhist Philosophy from 350 to 600 A.D.*, ed. Karl Potter, Delhi, Motilal Banarsidass, pp. 217–254. (Not at oxford.academia.edu).

2011. 'Abhidhamma Studies I: Jotipāla and the *Abhidhamma Anuṭīkā*', *Thai International Journal for Buddhist Studies*, 2, pp. 1–36: on a neglected medieval *ṭīkā* text.

2013 [Buddhist era 2556]. 'Abhidhamma Studies II: Sanskrit Abhidharma Literature of the Mahāvihāravāsins', *Thai International Journal for Buddhist Studies*, 4, pp. 1–61, with a possibly amended version published in 2016 as 'Sanskrit Abhidharma Literature of the Mahāvihāravāsins' in *Text, History and Philosophy: Abhidharma across Buddhist Scholastic Traditions*, edited by Bart Dessein and Weijen Teng, 169–222. Leiden: Brill: on the influence of Sri Lankan Abhidhamma ideas in mainland India, especially through the works of Jotipāla (sixth–seventh century). (oxford.academia.edu only has the abstract.)

2015. 'Abhidhamma Studies III: Origins of the Canonical Abhidha(r)mma Literature', *Journal of the Oxford Centre for Buddhist Studies*, 8: http://jocbs.org/index.php/jocbs/article/view/108/125

2015. 'The Case of the Abhidhamma Commentary', *Journal of the International Association of Buddhist Studies*, 36-37/1-2 (2013-2014[2015]), pp.389–422: on this literature in general but particularly the *Aṭṭhasālinī*, whose sources he traces back to the late second century and earlier. (Not at oxford.academia.edu).

Forthcoming. 'The *sacca-saṅkhepa* and its commentaries': planned to be published in the *Journal of the Pali Text Society*.

1. In 'Buddhist Studies in Britain', *The State of Buddhist Studies in the World 1972–1997*, ed. Donald K. Swearer and Somparn Promta, Bangkok, Chulalongkorn University, 2000, p.182.

Buddhist meditation

1973. 'Buddhist *Jhāna:* its Nature and Attainment According to the Pali Sources', *Religion*, 3, pp. 115–31: a key early study of this meditative state central to *samatha* meditation, with which he was greatly involved. (A paper of the same title also appears in *Medagoda Sumanatissa Felicitation Volume*, ed. D. Dorakuṇḍura, C. Wikramagamage and A. Guṇasiṃha, Colombo, Medagoda SumanatissaFelicitation Committee, 1996, pp. 105–116.)

1984. '*Samatha-yāna* and *Vipassanā-yāna*' in *Buddhist Studies in Honour of Hammalava Saddhatissa*, ed. Gatare Dhammapala *et al.*, Nugegoda, Sri Lanka, University of Sri Jayewardenapura, pp. 56–68: a key discussion of the various ways in which *samatha* and *vipassanā* meditation can be combined.

1992. '*Vitakka/vitarka* and *Vicāra*: Stages of *Samādhi* in Buddhism and Yoga', *Indo-Iranian Journal*, 35(2–3), pp. 135–157: on key ingredients of the first *jhāna* and also certain stages of Patañjali's yoga.

1996. 'The Origins of Insight Meditation' in *The Buddhist Forum, Volume 4*, ed. Tadeusz Skorupski, London, School of Oriental and African Studies, pp. 35–58: on the relation of *samatha* and *vipassanā* in ancient and recent times: https://www.academia.edu/15726724/The_Buddhist_Forum_IV

1997. 'Aspects of Esoteric Southern Buddhism' in *Indian Insights: Buddhism, Brahmanism and Bhakti*, ed. Peter Connolly and Sue Hamilton, London, Luzac Oriental, pp. 185–208: an exploration of kinds of Theravāda meditation side-lined in modern times, involving visualisations and use of mantra-like verbal formulae in Pali.

2009. 'Scholar Monks and Meditator Monks Revisited', in *Destroying Māra Forever: Buddhist Ethics Essays in Honor of Damien Keown*, ed. John Powers and Charles S. Prebish, Ithaca, N.Y., Snow Lion, pp. 31–46: reflections of the relation of scholarship and meditation, two key focusses of his own life.

2015. 'The Sutta on Mindfulness with In and Out Breathing' in *Buddhist Meditative Praxis: Traditional Teachings and Modern Applications*, ed. K.L. Dhammajoti, University of Hong Kong, Centre of Buddhist Studies, pp. 1–24. This is on the sixteen stages of Ānāpāna-*sati* meditation, both in its original meaning and later interpretation. (Not at oxford.academia.edu)

Buddhist ethics

1974. 'Ethical Standards in World Religions: III. Buddhism', *The Expository Times*, 85(4), pp. 100–104: a brief but excellent overview of Buddhist ethics.

1996. 'Good or Skilful? *Kusala* in Canon and Commentary', *Journal of Buddhist Ethics*, 3, pp. 136–164: http://blogs.dickinson.edu/buddhistethics/files/2010/04/cousins12.pdf An exploration of the meanings of this term which is central to both Buddhist ethics and meditation.

Buddhism in the West

1994. 'Theravāda Buddhism in England', in *Buddhism into the Year 2000: International Conference Proceedings,* (no named editor), Bangkok and Los Angeles, Dhammakaya Foundation, pp. 141–150: an overview of a topic that he was himself much involved in.

Buddhist overall

1984. Fifty-five entries in J.R. Hinnells, *Penguin Dictionary of Religions*, Harmondsworth (not at oxford.academia.edu). On Buddhism: '*abhidhamma*', '*ālaya-vijñāna*', '*anukampā*', '*bhāvanā*', '*bodhi-pakkhiya-dhamma*', 'Buddhaghosa', 'Buddha image', 'Central Asian Buddhism', 'Dhammapāla', '*diṭṭhi*', 'emptiness', '*kamma-ṭṭhāna*', '*lokuttara*', '*nibbāna*', 'Pali', '*pāramitā*', '*samatha*', 'Sinhalese Buddhism', 'skilful means', 'South-East Asia, Buddhism in', '*Śūnyatāvāda*', '*suttanta*', 'Theravāda', 'Vaibhāṣika', '*vipassanā*', 'Western Buddhism', 'Yogācāra'. On Indian philosophy: 'Advaita Vedānta', 'Advaitin cosmology', 'Ājīvaka', '*bhakti-yoga*', '*Brahmasūtra*', '*darśana*', '*dhyāna-yoga*', 'Gosāla', '*guṇa*', '*haṭha-yoga*', '*karma-yoga*', '*jñāna-yoga*', '*līlā*', 'Lokāyata', '*māyā*', 'Mīmāṃsā', '*nāstika*', 'Nyāya', '*prakṛti*', 'Rāmānuja', 'Sāṃkhya', '*saṃsāra*', '*Śaṅkara*', 'Vaiśeṣika', 'Vaiṣṇava Vedānta', 'Vedānta', '*yoga*', 'Yoga-darśana'. (All retained in: John R. Hinnells, *A New Dictionary of Religions*, Blackwell, 1995.)

1984. 'Buddhism in *Handbook of Living Religions*, ed. J.R. Hinnells, Harmondsworth, Penguin, New York, Viking, 1984, pp. 273–343. An expanded version of this is in *A New Handbook of Living Religions,* ed. J.R. Hinnells, Oxford, Blackwell, 1997, pp. 369–444: perhaps the best concise overview of Buddhism. (Not at oxford.academia.edu).

1995. 'Introduction', in Ven. B. *Ānandamaitreya* Mahānāyakathera, *Nine Special Qualities of the Buddha & Other Essays*, London, World Buddhist Foundation, pp. i–ix. (Not at oxford.academia.edu).

1998. 'Buddha' and 'Nirvāṇa', in *Routledge Encyclopedia of Philosophy*, Chief Editor Edward Craig (Not at oxford.academia.edu, but at: https://www.rep.routledge.com/articles/biographical/buddha-6th-5th-century-bc/v-1 and https://www.rep.routledge.com/articles/thematic/nirvana/v-1/sections/origins-and-etymology-of-the-word-nirvana

2018. '*Cetiya* and *Thūpa*: the Textual Sources', chapter 2 in *Relics and Relic Worship in Early Buddhism: India, Afghanistan, Sri Lanka and Burma*, edited by Janice Stargardt and Michael Willis, 18–30. London: British Museum Publications

Mysticism

1972. 'Annotated Bibliography of Mysticism' in Community Relations Commission, *Education for a Multi-Cultural Society III*, 1972, pp. 80–83. (Not at oxford.academia.edu).

1989. 'The Stages of Christian Mysticism and Buddhist Purification: *Interior Castle* of St Theresa of Avila and the *Path of Purification* of Buddhaghosa', in *The Yogi and the Mystic: Studies in Indian and Comparative Mysticism*, ed. Karel Werner, London, Curzon, pp. 103–120: traces similarities of experience through differences of language and culture.

Book reviews

Of his 45 book reviews, those available from oxford.academia.edu are of these books (dates are of the reviews, not the books):

1974. B.C. Olschak, *Mystic Art of Ancient Tibet,* reviewed in *The Expository Times* 85, p. 286.
1976. Lynn de Silva, *The Problem of the Self in Buddhism and Christianity*, reviewed in *The Expository Times* 87, p. 92
1976. R. Puligandla, *Fundamentals of Indian Philosophy*, reviewed in *The Expository Times,* 87, p.349.
1976. Oscar Shaftel, *An Understanding of the Buddha,* reviewed in *The Journal of Asian Studies,* 36 (1), pp. 120–121.
1978. Irmgard Schloegel, *The Zen Way*, G. Parrinder, *Wisdom of the Early Buddhists,* and Ernest Wood, *Zen Dictionary*, reviewed in *The Expository Times,* 89, p. 154
2001. Carol S. Anderson, *Pain and its Ending: The Four Noble Truths in the Theravāda Buddhist Canon,* reviewed in *Journal of Buddhist Ethics,* 8, pp. 36–41: http://blogs.dickinson.edu/buddhistethics/files/2010/04/cousins0111.pdf

Other reviews of his include ones of:

1972. H. Saddhatissa, *The Buddha's Way,* reviewed in *Religion*, 2.
1974. Melford E. Spiro, *Buddhism and Society: A Great Tradition and its Burmese Vicissitudes,* reviewed in *Religion* 4.
1974. S.M. Stern and Sofie Walzer, *Three Unknown Buddhist Stories in an Arabic Version*, reviewed in *Journal of Semitic Studies* 19.
1976. Tenzin Gyatso, the XIVth Dalai Lama, *The Buddhism of Tibet and the Key to the Middle Way*, reviewed in *The Expository Times* 87.
1976. Nāgārjuna, *The Precious Garland and the Song of the Four Mindfulnesses*, reviewed in *The Expository Times* 87.
1979. The Open University, '*Man's Religious Quest: The Noble Path of Buddhism*, reviewed in *Religion* 9(1), pp. 125–127.
1979. Hee-Jin Kim, *Dōgen Kigen: Mystical Realist*, reviewed in *Religion* 9(2).
1980. Joseph Head and S. L. Cranston, *Reincarnation: The Phoenix Fire Mystery*, reviewed in *Religion* 10(2), pp. 224–225.
1980. Giuseppe Tucci, *Religions of Tibet,* translated by Geoffrey Samuel, reviewed in *The Tablet.*
1980. Amaury de Riencourt, *The Eye of Shiva*, reviewed in *The Tablet.*
1980. Confucius, *The Analects*, translated by D.C. Lau, reviewed in *The Tablet*.

1981. Fumimaro Watanabe, *Philosophy and its Development in the Nikāyas and Abhidhamma*, reviewed in *Bulletin of the School of Oriental and African Studies*, 48(1), p. 156.
1982. Winston L.King. *Theravāda Meditation: The Buddhist Transformation of Yoga*, reviewed in *Religion* 10(2), pp. 185–186.
1985. Bhikkhu Ñāṇamoli, *The Path of Discrimination*, reviewed in *Indo-Iranian Journal*, 28.
1985. C.E. Godakumbura & U Tin Lwin, *Catalogue of Cambodian & Burmese Pali manuscripts*, reviewed in *Bulletin of the School of Oriental and African Studies*, 48(3), pp. 620–21.
1985. K.R. Norman translation, with alternative translations by I.B.Horner and Walpola Rāhula, *The Group of Discourses (Sutta-nipāta) Vol.I.*, reviewed in the *Journal of the Royal Asiatic Society*, 117(2), pp. 219–220:
1987. Sangharakshita, *The Eternal Legacy*, reviewed in *Studies in Comparative Religion*, 19.
1987. Peter Masefield, *Divine Revelation in Pali Buddhism*, reviewed in *Studies in Comparative* Religion, 19.
1988. Paul J. Griffiths, *On Being Mindless: Buddhist Meditation and the Mind-body Problem*, reviewed in *Bulletin of the School of Oriental and African Studies*, 51(3), pp. 579–580.
1989. S.R. Goyal, *A History of Indian Buddhism*, reviewed in *Journal of the Royal Asiatic Society*, 121(1), pp. 168–169.
1992. David Seyfort Ruegg, *Buddha-nature, Mind and the Problem of Gradualism*, reviewed in *Bulletin of the School of Oriental and African Studies*, 55(2), pp. 347–348.
1994. John S. Strong, *The Legend and Cult of Upagupta*, reviewed in *Journal of the Royal Asiatic Society*, 4(1), pp. 114–115.
1994. K.R. Norman, *The Group of Discourses, Vol. II*, reviewed in *Journal of the Royal Asiatic Society*, 4(2), pp. 291–292.
1994. Hirakawa Akira, *A History of Indian Buddhism*, reviewed in *Religion* 24.
1994. Uma Cakravarti, *The Social Dimensions of Early Buddhism*, reviewed in *Religion* 24.
1994. Damien Keown, *The Nature of Buddhist Ethics*, reviewed in *Religious Studies*, 30(2), pp. 252–254.
1995. David Seyfort Ruegg, *Earliest Buddhism and Madhyamaka*, reviewed in *Indo-Iranian Journal*, 38.
1995. Reginald Ray, *Buddhist Saints in India*, reviewed in *Bulletin of the School of Oriental and African Studies*, 59(1), pp. 172–173.
1996. Peter Masefield, *The Udāna Commentary*, Vols 1 and 2, reviewed in *Bulletin of the School of Oriental and African Studies*, 59(1), pp. 580–581.
1997. Oskar von Hinüber, *A Handbook of Pāli Literature*, reviewed in *Bulletin of the School of Oriental and African Studies*, 61(1), pp. 155–156.
1999. Richard Gombrich, *How Buddhism Began: The Conditioned Genesis of the Early Teachings*, reviewed in *Bulletin of the School of Oriental and African Studies*, 62(2), pp. 372–373.

2001. Bart Dessein, *Saṃyuktābhidharmahṛdaya. The Heart of Scholasticism*, reviewed in *Middle Way* 76(2): pp.119–122.
2000. Steven Collins, *Nirvana and other Buddhist Felicities,* reviewed in *Buddhist Studies Review*, 17(2), pp.236–39. (Downloadable from http://ukabs.org.uk/resources/journal-archives/buddhist-studies-review-vols-1-22/)
2002. Padmanabh S. Jaini, *Collected Papers on Buddhist Studies*, reviewed in *Nagoya Studies in Indian Culture and Buddhism*, 22, pp.244–245.
2006. Anālayo, *Satipaṭṭhāna: The Direct Path to Realization,* reviewed in *Buddhist Studies Review*, 23(1), pp.130–134.
2011. Richard Saloman (with Andrew Glass), *Two Gāndhārī Manuscripts of the Songs of Lake Anavatapta (Anavatapta-gāthā),* reviewed in *Bulletin of the School of Oriental and African Studies*, 74(3), pp. 494–496.
2013 Primoz Pecenko, *Aṅguttaranikāyapurāṇaṭīkā*, reviewed in *Bulletin of the School of Oriental and African Studies*, 76(3), pp. 527–528.

Peter Harvey is Emeritus Professor of Buddhist Studies at the University of Sunderland. He co-founded, with Ian Harris, the UK Association for Buddhist Studies, has acted as its Secretary and President, and now edits its journal, *Buddhist Studies Review*. His books include *An Introduction to Buddhism: Teachings, History and Practices* (Cambridge University Press 1990 and 2013), *An Introduction to Buddhist Ethics: Foundations, Values and Issues* (Cambridge University Press 2000), and *The Selfless Mind: Personality, Consciousness and Nirvana in Early Buddhism* (Curzon, 1995), and he has published many papers on early Buddhist thought and practice and on Buddhist ethics. More recently, he edited an extensive integrated anthology of Buddhist texts, *Common Buddhist Text: Guidance and Insight from the Buddha* (2017) published for free distribution by Mahachulalongkorn-rajavidyalaya University, Thailand; in 2019, he published a booklet, *Buddhism and Monotheism* (Cambridge University Press).

Meditation and the Buddhist Path

— 2 —

The Four *Jhānas* and their Qualities in the Pali Tradition

Peter Harvey

A strong strand of the scholarship of Lance Cousins focussed on the *jhānas* and related matters, and he was also a practitioner and teacher of *samatha* meditation, which aims at the *jhānas*. In this dual tradition, this paper explores subtle questions about the nature of each *jhāna* as dealt with in the Pali *Nikāyas*, Abhidhamma and commentaries. Its aim is to help illuminate what it is like to be in any of these *jhānas*: what is going on in them, and what has been transcended? What do the similes for each *jhāna* convey about the overall situation in them? What kind` of thought and feelings are understood to occur in them? To what extent does breathing stop in deep *jhāna*? To what extent is hearing transcended in them? What happens in moving between them? How are they related to developing insight?

Introduction

Lance Cousins' writings on meditation began in 1973 with his influential 'Buddhist *Jhāna:* its Nature and Attainment According to the Pali Sources'. In this paper, I would like to further explore this topic, especially as based on the Pali *suttas*, but also on the *Abhidhamma-piṭaka* and later Pali literature and to an extent informed by my own experience.

Stilling the hindrances, and the arising of the *jhāna*-factors

Qualities particularly associated with the *jhānas* are ones which are also seen to occur, to a degree, in other skilful/wholesome states of mind. The process of moving towards the first *jhāna*, through what later came to be called 'access' (*upacāra*) concentration, is described in the *suttas* thus:

> When one sees that the five hindrances have been given up in oneself, gladness (*pāmujjaṃ*) arises, and when one is glad, joy (*pīti*) arises. When the mind is joyful, the body becomes tranquil (*pīti-manassa kāyo passambhati*), and with a tranquil body, one experiences happiness (*pasaddha-kāyo sukhaṃ vedeti*); the mind of someone who is happy becomes concentrated (*sukhino cittaṃ samādhiyati*). (DN I 73)

Here, in the *Sāmañña-phala Sutta*, this sequence of skilful qualities arises from sitting, setting up mindfulness and overcoming the five hindrances, after having previously restrained the mind from inappropriately relating to sense-objects and

Keywords: *jhāna, vitakka, vicāra, pīti, sukha, somanassa, domanassa*, breathing, hearing, masteries, insight being mindful of movements. In other places, this same sequence of states, from gladness onwards, arises from:

- non-regret (*avippaṭisāra*) from good ethical discipline and restraint (Vin V 164, AN V 1–2, Vism 12).
- faith (*saddhā*) from appropriate reflection on the *dukkha* aspect of life (SN II 30–1),
- unwavering confidence (*avecca-ppasāda*) in the Buddha, *Dhamma* and *Saṅgha* so as to gain inspiration in the goal and in the *Dhamma* (MN I 37–38, AN III 285).
- hearing *Dhamma*, teaching it, reciting it or studying it, *or* from a *samādhi-nimitta* being well held in the mind (DN III 241–242),

Lance Cousins (1973, 120) comments on the DN III 241 list: 'To these others can easily be added — worship of relics, recollecting the qualities of the Triple Gem, and in later times the cult of the image', citing Vibh-a 347–48, which talks of 'by arousing joy with the Buddha as object on seeing a shrine or Bodhi-tree ... or with the Saṅgha as object on seeing the Saṅgha ...'.

The mind free from the hindrances is said to be 'ready (*kalla-*), receptive/open (*mudu-*), uplifted/elated (*udagga-*), trustful/clear (*pasanna-*)' (MN I 380) and thus open to deep calm and insight into *Dhamma.*

First *jhāna*

The relieved gladness of being beyond — or 'secluded from' — the hindrances then gives an opportunity for moments, or longer stretches, when the first *jhāna* is entered, with the *jhāna*-factors at full strength:

> Completely secluded from sense-pleasures, secluded from unskilful states, he enters and dwells in the first *jhāna*, joy and happiness born of seclusion, accompanied by mental application and examining (*So vivicc'eva kāmehi vivicca akusala dhammehi savitakkaṃ savicāraṃ vivekajaṃ pīti-sukhaṃ paṭhama-jjhānaṃ upasampajja vihāreti*).
>
> He suffuses (*abhisandeti*), fills, soaks, and drenches this very body (*imam eva kāyaṃ*) with the joy and happiness born of seclusion, so that there is no part of his whole body that is untouched by that joy and happiness.
>
> (DN I 73, MN I 276, MN III 92, AN III 25)

It is said at MN I 294 that the first *jhāna* consists of five factors: mental application (*vitakka*), examining (*vicāra*), joy (*pīti*), happiness (*sukha*) and one-pointedness of mind (*citt'ekaggatā*), while an Abhidhamma-like passage at MN III 25 adds that also present when in first *jhāna* are: sensory contact, feeling, perception, volition, mind (*citta*), desire-to-do (*chanda*), decision (*adhimokkha*), vigour (*viriya*), mindfulness, equanimity (*upekkhā*) and attention (*manasikāra*).

Vitakka and *vicāra*

Lance Cousins helped elucidate the nature of *vitakka* and *vicā*ra in his 1992 article '*Vitakka/vitarka* and *Vicāra*'. He discusses (pp. 138–144) the *Dhammasaṅgaṇī* registers for them (Dhs 7 and 8), respectively:

1. *takka* 2. *vitakka* 3. *saṅkappa* 4. *appanā* 5. *vyappanā* 6. *cetaso abhniropanā* 7. *sammā saṅkappa* (as Dhs. 21 and 298 on *sammā saṅkappa* and at MN III 73 on noble *sammā saṅkappa*)

and

2. *cāra* 2. *vicāra* 3. *anuvicāra* 4. *upavicāra* 5. *cittassa anusandhanatā* 6. *anupekkhanatā*

After discussing all these terms in the literature of the relevant periods, he translates them (p.144) respectively as:

1. speculation 2. thought 3. thought formation 4. fixing 5. firm fixing 6. applying the mind 7. right thought formation

and

1. wandering 2. wandering about 3. repeated wandering about 4. frequenting, 5. explorativeness of mind 6. constant examination

He points out that in the early post-canonical *Peṭakopadesa* (p. 142), '*Vitakka* is defined as the first alighting (of the mind on an object), while *vicāra* is the exploration (*vicarana*) of what has been understood (by *vitakka*)' (1992, 144), and concludes (p.153):

> For the canonical *abhidhamma*, *vitakka* at its weakest results in a tendency to speculate and fix upon ideas. More strongly developed it is the ability to apply the mind to something and to fix it upon a (meditative) object. *Vicāra* at its weakest is simply the tendency of the mind to wander. More highly developed it is the ability to explore and examine an object. In one way we can say that *vitakka* is 'thinking of' something, whereas *vicāra* is 'thinking about' that same thing, but in fact the latter is probably intended to refer more to what we would now describe as the mind's associative faculty. [Note 81 adds here: It is not as such 'sustained application of mind' nor is it 'holding the mind' on an object — these are results of *vicāra*, not its nature].

As I see them, *vitakka* and *vicāra* in the first *jhāna* are a) engaging with the meditative object and b) getting to know it by carefully exploring it.

While *vitakka* and *vicāra* in grosser forms, as thinking and reflecting, are what normally precede speech (SN IV 293), in first *jhāna*, one cannot speak (SN IV 217): here they only exist in subtle forms, engaged in contacting and examining the object of meditation, such as the *nimitta* (sign/mental imprint or impression) of the breath.

Pīti and *sukha*

Vitakka and *vicāra* working in this way keeps things together, so that joy and happiness arise, like bubbles from kneaded soap powder, seeping into and flowing around one's experienced 'body':

> It is as if a skilled bath attendant or his pupil were to sprinkle bath powder into a bronze dish, and then knead it together adding the water drop by drop so that the ball of soap absorbed and soaked up the moisture until it was saturated with moisture, yet not quite dripping. (DN I 74, MN I 276, MN III 92, AN III 25)

The use of such a simile can be seen to both be to inform what a *jhāna* is like, and also, by bearing it in mind, to help a person enter it, or recognize that they are, or are not, in it.

The joy and happiness of *jhāna* is seen as of a non-sensual, spiritual (*nirāmisa*) nature (SN IV 236). In the first *jhāna* they are 'born of seclusion' from the hindrances, that is, they arise from the relief at not being burdened and hemmed in by these.

The quality 'joy', *pīti*, in *jhāna* is a feeling of satisfaction in the form of physical and mental zest and refreshing energization, felt, at first, as mild joyful tingles. Vism 143–144 says of *jhānic* joy:

> It refreshes (*pīṇāyati*), thus it is joy (*pīti*). It has the characteristic of endearing (*sampiyāyana-*). Its function is to refresh (*-pīṇana-*) body and mind; or its function is to pervade (*pharaṇa-*). It is manifested as elation (*odagya-*). But it is of five kinds as minor (*khuddikā*) joy, momentary (*khaṇikā*) joy, showering (*okkantikā*) joy, uplifting (*ubbegā*) joy, and pervading (*pharaṇā*) joy.
>
> Herein, minor joy is only able to raise the hairs on the body. Momentary joy is like flashes of lightning at different moments. Showering joy breaks over the body again and again, like waves on the sea shore. Uplifting joy can be powerful enough to levitate the body and make it spring into the air (*kāyaṃ uddhaggaṃ katvā ākāse langhāpanappamāṇappattā*). ... When pervading joy arises, the whole body is completely pervaded, like a filled bladder, like a rock cavern pervaded by a huge inundation.

While the *Visuddhimagga* goes on to give examples of 'uplifting' joy involving people moving some distance through the air between different locations, in contemporary experience it involves such things as bodily shaking, jerking, arm movements, and sudden leg movement that may propel the body upwards. Its particular effects vary considerably between individuals. Pervading joy is less intensely focussed at particular points in the body but more tranquilly pervades it all — as with water that fills all the crevices of a cave system. The *Vimuttimagga* (Ehara *et al.* 1977, 89) compares the fifth level of joy to 'a thunder-cloud that is full or rain', and the fourth level is described in a different way to the above: 'Swiftly going joy is joy that spreads through the mind and vanishes not long after. It is comparable to the store of a poor man. ... [it] causes the arising of both the good and the bad, and depends on skill'. Indeed a person needs to learn the skill of working with strong joy and its effects on the body in a way akin to how a person breaking in an untamed horse learns to master it.

Of joy as a factor of awakening (*bojjhaṅga*), it is said:

> When a spiritual joy arises in one with aroused vigour, then joy as a factor for awakening becomes aroused. ... For one of joyous heart (*pīti-manassa*), the body grows tranquil and the mind grows tranquil. When the body and mind (*cittaṃ*) of a monk of joyous heart grow tranquil, then tranquillity (*passaddhi*) as a factor for awakening becomes aroused. (MN III 85–86)

Vism 144–145 continues on joy as a *jhāna*-factor:

> Now this fivefold joy, when conceived and matured, perfects the twofold tranquillity (*passaddhiṃ*), that is, bodily and mental tranquillity. When tranquillity is conceived and matured, it perfects the twofold *sukha*, that is, bodily and mental *sukha*. When *sukha* is conceived and matured, it perfects the threefold concentration, that is, momentary concentration, access (*upacāra-*) concentration, and absorption (*appanā-*) concentration (i.e. *jhāna*). ... pervading joy is the root of absorption and comes by growth into association with absorption. ...
>
> Pleasing, it is pleasure (*sukkhanaṃ sukhaṃ*). It thoroughly devours, consumes, bodily and mental affliction (*kāyacittābādhan*), thus is it *sukha*. It has agreeableness (*sāta-*) as its characteristic. Its function is to strengthen (*upabrūhaṇa-*) associated states. It is manifested as aid (*anuggaha-*).
>
> And wherever the two are associated, joy is the enjoyment at getting a desirable object, and *sukha* is the actual experiencing of it when got. Where there is joy, there is *sukha*; but where there is *sukha*, there is not necessarily joy.
>
> If a man exhausted in a desert saw or heard about a pond on the edge of a wood, he would have joy; if he went into the wood's shade and used the water, he would have *sukha*.

This sees *sukha* as a more easeful and restful feeling than *pīti*, arising from a state of bodily and mental tranquillity, a more harmonious state than the energized state of *pīti*. One can say that while joy arises from the gathering of energies that were previously scattered, *sukha* comes with a settling down of these energies. It is less obvious than *pīti*, somewhat like a person standing at the back of a room, less noticeably than a more energized person in the foreground. The above passage sees it as having both a physical and a mental aspect, thus including physical pleasure and mental pleasure, i.e. happiness.

To help clarify what *sukha* may refer to in the first *jhāna*, we see in the *sutta*s that:

> And what, monks, are the two kinds of feeling (*vedanā*)? Bodily and mental (*kāyikā ca cetasikā ca*). ...
>
> And what, monks, are the three kinds of feeling? Pleasant feeling, painful feeling and neither-pleasant-nor-painful feeling (*sukhā vedanā dukkhā vedanā adukkhamasukkhā vedanā*). ...
>
> And what, monks, are the five kinds of feeling? The pleasure faculty, the pain faculty, the happiness faculty, the unhappiness faculty, the equanimity faculty (*sukhindriyaṃ dukkhindriyaṃ somanassindriyaṃ domanassindriyaṃ upekhindriyaṃ*). ...
>
> And what, monks, are the six kinds of feeling? Feeling born of eye-contact ... of ear-contact ... of nose-contact ... of tongue-contact ... of body-contact ... of mind-contact (*cakkhu-samphassa-jā vedanā ... kāya-samphassa-jā vedanā, mano-samphassa-jā vedanā*). (SN IV 231–232)
>
> The pleasure faculty and the happiness faculty are to be seen as pleasant feeling (*sukhā vedanā*). The pain faculty and the unhappiness faculty are to be seen as painful feeling (*dukkhā vedanā*). The equanimity faculty is to be seen as neither-painful-nor-pleasant feeling. (SN V 210)

> And what, monks, is the pleasure faculty? Whatever bodily pleasure there is, whatever bodily comfort, the pleasant, comfortable feeling born of body-contact (*kāyikaṃ sukhaṃ kāyikaṃ sātaṃ kāya-samphassa-jaṃ sukhaṃ sātaṃ vedayitam*).
>
> And what, monks, is the pain faculty? Whatever bodily pain (*dukkhaṃ*) there is, whatever bodily discomfort, the painful (*dukkhaṃ*), uncomfortable feeling born of body-contact.
>
> And what, monks, is the happiness faculty? Whatever mental pleasure (*cetasikaṃ sukhaṃ*) there is, whatever mental comfort, the pleasant (*sukhaṃ*), comfortable feeling born of mind-contact (*mano-samphassa-jaṃ*).
>
> And what, monks, is the unhappiness faculty? Whatever mental pain (*cetasikaṃ dukkhaṃ*) there is, whatever mental discomfort, the painful (*dukkhaṃ*), uncomfortable feeling born of mind-contact.
>
> And what, monks, is the equanimity faculty? Whatever feeling there is, whether bodily or mental, that is neither comfortable nor uncomfortable. (SN V 209)

Together, these show that *sukha* is *sukha*/pleasant feeling that can be bodily (*kāyika*) or mental (*cetasika*), these being, respectively the *sukha* faculty (*indriya*) and the *somanassa*/happiness faculty, which arise, respectively from the bodily/tactile sense and mind-sense (*mano*). The *sukha* of the first *jhāna*, while it suffuses the body, arises not as such from the stimulation of the tactile sense, but from the mind's perception of a situation. Hence Vibh 257 explains it specifically as *mental sukha*: 'mental comfort, mental pleasure, comfortable, pleasant feeling, comfortable, pleasant feeling born of mental (*ceto-*) contact'. That is not to say, though, that physical pleasure may not accompany it, due to the effect of *jhāna* on the body. The *pīti* which it accompanies certainly has an effect on the body.

Both kinds of *sukha* have an easeful quality, though bodily *sukha* is less subtle than mental *sukha*. Either may occur in skilful or unskilful mind states.[1] It is largely the presence of mindfulness that ensures they are skilful.

Second *jhāna*

While the joy and happiness of the first *jhāna* come from the relief of being beyond the hindrances, in the second *jhāna* they come from the gathered, concentrated state produced by the first *jhāna*. As *vitakka* and *vicāra* have done their job, they fall away in order to enter second *jhāna*:

> From the subsiding of mental application and examining, a monk enters and dwells in the second *jhāna*, joy and happiness born of concentration, without mental application and examining and with inner calm confidence and mental unification (*bhikkhu vitakka-vicārānaṃ vūpasamā ajjhattam sampasādanaṃ cetaso ekodi-bhāvaṃ avitakkaṃ avicāraṃ samādhijaṃ pīti-sukhaṃ dutīya-jjhanaṃ upasampajja viharati*) (DN I 74, MN I 276, MN III 93, AN III 25)

1. Abhi-s 80: Bodhi 1993, 77–78, Wijeratne and Gethin2002, 55.

This stilling of *vitakka* or *vicāra* might be seen as like placing ones hands behind one's back after one has used them to adjust a microscope, which one now intently looks down. Without any *vitakka* or *vicāra*, one can simply *be* with the object, without a need to bring the mind back to it and get to know it. There is also a state of 'noble silence' (SN II 273), without even subtle mental talking, i.e., without any thinking. Joy and happiness continue to pervade:

> He suffuses, fills, soaks, and drenches this very body with the joy and happiness born of concentration (*samādhijaṃ*), so that there is no part of his whole body that is untouched by that joy and happiness.
>
> It is as if there were a pool where water sprang up (from below), but which has no water flowing into it from the east, the west, the north, or the south, and which the (rain) god did not fill with rain from time to time. Now when the cool waters sprang up in that pool they would suffuse, fill, soak, and drench that same pool with cool water, so that no part of that pool would be untouched by the cool water. (DN I 74, MN I 276–7, MN III 93, AN III 25–6)

That is, spiritual joy and happiness well up from deep within and flow around the meditator. There are also the qualities of 'inner calm confidence and mental unification'; that is, a bright clarity and calm confidence that trusts this state – *pasāda*, closely related to *sampasādana*, is the attitude a devotee has towards the Buddha, *Dhamma* and *Saṅgha* (e.g. SN V 342) – so that the mind can be well gathered within it.

Third *jhāna*

For the third *jhāna*, the energized joy that has been experienced in the first two *jhāna*s has fulfilled its role and is allowed to fade away, perhaps like a booster rocket falling away:

> With the fading away also of joy, a monk dwells equanimously and, mindful and clearly comprehending, he experiences with the body the happiness of which the noble ones speak saying, 'equanimous and mindful, he dwells happily'; he enters and dwells in the third *jhāna* (*bhikkhu pītiyā virāgā ca upekhako ca viharati sato ca sampajāno, sukhañ ca kāyena paṭisamvedeti yan taṃ ariyā ācikkhanti: upekhako satimā sukha-vihārī ti tatiya-jjhānaṃ upasampajja viharati)* (DN I 75, MN I 277, MN III 93, AN III 26)

Here, the feeling-tone calms down into a gentle, contented happiness. In the third *jhāna*, happiness does not *well up*, as in the second *jhāna*, but just *fills and pervades*:

> He suffuses, fills, soaks and drenches this very body with a happiness distinct from joy (*nippītikena sukhena*), so that there is no part of his whole body that is untouched by that happiness.
>
> It is just as if, in a pond of blue, red or white lotuses, there were some lotuses that had come into bud and grown in the water, never rising out of the water, but flourishing beneath its surface. Those lotuses would be suffused, filled, soaked, and drenched from root to tip with cool water, so that no part of those blue, red or white lotuses would be untouched by the cool water. (DN I 75, MN I 277, MN III 93–94, AN III 26)

While here the *feeling-tone* is happy, the *attitude* is one of even-minded, balanced equanimity. Moreover, being 'mindful and clearly comprehending' is particularly mentioned. MN III 25 includes equanimity and mindfulness as qualities present even in the first *jhāna,* but evidently they here come to the fore and are accompanied by clear comprehension (*sampajañña*) of a notable level (MN III 82–88, mentions clear comprehension as involved in all of the 16 stages of *ānāpānasati*). So, the third *jhāna* is a state of contented, balanced happiness with strong mindfulness and understanding.

Fourth *jhāna*

In the fourth *jhāna*, happiness gives way to a peaceful, neutral feeling:

> A monk, from the abandoning of *sukha* and the abandoning of *dukkha,* from the passing away of the previous happiness and unhappiness (or, from the previous passing away of happiness and unhappiness), enters and dwells in the fourth *jhāna,* neither painful nor pleasant, with purity of mindfulness by equanimity (*bhikkhu sukhassa ca pahānā dukkhassa ca pahānā pubb'eva somanassa-domanassānaṃ atthagamā adukkhaṃ asukhaṃ upekhā-sati-pārisuddhiṃ catuttha-jjhanaṃ upasampajja viharati*). (DN I 75, MN I 277, AN III 26–27)

I see the above as not wholly clear: are the *sukha* and *dukkha* of the first line to be identified as two of the three kinds of feeling (*sukha, dukkha* and neither) or two of the five kinds (*sukha, dukkha, somanassa, domanassa, upekkhā*), and how is *pubb'eva* best translated and applied here? These related issues will be discussed below. Here, note that the qualities of mindfulness and equanimity, which came to the fore in the third *jhāna*, are said to be purified, along with the mind:

> A monk sits suffusing this very body with a mind that is thoroughly purified and cleansed (*parisuddhena cetasā pariyodātena*), so that there is no part of his body that is untouched by that thoroughly purified and cleansed mind. (DN I 75–6, MN I 277, MN III 94, AN III 27)

The related simile is:

> It is as if a person were to be sitting covered from the head down with a white cloth, so there were no part of his whole body that is untouched by that white cloth (*puriso odātena vatthena sa-sīsaṃ pārupitvā nisinno assa, nāssa kiñci sabbāvato kāyassa* odātena *vaṭthena apphutaṃ assa*). (DN I 76, MN I 277–278, MN III 94, AN III 27)

The commentary on DN I 76 (DN-a I 219) says, as translated by Bodhi (1989, 152):

> In the simile for the fourth jhāna, the white cloth is mentioned for the purpose of showing suffusion by heat [*utu-pharaṇatthaṃ*]. For there is no suffusion by heat with a soiled cloth; with a clean cloth that has just been washed the suffusion by heat is strong. For in this simile the material body [*karaja-kāyo*] is like the cloth and the happiness [*-sukhaṃ*] of the fourth jhāna is like the suffusion by heat. Therefore just as when a man has bathed well and is sitting covered from head down by a clean cloth, the heat from his body suffuses the entire cloth so that there is no part of the cloth not suffused by heat, similarly there is no part of the bhikkhu's material body that is not suffused by the happiness of the fourth jhāna.

The new sub-commentary on DN-a I 219 argues that the *sutta*'s simile 'requires interpretation (*neyyatthato*)' (Bodhi 1989, 152). It also says that while the fourth *jhāna* lacks happiness as a pleasant feeling, its equanimity can be seen as a form of happiness due to its peacefulness, citing a passage at Vibh-a 171 on this. The commentaries' interpretation seems a little strained, but it is repeated in the commentaries on the simile at MN I 277 (MA-a II 323) and AN III 27 (AN-a III 234–235), which also suggest that 'the body of a monk is surely entirely touched by the subtle *rūpa* originating from the fourth *jhāna*'. Overall the explanation conveys an image of a cloth or towel, enveloping a warm, cleansed body, being pervaded by heat radiating from the body, this standing for the happy peacefulness and subtle physical effects of the fourth *jhāna* pervading a meditator's body.

The above interpretations aim to link the simile particularly with the suffusing aspects of the fourth *jhāna*. Alternatively, one could see it as about other aspects of this *jhāna*. The image of sitting enclosed by a white cloth suggests being contained within, set apart from the world in a cleansed, pure state; meditating under a cloth can produce this kind of feeling. Anālayo (2017, 60) also comments that the image:

> seems to exemplify the imperturbable nature of the mind reached at this juncture of meditative absorption. This condition is similar to a body that is well protected from the impact of cold or heat through this cloth[2] at the same time presumably also being protected from being bitten by mosquitoes, gad flies, etc.

Elsewhere (2011, 675), he cites SN I 167 and Sn p.80 as examples of the Buddha meditating when covered by his robe. The *Vimuttimagga* (Ehara *et al.* 1977, 112) says on the simile, the description of which includes 'so a bhikkhu covers his body and limbs with purified mindfulness':

> As the man who covers his body from head to foot with a white cloth is protected from extremes of heat and cold, experiences an even temperature and is undisturbed in body and mind, so the yogin who enters the fourth meditation, *jhāna*, experiences neither pain nor pleasure. This is the bliss of equanimity. With it he fills his body.

The simile is perhaps also suggestive of being 'dead to the (external) world', as with a body wrapped in a funeral shroud.[3] We know that this happens today in India, and DN II 141, on how the Buddha's body was to be treated as that of a *Cakkavatti* king, starts with, 'They wrap the mortal body (*sarīraṃ*) of a *Cakkavatti* king in a new cloth (*ahatena vatthena veṭhenti*) ...'.

In this connection, it can be noted that the fourth *jhāna* is said to be a state in which breathing has stopped (SN IV 217: *assāsapassāsā niruddhā honti*; for more on this, see below). Vism 283 says that there is no breathing (*assāsapassāsā*) in, amongst others, those who are in the fourth *jhāna*, dead, or in the womb. In line with this, as well as a possible allusion to being 'dead to the world', another possible allusion is to being in the womb: an enclosed state, cut off from the outside world, in which there is no breathing; and near the end of pregnancy it is a state of great potential

2. Curiously, he cites the MN-a II 323 passage in support here.
3. Thanks to Deven Patel, of the University of Pennsylvania, for suggesting this to me.

for future development, just as the fourth *jhāna* is a state from which the formless states, psychic powers and the other five *abhiññās*, including liberation from *saṃsāra*, can develop.

The four *jhānas* compared

The fourth *jhāna* simile, however exactly interpreted, builds on the earlier watery/purifying similes of working soap into a lather, water welling up, and water pervading. One can also see a progression, through the four *jhānas*, of: joy and happiness at *entering* the *jhānic* realm; joy and happiness at *being* there; contented happiness at resting at ease there; and complete mental unification in this realm.

A summary of key aspects of the *jhānas* is shown in table 1.

Table 1- The four *jhānas*.

Jhāna	*From*	*Qualities*	*Simile*
1	gladness at lack of hindrances > joy in mind > tranquillity of body > happiness > mind is concentrated.	secluded from sense-pleasures and from unskilful qualities, born of seclusion, and with mental application and examination, and with joy and happiness suffusing the body.	ball of moist cleansing agent kneaded together.
2	subsiding of mental application and examination	a state of inner calm confidence and mental unification, born of concentration, and with joy and happiness suffusing the body.	a cool pool with water welling up from a spring below.
3	fading of joy	a state of equanimity, mindfulness and clear comprehension, with happiness suffusing the body.	budding blue, red or white lotuses under the water and suffused by it.
4	being beyond any mental or physical pain or happiness	a mind purified by equanimity and mindfulness, that suffuses the body	a person sitting completely wrapped in a clean white cloth.

In comparing the *jhānas*, one can also draw on the nature of the deities that are seen to dwell in heavenly levels of existence paralleling each of the *jhānas*:[4]

4. Listed at Gethin 1998, 116–117. AN II 126–28 sees the Brahma-kāyika, Ābhassara, Subha-kiṇha and Vehappala gods as, respectively, the destiny of those who dwell often in one of the *jhānas*; ordinary people who desire and relish the *jhānas* then go on to a low rebirth, while noble disciples can attain enlightenment in the relevant heaven. Vibh 422–25 list the different kinds of

1. For the first *jhāna*, these are gods 'of the Brahmā group' (*brahma-kāyika*): the retinue and 'ministers of Great Brahmā', and Great Brahmā, the latter being full of lovingkindness (opposed to the hindrance of ill-will) and the other *brahma-vihāras*, and seen by some as an active creative force. These gods can be seen as suggestive of the subtle activity of *vitakka* and *vicāra*.
2. For the second *jhāna*, they are gods of limited, boundless or streaming *radiance* (*parittābha, appamāṇābha, ābhassara*), suggestive of a very bright state of mind and meditative *nimitta*.
3. For the third *jhāna*, they are gods of limited, boundless or complete *beauty* (*paritta-subha, appamāna-subha, subha-kiṇha*), suggestive of a very beautiful *nimitta*. The height of lovingkindness is also said to be in a state of 'beauty' (SN V 119), perhaps meaning the third *jhāna*.
4. For the fourth *jhāna*, they are the 'Very Fruitful' (*vehapphala*) gods, as this is a state of great potential; also at this level are heavens of great wisdom, where the almost-enlightened non-returners are reborn; another heaven at this level, though, is that of 'unconscious beings' (*asañña-satta*), who mishandled the fourth *jhāna* state by letting subtle perception to then fall into no perception, due to insufficient mindfulness.

Feelings in the third and fourth *jhānas*

How, then, as we to see the *sukha* and *somanassa* mentioned in the fourth *jhāna* description? Is the *somanassa* abandoned some time *prior* to entering fourth *jhāna*, or is it the (mental) *sukha* that is abandoned in the process of entering the fourth *jhāna*? The *Nikāyas* see the way the various feeling are abandoned in the *jhānas* thus (*Uppaṭipāṭika Sutta:* SN V 213–16): 1) The pain faculty (*dukkha indriya*, i.e. physical pain) ceases in the first *jhāna*, 2) the unhappiness faculty (*domanassa indriya* i.e. mental pain) ceases in the second *jhāna*, 3) the pleasure faculty (*sukha indriya*, i.e. bodily pleasure) ceases in the third *jhāna*, and 4) the happiness faculty (*somanassa indriya*) then ceases in the fourth *jhāna*. Thus, in the fourth *jhāna*, only neutral feeling remains, the faculty of equanimity, as well as equanimity as an attitude of mind.

This means that the *sukha* in the third *jhāna* (e.g. DN I 75) must be that aspect of *sukhā vedanā* that is <u>somanassa</u> – happiness or mental pleasure, while it is lacking in the other aspect of *sukhā vedanā* – the 'pleasure faculty', *sukha indriya*, i.e. bodily pleasure, pleasure in some way related to the tactile sense. This implies that bodily pleasure may thus have existed in the first two *jhānas*, along with mental pleasure, or at least it may exist *between jhāna* 1 and 2, and on leaving 2: Dhs 160, 161 and 163 says that the *somanassa* but not *sukha* faculty exists *in* the first three *jhānas*. The commentary on SN V 213–16 (SN-a III 243) says, 'The pleasure faculty is abandoned already in the access to the third *jhāna*, but it may arise when the body is touched by the sublime physical phenomena originating from joy (*pīti-samuṭṭhāna-*

---

devas linked to each *jhāna* and sees which level is attained as being due to the level at which is related *jhāna* is mastered.

paṇīta-rūpa-phuṭṭha-kāyassa siyā uppatti).' So, when one enters the third *jhāna*, both joy and physical pleasure fall away, but mental pleasure, happiness, remains, as a more subtle feeling.

Tse-fu Kuan (2005, 288) sees this as implausible as it is said that in the third *jhāna* the 'body' (*kāya*) is suffused with this *sukha*; but *kāya* is not used only to refer to the physical body,[5] also covering the broader sense of 'body' as a 'group'. At MN I 299, the term *sakkāya*, i.e. *sat* (existing) *kāya* is explained as the five *upādāna-kkhandhas*, i.e. the grasped-at processes of body *and mind*. At DN II 62, on the *nāma-rūpa nidāna*, talks of the 'mind-group' (*nāma-kāya*) and 'form-group' (*rūpa-kāya*), with SN II 3–4 explaining *nāma* as 'feeling, perception, volition, sense contact and attention'. Moreover, it is said that one senses with the *kāya* in the formless states, which are beyond input from the five physical senses (AN IV 426–28, MN I 293, cf. MN I 477–479). Hence when Vibh 259, on 'experiences *sukha* with the body (*kāyena*)' in the third *jhāna*, explains *kāya* as the *khandhas* of perception, volitional activities and consciousness, this is certainly plausible. What is meant is happiness spreading through the mentally experienced 'body'.

As *somanassa* then stops in the fourth *jhāna*, this surely implies that when it is said of this *jhāna*, 'from the abandoning of *sukha* and the abandoning of *dukkha*', this means that *two of the three* kinds of feeling, pleasant feeling and painful feeling, equivalent to *four of the five* feeling-faculties, are fully absent in this *jhāna*: bodily *sukha* has previously be abandoned — as has bodily and mental *dukkha* — and now mental *sukha* is abandoned. Hence *pubb'eva somanassa-domanassānaṃ atthagamā* would mean: not 1) 'from the previous passing away of happiness and unhappiness' but 2) 'from the passing away of the previous happiness and unhappiness'. Alternatively, 3) the *pubb'eva* may go with what precedes it, not follows it: *dukkhassa ca pahānā pubb'eva*, and mean 'from the abandoning, previously, of *dukkha*'.

Existing translations go variously with 1), 2) and 3) types of translations:

1. Ñāṇamoli and Bodhi (1995, 368, at MN I 277), 'and with the previous disappearance of joy and grief'; Bodhi (2000, 1277, at SN IV 226), 'and with the previous disappearance of joy and displeasure'; and Bodhi (2012, 649, at AN III 27), 'and with the previous disappearance of joy and dejection'; Kuan (2005, 289, 294–295) also sees the fourth *jhāna* description as meaning *somanassa* and *domanassa* have both previously ceased, in *jhāna* prior to the fourth.
2. T.W. Rhys Davids (1973 [1899], 86, at DN I 75), 'by the passing away alike of any elation, any dejection, he had previously felt'; I.B.Horner (1982 [1938], at Vin III 4), 'by the annihilation of the rejoicing and sorrowing I had before'; Maurice Walshe (1987, 103, at DN I 75), 'and with the disappearance of former gladness and sadness'; Rune Johansson (1981, 98, at DN I 183), 'his former feelings of ease and distress disappear'.

5. Harvey 1995, 116–118; Kuan 2008, 81–103.

3. Rupert Gethin (2008 29, at DN I 75), translates all of *sukhassa ca pahānā dukkhassa ca pahānā pubb'eva somanassa-domanassānaṃ atthagamā* as 'by the letting go of happiness and unhappiness, as a result of the earlier disappearance of pleasure and pain'.

Translation type 2) is supported by DN I 183, which immediately after the above fourth *jhāna* description, 'A monk, from the abandoning of *sukha* ... with purity of mindfulness by equanimity', continues, 'His previous subtle but real perception of equanimity and *sukha* cease' (*Tassa yā purimā upekkhā-sukha-sukhuma-sacca-saññā sā nirujjhanti*).

Now Vibh 260, on the fourth *jhāna*, takes *sukha* and *dukkha* as physical *sukha* and *dukkha*, and sees the *pubbeva* as grouped with the words that follow it, and Vism 165 says:

> Herein, 'with the abandoning of *sukha* and the abandoning of *dukkha*': with the abandoning of bodily *sukha* and bodily *dukkha*. With the previous: which took place before (*Pubb'evā ti tañ ca kho pubb'eva*), not in the moment of the fourth *jhāna*. 'From the passing away of happiness and unhappiness': with the previous passing away of the two, that is, mental *sukha* and mental *dukkha*; with the abandoning, is what is meant.
>
> But when does the abandoning of these take place? At the moment of access of the four *jhānas*. For happiness is only abandoned at the moment of the fourth-*jhāna* access, while (bodily) *dukkha*, unhappiness, and (bodily) *sukha* are abandoned respectively at the moments of access of the first, second, and third *jhānas*. So although the order in which they are abandoned is not actually mentioned, nevertheless the abandoning of the *sukha, dukkha,* happiness and unhappiness is stated here according to the order in which the faculties are summarized in the *Indriya Vibhaṅga* (Vibh 122: i.e. *sukha, dukkha, somanassa, domanassa*).

Here, while *somanassa* is seen as abandoned previously to the fourth *jhāna*, this is not in a lower *jhāna* but in the fourth *jhāna* access state.

Feeling in the first and second *jhānas*

SN V 213–14 sees physical *dukkha* as ending in the first *jhāna*, and unhappiness ending in the second *jhāna*. However, the probably Sarvāstivādin **Abhidharmāmṛta(rasa)-śastra* held that the unhappiness faculty ceases in the first *jhāna*, while the pain faculty is what ceases in the second *jhāna*, the same being said in the Dārṣṭāntika **Tattavasiddhi* and the *Yogācārabhūmi*, which attributes this idea to the *Aviparītaka Sūtra* (Kuan 2005, 289–290). Which is most plausible? As in the first *jhāna* the body is suffused with joy and pleasant feeling, completely at ease, how could it also experience either physical pain or unhappiness? Physical discomfort is a more obvious distraction, so is more likely to drop away before the first *jhāna*, but what of unhappiness. Could it still occur prior to entering the second *jhāna*?

If it can, this might mean that there can still be some kind of unpleasant mental feeling in first *jhāna*, perhaps due to seeing that the mind is not yet fully stilled. However, it is said (AN III 207) that 'in the joy of solitude' (*paviveka pīti*), which the commentary (AN-a III 303) plausibly sees as the first two *jhānas*, even 'pain and unhappiness connected with the skilful do not occur'; and Dhs 160 says *somanassa* but not *domanassa* exists in the first *jhāna*. That *domanassa* cannot exist in the first *jhāna* is the reason why Kuan (2005, 29) sees the view that it, and not physical pain, ceases in the first *jhāna*, as the most plausible one.

The other possibility is that there is no unpleasant mental feeling actually *in* first *jhāna*, but when the mind starts to move towards the second *jhāna*, it might briefly arise.

Relevant here is Lance Cousins' statement (1973, 127):

> It is apparently not possible to go directly from a lower *jhāna* to a higher.[96] In each case it is necessary to return to a more normal state of consciousness. The interpretation of this seems clear. *Jhāna* is conceived of as calming and purifying the normal consciousness. This achieved, a higher *jhāna* becomes possible, which in turn further purifies the normal state. The process obviously continues some way, but, although it could no doubt be quite long-lasting, it cannot achieve a permanent improvement.

His note 96 says:

> 96. The *Visuddhi-magga* description (Chaps. III, IV, X) is clear; at each stage the access *jhāna* has the factors of the *jhāna* below it. This view is clearly stated in the *Kathāvatthu* (Kv 565, 30–569, 14 [=Kvu XVIII.6]) and seems to be implied in the *nikāyas* by passages which juxtapose forms like *vuṭṭhahitvā* and *samāpajjitvā* [having emerged, having attained].

At Kvu XVIII.6, the Theravādin argues against the view that a meditator passes directly from one *jhāna* to the next, without any intervening process. It argues that there are processes of 'adverting (*āvaṭṭanā*), reflecting, co-ordinating, attending, willing, wishing and aiming (*paṇidhī*)' leading up to each *jhāna*, that concern the disadvantages of the qualities about to be dropped in the next *jhāna*.

The commentary on SN V 213–214 (SN-a III 243) says, 'The unhappiness faculty is abandoned in the access to the second *jhāna* but arises again when there is bodily fatigue and mental strain (*kāya-kilamatthe citt'upaghāte*) on account of mental application and examining.' Such strain might arise on deciding to leave the first *jhāna*, but before second *jhāna* access was established. This possibility seems supported by DN II 278, which says that *domanassa* which is beyond *vitakka* and *vicāra* is superior to *domanassa* which is not beyond them not. This perhaps implies that *domanassa* can exist not only prior to the first *jhanā*, but also *beyond* it, if not yet in the second *jhāna*.

In the Theravādin Abhidhamma, the only kinds of mind-states in which unhappiness is said to occur is in two kinds of unskilful *citta*s associated with aversion[6] (*paṭigha-sampayutta*), whether instigated (Dhs 421) or not (Dhs 413, 416–417) (and not in any karmically resultant state), and which only occur in the realm of sense-pleasures (Vism 493). Dhs 1389 says that, 'The two arisings of *citta* associated with unhappiness, body-consciousness associated with pain (*dukkha-*), neutral feeling (*vedanā upekkhā*), material form and *nibbāna*: these *dhamma*s are not to be seen as associated with joy, with pleasure (*sukha-*) or the neutral (*upekkhā-*)'. This implies

6. Abhi-s 8; Bodhi 1993, 17, Wijeratne and Gethin 2002, 77.

that any unhappiness associated with (joy-containing) first *jhāna* would occur when the mind actually dips out of *jhāna*, including when it is moving between first and second *jhāna*.

The kind of unhappiness that could occur between these *jhāna*s– the unhappiness connected with the skilful of AN III 207 — is perhaps suggested by these cases:

- A monk or nun who 'lives the complete and pure spiritual life, even with *dukkha* and *domanassa*' can be praised for the effort etc. put in to cultivating skilful states (AN III 4).
- At, MN III 218, seeing that six kinds of sense objects are impermanent and *dukkha* leads to longing (*pihaṃ*) for liberation, then unhappiness based on renunciation (*nekkhamma-sitaṃ domanassaṃ*), though at MN III 217, seeing that six kinds of sense objects are impermanent and *dukkha* leads to *happiness* based in renunciation.
- At MN III 220, one overcome *somanassa, domanassa* and *upekkhā* (in response to any of the six kinds of sense objects) based on the household life by relying on *somanassa, domanassa* and *upekkhā* based on renunciation. For the *somanassa, domanassa* and *upekkhā* based on renunciation, one relies on the *somanassa* to overcome *domanassa*, and *upekkhā* to overcome *somanassa.*

So on leaving the happiness of the first *jhāna*, there may be a small element of unhappiness prior to the skilful state of second *jhāna* being accessed (though not between higher *jhāna*s).

Does breathing fully stop in the fourth *jhāna*?

At MN I 301, in-breathing and out-breathing (*assāsapassāsā*) are said to be 'body-activity (*kāya-saṅkhāro*)', as they are 'bodily states, bound up with the body (*kāyikā ete dhammā kāya-paṭibaddhā*)', mental application and examination (*vitakka* and *vicāra*) are 'speech-activity' as they are what precede speech, and perception and feeling (*saññā* and *vedanā*) are 'mind (*citta-*) activity' as they are 'mental (*cetasikā*) states, bound up with the mind'. At SN IV 217 there is said to be a successive cessation (*nirodha*) of *saṅkhāras*, in which a succession of phenomena are ceased (*niruddha*): in the first *jhāna*, speech; in the second, *vitakka* and *vicāra*; in the third, joy (*pīti*), in the fourth, *assāsapassāsā*;[7] in the sphere of infinite space, the perception of form; in each of the remaining three formless state, the perception pertaining to the one below it; in the cessation of perception and feeling, perception and feeling.

Does this mean that there is literally no breathing in the fourth *jhāna*, just as there is no *vitakka* and *vicāra* in the second? MN I 243–244, on Gotama's ascetic period, says that he tried forceful stopping of breathing (which only led to great physical pain), whether through the mouth, nose *or ears.* While an ascetic pain-inducing *holding* of the breath is not what mindfulness of breathing involves, the

7. It is said that, in the fourth *jhāna*, 'body-activity is tranquilized (*passaddha-*)' (DN IV, 270, AN V 31); in-and-out breathing is a 'thorn' to the fourth *jhāna* (AN V 135).

idea that one might even breathe through the ears is interesting. Is even this transcended in fourth *jhāna*?

In discussing mindfulness of breathing, the *Visuddhimagga* explains that the breathing gets progressively more subtle from the first through to the fourth *jhāna*, in which 'it is so exceedingly subtle that it even reaches non-occurrence (*atisukhumo nappavattim eva pāpuṇātī ti*)' (p. 275). Vism 276–277 cites Patis I 184–186, which likens the stages of subtlety of the breath to the fading sounds of a gong, where a careful listener becomes progressively attuned to fainter sounds; and even when the faintest sound ceases, the mind still retains the mental impression (*nimitta*) of it.[8] Sometimes one needs to investigate whether breathing still exists, even though it does so faintly (Vism 274). This can be helped by reminding oneself that one must still be breathing if not in any of the states in which there are no breathing in and out (*assāsapassāsā*): in beings who are in the womb, submerged in water, an unconscious (*deva-*)being, dead, in the fourth *jhāna*, reborn in the form or formless realms, or in the cessation of perception and feeling (p.283). Of course for someone who is unsure if they are in the fourth *jhāna* or not, this would not help give them an answer, and indeed the arising of questioning on this would itself preclude them from being in fourth *jhāna*.

On the edge of fourth *jhāna*, breathing could have become very *slight* in depth, and very *slow*. It may also become *suspended* for periods if the pause between an in- and out-breath (or out- and in-) becomes extended as the mind is intently taken up with the *nimitta* of the breath, when the mind may dip into fourth *jhāna* for a short time. As the breath became even more slight and slow, this non-forceful suspension could then become even more extended, in more sustained fourth *jhāna*. As the body and mind are very still in fourth *jhāna*, they would require minimal energy-input, so this becomes plausible.

What does modern science say on how long a person can survive without breathing? With practice, a person might be able *hold* their breath for up to three minutes, after which consciousness would be lost, though for many this would happen earlier. Then:

> The brain can survive for up to *about six minutes* after the heart stops. The reason to learn cardiopulmonary resuscitation (CPR) is that if CPR is started within *six minutes* of cardiac arrest, the brain may survive the lack of oxygen. After *about six minutes* without CPR, however, the brain begins to die. [9]

Experienced free-divers can extend the survivable time without breathing, though there are relevant physiological changes when in cold water, with the heart slowing, that aides this. The world record for a free-diver's breath-holding is 22 minutes, but this was after 20 minutes of hyperventilating with pure oxygen. That said:

8. As mindfulness of breathing can take one through the four formless states to cessation (SN V 317–19), it must presumably work at this level with the remaining *nimitta* of a previously ceased breath, though some minimal breathing might perhaps arise while moving from one to another of them.

9. 'What is Brain Death? — How Brain Death Works' | HowStuffWorks https://science.howstuffworks.com/life/inside-the-mind/human-brain/brain-death1.htm

> free divers often report reaching a place of great relaxation during dives in order to minimize their metabolic functions and preserve oxygen. Metabolic function is especially important in cases where going without oxygen isn't quite so voluntary. [10]
>
> When US toddler Michelle Funk fell into an icy stream in 1986, she survived an estimated 66 minutes underwater, preserved by deep hypothermia that reduced her metabolic rate to almost nothing. [11]

This point about 'greater relaxation' is clearly relevant to *jhāna*.

Hearing in the *jhānas*

Lance Cousins makes a clear and explicit claim in his paper on *jhāna* (1973, 125):

> If we are to understand *jhāna* as being a trance state, it must be as a lucid trance. It is equally clear that it possesses many of the characteristics of trance. The mind does not perceive through the five senses and is incapable of speech from the first *jhāna*.[12] By the fourth all bodily activities have ceased.[13] The movement of the breath is explicitly mentioned and the heart-beat doubtless implied.[14]

There is some debate as to whether one can hear sounds in the *jhānas*, though it is only explicitly said in the *suttas* that this becomes impossible in the *formless* states, beyond the four *jhānas* (AN IV 426–428, MN I 293). That the formless states go beyond awareness of input of the five senses is also seen at DN II 130–132, where it is said that Āḷāra Kālāma — who taught the Buddha the sphere of no-thingness — once had not seen or heard 500 carts go by, even though he was not asleep, but was percipient (*saññī*), with the Buddha saying he had similarly once not seen or heard a thunderstorm that killed two farmers and four oxen. The Buddha's attainment is seen as a greater one, which implies that the shutting down of five-sense perceptions has degrees, such that a loud enough noise can rouse a person from formless states unless they have the greatest mastery of them. This seems similar to how noise can rouse a person from sleep, but a deeper sleep will need a louder noise to end it.

Some see the fact that even the first *jhāna* is 'Completely secluded from *kāmas* (*kāmehi*)' as entailing that there is no awareness of objects of the five senses in *jhāna*. However, *kāma* probably here means 'sense-*desire*', as it is explained at Vibh 256; so as to be equivalent to the first hindrance: *kāma-cchanda*. Even if its referent is to sensory-*objects*, the *kāma-gunas*, these are explained at AN III 411 as only *desirable* sense-objects:

> There are these five strands of sense-pleasure (*kāma-guṇā*): forms cognizable by the

10. *Medical Daily:* 'Breaking Point: How Long Can Someone Go Without Breathing?': http://www.medicaldaily.com/breaking-point-how-long-can-someone-go-without-breathing-364450
11. BBC, 'How long can you go without air?': http://www.bbc.com/future/story/20140714-how-long-can-you-go-without-air
12. A note here refers to SN IV 217, AN V 135, Kvu II.5, XVII.8.
13. A note here refers to e.g. DN III 270, AN V 31.
14. A note here refers to AN V 135, SN IV 217.

> eye that are wished for, desired, agreeable, pleasing, connected with sensual pleasure (*kām'ūpasaṃhitā*), tantalizing; ... sounds ... odours ... tastes ... tactile objects.... However, these are not sense-pleasures (*kāmā*); in the Noble One's discipline, these are called '*kāma-gūṇā*'. A person's sense-pleasure (*kāmo*) is lustful resolve (*saṅkappa-rāgo*)'.

Being free of desire for pleasant sense-objects does not in itself mean that one is unaware of them, or of neutral or unpleasant ones. It is even said that there are *samādhi*s in which one can see divine (*dibba*) forms and hear divine sounds (DN I 152), though these *samādhi*s are not specifically said to be *jhāna*s.

A relevant passage on whether one can hear in a *jhāna* is at AN V 133–134.[15] Here, some noted elder disciples move to a quieter place when a group of laypeople, come to see the Buddha, are making 'high and loud sounds' (*uccā-saddā mahā-saddā*)', because the disciples recall that the Buddha has 'called sound a thorn (*sadda-kaṇṭakā*) to the *jhānas*. Let us go to Gosiṅga Sal Woods. There we can dwell at ease, with few sounds (*appa-saddā*) and uncrowded (*appa-kiṇṇā*)'. The Buddha agreed with them and said:

> 1) Delight in company is a thorn to one who delights in solitude. 2) Pursuit of an attractive object is a thorn to one intent on meditation on the mark of the unattractive. 3) An unsuitable show is a thorn to one guarding the doors of the sense faculties. 4) Keeping company with women is a thorn to the celibate life. 5) Sound (*saddo*) is a thorn to the first *jhāna*. 6) Mental application and examination is a thorn to the second *jhāna*. ...

Given that the context of the above is a situation where there is sound that is 'high and loud', i.e. noise, does the above mean: a) *noise* makes it *difficult to attain, or remain in,* the *jhāna*s, or b) in *jhāna, no sounds are heard*? The context suggests a), though some of the other 'thorns' referred to, such as no 6), suggests b), as there is no *vitakka* and *vicāra* within second *jhāna*. Against b), it is not said that ear-consciousness, i.e. *hearing* a sound, is a thorn to the first *jhāna*. Vibh 251–52, on *jhāna*, says that the place to practise to attain *jhāna* is a place 'secluded' from crowds, and has 'little sound (*appa-saddhan ti*)', by being uncrowded with laypeople or monks, and 'little tumult' (*appa-nigghosa*), i.e. with little sound and 'free from the atmosphere of humans'. It thus talks of a quiet but not silent place, and has nothing on the issue of *hearing* within *jhāna*.

However, the *Kathāvatthu* (Kvu XVIII.8) discusses whether 'one who has attained (*samāpanno*) hears sound (*saddaṃ suṇātīti*)'. The discussion implies such 'attainment' concerns *jhāna*, and the Theravādin argues that sound cannot be heard by one who is 'attained'. Both the Theravādin and his opponent agree that one cannot see forms, smell, taste or feel any touch when 'attained'. Both agree that it is not case that 'the attained is endowed with ear-consciousness' and that *samādhi* is for one endowed with mind-consciousness. The Theravādin then argues that there can thus be no hearing in *samādhi*, as this would entail two sensory contacts (*phassa*) at the same time. The opponent then argues that sound cannot be a thorn to first *jhāna* if one cannot hear *in* it. Their implication seems to be that in *jhāna*, the mind, while gener-

15. Discussed, with *Āgama* parallels, at Anālayo 2016, 44–46 and 2017, 140–143.

ally taking a mental object, can sometimes take sound as an object. The Theravādin then emphasizes that other 'thorns' concern factors absent in the *jhāna* they are thorns to. The matter, though, was clearly a debated, controversial one. Kvu-a 175 says that 'sound is a thorn' was said because 'sound induces distraction, "When a loud sound strikes the ear, one is aroused from first *jhāna*". Hence the citation is inconclusive'. That is, a loud enough sound would disrupt the *jhāna* and end it, as it does with sleep. In deep sleep, one is not hearing sounds, but the hearing sense is in some sense operative, such that a loud enough sound can impinge on the sleeping mind. The *Vimuttimagga* (Ehara *et al.* 1977, 120) says: 'When the yogin enters into concentration, he hears sounds, but is unable to speak because the faculty of hearing and that of speech are not united. To a man who enters form concentration, sound is disturbing. Hence the Buddha taught: "To a man who enters concentration, *jhāna*, sound is a thorn"'.

The Kvu idea that the mind in *jhāna* has a mental object and so cannot be simultaneously be aware of a sound seems to be the basis of the *Visuddhimagga* (329–330) saying that there is no consciousness through any of the five physical senses in any *jhāna*. In the developed Theravādin *Abhidhamma* of the commentaries, the mind is seen to take only one kind of sense object in any micro-moment. So one does not see and hear simultaneously, but the attention rapidly dances between the objects of the six senses (the five physical senses and mind), building up a *seemingly* simultaneous picture of the world.[16] When aware of a specific sensory object, if the awareness is strong enough, the mind actively responds to it with seven moments of what is called *javana*. It then briefly reverts to the background state of *bhavaṅga*, a kind of sub-conscious state which occurs uninterruptedly in dreamless sleep, before adverting to another specific sensory object. In the full 'absorption' (*appanā*) of *jhāna*, however, the usual stretch of seven moments of *javana* is extended: 'When absorption concentration has arisen, the mind, having once interrupted the flow of *bhavaṅga*, carries on with a stream of skilful *javana* for a whole night and for a whole day' (Vism 126). As the mind is focussed on only one specific object at this time, the mental object that is the retained impression (*nimitta*) of the meditative object, it cannot be aware of anything else at that time.

At Vin III 109,[17] Mahā-Moggallāna is criticized by other monks for saying that he had entered imperturbable (*āneñja*) *samādhi*, but still heard the sound (*sadda*) of trumpeting elephants. The Buddha says that 'that was *samādhi*, but it was not wholly purified'. The commentary (Vin-a 513) says that, while Mahā-Moggallāna had the eight attainments (four *jhāna*s and four formless attainments), he heard the sound between different attainments. That said, the 'imperturbable' (*āneñja*) *samādhi*s are only the fourth *jhāna* (DN I 76) and the four formless ones. Indeed, Vibh 135 explains that 'imperturbable' volitional activities are ones that belong to the formless level.

As explained at MN I 190, to be conscious of a particular kind of sensory object that is in the range of the relevant sense-organ, there needs to be the 'appropri-

16. Harvey 1995, 145–148, 162–164, 252–258.

17. Anālayo 2016, 41–32 and 2017, 138–140 discusses this and parallel passages in the *Āgamas*.

ate act of attention (*samannāhāra*)'. The level of absorption in which one does not register sounds for a stretch of time is more likely to happen in the fourth *jhāna.*

Of course in any meditative sit, the level of absorption may vary in depth, so hearing some sounds still allows that there also may be a few or many moments when there is full absorption, full *jhāna*. When this is the case, of course, one does not know whether there are any sounds that are hearable but not being heard! – and if one *checks* if this is the case, absorption on the *nimitta* will be *lost*. I have noticed, though, that when in a very well-concentrated meditative state, and sound from a passing car is noticed, I can sometimes 'see' attention being drawn away from the *nimitta* to the sound. This indicates that *not* being drawn away is also possible.

Overall, I would say that in the four *jhāna*s, when there is full, intent one-pointed concentration on the *nimitta* for a stretch of time, sounds may not be registered, just as they are not when one is intently absorbed in a book or a task. For example, when I was a postgraduate and was just about to give my first conference paper, I was intently concentrating, reading over my paper to get ready to give the talk. Lance Cousins crept up behind me and said 'Peter' three times, with increasing volume; I heard nothing until the third time he said it.

It is interesting that Bhikkhu Anālayo (2016, 40–46), while he argues that many early schools held that one cannot hear in *jhāna,* says (2016, 41):

> In what follows, my discussion of the possibility of 'hearing sound' intends the mental processing of externally created sound waves in such a way that these are understood for what they are. The question at stake is thus whether a mind immersed in the second absorption can at the same time recognize, for example, the sound of a bell being rung for being the sound of a bell.

This implies that, for him, the non-hearing of sound in *jhāna* is actually about not *recognising* any sound that is heard. However, his 2016 discussion of the matter is further developed in his 2017 work (137–150): here the wording of the above footnote, after 'at the same time', is changed to: 'while remaining in the absorption attainment, be conscious of a particular sound' (2017, 137). This means that there is no recognition of a specific sound as there one is not even *conscious* of it. Analāyo also helpfully comments:

> With the above discussion I certainly do not intend in any way to be devaluing experiences where absorption factors are present and one is still able to hear or think, which can indeed be very powerful and subjectively empowering. My intention is only to enable the drawing of a clear distinction between absorption proper of the type described in the early discourses and states bordering on this type of absorption. Such a distinction has considerable practical significance, simply because overestimating the absorbed condition of the mind that one has been able to reach can lead to underestimating the potential of going deeper. (2017, 146).

Moving between *jhānas* and developing the masteries

It is said that if one tries to move from one *jhāna* to the next without first having 'pursued, developed, cultivated and focussed well on the *nimitta*' of the *jhāna* one is in, one may not successfully enter the next *jhāna*, and also lose the one that one is in, like an inexperienced mountain cow venturing carelessly up into a higher area to eat, and losing her footing (AN IV 418–419). Analāyo (2014, 71) also cites a parallel *Āgama* passage[18] in Chinese which adds that someone who progresses to the second *jhāna* without realising it, and then worries about having lost first *jhāna*, then loses both.

Cousins says (1973, 123–124), 'It would appear that for the beginner absorption is only achieved for a very brief period', citing passages such as Vism 138–139, which says it initially lasts only one mind-moment. Indeed AN I 38 says that one can be in *jhāna* for a period as short as a finger snap. Cousins continues:

> The length of time depends at first upon the quality and length of the preliminary exercises but ultimately upon the skill acquired in the exercise of the five masteries (*vasitā*). These are first recorded as a list in the *Paṭisambhidā-magga*, but they have a much greater antiquity.[19] The intention appears to be to habituate the process of entry into (trance-like) absorption and to bring it completely under voluntary control.

Each *jhāna* is seen as a *vihāra* or 'dwelling' (DN III 265). To 'dwell' in or inhabit such a state for a time surely enables its qualities to strengthen, and to suffuse a person's body and mind. This helps them get to *know* each *jhāna*, how it feels, and the mode of being in it — which is a real contrast from the feel of the everyday mind, especially in a negative mode. This then enables a person to mindfully recall the qualities experienced in *jhāna* from everyday consciousness, and also to re-enter it more easily.

The five masteries, also called *vasīs*, are described at Patis I 99–100 and Vism 154–155. They involve gaining greater control over the experience of *jhāna*, lengthening its duration, and enabling one to enter and leave it at will. Lance Cousins compared the masteries to the ability that some people have of going to sleep at will and then waking after a set time. Their exercise is also like the mastery of a skill such as playing a piece of music.

The masteries are those of:

1. adverting (*āvajjanā*): the ability to quickly switch from one's normal everyday state so as to bring 'on-line' the factors needed for *jhāna*.
2. attaining (*samāpajjanā*): having entered a good meditative mode through adverting, the ability to enter and attain a particular *jhāna*. In time, this can be done quite quickly.
3. resolving (*adhiṭṭhānā*): the ability to remain in a *jhāna* for a predetermined period — comparable to the resolve to sit in meditation for a certain period of time, or to wake up at a certain time.

18. *Madhyama-āgama* 176 at *Taishō* I 714a2.

19. A reference here says: 'Patis I 100, 1–24 ; the *vasitā* are referred to with a somewhat variant terminology at SN III 263, 21–278, 17 ; AN III 311, 27-30 ; 427, 22–428, 6 . Also DN III 212, 17 ; AN I 94, 21 . Commentarial account at Vism IV 131–136.'

4. emerging (*vuṭṭhānā*): the ability to quickly and effectively withdraw from a *jhāna* at the end of a practice, and to do this with clear comprehension.
5. reviewing (*paccavekkhaṇā*): the ability to recall and review a practice one has just left and states attained in it. If the recollected state was a *jhāna*, one recollects the *jhāna* factors in turn, which aids later adverting to them due to making them more familiar, accessible and understood. It also involves detecting any flaws or defects in the meditation object or one's mental state. This helps in avoiding attachment and in preparing for the next stage. It is said to be like a person standing considering a person sitting, or sitting, considering a person lying down: observing, reflecting and understanding.

The masteries concern gaining the facility to enter and leave any meditative state. The aim is to develop them so that they can be exercised 'where, when, and for as long as one wishes, without difficulty' (Patis I 100), so that one could even enter and leave *jhāna* over a few seconds, perhaps even when pausing between movements and activities once strong mastery of *jhāna* is developed.

The five masteries relate to items found in the *suttas*. At AN IV 34, it is said that a monk having seven qualities 'exercises mastery over his mind (*cittaṃ vase vatteti*) and is not a servant of his mind', namely being skilled (*-kusala*) in: 1) *samādhi*, 2) attainment (*samāpatti-*) of *samādhi*, 3) duration (*ṭhiti-*) of *samādhi*, 4) emergence (*vuṭṭhāna-*) from *samādhi*, 5) pliancy (*kallita-*) for *samādhi*, 6) the range (*gocara-*) of *samādhi*, and 7) resolution (*abhināhāra-*) regarding *samādhi*. At AN III 427–428 six qualities that enable a monk to attain strength (*balata*) in *samādhi* are 2), 3), 4) plus practising carefully (*sakkaccakārī*) and persistently (*sātaccakārī*), and doing what is suitable (*sappāyakārī*). At AN III 111, 2) to 7) makes a monk able to split asunder ignorance. DN III 212 includes, in a list of pairs of qualities, skill (*kusalatā*) in attainment and emergence from attainment, two qualities also referred to at AN I 94. Similar qualities are discussed at SN III 263–278 in various combinations.

Jhāna and insight practice

The mind in fourth *jhāna* state is said to be:

> concentrated ... thoroughly purified and cleansed — stainless, without defilements, having become sensitive, workable, and steady, reaching a state that is imperturbable (*samāhite citte parisuddhe pariyodāte anaṅgaṇe vigātūpakkilese mūdū-bhūte kammaniye ṭhite ānejjappatte*) (DN I 76)

This is an extremely sensitive and potent state that can be used as a basis for various explorations and investigations, 'applied and directed to knowledge and vision'. It can be followed by: the six higher knowledges (*abhiññā*) or directly to the three knowledges (*tevijjā*), the last three of these, culminating in liberation; the four formless states then the cessation of perception and feeling — in the formless states, perception (*saññā*) becomes the focus of work, paralleling the work on feeling (*vedanā*) in the four *jhānas* (Cousins forthcoming, chs. 2 and 3).

Both the *jhānas* and other meditative states can also be used as the basis for, and the focus of, attention to the limitations of any conditioned state, even sublime ones. It is said that the four *jhānas*, the four immeasurables and first three formless states are 'doors to the deathless' (MN I 350–353 and AN V 343–347), like eleven exits from a burning house. One can contemplate any of these as 'conditioned and volitionally shaped (*abhisaṅkhataṃ abhisañcetayitaṃ*) ... impermanent and subject to cessation (*nirodha-dhammaṃ*)', so as to open the mind towards *Nibbāna*, which can lead to becoming an *Arahat* or Non-returner, as in these passages. In a similar way (MN I 435–436), one can review each of the *khandhas* in any of the *jhānas* or first three formless states (the last has too little operating perception to do a contemplation in it) as subject to the three marks, so that the mind turns away from these states towards the 'deathless element' as, 'This is the peaceful, this is the excellent, that is the stilling of all *saṅkhāras*[20] (*sabba-saṅkhāra-samatho*), the relinquishing of all attachments (*sabbūpadhi-paṭinissago*), the destruction of craving, dispassion, stopping, *Nibbāna*'.

To do such contemplations, the mind would need to step slightly aside from the relevant *samādhi*, to shift the focus from the *samādhi*'s object to the *samādhi* itself, and then to the 'deathless', while retaining most of the qualities of concentration, calm, mindfulness, etc. of the relevant state.

Conclusion

We have thus seen how the four *jhānas* are kinds of deep mental engagement in which great joy and happiness arise and are then transcended, a process of cleansing and purification. The mind lets go of negative qualities, develops positive ones, then progressively lets go of these to enter levels of greater subtlety. Doing this requires keen mindfulness, so that the process leads to the mind becoming very concentrated, gathered, unified, but also very alert, bright and sensitive. The concentration means that the focus can be entirely internal, with no input from the five senses, and the stilling of the body and mind mean that breathing can stop. *Jhāna* is at first only dipped into for short periods, but these can be extended as mastery is developed. In moving from one *jhāna* to another, there is a non-*jhānic* transition period. Also, the purifying effect of *jhāna* means that most of its gathered, alert stillness remains when the mind steps slightly aside from it into a more probing, exploratory mode, to develop incisive insight into the limitations of all conditioned states, including even the *jhānas*. Practising the *jhānas* schools the mind in letting go, and gathers and strengthens the resources for seeing the limitations of *any* conditioned state, however subtle. As with physical travel, inner 'travel' broadens the mind. One can discover new wonders, but also see that wherever one goes, the 'culture' there is conditioned and limited.

20. Which could here mean either volitional activities or conditioned things.

Abbreviations

Abhi-s	*Abhidhammathasaṅgaha*
AN	*Aṅguttara Nikāya*
AN-a	*Aṅguttara Nikāya* commentary
Dhp	*Dhammapada*
Dhs	*Dhammasaṅgaṇī*
DN	*Dīgha Nikāya*
DN-a	*Dīgha Nikāya* commentary
Kvu	*Kathāvatthu*
Kvu-a	*Kathāvatthu* commentary
Miln	*Milindapañha*
MN	*Majjhima Nikāya*
MN-a	*Majjhima Nikāya* commentary
Patis	*Paṭisambhidāmagga*
SN	*Saṃyutta Nikāya*
SN-a	*Saṃyutta Nikāya* commentary
Sn	*Sutta-nipāta*
Vibh	a *Vibhaṅga* commentary
Vibh-a	*Vibhaṅga* commentary
Vin	*Vinaya Piṭaka*
Vin-a	*Vinaya Piṭaka* commentary
Vism	*Visuddhimagga*

Bibliography

Anālayo, Bhikkhu. 2011. *A Comparative Study of the Majjhima-nikāya.* Taipei: Dharma Drum.

———. 2014. 'The First Absorption (*Dhyāna*) in Early Indian Buddhism: A Study of Source material from the *Majjhima-āgama*'. In *Cultural Histories of Meditation*, edited by H Eifring, 69–90. Oslo: University of Oslo.

———. 2016, 'The Second Absorption in Early Buddhist Discourse'. In *Buddhist Meditative Traditions: Dialogue and Comparison*, edited by Chuang Kuo-pin, 25–58. Taiwan: Dharma Drum Publishing Corporation.

———. 2017. *Early Buddhist Meditation Studies*, Barre, Barre Center for Buddhist Studies.

Bodhi, Bhikkhu. 1989. *The Discourse on the Fruits of Recluseship: The Sāmaññaphala Sutta and its Commentaries.* Kandy: Buddhist Publication Society.

———. 1993. *A Comprehensive Manual of Abhidhamma.* Kandy: Buddhist Publication Society.

———. 2000. *The Connected Discourses of the Buddha: A New Translation of the Saṃyutta Nikāya*, Boston, MA: Wisdom.

———. 2012. *The Numerical Discourses of the Buddha: A Translation of the Aṅguttara Nikāya*, Boston, MA: Wisdom.

Cone, Margaret. 2001. *A Dictionary of Pāli*, Part I. Oxford: Pali Text Society.
Cousins, L. S. 1973. 'Buddhist *Jhāna*: Its nature and attainment according to the Pali sources'. *Religion*, 3: 115–131. https://doi.org/10.1016/0048-721X(73)90003-1
———. 1992. '*Vitakka/vitarka* and *Vicāra*: Stages of *samādhi* in Buddhism and yoga'. *Indo-Iranian Journal* 35: 137–157. https://doi.org/10.1163/000000092794742673
———. forthcoming. *Buddhist Meditation: Old and New*. Edited by Sarah Shaw.
Ehara, N.R.M. Soma Thera and Mahinda Thera. 1977. *The Path of Freedom (Vimuttimagga)*. Kandy: Buddhist Publication Society.
Gethin, Rupert. 1998. *The Foundations of Buddhism*. Oxford: Oxford University Press.
———. 2008. *Sayings of the Buddha: New Translations by Rupert Gethin from the Pali Nikāyas*, Oxford: Oxford University Press.
Harvey, Peter. 1995. *The Selfless Mind: Personality, Consciousness and Nirvana in Early Buddhism*. Richmond: Curzon.
Horner, I. B. 1982 [1938]. *The Book of the Discipline, Vol. I*. London: Pali Text Society.
Johansson, Rune E. A. 1981. *Pali Buddhist Texts: An Introductory Reader and Grammar*. Richmond: Curzon.
Kuan, Tse-fu. 2005. 'Clarification of feelings in Buddhist *dhyāna/jhāna* meditation'. *Journal of Indian Philosophy* 33: 285–319. https://doi.org/10.1007/s10781-004-7378-6
———. 2008. *Mindfulness in Early Buddhism: New Approaches Through Psychology and Textual Analysis of Pali, Chinese and Sanskrit Sources*. London: Routledge.
Ñāṇamoli, Bhikkhu and Bhikkhu Bodhi. 1995. *The Middle Length Discourses of the Buddha: A New Translation of the Majjhima Nikāya*. Boston, MA: Wisdom.
Rhys Davids, T. W. 1973 [1899]. *Dialogues of the Buddha, Part I*. London: Pali Text Society.
Walshe, Maurice. 1987. *Thus Have I Heard: The Long Discourses of the Buddha*. London: Wisdom.
Webster, David. 2005. 'The weary Buddha, or why the Buddha nearly couldn't be bothered'. *Buddhist Studies Review* 22(1): 15–25.
Wijeratne, R.P. and Rupert Gethin. 2002. *Summary of the Topics of Abhidhamma and Exposition of the Topics of Abhidhamma*. Oxford: Pali Text Society.

Peter Harvey is Emeritus Professor of Buddhist Studies at the University of Sunderland. He co-founded, with Ian Harris, the UK Association for Buddhist Studies, has acted as its Secretary and President, and now edits its journal, *Buddhist Studies Review*. His books include *An Introduction to Buddhism: Teachings, History and Practices* (Cambridge University Press 1990 and 2013), *An Introduction to Buddhist Ethics: Foundations, Values and Issues* (Cambridge University Press 2000), and *The Selfless Mind: Personality, Consciousness and Nirvana in Early Buddhism* (Curzon, 1995), and he has published many papers on early Buddhist thought and practice and on Buddhist ethics. More recently, he edited an extensive integrated anthology of Buddhist texts, *Common Buddhist Text: Guidance and Insight from the Buddha* (2017) published for free distribution by Mahachulalongkorn-rajavidyalaya University, Thailand; in 2019, he published a booklet, *Buddhism and Monotheism* (Cambridge University Press).

— 3 —

Paths of Monastic Practice from India to Sri Lanka: Responses to L.S. Cousins' Work on Scholars and Meditators

Bradley S. Clough

In 1996, L. S Cousins published a groundbreaking piece on paths of monastic practice titled 'Scholar Monks and Meditator Monks Revisited' (Powers and Prebish 2009, 31–46). As the title suggests, this work reconsiders the role of two types of monks, doing so by closely analyzing a famous *sutta* (*Mahācunda Sutta*, A III 355–356) that depicts a strong dispute between *jhāyins* or 'meditators' and *dhammayogas*, whom scholarship has almost universally defined as 'scholars'. Because of this, almost all have interpreted this debate as the first sign in early Indian Buddhism of a great bifurcation in the *saṅgha* between those concentrating on book learning (*pariyatti*) and those concentrating on practice (*paṭipatti*) — a split that became more and more marked over the centuries until the division became more or less official in medieval Sri Lanka. Cousins convincingly contests this history, with one of his main points being that the *dhammayogas* were not at all just scholars. Like the meditators, theirs was a practical path that resulted in profound realization of the *Dhamma*, albeit a different path from that of the meditators. Cousins then goes even further, arguing that the split between scholars and meditators is not very evident in South Asian Buddhist history until the time of Buddhaghosa and thereafter. My intention here is to respond as fully as possible to Cousins' methods and conclusions, by offering evidence and arguments that sometimes support his work further and sometimes critique his work. This is done in the spirit of spurring on more discussions on this important, complex, and contested issue.

As this collection's title indicates, L. S. Cousins' scholarship gave special attention to issues pertaining to *magga* (in the sense of practical paths to *Nibbāna*) and *Dhamma* (in the sense of Buddhist teachings). Due to the work of Cousins and others, it is well accepted today that *Dhamma* does not refer only to scholastic teaching of doctrine, but also to teaching that applies doctrine to practical pursuits of *Nibbāna*. So, *magga* and *Dhamma* are intimately related. That said, it also seems apparent that modern Western scholarship on the Pali *suttas* and commentaries has led to a consensus that the well-known bifurcation of the monastic *saṅgha* into the separate vocations of scholar monks and meditator monks — with the former focusing fairly exclu-

Keywords: *dhammayoga, dhammakathika, jhāyin*, Mahācunda, *Nibbāna, Arahat, arahatta, bhāṇaka, atthapada, dhammānusārin, diṭṭhippatta, paññāvimutta, kāyasakkhin, ubhātobhāgavimutta*, learning, meditation, path, practice, tranquillity, wisdom, insight

sively on learning (*pariyatti*) and the latter on practice (*paṭipatti*) — that began to emerge in Sri Lanka perhaps as early as shortly after the time tradition has assigned to the first writing down of what became later known as the *Tipiṭaka* (*c.* 35 BCE), clearly has roots in several *suttas* that reflect relatively earlier events in India and Sri Lanka. So, put slightly differently, there is seen to be a significant separation between *magga* and *Dhamma* after all! This position is partially based on another event assigned by tradition to this time, namely a controversy between monks called *dhammakathikas* (*Dhamma*-preachers) and *paṁsukūlikas* (rag-robe wearers) (Mp I.92–3). I will argue that there are some good reasons for the scholarly consensus on this matter. However, I also maintain that Cousins' analysis of this issue, found primarily in his piece titled 'Scholar Monks and Meditator Monks Revisited' (Powers and Prebish 2009, 31–46), convincingly compels us to question the received wisdom here. His novel interpretations of a much-referenced dialogue found in one *sutta* (*Mahācunda Sutta*, A III 355–356) and careful exegeses of certain commentarial passages lead him to conclude that (1) a key encounter between two factions of monks called *dhammayogas* (Cousins (2009, 35) translates this as '[those] devoted to the *dhamma*') and *jhāyins* (meditators), which was mediated by the *Arahat* elder Mahācunda, is not at all a dispute between scholars and practitioners; and (2) this supposed dispute and split probably did not occur until several centuries after the events assigned to first century BCE. My intention here is to substantially respond both supportively and critically to Cousins' methods, arguments, and conclusions in this essay of his, with the hope of spurring on even further discussions about paths of monastic practice.

Cousins focuses first on three *suttas* from the *Aṅguttara-nikāya* that are attributed to this elder Mahācunda. Here he persuasively shows that these discourses are of special import, because (a) Mahācunda is consistently singled out as one of the Buddha's most outstanding disciples; and (b) the Buddha, quite unusually, is not present in them. Cousins allows that Mahācunda's pronouncements may be post-*parinibbāna*. In any case, he firmly establishes that Mahācunda was among the few leading authorities in the early *saṅgha* (pp. 31–34). With respect to the first two sermons of Mahācunda (*Katthī Sutta*, A V 157–161 and *Cunda Sutta*, A V 41–45), Cousins points to what he sees as Mahācunda's main concern, based in the *Vinaya*'s establishment of the fourth *parājīka* rule, with false and true claims about (1) having knowledge of *Dhamma*; (2) accomplishing self-development (*bhāvanā*) of body, morality, mind, and wisdom; and (3) attaining the first two combined (pp. 34–35).

These claims of attainment are the focus of the famous third of these *suttas* (*Mahācunda Sutta*, A III 355–356), which tells of a clearly hostile encounter between some monks 'devoted to the *dhamma*' (*dhammayoga*) and meditator (*jhāyin*) monks. Cousin's first ground-breaking argument challenges the practically unanimous scholarly interpretation, which simply echoes the commentator Buddhaghosa's glossing of the *dhammayoga* as a *dhammakathika* (*dhamma*-preacher). Most interpreters have also gone on to another uncritical assumption, which is that the word *Dhamma* in this discourse has the limited meaning of 'book knowledge', when closer examination would show that even Buddhaghosa, in his definition of *dhammakathika*, understood *Dhamma* in a much broader sense (p. 36). Cousins' assertion that scholars have incorrectly imposed a much later commentarial type upon a kind of practitioner presented in an early *sutta* could be construed as misleading, for it has been observed that the term *dhammakathika* appears frequently in the *suttas* and *Vinaya* (Deegalle 2006, 46). However, the term is almost always applied to the Buddha and his major *Arahat* disciples, who clearly were not mere scholastic teachers. Later on, Cousins will argue that it is not until after Buddhaghosa that the term *dhammakathika* became fairly synonymous with the monk whose duty was (more or less) books (*ganthadhura*).

I want to support Cousins' cautionary stance about scholarship that interprets an early *sutta* through the eyes of Buddhaghosa as an important response to a problematic in Buddhist studies that has been most fully identified by Charles Hallisey in a relatively recent discussion of the state of research on Theravāda traditions (Hallisey 1995). Hallisey addresses how Western Orientalists and Theravādins themselves have read ancient texts in modern times, pinpointing how Western pioneers in the field, originally and out of necessity, imitated traditional Buddhist hermeneutic patterns in their investigations by using commentarial literature primarily as a guide to the meaning of canonical texts. He labeled this tendency an 'elective affinity' between positivist Western historiography and Theravādin modes of self-representation. Another leading scholar of Theravāda traditions, Steven Collins, had identified the same problematic a few years earlier as a 'metaphysics of origins', wherein historians and Buddhists share the orientation that commentaries are not records of the growing understanding of a text; instead they are signposts for those in the present to recover meanings already promulgated in the past (Collins 1990, 43).[1]

Cousins next looks at the criticisms that the *dhammayogas* and the *jhāyins* level at each other. His interpretations of these critiques is based on a skill in which he was perhaps unsurpassed, a skill that combined an unmatched knowledge of the breadth of Pali literature with careful and precise etymological analyses that revealed a greater complexity and nuance in textual passages than had been recognized before. Here he says that the *dhammayogas*' criticism of the *jhāyins* is hard to translate because it plays on different meanings of the verb *jhāyati*, which can mean either to practice meditation or to think, often in an obsessive or imaginative way (p. 36). Cousins' analysis of this verb to reach a more precise understanding is novel and illuminating. In my own reading of this *sutta*, I have benefited from and share his perspective. If we look closely at the *dhammayogas*' criticism of the *jhāyins*, they are clearly pointing to the latter's repeated focus on the egocentric, prideful thought, 'We are meditators'. Based on his own take on the verb, Cousins' conclusion is that the *dhammayogas* were saying in effect that these so-called thinkers don't really think! I would suggest that an equally valid reading, also based on Cousins' revealing exposition on *jhāyati*, would be that these other monks

1. That this trend in the study of Pali materials extends into Buddhist Studies more widely is evidenced by discussions by two noteworthy scholars of Chan/Zen, Bernard Fauré (1994, 94 and 113) and Steven Heine (1995, 68).

imagine that they practise absorption in meditation, but actually they think obsessively about themselves. In Bhikkhu Bodhi's translation of this *sutta*, he too notes (pp. 1760–1761) that to see the *dhammayogas* as mere scholars/preachers is to read the considerably later split of the *saṅgha* into scholars and meditators back onto this earlier text, and he then goes on to suggest that they simply took a more cognitive approach to mastering the *Dhamma*. This suggestion supports my reading that the *dhammayogas* insinuate that the meditators should be thinkers like us (seeking union with the *Dhamma*), but their mode of thought is too self-obsessed. Based on my rendering here, I would suggest that perhaps a better translation of the *dhammayoga* than Cousins' 'devoted to *dhamma*' would be 'united (in the sense of "yoked") with *dhamma*'. 'Devoted' might be too suggestive of a faith-based path, such as that of the ideal type of practitioner known as the *saddhānusārin* ('follower of faith'), who is defined (M I 479) as one who has neither experienced (lit. 'touched with the body'; more on this key phrase later) the peaceful formless meditative liberations (*vimokhas*) nor eliminated any impure influxes (*āsava*) with insight, but does have faith in and love for the Tathāgata (often faith in and love for the *Dhamma* is added as well). And Cousins' own eventual conclusion that the *dhammayoga* achieves an important type of practical realization himself/herself also leads me to prefer 'united with (or even "practised in") the *dhamma*'.

As for the *jhāyins*' response to the *dhammayogas*, I share Cousins' interpretation that its long list of the negative mental qualities of the latter amounts to saying that these other monks are profoundly uncomposed. Cousins says the meditators are basically accusing them of not practising the *Dhamma*. I concur, but there is a problem here in that the main, overriding thesis of his piece is that the split between a group of practitioners whose duty is meditation (*vipassanādhura*) and scholars whose duty is books (*ganthadhura*) is nowhere found in the *Tipiṭaka* and isn't fully identified until Buddhaghosa at the earliest. But oddly, here he seems to quite explicitly acknowledge that in the minds of some early meditators, such a division already existed. He then goes even further, asserting that the meditators indeed intended to contrast practice (*paṭipatti*) and study (*pariyatti*). This also seems to contradict his main thesis. Indeed, he argues later that the issue of whether to prioritize *pariyatti* or *paṭipatti* does not arise until that famous first century BCE debate between the *paṁsukūlikas* and *dhammakathikas* in Sri Lanka, and even that event is barely mentioned in commentaries composed prior to the twelfth century CE (p. 41).

As I stated at the outset, there are some good reasons to support the scholarly consensus, opposed by Cousins, that there is some solid evidence in the *suttas* and *Vinaya* of a nascent vocational division between scholars and meditators. Again, one piece of evidence for this is Cousins' own point about the meditators in the *Mahācunda Sutta* accusing their opponents of failing to practise the *Dhamma*. Furthermore, if we find any indications of scholar monk versus meditator monk divergences before Buddhaghosa, his thesis is diminished. If we accept the traditional accounts that Buddhaghosa primarily relied upon the somewhat earlier Sinhalese commentaries, we could modify things a bit and say that any textual evidence for conflict prior to the first centuries CE would work against his case. Let us briefly consider a few such pieces of evidence.

Dhp 19–20 states that one who recites much of texts but does not put them into practice does not partake in the religious quest. Such a person is likened to a cowherd who counts other people's cattle. By contrast, one who recites little but knows that his/her mind is liberated, through the elimination of passion, ill-will, and unawareness, lives in accord with the *Dhamma* and partakes in the religious quest. These verses clearly indicate that the person of practical realization is far superior in progress along the path to the person of much learning but no practical realization. This is echoed by even more straightforward declarations found in the Dhp, such as verse 372, which indicates that the highest realization of liberating gnosis is only achievable within the experience of meditative absorption:

> There is no *jhāna* for one without wisdom (*apaññassa*),
> And no wisdom for one who does not practice *jhāna* (*ajhāyato*).
> For whom there is both *jhāna* and wisdom,
> He is surely in the presence of *nibbāna*.[2]

S II 115–118 compares the monk who sees dependent origination and *Nibbāna* but is not quite an *Arahat* to a thirsty person who knows there is water in the well but has no bucket or rope to taste it. Here 'tasting water' almost certainly indicates fully experiencing *Nibbāna* (or 'knowing that the mind is liberated', as our Dhp passage put it). Later we will examine further how sometimes sensory activities like 'tasting' or 'touching' can be metaphors for 'experiencing', even up the point of *Nibbāna*. Likewise, statements about knowing water is present but not being able to taste it indicate the condition of understanding *Nibbāna* or mental liberation but not fully experiencing it. Again, one who practically embodies the *Dhamma* is superior to the one who understands the nature of it. However, we must also consider here another key conclusion that Cousins will reach in his analysis of the *Mahācunda Sutta*, which is that both the *dhammayoga* as a person who knows the *Dhamma* and the *jhāyin* as a person who experiences at least a taste of *Nibbāna* as part of absorption in meditative states, have gained profound realizations. The clear implication here is that they engage in different practices, but in the end reach very important transformational attainments; the difference between them is only a matter of degree or level of understanding. Whereas in our Dhp passage the difference between the reciter and the meditator is quite significant, in S II 115–118 all that is said about the monk of knowledge is that he is not quite an *Arahat*![3]

At D III 219 and 305 and elsewhere (Netti 7; Vibh 324 and 753), there is a well-known epistemological distinction made between (1) wisdom based on hearing or learning (*sutamayā-paññā*), which comes from another's testimony; (2) wisdom based on thinking (*cintāmayā-paññā*), which arises from personal reflection; and (3)

2. I am indebted to Peter Harvey for this rendering of the verse.
3. Bhikkhu Bodhi, in his exegesis of this text, has also concluded that the difference here is only a matter of slight degree (2003, 51 ff.)

wisdom based on mental cultivation or meditation (*bhāvanāmayā-paññā*). The clear superiority of the third kind of insight over the first two is emphasized by the Netti's statement that it only comes about after the path is completed and the Vibh shows us that *bhāvanā* here definitely means meditation (and not some other form of self-cultivation) by saying that the third level of wisdom can only be achieved by one practised in the eight states of meditative attainment (*samāpanna*). So here again we see distinctions drawn between those whose understanding is limited because it is only heard from others (like the reciter counting another's cows), those whose understanding is higher because of a personal grasp of the *Dhamma* (like the not-quite *Arahat* whose understands *Nibbāna*, etc.), and those whose understanding is even higher (perhaps even complete) because it stems from meditative experience (like the one who touches *Nibbāna* or knows their own mind is liberated). Alternatively, one could say again that these distinctions are only ones of degree, in that all three have achieved some level of transformative insight (*paññā*).

To get back to our Dhp passage's sharp distinction between reciters and those who put the *Dhamma* into practice, there is one last area of evidence that indicates a vocational choice made by some members of the early *saṅgha* to focus on learning and preservation of the *Dhamma* to such an extent that meditation practice was almost surely elided. In the *suttas* and *Vinaya* there are many references to reciters (*bhāṇakas*), who appear to be scholarly specialists focused almost entirely if not exclusively on textual (first oral, then written) knowledge. In the main account of the First Council shortly following the Buddha's *parinibbāna* (Vin II 284–308), which describes his disciples' efforts to preserve his *Dhamma*, it is said that the *Vinaya* and four *nikāyas* (the *Khuddaka-nikāya* is not mentioned) were each assigned separately to a leading *Arahat* elder, who then began his task by regularly reciting his section with his pupils. This is perhaps our best piece of evidence that a marked degree of specialization was present at an early stage. This account is also one of many places in the early texts where there is reference to specialization in the memorization and recitation of three kinds of scriptural traditions, namely the preacher of or expert in the *Dhamma* (*dhammakathika* or *dhammadhara*; this indicates specialization in the *suttas*, since the terms appear to be synonymous with *suttantika* and *suttadhara*), expertise in the *Vinaya* (*vinayadhara*) and expertise in classificatory lists (*mātikādhara*[4])[5] Most scholars agree that the classification of scripture into three collections attests to the existence in the *saṅgha* of three types of specialists (Frauwallner 1956, Lamotte 1958, 164 and Collins 1990, 91). This position is supported by inscriptional evidence from Bhārhut, Sāñcī, Kārlī, Bodh-Gāyā, and Amarāvatī (all dating to roughly second century BCE) that distinguishes between *sutta* experts and *Vinaya* experts (Lamotte 1958, 164). Furthermore, when we look at early inscriptions from Sri Lanka (third century BCE to first century CE), we

4. These lists were most likely the basis for the later *Abhidhamma* literature, although commentaries define experts in these as 'experts on two lists', which are the *Vinaya*'s *pātimokkhas* for monks and nuns.

5. M I 221 and 223: A I 117, A II 169–70, A III 179, A V 16, 349, and 352; Vin I 119, 127, 337, and 339, Vin II 8, 55, 75–6, and 299.

find more evidence of even greater specialization, in their references to *Saṃyutta-*, *Majjhima-*, and *Aṅguttara-bhāṇakas* (Deegalle 2006, 42). Back in India, inscriptions at Nāgārjunakoṇḍa refer to 'masters (ācariyas) who are preachers (*osakas* [=*desakas*]) and reciters (*vācakas*)' of the *Dīgha-* and *Majjhima-nikāyas*, as well of the five *mātukas* (=*mātikās*) (Deegalle 2006, 41). While the dating of the Nāgārjunakoṇḍa inscriptions (third to fourth centuries CE) is prior to Buddhaghosa, it is roughly contemporaneous with the Sinhalese commentaries, so it is a bit uncertain if we can use them to contest Cousins' dates for the beginnings of textual specialization. When we get to Buddhaghosa, we find his commentaries filled with more references to this higher degree of textual specialization. But this is when Cousins says that textual specialization really began, so we cannot use these works to refute his thesis further. Still, one cannot resist citing the best piece of evidence that some textualists definitely did not meditate, which is a story in Vism 95–97 that tells of a *Majjhima-bhāṇaka* in Sri Lanka who spends all of his days memorizing *suttas*. But, when he finally takes up meditation, he vows to never look at the *suttas* again! This could be an old story predating Buddhaghosa and the Sinhalese commentaries, but we cannot say for sure.

It is also seen that by the second century BCE there were monks who focused on all three collections or at least all of the *nikāyas* together! Inscriptions from Bhārhut, Sāñcī, Mathurā, and Kānheri refer to *bhāṇakas*, (in a generic sense, not as reciters of a particular collection), knowers of the *Tipiṭaka*, and knowers of the (four or five) *nikāyas* (Lamotte 1958, 164, Schopen 1997, 30–31, and Deegalle 2006, 40–41). It is almost inconceivable that experts in such a wide range of scripture could have had any time for meditation.

It is hoped that a strong case has now been made that points to the fairly early existence of institutions in Buddhism where many monks focused probably exclusively on preservation of substantial textual traditions.[6]

To get back to analyses of the *Mahācunda Sutta*, we are at the point of the end of the text, where Mahācunda himself responds to the feud by admonishing the two groups for their harsh criticisms, to the point where they undermine each other and betray the monks' mission of the welfare and happiness of humans and gods. He preaches complimenting each other, with the *jhāyins* being praiseworthy as rare ones who 'dwell touching the deathless' (more on this interesting phrase later) and the *dhammayogas* being praiseworthy as rare ones who 'pierce meaningful terms and see'.

Curiously, Cousins offers no interpretation of the phrase about the *jhāyins*. His focus on this last part of the *sutta* is almost entirely on the phrase describing the *dhammayogas*, with special attention to the word 'meaningful terms'[7] (*atthapada*). His analysis of this exemplifies one of Cousins' great strengths: careful, rigorous,

6. Further bolstering of this case is the common position held by Finot (1901), Bareau (1963), Frauwallner (1956), Ray (1994), and Gombrich (1988 and 1990) that from a very early stage, there was a priestly elite in Buddhism, based on Brahmanical models, whose sole task was custodianship of the texts.

7. In his editing of this article, Peter Harvey correctly noted that *atthapada* is in the singular in this passage.

and deeply learned philologically-based explication that yields ground-breaking results with respect to both a more precise understanding of texts and a clearer understanding of early Buddhist history.

We will turn to his exegesis of this key phrase shortly, but let us first turn to Cousins' reading of the *sutta*'s conclusion, where he assigns great importance to Mahācunda's reconciliatory response above all else. For Cousins, the significance of this *sutta* lies almost entirely in Mahācunda's indications that the practices of the *dhammayogas* and *jhāyins* are not at all irreconcilable. On the contrary, these seemingly disparate approaches both eventuate in profound realizations of the *Dhamma*. Cousins argues that what is noteworthy here is this great *thera*'s conclusion that the two practices are not in conflict with each other. Therefore, the upshot is that this *sutta* provides key evidence that there was as yet no significant split between these two groups within the *saṅgha*.

In my analysis, this conclusion problematically ignores some of what takes place earlier in the *sutta*. While I think that his revealing of the likely meaning of *atthapada* compels us to rethink interpretations of this *sutta* that point only to conflict with no resolution, to me one cannot put aside the situation described earlier in the *sutta* where the two groups in this setting very divisively voice major points of contention and stark opposition to each other. While we will never know for certain if Mahācunda's attempt at reconciliation convinced the two sides to accept each other's approaches to the *Dhamma* as valid and valuable, the fact that the *sutta* ends without any indication of responses by the two groups might well suggest that here no mutual acceptance was reached. The fact also remains that these two sides were at some point quite opposed to one another, at least in some places. Furthermore, if the practices of these two groups were meant to be complementary, why would Mahācunda simply urge them towards praise and not at least suggest the possibility of fulfilling the *Dhamma* by taking up each other's practices? Simply urging praise is yet another indication that this was more a matter of keeping different factions within the *saṅgha* at peace. Cousins says that those who see conflict here are being overly literal and speculative. I see no reason not to take the account at face value and also fail to see how his conclusions are any less speculative.

In regarding early scriptures like this as reflecting real historical events, which both Cousins and I are doing, we must take into account at least briefly recent trends in the study of Buddhism in South Asia (and elsewhere), which of course include the cases made by Gregory Schopen and others in his footsteps, who seek to establish that when we read scriptures, what is being presented to us is not at all descriptive of historical events, but is rather completely prescriptive of the highest ideals promoted by the religion. It is maintained that while other kinds of sources, such as archeological and inscriptional ones, do indeed show us what monks (and laypeople) were actually doing at one time, the concerns of the *Tipiṭaka* lie elsewhere. In terms of my own interpretation of the *sutta* under consideration, I would reply that if it were solely concerned with ideals, Mahācunda's response may well represent the cherished ideal in Buddhism of avoiding a split in the *saṅgha* (*saṅghabheda*). Indeed, Mahācunda's explicit concern here is that the monks not betray each other and thus compromise their mission. But as we have just noted, this *sutta* ends without any indication of whether or not communal harmony was reached. Furthermore, if *suttas* only prescribe ideals, why would this one spend so much time describing an evident case of genuine discord in the *saṅgha*? Disagreement and division are usually not ideals of a religious community, or at least they are not in this context, where we know that Buddhism frowns on *saṅghabhedas*. I would say that when we read the *Tipiṭaka*, we find it chock full of diversity and controversy concerning almost all issues, ranging from meditation and other forms of practice[8] to monastic disciple and doctrinal interpretation. This indicates to me that dismissing the possibility that these texts at least sometimes reflect historical developments in practice is far too drastic and uncritical,[9] and that if we read the texts with a nuanced eye, we will find both described histories of practice and prescribed ideals.[10] Buswell and Gimello (1992) address the relationship between ideals and historical practices in their influential work on Buddhist paths to liberation, where they maintain that even ideals of spiritual progress that mostly apply only analogically and normatively still prompt practitioners to mold their own experiences according to these ideals of their religious heritage (p. 11). They also say that,

> Ideal goals presumed to have been achieved by spiritual exemplars at the source of a tradition have often been objectified, codified, and made available to ordinary practitioners throughout Buddhist history. Ideals about the path provide detailed orderings of experience and serve as explicit guides to practitioners for achieving the archetypal goal (pp. 10–11).

Let us now turn back to Cousins' analysis of the phrase 'pierce meaningful terms (*atthapadaṃ*) and see', to see both how he might have replied to the Schopenian stance on scripture, and more importantly, how he shows that the *dhammayogas* went far beyond just a scholastic approach to understanding the *Dhamma*. First pointing to Buddhaghosa's reading of this phrase as connoting an understanding of the path with accompanying insight, Cousins maintains that Mahācunda implies that the *dhammayogas* achieve a profound experiential level of realization. To support this (and presumably also show that he is not simply imposing a later commentarial reading on this *sutta*), he goes on to examine the few times that *atthapada* is found in the *nikāyas*. In one case (A II 189–190), *atthapada* is defined as a peaceful wisdom beyond reasoning (*takka*), which reminds him of the frequent nikāyan definition of the phrase 'profound *dhamma* that is hard to see and awaken to' as something beyond doctrine in any superficial sense (Cousins 2009, 37). Indeed, when the

8. For a lengthy treatment of diversity and controversy with respect to Theravādin theory and practice of paths leading to *Nibbāna*, see Clough 2012.

9. Wynne (2007, 5) calls the position that all religious literature is strictly normative 'a dubious *a priori* assumption'.

10. Hallisey (1990, 208), in a discussion about the *Vinaya*, makes the important point that understanding the thought-world or *mentalité* of the larger texts is crucial to reconstructing the historical context of early Buddhist monasticism.

Buddha himself use this phrase, he seems to refer to nothing less than his experience of enlightenment itself! In a second case (A IV 362), 'piercing meaningful terms' refers to a stage of hearing and discussing the *Dhamma* that goes beyond the meaning of words. So again, it is clear that the *dhammayoga* goes beyond verbal knowledge. I might add here that this indicates going beyond *sutamayā-paññā* to *cintamayā-paññā* at the least. Finally, at Dhp 101–102, a single meaningful term is contrasted with thousands of senseless words by virtue of it bringing the peace of *Nibbāna*.[11]

So, Cousins concludes, the main point of the three *Aṅguttara-nikāya* discourses featuring Mahācunda is that both meditation and devotion to the *Dhamma* can lead to rarefied realizations of the Buddha's teaching. This conclusion is another reason why I would render *dhammayoga* as 'united with the *Dhamma*' or at least 'practised in the *Dhamma*'. His conclusion about *dhammayoga*s and *jhāyin*s in the third *sutta* also connects with the first two *sutta*s' concerns about the equal value of deep understanding of *Dhamma* and deep meditative experience. This interpretation also makes the common understanding — which is again that these *sutta*s are early indicators of division and even conflict between scholars and meditators that would surface even more markedly in later history — not quite impossible but speculative at best. To reiterate my position on this, I would still maintain that a clear conflict is described in the *Mahācunda Sutta*. However, due to Cousins' careful, learned and convincing work on this, I would say that this conflict was not between scholars and meditators, but between two different kinds of practical path-followers who both can achieve profound (and perhaps nibbānic?) experiential realizations of the *Dhamma*.

Cousins goes on to say that regardless of when one thinks the *sutta*s were collected (be it right after the *Mahāparinibbāna*, not until fifth century CE, or somewhere in between), these three *sutta*s show that a scholar versus meditator split was certainly not a reality in or shortly after the Buddha's time and perhaps may not even have been the case several centuries later. At the very least we have one very important elder who held that both cognitive insight and meditative experience are valuable to Buddhism. Perhaps with conscious attention to the Schopenian stance, Cousins concludes that these *sutta*s may well present an ideal that values both cognitive and meditative approaches to the *Dhamma*, but that ideal is found throughout South Asian Buddhist history.

In support of Cousins' insightful case, I would put forth that the *dhammayoga*s' approach bears a striking similarity to the path to *Nibbāna* associated in the *nikāya*s with a type of practitioner who begins the path as a '*dhamma*-follower' (*dhammānusārin*), continues it as a 'vision-attainer' (*diṭṭhippatta*), and completes it as 'one liberated by wisdom' (*paññāvimutta*). I acknowledge at the outset that path schemes assigned to such noble persons (*ariya-puggala*) may well represent ideals, but here I would simply point the reader back to our discussion of the relationship

11. Cousins' interpretation of these verses is based on his reading of the verb *upasammati* and the Dhp commentary's explanation of the verses. Cousins also points out that in Pali *attha* usually means both 'meaningful' and 'connected to the goal'.

between ideals and historical practices. I base the parallel I'm drawing on the similarities between Cousins' *dhammayoga* and the *dhamma*-follower/vision-attainer, and on the connections between the *dhammayoga* as one who 'sees the path by penetrating it with insight' (*paññāya ativijjha*) and the *paññāvimutta*. Just as Cousins showed the false equation of the *dhammayoga* and the scholar, I would like to critique the modern scholarly tradition, which began with de la Vallée Poussin's definition of this type as 'purement et surtout intellectuelle', and completely lacking in experiential verification of Buddhist truths (de la Vallée Poussin 1937, 189–190). This misreading is almost surely based on reading the purely commentarial category of the *sukkhavipassaka* ('one whose wisdom is dry', Vism 666, 702) back onto this canonical type. The *Kīṭāgiri Sutta* (M 70), the *locus classicus* on noble persons' paths, describes the *dhamma*-follower as one without both experience of the formless states of liberative absorption reached through tranquillity meditation (*samatha-bhāvanā*) and any destruction of the impure influxes (*āsavas*).[12] Nevertheless, this person's wisdom has been cultivated to the point of complete acceptance of the *Dhamma* with a measure of appreciative understanding (S V 377).[13] With continued development of wisdom, the *dhamma*-follower will acquire the *dhamma*-eye (*dhammacakkhu*), the key realization that all things both arise and fall, so as to be a stream-enterer (*sotāpanna*), one in the stream that inevitably results in *Nibbāna*. This person still lacks joyous wisdom (*nahaspaññā*), swift wisdom (*javanapaññā*), and liberation (*vimutti*), but is bound for complete awakening (*saṁbodhiparāyana*).

According to the *Kīṭāgiri Sutta*, one at the stage of a vision-attainer has destroyed some *āsavas* and 'penetrated the *Tathāgata*'s teaching by means of wisdom'. Again, this is extremely reminiscent of the *dhammayoga* who 'sees the path by penetrating it with wisdom', just mentioned above. Furthermore, the vision-attainer fully understands anything that the Buddha has declared and can implement any teaching in practice. Hopefully it is clear by now that this noble person has profound practical realization of the *Dhamma* that is in line with Cousins' depiction of the *dhammayoga*. Such a one is far beyond a scholastic or 'purement intellectuelle' grasping of the *Dhamma*.

When the vision-attainer achieves the *Arahat*'s fruit (*arahattaphala*), this noble person becomes a *paññāvimutta*. Many points in the *nikāyas* (such as S II 119–123 and A II 83) establish that the main practice leading to *paññāvimutti* is meditation on the arising and passing away of the five aggregates. There is a further connection (though it is not one made by the *suttas* themselves) that I would like to make, which is that this meditation is well known as part of the fourth and final foundation of mindfulness (*satipaṭṭhāna*) discussed in other *suttas*. So, one could argue that

12. I wish to thank Peter Harvey (personal communication, April 12 2018) for correcting a mistake of mine here. I had taken the reference to 'states of liberative absorption' (*vimokhā*) to refer to the entire series of eight states, but Harvey made it clear the text specifies only the formless ones.

13. I am indebted to Peter Harvey (personal communication) for help with the phrase *dhammā paññāya mattaso nijjhānaṃ khamanti*. For his full treatment of the *dhamma*-follower, see Harvey 2013, pp. 30ff.

the practical path of the *dhammayoga* culminates in insight meditation (*vipassanā-bhāvanā*), which is far beyond the practice of scholarship alone.

Many *suttas*, including the *Kīṭāgiri*, say that the *paññāvimutta* destroys all *āsavas* by means of great wisdom. However, when it comes to the first five of the six higher knowledges (*abhiññā*) and peaceful formless liberations stemming from tranquillity meditation, this one has never 'touched [them] with the body' (S II 119–123). This phrase indicates experiencing the highest *jhāna*-based states,[14] and quite closely matches the terminology that Mahācunda uses to praise the attainments of the *jhāyins*! The only difference is that the first phrase refers to experiencing the higher knowledges and formless liberations (*vimokhas*), whereas the second phrase refers to experiencing the 'deathless' or *Nibbāna* itself. But we will see momentarily that the type of noble person that I associate with the *jhāyin* first touches the formless *vimokhas* with the body and then at the end of the path touches *Nibbāna* with the body. This touching of the deathless or *Nibbāna* with the body is somewhat reminiscent of tasting the water from the proverbial well of the *Arahat*'s *Nibbāna*, as found in the *Kosambī Sutta* discussed earlier. To me is it clear that these sensory metaphors point to tangible experiences of meditative states like the formless *vimokhas* and the meditative realization of *Nibbāna*.

The type of noble person that I see paralleling the path of the *jhāyin* is that of the 'body-witness' (*kāyasakkhin*), who eventually becomes 'one liberated in both ways' (*ubhātobhāgavimutta*). This path of the *jhāyin* is quite different from that of the *dhammayoga*, but our analysis here will further support Cousins' conclusion that both paths lead to profoundly realized understanding of the *Dhamma*. However, we must also recognize significant difference here, in that one arrives via knowledge (but not mere intellectual book-knowledge) and the other via meditative cultivation of body and mind. As the name indicates, the body-witness has the central accomplishments of 'bodily' touching or deeply experiencing either the four *jhānas* and four formless *samāpattis* (according to A IV 451–453) or the previously mentioned (*jhānas* then) formless *vimokhas* (according to the *Kīṭāgiri Sutta*). Despite the slight discrepancy in definitions, the important point here is that these attainments are more based in *samatha-bhāvanā* and less based in *vipassanā-bhāvanā* than is the case of the path of practice culminating in *paññāvimutti*. Remarkably, one relatively early *nikāya* passage says that the body-witness achieves nothing less than the destruction of all *āsavas* (in other words, attains *Nibbāna*) simply by dwelling in the *samāpatti* of cessation of perception and feeling (*saññā-veditā-nirodha-samāpatti* or *nirodha-samāpatti* for short) that immediately succeeds the formless ones (A IV 451–453).[15] Some com-

14. Since the first five *abhiññās* are only attained in the fourth *jhāna*, one can assume that this type of practitioner never goes higher than the third *jhāna* and, as we will see, there are good reasons to think that s/he doesn't typically gain absorption into any of the *jhānas* at all.

15. As Peter Harvey points out (personal communication), these passages state that destruction of the *āsavas* in this state also involves the practitioner's 'seeing with wisdom'. This is certainly true, but here we should also note previous scholarship that has raised concerns about how any kind of *paññā*, in the sense of discriminating insight, is possible when the mind is said to be entirely without perception and feeling! For a key discussion of this dilemma, see Paul Griffiths 1981.

mentaries say the same (Sv 514 and Ps 188-189[16]). Likewise, a later *nikāya* passage and several commentaries speak of the body-witness as one who 'touches *jhāna* and afterwards attains *Nibbāna*' (Patiș V 58-61 and 63; Ps III 188–189; Vism 660; and Mp II 190). So, the body-witness seems here to be the exact equivalent of the *jhāyin*: both touch *Nibbāna* (cessation, the deathless) with their bodies! It appears that according to these texts at least, the final goal can be reached primarily through *samādhi* and *samatha–bhāvanā*. These texts also say that body-witnesses are those of great tranquillity who meditate on *dukkha* with the *samādhi*-factor being outstanding. So, here we see a clear distinction between the path of the *jhāyins* or body-witnesses and that of the *dhammayogas* or *paññāvimuttas*.

A IV 454 gives even more evidence that some felt that *Nibbāna* could be realized in the midst of meditative absorption, when it defines *nirodha-samāpatti* as '*Nibbāna* in this life'. M I 203–204 describes the four *jhānas* and four formless *samāpattis* culminating in *nirodha-samāpatti* as higher and more excellent than all other attainments, including knowledge and vision acquired through insight. M I 456 says that in *nirodha-samāpatti* the ten fetters (*saṁyojanas*) are removed.[17] The removal of all fetters indicates that *arahatta* and *Nibbāna* have been achieved. The *Bahuvedanīya Sutta* (M I 396) also presents *nirodha-samāpatti* as the culmination and epitome of the path to liberation; the Buddha calls it the most extreme and refined pleasure.

Getting back to the body-witness, it must be acknowledged that despite the plethora of evidence just given, the most frequent description of this noble person in other *suttas* (e.g. M I 477–479) is that while such a one does destroy some *āsavas*, this one is still a trainee (*sekha*) with much diligent effort remaining before detachment and *Nibbāna*, which only come when one is beyond training (*asekha*) and has become 'liberated in both ways' (*ubhātobhāgavimutta*).

Regarding the one with two liberations, there are also a wide variety of differing definitions in the *suttas* and commentaries.[18] The most frequent view is that the first liberation comes when one frees oneself from the form-realm *jhānas* and goes on to master the more peaceful formless-realm *samāpattis*. The second and final liberation comes when the *ubātobhātobhāga* sees with insight that these *samāpattis* too are unsatisfactory, impermanent, and without self, and are thus unworthy of attachment. Only in this way are the *āsavas* destroyed. But interestingly, this goal is primarily reached by first touching with the body (that key phrase again!) each of the *jhānas* and *samāpattis*. Only then does one detach oneself from them by means of wisdom. To be clear, this very same process is said to result in experiencing the 'deathless' and 'directly visible *Nibbāna*' (see A IV 453–455 and elsewhere). Once again, we see that like the *jhāyin* who 'touches the deathless with the body, the

16. Interestingly, this latter reference is to the *Kīṭāgiri Sutta* itself, which in contrast to A V 451–453 says that the body-witness destroys only some *āsavas* because of limited wisdom.

17. Peter Harvey (personal communication) notes that in some passages (e.g. A III 194) practitioners emerge from *nirodha–samāpatti* as non-returners, not *arahants*.

18. See Clough 2012, 35–38 for a full treatment of the varying definitions.

ubhātobhāgavimutta also is one who tangibly realizes the deathless (as is indicated by another sensorial phrase that indicates experience, 'directly visible *Nibbāna*').[19]

In comparing the *dhammayoga/paññāvimutta* type with the *jhāyin/ubhātobhāgavimutta* type, the paths are ultimately similar in the end, in that they both culminate with deep insight into the three marks of existence (*tilakkhaṇa*). This supports Cousins' conclusion about the paths of both the *dhammayoga* and the *jhāyin* having profound realizations of the *Dhamma*. However, the two paths are otherwise notably disparate, in that one path leads to the goal almost exclusively through cognitive *vipassanā*-based insights, whereas on the other path one travels almost entirely through *samatha*-based experiences. Gombrich (1997, chapter IV) points further to the conflicting nature of these paths, speculating that the presence of the wisdom-based path threatened the viability of the tranquillity-based path. He rhetorically asks: why would one continue the very hard work of pursuing entrance into each *vimokha* when one could realize their true nature through wisdom alone? When we combine these last points with all of the other evidence that we have marshalled throughout this chapter, we must challenge Cousins' conclusion that the three *Aṅguttara-nikāya suttas* under examination point to a reconciliation between two monastic groups. There is little doubt that when one surveys all of the early Pali works and the second *sutta* (*Cunda Sutta*, A V 41–45) under consideration here, one finds plentiful support for combining absorption in the *jhānas* and *samāpattis* and wisdom. However, when one looks at the first *sutta* under consideration here (*Katthī Sutta*, A V 157–161, which portrays one monk questioning the authenticity of another monk's claimed meditative attainment) as well as the third *sutta* under consideration (*Mahācunda Sutta*, A III 355–356, where the *dhammayogas* and *jhāyins* have a major dispute), and then combines them with the ample evidence I have given here about tensions and differences between knowledge-based paths and paths based on tangibly experiencing states of meditative absorption, it is also quite clear that there were strong opposing voices in the *saṅgha* which opposed reconciling the paths of emphasizing concentration and that of emphasizing wisdom.[20] I fully concur with Cousins that the divisions I have pointed out are for the most part not between scholars and meditators, with the notable exceptions of monks who from early times specialized in recitation and memorization of texts to the point of probably eliding meditation completely. I also agree with him that the divisions are between two different practical ways of entering and following paths that both culminate in the most profound realization of *Nibbāna* by means of wisdom.

There is much else to commend in Cousins' further treatment of the scholar and meditator issues in his chapter. His arguments on the whole are so persuasive to me that I have little to add in the space I have remaining. So, I will limit myself to brief summaries. The next issue that he discusses is the famous first century BCE Sri

19. For another important discussion of how the *kāyasakkhin/ubhātobhāgavimutto* are defined in Pali texts, see Wynne 2002.

20. Peter Harvey (personal communication) offers an interesting possibility, which is that at least some disputes like this may have been caused by lesser members of different groups who were not yet free of the fetter (*saṃyojana*) of clinging to their own practices (*sīlabbata-parāmāsa*)!

Lankan encounter between the *dhammakathikas*, who promoted learning (*pariyatti*) above all else, and the *paṁsukūlikas*, who advocated practice (*paṭipatti*) above all (Cousins 2009, 41). He convincingly challenges the scholarly consensus that this event marked the victory of learning and the rejection of practice. Both parties strongly and commonly agreed that in that troubled time, the very survival of the *saṅgha* was at stake, and so they absolutely needed to debate for the sake of both preserving the institution of Buddhism (*sāsana*) and ensuring that practical realization (*paṭivedha*) of the *Dhamma* would be possible in the future. Cousins also rather newly points out that the account may overemphasize divisions between the two groups because it was largely composed in the twelfth century CE by scholar monks, who by that point were indeed much at odds with practising meditators. But while the learning of texts certainly did become the much-preferred vocation over meditation in Sri Lanka's future, there is much indisputable evidence that both vocations survived well for a very long time.[21]

Finally (pp. 42–43), Cousins investigates when the tradition in Sri Lanka first clearly drew lines between the practice of village-dwelling monks specializing in book-learning and teaching and that of forest-dwelling monks specializing in insight meditation. Through a careful and thorough surveying of the Pali commentaries, he shows that this formal vocational division was not much recognized prior to Buddhaghosa. He also observes in Buddhaghosa's writing something pertinent to my arguments here, which is that this great commentator at at least one point (Ps III 147) speaks of a formal division between meditators specializing in *samatha* and those specializing in *vipassanā*.[22] So, the division I have argued for still existed at this time. However, Cousins, following his line of argument, asserts that there is no real difference here, since the two approaches must be combined to realize *arahatta*. The examples of no less illustrious figures than Moggallāna and Sāriputta show that at least some did combine the two since the early days, even if the combination didn't occur until the culmination of paths that started out very differently.

In conclusion, I would simply say that it is clear that in addressing contested issues about the relationship between scholar and meditator monks in South Asian Buddhism, as it is presented in Pali literature, Cousins has done much remarkably ground-breaking work, especially considering that his focus is more or less on one rather short *sutta*! This is further testimony to the great importance of his scholarship not only on *magga* but also on related topics such as the origins of Buddhist meditation and the nature of the *jhānas* (Cousins 1973, 1984, and 1996). I hope I have contributed to furthering conversation on this issue, by responding to Cousins' work on this with well-evidenced arguments that mostly support but occasionally

21. Please see Clough 2012, chapter five, for an in-depth examination of the history of vocational diversity in the Sri Lankan *saṅgha*. There is much there that would further support Cousins' position on this issue.

22. Cousins does also note, however that in Buddhaghosa's *Paramatthajotikā*, there is a sharp distinction made between the village-dweller who lives with his teachers and spends his time memorizing large parts of the *sutta*- and *Vinaya-piṭakas* and the forest-dweller completely focused on realization (*sacchikiriyā*).

critique his methods and conclusions. In the end, I think we agree on much more than we disagree. While he chose to emphasize the end of different paths which finally must culminate in wisdom, I have cited most of the fairly rare examples where the role of wisdom seems diminished. I have chosen to emphasize the varying approaches taken right up to just before the realization of *arahatta* or *Nibbāna*, the final goal that in almost all cases does require insight into the *tilakkhaṇas*. May discussions on this rich, complex, and important topic be continued!

Abbreviations

A	*Aṅguttara-nikāya*
Mp	*Aṅguttara-nikāya* commentary (*Manoratha-pūraṇī*)
Dhp	*Dhammapada*
D	*Dīgha-nikāya*
M	*Majjhima-nikāya*
Ps	*Majjhima-nikāya* commentary (*Papañca-sūdanī*)
Netti	*Nettipakaraṇa*
Paṭis	*Paṭisambhidāmagga*
S	*Saṃyutta-nikāya*
Sv	*Dīgha–nikāya* commentary (*Sumaṅgala-vilāsinī*)
Vibh	*Vibhṅga*
Vin	*Vinaya-piṭaka*
Vism	*Visuddhimagga*

Bibliography

Bareau, Andre. 1963. *Recherches sur la Biographie du Buddha dans les Sūtrapiṭaka et les Vinayapiṭaka Anciens*. Paris: Publications de l'Ecole Francais d'Extreme-Orient.

Bodhi, Bhikkhu. 2003. 'Musīla and Nārada Revisited: Seeking the Key to Interpretation'. In *Approaching the Dhamma: Buddhist Texts and Practices in South and Southeast Asia*, edited by Anne M. Blackburn and Jeffrey Samuels, 47–68. Seattle: Pariyatti Editions.

———. 2012. *The Numerical Discourses of the Buddha: A Translation of the Aṅguttara Nikāya*. Boston, MA: Wisdom Publications.

Buswell, Robert and Robert Gimello, eds. 1992. *Paths to Liberation: The Mārga and Its Transformations in Buddhist Thought*. Honolulu: University of Hawaii Press.

Clough, Bradley S. 2012. *Early Indian and Theravāda Buddhism: Soteriological Controversy and Diversity*. Amherst, NY: Cambria Press.

Collins, Steven. 1990. 'On the Very Idea of the Pāli Canon'. *Journal of the Pāli Text Society* XV: 89–126.

Cousins, L.S. 1973. 'Buddhist Jhāna: Its Nature and Attainment According to the Pali Sources'. *Religion* 3: 115–131. https://doi.org/10.1016/0048-721X(73)90003-1

———. 1984. 'Samatha-yāna and Vipassanā-yāna'. In *Buddhist Studies in Honor of Hammalava Saddhatissa*, edited by Gatare Dhammapala, Richard Gombrich and K. R. Norman, 56–68. Nugegoda, Sri Lanka: University of Sri Jayewardenpura.

———. 1996. 'The Origins of Insight Meditation'. In *The Buddhist* Forum *Vol. IV*, edited by Tadeusz Skorupski, 35–58. New Delhi: Heritage Publishers.

———. 2009. 'Scholar Monks and Meditator Monks Revisted'. In *Destroying Māra Forever: Buddhist Ethics Essays in Honor of Damien Keown*, edited by John Powers and Charles S. Prebish, 31–46. Ithaca, NY: Snow Lion Publications.

Deegalle, Mahinda. 2006. *Popularizing Buddhism: Preaching as Performance in Sri Lanka*. Albany: State University of New York Press.

Fauré, Bernard. 1994. *Chan Insights and Oversights: An Epistemological Critique of the Chan Tradition*. Princeton, NJ: Princeton University Press.

Finot, Louis. 1901. *Rāṣṭrapālaparipṛcchā*. Saint Petersburg: Imperial Academy of Sciences.

Frauwallner, E. 1956. *The Earliest Vinaya and the Beginnings of Buddhist Literature*. Rome: ISMEO.

Gombrich, Richard. 1988. *Theravāda Buddhism: A Social History from Ancient Banares to Modern Colombo*. London: Routledge and Kegan Paul. https://doi.org/10.4324/9780203310878

———. 1990. 'Recovering the Buddha's Message'. In *The Buddhist Forum*, edited by Tadeusz Skorupski, 5–20. London: SOAS.

———. 1997. *How Buddhism Began: The Conditioned Genesis of the Early Teachings*. New Delhi: Munshiram Manoharlal Publishers.

Griffiths, Paul. 1981. 'Concentration or Insight: The Problematic of Thervāda Buddhist Meditation-Theory'. *Journal of the American Academy of Religion* 49(4): 606–624. https://doi.org/10.1093/jaarel/XLIX.4.605

Hallisey, Charles. 1990. 'Apropos the Pāli Vinaya as a Historical Document'. *Journal of the Pali Text Society* XV: 197–208.

———. 1995. 'Roads Taken and Not Taken in the Study of Theravāda Buddhism'. In *Curators of the Buddha: The Study of Buddhism Under Colonialism*, edited by Donald Lopez, 31–61. Chicago, IL: University of Chicago Press.

Harvey, Peter. 2013. 'The *Saṅgha* of the Noble *Sāvaka*s, with Particular Reference to Their Trainee Member, the Person "Practising for the Realization of the Stream-entry-fruit"'. *Buddhist Studies Review* 30(1): 3–70. https://doi.org/10.1558/bsrv.v30i1.3

Heine, Steven. 1995. *Dōgen and the Koan Tradition: A Tale of Two Shobogenzo Texts*. Albany: State University of New York Press.

Lamotte, Etienne. 1958. *Histoire du Bouddhisme Indien des Origines a l'ere Saka*. Louvain: Publications Universitaires, Bibliotheque Du Museon.

Ray, Reginald A. 1994. *Buddhist Saints in India: A Study in Buddhist Values and Orientations*. Oxford: Oxford University Press.

Schopen, Gregory. 1997. *Bones, Stones and Buddhist Monks: Collected Papers on the Archaeology, Epigraphy, and Texts of Monastic Buddhism in India*. Honolulu: University of Hawaii Press.

Wynne, Alexander. 2002. 'An Interpretation of Released on Both Sides (*ubhāto-bhāga-vimutti*) and the Ramifications for the Study of Early Buddhism'. *Buddhist Studies Review* 19(1): 31–40.

———. 2007. *The Origin of Buddhist Meditation*. New York: Routledge. https://doi.org/10.4324/9780203963005

Bradley Clough is an independent scholar who previously held positions in Buddhist Studies at Bard College and the University of Montana and an endowed chair in Comparative Religion at the American University in Cairo. His primary research interests in soteriology and monasticism led to his book, *Early Indian and Theravada Buddhism: Soteriological Controversy and Diversity* (Cambria Press 2012), as well as many other publications. Other South Asian Buddhist themes he has addressed in his work are pilgrimage and sacred space, nonviolence and altruism, textual authority, family life, spiritual biography, just-war theory, and meditative accomplishment. He also co-edited with David Blanks the volume titled *Humanist Perspectives on Sacred Space* (American University in Cairo Press, 2011).

— 4 —

'I'm Not Getting Anywhere with my Meditation ...': Effort, Contentment and Goal-directedness in the Process of Mind-training

AMARO BHIKKHU

This article draws on the teachings of the Pali Canon and the contemporary lineages that are guided by its principles. In particular, reference is made to the author's mentors in the Thai Forest Tradition. It explores the respective roles of goal-directed effort and contentment in the process of meditative training, and skilful and unskilful variations on these. Effort is needed, but can be excessive, unreflectively mindless, unaware of gradually developed results, or misdirected. Contentment can be misunderstood to imply that skilful desire has no role in practice, and lead to passivity; though it is needed to dampen down an over-energized mind, or motivation rooted in aversion or ambition, and comes from insight-based non-attachment. Right effort avoids the craving to become or to get rid of, but is associated with a skilful *chanda*/desire that is an aspect of the *iddhi-pāda*s, the Bases of Spiritual Power. Mindfulness aids the balance of energy and concentration in the Five Faculties, and the energizing and calming qualities in the Seven Factors of Enlightenment. In the end, from practising Dhamma in a way that is truly in accordance with Dhamma (*dhammānudhamma-paṭipatti*), progress naturally flows from seeing and becoming Dhamma.

1. Introduction

The words that form the start of the title of this article will be familiar to most people practising meditation as well as those who are also teaching it in the West. We are a pragmatic and goal-oriented culture, in the main part, so we put effort into our jobs, our education, even our holidays and we expect to get certain results. We can even assume that such results are our right: 'I've paid my fee, now I want my product.' In many circumstances this is a fair enough assumption, but when it comes to mind-training things are far less predictable. We can put in years of effort, faithfully and with vigour, yet feel that we are 'not getting anywhere'. Our experiences fail to match the glorious simplicity and fluidity of the stages of accomplishment as described in the *suttas*, or the colourful and insightful stages of realization as described by our mentors or by contemporary popular authors. 'What's going wrong?' we ponder, 'why am I still struggling with *x*, *y* or *z* after all these years?'

Keywords: Right Effort, right and wrong striving, expectation, contentment, goal-directedness, passivity, *chanda*, *bhava-taṇhā*, *vibhava-taṇhā*, *dhammānudhamma-paṭipatti*, *iddhi-pāda*, *bojjhaṅga*

As this is such a common experience it seems worthy of exploration and elucidation. This essay will investigate some of the aspects of the relationship between Right Effort (*sammā-vāyāma*), and the related qualities (at least within Buddhist practice) of being focused on and directed towards a goal (*niṭṭhā*), and contentment (*santosa*). Both halves of this pair have positive and negative characteristics, according to the Buddha's teachings, thus it will be helpful to begin by clarifying what these various attributes are.

2. The positive aspects of exertion and goal-directedness

2.1. *Sutta* quotes regarding striving

Throughout the *suttas* of the Pali Canon there are abundant passages that highlight the fact that the Buddha's Path is one pursued through making effort. For example (at S 43.12):

> And what, bhikkhus, is the path leading to the unconditioned? Here, bhikkhus, a bhikkhu generates desire (*chandaṃ*) for the nonarising of unarisen evil unwholesome states; he makes an effort (*vāyamati*), arouses energy (*viriyaṃ*), applies his mind and strives (*padahati*) ... for the abandoning of arisen evil unwholesome states ... for the arising of unarisen wholesome states ... for the continuance of arisen wholesome states, ... he makes an effort, arouses energy, applies his mind and strives: this is called the path leading to the unconditioned.
>
> (Bhikkhu Bodhi trans., p. 1376, Pali added)[1]

There are these four right strivings or exertions (*sammā-ppadhāna*); they are the four qualities that constitute the fabric of Right Effort. In another discourse (S 49.1), after describing these four, the Buddha uses the compelling image of the sloping of the River Ganges inexorably toward the sea: 'Bhikkhus, just as the River Ganges slants, slopes and inclines towards the east, so too a bhikkhu who develops and cultivates the four right strivings, slants, slopes and inclines towards Nibbāna.' (Bhikkhu Bodhi trans., p. 1709).

In the *Cetokhila Sutta*, 'The Wilderness of the Heart' (M 16.26 (M I 103)), the Buddha describes the energetic engagement required in the development of the 'Four Bases of Spiritual Power' or 'Roads to Success' (*iddhi-pāda):*

> He develops the basis for spiritual power consisting in concentration due to zeal (*chanda*) and determined striving (*-padhāna-saṅkhāra-*); ... consisting in concentration due to energy (*viriya*) and determined striving; ... consisting in concentration due to [purity of] mind (*citta*) and determined striving; ... consisting in concentration due to investigation (*vimaṃsa*) and determined striving. And enthusiasm (*ussoḷhi*) is the fifth. (Ñāṇamoli and Bhikkhu Bodhi trans., p. 197)

2.2. 'Just do it!'

As a more colloquial expression of the same principle, of the necessity for application of effort in the realization of one's spiritual aspirations, here are some words

1. Except where otherwise stated, translations are the author's own.

from Ajahn Chah, one of the twentieth century's masters of Buddhist meditation:

> So, do it. Follow it until you know in pace with the breath, concentrating on the breath using the mantra '*Buddho*'. Just that much. Don't let the mind wander off anywhere else. At this time have this knowing. Do this. Study just this much. Just keep doing it, doing it in this way. If you start thinking that nothing is happening, just carry on anyway. Just carry on regardless and you will get to know the breath. ...
>
> Our practice of the heart is like this. After a moment, it's thinking of this and thinking of that. It is agitated and mindfulness is not continuous. But whatever it thinks about, never mind, just keep putting forth effort. It will be like the drops of water that become more frequent until they join up and become a stream. Then our knowledge will be encompassing. Standing, sitting, walking or laying down, whatever you are doing, this knowing will look after you.
>
> Start right now. Give it a try ... if you try too hard, you won't be successful; but if you don't try at all, then you won't be successful either.
>
> (*The Collected Teachings of Ajahn Chah*, pp. 259-262)

3. The negative aspects of exertion and goal-directedness

The application of energy and goal-directedness are, accordingly, shown to be essential elements of the Buddhist Path, so why do so many long-term meditators report disappointment with their efforts in their practice?

3.1. Excessive 'wrong striving'

A pertinent example to begin this section is the story of Bhikkhu Ānanda. On the eve of the First Council, he needed to be liberated himself before he could attend, and he had not yet attained full liberation. So he meditated strenuously in order to end all traces of greed, hatred and delusion. Though, try as he might, he could not do so. So he decided to lie down to sleep. Before his head hit the pillow and after his feet left the ground, in the few moments when he had relaxed his trying-too-hard mind-set, he attained liberation (CV XI.1.3.6).

The first problem is thus that of attaching to the idea of liberation, and 'trying too hard' to achieve it. The Buddha described his own zealous but ultimately fruitless efforts (for example at M 36.20-30 (M I 242–246)), culminating in the insight that:

> I thought: 'Whatever brahmans or contemplatives in the past ... in the future ... in the present are feeling painful, racking, piercing feelings due to their striving, this is the utmost. None is greater than this. But with this racking practice of austerities I haven't attained any superior human state ... Could there be another path to Awakening?' (Bhikkhu Ṭhānissaro trans.)[2]

In a similar vein there is the story in the Vinaya discipline (MV V.1.14–17) where the delicately reared Soṇa Koḷivisa goes at his walking meditation with such gusto that his feet are torn open and bleeding. The Buddha summons him to offer advice

2. https://www.accesstoinsight.org/tipitaka/mn/mn.036.than.html

and uses the example of tuning the strings of a *vīṇā*:

> '[W]hen the strings of your *vīṇā* were neither too stretched nor too loose, but fixed in even proportion, did your *vīṇā* have a good sound then ...?'
>
> 'Yes, venerable sir.'
>
> 'Just so, Soṇa — too eager a determination conduces to agitation, and too weak a determination to slothfulness (*accāraddhaviriyaṃ uddhaccāya saṃvattati, atilīnaviriyaṃ kosajjāya saṃvattati*).
>
> Therefore, Soṇa, be steadfast in cultivating evenness of determination, establishing harmony of your mental powers. Let that [balancing] be the object of your contemplation.'

Venerable Soṇa realized arahantship after receiving this teaching.

Even though roughly 2,500 years have gone by since that incident, we are still making the same mistakes. Here is some advice from some experienced teachers of this era, addressing the area of misdirected urgency and enthusiasm. Firstly, Ajahn Mun, the reviver of the Forest Meditation tradition in Thailand, in the late nineteenth and early twentieth century:

> Wanting what's good, without stop:
> That's the cause of suffering.
> It's a great fault: the strong fear of bad.
> 'Good' and 'bad' are poisons to the mind,
> like foods that enflame a high fever.
> The Dhamma isn't clear
> because of our basic desire for good.
> Desire for good, when it's great,
> drags the mind into turbulent thought
> until the mind gets inflated with evil,
> and all its defilements proliferate.
> The greater the error, the more they flourish,
> taking one further and further away
> from the genuine Dhamma.
>
> *The Ballad of Liberation from the Five Khandhas*, (Bhikkhu Ṭhānissaro trans.)

And then his student, Ajahn Chah:

> [W]e're all impatient, we're in a hurry. As soon as we begin we want to rush to the end, we don't want to be left behind. We want to succeed. When it comes to fixing their minds for meditation some people go too far. They light the incense, prostrate and make a vow, 'As long as this incense is not yet completely burnt I will not rise from my sitting, even if I collapse or die, no matter what, I'll die sitting.' Having made their vow they start their sitting. As soon as they start to sit, Māra's hordes come rushing at them from all sides. They've only sat for an instant and already they think the incense must be finished. They open their eyes for a peek, 'Oh, there's still ages left!' ...
>
> Actually it isn't necessary to go through all that. To concentrate means to concentrate with detachment, not to concentrate yourself into knots. But maybe we read the scriptures about the life of the Buddha, how he sat under the Bodhi tree and determined to himself:

> 'As long as I have still not attained Supreme Enlightenment I will not rise from this place, even if my blood dries up.'
>
> Reading this in the books you may think of trying it yourself. You'll do it like the Buddha. But you haven't considered that your car is only a small one. The Buddha's car was a really big one, he could take it all in one go. With only your tiny, little car, how can you possibly take it all at once? It's a different story altogether.
>
> Why do we think like that? Because we're too extreme. Sometimes we go too low, sometimes we go too high. The point of balance is so hard to find.
>
> (*The Collected Teachings of Ajahn Chah*, pp. 281–282)

Lastly Ajahn Sumedho, Ajahn Chah's senior Western student, offers his perspective on this area:

> The religious journey is what we call 'inclining to Nibbāna': turning away, inclining away from the sensory world to the unconditioned. So it's a very subtle kind of journey. It's not something you can do as an act of will; you can't just say, 'I'm going to realize the truth' or: 'I'm going to get rid of all my defilements and hindrances, get rid of lust, hatred, all my weaknesses!' — and actually do it. People who practise like that usually go crazy. ... (Ajahn Sumedho, *The Anthology*, Vol. 1. p. 75)

3.2. Mindless/unreflective 'wrong striving'

The second aspect of what can be called 'wrong striving' is not trying too hard but rather making effort in an unreflective, unmindful way. In this mode, persistence is applied in a more balanced way but it is non-reflective insofar as it is based on obedience to a method out of blind devotion: 'The teacher taught me to do mindfulness of breathing so I have been doing it this way for twenty years, even though I don't see any benefits'; or 'I have been a monk now for thirty years so I must be closer to liberation, mustn't I? After all, the Buddha said, "Patient endurance is the supreme practice for incinerating defilements"' (D 14.3.28).

There is a laudable patience and well-intentioned subservience to a system but, lacking wise reflection (*yoniso manasikāra*), investigation of qualities (*dhamma-vicaya*) or examination of results (*vimaṃsa*), those patient efforts can well be experienced as fruitless. To use the Buddha's words, when describing the fruitlessness of his own ascetic practices (at S 4.1):

> I know these penances to gain the deathless —
> Whatever kind they are — to be as vain
> As a ship's oars and rudder on dry land.
>
> (*The Life of the Buddha*, Bhikkhu Ñāṇamoli trans., p. 36)

It is like the gentleman who recently spent many hours driving round and round the M25 (the 117 mile long motorway that circles London) whilst believing he was on his way from London to Liverpool; he kept waiting for the familiar signs of approaching home territory but lacking them he just kept going until exhaustion overtook him. He failed to notice that the signs were repeating themselves. It is very easy with meditation practice to be similarly driving long and hard down the wrong road, failing to read the signs and taking appropriate action.

Another example is diligently boiling sand in the hope of getting rice; no matter how much effort we expend, or how careful we are in measuring it out and placing it on the hob, the efforts will not produce rice because the ingredients do not provide that possibility.

Thus if a meditation practice is labelled 'liberating' or if a teacher tells us 'this is right for you' or that 'this is the best method for the development of insight', it should be recognized that these are only words. It is up to the individual to test them out and see if the process does indeed work that way — is it rice or sand in the packet?

3.3. Perception of poor or absent results

The third aspect of 'wrong striving' is believing in the perception of having received poor results, or indeed that the mind is worse since beginning to practise meditation. A frustrated or disappointed meditator can judge their practice as having been fruitless when, without their realizing it, the truth is far from that. As a culture we have strong habits of self-deprecation, and anything like acknowledging one's achievements or reflecting on one's success (as in *cāgānussati,* recollection of one's generosity) is regarded with suspicion and looked upon with distaste as self-praise, inflatedness or pomposity. For example, there was a dedicated and long-term practitioner in the UK who habitually introduced himself as 'a failed Buddhist', albeit with a smile.

The Buddha, however, pointed out that progress can be happening without our realizing it. He gives a telling simile for this of the impressions slowly formed in the handle of a tool (at A 7.71):

> When a carpenter sees the impressions of their fingers and their thumb on the handle of their adze, they do not know, 'I have worn away so much of the adze handle today ...' but when it has worn away, they know that it has worn away. So too, when one is intent upon development, even though one does not know, 'I have worn away so much of the mental outflows (*āsava*) today ... but when they are worn away, one knows that they have worn away.'

One of the key elements in this simile is the noticing of the marks on the handle; it seems we fail to appreciate these, usually because we are too busy attending to the affairs of the day. For a meditator who makes the judgment that, 'I'm not getting anywhere in my practice', it is often enough to ask them, 'If you think back five years, ten years, and you compare how you receive criticism, or how you deal with angry feelings now, as compared to then — how do they compare? Has there been a change?' It is like asking the carpenter to look at the handle of the tool that they have used for many years; they usually see at once, 'Oh yes! I am much less defensive/reactive than I used to be.' It can be as obvious and distinctive as the fingermarks pressed into the wood.

Another common experience is: 'Since I started practising my mind has been getting worse.' Here is Ajahn Sumedho giving a description of the effects of meditation in the opening stages of a year-long solitary retreat in Thailand:

> I remember an experience I had in my first year of meditation in Thailand. I spent most of that year by myself in a little hut and the first few months were really terrible. All kinds of things kept coming up in my mind; obsessions, fears, terror and hatred. I'd never felt so much hatred. I'd never thought of myself as someone who hated people, but during those first few months of meditation it seemed I hated everybody. ... Then one afternoon I started having this strange vision — I thought I was going crazy, actually — I saw people walking off my brain. I saw my mother just walk out of my brain and into emptiness, disappear into space. Then my father and my sister followed. I actually saw these visions walking out of my head. I thought, 'I'm crazy! I've gone nuts!', but it wasn't an unpleasant experience. The next morning, when I woke from sleep and looked around, I felt that everything I saw was beautiful. Everything, even the most unbeautiful detail, was beautiful. I was in a state of awe. The hut itself was a crude structure, not beautiful by anyone's standards, but it looked to me like a palace. The scrubby-looking trees outside looked like a most beautiful forest. Sunbeams were streaming through the window onto a plastic dish, and the plastic dish looked beautiful! (Ajahn Sumedho, *The Anthology*, Vol. 1 p. 157)

Such accounts demonstrate that the process of spiritual development can be a struggle, but its fruits, in a mind-clearing letting go, can arise when one does not expect them.

3.4. Misdirection of effort

The last of the negative aspects of energy and goal-directedness to address is what might best be termed 'misdirection of effort'.

3.4.1. 'I shouldn't be experiencing anger etc. ...' — the need for peaceful coexistence/ radical acceptance

This misdirection has a couple of different dimensions, the first of which is more mundane and can be summed up in the assumption, for example: 'I shouldn't be experiencing this anger, this restlessness, and busy thoughts; I have to get rid of them so I can practise properly. After all, it says this in the *suttas* repeatedly ...'; such as in the many passages describing the mindful overcoming of the five hindrances and entry into the four *jhānas* (e.g. at M 27.18 (M I 181)).

Essentially what we are doing when we formulate such intentions ('I have to get rid of the hindrances (*nīvaraṇa*) so I can practise properly') is that we are endeavouring to climb over *this* in order to get to *that*; that is to say we unconsciously cultivate fear and aversion towards the hindrances that we think of as 'ours', with the aim of overcoming them and becoming a 'me' in some imagined better place beyond 'them', purified, happy and free.

This rejection based on fear and aversion tends to exacerbate and reify the perceived obstacles. In contrast, ironically, the best way to respond to the arising of the hindrances is to begin by radically, whole-heartedly accepting their presence — essentially to have loving-kindness (*mettā*) for them. In understanding the use of the word 'accepting' here, it is important to distinguish between 'liking' and 'loving'. Ajahn Sumedho speaks on this issue thus:

> *Mettā* means you love your enemy; it doesn't mean you like your enemy. If somebody wants to kill you and you say, 'I like them', that is silly! But we can love them, meaning that we can refrain from unpleasant thoughts and vindictiveness .... That's what we mean by *mettā*.
>
> *Mettā* means not creating problems around existing conditions, allowing them to fade away, to cease. For example, when fear comes up in your mind, you can have *mettā* for the fear — meaning that you don't build up aversion to it, you can just accept its presence and allow it to cease. ...
>
> But with *mettā*, you are not blinding yourself to the faults and flaws in everything. You are just peacefully co-existing with them. You are not demanding that it be otherwise. So *mettā* sometimes needs to overlook what's wrong with yourself and everyone else — it doesn't mean that you don't notice those things, it means that you don't develop problems around them. You stop that kind of indulgence by being kind and patient — peacefully co-existing. (Ajahn Sumedho, *The Anthology*, Vol. 2, pp. 33–36)

Such peaceful co-existence, not dwelling in aversion, is an embodiment of the radical acceptance of the way things are in the present (*paccuppanna-dhamma*). Again ironically, it is through this kind of radical acceptance that the hindrances seem to be most effectively met, counteracted and transcended.

3.4.2. 'We are not doing something now in order to become ...'

The second type of misdirection of effort has a more supramundane focus, to do with attachment to and identification with time, place and feelings of self (*ahaṃ-kāra*, 'I-making', *mamaṃ-kāra*, 'mine-making'). It can be best characterized by the idea that: 'I need to do something now in order to become enlightened in the future'. Ajahn Sumedho reflects on this area:

> 'If I practise hard, I might get enlightened in the future' is another self-illusion, isn't it? ... This is a creation: words, concepts about me as a person, what I think I am and what I should do in order to become. This is all about time and personality, not Dhamma. When I get caught in personality and the sense of time, there is no *sati* anymore, but there is judgment, hope, despair — all this arises. So then *sati* is the gate to the Deathless. That is why learning to recognize, to realize this natural state of being, isn't about becoming enlightened in the future. It is about being: being the light itself, being awareness itself now, recognizing, not trying to become someone who is aware anymore, but just this, this sense of openness, receptivity, attentiveness. (Ajahn Sumedho, *The Anthology*, Vol. 4, p. 90)

4. The negative aspects of contentment

4.1. 'Buddhists shouldn't have desires'

In the *Dhammacakkappavattana Sutta* (S 56.11), and in many other places, the Buddha points to craving (*taṇhā*) as being the cause of suffering, the painful and stressful (*dukkha*):

> This is the Noble Truth of the cause of *dukkha*: it is craving that leads to new birth and is bound up with pleasure and lust, ever seeking fresh delight, now here, now there;

namely craving for sense pleasure, craving for existence/becoming, and craving for non-existence/annihilation (non-becoming).

On account of *taṇhā* being named as the cause of *dukkha*, the erroneous message gets transmitted that all forms of intending, directing of attention, desiring, choosing, initiating of action, decision-making, indeed goal-directedness in all its forms should be demonized; they are all grouped together as aspects of *taṇhā* and thereby condemned as part of the problem of suffering. It as if by getting involved and choosing some action one pollutes reality; as Shelley puts it in Adonaïs:

> Life, like a dome of many-coloured glass,
> Stains the white radiance of Eternity

Or as in T.S. Eliot's poem 'The Love Song of J. Alfred Prufrock':

> Do I dare
> Disturb the universe?

It is a commonplace for teachers of Buddhism to be asked, often with plaintive earnestness, 'Buddhists shouldn't have desires, should they? I'm not supposed to want anything, isn't that right?' Or in the workplace, when one's colleagues are aware that one is a practitioner of Buddhism, 'You can't ask for a raise — you're supposed to be a Buddhist!' In the media Buddhist values are regularly represented as fundamentally passive; for example, Buddhist teacher Ethan Nichtern describes the views of the philosopher and cultural critic Slavoj Žižek:

> [F]or Žižek, Buddhism, in the context of a Western consumer culture, allows the individual to believe he is transforming his mind without actually changing the conditions of suffering that shape the individual's society.
> (Ethan Nichtern, *Huffington Post*, 20-8-2010)

The demonizing of all forms of volition and desire then makes it seem as though Buddhist practice should be thoroughly passive, a quietist one of only watching and 'not doing', as if any action was interfering with 'the way things are'. This misinterpreting can then easily lead to, again, a well-intentioned but ultimately harmful result — to wit a freezing of one's natural responsivity to time, place and situation, creating a falsely abstracted would-be observer who is unable to adjust that which is being observed without feeling as though they are doing something wrong and 'not following the practice'.

This is an unfortunate misunderstanding but, even though it is common, it should be surprising that it happens at all. Why? Because of the evidence of the life of the Buddha himself — the most eminent of enlightened beings. To be enlightened is not to be devoid of intentions and interests, or the ability to act, otherwise the Buddha would have never moved from the foot of the Bodhi tree and spent decades teaching others. This fact is clear evidence that our intentionality is part of 'the way things are' rather than an intrusion upon it.

In addition — as with the reification of the hindrances through aversion toward them — with respect to activity, contending against it to try to achieve some sort of über-abstracted observer state only serves to reify the role of action and engagement as the apparent disturber. One fails to realize that it is the attitude of contention that is causing the disturbance rather than the sense objects themselves. As Ajahn Chah puts it:

> It's the same with *saṅkhārā*. We say they disturb us, like when we sit in meditation and hear a sound. We think, 'Oh, that sound's bothering me.' If we understand that the sound bothers us then we suffer accordingly, if we investigate a little deeper, we will see that it's we who go out and disturb the sound! The sound is simply sound, if we understand like this then there's nothing more to it, we leave it be. (*The Collected Teachings of Ajahn Chah*, pp. 6-7)

So, the sounds of the world and action in the world need not be a disturbance. Or, to put it another way and to quote Seng-ts'an, in his 'Verses on the Faith Mind': 'When you try to stop activity to achieve passivity your very effort fills you with activity.' (Richard B. Clarke trans.)

4.2. Passivity/habituation/numbness

There is another aspect of the unskilful application of contentment that will be instructive to explore, this one related to the subject of §3.2, above — the making of efforts in an unreflective, unmindful way.

This is the issue of habituation to following a practice in a state of spiritual numbness — a blind belief that the method or practice will liberate and purify one if one just adheres to the behaviours required. It is a plodding along half-heartedly, dully content with the apparent lack of benefit. Whereas the subject of §3.2, above, dealt with making vigorous effort but in a fruitless way, and was thus related to the *nīvaraṇa* of restlessness (*uddhacca*), the present subject addresses practising with an unskilfully placid contentment and is thus related to the *nīvaraṇa* of sloth and torpor (*thīna-middha*). It is a kind of contentment but it is one that can be obstructive since it eschews reflection on experience; it leads to engaging with meditation as a learnt behaviour that is followed out of mere habit, rather than being a method of genuine transformation. It is a kind of inept *saddhā* unbalanced by the faculty of *paññā*.

That said, there are times when a lessening of mental sharpness can be appropriate:

> I also used to think: 'My mind is too alert and bright; I've got so much restless movement in my mind.' Because I had always wanted to have an interesting personality, I trained myself in that direction and acquired all sorts of useless information and silly ideas, so I could be a charming, entertaining person. But that doesn't really count, it's useless in a monastery in North-East Thailand. ... Instead of becoming fascinating and charming ... I started looking at the water buffaloes, and wondering what went on in their minds. ... I'd think: 'That's what I need, to sit in my kuti, sweating through my robes, trying to imagine what a water buffalo is thinking.' So I'd sit and create in my

> mind an image of a water buffalo, becoming more stupid, more dull, more patient and less of a fascinating, clever and interesting personality.
> (Ajahn Sumedho, *The Anthology*, Vol. 1, p. 57)

Similarly, Venerable Sāriputta once observed:

> Having attained the perfection of wisdom, having great discernment and great thought, not dull (but) as though dull, he always wanders, quenched. (Thag. 1015, Norman trans.)

To the undiscerning, a person of great calm and equanimity can *seem* to have a dull mind.

5. The positive aspects of contentment

5.1. *Aggi Sutta*: the roles of tranquillity, concentration and equanimity

The Buddha describes the Seven Factors of Enlightenment *(bojjhaṅga)* using the symbol of tending a bonfire (S 46.53):

> 'On an occasion, bhikkhus, when the mind is excited, that is the wrong time to develop investigation of qualities ..., energy ..., rapture as a factor of enlightenment. Why is that? The excited mind is difficult to calm down by those things. Just as if a person, wanting to extinguish a great bonfire, were to place dry grass, dry cowdung and dry sticks on it ... Is it possible that they would be able to extinguish that great bonfire?'
>
> 'No, venerable sir.' ...
>
> 'On an occasion, bhikkhus, when the mind is excited, that is the right time to develop tranquility ..., concentration ..., equanimity as a factor for enlightenment. Why is that? The excited mind is easy to calm down by those things. Just as if a person, wanting to extinguish a great bonfire, were to place wet grass, wet cowdung and wet sticks on it ... Is it possible that they would be able to extinguish that great bonfire?'
>
> 'Yes, venerable sir.'

Thus these three mental attributes — tranquillity (*passaddhi*), concentration (*samādhi*) and equanimity (*upekkhā*) — embody the calming and peaceful aspects of the enlightened mind, the mind that is free of all greed (*lobha*), hatred (*dosa*) and delusion (*moha*). This shows that, though contentment can have its drawbacks when wrongly applied, such calm and peaceful qualities must necessarily be in accord with Dhamma as well and, accordingly, should be considered as a *sine qua non* of the Buddhist path and goal.

5.2. *Dhammānudhamma-paṭipatti* — means and ends unified in Dhamma

The Buddha defines the first stage of enlightenment by using various criteria in the Pali Canon. One format that he employs is to speak of 'the four factors for stream entry'. These are listed (at S 55.5) as:

> Association with superior persons, Sāriputta, is a factor for stream-entry. Hearing the true Dhamma .... Careful attention .... Practice in accordance with the Dhamma is a factor for stream-entry. (Bhikkhu Bodhi trans., p. 1792)

The fourth on this list is *dhammānudhamma-paṭipatti*. This quality is of particular significance here as it echoes the point made above at §3.4.2, of not practising Dhamma with attitudes based on worldly principles. In the political and other spheres it is often touted that 'the end justifies the means', alongside such chestnuts as 'you have to be cruel to be kind' and 'all's well that ends well'.

According to the principle of *dhammānudhamma-paṭipatti* ('practising Dhamma in accordance with Dhamma') the opposite is held to be true; that is to say, if you use a forceful, contentious, agitated means, you cannot receive a peaceful result. The means and the end are directly related, unified, so that if a peaceful and energetic result is wished for, a means that matches that must be employed.

We can, correspondingly, go about our meditation with the same conflictive attitudes and find a similar result. If we try to wipe out the hindrances with aversion, or to become enlightened through ambitiousness, we will surely experience weariness and disappointment. Instead, if the qualities of contentment and goal-directedness are fully balanced and embodied in accordance with Dhamma — i.e. devoid of the biases (*agati*) of desire (*chanda*), hatred (*dosa*), delusion (*moha*) and fear (*bhaya*; D 33.19) — one is using a peaceful and harmonious means so a corresponding result is likely to follow.

5.3. Contentment through seeing all wholesome states as impermanent and subject to cessation, that is, via insight

As the *suttas* indicate, one way that the mind can be trained both energetically and contentedly is through the direct application of reflective wisdom (*yoniso manasikāra, paññā*) — the wisdom that keeps the making of effort in the context of Dhamma. This process is described in the *Aṭṭhakanagara Sutta* (M 52.4–14 [M I 350–352]).[3] Here the teaching elucidates how a deep contentment is continually refreshed through seeing all the wholesome states, of increasing refinement, as 'impermanent and subject to cessation' and thereby the mind is freed from attachment to them:

> Here, householder ... a bhikkhu enters upon and abides in the first *jhāna* .... He considers that and understands it thus: 'This first *jhāna* is conditioned and volitionally produced (*abhisaṅkhataṃ abhisañcetayitaṃ*), but whatever is conditioned and volitionally produced is impermanent, subject to cessation.' Standing upon that, he attains the destruction of the *āsavas* (mental outflows).

This pattern is repeated in the *sutta* for all the *jhānas*, up to the third of the *arūpa-jhānas*, as well as including the sublime abidings (*brahma-vihāra*). All the way along, as the mind deepens its concentration, those states are mindfully recollected in the context of their essential nature — as impermanent (*anicca*), unsatisfactory (*dukkha*) and not-self (*anattā*) — as defined by the analysis of the Buddha in the 'Discourse on the Characteristic of Not-Self', the *Anattālakkhaṇa Sutta* (S 22.59, MV I.6.38–47). The reminder that each state is impermanent, unsatisfactory and empty of self and what belongs to a self brings a cooling, settling quality, even as the states develop

3. Cf. Harvey paper in this collection, p. 41.

in splendour and vastness.

This is a contentment founded upon penetrative wisdom. Since it is based upon and incorporates wisdom, it embodies a subjective calmness, a coolness in the attitude, as well as a mundane calmness due to lack of disturbance in the objective world.

6. Right Effort (*sammā-vāyāma*) as the skilful alternative to *bhava-taṇhā* and *vibhava-taṇhā*

6.1. Four aspects of Right Effort — right/left hand analogy

The presence of the positive aspects of goal-directedness and contentment outlined above (in §2 and §5 respectively) indicate that there are ways that effort can be made that are in accord with Dhamma and that don't contribute to greater discontent. The factor of the Noble Eightfold Path called Right Effort (*sammā-vāyāma*) comprises the essence of these ways.

Right Effort is made up of four qualities called, as mentioned above (S 43.12 and S 49.1 in §2.1), the four Right Strivings or Exertions (*samma-ppadhāna*). They are summarized as follows:

i. 'restraining'; directed at the nonarising of unarisen unwholesome states (*saṃvara-padhāna*)
ii. 'letting go'; directed at the abandoning of arisen unwholesome states (*pahāna-padhāna*)
iii. 'developing'; directed at the arising of unarisen wholesome states (*bhāvana-padhāna*)
iv. 'maintaining'; directed at the continuance of arisen wholesome states, for their nondecay, increase, expansion and fulfilment by development (*anurakkhana-padhāna*)

In the exploration of the negative effects of misapplied goal-directedness and contentment, there are two qualities that can be identified as underpinning most of these unsatisfying outcomes. These two are 'craving for existence/becoming' (*bhava-taṇhā*) and 'craving for non-existence/becoming or annihilation' (*vibhava-taṇhā*). The four *samma-ppadhāna* are the liberating counterpoint to the afflictive *bhava-taṇhā* and *vibhava-taṇhā*.

Whereas *bhava-taṇhā* and *vibhava-taṇhā* are permeated by conceit (*māna*) and self-view (*sakkāya-diṭṭhi*), the four Right Strivings are free of them, otherwise they would not be 'Right' (*sammā*). *Vibhava-taṇhā* is an unskilful parallel to the first two of the Right Strivings; there is a restraining of the unwholesome that has not yet arisen and a letting go of anything unwholesome that has arisen, but no sense of I-making or mine-making obtrudes. It is not 'me' restraining or letting go, rather those actions are guided by mindfulness and wisdom (*sati-paññā*) attuned to the present reality. Similarly, *bhava-taṇhā* is an unskilful parallel to the second two of the Right Strivings; there is a deliberate bringing of the wholesome into being and the effort to maintain wholesome qualities that have arisen. Again, it is not 'me' rousing and sustaining anything in order for 'me' to get somewhere or be something but, guided by *sati-paññā*, those efforts are made according to time and place and situation, conducing all the while to liberation.

Even though these qualities can bear a striking resemblance to each other – restraining and letting go can look like the desire to get rid of, while developing and maintaining can seem identical to the desire to become – they are rather understood to be like the leaves of the stinging and the dead nettle, they look alike but they are quite different plants. Perhaps a better simile is that of being like the left and right hand, exactly like each other in one way yet completely opposite in another.

6.2. *Chanda* compared to *taṅhā* and related to the four *iddhi-pādas*

It was suggested above (in §4.1) that it was a mistake to consider all forms of intending, directing of attention, desiring, initiating of action or decision-making as being inimical to peace and liberation – even though that is a common misconception. This confusion has been exacerbated by the fact that two different words in the Pali have historically been translated into English as 'desire'. These are *taṇhā*, which we have already been looking at closely, while the other word is *chanda*. This latter term has variously been translated as 'desire', 'zeal', 'intention', 'will', 'interest', 'impulse', 'excitement', 'resolution', 'wish for' and 'delight in'. *Chanda*, in contrast to *taṇhā*, is essentially a neutral term, it signifies a directedness of interest or action but one that can be wholesome (e.g. *dhamma-chanda*, 'virtuous desire'), unwholesome (e.g. *kāma-chanda*, 'excitement of sensual pleasure', or *chanda* as one of the *agatis*, see above, §5.2) or neutral (e.g. as consent to the results of a community meeting). Thus one can have a wholesome desire for liberation, for example.

Since *taṇhā* is almost invariably unwholesome in nature, a better English word to use for it would be 'craving' as this latter term conveys a sense of self-centred agitation. One can have a craving for food or a cigarette but, if one is 'practising Dhamma in accordance with Dhamma' (*dhammānudhamma-paṭipatti*), one can't have a craving for enlightenment, at least not in the author's understanding of English usage.

Some of the misunderstandings about desire, goal-directed action, and their relationship to liberation have come about through the effects of translation but some have been there since ancient times. Here is a dialogue that took place in Kosambi between Ānanda and a layman called Uṇṇābha (at S 51.15). The layman asks Ānanda what the purpose of the holy life taught by the Buddha is. Ānanda explains that it is for the abandoning of 'desire' (*chanda*), and that the path that leads to this is the Four Bases of Spiritual Power, namely striving and concentration due to either desire (*chanda*), energy, mind or investigation. The laymen responds by saying, 'Such being the case, Master Ānanda, the situation is interminable, not terminable. It is impossible that one can abandon desire by means of desire itself.' Ānanda replies by asking him whether, before coming to the park where they were, did he not have a desire, energy, thought and investigation related to going to the park, which then all subsided once he had reached the park? The layman accepts that this was so, and Ānanda then says that it is the same with the desire etc. for arahantship.

The four qualities that Ānanda highlights here, when questioning Uṇṇābha and elucidating this area so skilfully, are the 'Four Bases of Spiritual Power' or 'Roads to Success' (*iddhi-pāda*) mentioned above in §2.1 (M 16.26 [M I 103]):

i. *chanda* = desire, zeal, interest
ii. *viriya* = energy, persistence
iii. *citta* = consideration, examination, planning
iv. *vimaṃsa* = investigation, review, reflection on results

In order to succeed at any task, the Buddha's teaching suggests that four factors need to be employed; (i) we need to be interested in the matter, (ii) we need to apply energy to getting it done, (iii) we need to think about how to best go about achieving the wished for result, and last and by no means least, (iv) we need to investigate if we have achieved our goal — this final factor provides the crucial feedback as to whether the action can be beneficially repeated in the future or some other action taken instead. These principles apply, again, irrespective of whether the task is wholesome (e.g. freeing the *citta* all of greed hatred and delusion), unwholesome (e.g. setting a bomb to go off in a public place) or neutral (e.g. baking a cake or going to visit a park).

6.3. The role of *sati* in the *bojjhaṅgas* and *indriyas*

As referred to above (at §3.4.2 and §6.1) mindfulness (*sati*) is a significant agent in the chemistry of liberation. Along with its role previously described, in the guiding of action that is free from self-view and conceit, it is the factor that balances the seven factors of enlightenment (*bojjhaṅga*): the three rousing ones — investigation of qualities (*dhamma-vicaya*), energy (*viriya*) and rapture (*pīti*); and the three calming ones — tranquillity (*passaddhi*), concentration (*samādhi*) and equanimity (*upekkhā*). In the *Aggi Sutta* (S 46.53 — at §5.1), the discourse employing the image of tending the bonfire and the pertinence of particular enlightenment factors in different situations, at its very end the Buddha concludes his description by declaring that: 'But mindfulness, bhikkhus, I say is always useful.' (Bhikkhu Bodhi trans., p. 1607). In his endnote to this sentence (p. 1910), Bhikkhu Bodhi quotes the *Sāratthappakāsinī*, the Commentary to the *Saṃyutta Nikāya*:

> It is desirable everywhere, like salt and a versatile prime minister. Just as salt enhances the flavour of all curries, and just as a versatile prime minister accomplishes all tasks of state, so the restraining of the excited mind and the exerting of the sluggish mind are all achieved by mindfulness, and without mindfulness this could not be done.

Another instance of mindfulness (*sati*) being the great balancer is in the functioning of the Five Faculties, the *indriya*. The group is traditionally divided into the pairs of:

i. faith (*saddhā*) and wisdom (*paññā*)
ii. energy (*viriya*) and concentration (*samādhi*)

Mindfulness has the role of balancing the effects of these faculties with each other (*Visuddhimagga* IV.45–49). Thus it integrates how faith and wisdom need to inform each other; likewise it orders how energy and concentration work together to help the mind be both alert and tranquil simultaneously. The five together are sometimes compared to the wings of a bird, with faith and energy as one wing, while concentration and wisdom form the other, and with mindfulness in the centre as the life-source and integrative principle.

In the context of working with Right Effort and the Bases of Spiritual Power, it is mindfulness (*sati*) — often conjoined with its supportive collaborators 'full awareness' or 'clear comprehension' (*sampajañña*), and wisdom or understanding (*paññā*) — that interprets the moment-by-moment changes in subjective attitude and objective experience. It attunes the mind to the present experience and continually guides its intentions and actions, in order that all efforts made conduce to realization and liberation.

7. Making progress in accordance with Dhamma

7.1. Progress along the path: Being Dhamma

The progress along the path that most of us are familiar with, at least in its initial stages, is described in the *Kīṭāgiri Sutta* (at M 70.23 (M I 479–480)):

> Monks, I do not say that the attainment of final knowledge is all at once. Rather, the attainment of final knowledge is after gradual training, gradual practice, gradual progress. ... There is the case where, when faith has arisen, one visits [a teacher]. Having visited, one grows close. Having grown close, one lends an ear. Having lent an ear, one hears the Dhamma. Having heard the Dhamma, one remembers it. Remembering it, one gains a reflective acceptance of those Teachings. When one has gained a reflective acceptance of those Teachings, zeal arises. When zeal has arisen, one applies one's will. When one applies one's will, one contemplates. Having contemplated, one strives. Having striven, one realizes with the body the ultimate truth and, having penetrated it with wisdom, sees it.

This description shows the natural unfolding of progress, based on interest, faith, reflection and effort. It was characteristic of Ajahn Chah to take a classical formulation like this from the scriptures and to add his own flavour to it:

> First one learns Dharma, but does not yet understand it; then one understands, but has not yet practiced. One practices, but has not seen the truth of Dharma; then one sees Dharma, but one's being has not yet become Dharma. (*Being Dharma*, p. *xx*, Paul Breiter trans.)

This insightful addition is of such significance that it provided the title to this particular collection of Ajahn Chah's teachings. It underscores the relative nature of all concepts of progress and degeneration and articulates the need for the realization of Dhamma to ripen to the point where, as it were, it is 'the Dhamma realizing what this apparent "me" is, rather than "me" realizing the Dhamma.'

7.2. How to embody this principle?

So, how can one best embody this principle, use it to inform one's efforts and facilitate progress in accordance with Dhamma? The Buddha summed the core issue up in four words, for example in the 'Shorter Discourse on the Destruction of Craving', the *Cūḷataṇhāsankhaya Sutta* (at M 37.3 (M I 251), cf A 7.61 and S 35.80):

> Here, ruler of gods, a bhikkhu has heard that nothing is worth adhering to (*sabbe dhammā nālaṃ abhinivesāya*). When a bhikkhu has heard [this], he directly knows everything; ... he fully understands everything; ... whatever feeling he feels, ... he abides contemplating impermanence in those feelings ... Contemplating thus, he does not cling to anything in the world. When he does not cling, he is not agitated. When he is not agitated, he personally attains Nibbāna.
>
> (Bhikkhu Ñāṇamoli and Bhikkhu Bodhi trans., p. 344)

As long as that principle of non-grasping is sustained, and applied in every dimension, then progress will develop as fully and swiftly as possible and will be enacted with an attitude of restful ease along the way. The urge to grasp anything should be restrained (*saṃvara*) and if anything has been grasped, in the sense of clung to, it should be let go of (*pahāna*).

If the ideas of 'me progressing' or 'not progressing' are let go of with wisdom, then progress happens in accordance with Dhamma. Eventually all that remains is Dhamma aware of its own nature, the felt sense of which is called *Nibbāna*. This is the end.

Abbreviations

A *Aṅguttara Nikāya*; translated by Bhikkhu Bodhi, *The Numerical Discourses of the Buddha*, Boston, Wisdom, 2012.

CV *Cullavagga*; translated by I. B. Horner, *The Book of the Discipline*, Part 5, London, Pali Text Society, 1952.

D *Dīgha Nikāya*; translated by M. Walshe, *Long Discourses of the Buddha*, 2nd revised edition, Boston, Wisdom, 1996.

M *Majjhima Nikāya*; translated by Bhikkhu Ñāṇamoli and Bhikkhu Bodhi, *The Middle Length Discourses of the Buddha*, Boston, Wisdom, 1995.

MV *Mahāvagga*; translated by I. B. Horner, *The Book of the Discipline*, Part 4, London, Pali Text Society, 1951.

S *Saṃyutta Nikāya*; translated by Bhikkhu Bodhi, *The Connected Discourses of the Buddha*, Boston, Wisdom, 2005.

Thag. *Theragāthā*; translated by K.R. Norman, *Elders' Verses I: Theragāthā*, London: Pali Text Society, 1969.

References to A and S are to *nipāta* or *saṃyutta* and *sutta* number. References to D and M are to *sutta* number and section within these as demarcated in the Walshe and Ñāṇamoli and Bodhi translations. As the M section numbers are not marked in other translations and the PTS Pali edition, Pali volume and page number are also given for M references. References to MV are to chapter, section and sub-section as marked in Horner's translation.

Bibliography

Chah, Ajahn. 2001. *Being Dharma*, trans. Paul Breiter. Berkeley: Shambhala Publications.

———. 2011. *The Collected Teachings of Ajahn Chah.* Belsay, Northumberland: Aruna Publications. Downloadable for free from: www.forestsanghapublications.org in a single volume or three separate ones.

Mun, Bhuridatta Mahathera, Phra Ajaan. 1995. *The Ballad of Liberation from the Five Khandhas*, trans. Bhikkhu Ṭhānissaro, Access to Insight: http://www.accesstoinsight.org/lib/thai/mun/ballad.html

Ñāṇamoli, Bhikkhu. 1972. *The Life of the Buddha: As it appears in the Pali Canon the Oldest Authentic Record.* Kandy: Buddhist Publication Society.

Nichtern, Ethan. 2010. *Huffington Post*, 20-8-2010.

Pasanno, Ajahn and Amaro, Ajahn. 2009. *The Island: An Anthology of the Buddha's Teachings on Nibbāna.* Redwood Valley, California: Abhayagiri Monastic Foundation: http://www.amaravati.org/dhamma-books/the-island/

Seng-ts'an. 'Verses on the Faith Mind' (*Hsin Hsin Ming*), trans. Richard B. Clarke: http://www.soul-guidance.com/houseofthesun/hsin.htm

Sumedho, Ajahn. 2014. *The Anthology Vol. 1 — Peace is a Simple Step.* Great Gaddesden: Amaravati Publications: http://www.amaravati.org/dhamma-books/anthology-vol-1-peace-is-a-simple-step/

———. 2014. *The Anthology Vol. 2 — Seeds of Understanding.* Great Gaddesden: Amaravati Publications.

———. 2014. *The Anthology, Vol. 4 — The Sound of Silence.* Great Gaddesden: Amaravati Publications; also by Wisdom Publications, 2007.

Amaro Bhikkhu is a Theravāda Buddhist monk and abbot of the Amaravati monastery in Hertfordshire. He has taught all over the world and is author of several books published by the monastery or associated ones: *Small Boat, Great Mountain* (2003), *Rain on the Nile* (2009) and *The Island — An Anthology of the Buddha's Teachings on Nibbāna* (2009) co-written with Ajahn Pasanno, and a guide to meditation called *Finding the Missing Peace* (2011).

Comparative Mysticism

— 5 —

John of the Cross, the Dark Night of the Soul, and the *Jhānas* and the *Arūpa* States: A Critical Comparative Study

ELIZABETH J. HARRIS

This paper examines function and structure within the religious paths advocated by John of the Cross (1542–1591), and the Buddha, with particular reference to the *jhānas* and the *arūpa* states, as represented in selected *suttas* within the Pāli texts. First, John of the Cross and the *jhāna* and *arūpa* states are contextualised. The teaching in *The Ascent of Mount Carmel* and *The Dark Night* (John of the Cross), and the *Sāmaññaphala Sutta*, the *Nivāpa Sutta* and the *Anupada Sutta* (*Sutta Piṭaka*) is then summarised. The two are then brought into conversation with each other to examine the extent to which the religious paths described move within the same landscape of spiritual practice. Differences in context and metaphysical underpinning are recognised. The paper argues, nevertheless, that similarities are more than evident, particularly with reference to attachment to sensory objects, discursive thought, and the idea of the self or the 'I'. The paper demonstrates that the two speak of mystical paths, which share many of the same practices and fruits, although couched in different metaphors.

> O house-maker [*taṇhā* craving], you are seen. You will not make the house again. All these rafters are broken, the house-ridge destroyed. The mind, set on the destruction (of material things), has attained the termination of the cravings.
>
> (*Dhammapada* v. 154; Norman 1997, 22)

> One dark night
> Fired with love's urgent longings
> — Ah the sheer grace!-
> I went out unseen,
> My house [the passions or voluntary appetites] being now all stilled;
>
> (St John of the Cross, *Stanzas of the Soul*; Kavanaugh and Rodriguez 1979, 68)

Introduction

Sr Nyanasiri (Helen Wilder d. 2004), a western woman who took the ten precepts of a contemporary nun in Sri Lanka, told me in one of our many conversations in the 1990s that the western scholar monk, Nyanaponika Mahāthera (1901–1994), for whom she acted as editorial assistant, had once told her that the best descriptions of the Buddhist *jhānas* were to be found in the writings of John of the Cross (1542–1591), a Spanish Christian mystic. When I was asked to contribute to this

Keywords: *jhāna*, *arūpa* states, *pīti*, *sukha*, meditation, contemplation, comparative spirituality, dark night, union with God

volume, this re-surfaced in my mind in the light of one of Lance Cousins' interests – comparative mysticism. In 1989, he wrote a seminal article that compared the meditative and mystical stages in the writings of Teresa of Avila (1515–1582), a contemporary of and close collaborator with John of the Cross in the reform of the monastic Carmelite Order, and in Buddhaghosa's *Visuddhimagga* (Cousins 1994). My study takes inspiration from this area within Lance's work, through a comparative study of two of the writings of John of the Cross, *The Ascent of Mount Carmel* and *The Dark Night*, and the descriptions of the *jhāna*s and *arūpa* (immaterial) states in three discourses in the Pāli Canon: the *Sāmaññaphala Sutta* (The Fruits of the Homeless Life, *Dīgha-nikāya* I 47–86), the *Nivāpa Sutta* (The Bait, *Majjhima-nikāya* I 153–160) and the *Anupada Sutta* (One by One as They Occurred, *Majjhima-nikāya* III 25–29).

Lance rightly claimed, in the above-mentioned article, that 'in certain respects' it would be misleading to 'think of a single transcendental mystical experience' present across different religious traditions (Cousins 1994, 103). He preferred to see 'the phenomena of mysticism' as a 'mystical way, involving a series of experiences, some quite distinct from others' (Cousins 1994, 103). Whilst highlighting parallels between Teresa of Avila and Buddhaghosa, he avoided matching concepts 'on a one to one basis', finding instead, 'parallel clusters of concepts functionally similar in their psychological effects' (Cousins 1994, 108). As he continued with his comparison, however, he went beyond function to structure and found that 'the general structure' of the path was 'remarkably similar' in both Teresa of Avila and Buddhaghosa (Cousins 1994, 120).

In this paper, I also concentrate on function and structure within the paths advocated by John of the Cross and the Buddha in his teaching on the *jhāna*s and the *arūpa* states and use spatial vocabulary to ask whether the two move within the same spiritual landscape. The only other detailed comparison between John of the Cross and Buddhism of which I am aware is by Peter Feldmeier (2006), although the Buddhist feel of some of the teachings of John of the Cross has not been lost on Christian theologians (Williams 1990, 163). Feldmeier, a Roman Catholic theologian, attempted, through his comparison, to propose a new model for interreligious dialogue, namely one that focussed on key themes such as the human being, how we become holy and the ultimate horizon (Feldmeier 2006, 6–7). His study was as much about this as about Buddhaghosa and John of the Cross. He concluded that, although there were many parallels between the two, the ultimate experiences advocated by them could not 'be farther apart', in that the former spoke of 'impersonal insight' and the latter of a mysticism of love and personal relationship (Feldmeier 2006, 73). Nevertheless, he suggested that, in terms of method, Buddhist and Christian teaching about religious practice could be complementary (Feldmeier 2006, 110).

Feldmeier was concerned that comparative studies could trivialise one or other of the traditions being compared, if difference was not respected and recognised. I agree with him but would want to go further than him in recognising similarity, treading a middle path between those who prioritise difference and those who prioritise similarity in comparative religious studies. This middle path accepts that

Buddhism and Christianity locate themselves within different models of ultimate meaning. John of the Cross's model of loving union with a personal God is different from the realisation of the Four Noble Truths and the goal of *nibbāna* as represented in the Pāli Canon. And the concepts of 'soul' and 'spirit' in John of the Cross differ from that of *anattā* (non-self) within Buddhism, although I will argue with Lynn de Silva, on the basis of mystics such as John of the Cross, that the differences are not so great as some would insist (de Silva 1979).

The religious contexts that shaped the Pāli texts and the writings of John of the Cross also differed. The Buddha was in debate with Brahmanism and other renunciant groups about the nature of the self, caste, ritual, morality and ultimate reality. He criticised moral judgements made on the basis of caste (see for instance the *Assalāyana Sutta*, *Majjhima-nikāya* II 147–157) and the belief that ritual, divorced from morality, could be efficacious (see for instance the *Kūṭadanta Sutta*, *Dīgha-nikāya* I 127–149). John of the Cross wrote within a Christian monastic milieu. He entered discussions about the importance of religious visions and the correct modes of performing rituals and decorating oratories, by dissuading people from attaching importance either to supernatural experiences or to the decoration of spaces for prayer (see for example *The Ascent of Mount Carmel* II. 10–11 and III. 35–36: Kavanaugh and Rodriguez 1979, 130–136 and 274–278)

These differences in doctrine and context must be respected. However, undertaking this study has brought me face to face with the surprise of similarity, the extent of which almost transcends the differences. John of the Cross, for instance, in a repetitive, clear and insistent style, speaks of the application and commitment needed to reach stages of consciousness where discursive reasoning and the work of the senses cease, which would seem to touch the interior landscape of the *jhānas*.

In this paper, I first place John of the Cross and the *jhānas* and the *arūpa* states in their respective contexts. I then summarise my three chosen *suttas* from the Pāli texts and the teachings of John of the Cross in *The Ascent of Mount Carmel* and *The Dark Night*. In these sections, I refrain from highlighting differences and similarities between John of the Cross, and the *jhānas* and the *arūpa* states, although these will no doubt arise in the reader's mind. It is in the last section that I bring the two into conversation and reflect on the extent to which they move within the same landscape of spiritual practice.

John of the Cross in context

John of the Cross was born in 1542 at Fontiveros, Spain, as Juan de Yepes y Alvarez into a family reduced to poverty.[1] In 1563, he joined the Carmelite Order, changing his name to Juan de Santo Matía (John of St. Matthias), and was ordained into the priesthood in 1567, after excelling in higher education in Salamanca. A meeting with Teresa of Avila in 1567, a woman twenty seven years his senior, led to them collaborating closely in the reform of the Carmelite Order, which had become lax in

1. I draw these biographical facts from Kavanaugh and Rodriguez 1979, 1–26 and Allison Peers 1943.

terms of discipline. The Discalced (barefooted) Carmelites resulted with an emphasis on simplicity, poverty to the extent of asceticism, and contemplative solitude or enclosure (McMahon 2000, 241). The history of this reform movement became turbulent. John of the Cross was imprisoned at one point, suffering torture, and food and light deprivation (Allison Peers 1943, 33–48), before the Discalced Carmelites gained independence of jurisdiction. His roles within the reformed Carmelite Order were various: vicar, prior, confessor, spiritual director, Rector of the Carmelite College in Baeza, Vicar Provincial of Andalusia, Prior of Granada and more. Internal dispute within the Order, however, led to him being stripped of office towards the end of his life. He died at the age of 49 in 1591. He was canonized in 1726 and declared a Doctor of the Church in 1926. Throughout his life, he combined administrative duties within the Order with spiritual practice, and gained a reputation for sanctity and his ability for spiritual direction. It is said that he directed Teresa of Avila, although his senior by many years, towards the highest forms of union with God.

Throughout his life, he maintained a lifestyle marked by the poverty and simplicity that informed the Discalced Carmelites. Allison Peers, for instance, described his first monastic dwelling as bare, wind-swept, cold and adorned only with rude crosses and skulls (Allison Peers 1943, 23–27). Kavanaugh and Rodriguez stressed his simple dress — 'an old, rough, brown habit and a white cloak so coarse it seemed to be made of goat's hair' — his concern for the poor and the sick, and his willingness to do manual work (Kavanaugh and Rodriguez 1979, 2)

The writings of John of the Cross that I have chosen to examine were directed towards those who already had experience of contemplation (e.g. Kavanaugh and Rodriguez 1979, 214). They began as commentaries on a poem, *Stanzas of the Soul*, which was probably written whilst he was in prison. In effect, they are down-to-earth manuals, rich with metaphor and illustration, about how to progress on the spiritual path towards union with God, written in vernacular Spanish (Howe 2000, 702). I agree with Merton that John was 'a remarkably lucid and simple writer', who was 'almost brutally clear'. Merton added, 'And that is the trouble. His simplicity is too radical. He never wastes time attempting to compromise' (Merton 1951, 39).

The Ascent of Mount Carmel, hereafter AMC, contains three books, each of which is divided into chapters. *The Dark Night*, hereafter DN, contains two books, each of which, again, is divided into chapters.

The *jhānas* and the *arūpa states* in context

The discourses in the *Sutta Piṭaka* of the Pāli Canon were also originally offered in a vernacular dialect both to those who were experienced in following the path of the Buddha and to those who were new to it. I respect Sarah Shaw's point that, although the discourses on meditation are usually addressed, '*bhikkhave*', namely to ordained monastics, this did not exclude others and was more likely to have been 'a formal generic term based upon the most usual kind of practitioner' (Shaw 2006, 13–14). Similar to the works of John of the Cross, they also grew out of a spirituality that stressed renunciation, simplicity and the need for meditative solitude, although the asceticism of John of the Cross went beyond what the Buddha might have judged necessary.

Both John of the Cross and the Buddha also taught out of their own experience and illustrated their teaching with down-to-earth illustrations and narrative. For the Buddha, the methods of meditation that he communicated, 'were forged by him in the course of his own quest for enlightenment' (Gunaratana 1995, 2). The term *jhāna* has usually been translated as 'meditative absorption' or 'trance'. Obeyesekere combines the two as 'meditative trance' (Obeyesekere 2012, 43). Others, for example Shaw and Gunaratana (Shaw 2006; Gunaratana 1995), refuse to translate the term. I align myself with these. The meaning of the term *jhāna* yields neither to 'absorption' nor 'trance', unless, as Cousins argues, it is a lucid trance (Cousins 1973, 125). As Shaw points out, it is linked to the term *jhāyeti*, imperfectly translated as to meditate or to contemplate (Shaw 2006, 18). The *jhāna*s are refined forms of consciousness that are reached through the cultivation of one-pointedness of mind in meditation.

The *jhāna*s and the *arūpa* states are usually linked with *samatha* (tranquillity) meditation rather than *vipassanā* (insight), since *samatha* develops through concentration on an object in order to gain one-pointedness of mind rather than through discursive thought. For this reason and the fact that the Buddha is believed to have been taught the last immaterial (*arūpa*) state, by a teacher he rejected before his enlightenment, because his methods did not lead to an awakening to truth, has led some to conclude that the *jhāna*s and the *arūpa* states have nothing to do with *nibbāna* and, therefore, have a subordinate position within Buddhist meditation.

Feldmeier, for instance, insists that the only way within Buddhism to escape the round of birth and rebirth is through *vipassanā* meditation and, therefore, that the *jhāna*s are not as important as the former (Feldmeier 2006, 62–64). Neither Cousins nor Shaw, however, would agree with him. Cousins demonstrated that there is no hard and fast rule about which form of meditation was prioritized within different schools of Buddhism (Cousins 1984) and Shaw, drawing on Cousins, states, 'I can find no grounds to suggest that the Buddha intended either to be underplayed or negated' (Shaw 2006, 196). I agree with Shaw. The *jhāna*s do not in themselves embody the insight needed for liberation but, as the discourses I will examine in this paper demonstrate, they directly open the window to insight. I would go further than Nyanaponika when he stated, 'Absorptions [i.e. *jhāna*] are only means to an end and cannot lead by themselves, to the highest goal of liberation, which is only attainable through Insight' (Nyanaponika 1992 102). There is much more to them than Nyanoponika's 'only' suggests.

The Pāli texts refer to four *jhāna*s, each of which is linked with different factors, which I will explore later. They culminate in absolute equanimity, devoid of conceptual thought or ecstasy. The fourth *jhāna* can then lead on to four or five more states that are formless or immaterial (*arūpa*). These are sometimes considered to be 'modes of the fourth jhana', since they are all 'constituted by one-pointedness' and equanimity (Gunaratana 1995, 23) and in later non-*sutta* texts as *jhāna*s in their own right. They are not numbered but are labelled according to 'the nature of the attention that is placed on the meditation object, or to develop the insight': boundless space; boundless consciousness; nothingness; and neither-perception-nor-non-perception (Shaw 2006, 19). A fifth state appears in two of the *suttas* in my study: the cessation of perception and feeling.

The *jhānas* in the Pāli texts

The three discourses that I have chosen offer slightly different accounts of the structure, progression and fulfilment of *jhāna*. The *Sāmaññaphala Sutta* holds the normative description of the four *jhānas*, placing them within a larger context of spiritual practice. Within this context, perfecting morality, for instance through the practice of lay and monastic precepts, comes first, followed by guarding the doors of the senses (*indriya saṃvara*), namely noticing and developing non-attachment to that which enters the consciousness through the six senses: eyes, ears, nose, tongue, the tactile sense and mind. After this comes the practice of mindfulness of body (*kāyānupassanā*) and of contentment (*appicchatā*), namely satisfaction with robes to cover the body and alms to meet the pangs of hunger. With this preparation, the practitioner finds a solitary place, either in the natural world or a cemetery, and, having eaten and adopted a suitable posture for meditation — sitting cross-legged with back erect — develops what has been termed mindfulness (*sati*). The next step is the abandonment of the five hindrances (*nīvaraṇa*): worldly or sensual desires (*kāmacchanda*); ill-will or hatred (*vyāpāda*), through developing compassion for the welfare of all; sloth and torpor (*thīna-middha*), through apprehending light; worry and restlessness (*uddhacca-kukkucca*) through developing a calm mind; and doubt (*vicikicchā*) (D I 71; Gethin 2008, 26-27)). Numerous similes are then offered to describe the psychological effect of this abandonment: paying off debts; recovering from illness; being freed from prison or slavery; and reaching security after travelling through the desert. Gladness, joy and a tranquillised body then arise, paving way for the *jhānas* and I quote the whole of the normative description of them:

> When he sees that the five hindrances have been given up in himself, gladness arises, and when one is glad, joy arises. When the mind is joyful, the body becomes tranquil, and when the body is tranquil one experiences happiness; the mind of someone who is happy becomes concentrated.
>
> Completely secluded from sense desires and unwholesome qualities, he lives having attained the joy and happiness of the first absorption, which is accompanied by thinking and examining, and born of seclusion. He suffuses, fills, soaks, and drenches this very body with the joy and happiness that comes from seclusion, so that there is no part of his body that is untouched by that joy and happiness. ...
>
> Furthermore, your majesty, by stilling thinking and examining, a monk lives having attained the joy and happiness of the second absorption, a state of inner clarity [or inner tranquillity] and mental unification that is without thinking and examining, and is born of concentration. He suffuses, fills, soaks, and drenches this very body with the joy and happiness that comes from concentration, so that there is no part of his body that is untouched by that joy and happiness. ...

> Furthermore, your majesty, by having no desire for joy a monk lives equanimously, mindful and fully aware; he experiences the bodily happiness of which the noble ones speak saying 'equanimous and mindful, one lives happily', and so he lives having attained the third absorption. He suffuses, fills, soaks, and drenches this very body with a happiness distinct from joy, so that there is no part of his body that is untouched by that happiness. ...
>
> Furthermore, your majesty, by letting go of happiness and unhappiness, as a result of the earlier disappearance of pleasure and pain, a monk lives having attained the pure equanimity and mindfulness of the fourth absorption, which is free of happiness and unhappiness. He sits suffusing this very body with a mind that is thoroughly purified and cleansed, so that there is no part of his body that is untouched by that thoroughly purified and cleansed mind. (Gethin 2008, 28–29)

Natural metaphors are used to describe each of these stages, most particularly the image of being suffused with cool water. The fourth *jhāna* is likened to being covered from top to toe in a freshly washed cloth. After reaching the fourth *jhāna*, in this particular discourse, the meditator, having 'gained a state that is unshakeable', then 'inclines and directs his mind towards knowledge and vision', with reference to the impermanence and non-essentiality of the body and the dependence of consciousness on it. The next stage is the development of *iddhi* or supernormal knowledges and powers: producing a 'mind-made body' by 'drawing that body out of this body'; developing psychic powers such as becoming many, passing through walls and mountains, walking on water and flying through the sky; gaining the divine ear and hearing distant human and divine sounds; knowing other people's minds; knowing one's own past lives; with a divine eye, seeing other beings passing from one life to another according to their *kamma*. The culmination of this sequence is knowing the Four Noble Truths and gaining liberation, the end of birth and rebirth. The same progression is found in several other discourses, for instance the *Mahāsakuludāyi Sutta* (M II 1–22). It is significant, in this *sutta,* that the *jhāna*s lead on to insight into impermanence (*anicca*) and that the practice of supernormal knowledges, which include insight into the principle of *kamma* (action) through seeing oneself and other beings passing from one life to the next, culminates in realisation of the Four Noble Truths and to liberation or arahantship.

In the *Nivāpa Sutta*, the Buddha narrates a metaphorical story of a deer-trapper (Māra or Evil One), who lays down some bait in the form of food (sensual pleasure) for his deer (renunciants and brahmins). His hope is that he will trap them, so he can better control them. Three herds of 'deer' are trapped, for different reasons. The first are simply tempted by the sensual pleasure of the food. The second attempts to avoid the food by adopting an austere lifestyle in the forest but are led back to it when in danger of starvation. The third are also caught, this time by profitless speculation about the undetermined questions on the world, the life principle and mortal body, and the state of an enlightened person after death. Only the fourth escape Māra, the deer-trapper, and they do this through reaching the four *jhāna*s, the four immaterial states and cessation. The preliminary discipline found in the *Sāmaññaphala Sutta* is given in shorthand with a phrase that embraces moral discipline and the suspension of the hindrances: 'secluded from sensual pleasures, secluded from unwholesome states' (M I 159; Ñāṇamoli and Bodhi 1995, 250). It is when the 'deer', or renunciants, are thus secluded, that they enter the first *jhāna*. The descriptions of the four *jhāna*s are short, without illustration and metaphor, but the jhānic factors are, not unsurprisingly, identical to those in the *Sāmaññaphala Sutta*. The immaterial states, where all sensory impact is transcended and one-pointedness or unification of mind is maintained, seem to follow seamlessly from the fourth *jhāna*. In succession, each mode of attention is transcended by the next, so that this group of renunciants becomes aware that 'space is infinite', then 'consciousness is infinite' and that 'there is nothing'. It then rests 'in the base of neither-perception-nor-non-perception', moving finally to 'the cessation of perception and feeling' (M I 159–160; Ñāṇamoli and Bodhi 1995, 251–252). On reaching the final state, the discourse then affirms that the cankers (*āsava*) are destroyed in these recluses through their seeing with wisdom. The group, therefore, attains arahantship (Ñāṇamoli and Bodhi 1995, 251). Significantly, after each *jhāna* and immaterial state, the discourse states, a bhikkhu of this kind is said 'to have blindfolded Māra, to have become invisible to the Evil One by depriving Māra's eye of its opportunity'.

The short *Anupada Sutta* is a peon of praise for the spiritual achievements of one of the Buddha's foremost disciples, Sāriputta, who was known for his wisdom. Sāriputta is first praised for entering and knowing the first *jhāna*. As in the *Nivāpa Sutta*, no preliminary training is described, except for seclusion from sensual pleasures and unwholesome states. In Sāriputta's case, however, the first *jhāna* is not only linked with detachment, thinking and examining, joy, happiness and one-pointedness of mind but also with watching 'the contact, feeling, perception, volition and mind; the zeal, decision, energy, mindfulness, equanimity and attention' connected with it, during which Sāriputta remains 'unattracted, unrepelled, independent, detached, free, dissociated with a mind rid of barriers' (M III 25; Ñāṇamoli and Bodhi 1995, 899). In other words, Sāriputta is envisioned as adopting an analytical, insight-led, approach to his experience of the *jhāna*, anticipating, according to Ñāṇamoli and Bodhi, a form of investigation linked with Abhidhamma (Ñāṇamoli and Bodhi 1995, 1315n). The second, third and fourth *jhāna*s are described in a similar way. Each *jhāna* has the same jhānic factors as in other discourses but Sāriputta is seen, each time, noting the 'the contact, feeling, perception, volition and mind; the zeal, decision, energy, mindfulness, equanimity and attention' connected with it. After the fourth *jhāna* has been attained, Sāriputta is praised for entering the immaterial states and cessation and the description of these is similar to that in the *Nivāpa Sutta*. Again, however, with each of the first three of these, Sāriputta is described as watching the 'the contact, feeling, perception, volition and mind; the zeal, decision, energy, mindfulness, equanimity and attention' connected with each. And, as in the *Nivāpa Sutta*, Sāriputta gains supreme insight and arahantship at the end of the process. In this discourse, the *jhāna* are used to chart the path to liberation in a disciple that not only experienced them but also deconstructed their nature through applying insight. The end result, however, is the same as in the *Nivāpa Sutta*. The *jhānas* lead on to or, as Harvey argues in this collection (p. 41, and see Amaro, p. 74), are doors to, insight and liberation (M I 350–53).

The descriptions of the *jhānas* in the three discourses I have chosen are formulaic and compact. Each rely on numerous other discourses that, for instance, describe in far greater detail the dangers of the five hindrances. The *Mahā-dukkha-kkhandha Sutta* (M I 83–95), for example, focusses on the dangers of sensual pleasures, and attachment to material form and feelings. When craving for sensual pleasures is present, it states, there is the pain of protecting possessions, quarrels between rulers and within families leading to outright war and multiple deaths, crimes that are dealt with through torture, and misconduct of body, speech and mind that leads to rebirth in hell. The *Saḷāyatana-saṃyutta*, without metaphor or illustration, includes a *sutta* (S 35.19) which gives this message with absolute directness: 'Bhikkhus, one who seeks delight in the eye seeks delight in suffering. One who seeks delight in suffering, I say, is not freed from suffering' (S IV 13; Bodhi 2000, 1139). The same is said of the other senses with the message that liberation is impossible if attraction to sensual pleasures remains.

Significant for my comparison are: the hindrances that need to be suspended before the *jhāna* can arise (worldly or sensual desires; ill-will or hatred; sloth and torpor; worry and restlessness; doubt); the factors linked with each *jhāna* (detachment, joy and happiness, discursive thought, inner tranquillity, one-pointedness, happiness without joy, equanimity and mindfulness); and the corruptions or cankers that need to be overcome if liberation is to be attained (sense desire — *kāmāsava*; desire for existence — *bhavāsava;* wrong views — *diṭṭhāsava*; ignorance — *avijjāsava*).

The Ascent of Mount Carmel and *The Dark Night*

It is often assumed that *The Ascent of Mount Carmel* and *The Dark Night* are two separate treatises but it is better to see them as one. Both were unfinished. Both purport to be commentaries on the same poem — *Stanzas of the Soul*, one verse of which appears at the head of this paper. Both elucidate the path to union with God through what John of the Cross labels the dark night of the senses and the dark night of the spirit, the latter containing an active and a passive night.

The dark night of the senses arises as the contemplative seeks to move beyond any attraction to or voluntary appetite for objects of the senses, in the awareness that 'freedom cannot abide in a heart dominated by the appetites — in a slave's heart' (AMC I. 4; Kavanaugh and Rodriguez 1979, 80). This has to be done, according to John of the Cross, by an expulsion 'of the form already there', namely sensual appetites, which 'weary, torment, darken, defile and weaken' a person. The appetites are like children, he continues, 'restless and hard to please, always whining to their mother for this thing or that, and never satisfied', making the person subject to them, 'dissatisfied and bitter, like someone who is hungry' (AMC, I. 6; Kavanaugh and Rodriguez 1979, 84–86). These 'appetites' need not be for 'venial sins'. They are far more likely to be attractions to ordinary things — to 'a person, to clothing, to a book or a cell, or to the way food is prepared, and to other trifling conversations and little satisfactions in tasting, knowing, and hearing things, etc' (AMC I. 11; Kavanaugh and Rodriguez 1979, 97). Or they can be to a particular 'overdecorated rosary', for a particular statue or for ever more adorned oratories for prayer (AMC III. 35; Kavanaugh and Rodriguez 1979, 276–282).

Frequent mention of the five senses is made in AMC and, within this 'night', the aim is to 'leave the senses as though in darkness, mortified, empty of pleasure' (AMC I. 13; Kavanaugh and Rodriguez 1979, 102). For, as John of the Cross declares 'Our vain covetousness is such that it clings to everything. It is like the wood borer which gnaws at both good and bad objects' (AMC III. 35; Kavanaugh and Rodriguez 1979, 276).

John of the Cross also speaks of four natural passions, rendered in English by Kavanaugh and Rodriguez as joy, hope, fear and sorrow, with 'joy' having the connotation of attachment to objects of the senses, including the mind. Within this 'night' these also have to be mortified and pacified. 'At the first movement of joy toward things, the spiritual person ought to repress it', John of the Cross declares (AMC III. 20; Kavanaugh and Rodriguez 1979, 248). Advice to this end is given in a series of maxims that include:

> Endeavour to be inclined always:
> not to the easiest but to the most difficult;
> not to the most delightful, but to the harshest; ...
> not to wanting something, but to wanting nothing; ...
> the desire to enter for Christ into complete nudity, emptiness and poverty
> in everything in the world. (AMC I. 13; Kavanaugh and Rodriguez 1979, 102–103)

Whether it is joy in our 'beauty, grace, elegance', in 'good intelligence, discretion and other talents pertinent to the rational part of man' or in 'the delights of food' and 'soft objects', joy should be eradicated, since it produces pride, vainglory, 'spiritual torpor' and 'disgust for the poor' (AMC III. 21–22: Kavanaugh and Rodriguez 1979, 248–257). Even joy in one's good works should be destroyed, since, among other fruits, it engenders clinging to the satisfaction these produce, and a desire for thanks and praise (AMC III. 28: Kavanaugh and Rodriguez 1979, 262–265).

In DN, John of the Cross itemises 'imperfections' that hinder those who are moving from being beginners in contemplation to being proficient and these demonstrate that the night of the senses is also about eradicating any kind of joy or satisfaction in spiritual achievements. The 'imperfections' are: pride; spiritual avarice; spiritual lust, namely lust that springs from the sensory pleasure found in spiritual practices; anger because spiritual satisfaction does not last; spiritual gluttony, arising from the delight of spiritual exercises; and spiritual envy and sloth, when spiritual practices lack satisfaction or interest (DN I 1–7; Kavanaugh and Rodriguez 1979, 297–311). At a later point, he compares the destruction of these to the action of fire on wood:

> These imperfections are the fuel which catches fire, and once they are gone there is nothing left to burn. So it is here on earth; when the imperfections are gone, the soul's suffering terminates, and joy remains.
> (DN II 10; Kavanaugh and Rodriguez 1979, 351)

It is worth stressing that the emphasis on the eradication of joy in the night of the senses is not a complete denial of all forms of joy. Joy in mundane objects, worldly achievements or even spiritual experiences has to be eradicated as a sensory joy that causes grief and distress. But there is another joy, a spiritual joy, as the above quote shows, when sensory joys have been overcome –'the serenity of habitual joy in God' (AMC III. 26; Kavanaugh and Rodriguez 1979, 259). There is also peace and tranquillity: 'the delight of peace; a habitual remembrance of God, and solicitude concerning Him; cleanness and purity of soul; and the practice of virtue' (DN I 13; Kavanaugh and Rodriguez 1979, 325).

Significantly, in the night of the senses, intellectual thought and reasoning remains, as the person actively reflects on his or her attractions to objects of sense and seeks to transcend them. In fact, John of the Cross gives considerable importance to human reason as a means of spiritual progress (e.g. AMC I. 22: Kavanaugh and Rodriguez 1979, 184). He is also, however, aware of the human capacity to be deceived by the intellect into thinking, for instance, that some thoughts entering the mind come from God rather than the self, leading to attachment to these thoughts, and 'more vanity of speech and impurity of soul than humility and mortification of spirit' (AMC II. 29: Kavanaugh and Rodriguez 1979, 204). He is equally critical of those who are greedy for supernatural visions and experiences, by stressing that the senses that create these visions, imaginative power and phantasy, must die, since they nurture vanity and greed, and draw people away from union with God (AMC II. 11–12; Kavanaugh and Rodriguez 1979, 131–140).

Turning to the night of the spirit, when practitioners become 'proficient', having gone through the 'purgation of the senses', a form of contemplation is entered, in which the senses yield nothing. They become arid. In this stage, the intellect, attachment to knowledge, reasoning powers and the discursive nature of the imagination are also annihilated, as are human memory and will, to be replaced by faith and love alone. The spiritual journey, therefore, becomes one of unknowing. John of the Cross stresses that this path is for the few: 'Few there are with the knowledge and desire for entering on this supreme nakedness and emptiness of spirit' (AMC, chapter 7; Kavanaugh and Rodriguez 1979, 122). It is so different a path that any work with the 'faculties' is now a hindrance:

> The reason is that now in this state of contemplation, when the soul has left discursive meditation and entered the state of proficients, it is God who works in it. He therefore binds the interior faculties and leaves no support for the intellect, nor satisfaction in the will, nor remembrance in the memory. At this time a person's own efforts are of no avail, but an obstacle to the interior peace and work God is producing in the spirit through that dryness of sense. Since this peace is something spiritual and delicate, its fruit is quiet, delicate, solitary, satisfying, and peaceful, and far removed from all these other gratifications of beginners, which are palpable and sensory. (DN I 9: Kavanaugh and Rodriguez 1979, 315)

These fruits, however, are not easily identified in this 'night', for it is described as 'narrow, dark and terrible' with 'obscurities and trials' that cannot compare to the night of senses, since there are literally no senses to give satisfaction (DN I 11; Kavanaugh and Rodriguez 1979, 320). Desolation and a sense of imprisonment, John of the Cross explains, can last for several years, leaving 'an individual's spiritual and natural faculties not only in darkness but in emptiness too' (DN II 8; Kavanaugh and Rodriguez 1979, 345). The practitioner feels naked and exposed in spirit for what happens is nothing less than an abandonment and annihilation of the self and of all human conditioning: 'true self denial, exterior and interior, through surrender of self both to suffering for Christ and to annihilation of all things' (AMC chapter 7; Kavanaugh and Rodriguez 1979, 124; see also DN II 18; Kavanaugh and Rodriguez 1979, 372).

Self-knowledge, nevertheless, grows:

> Now that the soul is clothed in these other garments of labor, dryness, and desolation, and that its former lights have been darkened, it possesses more authentic lights in the most excellent and necessary virtue of self-knowledge. It considers itself to be nothing and finds no satisfaction in self because it is aware that of itself it neither does nor can do anything. (DN I 12; Kavanaugh and Rodriguez 1979, 321)

What is actually happening in this darkness, according to John of the Cross, is that God is working in the soul, protecting it, even whilst the soul believes itself to be in darkness, because the intellect, being itself in darkness, cannot understand what is happening. This leads eventually to aridity and loss giving way to a purification and an emptiness of self, within which only love of God remains.

The end point of this path, union with God, is described in diverse ways in AMC and DN, including the following:

> Since this transformation and union is something that falls beyond the reach of the senses and of human capability, the soul must empty itself perfectly and voluntarily — I mean in its affection and will — of all the earthly and heavenly things it can grasp. It must through its own efforts empty itself insofar as it can. As for God, who will stop Him from accomplishing His desires in the soul that is resigned, annihilated, and despoiled. (AMC chapter 4; Kavanaugh and Rodriguez 1979, 112)

This passage combines own power and other power. Throughout the treatises, effort, discipline and rigorous determination are encouraged, with a recognition that other power, God, is active in drawing the contemplative forwards.

John of the Cross claims that contemplatives at the point when they are reaching union with God cannot give an account of what is happening to their spiritual directors because what they are experiencing is 'secret' and 'ineffable'. The contemplative may feel that he has been brought 'into a place far removed from every creature'. His description of this is worth quoting in full:

> He [the contemplative] will accordingly feel that he has been led into a remarkably deep and vast wilderness, unattainable by any human creature, into an immense, unbounded desert, the more delightful, savorous, and loving, the deeper, vaster, and more solitary it is. He is conscious of being so much the more hidden the more he is elevated above every temporal creature.
>
> A man is so elevated and exalted by this abyss of wisdom, which leads him into the

> veins of the science of love, that he realizes that all the conditions of creatures in relation to this supreme knowing and divine experience are very base, and he perceives the lowliness, deficiency, and inadequacy of all the terms and words used in this life to deal with divine things. He will also note the impossibility, without illumination of this mystical theology, of a knowledge or experience of these divine things as they are in themselves through any natural means, no matter how wisely or loftily one speaks of them. (DN II 17; Kavanaugh and Rodriguez 1979, 370)

In this process of purgation and the arising of states of consciousness beyond the senses, there is also a hiding from the devil. The devil was very real to John of the Cross and is mentioned throughout his writings, as a force that can tempt the practitioner away from the path. The person, however, who walks in faith rather than at the mercy of the senses is 'hidden from the devil' (AMC II 1; Kavanaugh and Rodriguez 1979, 107–108; DN II 23; Kavanaugh and Rodriguez 1979, 386). And when the goal has been reached, memory and will are restored but in accordance with the will of God.

AMC and DN do not spend much time on the joy of union with God or the perfection of love that this embodies. In another writing, *The Spiritual Canticle*, which is beyond the scope of this study, John of the Cross gives voice to this.

Comparing the *jhānas* and John of the Cross, and concluding thoughts

Similarities within the landscapes of the Buddha's teaching on the *jhāna*s and the spiritual commentary of John of the Cross are more than evident. One of the most obvious is the conviction in each that sustained spiritual practice moves the practitioner out of reach of the devil/Māra, or those interior and exterior forces that tempt the human away from spiritual progress with promises of selfish and sensual gratification. Moving deeper, the first of the hindrances that have to be overcome if someone is to attain the *jhāna*s is attachment to sensual pleasures. The first task for the Christian practitioner who is following the advice of John of the Cross is to enter a night of the senses, where all joy in the objects of the senses is eradicated. There are hints of the other Buddhist 'hindrances' in the description of this 'night'. Joy in objects of the senses produces, 'spiritual torpor'. 'Spiritual avarice' and anger are 'imperfections' that have to be burnt away. When they are destroyed, a new kind of joy arises, one of the factors present in the first two *jhāna*s.

The similarities go further. There is a recognition in both that discursive thought has to be transcended along the meditative path so that other ways of apprehending and knowing can arise. This happens when the second *jhāna* is reached in Buddhism and when the night of the senses gives way to the night of the spirit in John of the Cross. Inner tranquillity, a factor of the second *jhāna*, is also stressed by John of the Cross as a product of the night of the senses. The landscape of the night of the senses, in fact, seems to move in and out of the first two *jhāna*s, although John of the Cross is wary of delight and ecstasy, warning contemplatives that it can lead to self-indulgence.

The night of the spirit leads the meditator away from joy. So do the third and the fourth *jhānas*, although contented happiness remains in the third. Yet, within this 'night' there is, at first, no equanimity within John of the Cross's model. There is a thrusting of the contemplative into mental pain and aridity, as all of the faculties, conditioned previously by memories, imaginations and intellectual goods, are denuded. This appears very different from canonical evidence that mental pain is transcended in the second *jhāna* (S V 213–214). Yet, what emerges from the night of the spirit is, firstly, a peace that seems similar to equanimity –'its fruit is quiet, delicate, solitary, satisfying and peaceful' — and, secondly, a form of consciousness that touches the first two immaterial states — 'He will accordingly feel that he has been led into remarkably deep and vast wilderness, unattainable by any human creature'. That these states are beyond human vocabulary comes through in both the Buddhist and Christian descriptions.

A further area where the Buddhist and Christian landscapes touch is in the transcending of self-centredness or the 'I am' conceit. The corruptions (*āsava*) that have to be destroyed for liberation to be achieved, mentioned in the *Nivāpa Sutta*, are all linked with the delusion of self, the non-appreciation of *anattā* (non-self). The one who seeks sensory delights and clings to existence does this to protect their idea of what the self needs. One wrong view, an expression of ignorance, is that there is a permanent, unchanging self. Attachment to what a person identifies as 'self' and craving for material or immaterial existence for oneself are among the most insidious of fetters (*saṃyojana*) that tie beings to *saṃsāra*. The descriptions of the *jhānas* that I have given do not specifically mention these fetters but they are implicitly relevant. For instance, the insight gained after the fourth *jhāna* in the *Sāmaññaphala Sutta* is into impermanence and the interconnectedness of the *khandhas*, the five material and immaterial 'bundles' that make up the human person and leave no room for an unchanging soul, and even in the four *jhānas* themselves, intrusion of ego-centred thoughts hinders the process of mental stilling. In John of the Cross, the 'annihilation' of the self or of any idea that one is an 'I' in the night of the spirit is explained at length. Although the metaphysical underpinning is different, the function of *anattā* and this annihilation is similar, namely to pave the way for freedom, envisioned in Christianity as unity with a higher force of love, although wisdom is not absent, and, in Buddhism, as a liberation into wisdom and compassion.

All of this would suggest that the similarities might transcend the differences and that, in John of the Cross, there is an experiential awareness that touches what Buddhists call the *jhānas*. What we have, to echo Nyanaponika, is a description that even amplifies the Buddhist texts, or, in the vocabulary or this paper, two religious traditions moving within the same landscape.

However, Lance's words must also be remembered, that it is misleading 'to think of a single transcendental mystical experience'. That John of the Cross and the descriptions of the *jhānas* move in the same spiritual landscape and speak of similar paths does not mean that they are identical. The factors linked with each of the *jhānas* cannot be mapped exactly on the two 'nights' of John of the Cross. The 'darkness' of John of the Cross, for instance, is not replicated in the Pāli texts, namely his descriptions of anguish, when the senses are purged of attachment to external and internal objects, and of aridity, when memory, intellectual possessions and imagination are stripped away, which contrast with the images of coolness, lightness and whiteness present in the Buddhist texts. And, again, the differences in the metaphysical underpinning of the goals of spiritual practice in each must not be overlooked: a personal God and an impersonal *nibbāna*. It is at this point that the vocabulary of each diverges most dramatically.

However, it is worth considering whether the 'darkness' of John of the Cross actually touches a side of Buddhist experience that is not voiced in the texts I have chosen but that teachers of meditation recognise in their pupils: the cost of reaching the state where the *jhāna* and the immaterial states are possible, namely the anguish and pain that can arise when deeply buried conditioning comes to the surface of the consciousness in the process of meditation. For there is no doubt that memory, intellectual possessions and imagination have to be let go of within the *jhānas*. Perhaps this is what Nyanaponika glimpsed. If this is recognised, the two would then speak of mystical paths that share many of the same practices and fruits, although couched in different metaphors.

As for the ultimate goal, due to the differences in vocabulary and metaphysical underpinning, divergence has to be recognised. Nevertheless, I cannot help speculating that the experience that Christian mystics call union with the love of God is not so very different from the experience of absolute wisdom and compassion that Buddhists call *nibbāna*, since, in both, the psyche is liberated from any sense of self-identity and moves into a space that is beyond the reach of human vocabulary. In speculating this, however, I move beyond the remit of academic scholarship.

Abbreviations

AMC	*The Ascent of Mount Carmel.*
D	*Dīgha-nikāya.*
DN	*The Dark Night of the Soul*
M	*Majjhima-nikāya.*
S	*Saṃyutta-nikāya.*

Bibliography

Allison Peers, E. 1943. *The Spirit of Flame: A Study of St. John of the Cross.* London: Student Christian Movement.

Bodhi, Bhikkhu (transl.). 2000. *The Connected Discourses of the Buddha: A Translation of the Saṃyutta Nikāya.* Somerville, MA: Wisdom.

Cousins, Lance. 1973. 'Buddhist *Jhāna*: Its nature and attainment according to the Pali sources'. *Religion*, 3: 115–131. https://doi.org/10.1016/0048-721X(73)90003-1

———. 1994 [1989]. 'The Stages of Christian Mysticism and Buddhist Purification: Interior Castle of St Teresa of Ávila and the Path of Purification of Buddhaghosa'. In *The Yogi and the Mystic: Studies in Indian and Comparative Mysticism*, edited by Karel Werner, 103–120. Richmond, Surrey: Curzon.

———. 1984. 'Samatha-yāna and Vipassanā-yāna'. In *Gatare Dharmpala: Buddhist Studies in Honour of Hammalawa Saddhatissa*, edited by Richard Gombrich and K. R. Norman, 56–68. Nugegoda, Sri Lanka: Hallamalawa Saddhatissa Felicitation Volume Committee.

De Silva, Lynn. 1979 [1975]. *The Problem of the Self in Buddhism and Christianity*. London and Basingstoke: Macmillan. https://doi.org/10.1007/978-1-349-03729-2

Feldmeier, Peter. 2006. *Christianity Looks East: Comparing the Spiritualities of John of the Cross and Buddhaghosa*. Mahwah, NJ: Paulist Press.

Gethin, Rupert. 2008. *Sayings of the Buddha: New Translations by Rupert Gethin from the Pali Nikāyas*. Oxford: Oxford University Press.

Gunaratana, Henepola. 1995. *The Jhanas in Theravada Buddhist Meditation*. www.accesstoinsight.org/lib/authors/gunaratana/wheel351.html (originally published by The Buddhist Publication Society, Kandy)

Howe, Elizabeth Teresa. 2000. 'John of the Cross, St.'. In *Encylopedia of Monasticism*, edited by W. J. Johnston, vol I: 701–702. Chicago, IL: Fitzroy Dearborn.

Johnston, William M., ed. 2000. *Encylopedia of Monasticism*, 2 vols. Chicago, IL: Fitzroy Dearborn.

Kavanaugh, Keiran and Otilio Rodriguez, trans. 1979. *The Collected Works of St. John of the Cross*. Washington, DC: Institute of Carmelite Studies.

McMahon, Patrick Thomas. 2000. 'Carmelites, Female'. In *Encylopedia of Monasticism*, edited by W. J. Johnston, vol I: 240–242. Chicago, IL: Fitzroy Dearborn.

Merton, Thomas. 1951. *The Ascent of Truth*. Hollis and Carter: London.

Ñāṇamoli, Bhikkhu and Bhikkhu Bodhi. 1995. *The Middle Length Discourses of the Buddha: A New Translation of the Majjhima Nikāya*. Boston, MA: Wisdom.

Norman, K. R., trans. 1997. *The Word of the Doctrine (Dhammapada)*. Oxford: Pali Text Society.

Nyanaponika, Thera. 1992 [1962]. *The Heart of Buddhist Meditation: A handbook of Mental Training Based on the Buddha's Way of Mindfulness*. Kandy: Buddhist Publication Society.

Obeyesekere, Gananath. 2012. *The Awakened Ones: Phenomenology of Visionary Experience*. New York: Columbia University Press.

Peers, E. Allison, ed. 1943. *Complete Works of Saint John of the Cross*. Translated from the Edition of P. Silverio De Santa Teresa. London: Burns Oates.

Shaw, Sarah. 2006. *Buddhist Meditation: An Anthology of Texts from the Pāli Canon*. London: Routledge.

Williams, Rowan. 1990 [1979]. *The Wound of Knowledge: Christian Spirituality from the New Testament to St John of the Cross*. London: Darton, Longman and Todd.

Elizabeth Harris is an Honorary Senior Research Fellow within the Edward Cadbury Centre for the Public Understanding of Religion, University of Birmingham, UK, having recently retired from being Associate Professor in Religious Studies at Liverpool Hope University. Her primary research interests are Theravāda Buddhism, Buddhist-Christian encounter and Buddhism in Sri Lanka, and she is a former President of the European Network of Buddhist-Christian Studies. Her works include *What Buddhists Believe* (Oneworld 1998), *Theravada Buddhism and the British Encounter* (Routledge 2006), as editor, *Hope: A Form of Delusion? Buddhist and Christian Perspectives* (EOS 2013) and *Religion, Space and Conflict in Sri Lanka: Colonial and Postcolonial Perspectives* (Routledge 2018).

— 6 —

Emptiness and Unknowing: An Essay in Comparative Mysticism

RUPERT GETHIN

Over the last fifty years the study of mysticism has been shaped by the debate between 'perennialists', who claim that mystical experiences are the same across different cultures, and 'constructivists', who claim that mystical experiences are shaped by, and hence specific to, particular religious traditions. The constructivist view is associated with the 'discursive turn' that has dominated the humanities for the last half century, emphasising cultural relativism. Nonetheless, the constructivist position is not without problems. Inspired in part by Lance Cousins' 1989 comparison of Buddhaghosa's *Path of Purification* and Teresa of Ávila's *Interior Castle*, the present article seeks to bring out parallels in the contemplative exercises and the progress of the 'spiritual life' found in Buddhist accounts of meditation (such as the *Cūḷa-Suññata-sutta*) and Christian apophaticism (as presented in *The Cloud of Unknowing*). The article seeks to establish specific parallels in the techniques of and approaches to contemplative practice in both traditions, as well as in the phenomenology of the experiences of the meditator (*yogāvacara*) or contemplative at different stages in the work of meditation and contemplation.

1. Comparative mysticism

In the autumn of 1978 as a second-year undergraduate at the University of Manchester I signed up for a course called 'Mysticism'. The course was principally taught by Lance Cousins, but included a contribution on Jewish mysticism from Alan Unterman. At the first class Lance announced that everyone doing the course would be required to give a full fifty-minute lecture — he paused and repeated, 'yes, I do mean *lecture*' — on a Christian mystic. There were murmurings in the room. Even then I realised that this was something of a ploy to make sure the students on the course remained low in number yet committed. It worked. There were in the end just seven of us.

While I had attended Lance's introductory lecture series on Buddhism in my first year, for me personally this course on mysticism represented the start of a period of more or less ten years during which I studied closely with Lance, first as an undergraduate and then as his doctoral student, completing my PhD under his supervision in 1987. Certainly I owe my approach towards and understanding of Buddhist

Keywords: mysticism, meditation, emptiness, Buddhism, apophaticism, *Cūḷa-Suññata-sutta*, *The Cloud of Unknowing*, perennialism, constructivism

texts, thought, and practice to Lance. But I also learnt from Lance an appreciation of other traditions of religious thought and practice.

The text I was allocated for my lecture on Christian mysticism was *The Cloud of Unknowing*. The beneficial result, as far as I am concerned, was that the pressure of having to prepare a 'lecture' meant that I read carefully through *The Cloud* and made detailed notes. The downside – one that will be familiar to all students and ex-students – was that I ended up knowing a lot about *The Cloud* but rather little about Richard of St Victor, Walter Hilton, Ruysbroeck, Teresa of Ávila, and John of the Cross. Had I been allocated a different Christian mystic, what follows would no doubt take a rather different form.

Over the course we talked about things we called 'Christian mysticism', 'Jewish mysticism' and 'Buddhist mysticism', while avoiding for the most part discussing precisely what constituted the thing called 'mysticism' that unified all these different mysticisms. Not that the course neglected this issue. But the issue was assigned to an essay question: How far is mysticism a universal phenomenon?

For this question we were assigned readings by Zaehner (1957), Stace (1960) and especially Katz's then newly published collection *Mysticism and Philosophical Analysis* (Katz 1978a). What I learned from this reading was that the position I was temperamentally and intuitively predisposed to – no doubt by my intellectual upbringing and conditioning – namely, the perennialist universalist position, that somehow mysticism *is* a universal phenomenon, that mystics in different times and different places somehow by their different paths reach the same place, was considered intellectually problematic, deeply so.

The chapters assigned from Katz's book forcefully challenged the suggestion that mystics by their different paths, Christian, Buddhist, Jewish, or even drugs, all arrive at some single experience which they all subsequently interpret as different in accordance with their doctrinal predispositions as God, Brahman, Nirvana, or even just a pleasant trip. From this perspective, then, there is not just one mountain with many different routes leading to the single summit, but rather there are many different paths ascending quite different mountains. That Christians experience God is because they follow a Christian path up a Christian mountain which precisely has God at its summit and not Nirvana. Buddhists, on the other hand, follow a Buddhist path up a Buddhist mountain which precisely has Nirvana at its summit.

What Katz argued at some length in his own contribution (Katz 1978b) to the volume was that there was no such thing as pure, raw, unmediated experience that can be separated and distilled from prior conditioning and posterior interpretation. All experiences are informed and shaped by their prior conditioning, and the manner in which they are subsequently presented cannot simply be dismissed and discounted as some wilful imposition on the experience after the event. This then is the constructivist position as opposed to the perennialist. Moreover, Katz argued that there is an inherent arrogance in the perennialist position (Katz 1978, 32, 40). If the Christian claims to have experienced being unified with God, who are we to come along subsequently and explain to him or her that, no, what you thought was

God was in fact Nirvana. Or that what the Buddhist thought was the selfless Nirvana was in fact the Advaita-Vedānta Ātman-Brahman.

The perennialists, such as Stace, as well as those such as Zaehner (who viewed mystical experience in terms of a hierarchy of nature, monistic and theistic mysticism) tended to see in mystical experience evidence of an encounter with the same ultimate reality across religions; for the Catholic Zaehner the highest mystical experience was a direct encounter with the reality of a divine being, for Stace, who seems to have become interested in Buddhism and Hinduism while serving in the Ceylon Civil Service, it was an experience of oneness with the absolute. The constructivists, resisting the accusation of reductionism, tended to adopt either an agnostic openness about the question of ultimate reality or a pluralistic position.

Thus Katz himself claimed to be agnostic on the question of whether mystical experiences are veridical or not, and suggested that his constructivist reading should not be taken as reducing mystical experience to 'mere projected psychological states' (1978b, 23). Yet it is not entirely clear that he can coherently avoid reductionism without committing to the position that only one account can be true, although there are no grounds on which to determine which one that might be. For Katz claims to take what mystics actually say about what they have experienced seriously (Katz 1978b, 40), and part of what they say is that they have encountered a final reality beyond their psychological state. But since their accounts of that reality differ, they cannot all be right in this. Thus if we wish to avoid the conclusion that some at least are talking of 'projected psychological states', then we must conclude that some at least are confused about either the nature or the finality of that reality — or if not confused, talking about the same final reality using different language. Yet this is effectively to move away from the radical constructivist position and return to something akin Zaehner's or Stace's position.

The arguments of the constructivist certainly carry some weight, yet they are also not without various objections. In 1990 Forman edited a collection of essays that were presented as a counter to the constructivist position, *The Problem of Pure Consciousness*. In his introduction, he criticised Katz's constructivist arguments in some detail and defended the reality of what he termed a 'pure consciousness event' as a cross-cultural phenomenon (Forman 1990b, 9–25).[1] This collection also included a contribution by Almond (1990) which made the point that the constructivist position is itself constructed. That is, it is informed and determined by certain specific intellectual trends and fashions that held sway in the latter half of the twentieth century.

What has been called 'the discursive turn in the humanities' is perhaps complete and, as far as the study of religious and mystical experience is concerned, we are perhaps now in the age of neuroscience (cf. Taves 2009, 56–57). Yet much of the force of the last fifty or more years of intellectual endeavour in the humanities has been directed towards persuading us of the extent to which we live in a world where there are no universal truths and no universal values. In reality there are a number

1. For summaries of the objections to the constructivist position see Marshall 2005, 181–97; Gellman 2017.

of different worlds, each with its own set of truths and values; trying to position ourselves outside all these worlds in a super world where we can gaze down from on high from a single, absolute vantage point is futile.

As scholars, then, we tend to retreat into the world of our own scholarly specialisms, a world where we feel we can have some hope of learning the values and mastering the rules of what determines truth. In my case this became the world of Indian Buddhist texts. But the questions raised by apparent cross-cultural parallels do not go away and in many ways remain the most interesting and intellectually challenging. The problem is that these questions may lead one into strange in between worlds occupied by the ghosts and demons of critical theory and methodology where real scholars anyway do not venture and those who do are in danger of becoming hopelessly lost. Even worse, comparative studies involve venturing into the kingdoms of others where strangers who dare to enter risk arrest and summary trial. Yet one of the scholarly and academic virtues that I think Lance liked to encourage in his students was not to be in thrall of intellectual and academic fashions.

During the undergraduate 'Mysticism' course, while Lance's openness to and appreciation of Christian and Jewish mystical literature was certainly apparent, his own position in the emerging debate between perennialists and constructivists was not quite clear. But he did draw our attention to the essay by Peter Moore (1978) in Katz's collection. One of the points that Moore makes is that '[a]ny adequate account of mystical practices would have to include the whole programme of ethical, ascetical, and technical practices typically followed by mystics within religious traditions' (Moore 1978, 113). One of the problems of the constructivist thesis is perhaps that it is put forward by those who are too invested in the view that words are everything; the lives of yogins and contemplatives, by contrast, are informed not just by texts and doctrines but by a whole way of life that includes various kinds of spiritual exercise: thus 'mystics' may not *believe* the same things, but they often *do* similar things.

In 1989 Lance published an article comparing Buddhaghosa's *Path of Purification* and Teresa of Ávila's *Interior Castle* in which he in part tried to take the approach advocated by Moore. He begins by alluding to the different positions and suggesting that the search for a single transcendental mystical experience is unhelpful; what he wishes to argue is that 'there is considerable *similarity* in the structure and stages of the mystical way as conceived in different traditions' (Cousins 1989, 103). He goes on to argue for a number of quite specific parallels in the structure and stages of the mystical path of Teresa'a *Interior Castle* and Buddhaghosa's *Path of Purification*. Whether or not one is convinced by all of these, the overall point that their 'models of the path [...] run parallel' seems persuasive:

> Each begins with purification, each moves on to states of interiorization, joy and peace, then to trance phenomena, then to rejection of the world combined with non-normal acquisitions of knowledge, and each finishes with a transformatory knowledge which remains permanently accessible. (Cousins 1989, 120)

This structural similarity seems to me something that a hard constructivist account of mysticism tends to bypass. Thus, as Lance suggested, one of the shortcomings in the comparative study of mysticism has been the overemphasis on the ultimate mystical experience and a preoccupation with identifying a special kind of experience to be labelled and categorised as mystical. The tendency to proceed in this manner goes back, I think, to William James who, in his chapter on mystical experience in his *The Varieties of Religious Experience*, listed its characteristics: ineffable, noetic, transient, passive (James 1902, 379–82). James saw this type of experience as encountered in a variety of different contexts. For James there may be all sorts of mystical experience, but he wants to see them all as sharing certain essential qualities. The mystical experience induced by alcohol or laughing gas shares certain essential features with the mystical experience encountered in prayer or expressed by the poet moved by a sunset. The difference between mystical experiences becomes one of intensity, not of essential quality.

Of course, part of the problem here is simply the word *mysticism* itself. 'Mysticism' is a word with a specifically Christian but complex cultural and religious history that is then abstracted from that context and applied as a universal cross-cultural category, often with an undue assumption that we all know what it means. It is a word that is used by different writers sometimes technically, sometimes vaguely and often inconsistently. The problem of the meaning of 'mysticism' and 'the mystical' becomes apparent if we try to render it in, say, Sanskrit or Pali. What is the Buddhist category that corresponds to 'mysticism'? Perhaps *paramārtha*, the ultimate or highest sense, perhaps *guhya*, 'private' or 'secret', perhaps just *yoga*, 'spiritual work', perhaps *samādhi*, deep meditative and transforming thought.

As Lance also implied in his article, the tendency to focus on the special category of 'mystical experience' and its quality of ineffability suggests that we are dealing with something that bears no comparison to other experiences, yet much of what the mystics talk of has nothing of the ineffable about it: 'Difficulties in description are the same as those which normally accompany any attempt to describe inner experience.' (Cousins 1989, 109). This suggests that the problems of comparative mysticism are not so different from the problems of comparing experience cross-culturally more generally.

Falling in love is clearly to some extent a socially constructed experience. Some might argue that it is entirely so (Beall and Sternberg 1995), and that falling in love in southern India, say, in the sixth century has little in common with the experience of falling in love in northern Europe in the twenty-first. Yet when reading classical Tamil love poetry, admittedly in translation, I find it hard to dissuade myself that I do not recognise something of the experiences described. Here's an example by the anonymous 'Poet of the Foam on the Rocks' from the *Kuṟuntokai* anthology:

> People say, 'You will have to bear it.'
> Don't they know what passion is like,
> or is it that they are so strong?
> As for me, if I do not see my lover

grief drowns my heart,
and like a streak of foam in high waters
dashed on the rocks
little by little I ebb and become nothing.

(Ramanujan 2014, 68)

The 'interior landscape' of the tradition of classical Tamil love poetry is highly stylised with a sophisticated conventional symbolism (Ramanujan 2014, 79–102), yet nonetheless appears to cross the bounds of culture. It also, as Fred Hardy demonstrated, fed into the emotionalism of Indian devotional 'mysticism' as expressed in the *Bhāgavata-purāṇa* (Hardy 1983).

In sum, rather than thinking that we are dealing with the special problems of some peculiar category of experience — call it 'religious' or 'mystical' — a more pragmatic and fruitful approach to comparative 'mysticism' might be to approach matters with the view that we are dealing with the problems of talking about interiority more generally. Certainly it seems to me that there are undeniable parallels and points of contact between the contemplative life as set out in certain medieval Christian texts and the *brahmacariya* or religious life set out in certain Buddhist texts. But these points of contact, these parallels, are not usefully explored by immediately appealing to the category of mystical experience, and thereby by seeking to identify the experience of Nirvana as merely an alternative interpretation of the experience of oneness with God. Rather they emerge when we begin to consider (a) specific techniques of and approaches to the contemplative life and Buddhist meditation, (b) the structure and progress of the contemplative life, and (c) the effect of that life on the one who follows it to its end. In short, the religious life as envisaged by certain Christian texts and Buddhist texts is considered to comprise meditative exercises, to be progressive and to be transformative. With this in mind I want to turn initially to one specific short Buddhist text, the *Cūḷa-Suññata-sutta*, or 'Shorter discourse on emptiness', as an example of an early Buddhist account of the method and progress of contemplation that bears some comparison with what is found in *The Cloud of Unknowing*.

2. Emptiness

Like the other 152 discourses of the *Majjhima-nikāya* the *Cūḷa-Suññata-sutta* (M III 104–109) is the end product of a process of oral composition and transmission of uncertain nature and length.[2] The substance of its content is put into the mouth of the Buddha, but in the form in which it comes down to us its relationship to a particular author is problematic. It is written in a formalized and elliptic style that

2. Cousins 1983 has, of course, been particularly important in informing the debate on the oral composition and transmission of early Buddhist literature. In the case of the *Cūḷa-Suññata-sutta*, essentially two recensions of the discourse survive, the Pali text of the Theravādins alongside Chinese and Tibetan translations of the Sarvāstivādin text. For a discussion of the differences and further references, see Anālayo 2011, II.683–88. The principal differences are (1) in the Sarvāstivāda version the move from the meditation on 'nothingness' directly to the 'signless' meditation, without the intervening stage of 'neither perception nor non-perception', and (2) in the Theravāda version a second account of 'signless' meditation.

renders its precise meaning obscure and open to interpretation. In reading the discourse we are thus in part at least dependent on other discourses as well as the Theravāda exegetical tradition to arrive at an understanding of the path of meditation it describes.

The *Cūḷa-Suññata-sutta* takes the form of a dialogue between the Buddha and Ānanda. In truth it is more of a monologue than a dialogue. For Ānanda, having asked his initial question, remains respectfully silent for the rest of the discourse, taking in the instruction that the Buddha delivers. The Buddha describes to Ānanda how a monk might live 'dwelling in emptiness' (*suññatā-vihāra*). This practice of dwelling in emptiness is progressive. It begins by assuming the life of a Buddhist monk as part of a community in the forest. Removed from the town and people, the monk can live paying no attention to the town and people. His mind thus becomes empty of any consciousness of the town and people; it settles in a simple and unified awareness of the forest. It is free of all disturbances and distractions save those related to his awareness of the forest. This is characterized as a true, undistorted, and pure entry into emptiness.

The practice of dwelling in emptiness now proceeds by progressively simplifying the contents of thought. At each stage the mind is emptied of some relatively gross thought in order to pay attention to one that is subtler and simpler. At each stage the monk is described as becoming aware that his mind is empty of all disturbances save those that are connected with the simple idea his attention rests on. Thus the monk empties his mind of awareness of the forest to settle his attention in the unified awareness (*ekatta*) that is dependent simply on the perception of earth. He empties his mind of his awareness of earth to settle it in the unified awareness dependent on the perception of the sphere of infinite space; he empties his mind of awareness of the sphere of infinite space to settle it in the unified awareness dependent on perception of the sphere of infinite consciousness; he empties his mind of awareness of the sphere of infinite consciousness to settle it in the unified awareness dependent on the perception of the sphere of nothingness; he empties his mind of awareness of the sphere of nothingness, to settle it in the unified awareness that is dependent on perception of the sphere of neither perception nor non-perception.

At this point he has reduced his mind to such a subtle state of awareness that he can go no further. And yet he does. Emptying his mind of awareness of the sphere of neither perception nor non-perception, his mind settles in the unified awareness that is dependent on 'a concentrated state of mind that is without sign' (*animitta-cetosamādhi*). This is empty of all disturbances save the subtlest disturbance connected with the body and its six senses because of being alive (M III 107.34–108.1: *imam eva kāyaṃ paṭicca saḷāyatanikaṃ jīvitapaccayā*).

Now it seems the monk truly has gone as far as he can go. And at this point something happens: an inner transformation that is described in more recognizably and explicit Buddhist doctrinal terms. A knowledge arises that this place that he has brought his mind to is constructed (*abhisaṃkhata*), willed (*abhisañcetayita*), and that whatever is so constructed and willed is impermanent (*anicca*) and subject to cessation (*nirodhadhamma*). And with the arising of this knowledge all the defilements, all destructive emotions, the taints of greed, hatred and delusion are destroyed. He becomes awakened.

Certainly this short and schematic account of the practice of emptying the mind needs to be read alongside other discourses and accounts of Buddhist meditation found in the corpus of early Buddhist texts, as well as exegetical texts. In the *Cūḷa-Suññata-sutta* the progression through each successive emptying of the mind is presented as unproblematic, almost routine. Elsewhere, however, it is made clear that the work of coaxing the mind to pay attention to the desired object of meditation, and only that object, is all but straightforward. The mind must overcome a number of obstacles. The list of obstacles most often mentioned in the texts is, of course, that of the five hindrances: desire for objects of the senses, which makes things other than the meditative object seem more attractive and interesting to the mind; ill will, which causes the monk to become irritable at the thought of having to continue with his meditations; dullness and sleepiness, when the task of meditation produces in the monk lethargy and drowsiness; excitement and anxiety, when the monk becomes alternately excited at his progress and dejected at his lack of progress; doubt, when the monk begins to doubt that the work of meditation is a worthwhile pursuit at all.[3] The *Vitakkasaṇṭhāna-sutta* (M I 118–22), or 'Discourse on stilling thoughts', sets out five progressive strategies for dealing with distracting and disturbing thoughts: (1) plagued by thoughts connected with greed or anger, try to direct the mind towards thoughts connected with desirelessness and friendliness; (2) if this fails consider how such thoughts are harmful to you; (3) if this fails, do not pay attention to them, distract yourself by doing something, such as chanting memorized texts; (4) if this fails, try to analyse just why you are thinking in this way; (5) and finally, if all else fails, grit your teeth and with an act of determination, force the thoughts from your mind.

3. Unknowing

I now turn to *The Cloud of Unknowing*. Such a leap is from a certain perspective somewhat arbitrary — a result of the circumstances that meant *The Cloud* was a text that I read almost forty years ago and whose account of the contemplative life I found strangely compelling, and which has thus stayed with me, from time to time coming to mind as I have worked on texts concerned with Buddhist meditation. But beyond that, as both Lance Cousins and Ninian Smart have suggested, there seems a special interest in trying to explore and articulate just what might be similar in accounts of meditative and contemplative practice from what are very different religious traditions (Cousins 1989, 103–04; Smart 1992, 103–04). In his attempt to read *The Cloud* through the eyes of Buddhaghosa, Smart tried 'to get at the phenomenology behind the language' (Smart 1992, 103). Smart essentially attempts to translate *The Cloud* into a less ramified idiom that Buddhaghosa might have been able to understand.

3. For the standard account of the hindrances and their removal, see D I 71–73.

Some of the correspondences I suggest are also indicated by Smart, but by taking as my starting point the specific account of the *Cūḷa-Suññata-sutta*, I think it is possible to bring out several further parallels of meditative technique that highlight similarities in approach and structure.

A book of contemplation the which is called the Cloud of Unknowing in the which a soul is oned with God is the heading of a text written in Middle English sometime in the second half of the fourteenth century. The text amounts to some ninety pages in modern editions. It is of a very different character from the *Cūḷa-Suññata-sutta*. It is a personal and intimate set of instructions and advice written by someone clearly of some experience in the work of contemplation and apparently addressed to a young man of twenty-four who is a novice in the work. The author is unknown, as is his precise background; and while he draws on well established traditions of Christian apophaticism that look back to Denys the Areopagite, the progress of the work is largely unsystematic.[4]

Nonetheless *The Cloud* begins by setting out the general scheme of the four degrees and forms of Christian men's living: (1) the common, (2) the special for those who have taken religious vows, (3) the singular for those following the contemplative life, and (4) the perfect for those who are in union with God. In addition the author works with the basic distinction between the active and contemplative lives. These are each divided into a lower and a higher, and in this division there is an overlap between the higher active life and the lower contemplative life (Underhill 1922, 98–100).

In the lower contemplative life it is quite acceptable to contemplate and meditate on God's works and attributes, on man's wretchedness and the passion of Christ, on his pity and compassion. Yet in the higher contemplative life the contemplative is striving after knowledge of God, and oneness with God. In this work such meditations become inappropriate and even a distraction. The contemplative must turn his mind away from them; he must cover them with a thick cloud of forgetting and enter into the darkness of the cloud of unknowing (Underhill 1922, 85–89).

The author of *The Cloud* addresses the practical problem of how to stop thinking about God's works and turn the mind elsewhere so as to enter the cloud of unknowing. The method is not to try immediately to empty the mind of any thoughts of God whatsoever. Rather one should avoid the temptation to think discursively about such matters. In order to help him in this task, the contemplative should take a single simple word of one syllable — love, God, sin — as the object of contemplation (Underhill 1922, 93, 188–96). But he should not attempt to analyse the word and reflect discursively on the concepts that it embraces. You should rather 'hold them all whole these words; and mean by sin, a *lump*, thou wottest never what, none other thing but thyself' (Underhill 1922, 189).[5]

4. On the work generally, see Hodgson 1944, li–lxxxvi. Hodgson 1944 is the standard scholarly edition; I quote the text as it appears in Underhill 1922, which modernizes English spelling but otherwise leaves the fourteenth-century English largely unchanged.

5. Wolters (1978, 103) renders this, 'Mean by "sin" the whole lump of it, not particularizing about any part, for it is nothing other than yourself.'

4. Emptiness and unknowing

In all this there seem to me to be real parallels with certain Buddhist approaches to meditation and contemplation. As we have seen in the case of the *Cūḷa-Suññata-sutta*, these are based in the first place on trying to narrow the focus of attention and to limit the proliferation of discursive thought.

The Theravāda commentarial tradition understands there to be thirty-eight objects for meditation handed down in the canonical texts, and two additional objects (Vajirañāṇa 1975, 69–70, 71). In setting out the different topics of meditation in his *Visuddhimagga* Buddhaghosa explains that certain subjects can be developed to the point of 'access' (*upacāra*) concentration but are not suited to the further development of concentration to the point of full 'absorption' (*appanā*). The underlying reason for this appears to be that certain topics are precisely too discursive in nature, for the development of concentration involves first the focusing of discursive thinking (*vitakka*) and examination (*vicāra*), and eventually their stilling altogether.[6]

Thus such meditations as recollection of the qualities of the Buddha, the Dharma and the Sangha are practised in the first place by reciting and contemplating short formulas listing their various qualities. While these types of meditation are suitable for initially steadying the mind in access concentration, they are not suitable for the higher stages of *jhāna* practice. To go beyond access concentration the meditator (*yogāvacara*) must take simpler objects of meditation, the breath, the concepts of earth, fire, water, or air in the form of 'the spheres of totality' (*kasiṇāyatana*); the emotions of kindness, compassion, and sympathetic joy. Significantly from the point of view of the present comparative exercise, these simpler meditation subjects may begin with the silent repetition of a simple word for 'earth', for example, in order to bring the mind towards resting on the simple concept of earth (Vism 125 (IV.29)). It is this approach to meditation that we must understand in the *Cūḷa-Suññata-sutta* when it talks of the meditator's consciousness being empty of all but the forest, all but the earth. This kind of meditation on certain simple non-discursive objects leads progressively through the first three stages of *jhāna* to the fourth. Here all discursive thought is said to have ceased and the mind settles in perfect balance and equilibrium, temporarily untroubled. The fourth *jhāna* or absorption is taken by the commentaries as the immediate basis for emptying the mind still further, by progressively attenuating the conceptual apparatus of the mind through meditation on the spheres of infinite space, infinite consciousness, nothingness, and neither perception nor non-perception, as described in the *Cūḷa-Suññata-sutta*. These 'formless' meditations are thus taken as advanced forms of meditation based on the fourth *jhāna*, and the Theravāda exegetical tradition reads the *Cūḷa-Suññata-sutta*'s account of the monk's emptying his mind of awareness of the forest to become aware of the notion of earth as indicating progressive meditation using the earth *kasiṇa* (Ps IV 154).

6. See Vism 111 (III.106–107), 212 (VII.66), 217 (VII.87), 221 (VII.91).

There is in this meditation practice no overt or formal attempt to cultivate knowledge of Buddhist philosophy, metaphysics and doctrine. It is presented as a process of emptying the mind. Yet it is apparent from the account of the *jhānas* found elsewhere in the *Nikāyas* that this emptying of the mind is not a mere blanking out of the mind and its emotions,[7] but involves purifying the mind and making it sensitive and receptive (*mudu*) in preparation for the liberating knowledge of awakening. The mind that reaches the fourth *jhāna* is described as purified (*pārisuddha*) and cleansed (*pariyodāta*), stainless (*anaṅgaṇa*), without defilements (*vigatūpakkilesa*), sensitive (*mudubhūta*), workable (*kammaniya*), steady (*ṭhita*), unshakable (*āneñja-ppatta*) (D I 76.13–15).

Returning to *The Cloud*, its tenth chapter describes how, as one tries to push down all discursive thoughts of God and his works below the cloud of forgetting and enter into the cloud of unknowing, the contemplative's thoughts may be taken over by thoughts of liking or grumbling with regard to some men or women. Thoughts may be connected with wrath, envy, sloth, pride, covetousness, gluttony and lechery. These are, of course, the seven deadly sins but they are presented here in line with their original conception as the eight *logismoi* in the writings of Evagrius, that is, thoughts that come to distract and plague the ascetic as he struggles in his work of contemplation.[8] In this sense they have a direct affinity with the five hindrances set out in Buddhist texts mentioned earlier (desire for the objects of the senses, ill will, dullness and sleepiness, excitement and anxiety, doubt). It is worth noting here also that the method of looking over the shoulder, as it were, of unwanted thoughts, described in chapter thirty-two of *The Cloud*, bears some resemblance to the methods for dealing with distracting thoughts found in the *Vitakkasaṇṭhāna-sutta*, also mentioned earlier.

We are told in *The Cloud* that as the contemplative struggles and strives in his work to penetrate the darkness of the cloud of unknowing that lies between him and his God, then God will

> [S]ometimes peradventure send out a beam of ghostly light, piercing this cloud of unknowing that is betwixt thee and Him; and shew thee some of His privity, ... Then shalt thou feel thine affection inflamed with the fire of His love, far more than I can tell thee, or may or will at this time. (Underhill 1922, 164)[9]

7. See Cousins 1973, 120 , and Harvey pp. 21–24 in this collection, on the role of 'joy' (*pīti*) in *jhāna*.

8. See, for example, Evagrius, 'On the eight thoughts' (Sinkewicz 2003, 66–90).

9. Marshall (2005, 3–4) briefly refers to scholars who 'take issue with the prominence given to intense, private experience in the study of religion and mysticism', among them Turner (1995). With reference to what he calls the 'informal view around' that the 'mystical' has 'something to do with the having of very uncommon, privileged "experiences"', Turner (1995, 2) comments: 'when I read any of the Christian writers who were said to be mystics I found that many of them—like Eckhart or the Author of *The Cloud of Unknowing*—made no mention at all of any such experiences and most of the rest who, like John of the Cross or Teresa of Avila, did make mention of "experiences", attached little or no importance to them and certainly did not think the having of them to be definitive of the mystical.' At the risk of simplifying Turner's complex argument, I find it difficult to read a passage such as the one here quoted from *The Cloud* as not in some sense a description of an 'uncommon, privileged experience'. Of course, it is possible to problematize what precisely is meant by 'uncommon', 'privileged', 'experience' and 'mystical'.

The imagery of light in mystical literature is, of course, widespread. But this passage suggests to me something rather more than the use of imagery or metaphor. I am tempted to suggest a more specific correspondence with Buddhist accounts of the stages of meditation. Buddhist manuals devote considerable space to the discussion of *nimittas*, the 'signs' (*nimitta*) that appear in various forms at various stages of meditation practice.[10] Technically *nimittas* are regarded as the simple conceptual objects of meditation. But at certain points they take the form of visual images seen with the mind's eye — that is, precisely 'ghostly', as opposed to material, light. At the stage of the arising of access concentration in preparation for full absorption a significant transformation is said to take place in the *nimitta*. What is called the counterpart sign arises. Up to this point the meditator has been working to keep attention on the ordinary learning or training object of meditation (*uggaha-nimitta*). Eventually as the meditator works at keeping his or her attention on the object of meditation, the obstacles and hindrances that the mind puts in the way of contemplation subside and then the 'counterpart sign' arises. One should not be misled by this technical sounding terminology. The arising of the counterpart sign is understood as having an emotionally transforming and fulfilling effect on the meditator: it is described in vivid terms as bursting out of the acquired sign like the circle of a looking-glass drawn from its cover, like mother of pearl when well washed, like the circle of the moon emerging from behind a dark cloud, a hundred or a thousand times more purified. The arising of the counterpart sign is also associated with the arising of the particular kind of joy or happiness termed 'suffusing joy' (Cousins 1973, 120), which suffuses the whole body:

> It is as if a skilled bath attendant or his pupil were to sprinkle bath powder into a bronze dish, and then knead it together adding the water drop by drop so that the ball of soap absorbed and soaked up the moisture until it was saturated with moisture, yet not quite dripping. In exactly the same way the monk suffuses, fills, soaks, and drenches this very body with the joy and happiness that come from seclusion, so that there is no part of his body that is untouched by that joy and happiness. (D I 74.1–9)

The author of *The Cloud* presents contemplative practice as involving an interplay between the hard work of contemplation and the grace of God. The hard work of contemplation lies in the struggle to put the distracting and inappropriate thoughts beneath the cloud of forgetting and to keep them there, preventing them from rising up above it. The rest is God's work — the stirring of love arising from the naked intent on God.

In the context of comparison with Buddhist meditation, one of the most striking aspects of the work of keeping unnecessary and distracting thoughts beneath the cloud of forgetting is the manner of dealing with thoughts occupied with oneself. This is dealt with most clearly in chapter forty-three:

> Thus shalt thou do with thyself: thou shalt loathe and be weary with all that thing that worketh in thy wit and in thy will unless it be only God. For why, surely else, whatsoever that it be, it is betwixt thee and thy God. (Underhill 1922, 208)

10. Vism 124–27 (IV.27–31); Cousins 1973, 118–20. On *obhāsa* and the seeing of forms in meditation, see also M III 157–60.

The problem is that it is precisely oneself that gets in the way of coming closer to God:

> [T]he proof, thou shalt find when thou hast forgotten all other creatures and all their works—yea, and thereto all thine own works—that there shall live yet after, betwixt thee and thy God, a naked witting and a feeling of thine own being: the which witting and feeling behoveth always be destroyed, ere the time be that thou feel soothfastly the perfection of this work. (Underhill 1922, 209)

What the author of *The Cloud* says here is that after the contemplative has pushed down thoughts of everything else below the cloud of forgetting, there still remains a bare awareness of one's own self, and that this must be got rid of to complete the work of contemplation.

There is a clear correspondence here with Buddhist notions of 'not-self' (*an-attan*). The Buddhist doctrine of not-self is routinely presented in Buddhist text-books as a philosophical and metaphysical position. That is, it is seen as equivalent to a Humean reduction of the self to fleeting impersonal mental phenomena behind which there is no enduring self. While it would be quite wrong in my view to deny that in Indian Buddhist systematic thought the doctrine of not-self does in significant respects indeed operate in this manner, the way in which the Buddhist doctrine of not-self in addition operates as a contemplative device to challenge, break down and undermine our sense of self-importance can be neglected in many modern presentations of Buddhist thought. The doctrine of not-self tends to be treated as if it were merely an intellectual position and a metaphysical stance. Meditation on not-self is treated as if it were merely a matter of the intellect, when in truth it must be the most emotionally and psychologically challenging meditation there is: the meditation that brings home to us that there is nothing in the world of which we can truly say, 'I am this. This is mine.'

When Christianity and Buddhism are contrasted doctrinally, the two points that are routinely highlighted are the understanding of self and belief in God: Buddhism denies the existence of self, while Christianity affirms the existence of an immortal soul; Buddhism has no interest in God, while Christianity is all about God. I have suggested that at least in a contemplative text such as *The Cloud* there is a clear practical contemplative counterpart to the Buddhist notion of not-self. That is, affectively, in a practical contemplative and meditative context the two traditions may be much closer than might first appear.

Following the lead of an essay by Mahinda Palihawadana, 'Is there a Theravada Buddhist idea of grace?' (Palihawadana 1978), I shall conclude by drawing attention to the manner in which there may also be an affective and practical counterpart in the Buddhist vision of the meditative path to the notion of God's grace. As outlined here, at least some accounts of the Buddhist path can be understood as a series of successive meditations that constitute a step-by-step emptying of the mind and emptying of the heart. I use the word *heart* because the process indicated here cannot but involve a profound restructuring of the meditator's emotional being. The emptying of the mind brings the meditator to a point where he or she can go no further, and can do no more. As Palihawadana points out, it is precisely when the meditator has arrived at this point that the final awakening, the final purification, takes place. But it takes place not as a result of an act of will, but rather as consequence of the will's giving up, as a consequence of the realization of the will's limitations (Palihawadana 1978, 193).

This is not, of course, to suggest that Christians — at least those who pursue the contemplative life envisaged by *The Cloud* — must really believe in the doctrine of no self, nor that Buddhists must really believe in God's grace. But what we can say is that both traditions sometimes present the contemplative path, the path of purification, as a turning away from ordinary discursive thought by means of techniques of simplifying and emptying the mind. This process is not just an abstract dry and intellectual exercise, but in both traditions has profound emotionally transformative effects. The process becomes a struggle not just to keep certain thoughts at bay, but a struggle with one's own sense of self at the deepest and profoundest levels of one's being. Taken to its ultimate conclusion this process is transformative: one does not emerge from it the same person. For both the contemplative of *The Cloud* and the Buddhist meditator their relationship with the world, with self and with others is transformed. For a contemplative of *The Cloud* such a transformation is associated with being 'oned with God'. For the Buddhist meditator it is associated with the final going out of the fires of greed, hatred and delusion.

Acknowledgements

I am grateful to Peter Harvey, Rita Langer and David Leech for their comments and suggestions on an earlier draft of this article.

Abbreviations

D	*Dīgha-nikāya*
M	*Majjhima-nikāya*
Ps	*Papañcasūdanī*
Vism	*Visuddhimagga*

Bibliography

Almond, Philip C. 1990. 'Mysticism and Its Contexts'. In *The Problem of Pure Consciousness*, edited by Robert K. C. Forman, 211–219. Oxford: Oxford University Press.

Anālayo. 2011. *A Comparative Study of the Majjhima-Nikāya*. 2 vols. Taipei: Dharma Drum.

Beall, Anne E. and Robert J. Sternberg. 1995. 'The social construction of love'. *Journal of Social and Personal Relationships* 12: 417–438. https://doi.org/10.1177/0265407595123006

Cousins, L. S. 1973. 'Buddhist *Jhāna*: Its Nature and Attainment according to the Pāli Sources'. *Religion* 3: 115–131. https://doi.org/10.1016/0048-721X(73)90003-1

———. 1983. 'Pāli Oral Literature'. In *Buddhist Studies: Ancient and Modern*, edited by P. Denwood, and A. Piatigorsky, 1–11. London: Curzon Press.

———. 1989, 'The Stages of Christian Mysticism and Buddhist Purification: Interior Castle of St. Teresa of Ávila and the Path of Purification of Buddhaghosa'. In *The Yogi and the*

Mystic: Studies in Indian and Comparative Mysticism, edited by Karel Werner, 103–120. London: Curzon.
Forman, Robert K. C., ed. 1990a. *The Problem of Pure Consciousness*. Oxford: Oxford University Press.
———. 1990b. 'Introduction: Mysticism, Constructivism, and Forgetting'. In *The Problem of Pure Consciousness*, edited by Robert K. C. Forman, 3–49. Oxford: Oxford University Press.
Gellman, Jerome. 2017. 'Mysticism', in *The Stanford Encyclopedia of Philosophy* (Spring 2017 Edition), edited by Edward N. Zalta https://plato.stanford.edu/archives/spr2017/entries/mysticism/
Hardy, Friedhelm. 1983. *Viraha-Bhakti: The Early History of Kṛṣṇa Devotionalism in South India*. Oxford: Oxford University Press.
Hodgson, Phyllis, ed. 1944. *The Cloud of Unknowing, and The Book of Privy Counselling*. London: Early English Text Society.
James, William. 1902. *The Varieties of Religious Experience: A Study in Human Nature*. New York: Longmans, Green, and Co. https://doi.org/10.1037/10004-000
Katz, Steven T., ed. 1978a. *Mysticism and Philosophical Analysis*. London: Sheldon Press.
———. 1978b. 'Language, Epistemology, and Mysticism'. In *Mysticism and Philosophical Analysis*, edited by Steven T. Katz, 22–74. London: Sheldon Press.
Marshall, Paul. 2005. *Mystical Encounters with the Natural World: experiences and explanations*. Oxford: Oxford University Press. https://doi.org/10.1093/0199279438.001.0001
Palihawadana, Mahinda. 1978. 'Is There a Theravāda Buddhist Idea of Grace?' In *Christian Faith in a Religiously Plural World*, edited by Donald G. Dawe, and John B. Carman, 181–195. Maryknoll: Orbis Books.
Ramanujan, A. K. 2014. *The Interior Landscape: Classical Tamil Love Poems*. New York: New York Review of Books.
Sinkewicz, Robert E. 2003. *The Greek Ascetic Corpus: Evagrius of Pontus: Translation, Introduction, and Commentary*. Oxford: Oxford University Press. https://doi.org/10.1093/acprof:oso/9780199259939.001.0001
Smart, Ninian. 1992. 'What Would Buddhaghosa Have Made of *The Cloud of Unknowing*?' In *Mysticism and Language*, edited by Steven T. Katz, 103–121. Oxford: Oxford University Press.
Stace, W. T. 1960. *Mysticism and Philosophy*. London: Macmillan.
Taves, Ann. 2009. *Religious Experience Reconsidered: A Building Block Approach to the Study of Religion and Other Special Things*. Princeton, NJ: Princeton University Press.
Turner, Denys. 1995. *The Darkness of God: Negativity in Early Christian Mysticism*. Cambridge: Cambridge University Press.
Underhill, Evelyn, ed. 1922. *A Book of Contemplation the Which is Called the Cloud of Unknowing, in the Which a Soul is Oned With God*. London: J. M. Watkins.
Vajirañāṇa, Paravahera Mahāthera. 1975. *Buddhist Meditation in Theory and Practice: A General Exposition According to the Pāli Canon of the Theravāda School*. Kuala Lumpur: Buddhist Missionary Society.
Wolters, Clifton. 1978. *The Cloud of Unknowing, and Other Works*. Harmondsworth: Penguin.
Zaehner, R. C. 1957. *Mysticism Sacred and Profane: An Inquiry Into Some Varieties of Praeter-Natural Experience*. Oxford: Clarendon Press.

Rupert Gethin is Professor of Buddhist Studies at the University of Bristol, where he has taught since 1987. His primary research interest is in the history and development of Indian Buddhist thought in the Pali Nikāyas and exegetical literature. He is the author of *The Buddhist Path to Awakening* (Brill 1992; Oneworld 2001), *The Foundations of Buddhism* (Oxford University Press 1998), *Sayings of the Buddha: A selection of suttas from the Pali Nikāyas* (Oxford University Press 2008) and, with R.P. Wijeratne, *Summary of the Topics of Abhidhamma and Exposition of the Topics of Abhidhamma* (Pali Text Society 2002). He has also published a number of scholarly articles especially on the theory of Buddhist meditation and Abhidharma. He has been President of the Pali Text Society since 2003.

Interpreting Buddhist Teachings

— 7 —

Ambiguity and Ambivalence in Buddhist Treatment of the Dead

RICHARD GOMBRICH

Every culture is concerned about what happens to people when they die. Even when the dominant religion/ideology provides an answer, an examination of what people actually say and do generally discloses various inconsistences, for example between what they claim to believe and what their actions (notably rituals) suggest that they believe or at least consider possible. In every traditional Buddhist society, adherents are supposed to believe in rebirth, a fate which only those who achieve enlightenment escape, and yet in both the Indian and the Chinese Buddhist traditions people worship and to some extent interact with their dead ancestors and in doing so preserve local pre-Buddhist beliefs and customs. In both traditions there are likewise inconsistencies between what people believe about themselves and what they believe about others, as well as beliefs about how to treat dead parents and how to treat dead strangers. Much in the observ able mixture of beliefs and practices may be ascribed to the Buddha himself.

Though studies of human culture are not particularly fond of saying so, probably the outstanding feature of human beliefs is their inconsistency. Naturally enough, this inconsistency is particularly noticeable in beliefs concerning matters on which the evidence is inadequate to provide clear or incontestable answers; and of this beliefs concerning what happens to us when we die offer an excellent example.

In the abstract of her magnificently informative doctoral thesis, Dr. Gillian Evison writes: 'the relative is loved and honoured but the corpse is frightening and quickly becomes disgusting', and this ambivalence towards death is a 'recurrent theme both in ritual and its interpretation'.[1] Her thesis deals only with Hindu communities, but this observation is no less valid for Buddhists. Scholars frequently write that beliefs in this area are inconsistent, and some then add that this inconsistency does not seem to bother the participants. While I agree with this view,

1. Evison 1989, 3. Evison has recorded Hindu funeral practices in three periods: the ancient brahminical/Vedic period, that recorded in the *Purāṇas* (lengthy Sanskrit texts which one can broadly think of as 'mediaeval'), and that recorded in modern ethnographic literature. The Brahminical evidence concerns only brahmins and gives us no information about other castes; the ethnographic literature embraces various castes at every level; the *Purāṇas* specify next to nothing about the time, place, or social milieu of their composition (which in many cases stretched over long periods), and thus fall between the two. Early Buddhism falls at the end of the Vedic period.

Keywords: Indian and Chinese Buddhist traditions, karma, rebirth, ancestors, mortuary rites, ambivalence

I suggest that we may gain more insight if we speak of ambiguity and ambivalence rather than simply of inconsistency.

Within the range of Lance Cousins' interests and expertise, even if we confined ourselves to one culture or one religious tradition, this theme would provide more than enough material for a full-length volume. For that, however, I now have neither time nor space. What I have chosen to do is to consider the two most widespread theories in the Buddhist world about the fate of the dead, theories which have for more than two millennia guided the behaviour of vast populations. One of these two theories is that the dead require regular recognition and worship from their direct descendants. The other is the theory which can be referred to as *karma*.

A few remarks about each may help to clarify the necessarily succinct material which follows. In both theories, death is not the final end of an individual, but everyone who is not enlightened undergoes at least one form of rebirth.

First, ancestor worship. Both in India and in China, the two main cultures which contain, or have contained, many Buddhists, most of society is patrilineal, so that social identity is determined by the males. Sons, particularly eldest sons, dominate funeral rites, as they do most features of family life, and are responsible for maintaining the rituals they inherit. What happens to women when they die is considered very little or not at all. In order to benefit from the offerings and to protect their dutiful descendants, the souls of adult males must have some attributes of a living being, and how this comes about is variously explained; but the entire emphasis of the Hindu and Confucian traditions is not on such explanatory theories but on ritual performances, which tend to be prescribed in minute detail. At least initially, the dead follow the same course, though after a while they may go to a heaven or a hell; ethical considerations enter only at the point where there seems to be such a bifurcation.

Karma (Sanskrit: *karman*) means 'action'; the word hardly ever refers to a purely physical movement, but means an action which is significant, whether it be a rite, or an act which has a moral quality, whether good or bad. Such an act is deemed to entail consequences, pleasant or unpleasant, for the doer, whether in this life or in a future life. The basic metaphor is agricultural: planting a seed and reaping a harvest. This theory is gender-blind: it applies to women in just the way that it applies to men. In contrast to the ancestor theory, this theory *ethicizes* the world, in particular human beings: one's fate after death is determined by one's ethical record.

According to the Buddha, the ethical quality of an act lies in the motive behind it; at one point he even says, 'I say that karma is intention' (A III 415). In the Brahminism of his day, *karman* primarily referred to an enjoined ritual act (and a bad *karman* was a prohibited act), but the Buddha turned this on its head and considered ritual *per se* ethically neutral. Buddhism came to influence Brahminism and Hinduism, but they have never fully differentiated ethics from ritual.

That is not the only reason why it is not surprising that the word *karman* has been used in confusing ways, with divergent implications. In many contexts karma is understood to refer not to an action but to the *results* of an action (in Sanskrit:

karma-vipāka — *vipāka* means 'maturation'). To advert to my main theme: the anthropologist of India David Pocock wrote that 'few Westerners accept fully the finiteness of their own existence, so that death tends to be thought of as something that happens to others', and in the same way the Gujarati peasants whom he studied thought of rebirth as 'primarily for other people' (Pocock 1973, 38–9).[2] Similarly, anyone who knows anything about Buddhism knows that Buddhists believe in rebirth, which may occur anywhere in the universe and in any animate form, and at the same time everyone in traditional Buddhist societies is familiar with beliefs and practices, many of them obligatory, which put them in touch with the recently dead members of their own families.

***

My main aim is to discuss attitudes to dead relatives among Buddhists, starting with the Buddha himself; but I think it would be helpful if I began with the history of how those attitudes developed. When I was first learning about ancient India, it was accepted by scholars that in the *Ṛg Veda*, the text which supplied the earliest evidence, there was no trace of the doctrine of rebirth. Since the doctrine of karma requires a belief in rebirth, it was likewise thought that no idea in any way related to karma existed in India at that period. It was generally known that ancestor worship was widespread in human societies, and the *Ṛg Veda* did briefly allude to *pitaras*, literally 'fathers', former members of one's patrilineage, but they appeared to have no connection to karma or rebirth.

This has all changed since Joanna Jurewicz of the University of Warsaw showed that in the hymn in the *Ṛg Veda* known as the 'Funeral Hymn' (X.16), the cremation fire is asked to allow the dead man to return and rejoin his descendants.[3] At about the same time as she made this discovery, the anthropologist Gananath Obeyesekere published a brilliant book, *Imagining Karma* (2002) in which he surveyed beliefs about what happens after death in a range of societies, and showed that the belief that the dead are somehow reborn is very widespread indeed. 'The fundamental idea of reincarnation is that at death an ancestor or close kin is reborn in the human world, whether or not there has been an intermediate sojourn in another sphere of existence or after-world. ... [E]ventually I must ... be reborn in the world I left' (Obeyesekere 2002, 15). The person reborn is usually expected to rejoin the same family or clan. In small-scale societies this has nothing to do with ideas of right and wrong; if there is any factor necessary for this process to take place, it is usually being given a proper funeral.

Jurewicz has shown that the *Ṛg Veda* fits this pattern. The dead man goes to live in the sun, regardless of his moral record. After a time, he returns in the rain, which is 'sown' and produces barley, which in turn creates semen, and this leads

2. The whole passage is well worth reading.

3. Jurewicz 2004, 45–60. She translates: 'Release him, Agni, from his fathers.' The translation given by P.V. Kane (1953, 196) though generally accepted, is thus wrong: 'O Agni! Discharge again towards the pitṛs this deceased.'

to his being reborn in his original family and starting the same cycle over again.

The idea that the form in which one is reborn depends on the moral quality of one's karma appears in the earliest *Upaniṣads* (notably the *Bṛhad-āraṇyaka*), in Jainism and in Buddhism. Though it has so far not been possible to date these three with any precision, the first two seem to be a bit earlier than Buddhism, since the Buddha responds to some of their teachings (without naming his sources). Obeyesekere calls this 'ethicizing' rebirth — which in the cases of Jainism and Buddhism leads to ethicizing the universe.

When rebirth is first ethicized, the basic model remains simple. This world is the arena of action, the other world is the arena of pay-off (*karma-vipāka*). When the pay-off is complete, you come back to this world and start again. However, what comes to characterize all the Indian soteriologies — Brahminical/Hindu, Jain and Buddhist — is that they add to rebirth the idea that in this life one can escape from the cycle, and it is such an escape, 'liberation', that constitutes salvation. As Obeyesekere writes (2002, 79): 'There can no longer be a single place [after death] for those who have done good and those who have done bad. The other world must minimally split into two, a world of retribution ('hell') and a world of reward ('heaven').' All the traditions mentioned come to agree that since all lives are finite and a good rebirth will inevitably come to an end, the best solution — because the only final one — is liberation. While all these traditions complicate their cosmology by multiplying heavens and hells, thus providing much lurid material for myths and sermons, these sub-divisions do not change the overall picture.

In cosmology Hindus keep the underlying binary model. It is humans and the higher animals who are the moral agents, and at death they go to a heaven or a hell to be rewarded or punished. Though escaping rebirth is seen as ultimately the best destiny, most people aim for a good rebirth in heaven or in a good station on earth — and ethnography suggests that despite their different 'official' doctrines, very many Jains and Buddhists have the same attitude, which leads to much inconsistency.

For Hindus, it is in general impossible to alter one's place in the world after death, and therefore one's enjoyment or suffering, because that existence is only for pay-off. They do not believe that those born in a heaven can continue to do good. In post-Vedic texts, the general picture is 'that sins, when not expiated by penances or by State punishment, lead to hell, and then, owing to some remnants of the evil deeds, to birth as lower animals, and then as decrepit or diseased human beings' (Kane 1953, 154).[4] Kane (1953, 177) writes:

> The teaching of the works on *karma-vipāka*, though dismal and terrifying, comes to this: that no soul need be without hope provided it is prepared to wait and undergo torments for its misdeeds, that it need not be appalled by the numerous existences foreshadowed in those works, and that the soul may in its long passage and evolution be ultimately able to discover its true greatness and realize eternal peace and perfection.

The Buddhists, by contrast, went to the extreme of ethicizing the entire universe. According to Buddhism, all sentient beings, however situated, from gods at the

4. In quoting this great work, I have often taken the liberty of improving the punctuation.

top, down through human beings, animals, ghosts, and ultimately even those suffering in hell are part of one moral community capable of good and bad moral intentions which will inevitably affect the character of their future rebirths. In this they resemble human society, including all castes and both genders. The Buddha's version of karma doctrine brought this about through his radical pronouncement (already mentioned above) that karma is created by intention. This of course means that any individual's moral standing, which could be said to be the most important thing about them, is entirely due to what has gone on in their head.

It follows from this that, unlike in Hinduism, any sentient being, whether human, animal, god or ghost, continues to have moral responsibility, and can, for example, be influenced by preaching.

However, we shall see below that in the context of death and mortuary rituals there are important exceptions, or at least ambiguities, to this pattern.

***

The above is a thumbnail sketch of how *karma* as a theory of rebirth according to ethical rules developed, until it became full grown, and consistent, either in the Buddha's teaching during his lifetime, or at least very soon after his death (which I believe took place shortly before 400 BC). But what was meanwhile happening to the ancestral spirits? I cannot entirely answer this without any mention of the karma theory; and I shall also need to advert to my topic of inconsistency.

In her final summary, Evison writes (1989, 426):

> Although the ritual structure of funeral ceremony has remained unchanged since Vedic times, a major change in ideology has taken place. In the Vedic material the world is created and sustained by sacrifice. If a person spends his life performing Vedic sacrifices he is cremated in a self-sacrifice resembling the cosmic sacrifice which creates and sustains the world. Through this, he escapes going to the world of Ancestors and eventual rebirth but instead goes to the Brahma worlds from which there is no return. Vedic funeral ritual also contains another ideology, inconsistent with sacrificial theory, in which the deceased becomes an Ancestor in the world of Ancestors, from whence he is summoned by regular śrāddhas.[5] In Purāṇic literature death is instead a journey through a mythological landscape to the kingdom of Yama, where the deceased is judged according to his deeds and allotted an appropriate rebirth. At the same time Purāṇic texts also hold the inconsistent belief that the deceased is an Ancestor in the Ancestor world, who can be summoned to partake in śrāddha rites. It is this Purāṇic ideology which is held by most Hindus recorded in the ethnography.[6]

If we compare the data in the *Ṛg Veda* 'Funeral hymn' with the voluminous information which we have in ritual handbooks for Brahmins over the next few centuries, down to the time of the Buddha and even beyond, setting both against

5. A *śrāddha* is an offering to benefit male ancestors. *Piṇḍas*, balls of rice and sesame seeds, are offered to Brahmins on prescribed occasions, ideally by the son of the deceased, and water is offered daily by sprinkling it. More on this below. [Fn by RG.]

6. Evison continues: '[W]hile the Vedic ideology has little in common with other Indo-European cultures, the Purāṇic picture of death corresponds closely with the Hades of the Greco-Roman world ...' (427). She shows this in detail on pp.424–426.

Obeyesekere's remarks, we can draw a few useful conclusions.

1. The *Ṛg Vedic* belief that the dead man will return, in other words, be reborn, in the same family, which is found in very many small scale societies, seems to become obsolete – presumably as the society increases in scale. 'The Vedic sutras contain no reference to any ceremony whereby a family ascertains the identity of the Ancestor who has been reborn into the family in the form of a new child' (Evison 1989, 397).
2. The word *pitṛ* means 'father', but Kane (1953, 340) explains that in the plural it 'is used in two senses, viz. (i) a man's three immediate deceased ancestors; (ii) the early or ancient ancestors of the human race that were supposed to inhabit a separate world (*loka*) by themselves.' It can be imagined that this dual use caused confusions and a variety of theories, particularly since the two might also be identified. Besides, as I have shown elsewhere (1971, 163), further confusion arose because derivatives from a common word for a dead person, *preta*, could easily be confused with derivatives from *pitṛ*, especially in Pali.
3. The *Ṛg Vedic* association of dead ancestors with the sun gives way to an association with the moon, which is seen as (among other things) a vessel full of the life-giving liquid *soma*. The two longest, and perhaps oldest, *Upaniṣads*, the *Bṛhad-āraṇyaka* and the *Chāndogya*, both contain (with minor variants between them) a doctrine called the 'Five fire knowledge' (*pañcāgni-vidyā*). This holds that at death men (women are still not mentioned) divide into three groups. The best, who have understood that ultimately they are *brahman*, go on a kind of tour of the cosmos which culminates in visiting the world of the gods, then the sun, then the lightning, and finally merging into *brahman*; these are not reborn. The second group are those who have performed sacrifices, given gifts and performed austerities; their parallel tour takes them to the world of the fathers, thence into the moon, and after further stages they come back to earth in the rain, as happens according to the *Ṛg Veda*. Of the third group we are told only that they do not follow either of those two paths but become worms, insects or snakes and constantly die and are reborn. This account of three destinies only partially matches what is enacted in ritual.
4. The ambivalence highlighted by Evison is most notable in the treatment of the recently dead. However, Kane points out that although in the *Ṛg Veda* and *Atharva Veda* '*pitṛ*s are invoked with affection and regard for conferring various boons' (Kane 1953, 346), fear is also expressed, for example: 'Whatever fault we may commit in reference to you through our being (erring) men, do not injure us for that' (RV X.15.6) (Kane 1953, 347).

The Brahmin/Hindu view, which provides a kind of framework for all mortuary rituals, is that the dead person (initially referred to as the *preta*) goes through three phases. The first, which follows death immediately, is very like what we are used to thinking of as a ghost. It is in this form that the dead person inspires most fear and/or disgust.

Evison writes (1989, 363): 'When the relatives return to the house after the cremation, they usually perform the *nagna-prachādana* (the covering of nakedness).' A Brahmin is offered a garment (and some other things), with the words: 'For N.N. of the family N.N., who is now going from the world of men to the world of *pretas*. To free him from the condition of being a ghost, I give today the *nagna-prachādana* for clothing along the way.' A hole is dug in the ground by the entrance to the house, and a stone placed in it. This stone stays there until the *piṇḍa* on the tenth day has been offered. The dead person is offered a *piṇḍa*, which is a small ball of boiled rice with sesame seeds, each day; they are considered his food and constitute his body, though it is a temporary body. When mortuary offerings are made, the ritual is enacted by offering them to a Brahmin, who acts as a surrogate for the departed. While such a Brahmin performs an essential function, his close association with death and thus with impurity means that he is socially classified as the very lowest kind of Brahmin. 'The picture of the deceased appears to be fluid: the dead person inhabits a stone, is an aerial spirit, and is also present in Brahmins, and an offering may cover more than one of these categories' (Evison 1989, 365).

Offerings to ancestors are known as *śrāddha*. They are of many types, of which none is more important than the first. This is called *sapiṇḍī-karaṇa*, and has the effect of permitting the dead person to join his ancestors in the 'world of the fathers', however that may be conceived. It is performed on the eleventh day after death for a Brahmin, later for lower castes, up to a month for a *śūdra*. After this, timetables vary, but the general picture is that on the anniversary of the death there is another important *śrāddha*, which marks the point at which the dead man joins his ancestors and moves from being a *preta* to being a *pitṛ*. The word *sapiṇḍī-karaṇa* means 'making (someone) into one who participates in the same offering of (funerary) rice-balls (as oneself)', in other words, making him into a kinsman. This indicates that by dying the man left your kin group, and now you have restored him to it (by making him an ancestor). As Evison writes (1989, 79):

> The mourners' picture of the ghost in this intermediate period is extremely fluid. It is thought to inhabit a body provided by the mourners, yet it is also a disembodied spirit and may also be present in a person or animal. This diversity of form provides the relatives with the opportunity to feed the ghost through several different channels, thus minimising the risk of failure and providing them with greater peace of mind.

***

We come now to the intersection between the theory of karma and the theory of ancestors. First we look at this intersection in Brahminism/Hinduism, where karma theory is very much the weaker of the two systems.

Evison writes (1989, 4):

> Virtually all Hindus pay some lip service to the ethical law of karma but it figures only in the interpretations of what people do and not in determining the acts them-

selves, which seem to express other things, like a fear of ghosts or the belief that ritual intervention can determine the deceased's fate after death.

Kane writes (1953, 335):

> A firm believer in the doctrine of *karma, punarjanma* (re-incarnation) and *karma-vipāka* may find it difficult to reconcile that doctrine with the belief that by offering balls of rice to his three deceased paternal ancestors a man brings gratification to the souls of the latter. According to the doctrine of *punarjanma* ... the spirit leaving one body enters into another and a new one. But the doctrine of offering balls of rice to three ancestors requires that the spirits of the three ancestors, even after the lapse of 50 or 100 years, are still capable of enjoying in an ethereal body the flavour or the essence of the rice balls wafted by the wind. Further, [the texts] provide that the grandfathers, being themselves gratified (by the offerings of food in śrāddha), bestow on men (their descendants) long life, progeny, wealth, learning, heaven, *mokṣa* (final beatitude), all happiness and kingdom.

For Buddhists, the theory of karma and rebirth according to one's moral record is all-important (as I have argued in my book *What the Buddha Thought*, 2009). Someone who comes from a non-Indian cultural background, such as a modern Westerner, and accepts the Buddha's teachings on karma, may see no logical reason why one of the kinds of being which one may be reborn as is a 'hungry ghost', in other words what in Pali is called a *peta* and in Sanskrit a *preta*. There are two books in the *Khuddaka Nikāya* of the Pali canon, the *Peta-vatthu* and the *Vimāna-vatthu*, which to the Westerner may well seem crude and superfluous. Surely the sufferings of the *peta* could be accommodated in hell? And why are the subjects of the *Vimāna-vatthu*, in their stereotyped celestial carriages, singled out from others who are reborn in a heaven?

The answer is historical, and it centres on mortuary rites. While the Buddha taught that rituals were pointless, and laid out a life for the ordained (monks and nuns) in which the part played by ritual was minimal, he did not try to interfere with any lay customs which did not involve violence, as did animal sacrifice. Though there is very little mention in the canon of lay ritual, one can probably deduce from Asoka's edicts[7] that rituals involving extravagant expenditure also met with his disapproval.

The beliefs sketched above about the fate of the dead and the need to perform rituals to help them were evidently deeply ingrained in the population. In one text[8] a Brahmin says to the Buddha that Brahmins practise funerary rituals in which they pray that the gifts which they give to the officiating Brahmins may by this means be enjoyed by the dead, and he asks whether this really works. The Buddha's initial reply is that it does not work if the dead relative is reborn in hell, as an animal, as a human or as a god, but it does work if he is reborn as a *preta*, in which case he lives on what his kinsmen supply. This is of course Brahmin orthodoxy. When asked further, the Buddha says that if the particular relative the donor had in mind is not in fact a *preta*, other relatives who are *preta*s will enjoy the offering instead, and it can

7. Notably Rock Edict IX.

8. A V 269–73 = *sutta* 177.

never be the case that one has no relatives who have been reborn as *pretas* — but in any case no act of giving can fail to have a result. This implies that the custom should be continued. In this text there is no mention of the transfer of merit, so the Buddha is simply telling the Brahmin what he expects and hopes to hear: that the objects donated do pass to the dead and are enjoyed in much the same way as they would be by living human beings.

This suggests that what became the standard Buddhist response to this situation, the transfer of merit, was probably devised and followed towards the end of the Buddha's life. The transfer of merit is an ingenious doctrine which came to permeate the whole of Buddhist practice in every Buddhist tradition, including every form of the Mahāyāna. It is based on the Buddha's dictum that the moral quality of an act resides solely in the intention behind it. From this one might deduce that if I sincerely wish to give someone a dollar, the good karma I have thereby earned is not affected by whether in the end I give it or not. That would not in fact be a correct interpretation, because, just as in English law, whether an intention is carried out cannot be left out of account, and it is assumed that the intention was greater if it was acted on — just as murder is a worse crime than manslaughter.

This aspect need not concern us here. What does concern us is that a good intention may evoke a similar good intention in an onlooker, and the latter thereby earns as much merit as the first intender.[9] Thus, if I intend to give a poor man a dollar, someone who learns of my intention may come to feel equally generous and thus develop an intention just like mine — regardless of whether the intention is finally carried out.

The result recalls the English expression of 'having your cake and eating it'. If I want to feed my parents, whether they be alive or dead, that good intention contributes to my store of merit. If someone then learns of my feelings and is inspired to imitate them, they acquire merit too — though this takes away none of my merit. The practical consequence is that when I do something good, or even just intend to do it, I should inform others about my feelings, because that will inspire them to earn merit for themselves. To hide one's light under a bushel is thus worse than pointless. The English term 'transfer of merit' is however seriously misleading, because nothing gets transferred; but it is just like lighting one candle from another. One must remember that in Brahminism/ Hinduism one can expunge bad karma from one's record by performing a penance, but this is not so in Buddhism: to avoid paying for bad karma, one can only acquire enough good karma to outweigh it, and mortuary rites give the dead an opportunity for creating good karma by witnessing generous acts and emulating the intentions behind them.

When this topic of merit transference is mentioned, it is very easy to be misled by the metaphor into talking as if merit were like money, something one can accumulate in a bank account — and many Buddhists do appear to think of it like that. The historian Richard Seaford has argued that the widespread use of money in ancient India came about in the same period as the Buddhist teaching of karma.

9. In Pali doing an act of merit which is aimed to inspire another is called *patti*, gratefully accepting that opportunity is called *pattânumodanā*.

He writes that the 'metaphysics of money' involves 'the belief that we are primarily individual agents and only secondarily (if at all) members of a larger [social] entity ...'. 'The power of money can increase independence even from deity; ...'.[10] It is possible that there is an element of coincidence here, because both the teaching of 'the transfer of merit' and the increase in the use of money can be explained independently; nevertheless, the fact that both seem to have occurred in the Buddha's environment late in his lifetime, towards the end of the fifth century BC, cannot but impress the historian.

It is customary for Buddhists to feed monks, if possible in one's own home, at certain fixed intervals of time after the death of a relative. In Sinhala this is called a *dānē* (literally: 'giving'). 'A *dānē* on the seventh day after the death is obligatory, and one three months after the death is almost equally common, while annual *dānē*s on the anniversary of the death are very common, especially for dead parents' (Gombrich 1971, 229).[11] These are all called *mataka dānē*s, meaning that they are given for the dead.

Though the food is offered to the monks with the thought that their consuming it is tantamount to its being consumed by the *preta*(s), giving to the Saṅgha and transferring the merit of that act came to be seen as more reliable than the simple act of providing food and drink. 'The stated purpose of the *Petavatthu* was 'to establish the superior merit of making gifts to the Buddhist Holy Order and their efficacy as a means of releasing the *preta*s from their state of woe.'[12]

> The word *preta* was and is ambiguous. Anyone who had died could be called a *preta*, which never lost its original sense of 'the departed'. Thus the Buddha said that parents normally desired to have children in the expectation that children would make offerings to them when they (the parents) became *preta*s. Everyone was due to become a *preta* in this sense, and even today in Ceylon the dead can be so termed.[13] So the practice of offerings to *preta*s has been filled with ambiguity and uncertainties from the earliest times.[14] When such offerings were made by a Buddhist to his ancestors in ancient India, he was caring for his departed ancestors wherever they were. Perhaps they were *preta*s in the sense that they were in an intermediate state between rebirths. Perhaps they were *preta*s in the sense that they had already been reborn in the *pretaloka* [*preta* world] and were suffering for their evil deeds. To cover either contingency he would not only offer them food and drink, but also make gifts to the Saṅgha and dedicate the merit therefrom to relieve and release them.
>
> (Welch 1967, 181)

It is striking that in mortuary rituals, Buddhist monks take over the role played by Brahmins among the Hindus. Buddhists do not believe in impurity in the Brahmin/

10. Seaford 2004, 293, cited in my *What the Buddha Thought*, 2002, 24–25.
11. The next few pages describe and discuss *dānē*s for the dead at considerable length.
12. B. C. Law: *The Buddhist Conception of Spirits*, London, 1936, p.15, cited in Welch 1967, 181.
13. This does not quite capture my own experience in Sri Lanka. I write: 'the semantic overlap between *pitaras* and *preta*s is still a living reality ... [A]lthough logically *preta*s can be anyone's relations, the only *preta*s of whom people usually think and with whom they interact are their *own* dead relatives.' Gombrich 1971, 163. [Fn by RG.]
14. Cf. what is written above about Brahmin *pitaras*. [Fn by RG.]

Hindu sense, so that aspect is lost and no separate group of monks or nuns develops among Buddhists to take on these duties. There are however other striking facts about Buddhist monks which show how they play Brahmin-like roles for Buddhists. For example, in the standard liturgical formula describing the Saṅgha, its members are called *dakkhineyyo*, 'fit to receive a *dakṣiṇā*'. Sanskrit *dakṣiṇā* is the technical term for the fee that has to be paid to any officiating Brahmin for his role performance.

There seem to be inconsistences in the Buddhist system, some of them probably due to its heritage from the wider society, some more likely due to attempts to iron out problems with the new account of things. There is a certain symmetry between the *Vimāna-vatthu* and the *Peta-vatthu*: the characters in the former have done good on earth and are now enjoying their rewards in heaven, while those in the latter are in the opposite case, being wretched ghosts with no home. At first blush this looks just like the archaic binary system: both groups are simply receiving their pay-off, without continuing to perform karma themselves. However, the intervention of Buddhism has complicated the position of both.

Let me start with the wicked. That a man who dies with predominantly bad karma may either become a *preta* or be reborn in hell may look like a kind of duplication; but a historian can again explain it by referring to the Brahmin/Hindu background; in that system, as we have shown, the *preta* occupies a temporary status, before he goes to join his ancestors – except if he meets with the misfortune that his *sapiṇḍī-karaṇa* is not performed, in which case he roams around homeless forever. We shall see that in Buddhism too the status is basically temporary, though if things go wrong it may become permanent. Hell is difficult to explain, in that it is inhabited both by those who are being tormented as a result of their bad karma and by the demons who are doing the tormenting. Vasubandhu, in his *Viṃśatikā-kārikā* (v.7), argues that both the demons and their tortures are mental projections of the wicked.[15] Just as in Christianity there is a tradition, called 'the harrowing of hell', according to which Christ visited hell between his crucifixion and his Resurrection and released the righteous who had not known about him, in the Mahāyāna there are similar stories about *arhats* or *bodhisattvas*,[16] but these are not part of early Buddhism and no such feat is ever ascribed to the Buddha.[17]

The major exception to the ethicization of the Buddhist universe is that according to my Theravādin informants in Sri Lanka the gods who populate the heavens are not thought of as making merit – in which they resemble those suffering in hell. Their explanation for this (which does not seem to be discussed in any ancient text) is that life in heaven is too comfortable, causing heaven-dwellers to forget

15. I owe this information to Alexander Wynne. I also thank Peter Harvey for pointing out that he says the same in his *Abhidharma-kośa-bhāṣya* III.59 a-c, but there adds that on another view they are real beings.

16. In the Buddhist case, the visitor remitted the torments of the wicked, but this does not seem to be what Christ is believed to have done.

17. At one point in his life he is said to visit a heaven in order to preach to his late mother, but that does not seem to be relevant here.

the basic truth that all life is *dukkha* (unsatisfactory).[18] This then becomes used as a justification for the Theravādin custom of transferring one's merit to the gods after performing an act of piety; they cannot earn merit for themselves, so we must do it for them, drawing their attention to what we are doing so that they can gain merit by empathy.

This technique which permits the gods to acquire merit is just the same as is applied to the recently dead. The intended results, of course, are different: the gods in return are supposed to give people protection and grant their wishes for this life – all the boons listed above by Kane as what ancestors bestow on their descendants. So the positive functions which the Brahmin/Hindu ideology ascribes to ancestors (though gods may share these functions as well), the Buddhists firmly assign to gods. In the Buddhist interaction with *preta*s, however, the benefits flow the other way.

*Preta*s are, after all, one's relatives. Tradition puts the bereaved family in an awkward position emotionally. Even if this is not always a fact, parents are supposed to be deeply loved and honoured, and by the same token the assumption is that they are virtuous. In an unethicized world like that of the Brahmins, everyone gets the same treatment at death, regardless of their individual merits, and to think that one's dead father is now a *preta* makes no prejudicial assumptions about his character. In the passage quoted above the Buddha says that it can never be the case that one has no relatives who have been reborn as *preta*s, a statement which I think is rarely if ever cited, and which he seems almost to withdraw by saying that making a gift is always a good thing to do anyway.

The monk in charge of my local temple when I did fieldwork in Sri Lanka gave me an elaboration of the Buddha's statement which represents the received opinion among Theravādins:

> Death is primarily an occasion for doing merit oneself; secondarily for offering it in case the dead man is expecting it. He can, however, only rejoice and benefit from the merit if reborn as a *preta*, because if he is higher than that he does not need the merit, if he is lower, i.e., in hell, he cannot get it. But this does not mean that the relatives who are ceremonially feeding the monks assume that the dead man is now a *preta*, for if we pay a call we take food along as a gift, but if the person is out we eat it ourselves; similarly, our act of merit earns merit for the living whatever the fate of the dead.
>
> Gombrich 1971, 231[19]

In post-canonical sources there is a further refinement, which seems to be a scholastic embellishment: *preta*s fall into four classes, hierarchically ordered, and only the top class, called *para-dattôpajīvin* ('living on what is given by other people') are able to benefit. Another Theravādin refinement is a belief (again without canonical authority) that the life of a *preta* lasts only seven days, and if they can-

18. Similarly, it is believed that nirvana can only be attained while living in this human world – though here too there is an inconsistency: this restriction does not apply to those in the heavens higher than the heavens of the gods (*deva-loka*).

19. This explanation is found in the post-canonical Pali text, *Milindapañho*, ed. V. Trenckner, London: Williams and Norgate, p. 294.

not escape from that condition (through acquiring merit) they will be reborn even lower, in other words in hell. In other Buddhist traditions, this life span varies; and in the Sarvāstivāda tradition the gap before rebirth lasts 49 days. Again, the view of *preta* as a temporary status (as well as variants in timing) is obviously derived from the Brahmin/Hindu mortuary customs.

While a *preta* has little or no opportunity to perform meritorious actions independently, its[20] acquisition of merit through a thought process is not confined to a ritual occasion. In the *Majjhima Nikāya*, in a list of recommendations how a monk should behave, the Buddha says: 'If a monk should wish that it bring great advantage to his dead kinsmen to recollect him with faith in their hearts, he should fulfil the precepts, ... not neglect meditation, ...';[21] and the commentator says: 'If the dead relative acquires faith in the virtue of his monastic kinsman and just recollects him, that is capable of keeping the deceased from an evil rebirth for many thousands of *kalpas* and causing him finally to reach the deathless state.'[22] This surely adds a new dimension to the 'transfer of merit'.

***

In a recent article about modern Chinese Buddhism, Dr Yao Yu-Shuang and I quoted with approval the following paragraph about Buddhist ancestor worship by Francisca Cho:

> The way in which Buddhist ritual provided a way to enhance the indigenous practice of ancestor worship is particularly interesting. The institution of Buddhist monasticism, with its order of celibate monks, seriously clashed with the Chinese concern with preserving and perpetuating the family line. But in the Buddhist ritual system, supporting the monastic order with economic necessities created merit (good karmic fruit) for the donor that could be transferred to his ancestors, ensuring auspicious circumstances in their new lives. Hence an inherently offensive social institution was brilliantly transformed by the Buddhist cosmology of rebirth into a most potent site for the practice of filial piety. What is particularly noteworthy here is both the fact and irrelevance of the clashing conceptual structures brought about by this blending of Buddhist and Confucian practice. Buddhist merit was dedicated to ancestors in the belief that it would help them attain auspicious new births. But in Confucian practice, propitiation of ancestors was premised on the belief that ancestral spirits hovered and remained close to the living, with the power to bring them fortune or harm. Do ancestors remain with the living, or do they reincarnate? For the Chinese practitioners, resolving the question was of less importance than the added ritual technology for practicing filial piety, which assured the well-being of the living.[23]

Now that I have had occasion to return to my own publications, and others, on Buddhism in India and Sri Lanka, I realise that what she describes in China

20. Remember, a *preta* can be feminine, as befits a belief concerned with karma rather than with ancestors.

21. *Ākaṅkheyya Sutta*, M I 33, lines 20–23.

22. *Papañcasūdanī* I, 159–160.

23. Cho 2012, 277 as also cited in Gombrich and Yao 2013, 254.

could have been written almost word for word about Buddhism in India and the Theravāda tradition. For 'Chinese' read 'Indian', for 'Confucian' read 'Brahminical'; the variations are trivial. Her eloquence should not blind us to the fact that the 'brilliant transformation' she refers to took place almost a millennium earlier than she thinks, and it is highly probable that its main features can be ascribed to the Buddha himself.

If there is any merit in what I have written, may it accrue to Lance Cousins.

Bibliography

Cho, Francisca. 2012. 'Buddhism and Science: Translating and Re-translating Culture'. In *Buddhism in the Modern World*, ed. David L. McMahan, 273–288. Abingdon: Routledge.

Evison, Gillian. 1989. 'Indian Death Rituals: the Enactment of Ambivalence'. Unpublished PhD thesis, Oxford.

Gombrich, Richard. 1971. *Precept and Practice: Traditional Buddhism in the Rural Highlands of Ceylon*. Oxford: Clarendon Press.

———. 2009. *What the Buddha Thought*. London and Oakville, CT: Equinox.

Gombrich, Richard and Yu-Shuang Yao. 2013. 'A Radical Buddhism for Modern Confucians'. *Buddhist Studies Review* 30(2): 237–259. https://doi.org/10.1558/bsrv.v30i2.237

Jurewicz, Joanna. 2004. 'Prajāpati, the fire and the *pañcāgni-vidyā*'. In *Essays in Indian Philosophy, Religion and Literature*, edited by Piotr Balcerowicz and Marek Mejor, 45–60. Delhi: Motilal Banarsidass.

Kane, P. V. 1953. *History of Dharmaśāstra* IV. Poona: Bhandarkar Oriental Research Institute.

Obeyesekere, Gananath. 2002. *Imagining Karma: Ethical Transformation in Amerindian, Buddhist, and Greek Rebirth*. Berkeley: University of California Press. https://doi.org/10.1525/california/9780520232204.001.0001

Pocock, David. 1973. *Mind, Body and Wealth: A Study of Belief and Practice in an Indian Village*. Oxford: Basil Blackwell.

Seaford, Richard. 2004. *Money and the Early Greek Mind*. Cambridge: Cambridge University Press. https://doi.org/10.1017/CBO9780511483080

Welch, Holmes. 1967. *The Practice of Chinese Buddhism 1900–1950*. Cambridge, MA: Harvard University Press.

Richard Gombrich was Boden Professor of Sanskrit at the University of Oxford from 1976 to 2004, and went on to found the Oxford Centre for Buddhist Studies. He has published such works as *Precept and Practice: Traditional Buddhism in the Rural Highlands of Ceylon* (Clarendon 1971, and 1998 Motilal Banarsidass), *Theravāda Buddhism* (Routledge 1988 and 2006), *How Buddhism Began: The Conditioned Genesis of the Early Teachings* (Athlone 1996), and *What the Buddha Thought* (Equinox 2009); he has written extensively on early Buddhism and Pāli studies, and has served as President of both the Pali Text Society (1994–2002) and the UK Association for Buddhist Studies (2006–2013).

— 8 —

The *Alagaddūpama Sutta* as a Scriptural Source for Understanding the Distinctive Philosophical Standpoint of Early Buddhism

P. D. Premasiri

The *Alagaddūpama Sutta* is the 22nd discourse of the *Majjhima-nikāya* of the Pali canon. In the sutta itself it is mentioned that the Buddha's delivery of this discourse was necessitated by the need to refute a wrong view held by one of his disciples named Ariṭṭha. Parallel versions of the sutta are found preserved in the Chinese *Āgamas*. The two main similes used in the sutta, those of the snake and of the raft, are referred to in the scriptures of a number of non-Theravāda Buddhist traditions as well, showing that the Buddhist doctrine represented in it is early and authentic and the message contained in the sutta was considered to be extremely significant by many early Buddhist traditions. The *Alagaddūpama Sutta* shows the Buddha's role as one of the earliest thinkers in the history of philosophy who engaged in a critique of the craving for metaphysics and dogma frequently exhibited in those who propound worldviews. The Buddha did not value a belief or a worldview on grounds of the logical skill with which it was constructed but on grounds of the transformative effect it could have on the character of an individual and the sense of wellbeing it could promote. There are several discourses of the Pali canon which give prominence to this aspect of the Buddha's teaching. Among them the *Brahmajāla Sutta* of the *Dīgha-nikāya* and the *Aṭṭhakavagga* of the *Suttanipāta* need special mention. The Buddha is seen to have consistently avoided engagement in speculative metaphysics, pointing out that the goal of his teaching goes beyond all such engagement. The Buddha himself distinguished his own worldview as a Teaching in the Middle (*majjhena*) avoiding the common tendency of humankind to be trapped by either of the two extremes, Eternalism or Annihilationism. These distinctive standpoints of the Buddha are all seen to be amply represented in the *Alagaddūpama Sutta.*

The *Alagaddūpama Sutta* in different Buddhist traditions

I am extremely grateful to the editors of the Lance Cousins memorial volume for giving me the opportunity to contribute a paper by way of tribute to a scholar of the calibre of Lance, particularly in the field of Buddhist and Pali studies, and the practical aspects of the Oriental religious traditions in general. I believe that the illumination that he has brought to the field of textual studies in the Pali canonical

Keywords: simile of the snake, simile of the raft, dogmatic clinging, speculative reason, craving for metaphysics, *avyākata*, Eternalism, Annihilationism, Teaching in the Middle and post-canonical literature, and the interpretations of key Buddhist concepts contained therein, are of immense value to the future generations of scholars. As a close associate of Lance during a period of three years when both of us were students of the University of Cambridge in the mid-1960s, and ever since, although physically separated by the distance between Britain and Sri Lanka, I have had many opportunities to share my knowledge of the subject area of Pali studies that happened to be a major part of our common academic interests with him. It is in view of the indelible memories of such association both at the level of academic study and the practice of the methods represented in the Buddhist contemplative tradition that I made up my mind to contribute this paper to the proposed volume.

Non-Pali versions of the sutta are found in whole or in part in the *Āgama* collection of suttas preserved in Chinese. They were probably translations of an early Buddhist Sanskrit version which derived the material from a common early source which served as the basis for the Pali version as well. The fact that the same account is preserved in different Buddhist traditions provides substantial evidence for the antiquity of the Buddhist doctrines presented in it. The Chinese parallel in the *Madhyama Āgama* names it as 'The Discourse on Ariṭṭha' (Anālayo 2011, 147) as the Buddha's delivery of this discourse is mentioned as having been necessitated by the need to refute a wrong view held by one of the disciples of the Buddha named Ariṭṭha.

> The simile of the snake and the simile of the raft recur as discourses on their own in the *Ekottarāgama*; in addition to which parts of the discourse are also preserved in two discourses. The introductory part of the *Alagaddūpama Sutta*, which narrates the monk Ariṭṭha's obstinate adherence to his misunderstanding, recurs in the *Vinayas* of the Dharmaguptaka, Kāśyapīya, Mahāsāṅghika, Mahīśāsaka, (Mūla) Sarvāstivāda, Sarvāstivāda and Theravāda traditions as an exemplary case for unwillingness to give up a wrong view. (Anālayo 2011, 147)

All these references point to the importance attached to the sutta across a number of Buddhist traditions.

The principal message of the sutta happens to be emphasized and reiterated in the early *Prajñāpāramitā* literature which represents an attempt to rectify some of the misguided doctrinal tendencies that appeared in the historical development of Buddhist ideas within about the first two centuries after the demise of the Buddha. The *Vajracchedikā Prajñāpāramitā Sūtra*, for instance, refers to one of the two similes used by the Buddha in the sutta, namely the simile of the raft, in its attempt to deny the substantial existence of any real entities in the form of either Self or *Dharma* (*Na khalu punaḥ Subhūte bodhisattvena mahāsattvena dharma udgrahītavyo nādharmaḥ. Tasmād iyaṃ tathāgatena sandhāya vāg kolopamaṃ dharmaparyāyam ājānādbhir dharmā eva prahātavyā prāgevādharmā iti*: Mss 77). It is said in this context that Bodhisattvas entertain neither the conception of *dharmas* nor that of *adharmas*, for, if they were to entertain such conceptions they would also be involved in the grasping of a (real) self (*ātmagrāho*), being (*sattvagrāho*), soul (*jīvagrāho*) or person (*pudgalagrāho*). The Bodhisattva should neither grasp *dharmas* nor *adharmas*. Therefore, on account of this the *Tathāgata* spoke of the way of *Dharma* which is similar to a raft so that by those who understand, even *Dharmā* ought to be abandoned, while to begin with *Adharmā* ought to be. All these references point to the importance attached to the sutta across a number of Buddhist traditions.

The *Alagaddūpama Sutta* in the Pali Canon

As in the non-Theravāda versions of the *Alagaddūpama Sutta*, the version in the Pali canon too, which is our primary source for discussion, opens with mention of Ariṭṭha's firm commitment to the wrong view that in associating with practices that the Buddha had declared to be conducive to danger in safeguarding the principles of the holy life, such association (*ye te antarāyikā dhammā vuttā bhagavatā te paṭisevato*) really conduces to no danger (*nālaṃ antarāyā ti*). The commentarial explanation of 'practices conducive to danger' in this context is that it concerns sexual relationships (*methunadhamme doso natthīti:* Ps II 103). In the sutta itself, however, the Buddha draws attention not so much to the specific point about Ariṭṭha's view on sexual misconduct, but on the general point about the proper way to adopt and utilize his teachings. Ariṭṭha is initially reprimanded by the Buddha for holding on to a wrong view and in the ensuing discussion the Buddha focuses mainly on the possible abuses of his teaching.

According to the *Alagaddūpama Sutta*, having severely reprimanded Ariṭṭha, the Buddha drew attention to the wrong motives from which some may study what he taught. If anyone were to learn his *Dhamma* for the purpose of censuring or reproaching others who held different views with feelings of hostility (*upārambhānisaṃsaṃ*), or for the purpose of defending one's own dogma against the criticism of others (*itivādapamokkhānisaṃsaṃ*), the Buddha says that they make an abuse of the *Dhamma*. They are comparable to persons who take a snake by its tail, resulting in immediate harm to themselves. The simile of the snake is immediately followed by the simile of the raft (*kullūpama*) in which the Buddha compares the *Dhamma* taught by him to a raft used in order to cross over from insecurity to security and safety, keeping clearly in mind that the *Dhamma* should not be grasped with passion as a dogma. The *Alagaddūpama Sutta* belongs among other instances in which this theme of the Buddha's teaching distinguishing it from numerous worldviews known during his time. It shows the Buddha's role as one of the earliest thinkers in the history of philosophy who engaged in a critique of the craving for metaphysics and dogma frequently exhibited in those who propound worldviews. A belief or a worldview having no (positive) consequence upon the practical life of the individual believers, with no transformative effect upon the quality of their way of life, character traits, interpersonal relationships and sense of well-being, was considered as worthless. This feature of the Buddha's teaching has been presented as a distinguishing mark in several discourses as well as sections specially allocated in the canon for emphatically reiterating it.

References to the central message of the sutta in other Theravāda canonical sources

The very first discourse of the Buddha included in the *Sutta Piṭaka* of the Pali canon, the *Brahmajāla Sutta*, aims at a classified enumeration of all worldviews (*diṭṭhi*) that were known during the time of the Buddha with a view to emphasizing the fact that the Buddha's teaching transcended all those previously existing dogmas and was meant to serve a totally different purpose. The Buddha classified all the views known at that time into two main categories as (1) those propounded by speculators about the past (*pubbantakappikā*) and (2) those propounded by speculators about the future (*aparantakappikā*). The former are mentioned as those who made diverse illegitimate affirmations concerning the absolute beginning of the world and living beings, transcending the limits of all human experience (*pubbantaṃ ārabbha anekavihitāni adhivuttipadāni abhivadanti*). The latter made similar statements about the ultimate destiny (*aparantaṃ ārabbha*) of the world and its beings. In this context it is pointed out that the realities the Buddha realized and revealed to the world, having directly experienced them by himself through higher knowledge, were different (*aññeva dhammā ... ye tathāgato sayaṃ abhiññā sacchikatvā pavedeti*); they are profound, difficult to see, difficult to understand, calming, excellent, not conclusions derived from speculative reasoning, subtle and to be known by the wise (*gambhīrā duddasā duranubodhā, santā, paṇītā, atakkāvacarā, nipuṇā, paṇḍitavedanīyā:* D I 12). There are several characteristics common to these diverse views that the Buddha enumerated and considered objectionable. First, he pointed out that all those views were nothing but expressions of the sense of insecurity felt by persons who did not know and did not see, and were driven by craving, agitation and a sense of insecurity (*ajānataṃ apassataṃ vedayitaṃ taṇhāgatānaṃ paritasitavipphanditameva*; D I 41). Secondly, the foundation of each different view is given as the subjective sense experience of each individual with none of those views having a foundation other than sense impression (*phassa paccayā ... aññatra phassā paṭisaṃvedissantīti netaṃ ṭhānaṃ vijjati*; D I 43–4). Thirdly, the Buddha employed his vision into Dependent Arising to explain the destiny of those who depended on their subjective sense impressions and tried to cling to a world view objectified as the absolute truth due to their craving and attachment. He says that dependent on their craving arises clinging, and dependent on clinging the process of becoming, bringing about all the pains of a continuing flow of existence (D I 45).

The next noteworthy section in the Pali canon which draws attention to the same theme is the *Aṭṭhakavagga* of the *Suttanipāta*, the antiquity of which also can be established on strong evidential grounds.[1] The discourses in this section of the *Suttanipāta* emphasizing this particular theme are the *Duṭṭhaṭṭhaka, Suddhaṭṭhaka, Paramaṭṭhaka, Māgandiya, Pasūra,* the *Cūlaviyūha* and the *Mahāviyūha Suttas*. In the *Duṭṭhaṭṭhaka Sutta* the Buddha points out that people are inclined to grasp views

1. Regarding evidence for the antiquity of the *Aṭṭhakavagga* of the *Suttanipāta* see Norman 2001, Introduction; Pande 1983, 53–54; Jayawickrama 1948, 42–43.

with great tenacity and are unwilling to let go of them because they have taken them up due to the influence of strong desires and individual preferences:

> How could one go beyond one's own dogma to which one has been led in accordance with one's intense desire and preference (*sakaṃ hi diṭṭhiṃ katham accayeyya — Chandānunīto ruciyā niviṭṭho*). One would make one's own conclusive judgments depending upon (the confines of) one's knowledge (*Sayaṃ samattāni pakubbamāno — yathā hi jāneyya tathā vadeyya*). (Sn 781)

The Buddha points out how dogmas are a consequence of rationalizations of people's inclinations, desires, propensities, likes and dislikes. They are motivated and propelled by certain transient desires and they come to grasp a view strongly because they see some temporary advantage in holding it (*Yad attani passati ānisaṃsaṃ taṃ nissito kuppapaṭiccasantiṃ*; Sn 784). Due to the psychological fact that people have the latent tendency to cling to dogmas (*diṭṭhānusaya*) even if one dogma is given up they cling to another like monkeys who let go of one branch only to cling to another (*Te uggahāyanti nirassajanti — kapīva sākhaṃ pamuñcaṃ gahāya*; Sn 791). The dogmatism that goes with it usually results in interpersonal hostility, because one tends to look upon the views held by others as inferior. Whatever one exalts as the most superior view (*Yaduttariṃ kurute jantu loke*), in terms of that, one declares all other views as inferior (*hīnāti aññe tato sabbam āha*). Therefore, one cannot avoid conflicts and controversies (*Tasmā vivādāni avītivatto*; Sn 796). People call each other fools, each one clinging to their own dogma. The Buddha notes the ridiculous nature of such controversy, pointing out that if by virtue of rigidly conforming to a dogma one becomes wise then all of them could claim to be wise, and none among them is of inferior wisdom (*na tesaṃ koci parihīna pañño*; Sn 881), while by virtue of not conforming to one's own dogma, another person becomes a fool, then all those who do not conform to the dogmas of others will turn out to be fools (*sabbeva bālā sunihīnapaññā*; Sn 880) . The only reward they get from engaging in controversy in public debate regarding views is a boost to their pride and conceit, which in itself is morally damaging (Sn 829 and 883; see also 895–896).

The repeatedly emphasized message of the *Aṭṭhakavagga* of the *Suttanipāta* is that dogmatism is a product of an attempt to grasp a subjective construction of sense experience and affirm with strong conviction that one's construction is in accordance with the objective and absolute truth. The Buddha points out that this leads to a diversity of 'truths' that happen to be self-contradictory, resulting in disagreements and hostile debates about the nature of truth. People are attached to their individual subjective constructions in terms of *saññā* (perception) without realizing that *saññā* in itself is of an alterable nature. According to the Buddha, there cannot be diverse mutually contradictory eternal truths in the world other than due to *saññā* (*na heva saccāni bahūni nānā - aññatra saññāya niccāni loke*; Sn 886). It is persons who grasp *saññā* that come into conflict in the world clinging to dogmatic views (*saññañca diṭṭhiñca ye aggahesuṃ -te ghaṭṭayantā vicaranti loke*; Sn 847). One who is unattached to *saññā* has no bonds (*saññā virattassa na santi ganthā*; Sn 847). In the *Cūḷaviyūha Sutta* the Buddha speaks of one truth, the understanding of which puts an end to all disputation (*Ekaṃ hi saccaṃ na dutiyam atthi — yasmiṃ pajā no vivade pajānaṃ*; Sn 884). This statement of the Buddha is likely to be misunderstood as an affirmation of an absolute truth in terms of which nothing else can be considered as true. However, what was intended by the statement was that when one attained calmness and peace by the eradication of all corruptions of the mind, an attainment which was considered by the Buddha to be truly possible, there could no more be an inclination to enter into debates about truth (*no vivade*). This is further confirmed by the *Māgandiya Sutta* of the *Aṭṭhakavagga* where Māgandiya questions the Buddha to present his own dogma (*diṭṭhigataṃ ... vadesi kīdisaṃ*; Sn 836). In response, the Buddha presents no thesis as his judgment about absolute truth in the form 'This is what I affirm', having considered all the known dogmas (*idaṃ vadāmīti na tassa hoti dhammesu niccheyya samuggahītaṃ*). He further says that with vision, he does not cling to any view, but has seen the peace and tranquility within (*passañca diṭṭhīsu anuggahāya — ajjhattasantiṃ pacinaṃ adassaṃ*; Sn 837).

The Buddha used the term *pacceka-sacca*, 'individual truth' (Sn 824), signifying the subjective nature of opinions about truth that people affirmed primarily on the basis of speculative reason. It is observed that people get strongly attached to what they themselves conceive as the truth and due to being impassioned by their own dogmatic opinion (*sandiṭṭhirāgena hi te'bhirattā*; Sn 891) seek conformity of other persons also to the same viewpoint. Ten basic positions came to be identified in early Buddhism as dogmas pertaining to ultimate questions about the beginning and end of things (D I 187–188). The Buddha was sometimes found fault with for his refusal to commit himself to any one of those ten positions (D I 189). A disciple of the Buddha named Māluṅkyaputta threatened to leave the Buddha's order if the latter did not commit himself to a categorical position regarding those views (M I 426 f.). Sāriputta describes Buddhist monks with *ariyan* dispositions as those who have discarded the various subjective truths believed by diverse renunciants and brahmins, they have totally abandoned, thrown away, vomited them out, they are released from, have given up and relinquished them (*puthu samaṇabrāhmaṇānaṃ puthu paccekasaccāni nunnāni honti panunnāni cattāni vantāni muttāni pahīnāni paṭinissaṭṭhānāni*; D III 270). In the *Udāna* of the *Khuddaka Nikāya* those positions are compared to the descriptions of the reality of the nature of an elephant by persons born blind after experiencing with touch some limited part of the elephant's body (Ud 68f). The reasons given by the Buddha for not committing himself to any of those views were primarily of a pragmatic nature. They were considered as not productive of any beneficial outcome (*na atthasaṃhitaṃ*), not relevant to the objectives of his teaching (*na dhammasaṃhitaṃ*), not related to the fundamentals of the higher life (*na ādibrahmacariyakaṃ*), not conducive to disenchantment (*na nibbidāya*) with things that produce bondage, to dispassion (*na virāgāya*), to cessation (*na nirodhāya*), meaning the cessation of the continuing unsatisfactory process of existence, to calmness (*na upasamāya*), to higher understanding (*na abhiññāya*), to awakening to the immediately observable realities of existence (*na sambodhāya*) and to the peace of *Nibbāna* (*na nibbānāya*) (D I 188–189).

It is in the light of the Buddha's remarks represented in numerous discourses scattered in the Pali canon regarding the harmful consequences of dogmatic clinging to views resulting from the craving for grasping something as the absolute truth that the two similes occurring in the *Alagaddūpama Sutta* have to be understood. The importance of avoiding commitment to speculative views appears to be the central theme in the *Alagaddūpama Sutta.* This distinguishing feature of early Buddhism is consistently related and tied up in the sutta with other unique characteristics of the Buddha's teaching. In the *Saṃyutta-nikāya* the Buddha propounded his Philosophical Middle against two extreme positions held almost universally in human thought since the beginning of attempts on the part of humans to account for our experience of the world and its living beings. The Buddha's pronouncement of the Philosophical Middle was as a response to his own disciple Kaccāyanagotta's question regarding what is considered as the right view (*sammā diṭṭhi*). This brings us to the point that although the Buddha kept away from speculative views, he had a notion of a right view. The first extreme rejected in this context is that of Eternalism (*sassatavāda*) according to which both the self and the world are eternal (*sassato attā ca loko ca*) or everything exists (*sabbaṃ atthi*), in the sense that the underlying essence of everything is eternal. The second extreme was that of Annihilationism (*ucchedavāda*), according to which there is no continuity whatsoever and everything is just annihilated or destroyed at death including the life process of living beings (S II 17f.). The Buddha attributes both positions to craving and desire which take the two extreme forms of seeking for eternal existence due to intense attachment to life, or hoping for total destruction so that one does not have to care about how one lives one's life here and now.

The distinctive philosophical standpoint of early Buddhism as stated in the *Alagaddūpama Sutta*

In the *Alagaddūpama Sutta* after presenting the simile of the raft, the Buddha condenses the first extreme in the sphere of speculative views into a six-fold scheme (*cha diṭṭhiṭṭhānāni*) out of which the first five are attempts to see an eternal essence in one of the five aggregates of personality, namely, material form (*rūpa*), feelings (*vedanā*), perceptions (*saññā*), volitional constructions (*saṅkhārā*), and the totality of sensory consciousness inclusive of all its associations. The reference is to a mistaken identification of these processes superimposing an eternal essence on them and considering them as identical with a supposed eternal Self. The sixth is the view that the essence of the individual self is identical with the eternal essence of the cosmos and that departing from this world a person becomes one with the cosmic essence and survives to eternity (*so loko so attā so pecca bhavissāmi nicco dhuvo sassato avipariṇāmadhammo sassatisamaṃ tatheva ṭhassāmi*). In the history of human thought some philosophical conclusions relating to the nature of ultimate reality conform to this view point as in the monism of the *Upaniṣad*s and the monism of Spinoza, while in others such as Judaism, Christianity and Islam the saved soul is not seen to become one with God, but to be eternally in God's presence.

The Buddha recognized that those who entertained such views were agitated by the very thought of conceiving the non-existence of such a reality. However, the noble disciple who heeds the teaching of the Buddha is considered here as not being agitated by such a prospect (*so evaṃ passato asati na paritassati*). Agitation and dejection could occur due to the evanescent nature of things of the external world to one who is attached to those things, confirming the directly experienced truth about suffering caused by craving. Attention to this fact is drawn in the sutta by the Buddha saying that there would be suffering to a person due to the impermanence of external things (*siyā ... bahiddhā asati paritassanā*). In the case of a person who does not entertain thoughts associated with craving for such things, agitation does not occur. At this point the Buddha refers to his teaching which does not contain any view pertaining to eternity of any sort. The Buddha's teaching is for the total destruction of all dogmatic positions, and fixations of mind, the excitation and flaring up of all unwholesome emotions, and the latent tendency to strongly cling to things (*diṭṭhiṭṭhāna-adhiṭṭhāna-pariyuṭṭhāna-abhinivesa-anusayānaṃ paṭighātāya*). It is also for the appeasement of all volitional constructions (*sabba-saṅkhāra-samathāya*), for the giving up of all tendency to fix one's mind on things having approached them with craving (*sabbūpadhi-paṭinissaggāya*), for the destruction of craving (*taṇha-kkhayāya*), for dispassion (*virāgāya*), for cessation (*nirodhāya*) and for the tranquility of *Nibbāna* (*nibbānāya*). Those deeply immersed in the view that there was some kind of eternal life for the self were found to be intensely agitated when the Buddha or a disciple of the Buddha presented such a teaching. They suffered from the fear of annihilation of the Self and going into non-existence (*ucchijjissāmi nāma su vinassissāmi* nāma *su na hi nāma bhavissāmi*). A unique feature of the teaching of the Buddha among all religious philosophies consists in the negation of eternal life as the ultimate goal of the practice of the higher life. The aim is not to attain eternal life, but to understand the futility of aiming at such a goal, and liberating one's mind totally from craving and desire for the transient things of the world including the craving for continued existence in some form.

The section that follows the above in the *Alagaddūpama Sutta* clearly affirms the verifiable and non-authoritarian basis of the Buddhist teaching. In this section the Buddha compares the insights he had gained about reality with those of his disciples. He says that if there were to be any object of grasping that is permanent, fixed, eternal, not subject to change, and would stay as it is (*nicco dhuvo sassato avipariṇāmadhammo tatheva tiṭṭheyya*) one may grasp it. However, it is confirmed that neither in the personal experience of the Buddha nor in those of his disciples is such an object of grasping to be found. The Buddha also enquires about the possibility of clinging to a notion of self (*attavāda-upādānaṃ*), which by so doing would not give rise to grief, dejection and despair. Finally he asks whether there is any form of dependence on a dogma, depending on which the same consequence would not follow. There is common agreement on an experiential basis about the impossibility of this.

At the end of the discourse the Buddha points to the folly involved in the search for eternal life immersing oneself in the dogma of Eternalism and concludes that the view that one becomes eternal by merging with the Absolute Essence of the cosmos is entirely a foolish doctrine (*kevalo paripūro bāladhammo*). The Buddha's attention is drawn to the internal adjustment of the person resulting in a transformation at the cognitive and emotive levels of personality in such a way that the mind gets liberated from all defiling tendencies. Such a person is described in the sutta as one with a liberated mind (*vimuttacitto*). A person liberated in this manner is also described as one who has removed the cross-bar (*ukkhittapaligho*) signifying removing all the hindrances to insight, having destroyed ignorance altogether. He/she is also described as one who has filled the trench (*saṅkiṇṇaparikho*) in the sense that one has transcended altogether the possibility of becoming a victim of the cyclic process of existence which is productive of misery. He/she is one who has drawn out the arrow (*abbūḷhesiko*) in the sense that craving, which hurts like a poisoned arrow that has pierced the heart, causing existential suffering, has been altogether removed. Such a person is one who has been unlocked (*niraggalo*) in the sense that all the fetters belonging to the lower realms of existence have been broken asunder. He/she is a noble one who has thrown away the flag, laid aside the burden, and is undefiled (*ariyo pannadhajo pannabhāro visaṃyutto*) in the sense that all feelings of pride and conceit of the form 'I am' are altogether destroyed (*asmi māno pahīno*). Here, the Buddha says that a person with a liberated mind of that sort can be tracked by no other being in the world in such a way as to say 'his/her consciousness is fixed to (or leaning on) this' (*idaṃ nissitaṃ tathāgatassa viññāṇanti*).

A statement made by the Buddha in this context needs special attention because of the fact that the uniqueness of the Buddhist teaching implicit in the sutta tends to get blurred due to a misinterpretation of that statement by those who wish to bring back eternalist metaphysics into the teaching of the Buddha. The Buddha says that even in this life the *Tathāgata* cannot be known (*diṭṭhevāhaṃ dhamme tathāgato ananuvejjoti vadāmi*). The mistake occurs in attempting to interpret the Buddha's statement as a reference to the mysterious nature of the *Tathāgata*. The point is likely to get further confused when one relates this statement to other instances in which the Buddha speaks about the impossibility of categorically answering questions relating to the destiny of the liberated person after death.[2] However, little heed is paid to the simile of the fire that the Buddha used, in for instance, the *Aggivacchagotta Sutta*, because of the undue attention paid to the Buddha's use of words such as 'profound' (*gambhīro*), and 'immeasurable' (*appameyyo*) in describing the nature of the liberated person. The main point made in this context seems to be the meaninglessness of the questions raised regarding existence, non-existence etc. just as much as it is meaningless to question in which direction the fire has gone. There is no eternal essence in the flame which is a product of conditions. It goes on until the conditions consisting of the fuel last. The flame has come from no previous storehouse, nor will it be reabsorbed into an original essence from which it was produced. The conditions for its continuity have been removed or have ceased

2. This question is raised in the *Aggivacchagotta Sutta* in M I 486 f. where the Buddha attempts to explain the issue bringing in the simile of a fire.

to be. Consequently the fire is extinguished. This analogy suits well to explain the continuity of individuated existence through the five aggregates. It is only under the presupposition that there in an underlying essence that the questions relating to the after-death state of the liberated person could arise. There occurs in these instances a tendency towards the expression of the lurking metaphysical inclination in the minds of interpreters of religious doctrine to justify Eternalism.

There surely is an express denial by the Buddha in the concluding section of the *Alagaddūpama Sutta* of his association with any annihilationist view about the final destiny of living beings. The Buddha complains that some renunciants and brahmins falsely accuse him (*asatā tucchā musā abhūtena*) of being an Annihilationist, misrepresenting his position saying that he teaches about the annihilation, destruction and the disappearance (*ucchedaṃ vināsaṃ vibhavaṃ*) of a really existent being (*sato sattassa*). The emphasis here should be on the two terms '*sato sattassa*'. The Buddha's teaching is unique in this respect for not accepting the common assumption that there is a really existent being in the sense that there is an essence separable and apart from the observed transitory mental and material phenomena that constitute a living being, or indeed within these. The Buddha did not reject the notion of a living being as admitted in conventional language. What he rejected was that there is a hidden metaphysical reality which corresponds to terms used in our language for the purpose of identification through individuation the variety of sense impressions that impinge upon a person. According to the Buddha, the notion of a really existent being (*sato satta*) whose existence or non-existence needs to be predicated after death is based on an unwarranted assumption. It was due to that unwarranted assumption that the four questions pertaining to the after-death destiny of the liberated person were raised.

The above point is further clarified in the *Avyākata-saṃyutta* of the *Saṃyutta-nikāya*, where mention is made of Anurādha, a disciple of the Buddha being confronted with these questions by other religious teachers. Anurādha seeks the help of the Buddha himself in order to get a clarification. The Buddha then points out to Anurādha that all the aggregates of personality such as material form are characterized by change, unsatisfactoriness and absence of a soul essence. Having taught about the reality of each of the personality aggregates and shown that one should be disenchanted with them, the Buddha asks Anurādha whether the *Tathāgata* is identical with any of the aggregates (*rūpaṃ tathāgatoti samanupassasi ...*), whether the *Tathāgata* is conceivable within one of the aggregates (*rūpasmiṃ tathāgatoti samanupassasi ...*), whether the *Tathāgata* is conceivable apart from the aggregates (*aññatra rūpā tathāgatoti samanupassasi ...*), whether the *Tathāgata* is conceivable as the collection of the aggregates (*rūpaṃ vedanā saññā saṅkhārā viññāṇaṃ tathāgatoti samanupassasi*) and finally whether there is some entity without the possession of material form etc. who is conceivable as the *Tathāgata* (*ayaṃ so arūpī avedano ... tathāgatoti samanupassasi*) to all of which Anurādha responded in the negative. At this point the Buddha draws the attention of Anurādha to the fact that in truth and reality the *Tathāgata* cannot be obtained as an essence even in this immediate life (*diṭṭheva dhamme saccato thetato tathāgate anupalabbhiyamāne ...;* S IV 380–384). If that is so the questions pertaining to his existence etc. after his death become senseless. On the premises of the teaching of the Buddha, such questions become meaningless. They become meaningful only on the assumption of an essential person to begin with.

In the concluding section of the *Alagaddūpama Sutta*, the Buddha draws attention to the fact that throughout his career (*pubbe cevāhaṃ etarahi ca*, literally meaning both previously and now) he taught about suffering and its cessation (*dukkhañceva paññapemi dukkhassa ca nirodhaṃ*). The uniqueness of the Buddha's teaching rested on the fact that he was not engaged in the search for eternal life, but the understanding of suffering and eliminating it. The reason why the Buddha consistently refrained from committing himself to the existing viewpoints relating to the metaphysical questions raised, saying that they should be treated as undeclared or unexplained issues (*avyākata*) and that instead, there is a significant body of issues on which he provided explanations (*vyākata*), is amply clarified in the *Alagaddūpama Sutta.*

The real significance of the Buddha's claim that his teaching is in the middle, avoiding the extremes of Eternalism and Annihilationism, has often been undermined even in serious scholarly attempts made to interpret his teaching due to the weighty influence that the common ways of philosophizing about existence have had upon the human mind. One of the reputed Eastern scholars of the previous century who interpreted Buddhism as presenting the conception of an Absolute metaphysical Being as the ultimate goal to be attained is S. Radhakrishnan. According to him:

> Nirvāṇa is an eternal condition of being, for it is not a saṃskāra, or what is made or put together, which is impermanent. It continues while its expressions change. This is what lies behind the skandhas, which are subject to birth and decay. The illusion of becoming is founded on the reality of nirvāṇa. Buddha does not attempt to define it, since it is the root principle of all and so is indefinable. (Radhakrishnan 1929, 449)
>
> Nirvāṇa is timeless existence, and so Buddha must admit the reality of a timeless self. There is a being at the back of all life which is unconditioned, above all empirical categories, something which does not give rise to any effect and is not the effect of anything else. (Radhakrishnan 1929, 451–452)

It is not difficult to see that the above interpretation of Radhakrishnan goes completely against the spirit of the *Alagaddūpama Sutta.*

Two recent scholars who have interpreted the Buddhist concept of *Nibbāna* in a manner that is compatible with the present interpretation of the Buddha's message in the *Alagaddūpama Sutta* are D.J. Kalupahana and Asanga Tilakaratne. Kalupahana argues against Rune Johansson's view that what survives the death of the person who attains *Nibbāna* is *citta* or a kind of refined consciousness (Kalupahana 1976, 82–87). He also believes that K.N. Jayatilleke, who consistently argued the case for the attribution of an empiricist epistemology to the Buddha, finally compromised his position by admitting in connection with the concept of *Nibbāna* after the death of the person who attains it, the existence of something '"transempirical which cannot be empirically described and understood but which can be realized and attained"' (Kalupahana 1976, 87, citing Jayatilleke 1963, 476). Asanga Tilakaratne has attempted to interpret the notions of transcendence and ineffability in the context of Buddhist teachings could be understood in a way that obviates the necessity to affirm the notion of a persisting transcendental and ineffable reality beyond death (Tilakaratne, 1993).

As the Buddha pointed out, the people of the world are mostly stuck in one or the other of two viewpoints (*dvaya-nissita*), both of which are produced by the inability to see things with proper insight (*sammāppaññāya passati*) as they really come to be (*yathābhūtaṃ*). The most distinguishing feature of the Buddha's teaching is the avoidance of the dogma of an eternal Self or Being, while at the same time not falling into the extreme of materialistic Annihilationism. A close look at the *Alagaddūpama Sutta* shows that the message contained in it is in conformity with this distinctive characteristic of the Buddha's teaching.

Abbreviations

D I	*Dīgha-nikāya* Volume I. 1975. edited by T.W. Rhys Davids and J. Estin Carpenter. London: Pali Text Society.
M I	*Majjhima-nikāya* Volume I. 1979 edited by V. Trenckner. London: Pali Text Society.
M III	*Majjhima-nikāya* Volume III. 1977 edited by Robert Chalmers. London: Pali Text Society.
Mss	*Mahāyāna-sūtra-saṃgraha* Part I, 1961. edited by P.L. Vaidya. Mithila Institute of Post-Graduate Studies and Research in Sanskrit Learning.
Ps II	*Papañcasūdanī Majjhimanikāya-Aṭṭhakathā* Volume II. 1979 edited by J.H. Woods and D. Kosambi. London: Pali Text Society.
S II	*Saṃyutta-nikāya* Volume II. 1989 edited by M. Leon Feer. Oxford: Pali Text Society.
S IV	*Saṃyutta-nikāya* Volume IV. 1990 edited by M. Leon Feer. Oxford: Pali Text Society.
Sn	*Sutta-nipāta.* 1984 edited by Dines Anderson and Helmer Smith. London: Pali Text Society.
Ud	*Udāna.* 1982. edited by Paul Steinthal. London: Pali Text Society.

Bibliography

Anālayo Bhikkhu. 2011. *A Comparative Study of the Majjhima-nikāya.* Dharma Drum Buddhist College Research Series no. 3. Taipei: Dharma Drum Publishing.

Jayatilleke, K. N. 1963. *Early Buddhist Theory of Knowledge.* London: George Allen and Unwin.

Jayawickrama, N. A. 1948. 'The Criteria for the Analysis of the Sutta Nipāta'. *University of Ceylon Review* VI: 42–43.

Kalupahana, D. J. 1976. *Buddhist Philosophy: A Historical Analysis.* Honolulu: University Press of Hawaii.

Norman, K. R., trans. 2001. *The Group of Discourses (Sutta-Nipāta).* Oxford: Pali Text Society.

Pande, G. C. 1983. *Studies in the Origins of Buddhism.* Delhi: Motilal Banarsidass.

Radhakrishnan, S. 1929. *Indian Philosophy, Vol. I.* Second edition. London: George Allen and Unwin.

Tilakaratne, A. 1993. *Nirvāṇa and Ineffability: A Study of the Buddhist Theory of Reality and Language*. University of Kelaniya, Sri Lanka: Postgraduate Institute of Pali and Buddhist Studies.

P. D. Premasiri is Professor Emeritus at the Department of Pali and Buddhist Studies at the University of Peradeniya, Sri Lanka, and President of the Buddhist Publication Society and the Sri Lanka Association for Buddhist Studies. He has published numerous papers on Buddhist philosophy, Pāli literature, and Buddhist ethics, and *The Philosophy of the Atthakavagga* (Buddhist Publication Society 2008).

— 9 —

An *Ekottarika-āgama* Discourse Without Parallels: From Perception of Impermanence to the Pure Land

ANĀLAYO

With the present paper I study and translate a discourse in the *Ekottarika-āgama* preserved in Chinese of which no parallel in other discourse collections is known. This situation relates to the wider issue of what significance to accord to the absence of parallels from the viewpoint of the early Buddhist oral transmission. The main topic of the discourse itself is perception of impermanence, which is of central importance in the early Buddhist scheme of the path for cultivating liberating insight. A description of the results of such practice in this *Ekottarika-āgama* discourse has a somewhat ambivalent formulation that suggests a possible relation to the notion of rebirth in the Pure Abodes, *suddhāvāsa*. This notion, attested in a Pāli discourse, in turn might have provided a precedent for the aspiration, prominent in later Buddhist traditions, to be reborn in the Pure Land.

Introduction

The discourses found in the four Pāli *Nikāyas* and their counterparts in the Chinese *Āgamas* and at times in Gāndhārī and Sanskrit fragments or Tibetan translation, and on rare occasions even in Uighur, are the final product of centuries of oral transmission. According to the traditional account, these discourse collections hearken back to the first *saṅgīti* or 'communal recitation', to follow the terminology employed by Lance Cousins (1991, 27), the scholar in whose honour this article has been written.[1] Accounts of this *saṅgīti* in the Dharmaguptaka, Haimavata (?), Mahāsāṅghika, Mahīśāsaka, and Mūlasarvāstivāda *Vinayas* agree that at that time the corpus of orally transmitted discourses was divided into four main groups.[2] These allocate together long discourses, medium-length discourses, shorter discourses assembled by topic, and shorter discourses that involve some numerically arranged item between one and ten or eleven. The Theravāda *Vinaya* speaks of five such groups, adding a miscellaneous section now known as the *Khuddaka-nikāya*.[3]

1. Cf. also Gombrich 1990, 25 and the discussion in Tilakaratne 2000 and Skilling 2009, 55–60.
2. T 1428 at T XXII 968b19, T 1463 at T XXIV 820a23, T 1425 at T XXII 491c16, T 1421 at T XXII 191a24, T 1451 at T XXIV 407b27, and D 6 *da* 314a7 or Q 1035 *ne* 297a5.
3. Vin II 287,27. On the *Khuddaka-nikāya* cf., e.g., Abeynayake 1984, 33–46, Collins 1990, 108 note 11, von Hinüber 1996/1997, 42f, and Freiberger 2011, 218.

Keywords: Chinese *Āgamas*, discourse parallels, early Buddhism, impermanence, oral transmission, Pure Abodes, Pure Land

It seems indeed plausible that at a fairly early stage in the Buddhist oral tradition some such grouping would have come into being in order to facilitate a division of labour among reciters, not all of whom would have been able to memorize the entire corpus of texts in circulation at that time. In contrast, the *aṅga*s mentioned in several early discourses are probably best understood as referring to textual genres, rather than being a division of texts into groups.[4] As summed up by Lance Cousins (2013, 106), regarding the *aṅga*s, 'there is no indication anywhere that any of this has anything to do with an arrangement of the canonical literature in some kind of earlier recension.'

Whereas a basic division into groups, referred to as *Āgama*s or *Nikāya*s, appears to be a common starting point, the allocation of discourses to one of these groups seems to have been rather school-specific. In view of the ongoing demand to maintain the oral tradition, it is perhaps not surprising if different lineages of reciters took varying decisions in this respect, reflecting the need to ensure that each collection attracted sufficient prospective reciters willing to learn its contents and thereby ensure its transmission to future generations.

As a net result of these differing allocations, at present only one complete set of these four groups of discourses is extant, namely the Theravāda collection of the Pāli *Nikāya*s. Although it can safely be assumed that the reciter lineages of other Buddhist schools would have maintained comparable groupings of discourses, at present we only have access to parts of such collections, as the four main Chinese *Āgama*s do not belong to the same school. Besides resulting in some degree of overlap, in that a single Pāli discourse can have more than one parallel, found in different *Āgama*s, this situation also results in the existence of discourses without parallels, in the sense that a discourse is extant only from one of the reciter traditions to which we still have access.

The implications of a discourse having no known parallels are not necessarily straightforward. Although at first sight one might be tempted to conclude that this must reflect the comparatively late date of the coming into existence of this discourse, in actual fact the situation is more complex. An example in case would be the *Jīvaka-sutta* of the *Majjhima-nikāya*, which is without a parallel in the Chinese *Āgamas*.[5] Yet this does not imply that the Pāli discourse is late itself, or else that the reciters of the *Madhyama-āgama*, a collection probably transmitted within a Sarvāstivāda milieu,[6] dropped such a discourse from their collection of medium long discourses.[7] Instead, the reason is simply that the Sarvāstivāda reciters had allocated this text to their collection of long discourses; the recently discovered Sanskrit fragment *Dīrgha-āgama* does indeed have a version of this discourse.[8]

4. Cf. in more detail Anālayo 2016a.
5. MN 55 at MN I 368,17–371,22.
6. The general consensus among scholars on the school affiliation of the *Madhyama-āgama* has recently been called into question by Chung and Fukita 2011, 13–34, as well as Chung 2014 and Chung 2017; for critical replies cf. Anālayo 2012, 516–521 and Anālayo 2017b.
7. This has been assumed by Minh Chau 1964/1991, 31f.
8. Cf. the survey in Hartmann and Wille 2014, 141.

Nevertheless, the above-mentioned first-sight impression certainly carries considerable probability and in the case of the *Dīrgha-āgama* preserved in Chinese it seems that the three discourses in this collection that do not have a parallel are indeed of somewhat later origin.[9] In what follows I examine how far the same holds for a discourse in the *Ekottarika-āgama*, which to the best of my knowledge has so far not been translated or studied, at least in a Western-language publication.

A case study of a discourse without parallels from this collection is of particular interest, because the *Ekottarika-āgama* at times contains rather evolved manifestations of Mahāyāna thought (Anālayo 2013a).[10] In fact the *Ekottarika-āgama* even shows clear signs of a substantial reworking of the collection in China, resulting in the merging together of discourses that must have originally been distinct texts (Anālayo 2014/2015, 2015). Another remarkable feature is the apparent wholesale addition of a discourse, an addition evident from the distinctly different Chinese translation terminology, making it safe to conclude that this discourse would have been added in its Chinese form to the *Ekottarika-āgama* (Anālayo 2013b). This distinct character of the *Ekottarika-āgama* sets it apart from the other Chinese *Āgamas*, which show no signs of having gone through a comparable development in China. In view of this, one would easily suspect a discourse without parallel in this collection to be indeed distinctly late. Yet, as I hope to show in the remainder of the present article, this is not necessarily the case. In what follows I first translate the discourse in question.[11]

Translation

Thus have I heard. At one time the Buddha was at Sāvatthi in Jeta's Grove, the Park of Anāthapiṇḍika. At that time the Blessed One said to the monastics:[12]

'You should give attention to the perception of impermanence, widely [cultivate] the perception of impermanence. Having given attention to and widely [cultivated] the perception of impermanence, you will completely eradicate craving for the sen-

9. Cf. in more detail Anālayo 2014.

10. This to some extent relates to the challenging question of the school affiliation of this collection. Several scholars have argued for a Mahāsāṅghika affiliation of the *Ekottarika-āgama*; cf. Mayeda 1985, 102f (offering a survey of opinions in this respect by Japanese scholars), Pāsādika 2010, Kuan 2012, Kuan 2013a, Kuan 2013b, and Kuan 2013c; on the suggestion by Bareau 1955, 57 that the introduction to the collection points to such an affiliation cf. Anālayo 2013b, 15–19. Hiraoka 2013, however, points out narrative affinities between texts found in the *Ekottarika-āgama* and in the Sarvāstivāda tradition(s); cf. also points raised in Palumbo 2013, 297ff. Yet, as far as I can see, Harrison (2002, 19) is quite right when he states that the *Ekottarika-āgama* 'can hardly be Sarvāstivādin' (*pace* Palumbo 2013, 102 note 8); in fact, according to Kuan 2017, 446f, a central argument raised by Palumbo 2013 in favour of a Sarvāstivāda affiliation is based on a misunderstanding of a Chinese idiom. In view of the compositional history of the collection and the clear evidence for substantial Chinese influence on its final state, it seems to me that the school affiliation of this collection, at least in its present state, can no longer be determined; cf. Anālayo 2016b, 211–214.

11. The translated discourse is EĀ 38.2 at T II 717b28 to 717c17.

12. Here and elsewhere, I translate counterparts to the Pāli *bhikkhu* or Sanskrit *bhikṣu* with the gender-neutral 'monastic', in order to reflect the fact that in its general usage in the early discourses *bhikkhu* or *bhikṣu* can include female monastics; cf. in more detail Collett and Anālayo 2014.

sual sphere, and craving for the material sphere and the immaterial sphere, and you will also eradicate ignorance and conceit.

It is like a fire used to burn grass and sticks, which exhausts them forever and without a remainder, just without traces left behind. It is just like this when, on cultivating the perception of impermanence, one completely eradicates craving for the sensual [sphere] and craving for the material [sphere] and the immaterial [sphere], and ignorance and conceit, [eradicating them] forever and without a remainder.

The reason is, monastics, that at the time you cultivate the perception of impermanence your mind becomes dispassionate. By having a dispassionate mind, one in turn is capable of analyzing the *Dharma* and giving attention to its meaning, without there being worry, sadness, pain, and vexation. By having given attention to the meaning of the *Dharma*, one is not deluded or mistaken in one's practice. If one sees that there is a quarrel, one in turn has this thought:

"Those venerable ones do not cultivate the perception of impermanence, do not widely [cultivate] the perception of impermanence, for this reason they devote themselves to this quarrel. By quarrelling, they do not contemplate the meaning [of the *Dharma*]. By not contemplating its meaning, their minds are consequently confused. By persisting in this delusion, with the ending of life they will enter the three evil destinies: that of hungry ghosts, of animals, [or] of being in hell."

Therefore, monastics, you should cultivate the perception of impermanence, widely [cultivate] the perception of impermanence, and in turn become free from perceptions of ill will or delusion, becoming capable of contemplating the *Dharma* and contemplating its meaning. After the end of life, three good conditions will arise: being reborn in heaven or among humans, or the path to *Nirvāṇa*. Monastics, it is in this way that you should train.'

At that time the monastics, hearing what the Buddha had said, were delighted and received it respectfully.

Study

The gist of the above discourse is well in line with the importance given to contemplation of impermanence elsewhere in the early discourses. For example, according to a discourse in the *Saṃyutta-nikāya* and a parallel in the partially preserved *Saṃyukta-āgama*, insight into impermanence applied to the five aggregates of clinging is a way of cultivating insight that will bring lust or craving to an end and lead to liberation.[13] This accords well with the indication made in the passage translated above that the perception of impermanence will eradicate the three types of craving, namely those related to the sense-sphere, the material sphere, and the immaterial sphere. In this way, as far as the importance given to impermanence is concerned, the above translated text is well within the ambit of thought generally reflected in the early discourses.

An interesting contribution it makes is to relate the perception of impermanence to the arising of quarrels. The point appears to be that those who get heated up in attack and counterattack in a debate or litigation have lost the overall picture of reality as a changing process, which due to lacking permanence inevitably lacks the potential to provide true satisfaction or to be in some way or another something

13. SN 22.51 at SN III 51,15 speaks of the destruction of lust (*rāga*) and delight (*nandi*), and its parallel SĀ³ 12 at T II 496b27 of the destruction of craving (愛) and lust (貪).

one can truly grasp and appropriate as one's own. In other words, what is impermanent consequently must be *dukkha* and what is *dukkha* is certainly empty, a view of things that indeed would leave little room for the type of self-righteous attitude that fuels quarrels and litigations.[14]

Another dimension of the discourse above that requires further comment is the passage that I have translated as 'three good conditions will arise: being reborn in heaven or among humans, or the path to *Nirvāṇa*.' The term I have rendered as 'to arise' is 生, which could equally well be translated as 'birth'. In fact, to some extent such a translation would fit the context better, since the preceding passage speaks of entering the three evil destinies and thus is clearly concerned with forms of rebirth. Given that the present passage also has three different options, it would be natural to assume that it intends to present a contrast to what has been said earlier. The only problem with such an understanding, which has motivated me, after some hesitation, to opt for the translation 'arise', is that the third of these three options speaks of the 'path to *Nirvāṇa*'.

However, the idea of being born on the path to *Nirvāṇa* could be made sense of as referring to the taking of birth in a Pure Abode. These are heavens in Buddhist cosmology where only non-returners dwell and thus indeed a realm of rebirth that one could consider to be a 'path to *Nirvāṇa*', since all of its inhabitants are invariably destined to reach the final goal in those very realms. Moreover, given that all the inhabitants in a Pure Abode are, as non-returners, by definition free from desire and aversion, it would be a place that offers ideal conditions for further progress to the final goal. Thus being reborn in a Pure Abode could indeed be suitably reckoned a form of rebirth 'on the path to *Nirvāṇa*', by dint of the ideal conditions for progress along the path to the final goal combined with the certainty of reaching the goal in that same life time.

The idea of an actual aspiring to rebirth in the Pure Abodes can be found in the *Saṅkhārupapatti-sutta* of the *Majjhima-nikāya*. This discourse describes a monastic who is in possession of the five qualities of faith, virtue, learning, renunciation, and wisdom. Endowed with these five qualities, the monastic will be able to achieve various rebirths aspired to, ranging from the human realm to various heavens, including the Pure Abodes. The relevant passage proceeds as follows:[15]

> A monastic who possesses faith, possesses virtue, possesses learning, possesses renunciation, and possesses wisdom hears that the *devas* of radiance (*vehapphalā*) are long lived and beautiful, with abundant happiness. [The monastic] thinks: 'Oh, that on the breaking up of the body after death I might reappear in the company of the *devas* of radiance!' [The monastic] fixes the mind on it, resolves the mind on it, and develops the mind for it. These aspirations and this abiding, developed and cultivated in this way, lead to [the monastic's] reappearance there.

14. As Deshung Rinpoche 1995, 162 explains: 'someone who recollects the teachings on impermanence can very quickly decide what is worthwhile and what is not, and will soon become discriminating about his actions.'

15. The translation is based on MN 120 at MN III 103,1 (the abbreviated parts are supplemented from a previous section of the discourse); for a comparative study cf. Anālayo 2011, 679–681.

The *Saṅkhārupapatti-sutta* continues, after having taken up the *vehapphalā devas*, by making similar stipulations for rebirth among the *avihā, atappā, sudassī*, and *akaniṭṭhā devas*, thereby covering the different realms of the Pure Abodes recognized in early Buddhist cosmology. Each time the attraction of the long life, beauty, and happiness of these celestial beings leads the monastic to aspire for rebirth in the respective realm, and due to having such aspiration as well as the five qualities mentioned at the outset, such rebirth will indeed be accomplished.

Another Pāli discourse of relevance to my present exploration and from the same *Majjhima-nikāya* is the *Alagaddūpama-sutta*. After listing several levels of awakening attained by disciples of the Buddha in descending order, the discourse closes off with the asseveration that all those who have sufficient faith and love (*pema*) for the Buddha are bound for heaven:[16]

> In the *Dharma* thus well-proclaimed by me, being manifest, open, evident, and free of patchwork, those who have sufficient faith and sufficient love for me are all bound for heaven.

The *Madhyama-āgama* parallel to the *Alagaddūpama-sutta* has a similar statement:[17]

> My *Dharma* being in this way well proclaimed, revealed, and disseminated without deficiency, transmitted and propagated to *devas* and human beings, those who have faith and who delight in me will, on passing away, all be reborn in a good realm.

Combining this indication with the *Saṅkhārupapatti-sutta* to my mind shows that already among the early discourses ideas can be found that might well have served as a precedent for the notion in later tradition of aspiring to rebirth in the Pure Land.[18] I would contend that the similarities between the Pure Abodes and the Pure Land as celestial realms that afford ideal practice conditions, as well as the importance of an aspiration to such rebirth (notably by monastics) in the *Saṅkhārupapatti-sutta* and the reference to faith and love for the Buddha in the *Alagaddūpama-sutta* and its parallel are striking enough to allow for such a suggestion.

The passages just mentioned would in fact be better candidates for such a hypothesis than the discourse from the *Ekottarika-āgama* translated earlier. Besides the fact that the passage in question is ambiguous and allows for different translations, it does not bring in the motif of an aspiration for rebirth in a particular realm nor does it take up the topic of faith and love for the Buddha.

In this way, the above translated *Ekottarika-āgama* seems to be well in line with the type of thought reflected in other early discourses and in the case of one possible reading of a somewhat ambivalent passage, two Pāli discourses take a more pronounced stance in this respect. In sum, the *Ekottarika-āgama* passage in question

16. The translated passage is found in MN 22 at MN I 142,5; for comments on or reference to this passage cf., e.g., de La Vallée Poussin 1927/2001, 233; Ludowyk-Gyomroi 1947, 32; Upadhyaya 1980, 352; Cruise 1983, 159; and Norman 1991/1993, 184.

17. The translated passage is found in MĀ 200 at T I 766b23; for a comparative study cf. Anālayo 2011, 158.

18. On Indian antecedents for Pure Land Buddhism cf., e.g., Eckel 2003, Nattier 2003, and Strauch 2010.

need not be reflecting developments substantially later than those evident in the four Pāli *Nikāyas* in general.

This in turn gives the impression as if the circumstance that the discourse translated above does not have a parallel need not imply that it must be late. Instead, it may well be a case comparable to that of the *Jīvaka-sutta* of the *Majjhima-nikāya*, discussed above, although with the difference that in this case no Pāli parallels is known from what by all means does appear to be a complete set of the four discourse collections. Yet, although complete from the viewpoint of the Theravāda reciter tradition, it clearly need not be seen as a complete reflection of early Buddhist discourse material.

The *Ekottarika-āgama* has in fact at times preserved early material. One example is the only textual description of an actual footprint of the Buddha among the early discourses. Here the *Ekottarika-āgama* description has preserved a version of this footprint that is not yet adorned by a wheel-mark and thus quite probably earlier than its parallels, including a discourse in the *Aṅguttara-nikāya* and a version extant in Gāndhārī belonging to the British Library Kharoṣṭhī fragments, all of which describe the footprint being adorned with a wheel-mark, which they depict with varying detail.[19]

All of the foregoing taken together thus serves to show the complexity of the processes of oral transmission and textual formation responsible for what we now have access to in the form of the *Āgamas* and their Pāli *Nikāya* parallels.

Conclusion

An *Ekottarika-āgama* discourse without parallels turns out on closer inspection to display no definite signs of lateness, corroborating the fact that the complexity of the transmission of the early discourses is such that it does not allow invariably equating lack of parallels with lateness. At the same time, however, the discourse has an intriguing passage which, on adopting one of its possible interpretations, would point to the idea of rebirth in the Pure Abodes. This idea is found in a more explicit form in a Pāli discourse. Together with the indication in another Pāli discourse that faith and love for the Buddha lead to heaven, such ideas might have set a precedent for the aspiration found in later Buddhist traditions to be reborn in the Pure Land.

Acknowledgements

I am indebted to Bhikkhunī Dhammadinnā and Michael Running for commenting on a draft version of this paper.

19. EĀ 38.3 at T II 717c21 and its parallels AN 4.36 at AN II 37,26, British Library Kharoṣṭhī fragment 12 line 4f, Allon 2001, 120, SĀ 101 at T II 28a23, and SĀ² 267 at T II 467a29; cf. in more detail the discussion in Anālayo 2017a, 23–26.

Abbreviations

AN	*Aṅguttara-nikāya*
D	Derge
DN	*Dīgha-nikāya*
EĀ	*Ekottarika-āgama* (T 125)
MN	*Majjhima-nikāya*
Q	Peking
SĀ	*Saṃyukta-āgama* (T 99)
SĀ[2]	*Saṃyukta-āgama* (T 100)
SĀ[3]	*Saṃyukta-āgama* (T 101)
SN	*Saṃyutta-nikāya*
T	Taishō edition
Vin	*Vinaya*

Bibliography

Abeynayake, Oliver. 1984. *A Textual and Historical Analysis of the Khuddaka Nikāya.* Colombo: Tisara.

Allon, Mark. 2001. *Three Gāndhārī Ekottarikāgama-Type Sūtras, British Library Kharoṣṭhī Fragments 12 and 14.* Seattle: University of Washington Press.

Anālayo. 2011. *A Comparative Study of the Majjhima-nikāya.* Taipei: Dharma Drum Publishing.

———. 2012. *Madhyama-āgama Studies.* Taipei: Dharma Drum Publishing.

———. 2013a. 'Mahāyāna in the Ekottarika-āgama'. *Singaporean Journal of Buddhist Studies* 1: 5–43.

———. 2013b. 'Two Versions of the Mahādeva Tale in the Ekottarika-āgama, A Study in the Development of Taishō No. 125'. In *Research on the Ekottarika-āgama (Taishō 125)*, edited by Dhammadinnā, 1–70. Taipei: Dharma Drum Publishing.

———. 2014. 'Three Chinese Dīrgha-āgama Discourses Without Parallels'. In *Research on the Dīrgha-āgama*, edited by Dhammadinnā, 1–55. Taipei: Dharma Drum Publishing.

———. 2014/2015. 'Discourse Merger in the Ekottarika-āgama (2), The Parallels to the Kakacūpama-sutta and the Alagaddūpama-sutta'. *Journal of the Centre for Buddhist Studies, Sri Lanka* 12: 63–90.

———. 2015. 'Discourse Merger in the Ekottarika-āgama (1), The Parallel to the Bhaddāli-sutta and the Latukikopama-sutta, Together with Notes on the Chinese Translation of the Collection'. *Singaporean Journal of Buddhist Studies* 2: 5–35.

———. 2016a. 'Āgama and aṅga in the Early Buddhist Oral Tradition'. *Singaporean Journal of Buddhist Studies* 3: 9–37.

———. 2016b. *Ekottarika-āgama Studies.* Taipei: Dharma Drum Publishing.

———. 2017a. *Buddhapada and the Bodhisattva Path.* Bochum: Projektverlag.

———. 2017b. 'The "School Affiliation" of the Madhyama-āgama'. In *Research on the Madhyama-āgama*, edited by Dhammadinnā, 55–76. Taipei: Dharma Drum Publishing.

Bareau, André. 1955. *Les sectes bouddhiques du Petit Véhicule.* Paris: École Française d'Extrême-Orient.

Chung Jin-il. 2014. 'Puṇya-sūtra of the Ekottarikāgama in Comparison with the Fu-jing of the Chinese Madhyamāgama'. *Critical Review for Buddhist Studies* 16: 9–33.

———. 2017. 'Śrutānṛśamsa-sūtra of the Dīrghāgama in Comparison with the Wende-jing 聞德經 of the Madhyama-āgama'. In *Research on the Madhyama-āgama*, edited by Dhammadinnā, 113–146. Taipei: Dharma Drum Publishing.

Chung Jin-il and Fukita T. 2011. *A Survey of the Sanskrit Fragments Corresponding to the Chinese Madhyama-āgama, Including References to Sanskrit Parallels, Citations, Numerical Categories of Doctrinal Concepts and Stock Phrases*. Tokyo: Sankibo Press.

Collett, Alice and Anālayo. 2014. 'Bhikkhave and Bhikkhu as Gender-inclusive Terminology in Early Buddhist Texts'. *Journal of Buddhist Ethics* 21: 760–797.

Collins, Steven. 1990. 'On the Very Idea of the Pali Canon'. *Journal of the Pali Text Society* 15: 89–126.

Cousins, L. S. 1991. 'The "Five Points" and the Origins of the Buddhist Schools'. In *The Buddhist Forum Vol. II*, edited by T. Skorupski, 27–60. London: University of London, School of Oriental and African Studies.

———. 2013. 'The Early Development of Buddhist Literature and Language in India'. *Journal of the Oxford Centre for Buddhist Studies* 5: 89–135.

Cruise, Henry. 1983. 'Early Buddhism: Some Recent Misconceptions'. *Philosophy East and West* 33(2): 149–166. https://doi.org/10.2307/1399099

de La Vallée Poussin, Louis. 1927/2001. *La Morale Bouddhique*. Saint Michel: Éditions Dharma.

Deshung Rinpoche, Kunga Tenpay Nyima. 1995. *The Three Levels of Spiritual Perfection, An Oral Commentary on the Three Visions (Nang Sum) of Ngorchen Könchog Lhündrub*, translated by J. Rhoton. Boston, MA: Wisdom Publications.

Eckel, David. 2003. 'Defining a Usable Past: Indian Sources for Shin Buddhist Theology'. *Pacific World, Third Series* 5: 55–83.

Freiberger, Oliver. 2011. 'Was ist das Kanonische am Pāli-Kanon?'. In *Kanonisierung und Kanonbildung in der asiatischen Religionsgeschichte*, eds Max Deeg, Oliver Frieberger and Christoph Kleine, 209–232. Vienna: Verlag der Österreichischen Akademie der Wissenschaften.

Gombrich, Richard F. 1990. 'How the Mahāyāna Began'. *The Buddhist Forum* 1: 21–30.

Harrison, Paul. 2002. 'Another Addition to the An Shigao Corpus? Preliminary Notes on an Early Chinese Saṃyuktāgama Translation'. In *Early Buddhism and Abhidharma Thought, In Honor of Doctor Hajime Sakurabe on His Seventy-seventh Birthday*, edited by Sakurabe Ronshu Committee, 1–32. Kyoto: Heirakuji shoten.

Hartmann, Jens-Uwe and K. Wille. 2014. 'The Manuscript of the Dīrghāgama and the Private Collection in Virginia'. In *From Birch Bark to Digital Data: Recent Advances in Buddhist Manuscript Research*, edited by P. Harrison and J.-U. Hartmann, 137–155. Vienna: Verlag der Österreichischen Akademie der Wissenschaften. https://doi.org/10.2307/j.ctt1vw0q4q.9

Hiraoka Satoshi. 2013. 'The School Affiliation of the Ekottarika-āgama'. In *Research on the Ekottarika-āgama (Taishō 125)*, edited by Dhammadinnā, 71–105. Taipei: Dharma Drum.

Kuan, Tse-fu. 2012. 'A Geographical Perspective on Sectarian Affiliations of the *Ekottarika Āgama* in Chinese Translation (T 125)'. *Journal of the Oxford Centre for Buddhist Studies* 2: 179–208.

———. 2013a. 'Legends and Transcendence: Sectarian Affiliations of the *Ekottarika Āgama* in Chinese Translation'. *Journal of the American Oriental Society* 133(4): 607–634. https://doi.org/10.7817/jameroriesoci.133.4.0607

———. 2013b. 'Mahāyāna Elements and Mahāsāṃghika Traces in the *Ekottarika-āgama*'. In *Research on the Ekottarika-āgama (Taishō 125)*, edited by Dhammadinnā, 133–194. Taipei: Dharma Drum.

———. 2013c. 'The Pavāraṇā sutta and "Liberation in Both Ways" as against "Liberation by Wisdom"'. *Bulletin of the School of Oriental and African Studies* 76(1): 49–73. https://doi.org/10.1017/S0041977X12001437
———. 2017: [Review of Palumbo 2013], *Journal of the American Oriental Society* 137(2): 444–448. https://doi.org/10.7817/jameroriesoci.137.2.0444
Ludowyk-Gyomroi, Edith. 1947. 'The Valuation of saddhā in Early Buddhist Texts'. *University of Ceylon Review* 5(2): 32–49.
Mayeda, Egaku. 1985. 'Japanese Studies on the Schools of the Chinese Āgamas'. In *Zur Schulzugehörigkeit von Werken der Hīnayāna-Literatur, Erster Teil*, edited by H. Bechert, 1: 94–103. Göttingen: Vandenhoeck and Ruprecht.
Minh Chau, Thich. 1964/1991. *The Chinese Madhyama Āgama and the Pāli Majjhima Nikāya*. Delhi: Motilal Banarsidass.
Nattier, Jan. 2003. 'The Indian Roots of Pure Land Buddhism: Insights from the Oldest Chinese Version of the Larger Sukhāvatīvyūha'. *Pacific World, Journal of the Institute of Buddhist Studies* 5: 179–201.
Norman, K. R. 1991/1993. 'The Role of the Layman According to the Jaina Canon'. In *Collected Papers*, edited by K. R. Norman, 4: 175–185. Oxford: Pali Text Society.
Palumbo, Antonello. 2013. *An Early Chinese Commentary on the Ekottarika-āgama, The Fenbie gongde lun 分別功德論 and the History of the Translation of the Zengyi ahan jing 增一阿含經*. Taipei: Dharma Drum Publishing Corporation.
Pāsādika, Bhikkhu. 2010. 'Gleanings from the Chinese Ekottarāgama Regarding School Affiliation and Other Topics'. In *Translating Buddhist Chinese, Problems and Prospects*, edited by K. Meisig, 87–96. Wiesbaden: Harrassowitz.
Skilling, Peter. 2009. 'Redaction, Recitation, and Writing, Transmission of the Buddha's Teaching in India in the Early Period'. In *Buddhist Manuscript Cultures, Knowledge, Ritual, and Art*, edited by Stephen C. Berkwitz, Juliane Schober and Claudia Brown, 53–75. London: Routledge.
Strauch, Ingo. 2010. 'More Missing Pieces of Early Pure Land Buddhism: New Evidence for Akṣobhya and Abhirati in an Early Mahāyāna sūtra from Gandhāra'. *The Eastern Buddhist* 41(1): 23–66.
Tilakaratne, Asaṅga. 2000. 'Saṅgīti and sāmaggī: Communal Recitation and the Unity of the Saṅgha'. *Buddhist Studies Review* 17(2): 175–197.
Upadhyaya, K. N. 1980. 'The Impact of the Bhakti Movement on the Development of Mahāyāna Buddhism'. In *Studies in the History of Buddhism, Papers presented at the International Conference on the History of Buddhism at the University of Wisconsin, Madison, WIS, USA, August 19–21, 1976*, edited by A. K. Narain, 349–357. Delhi: B. R. Publishing Corporation.
von Hinüber, Oskar. 1996/1997. *A Handbook of Pāli Literature*. Delhi: Munshiram Manoharlal. https://doi.org/10.1515/9783110814989

Anālayo Bhikkhu is a Professor at the Numata Center for Buddhist Studies at the University of Hamburg. He is the author of numerous scholarly articles and books about aspects of early Buddhism, including *Satipaṭṭhāna: The Direct Path to Realization* (Windhorse 2003), *Perspectives on Satipaṭṭhāna* (Windhorse 2013), *The Genesis of the Bodhisattva Ideal* (Hamburg University Press, 2010), *The Dawn of Abhidharma* (Hamburg University Press 2014), *Rebirth in Early Buddhism and Current Research* (Wisdom 2018), and many translations from the Chinese *Āgamas*, with comparison to parallel suttas from the Pāli *Nikāyas*.

Abhidhamma

— 10 —

Equal-headed (*samasīsin*): An Abhidharma Innovation and Commentarial Developments

Tse-fu Kuan

The suicide accounts of three bhikkhus in *sutta* literature probably inspired the formulation of a particular type of person who attains Arahantship at death, later designated as an 'equal-headed' (*samasīsin*) person in the Abhidhamma. The Theravāda tends to depict those bhikkhus as non-Arahants before suicide. The Pali commentary explains that they did not attain Arahantship until their deaths and refers to two of them as each being an 'equal-header' (*samasīsī*). By contrast, the (Mūla-)Sarvāstivāda *sūtras* and Abhidharma portray them as Arahants during their lifetimes. The Sarvāstivādins deny the concept of *samasīsin* proposed by the Vibhājyavādins, which include the Theravāda and Dharmaguptaka schools. The Pali commentaries provide various explanations and classifications of *samasīsin*, which have one idea in common: the term signifies the concurrence of two events, and it denotes at least a person who only becomes an Arahant at death, and sometimes someone who becomes an Arahant at the same time as a certain kind of event occurs. The *Paṭisambhidāmagga*, a quasi-Abhidhamma text, has a chapter that expounds 'equal-head' (*samasīsa*) in an oblique way by enumerating various kinds of *sama* and of *sīsa* separately. The *Paṭisambhidāmagga* commentary tries to make sense of the term *samasīsa* by associating this textual exposition of *sama* and *sīsa* with the more commonly found term *samasīsin*.

1. Abhidharma formulation of *samasīsin*

In Buddhist literature a certain category (or categories) of sainthood is referred to as a *samasīsa* 'equal-head' or more frequently its derivative *samasīsin* 'equal-headed', namely *samasīsa* combined with the adjective suffix *-in*. Neither *samasīsa* nor *samasīsin* seems to be found in the *Vinaya-piṭaka* or the *Sutta-piṭaka* except in the *Paṭisambhidāmagga*,[1] which is a quasi-Abhidhamma text but is included in the *Sutta-piṭaka* (see Section 4). Such terminology probably first appeared in early Abhidharma literature as Chou (2008, 368) suggests. The *Puggalapaññatti*, among the earliest of the seven canonical Abhidhamma texts of the Theravāda school (Rhys Davids 1903, 188; Law 1933, 49; Norman 1983, 102; Mizuno 1997, 262; Willemen *et al.*

1. This information is yielded by searching the *Sutta-piṭaka* and the *Vinaya-piṭaka* in CST for *samasīsin* and *samasīsa* with different inflections. *Samasīsi* and *samasīsinā* appear respectively in the *Peṭakopadesa* and *Nettippakaraṇa*, which are not *sutta* literature but have been added to the *Khuddaka Nikāya* of the *Sutta-piṭaka* in Burma (von Hinüber 1997, 76).

Keywords: Abhidhamma, Abhidharma, *samasīsa*, *samasīsin*, Arahant, suicide, Theravāda, Sarvāstivāda, Dharmaguptaka, Vibhājyavādin

1998, 13), gives the following brief definition:

> What is an equal-headed person (*puggalo samasīsī*)? A person for whom the exhaustion of the taints (*āsava*) and the exhaustion of life occur simultaneously (*apubbaṃ acarimaṃ*, rendered literally as 'not before nor after'): he is called an equal-headed person.[2]

Here *samasīsī* is the masculine nominative singular of *samasīsin*. According to this definition, some particular type of people attain liberation from the taints, or Arahantship, at the time of death.

The **Śāriputra-abhidharma* 舍利弗阿毘曇論 (*Shelifu Apitan lun*,[3] T 1548), in all probability the Abhidharma of the Dharmaguptaka school (Mizuno 1966; Frauwallner 1995, 97; Mizuno 1996, 334–338; Willemen 2008, 37; Kuan 2017, 164–165), defines the 'equal-headed person' thus:

> What is an equal-headed person (**puggalo samasīsī*)? A person who does not yet practise the path, whose taints and life terminate simultaneously, or alternatively (**atha vā*)[4], [whose] life terminates immediately after the taints terminate, he is called an equal-headed person.[5]

Setting aside the expression 'does not yet practise the path', which will be discussed later, this definition consists of two parts. The first part is practically the same as the definition of a *samasīsin* person given in the *Puggalapaññatti*. The second part '[a person whose] life terminates immediately after the taints terminate' may be a later addition to the basic definition. This presumably later definition is relevant to the following passage in Buddhaghosa's (4th–5th century CE, von Hinüber 1997, 102–103) commentary to the *Aṅguttara Nikāya*:

> Here although [we say:] 'Exhaustion of the taints due to the path consciousness and exhaustion of life due to the death consciousness occur [simultaneously]', the two [exhaustions] do not really arise in one moment. But it is so said because his life ends immediately after the occasion on which he has reviewed the sheer destruction of the taints, and the interval is not perceived.[6]

This passage is intended to modify or clarify the preceding passage that defines a 'life equal-header' as a person whose exhaustion of life and destruction of the taints are simultaneous (see near the end of Section 3). This can also be seen as an

2. Pp 13: *Katamo ca puggalo samasīsī? Yassa puggalassa apubbaṃ acarimaṃ āsavapariyādānañ ca hoti jīvitapariyādānañ ca. Ayaṃ vuccati puggalo samasīsī.*

3. Transliterated in Pinyin.

4. BCSD 457 s.v. 復次: *atha vā* ...

5. T XXVIII 589b: 云何首等人？若人未行道，若有漏、若壽命一時俱斷，復次，斷漏無間命即斷，是名等首人。For the second occurrence of the term, I follow the *Shōgo zō*, which reads 等首 (equal head) as given in footnote 15 at T XXVIII 589, while the Taishō reads 首等 (head equal). The Taishō only gives the reading 首等 for the first occurrence of the term, which I suspect was originally also 等首 (equal head).

6. Mp IV 7: *Tattha kiñcāpi āsavapariyādānaṃ maggacittena, jīvitapariyādānaṃ cuticittena hotī ti ubhinnaṃ ekakkhaṇe sambhavo nāma n' atthi. Yasmā pan' assa āsavesu khīṇamattesu paccavekkhana-vārānantaram eva jīvitapariyādānaṃ gacchati, antaraṃ na paññāyati, tasmā evaṃ vuttaṃ.*

amendment to the definition of *samasīsin* given in the *Puggalapaññatti*, according to which a remarkable coincidence happens – a person is liberated from all his taints exactly at the time of death. In order to gloss this seemingly incredible coincidence, the *Aṅguttara Nikāya* commentary explains that an 'equal-headed' person attains liberation immediately before his death, but the interval between his liberation and death is so short that it seems as if his liberation and death occurred at the same moment. By contrast, the **Śāriputra-abhidharma*, while also referring to the idea of a person whose liberation occurs immediately before death, sees this as denoting a *second* kind of 'equal-headed person', the first one being as in the *Puggalapaññatti*: one whose liberation and death occur at the same moment.

2. *Sutta* basis for the concept of *samasīsin*

Although the terminology *samasīsin/samasīsa* is not found in the *suttas*, the concept does appear therein. In the *Aṅguttara Nikāya*, *sutta* 16 in the Book of the Sevens states:

> Some person dwells contemplating impermanence in all conditioned phenomena, perceiving impermanence, experiencing impermanence, constantly, continuously, and uninterruptedly focusing on it with the mind, fathoming it with wisdom. For him the exhaustion of the taints and the exhaustion of life occur simultaneously.[7]
>
> (trans. Bodhi 2012, 1006–1007)

In his commentary on the *Aṅguttara Nikāya*, Buddhaghosa says that here the equal-header (*samasīsī*) is being spoken of.[8] The last sentence of the above passage is almost identical to the definition of the 'equal-headed person' in the *Puggalapaññatti*. It is very likely that the 'equal-headed person' as formulated in this Abhidhamma text derives from the *Aṅguttara Nikāya* in view of the close affinity between the two texts as several scholars have noticed (Morris 1883, x–xi; Bodhi 2012, 58; Kuan 2015, 34–41). The term *samasīsin* was probably coined by the composers of early Abhidharma literature. Since this term appears in the Abhidharma works of the Theravādins and Dharmaguptakas as mentioned above, it could have already been created before the schism(s) that separated these two schools. It is generally held by various traditions that the original Buddhist Order first split into two fraternities, the Mahāsāṃghikas and the Sthaviras.[9] The present Theravāda and the extinct Dharmaguptaka schools are of Sthavira origin. Therefore, the term *samasīsin* may date back to the origi-

7. A IV 13: *idh' ekacco puggalo sabbasaṅkhāresu aniccānupassī viharati, aniccasaññī, aniccapaṭisaṃvedī satataṃ samitaṃ abbokiṇṇaṃ cetasā adhimuccamāno paññāya pariyogāhamāno. Tassa apubbaṃ acarimaṃ āsavapariyādānañ ca hoti jīvitapariyādānañ ca.*

8. Mp IV 6: *Idha samasīsī kathito.*

9. The Sthavira sect is also referred to as Sthaviravāda in Sanskrit and as Theravāda in Pali sources. The Theravāda school of today should not be confused with the original Theravāda (Sthavira[vāda]) sect. Yinshun (1994, preface, 36–38) identifies the present Theravāda school with the Tāmraśāṭīya school, an offshoot from the Vibhājyavādins. Choong (2000, 3) and Cousins (2001a, 168) hold a similar opinion. In this paper the term 'Theravāda' is used exclusively to refer to the extant Theravāda school, while the term 'Sthavira' refers to one of the two earliest sects formed through the first schism.

nal Sthaviras. Why did they create such terminology? A possible reason is that the Sthavira Ābhidharmikas coined this word to designate the foregoing type of person in a discourse equivalent or similar to the above *sutta* of the *Aṅguttara Nikāya*.

The above *sutta* (A 7:16) lists seven kinds of worthy people whose spiritual achievements are based on contemplation of impermanence. The next two *suttas* (A 7:17 and A 7:18) list the same seven kinds of people but replace impermanence with *dukkha* (suffering) and non-self respectively. Among the seven kinds of people listed in these three *suttas* of the *Aṅguttara Nikāya*,[10] six kinds other than the foregoing are all given designations in some *suttas*. These seven kinds of worthy people are listed in an order that 'represents a decreasing speed of spiritual attainment' (Harvey 1995, 100). The first kind of person, namely 'with the destruction of the taints, he has realized for himself with direct knowledge, in this very life, the taintless liberation of mind, liberation by wisdom ...' (trans. Bodhi 2012, 1006), is referred to as an Arahant (e.g. A I 109, S III 161). The third to seventh kinds are in turn called *antarā-parinibbāyī*, *upahacca-parinibbāyī*, *asaṅkhāra-parinibbāyī*, *sasaṅkhāra-parinibbāyī* and *uddhaṃsoto akaniṭṭhagāmī* (e.g. D III 237, S V 69–70), which refer to the five types of non-returner (*anāgāmin*).[11] Only the second kind of person, who attains Arahantship at the time of death, is given no designation in the *suttas*. This lack may have prompted the Ābhidharmikas to coin a new word to designate this unusual kind of person.

These seven kinds of worthy people correspond well to the seven fruits stated in a *sutta* of the *Saṃyutta Nikāya* (S V 69–70, in brief):

1. One attains gnosis early in this very life.
2. One attains gnosis at the time of death.
3. One becomes an *antarā-parinibbāyī*.
4. One becomes an *upahacca-parinibbāyī*.
5. One becomes an *asaṅkhāra-parinibbāyī*.
6. One becomes a *sasaṅkhāra-parinibbāyī*.
7. One becomes an *uddhaṃsoto akaniṭṭhagāmī*.

Two Chinese parallels in the *Saṃyukta Āgama*, SĀ 736 and SĀ 740, also talk about 'seven kinds of fruit/seven fruits' 七種果/七果 (*qi zhong guo/qi guo*), but curiously both *sūtras* enumerate only six fruits and leave out the description of the second fruit in the above list of seven fruits.[12] Such inconsistency as found in the two *sūtras*

10. These three Pali *suttas* have no parallels in the Chinese Āgamas or Sanskrit fragments (see SuttaCentral at https://suttacentral.net/an7). This does not signify that only the Theravāda Canon has these *suttas*. The *Dīrgha Āgama*, *Madhyama Āgama*, *Saṃyukta Āgama* and *Ekottarika Āgama* preserved in Chinese translation are attributed respectively to the Dharmaguptakas, Sarvāstivādins, (Mūla-)Sarvāstivādins and Mahāsāṃghikas (see Kuan 2013b, 628; Anālayo 2017: 67–71; Kuan 2013a, 51; Kuan 2013b, 611–627). None of these schools' four *Āgamas* are complete. Therefore, one or some of the above-mentioned schools might have included our three *suttas* in certain *Āgamas* that have been lost.

11. D III 237: *pañca anāgāmino: antarā-parinibbāyī, upahacca-parinibbāyī, asaṃkhāra-parinibbāyī, sasaṃkhāra-parinibbāyī, uddhaṃsoto Akaniṭṭha-gāmī.*

12. SĀ 736 at T II 196c and SĀ 740 at 197c: (1) SĀ 736: 現法智證樂, SĀ 740: 現法智有餘涅槃 (2) none (3) 中般涅槃 (4) 生般涅槃 (5) 無行般涅槃 (6) 有行般涅槃 (7) 上流般涅槃.

is not a mere coincidence. This deliberate omission of the second fruit was done by the school that transmitted the *Saṃyukta Āgama* now extant in Chinese translation. This school denied the second type of person listed above: 'One attains gnosis (*aññā*), namely Arahantship,[13] at the time of death', designated as *samasīsin* by other schools. Which schools upheld this notion? Which school rejected it? How did they argue for or against it? These issues are addressed below.

Three *suttas* in the Pali *Saṃyutta Nikāya* and their Chinese parallels in the *Saṃyukta Āgama* (one of the three also in the *Ekottarika Āgama*) record that three bhikkhus committed suicide and were not reproached for it, but on the contrary they were sanctioned by the Buddha as 'having attained nirvana (at his death/in his lifetime)' (*parinibbuta*)[14], or as 'blameless' (*anupavajja*) in the sense that the bhikkhu's death was not such that he laid down this body but took up another body (*tañ ca kāyaṃ nikkhipati aññañ ca kāyam upādiyati ... n'atthi*)[15] — he is liberated from rebirth.

In these three *suttas*, the three cases of suicide vary in terms of storyline. While Vakkali and Channa took their own lives from a wish to be free of unbearably painful illness, Godhika's suicide was motivated by his frustration of not being able to maintain 'temporary liberation of mind', or meditative attainment, despite his diligent practice. They all died an Arahant, but there is disagreement over when they attained Arahantship.

2.1 Godhika

The case of Godhika is less controversial. According to the *Godhika Sutta* of the *Saṃyutta Nikāya* (S I 120–122), he committed suicide from despair due to six consecutive failures to maintain his achievement of 'temporary liberation of mind' (*sāmayikā cetovimutti*), much less achievement of 'liberation', namely nirvana or Arahantship. Moreover, when Godhika was about to take his own life, Māra requested the Buddha to stop the suicide, referring to Godhika as a 'trainee' (*sekha*), which means one who is still on the path of training and has not yet reached the final goal or liberation (see A I 231). Therefore, the *sutta* implies that Godhika had not attained Arahantship until his death or the last moments before his death. Buddhaghosa's commentary makes this point clear and elaborates on it:

> The elder, it is said, thinking: 'What is the use of this life for me?', lay down on his back and cut his jugular vein with a knife. Painful feelings arose. The elder suppressed the feeling, comprehended that very feeling and set up mindfulness, contemplating on the main meditation subject, he reached Arahantship and attained nirvana as an equal-header (*samasīsī*).[16] (My translation mostly follows Bodhi 2000, 420 n. 312.)

13. The word *aññā* (Sanskrit *ājñā*), rendered as 'gnosis', is identified with Arahantship. See DOP I 48 s.v. *aññā* and BHSD 90 s.v. *ājñā*.

14. *parinibbuta* = 般涅槃. See S I 122 = T II 286b; S III 124 = T II 643a ≠ T II 347b.

15. *anupavajja* = 無大過. *tañ ca kāyaṃ nikkhipati aññañ ca kāyam upādiyati ... n'atthi* = 捨此身已餘身不相續. See S IV 60 = T II 348a.

16. Spk I 183: *Thero kira 'kiṃ mayhaṃ iminā jīvitenā?'ti uttāno nipajjitvā satthena gala-nāḷiṃ chindi. Dukkhā vedanā uppajjiṃsu. Thero vedanaṃ vikkhambhetvā, taṃ yeva vedanaṃ pariggahetvā, satiṃ upaṭṭhapetvā, mūla-kammaṭṭhānaṃ sammasanto arahattaṃ patvā samasīsī hutvā parinibbāyi.*

It is noteworthy that the commentary borrows the term *samasīsin* from the Abhidhamma and applies the concept to the case of Godhika. He is regarded as the kind of person whose taints and life terminate simultaneously. The Sarvāstivāda Abhidharma holds a different opinion, which is discussed in Section 2.5.

2.2 Channa

There are two almost identical versions of Channa's suicide in the Pali Canon: the *Channa Sutta* of the *Saṃyutta Nikāya* and the *Channovāda Sutta* of the *Majjhima Nikāya* (M III 263–266). According to the *Channa Sutta* (S IV 55–60), when Channa was gravely ill, Sāriputta and Mahācunda visited him. Channa expressed his intention of suicide, and Sāriputta tried to dissuade him from taking his life. Then Channa said: 'Remember this, friend Sāriputta: the bhikkhu Channa will use the knife blamelessly (*anupavajja*).' (trans. Bodhi 2000, 1165). After Channa's suicide, Sāriputta asked the Buddha about Channa's next birth, and the Buddha replied: 'Sāriputta, didn't the bhikkhu Channa declare his blamelessness (*anupavajjatā*) right in your presence?' (trans. Bodhi 2000, 1167). Bodhi (2000, 1407 n. 55) sees this dialogue as implying that Channa was already an Arahant when he declared: 'the bhikkhu Channa will use the knife blamelessly.' Similarly, Anālayo (2010, 131) comments: 'the Buddha reminds Sāriputta of Channa's earlier declaration, which in both versions involves an implicit claim to being an arahant. Such a reminder makes sense only as a way of confirming that Channa's earlier claim was justified.'

Disagreeing with the above views, Nawa (2011, 71–77) contends: (1) Whereas Channa's declaration insinuated his Arahantship, he actually hinted at his future nirvana. (2) Sāriputta and Mahācunda preached to Channa in such a way that Channa was not reckoned an Arahant, and in fact he was not. (3) Channa did not attain Arahantship and nirvana until his death, and so the Buddha indicated to Sāriputta that Channa's death represents the attainment of nirvana. Here, Nawa's opinion agrees with Buddhaghosa's assertion in the commentary that Channa was not an Arahant until his death. The commentary explains the phrase 'He used the knife' in the *sutta*:

> He used a knife which removes life; he cut his jugular vein. Then in that moment the fear of death possessed him, and the sign of his next birth arose. Knowing himself to be an ordinary person (*puthujjana*), with a mind moved by fear he established insight. Comprehending the formations, he reached Arahantship and attained nirvana as an equal-header (*samasīsī*).[17]

The commentary presents Channa as an ordinary man who, in the process of suicide, exerted himself so diligently that he luckily reached nirvana at the same time his life ended, just like the case of Godhika.

---

17. Spk II 373 (according to CST): *Satthaṃ āharesī ti jīvita-hāraka-satthaṃ āhari, kaṇṭha-nāḷaṃ chindi. Ath' assa tasmiṃ khaṇe maraṇa-bhayaṃ* (Ee omits *maraṇa*) *okkami, gati-nimittaṃ upaṭṭhāsi. So attano puthujjana-bhāvaṃ ñatvā, saṃviggacitto vipassanaṃ paṭṭhapetvā, saṅkhāre parigaṇhanto arahattaṃ patvā samasīsī hutvā parinibbuto.*

On the other hand, Nawa (2011, 76) points out that in the Chinese version (SĀ 1266), the Buddha's reply to Sāriputta's question denoted that Channa was already an Arahant before his suicide. Whereas, in the Pali version, the Buddha replied to Sāriputta: 'The bhikkhu Channa did indeed have these friendly families, Sāriputta, intimate families, hospitable families.' (my translation mostly follows Bodhi 2000, 1167), the Chinese counterpart of the Buddha's reply reads: 'A good man (**kulaputra*) rightly well liberated by gnosis (**samyag-ājñā-su-vimukta*) had hospitable families, intimate families, well-spoken families.'[18] In place of 'the bhikkhu Channa', the Chinese version here has 'a good man rightly well liberated by gnosis', hence indicating that Channa was already an Arahant before his suicide. It is inconceivable for an Arahant to break the precepts. Now, as Anālayo (2010, 132) points out, the *Vinaya* of the Sarvāstivādins explicitly states that suicide is not an offence,[19] but in the other *Vinaya*s an attempt to commit suicide or its successful completion constitutes an offence.[20] The *Saṃyukta Āgama* in Chinese translation is widely ascribed to the Sarvāstivāda or the Mūlasarvāstivāda (see Kuan 2013a, 51). Since the Sarvāstivādins did not regard suicide as an offence, they had no problem with depicting Channa as an Arahant who commits suicide in their *Saṃyukta Āgama*. In contrast, the Theravādins do not accept suicide as faultless in their *Vinaya*, and thus as Keown (1996, 28) says: 'By holding that Channa gained enlightenment only *after* he had begun the attempt on his life, the commentary neatly avoids the dilemma of an Arhat breaking the precepts.'

2.3 Vakkali

There are three different versions of Vakkali's suicide: the *Vakkali Sutta* of the Pali *Saṃyutta Nikāya*, *sūtra* 1265 of the Chinese *Saṃyukta Āgama*, and *sūtra* 10 in Chapter 26 of the *Ekottarika Āgama* in Chinese translation.

The *Saṃyutta Nikāya* and *Saṃyukta Āgama* versions are quite similar in storyline as follows. When Vakkali was gravely ill, the Buddha visited him and left. Then two deities each told the Buddha something about Vakkali. Agreeing with them, the Buddha sent some bhikkhus (in S, one bhikkhu in SĀ) to pass their remarks on to Vakkali. According to the Pali version, the second deity said: 'He will be liberated as one well liberated'[21] (trans. Bodhi 2000, 939), but in the *Saṃyukta Āgama* version this deity said: 'The venerable Vakkali has already, while being well liberated, attained liberation.'[22] The *Saṃyukta Āgama* version affirms that Vakkali was

18. T II 348a:正智正善解脱善男子有供養家、親厚家、善言語家。

19. T XXIII 382a: 自殺身無罪。

20. For references to the *Vinaya*s of different schools, see Anālayo 2010, 132 n. 36.

21. S III 121: *suvimutto vimuccissati*.

22. T II 346c14: 尊者跋迦梨已於善解脱而得解脱. This remark by the second deity is repeated verbatim at T II 346c20–21, and is repeated almost verbatim at T II 346c26–27 except that 已 (already) is missing. At T II 347a18–19 the deity's remark reads: 'The bhikkhu Vakkali has already, while being well liberated, attained liberation' 跋迦梨比丘已於善解脱而得解脱. Although 已 (already) is not found in one out of the four occurrences of the deity's remark, this could simply be an error that happened during translation or copying, as Anālayo (2011, 161 n. 27) suggests.

already an Arahant when the deities talked to the Buddha. This is in keeping with the Sarvāstivādin stance that an Arahant may take his own life since suicide is not an offence, just like the case of Channa presented by the *Saṃyukta Āgama* discussed above. The Theravāda version, however, uses a verb in the future tense, *vimuccissati* (will be liberated), to describe Vakkali, thereby suggesting the deity's prophecy that 'he will be liberated as one liberated by the liberation of the Arahantship fruit' as glossed in the commentary.[23] In other words, Vakkali was not yet an Arahant when the deities talked to the Buddha.

After the bhikkhus (in S, one bhikkhu in SĀ) had delivered the Buddha's message (including the two deities' remarks) to Vakkali, he asked the messenger(s) to tell the Buddha:

> Form is impermanent: I have no perplexity about this ... I do not doubt that whatever is impermanent is suffering. I do not doubt that in regard to what is impermanent, suffering, and subject to change, I have no more desire, lust, or affection. Feeling is impermanent ... Perception ... Volitional formations ... Consciousness ...[24]
>
> (trans. Bodhi 2000, 940)

In Bodhi's (2000, 1082 n. 172) opinion, the above message to the Buddha implies that Vakkali already considered himself an Arahant. The commentary, however, explains:

> The elder, it is said, overestimated himself. As he had suppressed the defilements by concentration and insight, he did not see [himself] assailed [by the defilements], thinking: 'I have destroyed the taints', 'What is the use of this painful life for me? I will use the knife and die.' Then he cut his jugular vein with a sharp knife, and painful feeling arose in him. In that moment, knowing himself to be an ordinary person, he quickly took up the main meditation subject, contemplating on it without loosening it, and attained Arahantship as he died.[25]
>
> (My translation mostly follows Bodhi 2000, 1082 n. 172.)

According to the commentary, Vakkali thought that he had destroyed the taints, which means that he thought that he was already an Arahant, but this was his delusion; he did not become an Arahant until he died, as a result of intensive meditation during the short period of excruciating pain caused by suicide. Although the commentary makes no mention of *samasīsī* in the case of Vakkali, he is indeed treated as a *samasīsī* in view of the commentarial description, which resembles the foregoing two cases in many respects.

23. Spk II 314: *arahatta-phala-vimuttiyā vimutto hutvā vimuccissati.*

24. S III 122–123: *Rūpam aniccaṃ tāhaṃ ... na kaṅkhāmi. Yad aniccaṃ taṃ dukkhan ti na vicikicchāmi. Yad aniccaṃ dukkhaṃ vipariṇāmadhammaṃ, n'atthi me tattha chando vā rāgo vā pemaṃ vā ti na vicikicchāmi. Vedanā aniccā ... Saññā... Saṅkhārā ... Viññāṇaṃ ...* This corresponds closely to its Chinese counterpart in SĀ 1265 at T II 347a: 我今日於色無常，決定無疑。無常者是苦，決定無疑。若無常、苦者、是變易法，於彼無有可貪、可欲，決定無疑。受、想、行、識亦復如是。

25. Spk II 314 (according to CST): *Thero kira adhimāniko ahosi. So samādhi-vipassanāhi vikkhambhitānaṃ kilesānaṃ samudācāraṃ apassanto, 'khīṇāsavo 'mhī' ti saññī* (Ee omits *saññī*) *hutvā 'kiṃ me iminā dukkhena jīvitena? Satthaṃ āharitvā marissāmī' ti tikhiṇena satthena kaṇṭha-nāḷaṃ* (Ee: *kaṇḍa-nāḷiṃ*) *chindi. Ath' assa dukkhā vedanā uppajji* (Ee: *uppajjati*). *So tasmiṃ khaṇe attano puthujjana-bhāvaṃ ñatvā avissaṭṭha-kammaṭṭhānattā sīghaṃ mūla-kammaṭṭhānaṃ* (Ee: *kammaṭṭhānaṃ*) *ādāya sammasanto arahattaṃ pāpuṇitvā va kālam akāsi.*

The *Ekottarika Āgama* version differs considerably from the other two versions.[26] Its position is however similar to the Theravāda commentary: Arahants are incapable of suicide. This version describes Vakkali's thoughts while performing the act:

> At that time, while stabbing himself with the knife, Vakkali thought: 'Among Śākyamuni Buddha's disciples, what has been done [by me] is contrary to the Dharma; it has evil results, not good results. Without having attained realization in the Dharma of the Tathāgata [I am] ending [my] life.'[27]
>
> (My translation mostly follows Anālayo 2011, 164)

This passage expresses that suicide is an offence and is detrimental from the Buddhist perspective. According to the *Ekottarika Āgama*, after the death of Vakkali, Ānanda said to the Buddha: 'This bhikkhu had been ill for a long time, originally being an ordinary man.' The Buddha replied: 'So it is, Ānanda, as you say.'[28] This conversation and the above passage both affirm that Vakkali was not an Arahant until his suicide, which then triggered a sense of urgency, and the ensuing endeavours dramatically led to the sudden attainment of liberation at his death.[29] Vakkali's action presented in this way raises few ethical or legal issues. To paraphrase the words of Keown (1996, 28), suicides by ordinary people afflicted by the distress of a serious illness are a sad but all too common affair.

2.4 Reflections on the three cases

Few of the different traditions' versions of the three *suttas* explicitly state whether the protagonist was an Arahant, one liberated from the taints, before his suicide. Given the ambiguity of the texts, they are liable to different interpretations.

Modern scholars also differ in their views. For example, Martin Wiltshire thinks that none of the three suicides were Arahants before their deaths whereas Louis de La Vallée Poussin gives the suicides of Vakkali and Godhika as examples of suicide by Arahants (Keown 1996, 26 and n. 49). Regarding the Theravāda tradition, two of the three bhikkhus are understood to be ordinary people (*puthujjana*) before death in Buddhaghosa's commentary. Keown (1996, 27) raises 'the question why the commentary should take such pains to establish that Channa was not an Arhat'. This question applies also to the other two cases. He explains: '... the tradition simply found it inconceivable that an Arhat would be capable of suicide ... it is often stated elsewhere that it is impossible for an Arhat to do certain things, the first of which is intentionally to kill a living creature.'[30] Anālayo (2010, 131), however, holds a different view:

> For the Pāli and Chinese versions of the present discourse to be describing the sui-

26. See the translation by Anālayo 2011, 164–166.
27. T II 642c: 是時婆迦梨以刀自刺，而作是念：「釋迦文佛弟子之中，所作非法，得惡利，不得善利，於如來法中不得受證而取命終。」
28. T II 643a: 阿難白佛：「此比丘抱病經久，本是凡人。」世尊告曰：「如是，阿難，如汝所言。」
29. T II 642c: 尊者婆迦梨便思惟是五盛陰 ... 彼於此五盛陰熟思惟之，諸有生法皆是死法。知此已，便於有漏心得解脫。爾時，尊者婆迦梨於無餘涅槃界而般涅槃。
30. D III 133, 235: *abhabbo ... khīṇāsavo bhikkhu sañcicca pāṇaṃ jīvitā voropetuṃ.*

cide of an arahant might at first sight seem to conflict with the canonical dictum that an arahant is incapable of intentionally depriving a living being of life. However, it is not clear whether this stipulation covers suicide, as it could be intended to cover only cases of depriving another living being of life.

Anyway, judging from the *suttas*, we are certain of one point common to the three monks: it was only after their deaths that their Arahantship was confirmed or pronounced by the Buddha in a retrospective fashion. This suggests that they were not recognized as Arahants in their lifetime, at least by their fellow monks and nuns.

An Arahant is one whose taints (*āsava*) are destroyed.[31] A stock formula on this recurs in many *suttas*: 'With the destruction of the taints, (someone) realizes for himself with direct knowledge, in this very life, the taintless liberation of mind, liberation by wisdom, and having entered upon it, he dwells in it'[32] (trans. Bodhi 2012, 318, 321, etc.). Thus, in normal cases, an Arahant is a person who has destroyed the taints in this very life and dwells in this taintless liberation while still alive. His fellow monastics may recognize and respect him as an Arahant during his lifetime, just like Sāriputta, Mahāmoggallāna, and so forth. None of the three bhikkhus discussed above enjoyed such status when they were still alive. Their Arahantship was seen (according to the Theravāda tradition) as concurrent with the end of life. So they could not be called an 'Arahant' in its usual and overt sense. This may be why the *sutta* compilers felt the need to classify such an unusual type of holy people under a different category, such as the second kind of person after the category of Arahant and before the five types of non-returners, among the seven kinds of worthy people listed in the *suttas* (A 7:16–18) of the *Aṅguttara Nikāya*, or among the seven fruits enumerated in a *sutta* of the *Saṃyutta Nikāya* and the two Sarvāstivādin parallels (although the description of the second fruit is omitted, see above). Then the Ābhidharmikas designated this special category with a new term 'equal-headed' (*samasīsin*, **samaśīrṣin*) as attested in the *Puggalapaññatti*, one of the earliest Abhidhamma work.

2.5 The Sarvāstivādins' non-acceptance of the idea of the *samasīsin*

As Chou (2008, 369–368) points out, the **Abhidharma-Mahāvibhāṣa* 阿毘達磨大毘婆沙論 (*Apidamo da piposha lun*, T 1545) of the Sarvāstivādins mentions the event of Godhika's suicide, but does not associate him with the idea of the *samasīsin*. He is simply referred to as an Arahant in this treatise:

> A *sūtra* states: 'There was an Arahant named Godhika. Having regressed from temporary liberation six times, out of fear of regressing again for a seventh time, he killed himself with a knife and attained nirvana (**parinirvāyin*, *ban niepan* 般涅槃, that is, he died without being reborn).'[33]

31. E.g. D III 83, M I 190, S III 161, A I 109: *arahaṃ khīṇāsavo*.

32. E.g. D I 156, II 251–252; M I 71, III 103; S II 214, V 203; A I 108–109, 232, II 87: *āsavānaṃ khayā anāsavaṃ ceto-vimuttiṃ paññā-vimuttiṃ diṭṭhe va dhamme sayaṃ abhiññā sacchikatvā upasampajja viharati.*

33. T XXVII 312b: 契經說：「有阿羅漢名瞿底迦，是時解脫六反退已，於第七時恐復退失以刀自害而般涅槃。」

This passage is preceded by a suspicious statement claimed to be canonical: 'As a *sūtra* states, there are two kinds of Arahant: one is subject to regression, the other is not subject to regression.'[34] This is actually a tenet held by the Sarvāstivādins, as stated in the **Samayabhedoparacanacakra* 異部宗輪論 (*Yibu zong lun lun*, T 2031), a Sarvāstivāda text on the process of schisms and the doctrines of the various schools.[35] From the context, it is clear that the **Abhidharma-Mahāvibhāṣa* invokes the story of Godhika to exemplify the kind of Arahant subject to regression during his lifetime.

Moreover, according to the above discussion of the cases of Channa and Vakkali, the Sarvāstivādins took the position that an Arahant may take his own life since suicide is not an offence. According to this school's *Saṃyukta Āgama*, Channa and Vakkali were indeed Arahants in their lifetime. Therefore, the Sarvāstivādins found no need to set up a category of noble ones like the *samasīsin*. On the contrary, they denied the theory of *samasīsin* proposed by the schools called the Vibhājyavādins 分別論者 (Fenbielunzhe). This is articulated in the **Abhidharma-Mahāvibhāṣa*:

> ... for the sake of refuting the Vibhājyavādins' [view]: 'There are defilements that can be destroyed without dependence on concentrative attainments (*samāpatti*).' They say thus: 'If a noble one is born in the sphere of neither-perception-nor-non-perception, since the noble path is not presently manifest to him, when his life ends, his defilements (**kleśa*,[36] Pali *kilesa*) are also exhausted, and he becomes an Arahant called "equal-headed" (**samaśīrṣin*).' For the sake of refuting their adherence [to this view] and elucidating that no defilement can be destroyed without dependence on a concentrative attainment, [we] argue this thesis.[37]

This text goes on to equate the noble path with (certain kinds of) concentrative attainments.[38] According to this passage, the Vibhājyavādins assume that one may eradicate some defilements without recourse to (concurrent) concentrative attainments, and illustrate this point by postulating that a noble one reborn in the sphere of neither-perception-nor-nonperception can become a '*samasīsin* Arahant' at death without practice of the noble path (concentrative attainments), which is not available there. The Sarvāstivādins made more arguments against this view in the following passage:

> A *sūtra* states: 'A bhikṣu can penetrate gnosis as far as[39] a concentrative attainment accompanied by perception [extends].'[40] 'Concentrative attainments accompanied by perception' (*saṃjñā-samāpatti*) refer to the four *dhyāna*s and the three formless

34. T XXVII 312b: 如契經說，阿羅漢有二種：一退法，二不退法。

35. T XLIX 16b: 阿羅漢有退義 'An Arahant may regress'.

36. BCSD 794 s.v. 煩惱: *kleśa* ...

37. T XXVII 310c: ......為遮分別論者：「有諸煩惱不依定滅。」彼作是說：「若有聖者生在非想非非想處，彼無聖道現在前義，壽量盡時煩惱亦盡，成阿羅漢，名為齊頂。」為遮彼執，顯無煩惱不依定滅，故作斯論。

38. T XXVII 310c: 此中定者顯對治道，謂對治道，或說為定，或說為道。

39. 乃至, rendered here as 'as far as', must be translated from *yāvat* (BCSD 74 s.v. 乃至: yāvat ...). See the next footnote.

40. This sentence means almost the same as '*yāvad eva saṃjñā-samāpattiḥ tāvad ājñā-prativedha iti*', which

> [attainments]. '[He] can penetrate gnosis (*ājñā*)[41]' means that [he] can develop wisdom to abandon the defilements and practise the path to exhaust the taints (*āsrava*). Some may doubt thus: 'Since there is no noble path in the sphere of neither-perception-nor-nonperception, if a disciple of the Blessed One is born there, in dependence on what can he exhaust the taints? ...' For the sake of resolving this doubt, [we] say that he attains Arahantship in dependence on the sphere of nothingness, [and we say so] for the sake of rejecting the Vibhājyavādins' contention that there are equal-headed (**samaśīrṣin*) Arahants. They say: 'A disciple of the Blessed One is born in the sphere of neither-perception-nor-nonperception. When he dies, his defilements, karma and life are exhausted all three together. It is not by the noble path that he attains Arahantship.' For the sake of rejecting their opinion and elucidating that [the three] are not exhausted together but must [be exhausted] by the noble path, [we] argue this thesis.[42]

This passage clarifies that the 'noble path' and 'concentrative attainments' mentioned in the previous passage actually refer to the four *jhāna*s and the three formless attainments, i.e. the sphere of infinite space, the sphere of infinite consciousness and the sphere of nothingness, in ascending order. The fourth formless attainment is the sphere of neither-perception-nor-nonperception. The four formless 'meditative' attainments correspond to the four realms or 'heavens' with the same names in Buddhist cosmology. This has to be understood in accordance with the Buddhist principle of 'the equivalence of cosmology and psychology' as Gethin (1998, 119) puts it. Accordingly, one can be reborn in a heaven/realm called 'the sphere of neither-perception-nor-nonperception'. This realm, beyond the four *jhāna*s and the three formless attainments, is said to be devoid of the noble path because it does not have a sufficient level of operative perception (*saññā*) in it to be able to develop insight (*vipassanā*). Therefore, from the Vibhājyavādins' viewpoint, it is impossible for someone reborn in the sphere of neither-perception-nor-nonperception to practise the noble path. He may be able to attain Arahantship or the destruction of his taints simultaneous with the end of his life — perhaps due to being a non-returner (*anāgāmin*) already destined for eventual Arahantship — and is specifically designated as an 'equal-headed (*samasīsin*) Arahant'.

For the Sarvāstivādins, however, it is inconceivable that one can become an Arahant without (concurrently) practising the noble path, which consists of concentrative attainments accompanied by perception (*saññā*), i.e. the four *jhāna*s and the three formless attainments. The **Abhidharma-Mahāvibhāṣa* contends that even a noble disciple reborn in the sphere of neither-perception-nor-nonperception can

is attributed to the Buddha in the *Abhidharma-samuccaya* (Abhidh-s 69). This Sanskrit sentence is equivalent to the Pali '*yāvatā saññā-samāpatti tāvatā aññā-paṭivedho*' cited for comparison below.

41. 聖旨 literally means 'holy meaning', but is apparently translated from *ājñā* (SJD 186 s.v. *ājñā*: 聖教, 勅旨). See the above footnote.

42. T XXVII 929b: 契經說：「苾芻乃至想定能達聖旨。」想定者，謂四靜慮、三無色。能達聖旨者，謂能起智斷煩惱，修道盡漏。或有生如是疑：「非想非非想處既無聖道，若世尊弟子生彼處者，依何能盡諸漏？......」為令此疑得決定故，說彼依無所有處得阿羅漢果，為止分別論者說有齊頂阿羅漢故。彼說：「世尊弟子生非想非非想處，於命終時，煩惱、業、命三事俱盡，不由聖道，得阿羅漢果。」為止彼意，顯盡非俱，必由聖道，故作斯論。

only attain Arahantship through a concentrative attainment accompanied by perception, in the sphere of nothingness, which is just one level below the sphere of neither-perception-nor-nonperception. To back up this argument, at the beginning of the above passage, the Sarvāstivādins quote a sentence from a certain *sūtra*: 'A bhikṣu can penetrate gnosis (*ājñā*) as far as a concentrative attainment accompanied by perception [extends].' This is a Sarvāstivāda counterpart of the following sentence in a *sutta* of the *Aṅguttara Nikāya*: 'There is penetration to gnosis (*aññā*) as far as a concentrative attainment accompanied by perception [extends].'[43] This sentence is preceded by an exposition of how the destruction of the taints (*āsava*) may occur in dependence on the four *jhānas* and the three formless attainments respectively, as follows. When a bhikkhu reaches one of the four *jhānas*, he then develops insight into the five aggregates (form, feeling, perception, volitional activities, consciousness) therein and directs his mind to the deathless element (i.e. nirvana), thereby attaining the destruction of the taints. When a bhikkhu reaches one of the three formless attainments, he develops insight into the four aggregates (excluding form) therein and directs his mind to the deathless element, thereby attaining the destruction of the taints. 'A concentrative attainment accompanied by perception' (*saññā-samāpatti*) in the foregoing sentence refers back to any of the four *jhānas* and the three formless attainments. The Sarvāstivādins apparently invokes a *sūtra* like the above *sutta* of the *Aṅguttara Nikāya* to support their argument that Arahantship (destruction of the taints/defilements) cannot be achieved without the practice of the noble path, and to refute what they see as the Vibhājyavādins' theory of *samasīsin*, because they understand this theory to only apply to one dying from the neither-perception-nor-nonperception rebirth, and they see a problem in Arahantship being attained from this level.

This theory of the Vibhājyavādins as delineated above in the **Abhidharma-Mahāvibhāṣa* accords well with part of the definition of *samasīsin* given by the **Śāriputra-abhidharma* as mentioned in Section 1: 'A person who does not yet practise the path, whose taints and life terminate simultaneously ...' It is most likely that this text belongs to the Dharmaguptaka school (see Section 1).[44] In his study of the Vibhājyavādins, Cousins (2001a, 168–169) concludes that the Dharmaguptakas (Dhammaguttikas) and Theravādins (Tambapaṇṇiyas) are among the main branches of the Vibhājyavādins (Vibhajjavādins). The Vibhājyavādins referred to in the above passages from the **Abhidharma-Mahāvibhāṣa* were probably the Dharmaguptakas rather than the Theravāda still thriving today. As we have seen so far, the Theravāda Abhidhamma and commentaries treat the *samasīsin* as a human being instead of a celestial being. More diverse ideas of the *samasīsin* conceived in the Pali commentaries are discussed below.

43. A IV 426: *yāvatā saññā-samāpatti tāvatā aññā-paṭivedho.*

44. However, Cousins (2015, 100) says: 'I believe that it was most probably the shared canonical text of the three Vibhajjavādin schools of the North-West, but it has usually been thought to belong specifically to one of them: the Dharmaguptakas.'

3. Commentarial developments of *samasīsin*

The commentary on the *Puggalapaññatti*, attributed to Buddhaghosa, says that there are three kinds of *samasīsin*: (1) posture equal-header (*iriyāpatha-samasīsī*), (2) illness equal-header (*roga-samasīsī*) and (3) life equal-header (*jīvita-samasīsī*). The 'posture equal-header' is described as follows:

> Here someone, having established insight and attained Arahantship exactly while walking, dies without being reborn[45] exactly while walking, like the Elder Paduma. Having established insight and attained Arahantship exactly while standing, he dies without being reborn exactly while standing, like the Elder Tissa who lived at Koṭapabbata Monastery. Having established insight and attained Arahantship exactly while sitting, he dies without being reborn exactly while sitting. Having established insight and attained Arahantship exactly while lying down, he dies without being reborn exactly while lying down. This is a posture equal-header.[46]

An example is provided in each of the first two cases only, namely one who dies without being reborn exactly while walking and one who does so exactly while standing, presumably because compared to death in a lying or sitting posture, to die while walking and to die while standing are so extraordinary that concrete examples are necessary for convincing the reader. This passage may be associated with the following passage from the *Visuddhimagga* by Buddhaghosa (trans. Ñāṇamoli 1975, 316):

> [Passage A] When a bhikkhu has attained Arahantship by developing some other meditation subject than this one, he may be able to define his life term or not. But when he has reached Arahantship by developing this mindfulness of breathing with its sixteen bases, he can always define his life term. He knows 'My vital formations will continue now for so long and no more'. Automatically he performs all the functions of attending to the body, dressing and robing, etc., after which he closes his eyes, like the Elder Tissa who lived at Koṭapabbata Monastery ... like the Elders who were brothers and lived at the Cittalapabbata Monastery.[47]

The Elder Tissa who lived at Koṭapabbata Monastery, described as one who 'dies without being reborn exactly while standing' in the *Puggalapaññatti* commentary, seems to be the same Elder Tissa who lived at Koṭapabbata Monastery as mentioned in the *Visuddhimagga* among examples of a bhikkhu who has reached Arahantship

45. CPED s.v. *parinibbāti*: dies without being reborn.

46. Pp-a 186: *Tattha yo cankamanto va vipassanaṃ paṭṭhapetvā arahattaṃ patvā caṅkamanto va parinibbāti Padumatthero viya. Ṭhitako va vipassanaṃ paṭṭhapetvā arahattaṃ patvā ṭhitako va parinibbāti Koṭapabbatavihāravāsī Tissathero viya. Nisinno va vipassanaṃ paṭṭhapetvā arahattaṃ patvā nisinno va parinibbāti. Nipanno va vipassanaṃ paṭṭhapetvā arahattam patvā nipanno va parinibbāti. Ayaṃ iriyāpathasamasīsī nāma.*

47. Vism VIII. 243, p. 241: *Ito aññaṃ kammaṭṭhānaṃ bhāvetvā arahattaṃ pattassa bhikkhuno hi āyu-antaraṃ paricchinnaṃ vā hoti aparicchinnaṃ vā. Idaṃ pana soḷasavatthukaṃ ānāpānasatiṃ bhāvetvā arahattaṃ pattassa āyu-antaraṃ paricchinnam eva hoti. So: ettakaṃ dāni me āyusaṅkhārā pavattissanti, na ito paran ti ñatvā attano dhammatāya eva sarīrapaṭijaggana-nivāsanapārupanādīni sabbakiccāni katvā akkhīni nimīleti, Koṭapabbatavihāravāsī Tissatthero viya ... Cittalapabbatavihāravāsino dve bhātiyattherā viya ca.*

by developing mindfulness of breathing and is able to define his life term. In both texts the Elder Tissa is said to have attained Arahantship in his lifetime: in the first, he attains Arahantship and then dies while in the same standing position; in the second, he is simply said to be an Arahant who knows how much longer he has to live.

Moreover, the Elder Paduma in the *Puggalapaññatti* commentary might be identified with one of the two Elders who were brothers mentioned above in the *Visuddhimagga*. Following the passage quoted above, the *Visuddhimagga* goes on (trans. Ñāṇamoli 1975, 316–317):

> [Passage B] ... one of the two Elders who were brothers went to his own dwelling place surrounded by the Community of Bhikkhus. As he stood on the walk looking at the moonlight he calculated his own vital formations, and he said to the Community of Bhikkhus 'In what way have you seen bhikkhus attaining nibbana (*parinibbāyantā*) up till now?'. Some answered 'Till now we have seen them attain nibbana sitting in their seats'. Others answered 'We have seen them sitting cross-legged in the air'. The Elder said 'I shall now show you one attaining nibbana while walking'. He then drew a line on the walk, saying 'I shall go from the end of the walk to the other end and return; when I reach this line I shall attain nibbana (*parinibbāyissāmi*)'. So saying, he stepped on to the walk and went to the far end. On his return he attained nibbana (*parinibbāyi*) in the same moment in which he stepped on the line.[48]

The words that Ñāṇamoli translates as 'attaining nibbana', 'shall attain nibbana' and 'attained nibbana' are different forms of the verb *parinibbāyati*, which can mean either 'to die without being reborn' or 'to become emancipated from all desire of life' (PED 428 s.v. *parinibbāyati*). Its cognate *parinibbāna* is better known since a famous *sutta* (D 16) is entitled '*Mahā-parinibbāna*', which depicts the Buddha's last days. In this context *parinibbāna* means 'final release from rebirth and transmigration' (PED 427 s.v. *parinibbāna*).[49] Now, in Passage B from the *Visuddhimagga*, the Elder 'attained nibbana' (*parinibbāyi*) at the moment he stepped on the line as he had foretold. As the passage concerns someone who is already an Arahant and who knows when he will die, here *parinibbāyi* means that he attained 'final release from rebirth and transmigration' or he died without being reborn.

As Nyanatiloka (1970, 126, 106) notes, *parinibbāna* is a synonym for *nibbāna* (nirvana), which has two meanings:[50]

48. Vism VIII. 244, pp. 241–242: *Dvebhātiyattherānaṃ kir' eko ... bhikkhusaṅghaparivuto attano vasanaṭṭhānaṃ gantvā caṅkame ṭhito candālokaṃ oloketvā attano āyusaṅkhāre upadhāretvā bhikkhusaṅghaṃ āha: tumhehi kathaṃ parinibbāyantā bhikkhū diṭṭhapubbā ti. Tatra keci āhaṃsu: amhehi āsane nisinnakā va parinibbāyantā diṭṭhapubbā ti. Keci: amhehi ākāse pallaṅkam ābhujitvā nisinnakā ti. Thero āha: ahaṃ dāni vo caṅkamantam eva parinibbāyamānaṃ dassessāmī ti. Tato caṅkame lekhaṃ katvā: ahaṃ ito caṅkamakoṭito parakoṭiṃ gantvā nivattamāno imaṃ lekhaṃ patvā va parinibbāyissāmī ti vatvā caṅkamaṃ oruyha parabhāgaṃ gantvā nivattamāno ekena pādena lekhaṃ akkantakkhaṇe yeva parinibbāyi.*

49. Nyanatiloka (1970, 126) points out that this term does not refer exclusively to the extinction of the five groups of existence (*pañca khandhā*, five aggregates) at the death of the Holy One, but is often applied to it.

50. For the two meanings of *parinibbāna*, see also PED 427 s.v. *parinibbāna*.

1. The full extinction of defilements (*kilesa-parinibbāna*),[51] which takes place at the attainment of Arahantship.
2. The full extinction of the groups of existence (*khandha-parinibbāna*), which takes place at the death of the Arahant.

According to Passage A from the *Visuddhimagga*, the two Elders who were brothers had reached Arahantship by developing mindfulness of breathing. They had thus attained nirvana in the sense of the full extinction of defilements (*kilesa-parinibbāna*). In Passage B from the *Visuddhimagga*, one of the two Elders who were brothers proclaimed: 'I shall now show you one attaining nibbana (nirvana) while walking', and then he attained nirvana at the moment he stepped on the line. On this occasion, 'he attained nirvana' (*parinibbāyi*) means that as an Arahant he died without being reborn due to the full extinction of the groups of existence, or the five aggregates (*khandha*). Accordingly, the exhaustion of his taints (defilements), or his attainment of Arahantship, did not occur simultaneously with the exhaustion of his life. Therefore, he was not an equal-headed person (*puggalo samasīsī*) as defined in the *Puggalapaññatti*, but strangely can be counted as a 'posture equal-header' (*iriyāpatha-samasīsī*) in the sense that he died without being reborn exactly while walking according to the *Puggalapaññatti* commentary, and may well refer to the Elder Paduma mentioned in this commentary, traditionally ascribed to Buddhaghosa[52] who composed the *Visuddhimagga*. He is a 'posture equal-header' not simply by dying and attaining extinction of his aggregates in a particular posture (as all Arahants die in *some* posture or other), but because this posture was the same as that in which he had earlier attained Arahantship.

Similarly, the Elder Tissa who lived at Koṭapabbata Monastery mentioned in Passage A of the *Visuddhimagga* can be identified with the Elder Tissa who lived at Koṭapabbata Monastery in the *Puggalapaññatti* commentary, which describes the elder as one who 'dies without being reborn exactly while standing' and names him to illustrate the 'posture equal-header'. In view of the foregoing discussion, a 'posture equal-header' posited in the *Puggalapaññatti* commentary is quite different from an equal-headed (*samasīsin*) person as defined in the Abhidhamma text that it comments on. It seems inappropriate to postulate the so-called 'posture equal-header' (*iriyāpatha-samasīsī*) and classify it under the category '*samasīsin*'.

There are similar problems with the second of the three kinds of *samasīsin* proposed in the *Puggalapaññatti* commentary. The 'illness equal-header' (*roga-samasīsī*) is explained as 'Someone contracts an illness. Having established insight and attained Arahantship in the midst of illness, he dies of that illness without being

51. As a metaphor, nirvana (*nirvāṇa* in Sanskrit, *nibbāna* in Pali) means 'blown or put out, extinguished (as a lamp or fire)', see MW 557 s.v. *nir-√vā*, *°vāṇa*, and cf. DOP II 580 s.v. *nibbāna*. Gombrich (1996, 65) points out that what is being blown out is the set of three fires: passion (greed), hatred and delusion. This amounts to 'the full extinction of defilements' as Nyanatiloka states, and is the basic meaning of *nibbāna* (nirvana) or *parinibbāna*.

52. von Hinüber (1997, 151) suggests that Buddhaghosa could be the initiator rather than the composer of the Abhidhamma commentaries.

reborn. This is an illness equal-header.'[53] Accordingly, an 'illness equal-header' has already attained Arahantship before he dies. For him the exhaustion of the taints (*āsava*) and the exhaustion of life does not occur simultaneously. Just like the 'posture equal-header', the 'illness equal-header' (*roga-samasīsī*) cannot be reckoned a *samasīsin* person as defined in the *Puggalapaññatti*. In sum, the first two kinds of *samasīsin* deviate from the basic Abhidhamma definition of *samasīsin*.

The third kind of *samasīsin* posited in the *Puggalapaññatti* commentary is the 'life equal-header' (*jīvita-samasīsī*). A large paragraph is devoted to the exposition of this kind of person. It includes a passage quoted from the *Paṭisambhidāmagga* and a gloss on part of this passage, which will be discussed in the next section. In its conclusion, *jīvita-samasīsī* refers to a person whose taints and life terminate simultaneously, and thus can be identified with the *samasīsin* person as defined in the *Puggalapaññatti*.

Apart from the three kinds of *samasīsin* in the *Puggalapaññatti* commentary, Buddhaghosa's commentary on the foregoing *sutta* of the *Aṅguttara Nikāya* (A 7:16) even talks about four types of *samasīsin* as follows:

1. While someone is affected by a certain illness, his recovery from the illness is simultaneous with his destruction of the taints. This is an illness equal-header.
2. While someone is experiencing a certain feeling, his removal of the feeling is simultaneous with his destruction of the taints. This is a feeling equal-header.
3. While someone is practising insight in a certain posture such as standing, his breaking the posture is simultaneous with his destruction of the taints. This is a posture equal-header.
4. Someone's exhaustion of life, due to attack or by natural causes, is simultaneous with his destruction of the taints. This is a life equal-header.[54]

Only the fourth type of *samasīsin*, the 'life equal-header' (*jīvita-samasīsī*), conforms to the basic Abhidhamma definition of *samasīsin* and fits in the context of the *sutta* passage from the *Aṅguttara Nikāya*. These four types of *samasīsin* are also explained in the *Puggalapaññatti* commentary except for the second type, the 'feeling equal-header' (*vedanā-samasīsī*). The description of this type is somewhat obscure. Bodhi (2012, 1773 n. 1465) translates it thus: 'One who has been afflicted with a severe painful feeling and attains the destruction of the taints at the same time that he overcomes the pain is called a "feeling same-header".' Anyway, this type of *samasīsin* is not one who attains Arahantship at the moment he dies, but has already attained

53. Pp-a 186: *Yo pana ekaṃ rogaṃ patvā antoroge yeva vipassanaṃ paṭṭhapetvā arahattaṃ patvā ten' eva rogena parinibbāti, ayaṃ rogasamasīsī nāma.*

54. Mp IV 6: *Yassa aññatarena rogena phuṭṭhassa sato rogavūpasamo ca āsavakkhayo ca ekappahāren' eva hoti, ayaṃ rogasamasīsī nāma. Yassa pana aññataraṃ vedanaṃ vediyato vedanāvūpasamo ca āsavakkhayo ca ekappahāren' eva hoti, ayaṃ vedanāsamasīsī nāma. Yassa pana ṭhānādīsu iriyāpathesu aññatarasamaṅgino vipassantassa iriyāpathassa pariyosānañ ca āsavakkhayo ca ekappahāren' eva hoti, ayaṃ iriyāpathasamasīsī nāma. Yassa pana upakkamato vā sarasato vā jīvitapariyādānañ ca āsavakkhayo ca ekappahāren' eva hoti, ayaṃ jīvitasamasīsī nāma.*

Arahantship, the destruction of the taints, before death. Such is also the case with the 'illness equal-header' and the 'posture equal-header'.

It is noteworthy that while the 'illness equal-header' and the 'posture equal-header' are also expounded in the *Puggalapaññatti* commentary, its descriptions of these two (mentioned earlier) diverge from those given in the commentary to the *Aṅguttara Nikāya* just listed above. Whereas the *Puggalapaññatti* commentary states that an 'illness equal-header' attains Arahantship in the midst of illness, according to the *Aṅguttara Nikāya* commentary an 'illness equal-header' attains Arahantship at the same time that he *recovers* from illness. In the *Puggalapaññatti* commentary a 'posture equal-header' attains Arahantship while maintaining the same posture, but in the *Aṅguttara Nikāya* commentary a 'posture equal-header' attains Arahantship at the moment he *changes* the posture in which he has practised insight.

Buddhaghosa's commentary on the foregoing *Godhika Sutta* of the *Saṃyutta Nikāya* expounds three kinds of *samasīsin*. The three terms and the order in which they appear in this commentary are exactly the same as those found in the *Puggalapaññatti* commentary, but its exegesis of the terms is closer to that in the *Aṅguttara Nikāya* commentary than to that in the *Puggalapaññatti* commentary. An abridged translation by Keown (1996, 25 n. 45) is as follows:

> i) *Iriyāpatha-samasīsī*: someone selects one of the four postures and resolves not to change posture until they attain Arhatship. The change of posture and Arhatship occur together. ii) *Roga-samasīsī*: someone recovers from an illness and attains Arhatship at the same time. iii) *Jīvita-samasīsī*: the destruction of the *āsavas* (*āsavakkhaya*) and the end of life (*jīvitakkhaya*) occur simultaneously.[55]

The above accounts give the impression that such diverse classifications and explanations of *samasīsin* were freely elaborated by various authors or even the same author. Nevertheless, these explanations have one idea in common: *samasīsa*, from which *samasīsin* is derived, always refers to the concept that two things happen at the same time. Therefore, *samasīsin* may be construed etymologically in this way: [one who is] possessed of (*-in*, possessive suffix [Warder 1991, 188]) both prominent features (*sīsa*, head) at the same time (*sama*, same/equal). In view of the above discussions, one of the features or events is always the attainment of either (1) Arahantship, that is, the destruction of the taints, or (2) *parinibbāna* in the sense of the extinction of the five aggregates (groups of existence), which takes place at the death of an Arahant. Therefore, according to the commentaries, the whole term denotes at least a person who only becomes an Arahant at death, and sometimes someone who becomes an Arahant at the same time as a certain kind of event occurs.

55. Spk I 183–184: *Samasīsī nāma tividho hoti: iriyāpatha-samasīsī, roga-samasīsī, jīvita-samasīsī. Tattha yo ṭhānādīsu iriyāpathesu aññataraṃ adhiṭṭhāya — imaṃ akopetvā va arahattaṃ pāpuṇissāmī ti vipassanaṃ paṭṭhapeti, ath' assa arahatta-ppatti ca iriyāpatha-kopanañ ca ekappahāren' eva hoti. Ayaṃ iriyāpatha-samasīsī nāma. Yo pana cakkhu-rogādīsu aññatarasmiṃ sati — ito anuṭṭhito va arahattaṃ pāpuṇissāmī ti vipassanaṃ paṭṭhapeti, ath' assa arahatta-ppatti ca rogato vuṭṭhānañ ca ekappahāren' eva hoti. Ayaṃ roga-samasīsī nāma ... Yassa pana āsava-kkhayo ca jīvita-kkhayo ca ekappahāren' eva hoti. Ayaṃ jīvita-samasīsī nāma.*

4. Equal-head (*samasīsa*) in the *Paṭisambhidāmagga*

In the Pali Canon, the *Paṭisambhidāmagga* is included in the *Khuddaka Nikāya* of the *Sutta-piṭaka* rather than in the *Abhidhamma-piṭaka*, but it is a quasi-Abhidhamma text and at some early date it was probably classed among the Abhidhamma works.[56] Chapter 36 (according to CST) of the *Paṭisambhidāmagga* (Paṭis 101–102) expounds on knowledge of 'the meaning of equal-head' (*samasīsaṭṭhe* < *samasīsa-aṭṭha*). It begins with a question: 'How is it that understanding of the complete cutting off of all *dhammas*, of their cessation, and of their non-reappearance, is knowledge of the meaning of equal-head?'[57] Accordingly, the meaning of 'equal-head' is seen as 'the complete cutting off of all *dhammas*, their cessation and their non-reappearance'. This lengthy expression implies nirvana or Arahantship on the following grounds.

In this chapter, 'all *dhammas*' is explained as 'the five aggregates, the twelve bases, the eighteen elements, things (*dhammas*) that are wholesome, unwholesome, indeterminate, in the sensual-desire sphere, in the form sphere, in the formless sphere, and unincluded things',[58] which must refer to all conditioned or worldly things because the text specifies the complete cutting off of all *dhammas*, the cessation and non-reappearance of all *dhammas*. The unconditioned or the supramundane things should not be cut off or brought to cessation.[59] The text elaborates on 'the complete cutting off [of all *dhammas*]' thus:

> He completely cuts off sensual desire through absence of desire, completely cuts off ill-will through non-ill-will, completely cuts off sloth-and-torpor through the conception of light, completely cuts off restlessness through non-distraction, completely cuts off doubt through definition of *dhammas*, completely cuts off ignorance through knowledge, completely cuts off aversion through gladness. He completely cuts off the hindrances through the first *jhāna* ... [and so on with the remaining three *jhānas* and formless attainments] ... He completely cuts off all defilements through the Arahantship path.[60]

This passage depicts how one cuts off all defilements and attains Arahantship. The explanations of 'cessation [of all *dhammas*]' and of 'non-reappearance [of all *dhammas*]' are modelled on the above passage and end in 'He causes the cessation of all defilements through the Arahantship path'[61] and 'No defilements reappear in one

56. Kimura 1968, 52; Norman 1983, 88–89; Buswell and Jaini 1996, 97; Mizuno 1997, 85, 87; Warder 1997, xxxiii–xxxv.

57. Paṭis I 101: *Kathaṃ sabba-dhammānaṃ sammā-samucchede nirodhe ca anupaṭṭhānatā paññā samasīsaṭṭhe ñāṇaṃ?* My translation largely follows Ñāṇamoli (1997, 99).

58. Paṭis I 101: *'Sabbadhammānan' ti pañcakkhandhā, dvādas' āyatanāni, aṭṭhārasa dhātuyo, kusalā dhammā, akusalā dhammā, abyākatā dhammā, kāmāvacarā dhammā, rūpāvacarā dhammā, arūpāvacarā dhammā, apariyāpannā dhammā.*

59. Paṭis-a I 324: *lokuttaradhammā hetusamucchedena samucchinditabbā na honti.*

60. Paṭis I 101: *'Sammāsamucchede' ti Nekkhammena kāmacchandaṃ sammā samucchindati. Abyāpādena byāpādaṃ sammā samucchindati. Āloka-saññāya thīna-middhaṃ sammā samucchindati. Avikkhepena uddhaccaṃ sammā samucchindati. Dhamma-vavatthānena vicikicchaṃ sammā samucchindati. Ñāṇena avijjaṃ sammā samucchindati. Pāmojjena aratiṃ sammā samucchindati. Paṭhamajjhānena nīvaraṇe sammā samucchindati ...pe... Arahatta-maggena sabba-kilese sammā samucchindati.*

61. Paṭis I 101: *Arahatta-maggena sabba-kilese nirodheti.*

who has obtained the Arahantship path'[62] respectively.

What follows is the exposition of the term *samasīsa*. It only explains *sama* and *sīsa* separately without explaining the whole compound:

> 'Equal (*sama*)': Absence of desire is equal to the abandoning of sensual desire. Non-ill-will is equal to the abandoning of ill-will. The conception of light is equal to the abandoning of sloth-and-torpor. Non-distraction is equal to the abandoning of restlessness. Definition of *dhammas* is equal to the abandoning of doubt. Knowledge is equal to the abandoning of ignorance. Gladness is equal to the abandoning of aversion. The first *jhāna* is equal to the abandoning of the hindrances ... [and so on with the remaining three *jhānas* and formless attainments] ... the Arahantship path is equal to the abandoning of all defilements.
>
> 'Head (*sīsa*)': Thirteen heads: (A) the head of impediments is craving, the head of bondages is conceit, the head of attachments is [wrong] view, the head of distractions is restlessness, the head of defilements is ignorance, (B) the head of determination is faith, the head of exertion is energy, the head of establishment is mindfulness, the head of non-distraction is concentration, the head of insight is understanding, (C) the head of transmigration is the life faculty, (D) the head of domains is liberation, the head of formations is cessation.[63]

This exposition, located towards the end of this chapter, is rather enigmatic. The whole chapter does not seem to elucidate the 'meaning of equal-head', but talks about it in an oblique way. The passage on 'equal (*sama*)' relates to the psychological attributes of an Arahant that result from abandoning all the unwholesome mental states. The passage on 'head (*sīsa*)' lists thirteen heads, i.e. leading items, which are divided into four groups and connected with the Four True Realities for the Noble Ones[64] (Four Noble Truths) in the *Paṭisambhidāmagga* commentary written by Mahānāma in 559 CE (von Hinüber 1997, 149). In my translation of this passage, these four groups are labelled as A, B, C and D, which refer respectively to the Reality of the origin (arising), Reality of the way, Reality of *dukkha* (suffering) and Reality of cessation according to the commentary.[65]

62. Paṭis I 102: *Arahatta-maggaṃ paṭiladdhassa sabba-kilesā na upaṭṭhahanti* (according to CST. Ee: *upaṭṭhanti*).

63. Paṭis I 102: *'Saman' ti Kāmacchandassa pahīnattā nekkhammaṃ samaṃ. Byāpādassa pahīnattā abyāpādo samaṃ. Thīna-middhassa pahīnattā āloka-saññā samaṃ. Uddhaccassa pahīnattā avikkhepo samaṃ. Vicikicchāya pahīnattā dhamma-vavatthānaṃ samaṃ. Avijjāya pahīnattā ñāṇaṃ samaṃ. Aratiyā pahīnattā pāmojjaṃ samaṃ. Nīvaraṇānaṃ pahīnattā paṭhamajjhānaṃ samaṃ ...pe... Sabba-kilesānaṃ pahīnattā Arahatta-maggo samaṃ.*
'Sīsan' ti Terasa sīsāni — palibodhasīsañ ca taṇhā, vinibandhanasīsañ ca māno, parāmāsasīsañ ca diṭṭhi, vikkhepasīsañ ca uddhaccaṃ, kilesasīsañ ca avijjā, adhimokkhasīsañ ca saddhā, paggahasīsañ ca vīriyaṃ, upaṭṭhānasīsañ ca sati, avikkhepasīsañ ca samādhi, dassanasīsañ ca paññā, pavattasīsañ ca jīvitindriyaṃ, gocarasīsañ ca vimokkho, saṅkhārasīsañ ca nirodho.

64. I follow this new translation by Harvey (2013, 13, 34, 46, etc.) for translating *catunnaṃ ariya-saccānaṃ* in this commentary (see footnote below). Cousins (2001b, 38) observes: '[I]t is unreasonable to say that the truth of arising should be abandoned ... The word *sacca*, however, means equally "reality" or "what is really there."'

65. Paṭis-a I 325: *taṇhādīni pañca sīsāni samudaya-saccaṃ, saddhādīni pañca magga-saccaṃ, pavattasīsaṃ jīvitindriyaṃ dukkha-saccaṃ, gocarasīsañ ca saṅkhārasīsañ ca nirodha-saccan ti imesaṃ catunnaṃ ariya-saccānaṃ ...*

The *Paṭisambhidāmagga* commentary tries to make sense of the term *samasīsa* by associating the above exposition of *sama* and *sīsa* with the more commonly found term *samasīsin*:

> The equal [consisting of] absence of desire, etc. and the head [consisting of] faith, etc.; alternatively [it means] there is of him the equal head (*samasīsa*), that is, an equal-header (*samasīsin*)[66] ... Someone who has a direct grasp of these Four True Realities for the Noble Ones in regard to an illness, a posture or a life faculty of the same sort, and has attained nirvana with no rebirth-substratum left — he is called an 'equal-header' (*samasīsin*) because of the aforesaid equals and those heads.[67]

This gloss deals with the above textual passage on *sama* and *sīsa* in such a way that the term *samasīsa* (equal-head) in the *Paṭisambhidāmagga* is identified with the term *samasīsin* (equal-header/equal-headed) frequently found in the commentaries and Abhidharma works. It should be noted that 'illness', 'posture' and 'life faculty' mentioned in this gloss allude to the 'illness equal-header', the 'posture equal-header' and the 'life equal-header' in the commentaries discussed above. Mahānāma's commentary on *samasīsa* draws upon the mainstream exegesis centred on *samasīsin* discussed above.

As mentioned in Section 3, the *Puggalapaññatti* commentary contains a paragraph devoted to the exposition of the 'life equal-header', which includes the above passage on thirteen heads quoted from the *Paṭisambhidāmagga* and glosses it as follows:

> Here the Arahantship path terminates ignorance, which is the head of defilements. The death consciousness (*cuti-citta*) terminates the life faculty, which is the head of transmigration. The mind that terminates ignorance is unable to terminate the life faculty. The mind that terminates the life faculty is unable to terminate ignorance. The mind that terminates ignorance is different from the mind that terminates the life faculty. For someone these two heads are terminated simultaneously (*samaṃ*, equally[68]), he is a 'life equal-header'. Why is this 'simultaneously' (*samaṃ*)? Because of equality in time (i.e. at the same time).[69]

Here 'ignorance' (*avijjā*) can be identified with 'taints' (*āsava*) in the *Puggalapaññatti*'s definition of the *samasīsin* person if the above passage is compared with a parallel in the *Aṅguttara Nikāya* commentary.[70] Thus a 'life equal-header' refers to a person

66. I am indebted to Professor Rupert Gethin (particularly), Dr Aleix Falqués and Dr William Pruitt for helping me translate the above difficult passage.

67. Paṭis-a I 325: *Nekkhammādikaṃ samañ ca, saddhādikaṃ sīsañ ca, samasīsaṃ vā assa atthī ti samasīsī ... imesaṃ catunnaṃ ariya-saccānaṃ ekasmiṃ roge vā ekasmiṃ iriyāpathe vā ekasmiṃ sabhāgajīvitindriye vā abhisamayo ca anupādisesa-parinibbānañ ca yassa hoti, so pubbe vuttasamānañ ca imesañ ca sīsānaṃ atthitāya samasīsī ti vuccati.*

68. *Samam* can mean 'equally' and 'at the same time with', see MW 1152 s.v. *sama*.

69. Pp-a IV 186–7: *Tattha kilesasīsaṃ avijjaṃ arahattamaggo pariyādiyati. Pavattasīsaṃ jīvitindriyaṃ cuticittaṃ pariyādiyati. Avijjā-pariyādāyakaṃ cittaṃ jīvitindriyaṃ pariyādātuṃ na sakkoti. Jīvitindriya-pariyādāyakaṃ cittaṃ avijjaṃ pariyādātuṃ na sakkoti. Avijjā-pariyādāyakaṃ cittaṃ aññaṃ, jīvitindriya-pariyādāyakaṃ cittaṃ aññaṃ. Yassa c' etaṃ sīsa-dvayaṃ samaṃ pariyādānaṃ gacchati, so jīvita-samasīsī nāma. Kathaṃ idaṃ samaṃ hotī ti? Vārasamatāya.*

70. Mp IV 7: *āsava-pariyādānaṃ maggacittena, jīvita-pariyādānaṃ cuticittena hotī ti* (Termination of the taints due to the path consciousness and termination of life due to the death conscious-

whose two heads, i.e. the taints and life, terminate simultaneously, and this is in fact an 'equal-headed person' as defined in the *Puggalapaññatti*. The *Puggalapaññatti* commentary puts this gloss on the foregoing *Paṭisambhidāmagga* passage in an attempt to decipher this cryptic passage in accordance with the *Puggalapaññatti*'s definition of *samasīsin*. This is done by the simple expedient of singling out just two heads among the thirteen heads enumerated in the *Paṭisambhidāmagga*, but the remaining eleven heads are left out as if not existing.

The discrepancy between the *Paṭisambhidāmagga* commentary and the *Puggalapaññatti* commentary in their interpretations of the *Paṭisambhidāmagga*'s passage on *samasīsa* reflects the following facts. First, different commentators interpreted the same passage at their discretion, just as different commentators or even the same commentator put forward various explanations and classifications of *samasīsin* in different commentaries. Secondly, as scholars have pointed out, the commentaries that have come down to us developed from older commentaries by different authors (von Hinüber 1997, 101; Norman 1983, 121), which were already heterogeneous before the commentators such as Buddhaghosa and Mahānāma mentioned above.

5. Conclusion

Several *suttas* enumerate seven kinds of worthy people in descending order:

1. One attains gnosis or the destruction of the taints in this very life = Arahant.
2. One attains gnosis or the destruction of the taints at the time of death.
3. *antarā-parinibbāyī.*
4. *upahacca-parinibbāyī*
5. *asaṅkhāra-parinibbāyī*
6. *sasaṅkhāra-parinibbāyī*
7. *uddhaṃsoto akaniṭṭhagāmī*

Among these seven kinds of people, six kinds are all given designations in certain *suttas*. Only the second kind of person, who attains Arahantship at death, is given no designation in the *suttas*. This lack may have prompted the Ābhidharmikas to coin a new word *samasīsin* to designate this unusual kind of person.

The Sarvāstivādin counterparts of such *sutta* passages leave out the description of the second kind in the above list of seven. They denied the concept of *samasīsin* proposed by the Vibhājyavādins, which include the Theravāda and Dharmaguptaka schools. The *Puggalapaññatti*, one of the earliest Abhidhamma texts of the Theravāda, defines the equal-headed person (*puggalo samasīsī*) as 'the person for whom the exhaustion of the taints (*āsava*) and the exhaustion of life occur simultaneously'. A similar definition appears in the **Śāriputra-abhidharma*, presumably the Abhidharma of the extinct Dharmaguptakas.

ness occur [simultaneously]). Here *āsava-pariyādānaṃ* (termination of the taints) is equivalent to *avijjā-pariyādāyakaṃ* (terminates ignorance) in the *Puggalapaññatti* commentary cited above while *jīvita-pariyādānaṃ* (termination of life) is equivalent to *jīvitindriya-pariyādāyakaṃ* (terminates the life faculty) in the *Puggalapaññatti* commentary.

The idea that some attain Arahantship at the time of death, which was later designated as a *samasīsin* person, may have originated from the suicide accounts of three bhikkhus in *sutta* literature. The Theravāda *sutta*s in Pali vaguely depict them as ordinary people before suicide or are ambiguous about whether they were Arahants before death. The Pali commentary unequivocally explains that they did not attain Arahantship until their deaths and refers to two of them as each being an 'equal-header' (*samasīsī*). By contrast, according to the (Mūla-)Sarvāstivāda *sūtra*s in Chinese translation, Channa and Vakkali were already Arahants before the event of suicide, and the **Abhidharma-Mahāvibhāṣa* of the Sarvāstivādins considers Godhika to be an Arahant during his lifetime. Since the Sarvāstivādins did not regard suicide as an offence, they had no problem with portraying these bhikkhus as Arahants taking their own lives, whereas the Theravādins do not see suicide as faultless and have to count them as a special type of noble ones, later called *samasīsin*, who committed suicide as ordinary people but dramatically reached Arahantship at death.

The Pali commentaries provide various explanations and classifications of *samasīsin*. These explanations have one idea in common: the term signifies that two things happen at the same time. *Samasīsin* may be construed etymologically thus: [one who is] possessed of (*-in*, possessive suffix) both prominent features (*sīsa*, head) at the same time (*sama*, same/equal). One of the features or events is always the attainment of either (1) Arahantship, namely the destruction of the taints, or (2) *parinibbāna* in the sense of the extinction of the five aggregates, which takes place at the death of an Arahant. According to the commentaries, *samasīsin* denotes at least a person who only becomes an Arahant at death, and sometimes someone who becomes an Arahant at the same time as a certain kind of event occurs.

The *Paṭisambhidāmagga*, a quasi-Abhidhamma text, has a chapter on knowledge of 'the meaning of equal-head'. The whole chapter expounds 'equal-head' (*samasīsa*) in an oblique way by enumerating various kinds of *sama* and of *sīsa* separately. The *Paṭisambhidāmagga* commentary tries to make sense of the term *samasīsa* by associating such textual exposition of *sama* and *sīsa* with the more commonly found term *samasīsin*. The *Puggalapaññatti* commentary also puts a sophisticated gloss on this cryptic *Paṭisambhidāmagga* passage in accordance with the *Puggalapaññatti*'s definition of *samasīsin*. 'The meaning of equal-head' (*samasīsaṭṭhe* < *samasīsa-aṭṭha*) as expounded in the *Paṭisambhidāmagga* implies nirvana or Arahantship, but seems irrelevant to the basic Abhidhamma definition of *samasīsin* as one who becomes an Arahant at death.

Acknowledgments

I owe a great deal to Professor Peter Harvey, who read through this paper carefully and provided many invaluable suggestions and corrections. I thank Mr Ken Su 蘇錦坤 for commenting on an earlier draft of this paper and Taiwan's Ministry of Science and Technology for the funding (MOST 104-2410-H-155-051-MY3). I am also grateful to Professor Rupert Gethin, Dr Aleix Falqués and Dr William Pruitt for helping me translate a difficult Pali passage. Special thanks are due to the late Mr L. S. Cousins, who taught me about Buddhism, including the Abhidhamma.

Abbreviations

References to Pali texts are to the Pali Text Society editions, unless otherwise stated.

A	*Aṅguttara Nikāya*
Abhidh-s	*Abhidharmasamuccaya*, input by members of the Sanskrit Buddhist Input Project, http://gretil.sub.uni-goettingen.de/gretil/1_sanskr/6_sastra/3_phil/buddh/asabhs_u.htm (29 April 2017).
BCSD	*Buddhist Chinese-Sanskrit Dictionary* 佛教漢梵大辭典, ed. Akira Hirakawa. Tokyo: The Reiyukai, 1997.
BHSD	*Buddhist Hybrid Sanskrit Grammar and Dictionary, Volume II: Dictionary*, ed. Franklin Edgerton, 1953. Delhi: Motilal Banarsidass. Reprint 1993.
CBETA	*CBETA Chinese Electronic Tripiṭaka Collection*, Version 2014. Taipei: Chinese Buddhist Electronic Text Association.
CPED	*Concise Pali-English Dictionary*, ed. A.P. Buddhadatta Mahāthera. Delhi: Motilal Banarsidass, repr. 2002.
CST	*Chaṭṭha Saṅgāyana Tipiṭaka*, Version 4.0 (digital version). Igatpuri: Vipassana Research Institute.
DOP I	*A Dictionary of Pāli*, Part I, ed. Margaret Cone. Oxford: Pali Text Society, 2001.
DOP II	*A Dictionary of Pāli*, Part II, ed. Margaret Cone. Bristol: Pali Text Society, 2010.
D	*Dīgha Nikāya*
DPPN	*Dictionary of Pāli Proper Names*, edited by G. P. Malalasekera. London: John Murray, 1937.
Ee	European edition (i.e. Pali Text Society edition)
M	*Majjhima Nikāya*
Mp	*Manorathapūraṇī* (Commentary on the *Aṅguttara Nikāya*)
MW	*A Sanskrit-English Dictionary*, edited by Monier Monier-Williams. Oxford: Clarendon Press, 1899.
Paṭis	*Paṭisambhidāmagga*
Paṭis-a	*Saddhammappakāsinī* (Commentary on the *Paṭisambhidāmagga*)
PED	*The Pali Text Society's Pali-English Dictionary*, edited by T. W. Rhys Davids and William Stede. London: Pali Text Society, reprint. 1986. (First published 1921–1925)
Pp	*Puggalapaññatti*
Pp-a	*Puggalapaññatti-Atthakathā* (*Puggalapaññatti Commentary*) from the *Pañcappakaraṇatthakathā*
SĀ	*Saṃyukta Āgama* (*Za ahanjing* 雜阿含經)
S	*Saṃyutta Nikāya*
SJD	漢訳対照梵和大辞典 (*A Sanskrit-Japanese Dictionary with Equivalents in Chinese Translation*), edited by Unrai Wogihara 荻原雲来. revised ed. Tokyo: 講談社, 1986.

Spk *Sāratthappakāsinī* (Commentary on the *Saṃyutta Nikāya*)

T *Taishō Shinshū Daizōkyō* 大正新脩大藏經, edited by Junjirō Takakusu 高楠順次郎 *et al.* Tokyo: Taishō Issaikyō Kankōkai, 1924–1934. (cited from CBETA)

Vism *Visuddhimagga of Buddhaghosācariya*, ed. Henry Clarke Warren. Delhi: Motilal Banarsidass. Reprint 1999. (First published 1950 Cambridge, MA: Harvard University Press)

Bibliography

English titles in parentheses are my translations.

Anālayo. 2010. 'Channa's Suicide in the *Saṃyukta-āgama*'. *Buddhist Studies Review* 27(2): 125–137. https://doi.org/10.1558/bsrv.v27i2.125

———. 2011. 'Vakkali's Suicide in the Chinese *Āgamas*'. *Buddhist Studies Review* 28(2): 155–170. https://doi.org/10.1558/bsrv.v28i2.155

———. 2017. 'The "School Affiliation" of the *Madhyama-āgama*'. In *Research on the Madhyama-āgama*, ed. Dhammadinnā, 55–76. Taipei: Dharma Drum Publishing Corporation.

Bodhi, Bhikkhu, trans. 2000. *The Connected Discourses of the Buddha: A New Translation of the Saṃyutta Nikāya*. Oxford: Pali Text Society.

———. trans. 2012. *The Numerical Discourses of the Buddha: A Translation of the Aṅguttara Nikāya*. Boston, MA: Wisdom Publications.

Buswell, Robert E., Jr. and Padmanabh S. Jaini. 1996. 'The Development of Abhidharma Philosophy'. In *Encyclopedia of Indian Philosophies, Volume VII: Abhidharma Buddhism to 150 A.D.*, edited by Karl H. Potter, 73–119. Delhi: Motilal Banarsidass.

Choong, Mun-keat. 2000. *The Fundamental Teachings of Early Buddhism: A Comparative Study Based on the Sūtrāṅga Portion of the Pāli Saṃyutta-Nikāya and the Chinese Saṃyuktāgama*. Wiesbaden: Harrassowitz Verlag.

Chou, Jouhan. 周柔含 2008. 齊頂(首)補特伽羅についての一考察 ('An Examination of the Samasīsī-puggala'). 印度學佛教學研究 *Journal of Indian and Buddhist Studies* 57(1): 373–367.

Cousins, L.S. 2001a. 'On the Vibhajjavādins: The Mahiṃsāsaka, Dhammaguttaka, Kassapiya and Tambapaṇṇiya branches of the Ancient Theriyas'. *Buddhist Studies Review* 18(2): 131–182.

———. 2001b. 'Review of *Pain and its Ending: The Four Noble Truths in the Theravāda Buddhist Canon* by Carol S. Anderson'. *Journal of Buddhist Ethics* 8: 36–41.

———. 2015. 'Abhidhamma Studies III: Origins of the Canonical Abhidha(r)mma Literature'. *Journal of the Oxford Centre for Buddhist Studies* 8: 96–145.

Frauwallner, Erich. 1995. *Studies in Abhidharma Literature and the Origins of Buddhist Philosophical Systems*, translated from the German by Sophie Francis Kidd. Albany: State University of New York Press.

Gethin, Rupert. 1998. *The Foundations of Buddhism*. Oxford: Oxford University Press.

Gombrich, Richard F. 1996. *How Buddhism Began: The Conditioned Genesis of the Early Teachings*. London: Athlone Press.

Harvey, Peter. 1995. *The Selfless Mind: Personality, Consciousness and Nirvāṇa in Early Buddhism*. Richmond: Curzon Press.

———. 2013. 'The *Saṅgha* of Noble *Sāvaka*s, with Particular Reference to their Trainee Member, the Person "Practising for the Realization of the Stream-entry-fruit"'. *Buddhist Studies Review* 30(1): 3–70. https://doi.org/10.1558/bsrv.v30i1.3

von Hinüber, Oskar. 1997 [1996]. *A Handbook of Pāli Literature.* 1st Indian ed. New Delhi: Munshiram Manoharlal Publishers.

Keown, Damien. 1996. 'Buddhism and Suicide: The Case of Channa'. *Journal of Buddhist Ethics* 3: 8–31.

Kimura, Taiken. 木村泰賢. 1968. 木村泰賢全集 第四巻 阿毘達磨論の研究 (*A Study of the Abhidharma Treatises*, vol. 4 of *Kimura Taiken Zenshū*). Tokyo: 大法輪閣.

Kuan, Tse-fu. 2013a. 'The *Pavāraṇā Sutta* and "liberation in both ways" as against "liberation by wisdom"'. *Bulletin of the School of Oriental and African Studies* 76(1): 49–73.

———. 2013b. 'Legends and Transcendence: Sectarian Affiliations of the *Ekottarika Āgama* in Chinese Translation'. *Journal of the American Oriental Society* 133(4): 607–634.

———. 2015. 'Abhidhamma Interpretations of "Persons" (*puggala*): with Particular Reference to the *Aṅguttara Nikāya*'. *Journal of Indian Philosophy* 43(1): 31–60. https://doi.org/10.1007/s10781-014-9228-5

———. 2017. 'From *Sūtra* to *Abhidharma*: An Important Transition in the History of Indian Buddhist Literature' 從經到論：管窺印度佛教文獻史上的重大變遷. *Cheng Kung Journal of Historical Studies* 53: 135–177.

Mizuno, Kōgen. 水野弘元 . 1966. 舍利弗阿毘曇論について ('On the *Śāriputra-abhidharma*'). In 金倉博士古稀記念印度学仏教学論集 (*Indian and Buddhist Studies: Festschrift on the Occasion of Dr Kanakura's 70th Birthday*), edited by 金倉博士古稀記念論文集刊行会, 109–134. Kyoto: 平楽寺書店.

———. 1996. 仏教文献研究. (*A Study of Buddhist Literature*). Tokyo: 春秋社.

———. 1997. パーリ論書研究. (*A Study of the Pali Abhidhamma Treatises*). Tokyo: 春秋社.

Ñāṇamoli, Bhikkhu, trans. 1975. *The Path of Purification.* 3rd edition. Kandy: Buddhist Publication Society. (First published 1956 Colombo)

———, trans. 1997. *The Path of Discrimination.* 2nd ed. Oxford: Pali Text Society.

Nawa, Ryūken. 名和隆乾. 2011. チャンナの自殺 ('Channa's Suicide'). 待兼山論叢: 哲学篇 *Machikaneyama ronsō: Tetsugaku hen* 45: 67–82.

Norman, K. R. 1983. *Pāli Literature: including the Canonical Literature in Prakrit and Sanskrit of All the Hīnayāna Schools of Buddhism.* Wiesbaden: Otto Harrassowitz.

Nyanatiloka. 1970. *Buddhist Dictionary: Manual of Buddhist Terms and Doctrines.* 3rd revised and enlarged edition. Singapore: Singapore Buddhist Meditation Centre.

Law, Bimala Churn. 2000 [1933]. *A History of Pāli Literature*. Varanasi: Indica Books.

Rhys Davids, T.W. 1903. *Buddhist India*, Indian repr. 1993. Delhi: Motilal Banarsidass.

Warder, A.K. 1991 [1963]. *Introduction to Pali*, 3rd edition. Oxford: Pali Text Society.

———. 1997. 'Introduction'. In *The Path of Discrimination.* 2nd edition. Translated by Bhikkhu Ñāṇamoli, v–lxiv. Oxford: Pali Text Society.

Willemen, Charles. 2008. 'Kumārajīva's "Explanatory Discourse" about Abhidharmic Literature'. *Journal of the International College for Postgraduate Buddhist Studies* 12: 37–83.

Willemen, Charles, Bart Dessein and Collett Cox. 1998. *Sarvāstivāda Buddhist Scholasticism.* Leiden: Brill.

Yinshun. 印順. 1994 [1971]. 原始佛教聖典之集成 (*Compilation of the Original Buddhist Scriptures*). 3rd revised edition. Taipei: 正聞出版社.

Tse-fu Kuan is Associate Professor in the College of General Studies at Yuan Ze University, Taiwan. He works on early Buddhist literature in Pāli and Chinese, and has published on topics relating to meditation, Abhidhamma, early Buddhist philosophy, and the *Ekottarika Āgama*, including *Mindfulness in Early Buddhism* (Routledge 2008).

– 11 –

Calligraphic Magic: Abhidhamma Inscriptions from Sukhodaya

Peter Skilling

The article presents five fifteenth- to sixteenth-century Pali inscriptions from Sukhodaya, Thailand. Three of them are engraved in the Khom alphabet on large square stone slabs, with considerable attention to format; they seem to be unique in Thai epigraphy. Two of these carry extracts from the *Abhidhamma*; the third gives a syllabary followed by the recollection formulas of the Three Gems. The other two epigraphs are written not on stone slabs but are inscribed on small gold leaves; they contain the heart formulas of the books of the *Tipiṭaka* and the qualities of the Buddha, Dhamma, and Saṃgha. The exact find-spots and functions of the slabs and gold leaves are not known. I suggest that they are the products of widespread and enduring Buddhist cultures of inscription, installation, and consecration, as well as of customs of condensation and abbreviation that have have been intrinsic to Thai liturgical and manuscript practices up to the present.

Lance Cousins' approach to Buddhist studies was holistic: his was a broad and boundless interest in the Dhamma as a living tradition with a deep history. One of his enduring passions was the Abhidhamma – not as a lifeless scaffolding of elaborate abstractions constructed in thin air, but as a living contemplative system that animated the intellectual history of the Buddhadhamma.[1] I offer in his memory a study of Abhidhamma inscriptions from Sukhodaya or Sukhothai.[2] In the popular Thai imagination, Sukhodaya is a fabled city, a golden and glorious age – the very dawn of Thai civilization. But in the world of hard facts, even post-truth, it is not easy to pin down exactly what Sukhodaya means. Does the name refer to a geobody, an autonomous state, an historical period, a literature, an architectural school, or styles and techniques of casting statues of the Buddha? All of these overlap and

1. 'Why were these Books, so dry and sterile-seeming to most, ever prized thus highly by our deeper thinkers? Only one who can appeciate the root of Buddha-dhamma and its message of Deliverance can understand the reason.' – Cassius A. Pereira, Foreword to Nyanatiloka 1971, xiii.

2. Sukhodaya is a Pali-Sanskrit word meaning 'source, origin, birth, or dawn of happiness'. The Indic word is spelt perfectly correctly in Thai as Sukhodaya (สุโขทัย), but according to the rules of Thai pronunciation it is pronounced 'Sukhothai'. In this article I tend to use Sukhodaya in historical contexts and Sukhothai in modern contexts, but the gentle reader should remember that they are the same word. It is same with Mahādhātu (มหาธาตุ), which is spelt perfectly according to Pali-Sanskrit rules but is pronounced Mahathat. In Thai there are many similar cases both among names and technical terms.

Keywords: Abhidhamma, Pali inscriptions of Thailand, Pali liturgy, Pali heart formulas, Sukhodaya/Sukhothai

interact but they are neither physically nor temporally coterminous. Sukhodaya was cosmopolitan and complex, an inland power centre that participated fully in the imaginaires of the age and at the same time forged its own identity. Simplistic nationalistic narratives do not do it justice.

The three stone inscriptions are from three different sites in the modern Tambon Meuang Kao ('Old City subdistrict') in Sukhothai province. One is from Wat Mahathat (วัดมหาธาตุ, Mahādhātu), the heart of the ancient moated city, a large cetiya set in a complex of subsidiary structures. The exact location of Wat Traphang Nak (วัดตระพังนาค), the source of the second inscription, is not known today, but near the southern Namo Gate (ประตูนโม) there is a pond still known locally as Traphang Nak. Today there is no temple named Traphang Nak but there is a ruined temple with a chedi named Wat Kon Laeng (วัดก้อนแลง) not far from the banks of the pond. The third find-spot is described as on the banks of the Nam Chon river, which is most probably the Khu Mae Chon (คู่แม่โจน), the moat that surrounds Wat Phraphai Luang (วัดพระพายหลวง) to the north of the ancient city, where there is a Mae Chon Temple (วัดแม่โจน). Clearly there is scope for further investigation. There is no information about the precise find-spots, and we cannot be certain whether these were their original locations; still, when we take the size and weight of the slabs into account, it is unlikely that they were moved for any distance. The gold leaves are, however, another matter. They are portable and could have come from anywhere. Here the weight of the evidence lies in the fact that the script is described as Khom Sukhothai and that the couple who presented them to the National Museum were from Sukhothai.

1. Stone slab from Wat Mahathat, Sukhothai

The large stone slab was found at an unrecorded date in a cetiya to the north of Wat Mahathat. No further details are available. Two parallel lines run along the outer border on all four sides to frame 19 lines of text written in the Khom Sukhothai script. The slab is broken vertically on the right side with the result that some letters are missing along the crack. The bottom line or lines — including the lower border — are broken off. In 2003 we were able to make an estampage of only the larger left-hand piece (Figure 1). The published transcription does not seem entirely accurate and a precise reading must wait for another occasion. The inscription given below for reference shows the layout and line breaks but not the details of the current condition of the slab.

The inscription opens with a circular punctuation mark flanked by double lines (|| ◎ ||) followed by *namo buddhāya*, 'homage to the Buddha'. The body of the text commences with the first 'matrix of the triads' (*tika mātikā*) of the *Dhammasaṅgaṇī*, the first of the seven books of the Abhidhamma. The second book, the *Vibhaṅga*, is represented by the *Paccayākāra-vibhaṅga* (No. 6, 'the modes of dependency') — the formula of the twelve links of dependent arising (*paṭiccasamuppāda*) in natural order in sutta style.[3] There follow the opening sentences of the *Dhātukathā*, the *Puggalapaññatti*, and the *Kathāvatthu*. Next come the components of the *Yamaka*:[4]

3. For the *Paccayākāra-vibhaṅga*, see Nyanatiloka, 1971, 34–37.

4. Abbreviated, with a few omissions.

Figure 1. Left-hand fragment of stone slab inscription from Wat Mahathat, Sukhothai. Estampage by Santi Pakdeekham, 2003. Courtesy Fragile Palm Leaves Foundation, Nonthaburi.

Script	Khom Sukhothai
Language	Pali
Date	CE 16th century (BE 21st century)
Support	Stone slab
Sides/lines	1 side with 19 lines
Dimensions	Width 71.5 cm; height 73 cm; thickness 5 cm
Registration no.	STh 30
Place of discovery	Cetiya to the north of Wat Mahathat, T. Meuang Kao, Meuang district, Sukhothai province (เจดีย์วัดมหาธาตุ ต. เมืองเก่า อ. เมือง จ. สุโขทัย)
Discoverer	Not known
Present location	Ramkhamhaeng National Museum, Sukhothai
Accession date	Not known
Photo/estampage	Estampage by Santi Pakdeekham/Fragile Palm Leaves Foundation, 2003
Publication	1) *Chareuk nai prathet thai*, Vol. 5, pp. 53–57. Read by Chaem Kaewkhlai. 2) Suphaphan Na Bangchang, *Wiwathanakan ngan khian phasa bali*, pp. 52–54.

the five aggregates (*khandha*: *Yamaka*, Section II), the twelve sense bases (*āyatana*: *Yamaka*, Section III), the eighteen elements (*dhātu*: *Yamaka*, Section IV), the four truths (*sacca*: *Yamaka*, Section V), the three formations (*saṅkhāra*: *Yamaka*, Section VI), and the seven biases (*anusaya*: *Yamaka*, Section VII), concluding with the titles of the last three (Sections VIII, IX, X: *citta-yamaka*, *dhamma-yamaka*, and *indriya-yamaka*). Finally come the twenty-four conditions of the *Mahāpaṭṭhāna*. In this way, a skeletal inventory of the seven books of the Abhidhamma is complete.

Inscription[5]

1. || ◎ || namo buddhāya || kusalā dhammā akusalā dhammā abyākatā dhammā ||
2. avijjā paccayā saṃkhārā saṃkhārapaccayā viññāṇaṃ viññāṇapaccayā nāmarūpaṃ
3. nāmarūpapaccayā saḷāyatanaṃ saḷāyatanapaccayā phasso phassapaccayā ve-
4. da(nā) vedanāpaccayā taṇhā taṇhāpaccayā upādānaṃ upādānapaccayā bhavo
5. bhavapaccayā jāti jātipaccayā jarāmaraṇaṃsokaparidevadukkhadomanassupā-
6. yāsā sambhavanti || saṅgaho asaṅgaho saṅgahitena saṅgahitaṃ || khandhapañña
7. tti āyatanapaññatti dhātupaññatti saccapaññatti indriyapaññatti puggalapa-ññatti ||
8. puggalo upalabbatti sacchikatthaparamatthenāti āmantā || pañcakkhandhā rūpakkhandho veda-
9. nākkhandho saññākkhandho saṅkhārakkhandho viññāṇakkhandho cakkhvāyatanaṃ sotāyatanaṃ
10. ghānāyatanaṃ jivhāyatanaṃ kāyāyatanaṃ manāyatanaṃ rūpāyatanaṃ saddāyatanaṃ
11. gandhāyatanaṃ rasāyatanaṃ phoṭṭhabbāyatanaṃ dhammāyatanaṃ || cakkhudhātu sotadhātu
12. viññāṇadhātu dukkhasaccaṃ dukkhasamudayasaccaṃ maggasaccaṃ kāyasaṅkhāro vacīsaṅkhāro
13. cittasaṅkhāro kāmarāgānusayo avijjānusayo cittayamakaṃ dhammayamakaṃ
14. indriyayamakaṃ || hetupaccayo āramaṇapaccayo adhipatipaccayo anantara-pacca-
15. yo samanantarapaccayo sahajātapaccayo aññamaññapaccayo nissayapaccayo u-
16. panissayapaccayo purejātapaccayo pacchājātapaccayo āsevanapacca-
17. yo kammapaccayo vipākapaccayo āhārapaccayo indriyapaccayo jhānapa-
18. ccayo maggapaccayo sampayuttapaccayo vippayuttapaccayo atthipaccayo
19. natthipaccayo vigatapaccayo avigatapaccayo

---

5. For each inscription I give an unedited transcription of the inscription based on the published readings. As far as possible it is an exact account of the document. The 'edition' that follows is not a critical edition but an edited and formatted version for ease of consultation. It shows what should be there, the standard text, formatted according to contemporary conventions.

I have not been able to read clearly the punctuation marks or determine the system. It has been difficult to ascertain whether there is *aṃ* or *aṅ*, and to what degree previous editors may have standardized these.

Edition

[HOMAGE] namo buddhāya ||
[DHAMMASAṂGAṆĪ] kusalā dhammā akusalā dhammā abyākatā dhammā ||
[VIBHAṄGA = PACCAYĀKARA-VIBHAṄGA NO. 6] avijjāpaccayā saṃkhārā, saṃkhārapaccayā viññāṇaṃ, viññāṇapaccayā nāmarūpaṃ, nāmarūpapaccayā saḷāyatanaṃ, saḷāyatanapaccayā phasso, phassapaccayā vedanā, vedanāpaccayā taṇhā, taṇhāpaccayā upādānaṃ, upādānapaccayā bhavo, bhavapaccayā jāti, jātipaccayā jarā-maraṇaṃ-soka parideva-dukkha-domanassupāyāsā sambhavanti ||
[DHĀTUKATHĀ] saṅgaho asaṅgaho saṅgahitena saṅgahitaṃ ||
[PUGGALAPAÑÑATTI] khandhapaññatti āyatanapaññatti dhātupaññatti saccapaññatti indriyapaññatti puggalapaññatti ||
[KATHĀVATTHU] puggalo upalabbatti sacchikatthaparamatthenā ti āmantā ||
[YAMAKA] pañcakkhandhā rūpakkhandho vedanākkhandho saññākkhandho saṅkhārakkhandho viññāṇakkhandho cakkhvāyatanaṃ sotāyatanaṃ ghānāyatanaṃ jivhāyatanaṃ kāyāyatanaṃ manāyatanaṃ rūpāyatanaṃ saddāyatanaṃ gandhāyatanaṃ rasāyatanaṃ phoṭṭhabbāyatanaṃ dhammāyatanaṃ || cakkhudhātu sotadhātu viññāṇadhātu dukkhasaccaṃ dukkhasamudayasaccaṃ maggasaccaṃ kāyasaṅkhāro vacīsaṅkhāro cittasaṅkhāro kāmarāgānusayo avijjānusayo cittayamakaṃ dhammayamakaṃ indriyayamakaṃ ||
[PAṬṬHĀNA] hetupaccayo āramaṇapaccayo adhipatipaccayo anantarapaccayo samanantarapaccayo sahajātapaccayo aññamaññapaccayo nissayapaccayo upanissayapaccayo purejātapaccayo pacchājātapaccayo āsevanapaccayo kammapaccayo vipākapaccayo āhārapaccayo indriyapaccayo jhānapaccayo maggapaccayo sampayuttapaccayo vippayuttapaccayo atthipaccayo natthipaccayo vigatapaccayo avigatapaccayo

2. Stone slab from Wat Traphang Nak, Sukhothai

This broken and chipped slab contains a 'syllabary inscription' of the vowels and consonants of an Indic alphabet. Officials from the National Library made estampages and took photographs in 1972 (2515). They learned that Phra Boranavatthachan (Thim), then abbot of Wat Ratchathani, Sukhothai, and Ecclesiastical Chief of Sukhothai Province, found the inscription at Wat Traphang Nak and presented it to the Ramkhamhaeng National Museum, Sukhothai. The registry does not record when it was discovered or when it entered the collection.

The inscription is carefully designed. The central square within which the inscription is placed is defined by a cross-hatch border between two pairs of lines. Outside of this the names of the four directions and the presiding kings of the group of four Great Kings are inscribed in larger letters facing outward on the four sides. Each name is set between a pair of radiating circles. The slab is chipped with the result that the end of lines 3 and 4 and the beginning of lines 6 to 8 have been obliterated. I have restored them on the assumption that the text follows the standard formulas.

Like that from Wat Mahathat, the Wat Traphang Nak inscription opens with *namo buddhāya*. This is a standard formula of homage that opens not only inscrip-

Script	Khom Sukhothai
Language	Pali
Date	CE 16th century (BE 21st century)
Support	Stone slab
Sides/lines	1 side with 14 lines
Dimensions	Width 66 cm; height 66 cm; thickness 5 cm
Registration no.	STh 33
Place of discovery	Wat Traphang Nak, T. Meuang Kao, Meuang district, Sukhothai province (วัดตระพังนาค ต. เมืองเก่า อ. เมือง จ. สุโขทัย)
Discoverer	Phra Boranavatthachan (Thim) (พระโบราณวัตถาจารย์ (ทิม))
Present location	Ramkhamhaeng National Museum, Sukhothai
Accession date	Not known
Photo/estampage	Estampage by Santi Pakdeekham/Fragile Palm Leaves Foundation, 2003
Publication	*Chareuk nai prathet* thai, Vol. 5, pp. 58–62. Read by Chaem Kaewkhlai.

Figure 2. Stone slab inscription from Wat Traphang Nak, Sukhothai. Estampage by Santi Pakdeekham, 2003. Courtesy Fragile Palm Leaves Foundation, Nonthaburi.

tions but also chants, *mantras* and *yantras*, and can itself be broken down to five syllables. At an uncertain date, Thai tradition equated the five syllables with sets of five: five precepts, five elements, five colours and lights – and the five Buddhas of the Fortunate Aeon (*bhadda-kappa*).[6] The association of *namo buddhāya* with the five Buddhas is given in a chant that is integrated into several texts, for example:[7]

na-karo kakkusandho ca
mo-karo konāgamano
bu-karo kassapo buddho
dhā-karo sakyapuṅgavo
ya-karo ariyametteyyo
pañcabuddhā ahaṃ namo.

The syllable *na* is Kakusandha;
The syllable *mo* is Konāgamana;
The syllable *bu* is Kassapa Buddha;
The syllable *dhā* is the scion of the Sākyas (that is, Siddhattha, Gotama);
The syllable *ya* is Ariya Metteyya:
To the five Buddhas I bow in homage.

The Wat Traphang Nak inscription continues with the word *siddhaṃ*, 'Success!' 'Accomplishment!'. *Siddhaṃ* often stands at the beginning of inscriptions in South and Southeast Asia, and of texts or textual divisions, as, for example, at the opening of the chapters of the Old Khotanese *Book of Zambasta* from Central Asia.[8] In the present inscription the words may be read as a unit, *namo buddhāya siddhaṃ*, which serves to open what follows – the syllabary, first the vowels and then the consonants. This is followed by the formulas of recollection of the Buddha, Dhamma, and Saṃgha, with the latter shortened.

Inscription

◎ pacchimavirūpaksa rājā ◎ [outer border, top]
◎ uttarakuvero rājā ◎ [outer border, left]
◎ purbādhaṭaraṭṭho ◎ [outer border, bottom]
◎ dakkhiṇaviruḷhako ◎ [outer border, right]

1. || ◎ || namo buddhāya siddhaṃ (a ā i ī u)[9] ū
2. e ai o au aṃ aḥ || ◎ ||
3. || ◎ || ka kha ga gha ṅa ca cha ja (jha ña)
4. ṭa ṭha ḍa ḍha ṇa ta tha da dha na (pa pha ba)
5. bha ma ya ra la va sa ha ḷa

6. See table of correspondences by Olivier de Bernon, *Fragile Palm Leaves Newsletter* 5 (May 2542/1999), p. 12.
7. From *Dvādasaparittagāthā*, a Mon chanting book published by Kittisāro at Pakklat in BE 2480 (CE 1937), p. 114, published in *Fragile Palm Leaves Newsletter* 5 (May 2542/1999), p. 3.
8. Maggi and Martini 2014, Table 1, p. 141.
9. The use of parentheses follows the published edition. I have not been able to verify it.

6. (i)tipiso bhagavā arahaṃ sammāsambuddho vi
7. (jjācaraṇa)sampanno sugato lokavidū
8. (anutta)ro purisadammasārathi satthā de
9. va manussānaṃ buddho bhagavāti s-
10. vākkhāto bhagavatā dhammo sandiṭṭhiko a
11. kāliko ehipassiko opanayiko pa
12. ccattaṃ veditabbo viññūhīti supaṭipa
13. anno ujupaṭipanno ñāyapaṭipanno sāmī
14. (ci)paṭipanno bhagavato sāvakasaṅgho || ◎

Edition

[FOUR MAHĀRĀJA]
◎ pacchima virūpaksa rājā ◎ [outer border, top]
◎ uttara kuvero rājā ◎ [outer border, left]
◎ purbā dhaṭaraṭṭho ◎ [outer border, bottom]
◎ dakkhiṇa viruḷhako ◎ [outer border, right]
[HOMAGE] || ◎ || namo buddhāya siddhaṃ
[VOWELS] a ā i ī u ū e ai o au aṃ aḥ ◎
[CONSONANTS] ka kha ga gha ṅa
ca cha ja jha ña
ṭa ṭha ḍa ḍha ṇa
ta tha da dha na
pa pha ba bha ma
ya ra la va sa ha ḷa
[BUDDHAGUṆA] itipiso bhagavā arahaṃ sammāsambuddho vijjācaraṇasampanno sugato lokavidū anuttaro purisadammasārathi satthā deva manussānaṃ buddho bhagavā ti
[DHAMMAGUṆA] svākkhāto bhagavatā dhammo sandiṭṭhiko akāliko ehipassiko opanayiko paccattaṃ veditabbo viññūhī ti
[SAMGHAGUṆA] supaṭipanno ujupaṭipanno ñāyapaṭipanno sāmīcipaṭipanno bhagavato sāvakasaṅgho || ◎

3. Stone inscription from Nam Chon River, Sukhothai

This is probably the longest Pali citation inscription in the Sukhodaya corpus. It takes up two sides with a total 57 lines, almost certainly engraved by the same hand. The recto is divided into two text areas, each of which is enclosed within double parallel lines. The inner square is reserved for the *Mātikā* of the twenty-four conditions of the *Paṭṭhāna*, which start in the upper left corner and run downwards. At the beginning is a circular symbol, a *fong man* (ฟองมัน); at the end is a *kho mut* (โคมูตร, *gomūtra*). The *Dhammasaṃgaṇī Mātikā* is engraved in the space between the inner box and the outer edges. It starts from the *Tikā Mātikā* and runs onto the verso, ending with the *upādāna-gocchakaṃ*. The words are written without separation, running clockwise in ascending order up to line 10; they are neatly written with few mistakes. The text ends at the top of the outer left line, part way through

Figure 3. Stone inscription from banks of Nam Chon River, Sukhothai. After *Prachum chareuk phak 8, Chareuk Sukhothai*, p. 373.

Script	Khom Sukhothai
Language	Pali
Date	CE 15th century (BE 20th century)
Support	Stone block
Sides/lines	2 sides: recto 22 lines, verso 35 lines
Dimensions	Width 71 cm; height 67 cm; thickness 5.5 cm
Registration no.	STh 19
Place of discovery	On the banks of the Mae Chon River, T. Meuang Kao, Meuang district, Sukhothai province (ริมฝั่งน้ำโจน, ต. เมืองเก่า อ. เมือง จ. สุโขทัย)
Present location	Ho Phra Samut Vajirañāṇa, National Library, Bangkok
Accession date	Not known
Photo	After *Prachum chareuk phak 8, Chareuk Sukhothai*
Read by	Chaem Kaewkhlai
Publication history	1) *Chareuk samai Sukhothai*, pp. 284–98. Read by Chaem Kaewkhlai. No rubbing or photo. 2) *Prachum chareuk*, Part 8, pp. 359–374. Reprint of previous reading. Good colour photograph of recto, p. 373. Poor photograph of verso, with sample close-up of text, p. 374. 3) Mention only in Supaphan Na Bangchang, *Wiwathanakan ngan khian phasa bali*, pp. 50–51.

the *saññojana-gocchakaṃ*, which continues on the verso. Regrettably no clear photograph or rubbing of the verso has been published. From the photograph in *Prachum chareuk* Part 8, it appears to be a straightforward text read from top to bottom, marked off by double lines around the edges. According to the transcription it has 35 lines. A photograph of the middle of the slab (*Prachum chareuk*, Part 8, p. 374) shows about 12 lines of text without the left- and right-hand portions.

Inscription[10]

Recto

[Text within central box]

1. ◎ hetupaccayo ārammaṇapacca-
2. yo adhipatipaccayo anantarapaccayo sa-
3. manantarapaccayo sahajātapaccayo a-
4. ññamaññapaccayo nissayapaccayo
5. upanissayapaccayo purejātapacca-
6. yo pacchājātāpaccayo āsevana-
7. paccayo kammapaccayo vipākapaccayo
8. āhārapaccayo indriyapaccayo
9. jhānapaccayo maggapaccayo sampayu-
10. ttapaccayo vippayuttapaccayo atthipa-
11. ccayo natthipaccayo vigatapaccayo a-
12. vigatapaccayo [*gomūtra symbol*]

[Text within outer area, starting from the first line of the top left corner above the inner box]

1a. ◎ kusalā dhammā akusalā dhammā abyāka-
1b. tā dhammā sukhāya vedanāya sampayuttā dha-
1c. mmā vedanāya sampayuttā dhammā adukkhama-
1d. sukkhāya vedanāya sampayuttā dhammā vipākā

2a. dhammā vipākadhammadhammā nevavipākanavopākadhamma-
2b. dhammā upādiṇṇupādāniyā dhammā anupādiṇṇupā
2c. dāniyā dhammā anupādiṇṇa-anupādāniyā dhammā
2d. saṃkiliṭṭhasaṃkilesikā dhammā asaṃkiliṭṭha-asaṃkile-
3a. sikā dhammā asaṃkiliṭṭha-asaṃkilesikā dhammā savitakka-
3b. savicārā dhammā avitakka-avicārā dha-
3c. mmā pitisahagatā dhammā sukhasam(!)agatā dhammā upekkhāsahaga-
3d. tā dhammā dassanena pahātabbā dhammā bhāvanāya pahātabbā
4a. dhammā nevadassanena na bhāvanāya pahātabbā dhammā dassanena
4b. pahātabbahetukā dhammā bhāvanāya pahātabbahetukā dhammā

10. The inscription given below for reference shows the layout and line breaks but no further details of the current state of the epigraph. I retain some of the parentheses of the published edition but am unable to verify them.

4c. nevadassanena na bhāvanāya pahātabbahetukā dhammā ā-
4d. cayagāmino dhammā apacayagāmino dhammā nevācayagā-

5a. mino nāpacayagāmino dhammā sekkhā dhammā asekkhā dhammā nevasekkhā nāsekkhā dhammā
5b. parittā dhammā mahaggatā dhammā appa(mā)ṇā dhammā parittārammaṇā dhammā maha-
5c. ggatārammaṇā dhammā appamāṇārammaṇā dhammā hīnā dhammā majjhimā dha-
5d. mmā paṇītā dhammā micchattaniyatā dhammā samattaniyatā dhammā aniyatā

6a. dhammā maggārammaṇā dhammā maggahetukā dhammā maggādhipatino dhammā uppa-
6b. nnā dhammā anuppannā dhammā upādino dhammā atītā dhammā anāgatā dhammā paccu-
6c. ppannā dhammā atītārammaṇā dhammā anāgatārammaṇā dhammā paccuppannārammaṇā
6d. dhammā ajjhattā dhammā bahiddhā dhammā ajjhattabahiddhā dhammā ajjhattārammaṇā dhammā

7a. bahiddhārammaṇā dhammā ajjhattabahiddhārammaṇā dhammā sanidassanasampaṭikhā dha-
7b. mmā anidassanasampaṭighā dhammā anidassana-apaṭighā dhammā hetudhammā nahe-
7c. tu dhammā sahetukā dhammā ahetukā dhammā dhammā hetusappayuttā dhammā hetuvippayuttā dha-
7d. mmā hetu ceva dhammā sahetukā ca sahetukā ceva dhammā na ca hetu hetu ceva

8a. dhammā hetusampayuttā ca hetusampayuttā ceva dhammā na ca hetu na hetu kho
8b. pana dhammā sahetukā ca ahetukāpi sappaccayā dhammā appacayā dhammā saṅkhatā
8c. dhammā asaṅkhatā dhammā sanidassanā dhammā anidassanā dhammā sampaṭighā dhammā appaṭi
8d. ghā dhammā rūpino dhammā arūpino dhammā lokiyā dhammā lokuttarā dhammā kenaci vi-

9a. ññeyyā dhammā kenaci na viññeyyā dhammā āsavā dhammā no āsavā dhammā sāsavā dhammā
9b. anāsavā dhammā āsavasampayuttā dhammā āsavavippayuttā dhammā āsavā ceva dhammā
9c. sāsavā ca sāsavā ceva dhammā no sasavā āsavā ceva dhammā āsavasampayuttā ca ā-
9d. savasampayuttā ceva dhammā no ca āsavā āsavavippayuttā kho pana ca dhammā sāsavāpi a-

[line 10 begins in the top left corner and runs clockwise]

10a. nāsavāpi saññojanā dhammā no saññojanā dhammā saññojaniyā dhammā asaññoja-
10b. niyā dhammā saññojani sampayuttā dhammā saññojanavippayuttā dhammā saññojanā ceva dhammā
10c. saññojaniyā ca saññojani sampayuttā dhammā saññojanavippayuttā dhammā saññojanā ceva dhammā
10d. saññojanasampayuttā ca saññojanasampayuttā ceva dhammā no ca saññojanā

Verso

1. saññojanasampayuttā dhammā saññojanavippayuttā dhammā sa-
2. ññojanā ceva dhammā saññojaniyā ca saññojaniyā ceva dhammā no
3. ca saññojanā saññojanā ceva dhammā saññojanasampayuttā ca sañño(jana)sa-
4. mpayuttā ceva dhammā no ca saññojanā saññojanāvippayuttā kho pana dhammā sañño-
5. janiyāpi asaññojaniyāpi ganṭhā dhamma no ganṭhā dhammā ganṭhaniyā dhammā ca ganṭhani-
6. dhammā ganṭhasampayuttā dhammā ganṭhavippayuttā dhammā ganṭhā ceva dhammā ganṭhaniyā ca ganṭhani-
7. yā ceva dhammā no caganṭhā ganṭhā ceva dhammā ganṭhasampayuttā ca ganṭhasampayuttā ceva dha-
8. mmā no ca ganṭhā ganṭhavippayuttā kho pana dhammā ganṭhaniyāpi aganṭhaniyāpi oghā dhammā no
9. oghā (dhammā oghaniyā) dhammā anoghaniyā dhammā oghasampayuttā (dhammā) oghavippayuttā dhammā oghā
10. (ceva dhammā ogha)niyā ca oghaniyā ceva dhammā no ca oghā oghā ceva dhammā oghas-
11. (mpayuttā ca ogha) sampayuttā ceva dhammā no ca oghā oghavippayuttā kho pana dhammā oghaniyāpi a-
12. (noghaniyāpi saññojanagocchakaṃ yogā dhammā no yogā dhammā yoganiyā dhammā ayoganiyā dha-
13. (mmā yogasampayuttā dhammā yogavippayuttā dhammā yogā ceva dhammā yoganiyā ca yoga(ni)yā ceva
14. (dhammā no ca yogā) yogā ceva dhammā yogasampayuttā ca yogasampayuttā ceva dhammā noca
15. (yogā yogā)vippayuttā kho pana dhammā yoganiyāpi ayoganiyāpi yogagocchakaṃ
16. nivaraṇā dhammā (no) nivaraṇā dhammā nivaraṇiyā dhammā anivaraṇā dhammā nivaraṇasampayuttā
17. dhammā nivaraṇavippayuttā dhammā nivaraṇā ceva dhammā nivaraṇiyā ca nivaraṇiyā ceva dhammā no
18. ca nivaraṇā nivaraṇā ceva dhammā nivaraṇasampayuttā ca nivaraṇasampayuttā ceva dhammā no
19. ca (nivaraṇā) nivaraṇā ceva dhammā nivaraṇasampayuttā ca nivaraṇasampayuttā ceva dhammā no
20. sā dhammā no parāmāsā dhammā parāmaṭṭhā dhammā aparāmaṭṭhā dhammā parāmāsasampayuttā dhammā parāmā-
21. savippayuttā dhammā parāmāsā ceva dhammā parāmaṭṭhā ca parāmaṭṭhā ceva dhammā no ca parāmāsā parāmā-
22. savippayuttā kho pana dhammā parāmaṭṭhāpi aparāmaṭṭhāpi parāmāsagocchakaṃ sārammaṇā dhammā anāramma-

23. ṇā dhammā cittā dhammā no cittā dhammā cettasikā dhammā acettasikā dhammā cittasampayuttā dha-
24. mmā cittavippayuttā dhammā cittasaṃsaṭṭhā dhammā cittavisaṃsaṭṭhā dhammā cittasamuṭṭhānā dhammā no cittasamuṭṭhānā
25. dhammā cittasahabhuno dhammā no cittashabhuno dhammā cittānuparivattino dhammā no cittānupa-
26. (rivatti) no dhammā cittasaṃsaṭṭhasamuṭṭhānā dhammā no cittasaṃsaṭṭhasamuṭṭhānā dhammā cittasaṃsaṭṭhasamaṭṭhānasaha-
27. bhuno dhammā no cittasaṃsaṭṭhasamuṭṭhānasahabhuno (dhammā) cittasaṃsaṭṭhasamuṭṭhānā parivattino dhammā no
28. cittasaṃsaṭṭhasamuṭṭhānānuparivatti (no dhammā ajjhattikā dhammā bā)hirā dhammā upādā dhammā no u-
29. pādā dhammā upādiṇṇā (dhammā anupādiṇṇā dhammā upā)dānā dhammā no upādānā dha-
30. mmā upādāniyā dhammā anupādāniyā (dhammā upādānasampayuttā dhammā upādāna)vippayuttā dhammā upādā-
31. nā ceva dhammā upādāniyā ca (upādāniyā ceva dhammā) no ca upādānā upā-
32. dānā ceva dhammā upādāna (sampayuttā ca u)pādānasampayuttā ceva
33. (dhammā no ca) upādānā (upādānavippayu)ttā kho pana dhammā
34. (upādāniyāpi anupādāniyāpi)
35. (upādānagocchakaṃ)

Edition

Recto

[Text within central box]

◎ hetupaccayo ārammaṇapaccayo adhipatipaccayo anantarapaccayo samanantarapaccayo sahajātapaccayo aññamaññapaccayo nissayapaccayo upanissayapaccayo purejātapaccayo pacchājātāpaccayo āsevanapaccayo kammapaccayo vipākapaccayo āhārapaccayo indriyapaccayo jhānapaccayo maggapaccayo sampayuttapaccayo vippayuttapaccayo atthipa-ccayo natthipaccayo vigatapaccayo avigatapaccayo [*gomūtra symbol*]

[Text within outer area, starting from the first line of the top left corner above the inner box]

kusalā dhammā akusalā dhammā abyākatā dhammā
sukhāya vedanāya sampayuttā dhammā [dukkhāya][11] vedanāya sampayuttā dhammā adukkhamasukkhāya vedanāya sampayuttā dhammā

vipākā dhammā vipākadhammadhammā nevavipākanavipākadhamma-dhammā upādiṇṇupādāniyā dhammā anupādiṇṇupādāniyā dhammā anupādiṇṇa-anupādāniyā dhammā

saṃkiliṭṭhasaṃkilesikā dhammā asaṃkiliṭṭha-asaṃkilesikā dhammāasaṃkiliṭṭha-asaṃkilesikā dhammā

11. Added according to context (Ed.).

savitakka savicārā dhammā avitakkavicārā [vicāramattā] dhammā avitakka-avicārā dhammā

pitisahagatā dhammā sukhasahagatā dhammā upekkhāsahagatā dhammā

dassanena pahātabbā dhammā bhāvanāya pahātabbā dhammā nevadassanena na bhāvanāya pahātabbā dhammā

dassanena pahātabbahetukā dhammā bhāvanāya pahātabbahetukā dhammā nevadassanena na bhāvanāya pahātabbahetukā dhammā

ācayagāmino dhammā apacayagāmino dhammā nevācayagāmino (nāpacayagāmino) dhammā

sekkhā dhammā asekkhā dhammā nevasekkhā nāsekkhā dhammā

parittā dhammā mahaggatā dhammā appamāṇā dhammā

parittārammaṇā dhammā mahaggatārammaṇā dhammā appamāṇārammaṇā dhammā

hīnā dhammā majjhimā dhammā paṇītā dhammā

micchattaniyatā dhammā sammattaniyatā dhammā aniyatā dhammā

maggārammaṇā dhammā maggahetukā dhammā maggādhipatino dhammā

uppannā dhammā anuppannā dhammā uppādino dhammā

atītā dhammā anāgatā dhammā paccuppannā dhammā

atītārammaṇā dhammā anāgatārammaṇā dhammā paccuppannārammaṇā dhammā

ajjhattā dhammā bahiddhā dhammā ajjhattabahiddhā dhammā

ajjhattārammaṇā dhammā bahiddhārammaṇā dhammā ajjhattabahiddhārammaṇā dhammā

sanidassanasappaṭighā dhammā anidassanaopaṭighā dhammā anidassana-apaṭighā dhammā

[bāvīsati tikamātikā][12]

hetudhammā nahetu dhammā
sahetukā dhammā ahetukā dhammā
dhammā hetusampayuttā dhammā hetuvippayuttā dhammā
hetu ceva dhammā sahetukā ca
sahetukā ceva dhammā na ca hetu
hetu ceva dhammā hetusampayuttā ca
hetusampayuttā ceva dhammā na ca hetu
na hetu kho pana dhammā sahetukā ca ahetukā pi

12. In the following, I add sectional titles in square brackets at end of the sections, based on *Syāmaraṭṭhassa Tepiṭakaṃ*. The inscription itself seems to supply at most five sectional titles. *Yoga-gocchakaṃ*, *nivarana-gocchakaṃ*, and *parāmāsa-gocchakaṃ* are clear, *saññojana-gocchakaṃ* is there but is misplaced, and *upādāna-gocchakaṃ* may be there but it is enclosed in parentheses.

[hetu-gocchakaṃ]

sappaccayā dhammā appacayā dhammā
saṅkhatā dhammā asaṅkhatā dhammā
sanidassanā dhammā anidassanā dhammā
sappaṭighā dhammā appaṭighā dhammā
rūpino dhammā arūpino dhammā
lokiyā dhammā lokuttarā dhammā kenaci viññeyyā dhammā kenaci na viññeyyā
dhammā

[cūlantara-dukaṃ]

āsavā dhammā no āsavā dhammā
sāsavā dhammā anāsavā dhammā
āsavasampayuttā dhammā āsavavippayuttā dhammā
āsavā ceva dhammā sāsavā ca
sāsavā ceva dhammā no sasāvā
āsavā ceva dhammā āsavasampayuttā ca
āsavasampayuttā ceva dhammā no ca āsavā
āsavavippayuttā kho pana ca dhammā sāsavā pi anāsavā pi

[āsava-gocchakaṃ]

saññojanā dhammā no saññojanā dhammā
saññojaniyā dhammā asaññojaniyā dhammā
saññojanasampayuttā dhammā saññojanavippayuttā dhammā
saññojanā ceva dhammā saññojaniyā ca
saññojanasampayuttā dhammā saññojanavippayuttā dhammā
saññojanā ceva dhammā saññojanasampayuttā ca
saññojanasampayuttā ceva dhammā no ca saññojanā

Verso

(saññojana-gocchakaṃ: continued)

saññojanasampayuttā dhammā saññojanavippayuttā dhammā
saññojanā ceva dhammā saññojaniyā ca
saññojaniyā ceva dhammā no ca saññojanā
saññojanā ceva dhammā saññojanasampayuttā ca
saññojanasampayuttā ceva dhammā no ca saññojanā
saññojanāvippayuttā kho pana dhammā saññojaniyā pi asaññojaniyā pi

[saññojana-gocchakaṃ]

gaṇṭhā[13]dhammā no gaṇṭhā dhammā
gaṇṭhaniyā dhammā ca gaṇṭhaniyā dhammā
gaṇṭhasampayuttā dhammā gaṇṭhavippayuttā dhammā
gaṇṭhā ceva dhammā gaṇṭhaniyā ca
gaṇṭhaniyā ceva dhammā no ca gaṇṭhā
gaṇṭhā ceva dhammā gaṇṭhasampayuttā ca
gaṇṭhasampayuttā ceva dhammā no ca gaṇṭhā
gaṇṭhavippayuttā kho pana dhammā gaṇṭhaniyā pi agaṇṭhaniyā pi

---

13. Syāmaraṭṭha has ganthā here and in following.

[gantha-gochakkaṃ]

ghā dhammā no oghā dhammā
oghaniyā dhammā anoghaniyā dhammā
oghasampayuttā dhammā oghavippayuttā dhammā
oghā ceva dhammā oghaniyā ca
oghaniyā ceva dhammā no ca oghā
oghā ceva dhammā oghasmpayuttā ca
ogha sampayuttā ceva dhammā no ca oghā
oghavippayuttā kho pana dhammā oghaniyā pi anoghaniyā pi

[ogha-gochakkaṃ]

yogā dhammā no yogā dhammā
yoganiyā dhammā ayoganiyā dhammā
yogasampayuttā dhammā yogavippayuttā dhammā
yogā ceva dhammā yoganiyā ca
yoganiyā ceva dhammā no ca yoga
yogā ceva dhammā yogasampayuttā ca
yogasampayuttā ceva dhammā no ca yoga
yogavippayuttā kho pana dhammā yoganiyā pi ayoganiyā pi

yoga-gocchakaṃ

nivaraṇā dhammā no nivaraṇā dhammā
nivaraṇiyā dhammā anivaraṇā dhammā
nivaraṇasampayuttā dhammā nivaraṇavippayuttā dhammā
nivaraṇā ceva dhammā nivaraṇiyā ca
nivaraṇiyā ceva dhammā no ca nivaraṇā
nivaraṇā ceva dhammā nivaraṇasampayuttā ca
nivaraṇasampayuttā ceva dhammā no ca nivaraṇā
nivaraṇavippayuttā kho pana dhammā nivaraṇiyā pi anivaraṇiyā pi

nivaraṇa-gocchakaṃ

parāmāsā] dhammā no parāmāsā dhammā
parāmaṭṭhā dhammā aparāmaṭṭhā dhammā
parāmāsasampayuttā dhammā parāmāsavippayuttā dhammā
parāmāsā ceva dhammā parāmaṭṭhā ca
parāmaṭṭhā ceva dhammā no ca parāmāsā
parāmāsavippayuttā kho pana dhammā parāmaṭṭhā pi aparāmaṭṭhā pi

parāmāsa-gocchakaṃ

sārammaṇā dhammā anārammaṇā dhammā
cittā dhammā no cittā dhammā
cetasikā dhammā acetasikā dhammā
cittasampayuttā dhammā cittavippayuttā dhammā
cittasaṃsaṭṭhā dhammā cittavisaṃsaṭṭhā dhammā
cittasamuṭṭhānā dhammā no cittasamuṭṭhānā dhammā
cittasahabhuno dhammā no cittashabhuno dhammā
cittānuparivattino dhammā no cittānuparivattino dhammā
cittasaṃsaṭṭhasamuṭṭhānā dhammā no cittasaṃsaṭṭhasamuṭṭhānā dhammā
cittasaṃsaṭṭhasamuṭṭhānasahabhuno dhammā no cittasaṃsaṭṭhasamuṭṭhānasa habhuno dhammā

cittasaṃsaṭṭhasamuṭṭhānā parivattino dhammā no
cittasaṃsaṭṭhasamuṭṭhānānuparivattino dhammā
ajjhattikā dhammā bāhirā dhammā
upādā dhammā no upādā dhammā
upādiṇṇā dhammā anupādiṇṇā dhammā

upādānā dhammā no upādānā dhammā
upādāniyā dhammā anupādāniyā dhammā
upādānasampayuttā dhammā upādānavippayuttā dhammā
upādānā ceva dhammā upādāniyā ca
upādāniyā ceva dhammā no ca upādānā
upādānā ceva dhammā upādānasampayuttā ca
upādānasampayuttā ceva dhammā no ca upādānā
upādānavippayuttā kho pana dhammā upādāniyā pi anupādāniyā pi

(upādāna-gocchakaṃ)

4. Heart formulas of the *Sutta-piṭaka, Phaya Kāsalak, Karaṇiya-metta-sutta, Traisaraṇagamaṇa*, plus *oṃ*

According to Cham Thongkhamwan's notes, Mr Somphong and Mrs Bunmi Phromwipha from the Phromwipha Pharmacy (ร้านขายยาพรหมวิภา) in the Sukhothai market donated the gold leaves to the National Museum on 3 February 1959.[14] The Ramkhamhaeng National Museum in Sukhothai was opened by King Bhumibol Adulyadej and Queen Sirikit only in 1962. Phra Ratchaprasitthikhun, abbot of Ratchathani Temple, donated more than 2,000 artifacts and local citizens also donated many objects to the new museum.

Script	Khom Sukhothai
Language	Pali
Date	CE 15th century (BE 20th century)
Support	Rectangular gold foil
Sides/lines	1 side with 2 lines
Dimensions	Not recorded
Registration no.	STh 42
Place of discovery	Sukhothai province
Present location	National Museum, Bangkok
Date of donation to museum	3 February CE 1959 / BE 2502
Donated by	Mr Somphong and Mrs Bunmi Phromwipha (นายสมพงษ์ และ นางบุญมี พรหมวิภา)
Photo/estampage	Not available
Publication history	1) *Chareuk nai prathet thai*, Vol. 5, pp. 47–49. Read by Cham Thongkhamwan 2) Supaphan Na Bangchang, *Wiwathanakan ngan khian phasa bali*, pp. 57–59.

14. Renowned epigraphist Cham Thongkhamwan (CE 1897–1969 / BE 2440–2512) was Professor at Silpakorn University. For his life and works, see *Prawat buraphachan dan chareukseuksa neuang nai ngan phithi 'khurubucha'*, 49–60.

Inscription

1. *dī(ma)saṃaṃ(khu)ca(bha)kasa*
2. *buddhasaṃmiuddhaṃadhomau*

Edition

dī ma saṃ aṃ khu ca bha ka sa
bud dha saṃ mi uddhaṃ adho ma a u

Interpretation

The first five syllables represent the titles of the five *Nikāyas*, the primary collections of the *Sutta-piṭaka*, by giving the first syllable of each.[15]

1. *dī* ***dī**ghanikāya*
2. *ma* ***ma**jjhimanikāya*
3. *saṃ* ***saṃ**yuttanikāya*
4. *aṃ* ***aṃ**guttaranikāya*
5. *khu* ***khu**ddakanikāya*

The next four syllables are the first syllables of the four lines of a verse known from the *Vajirasāratthasaṅgaha* and other sources.[16] This is known as the heart formula of (Phaya) Kāsalak (หัวใจกาสลัก):

> ***ca**ja **bha**ja **ka**ra **sa**ra*
>
> Drop it, stay with it, do it, remember!

The complete verse is:

> *caja dujjana-saṃsaggaṃ*
> *bhaja sādhu-samāgamaṃ*
> *kara puññam ahorattaṃ*
> *sara niccam aniccataṃ.*
>
> Drop it! — Stop mixing with bad people.
> Stay with it! — Keep the company of the good.
> Do it! — Make merit day and night.
> Always remember! — Everything is impermanent.

The verse is included in collections of moral and spiritual maxims like the Pali *Dhammanīti* and *Lokanīti*, and doubtless other texts.[17] There are Sanskrit parallels to the verse in Cāṇakya and elsewhere.[18] The Pali version and three Thai translations are included in the 'Anthology of *khlong* verses on worldy principles' (*Prachum khlong Lokanit*/ประชุมโคลงโลกนิติ, § 20) compiled in the reign of King Rama III (Phra Nangklao/พระนั่งเกล้า, reigned 1824 to 1851).

---

15. For the five *Nikāyas* see Norman 1983, 30–95; von Hinüber 1996, 23–64.
16. *Phra Khamphi Wachirasaratthasangkhaha*, 44–45.
17. Bechert and Braun 1981, 33 (*Dhammanīti* v. 411) and 75 (*Lokanīti* v. 42).
18. See Skilling 2555 [2012], 437–38.

The next four syllables are the 'heart formula of going for refuge' (หัวใจไตรสรณาคมน์, *hua chai traisaranakhom, traisaraṇagamaṇa*): I go to the Buddha, the Dhamma, and the Saṃgha for refuge (*buddhaṃ, dhammaṃ, saṃgham saraṇaṃ gacchāmi*).

bud ***bud****dha*
dha ***dha****mma*
saṃ ***saṃ****gha*
mi *saraṇaṃ gacchā****mi****.*

Going for refuge, entrusting oneself to the Buddha, is the basis of Dhamma practice. By taking refuge 'as long as one lives' (*yāva jīvaṃ*) one sets out on the path, and should take refuge, reciting the formula, at least once a day to reinforce and refresh one's practice. There are chants that elaborate on the refuges (such as *natthi me saraṇaṃ aññaṃ, buddho me saraṇaṃ varaṃ*). The assembly takes refuge, following the chants of the monks, at the beginning of all Thai ceremonies.

Next is a phrase 'above, below' from verse 8c of the *Karaṇīya-metta sutta*,[19] known in Thai as the หัวใจกรณีย์/*huachai karani*, 'heart formula of the *Karaṇīya*[*-sūtra*]':

mettañ ca sabbalokasmiṃ
mānasam bhāvaye aparimāṇaṃ
uddhaṃ adho *ca tiriyañ ca*
asambādhaṃ averaṃ asapattaṃ
tiṭṭhañ caraṃ nisinno vā
sayāno vā yāva tassa vigatamiddho
etaṃ satiṃ adhiṭṭhāya
brahmam etaṃ vihāraṃ idha-m-āhu.

Foster limitless love for the whole wide world in your mind,
Above, below, and all around, without obstruction, enmity, or rivalry.
Standing, walking, seated, lying down, keeping drowsiness at bay,
Setting mindfulness firm like this: they call it
A superbly divine way of life here in this world.

Last is the formula of *oṃ*, which is made up of three letters, *ma a u*.[20]

19. *Suttanipāta* (PTS) vv. 150–51 (*Uragavagga*, *Sutta* No. 8, verses 8–9). The *sutta* is also included in the *Khuddakapāṭha* (PTS, p. 8).

20. See Supaphan, *Wiwathanakan ngan khian phasa bali*, 59. There are numerous explanations and configurations of the three letters that make up *oṃ*.

5. Heart formulas of the *Buddhaguṇa*, the *Abhidhamma-piṭaka*, and the *Vinaya-piṭaka*

Script	Khom Sukhothai
Language	Pali
Date	CE 15th century (BE 20th century)
Support	Rectangular gold foil
Sides/lines	1 side with 2 lines
Dimensions	Not recorded
Registration no.	STh 45
Place of discovery	Sukhothai Province
Present location	National Museum, Bangkok
Date of donation to Museum	3 February CE 1959/BE 2502
Donated by	Mr. Somphong and Mrs Bunmi Phromwipha (see previous entry for details)
Photo/estampage	Not available
Publication history	1) *Chareuk nai prathet thai*, Vol. 5, pp. 47–49. Read by Cham Thongkhamwan.
	2) Supaphan Na Bangchang, *Wiwathanakan ngan khian phasa bali*, pp. 55–56.

Inscription

1. *asaṃvisulopusabu(bha)*
2. *saṃvidhāpukayapaā(pā)macupa*

Edition

a saṃ vi su lo pu sa bu bha
saṃ vi dhā pu ka ya pa āpāmacupa

Interpretation

The first nine syllables *asaṃvisulopusabubha* represent the *Buddhaguṇa*, the virtues or qualities of a Buddha. Recitation of the *Buddhaguṇa* is basic to practices of praising and recollecting the Buddha

a ***ara****haṃ*
saṃ ***sam****māsambuddho*
vi ***vi****jjācaraṇasampanno*
su ***su****gato*
lo ***lo****kavidū anuttaro*
pu ***pu****risadammasārathi*
sa ***sa****tthā devamanussānaṃ*
bu ***bu****ddho*
bha ***bha****gavā*

The next set of seven syllables *saṃvidhāpukayapa* represents the seven books of the Abhidhamma.[21]

saṃ ***saṃ****gaṇī*
vi ***vi****bhaṅga*
dhā ***dhā****tukathā*
pu ***pu****ggalapaññatti*
ka ***ka****thāvatthu*
ya ***ya****maka*
pa ***pa****ṭṭhāna*

The last set of five syllables *āpāmacupa* stands for the five books of the Vinaya.[22]

ā ***ā****dikamma*
pā ***pā****cittiya*
ma ***ma****hāvagga*
cu ***cu****lavagga*
pa ***pa****rivāra*

Comments

Inscriptions can be dated: they can be dated precisely when they bear a date, or they can be dated approximately when they have a clear stratigraphic context or association. The five inscriptions studied here have neither. Inscriptions can also be dated through palaeography, the comparative study of the shape of the letters to determine their age, but palaeography is a subjective art that needs to be grounded on a corpus of dated inscriptions. In the Siamese corpus, especially for the earlier periods, there are few uncontroversially dated records, and we end up running around in circles. We can say, but only very generally, that in this case the letters belong to the fifteenth to sixteenth centuries and are similar to the Khom Bali letters of other inscriptions.[23]

It is unlikely or even impossible that such large, heavy, carefully lettered and formatted stone slabs should have been produced after the middle of the sixteenth century when the population of the northern principalities (*chao meuang neua*)[24] — including that of Sukhothai and its neighbouring *meuang* — was uprooted and shifted to repopulate the central capital, Ayutthaya, which had been depopulated by the Burmese. This brought immense social and cultural disruption to the northern principalities, with the result that the archive of memory, the oral map of the landscape, was obliterated. The Luang Prasert chronicle states laconically that 'in that same year [CŚ 946, Year of the Monkey = 1584–1585], the households of the north-

21. For the seven books see Nyanatiloka 1971; Norman 1983, 96–107; von Hinüber 1996, 64–75.

22. For the five books see Norman 1983, 18–29 and von Hinüber 1996, 8–22. The titles and order of the European editions differ from those of the traditional Thai editions, but the contents are fundamentally the same.

23. See Pali inscription at Wat Si Chum from about the fourteenth century, unfortunately very fragmentary: Skilling 2008, 115.

24. At that time Meuang Neua meant the upper Chao Phraya basin, the cities listed in the Somdet Phra Phonarat chronicle.

ern *meuang*s were deported en masse down to Krung Phra Nakhon Si Ayutthaya'.[25] The royal chronicle of Somdet Phra Phonarat gives more details:[26]

> In the same ninth lunar month there was a royal command of his father the king [Phra Mahā Dhammarājā] to go up and flush the households of the northern cities down to the capital, Si Ayutthaya. When Somdet Phra Naresuan knew the command, he had the households of the *meuang*s Phra Phitsanulok, Phichai, Sawankhalok, Sukhothai, Kamphaeng Phet, Phichit, and all the smaller towns loaded onto boats and rafts, arranged flotillas of guard boats, and stationed detachments of soldiers as guards on both banks of the river, to prevent the households escaping before reaching the capital.[27]

The *Mātikā*s and the condensed *Tripiṭaka* must have been in circulation as autonomous extracts or as liturgical texts by this time at the latest. The Wat Mahathat stone slab is the earliest evidence that I know of for what is today known as the 'Seven books of the Abhidhamma' (พระอภิธรรม ๗ คัมภีร์/*Phra aphitham 7 kamphi*) — a selection of short extracts from each of the seven books of the Abhidhamma that stands for the complete set, whether through the medium of writing or that of recitation. In some details the Wat Mahathat inscription differs from those of other compilations of the 'Seven books of the Abhidhamma', but the inscription covers the full seven books, and that is the essential point. The installation of golden texts in the cetiyas at Wat Pho (Wat Phra Chetuphon) (see Skilling 2016) in nineteenth century Bangkok continued to follow the cultures of abbreviation and installation. The texts also have the social associations of the chanting of the condensed Tripiṭaka at funerary rites. The Cetiyas of the Four Reigns at Wat Pho were, after all, memorials dedicated to deceased kings. Whether the Sukhodaya slabs had funerary functions is not at present known.

The inscriptions belong to a period in Siamese cultural history during which Pali language and recitation had ritual, liturgical, and meditational functions that were all part of the broad and intangible stream of mental cultivation (*bhāvanā*). Their exact use is not known, but they might have been covers of stone relic caskets meant to protect the relics not only by their size and weight but by the magic power of the letters.[28] That is, they were produced within the Buddhist culture of inscription, installation, and consecration. The custom of installing the Buddha's word in *stūpa*s

25. *Phra ratchaphongsawadan krung kao chabap luang prasert*, 17.9, ในปีเดียวนั้น ให้เทครัวเมืองเหนือทั้งปวง ลงมายังกรุงพระนครศรีอยุทธยา. My translation; see also Frankfurter 1954, 59.

26. *Phra ratchaphongsawadan chabab somdet phra phonarat*, 98: translation by Chris Baker (11 May 2017). For another translation see Cushman and Wyatt 2000, 96–97.

27. ถึง ณะ วันอาทิตย์ เดือน 9 แรม 5 ค่ำ ขุนอินทรเดชะกลับลงมาถึงเมืองพระพิศณุโลก แลในเดือนเก้านั้น มีพระกำหนดสมเดจ์พระราชบิดาให้ขึ้นไปเทครัวอบพยบชาวเมืองเหนือทั้งปวงลงมายังพระนครศรีอยุทธยา สมเดจ์พระนเรศวรเปนเจ้าครั้นแจ้งพระราชกำหนดดังนั้น ตรัสให้เทครัวอบพยบในเมืองพระพิศณุโลก เมืองพิไชย เมืองสวรรคโลก เมืองศุโขไทย เมืองกำแพงเพ็ช เมืองพิจิตร์ เมืองเล็กน้อยทั้งนั้นลงบรรทุกเรือบ้างแพบ้าง แล้วแต่เรือคุมเปนหมวดเปนกอง แลแต่งกองทับป้องกรรสองฝั่งฟากน้ำลงมามิให้ครัวหนีได้ จนถึงกรุงเทพมหานคร.

28. The names of the four great kings are inscribed on the four sides of Inscription 2. The four kings were depicted on the four sides of the relic caskets of China, Korea, and Japan.

began in India nearly two thousand years ago; the practice was adopted in ancient Siam since the Dvāravatī period (seventh to eighth centuries CE if not earlier).

The formatting of the Sukhodaya stone slabs is a special feature. I do not know of any similar examples from other parts of the country or even the region, or from any period of Thai history. They link Sukhodaya to the cultures of word and alphabet and of magic diagrams (*yantra* and *maṇḍala*). These, like manuscripts, were made of perishable materials; they do not survive and the history of these cultures remains to be written. Ayutthaya society celebrated the majestic alchemy of letters in many alphabets: Khom Thai, Khom Bali, Thai, Mon, and Khmer, and delighted in intricate and refined poetics. Mastery of the alphabetic arts began with training in the *cintāmaṇī* manuals.

The layout of the slabs brings to mind the *dhāraṇī* amulets known largely from China, where they were written or painted on cloth and paper. Most are set within a square frame. A *dhāraṇī* of Mahāpratisarā has a 'two dimensional pyramid' design: the apexes of four triangular text blocs meet in the centre at a square space with a lotus (Drège 1999, fig. 54 and pp. 154–155). This compares with Inscription 3, where the four blocs meet at the centre. The *Mahāpratisarā* is one of the popular *dhāraṇīs* that spread throughout China and Southeast Asia. This example may date to the tenth century. Here the text is the Chinese translation. Another, found in Sichuan in 1944, is in Siddhamātṛka letters; the text is inscribed in a square running around a central square with a picture of the deity Mahāpratisarā. Around the border are figures of deities. In another from Dunhuang dated 980, the *dhāraṇī* is written in a circle also in Siddhamātṛaka.[29]

The slab inscriptions seem to link Sukhodaya to the broad stream of *Siddhaṃ* alphabetics — a mainstream that is not restricted to so-called esoteric or tantric Buddhism but rather goes beyond it. *Siddhaṃ* is the key to success — an interactive complex of educational and didactic practices that draw on the visual power of letters and the power of sound, the power of written and recited *buddha-vacana*. Most of the *Siddhaṃ* inscriptions in southern China and elswhere are earlier than the Sukhodaya slabs, but there may have been a long-term continuity — at least, this should not be ruled out. *Siddhaṃ* and *dhāraṇī* practices flourished in Dali and the kingdom of Nanzhao until the thirteenth century. A curious hybrid of the encounter between Pali Buddhism and *dhāraṇīs* is the Pali *Uṇhissa-vijaya*: a verse narrative that corresponds closely to the standard *Uṣṇīṣavijaya-dhāraṇī* narrative, but without the *dhāraṇī*. The Pali *Uṇhissa-vijaya* was widespread across central mainland Southeast Asia, and today is recited in ceremonies to prolong or fortify life-forces amongst the Thai, the various Tai, the Lao, and the Khmer.

On the other hand, the Sukhodaya inscriptions in Thai, Pali, and Khmer were well designed, and in the fourteenth century the massive project at Wat Si Chum to the north of the city engaged craftsmen to carve hundreds of stone slabs, many depicting *jātakas*. These were carefully formatted; the pictures were beautifully

29. For examples of *dhāraṇī* amulets, see Copp 2014, figs. 2.2, 2.3, 2.7, 2.11, 2.13, 2.16, 2.19, 2.10, 2.21. Drège 1999-2000, figs. 1–8; Hidas 2014; Wang 2011, passim.

etched, accompanied by brief Thai-language captions (see Skilling 2008). That is to say, the lapidary arts were well developed at Sukhodaya.

The last two inscriptions discussed above are on gold leaves. There are many inscribed gold leaves in Thai collections. The majority, perhaps, are *suvaṇṇapaṭ* (สุพรรณบัฏ) or *hiraññapaṭ* (หิรัญบัฏ), gold or silver foils that during the Ayutthaya period were inscribed in Thai with the royally bestowed names and titles of high-ranking monks and nobles. The term and custom continue to this day. A much smaller number give citations from Pali scriptures. Unfortunately there seems to be no study or even inventory of such artefacts. Deluxe editions of scriptures in gold were produced for centuries across Buddhist cultures.[30]

Written culture is more than tool of memory; the letters preserve canons but they also configure and consecrate. To understand the vibrant culture of *abhiṣeka* that has permeated Thai society from the time of the earliest records is one step towards the recovery of the cultural life of the Pali imaginary and the dynamics of Theravāda. Political power may have changed address — from Sukhodaya to Phitsanulok to Ayutthaya to Bangkok — but the spiritual and cultural dynamics live on.

Note

Throughout the preparation of this article, the National Museum and the National Library, both in Bangkok, have been undergoing renovation and moving to new buildings, with the result that I have not had access to the original objects. I have relied on the previous transcriptions and such estampages or photographs as are available to me. The result is that my readings are not ideal. The texts are well-known and formulaic, and they do not present significant variants or transmissional problems. The published editions place words or phrases within parentheses and compare them to the *Dhammasaṅgaṇī*. The parentheses usually mean that the editors have added the word or phrase on the basis of the canonical text. Because the available reproductions are not sufficiently clear for me to check all of the doubtful readings, and because no pictures of the two gold foils have been published, it seems futile to attempt a scrupulous edition until better materials are available.

We speak of Khom Sukhothai, but no palaeographic study exists in any European language. Such a study is a desideratum, as is an inventory of the Pali inscriptions of Sukhodaya and of Thailand. No matter what the date of the Pali epigraphic corpus may be, the Sukhodaya corpus is one of the most substantial Pali corpora in mainland Southeast Asia or Sri Lanka. There are no similar bodies of Pali inscriptions in Ayutthaya, Nakhon Si Thammarat, or Angkor Wat; the exceptions are the eleventh to thirteenth centuries corpus of Pukam or Pagan in Burma and King Dhammacedi's Kalyani Sima inscriptions outside of Pago in lower Burma dated to 1479.

30. For 'a scientific study of the gold from U Thong' see Bennett 2017; gold foil inscriptions are not, however, mentioned. Nor are they mentioned or illustrated in Namikawa's splendid *The Golden Figures of Buddha and Buddhist Sites in Thailand* (1987). Miksic's *Old Javanese Gold* (2011), has a chapter on gold in Southeast Asia; there are gold foil inscriptions in Java and Sumatra, but none, its seems in the *Yale University Art Gallery*.

Acknowledgements

I thank Santi Pakdeekham, Chris Baker, and Trent Walker for their help with this paper. I am grateful to Theerasak Thanusilp (Fine Arts Department, Sukhothai) for help in attempting to identify the find-spots of the inscriptions.

Bibliography

Thai sources

Chareuk nai prathet Thai Vol. 5. Bangkok: National Library/Fine Arts Department 2529 [1986] / จารึกในประเทศไทย เล่ม 5. กรุงเทพฯ: หอสมุดแห่งชาติ กรมศิลปากร. 2529 [1986].

Chareuk samai Sukhothai [Bangkok]: Fine Arts Department / จารึกสมัยสุโขทัย, กรุงเทพฯ: กรมศิลปาก, 2527 [1984].

Phra khamphi wachirasaratthasangkhaha. Edited and translated into Thai by Yaem Praphattong. Bangkok: Wat Suthat, 2512 [1969] / พระคัมภีร์วชิรสารัตถสังคหะ. แย้ม ประพัฒน์ทอง (แปลและเรียบเรียง). กรุงเทพฯ: วัดสุทัศน์, 2512 [1969].

Prachum chareuk phak 8 (Part 8), Chareuk Sukhothai. Bangkok: The Fine Arts Department, 2548 [2005]. ประชุมศิลาจารึก ภาค 8 จารึกสุโขทัย. กรุงเทพฯ: กรมศิลปากร, 2548 [2005].

Prachum khlong lokanit. Bangkok: Krom Wijakan, Krasuang Seuksathikan, 2543 [2002] / ประชุมโคลงโลกนิติ. กรุงเทพฯ: กรมวิชาการ กระทรวงศึกษาธิการ, 2543.

Phra ratchaphongsawadan chabab somdet phra phonarat Wat Phra Chetuphon truat sop chamra chak ekasan tua khian. Edited by Santi Pakdeekham. Bangkok: Munlanithi 'Tun Phra Phuttha Yotfa' nai Phra Boromorathchupatham, 2558 [2015]. พระราชพงศาวดาร ฉบับสมเด็จพระพนรัตน์ วัดพระเชตุพน ตรวจสอบชำระจากเอกสารตัวเขียน. ศานติ ภักดีคำ (บรรณาธิการ). กรุงเทพฯ: มูลนิธิ 'ทุนพระพุทธยอดฟ้าฯ' ในพระบรมราชูปถัมภ์, 2558 [2015].

Phra ratchaphongsawadan krung kao chabap luang prasert aksoranit, Rueng somdet phra boromasop kue chodmaihet ngarn phra meru krang krungkao kap phra ratchavicharn khong somdet phra puttachaoluang. Bangkok: Ton chabab, 2540 [1997] / พระราชพงศาวดารกรุงเก่า ฉบับหลวงประเสริฐอักษรนิติ์ และเรืองสมเด็จพระบรมศพ คือ จดหมายเหตุงานพระเมรุครั้งกรุงเก่า กับพระราชวิจารณ์ของสมเด็จพระพุทธเจ้าหลวง. กรุงเทพฯ: ต้นฉบับ. 2540 [1997].

Prawat buraphachan dan chareuk seuksa neaung nai ngan phithi 'khurubucha'. Bangkok: Section of Eastern Languages, Department of Archaeology, Silpakon University, 2546 [2003]. ประวัติบูรพาจารย์ด้านจารึกศึกษา เนืองในงานพิธี "คุรุบูชา". กรุงเทพฯ: ภาควิชาภาษาตะวันออก คณะโบราณคดี มหาวิทยาลัยศิลปากร. 2546 [2003].

Supaphan Na Bangchang. *Wiwathanakan ngan khian phasa bali nai Prathet Thai: chareuk tamnan phonsawadan san prakat*. Bangkok: Mahāmakuṭarājavidyālaya, 2529 [1986]. / สุภาพรรณ ณ บางช้าง. วิวัฒนาการงานเขียนภาษาบาลีในประเทศไทย: จารึก ตำนาน พงศาวดาร สาส์น ประกาศ. กรุงเทพฯ: มูลนิธิมหามกุฏราชวิทยาลัยฯ, 2529.

Syāmaraṭṭhassa Tepiṭakaṃ, Abhidhammapiṭake Dhammasaṅgaṇi. Bangkok: Mahāmakuṭarājavidyālaya, 2523 [1980].

Other sources

Bechert, Heinz and Heinz Braun. 1981. *Pāli Nīti Texts of Burma*. London: The Pali Text Society.

Bennett, Anna. 2017. *The Ancient History of U Thong, City of Gold*. Bangkok: Designated Areas for

Sustainable Tourism Administration (Public Organization) DASTA and Buddhadasa Indapanno Archives BIA.

Copp, Paul. 2014. *The Body Incantatory: Spells and the Ritual Imagination in Medieval Chinese Buddhism*. New York: Columbia University Press. https://doi.org/10.7312/copp16270

Cushman, Richard D., trans., and David K. Wyatt, ed. 2000. *The Royal Chronicles of Ayutthaya: A Synoptic Translation*. Bangkok: The Siam Society under Royal Patronage.

Drège, Jean-Pierre. 1999. 'Du texte à l'image: les manuscrits illustrés.' In *Images de Dunhuang. Dessins et peintures sur papier des fonds Pelliot et Stein*, edited by Jean-Pierre Drège, 105–159. Mémoires Archéologiques 24. Paris: École française d'Extrême-Orient.

———. 1999–2000. 'Les premières impressions des dhāraṇī de Mahāpratisarā.' *Cahiers d'Extrême-Asie* 11: 25–44. https://doi.org/10.3406/asie.1999.1149

Frankfurter, O., trans. 1954. 'Events in Ayuddhya from Chulasakaraj 686–966, A Translation from the Ratchphongsawadan krung kao chabap Luang Prasert Asksoranit'. In *The Siam Society Fiftiest Anniversary Commemorative Publication. Selected Articles from The Siam Society Journal*. Vol. I. 1904–29: 38–64. Bangkok.

Hidas, Gergely. 2014. 'Two *dhāraṇī* prints in the Stein Collection at the British Museum.' *Bulletin of the School Oriental and African Studies*, Vol. 77(1): 105–117. https://doi.org/10.1017/S0041977X13001341

von Hinüber, Oskar. 1996. *A Handbook of Pāli Literature*. Berlin and New York: Walter de Gruyter. https://doi.org/10.1515/9783110814989

Maggi, Mauro and Giuliana Martini. 2014. 'Annotations on the Book of Zambasta, III: Chapter 18 no more.' In *Scripta: An International Journal of Codiciology and Palaeography* 7: 139–158.

Miksic, John. 2011. *Old Javanese Gold. The Hunter Thompson Collection at the Yale University Art Gallery*. New Haven: Yale University Art Gallery/Yale University Press.

Namikawa Banri. 1987. *The Golden Figures of Buddha and Buddhist Sites in Thailand*. Tokyo: Nihonhōsōkyō kai.

Norman, K.R. 1983. *Pāli Literature, including the canonical literature in Prakrit and Sanskrit of all the Hīnayāna schools of Buddhism*. Wiesbaden: Otto Harrassowitz (Jan Gonda, ed., *A History of Indian Literature*, Volume VII Fasc. 2).

Nyanatiloka, Mahathera. 1971. *Guide through the Abhidhamma-Piṭaka, being a synopsis of the philosophical collection belonging to the Buddhist Pali canon followed by an essay on the Paṭicca-samuppāda*. Kandy: Buddhist Publication Society. Third Edition [First ed. 1938].

Skilling, Peter (ed.). 2008. *Past Lives of the Buddha. Wat Si Chum — Art, Architecture and Inscriptions* (with contributions by Pattaratorn Chirapravati, Pierre Pichard, Prapod Assavavirulhakarn, Santi Pakdeekham, Peter Skilling). Bangkok: River Books.

———. 2555 [2012]. 'At the Heart of Letters: Aksara and Akkhara in Thai Tradition.' In *80 that Mom Rajawong Suphawat Kasemsri* [Felicitation volume for MR Suphawat Kasemsri on his 80th Birthday] ed. Weerawan Ngamsantikul, 433–441. Bangkok: Rongphim Deuan Tula.

———. 2016. 'Chanting and Inscribing: The "Condensed Tripiṭaka" in Thai Ritual.' In *'Guiding Lights' for the 'Perfect Nature': Studies on the Nature and the Development of Abhidharma Buddhism. A Commemorative Volume in Honor of Prof. Dr. Kenyo Mitomo for his 70th Birthday.* Tokyo: Sankibo Busshorin, (1)–(35) = pp. 928–962.

———. 2017. 'The Many Lives of Texts: The *Pañcatraya and* the *Māyājāla Sūtras*.' In *Research on the Madhyama-āgama*, ed. Dhammadinnā, 269–326. Taipei: Dharma Drum Institute of Liberal Arts.

Wang, Eugene. 2011. 'Ritual Practice Without a Practitioner? Early Eleventh Century Dhāraṇī Prints in the Ruiguangsi Pagoda.' *Cahiers d'Extrême-Asie* 20: 127–160. https://doi.org/10.3406/asie.2011.1373

Peter Skilling retired from the French School of Asian Studies (EFEO) in 2016. He is a special lecturer at Chulalongkorn University, Bangkok, an honorary member of the Siam Society, Bangkok, and in 2017 he was elected an honorary fellow of the Asiatic Society of Mumbai. His expertise spans Sanskrit, Pāli, Thai and Tibetan literature, and South and Southeast Asian Buddhism, and he has published works including *Mahāsūtras: Great Discourses of the Buddha. Texts. Critical editions of the Tibetan Mahāsūtras* (2 vols, 1994 and 1997, Pali Text Society), *Beyond Worldly Conditions* (edited, 1999, Fragile Palm Leaves Foundation), *Pāli Literature Transmitted in Central Siam* (with Santi Pakdeekham, 2002, Fragile Palm Leaves Foundation), *Pāli and Vernacular Literature Transmitted in Central and Northern Siam* (with Santi Pakdeekham, 2004, Fragile Palm Leaves Foundation), *Buddhism and Buddhist Literature of South-East Asia: Selected Papers by Peter Skilling* (2009, Fragile Palm Leaves Foundation), *How Theravāda is Theravāda? Exploring Buddhist Identities* (co-edited, 2012, Silkworm).

— 12 —

The Relation of the *Saccasaṅkhepaṭīkā* Called *Sāratthasālinī* to the *Vinayavinicchayaṭīkā* Called *Vinayasāratthasandīpanī*

Petra Kieffer-Pülz

The present contribution suggests the common authorship of three Pāli commentaries of the twelfth/thirteenth centuries CE, namely the *Vinayavinicchayaṭīkā* called *Vinayasāratthasandīpanī* (less probably *Vinayatthasārasandīpanī*), the *Uttaravinicchayaṭīkā* called *Līnatthappakāsanī*, and the *Saccasaṅkhepaṭīkā* called *Sāratthasālinī*. The information collected from these three commentaries themselves and from Pāli literary histories concerning these three texts leads to the second quarter of the thirteenth century CE as the period of their origination. The data from parallel texts explicitly stated to having been written by Vācissara Thera in the texts themselves render it possible to establish with a high degree of probability Vācissara Thera as their author.

Introduction

Authorship attribution is necessary in the case of Pāli anonymous texts of premodern India. Cross-references are a safe instrument to attribute several interlinked works to one author,[1] and thus to broaden the textual basis for further investigations. But this does not automatically lead to the identification of the author. Nevertheless it is important, because authorship verification requires the analysis and comparison of larger quantities of text. Means to be applied may be, for instance, an author's writing style consisting of his lexical choices, syntactic constructions, structural features, or content-specific peculiarities. Nevertheless, in the case of these texts an author's writing style cannot always be safely identified, because of the extensive practice of reuse of text, because of the remodelling of earlier texts, and because of the translation into Pāli from Sanskrit[2] or Sinhalese templates.[3] The widening of the material base is helpful also with regard to the

1. For Saṅgharakkhita see Kieffer-Pülz 2017.
2. At least two cases are testified for Saṅgharakkhita Thera (twelfth/thirteenth century CE). See Kieffer-Pülz 2017, 34, 48.
3. Sumaṅgala Thera (twelfth/thirteenth century CE), for instance, for his *Abhidhammatthasaṅgaha-mahāṭīkā* translated larger portions from his teacher's *Abhidhammatthasaṅgaha-sannaya* (Kieffer-

Keywords: *Līnatthappakāsanī*, *Saccasaṅkhepaṭīkā*, *Sāratthasālinī*, *Sīmālaṅkārasaṅgaha*, *Thūpavaṃsa*, *Uttaravinicchayaṭīkā*, Vācissara Thera, *Vinayasāratthasandīpanī*, *Vinayavinicchayaṭīkā*

collection of information from the introductory and/or concluding portions of texts, from subheadings to chapters, and so on, and from secondary sources such as Pāli literary histories.

As a humble tribute to the memory of L. S. Cousins I contribute this paper tackling questions of authorship that also occupied Lance quite a bit in the last year of his life. I suggest the common authorship of the *Vinayavinicchayaṭīkā* (Vin-vn-ṭ) called *Vinayasāratthasandīpanī*, a commentary to Buddhadatta's Vinaya manual *Vinayavinicchaya* (Vin-vn; ca. fifth/sixth centuries CE), the *Uttaravinicchayaṭīkā* (Utt-vn-ṭ) called *Līnatthappakāsanī*, a commentary to Buddhadatta's Vinaya manual *Uttaravinicchaya* (Utt-vn), and the *Saccasaṅkhepaṭīkā* (Sacc-ṭ) called *Sāratthasālinī* a commentary to the Abhidhamma manual *Saccasaṅkhepa*[4] (Sacc; between seventh and twelfth centuries CE). In the first part I introduce the three commentaries; in the second I compare two similar passages in Vin-vn-ṭ and Sacc-ṭ.

1. The commentaries

1.1 The *Vinayavinicchayaṭīkā*

Regarding commentaries to Buddhadatta's Vin-vn, a *Vinayavinicchayaṭīkā* by Vācissara is mentioned in the *Gandhavaṃsa* (Gv 62,5–10), an undated work that originated in present day Burma, estimated to date from about the seventeenth century CE.[5] A *Vinayavinicchayaṭīkā* named *Vinayatthasārasandīpanī* by Mahā-Upatissa Mahāthera of Anurādhapura is listed in the *Piṭakat-samuiṅ* (Piṭ-sm 299), a bibliographical work produced in Burma in 1888. The mention of a commentary to Vin-vn called *Yogavinicchaya* in secondary literature[6] is based on a misunderstanding of Gv 62,10 (Kieffer-Pülz 2017, 26; 44f.). The mention of a *Vinayavinicchayaṭīkā* by Revata Thera in nineteenth-century sources from present day Burma and Sri Laṅka (Sās 34,15f.; Sās-dīp v. 1207) is based on a misunderstanding of the colophon added secondarily to Utt-vn-ṭ (see below, p. 221). In his edition of Buddhadatta's Vinaya manuals, A. P. Buddhadatta combines the two commentaries of Gv and Piṭ-sm, and makes them one. Though he probably is right, his argumentation is defective.[7]

Pülz 2016, 11); the author of the *Vinayavinicchayaṭīkā* examined here, states that he translated a Sinhalese commentary into Pāli, see below, pp. 215f. (vv. 10–17).

4. In Sacc-ṭ Ānanda is mentioned as its author; in later sources from Burma the name Dhammapāla is given. According to Cousins (unpublished) neither of them is a likely author, Cousins cautiously suggests Jotipāla.

5. For this and the next source see von Hinüber 1996: § 4.

6. See Malalasekera 1928, 198; Jayawardhana 1994, 183; Kitsudo 2015, 11.

7. '*Vinayasāratthadīpanī* (sic), the Commentary on *Vinayavinicchaya*, is written by a venerable Thera who was a pupil of the sub-commentator Sāriputta, the religious head of the Buddhist Order in Ceylon during the reign of Parākramabāhu the Great. The *Gandhavaṃsa* states that this Ṭīkā is a work of Mahāsāmi (sic) Vācissara, ...' (Buddhadatta 1928, xi). The title of the text corresponds neither to the one given in Piṭ-sm nor to the one in the seventeenth-century *Vinayālaṅkāraṭīkā*. Buddhadatta's designation of Vācissara as *mahāsāmi* is based on a misunderstanding of Gv 62,5ff. There *mahāsāmi* is simply the title of the *Subodhālaṅkāraporāṇaṭīkā*. The claim that the Gv states that this *ṭīkā* (i.e. the *Vinayasāratthadīpanī* (!)) is a work of Vācissara is not correct, since Gv does not give a title.

A single *ṭīkā* to Vin-vn is accessible in a Burmese edition. It is called *Vinayatthasārasandīpanī* (Vin-vn-ṭ) by the editors on the title page and in the subheadings of the chapters.[8] This corresponds to the title mentioned in Piṭ-sm for Mahā-Upatissa's *ṭīkā*. The printed *ṭīkā* is, however, found quoted in Tipiṭakālaṃkāra's *Vinayālaṅkāra* (Pālim-nṭ; present day Burma, between 1639 and 1651 CE) with the title *Vinayasāratthasandīpanī*,[9] that is with the words *sāra* and *attha* in reverse order, which probably is the correct title.[10] Vin-vn-ṭ does not have a colophon, but it has an introduction of nineteen verses. The first and last nine are in the Triṣṭubh metre, the tenth, forming the middle, is written in the Rucirā metre.[11]

Vin-vn-ṭ, ganthārambhakathā (see below pp. 214–216 for the text)

The first three verses contain a homage to the triple gem, followed by a homage to former teachers (v. 4), and to the author's own teacher, Sāriputta *mahāsāmi* (v. 5). The latter is characterized as an author (v. 6), revered even by King Parakkamabāhu I (1153–1186 CE) the unifier of the *nikāya*s in Sri Lanka (v. 7). V. 8 states that the author of Vin-vn-ṭ obtained great merit by paying homage to the triple gem, and thus succeeded in destroying all obstacles. V. 9 introduces Buddhadatta, the author of the *mūla*-text, with the names of his condensations mentioned subsequently (v. 10). Furthermore, the existence of a Sinhalese commentary (*vivaraṇa*) to them is stated (v. 10). Because it was written in Sinhalese it was not intelligible to monks in India.[12] This is one reason why the author was asked by the first of altogether five individuals,namely the forest dweller Sumaṅgala Thera,[13] to translate it into Pāli

8. Vin-vn-ṭ I 50,9; 132,8; 148,12; etc.

9. Pālim-nṭ I 37,23; 41,1; 43,18. This title is close to that of the *Vinaya* subcommentary written by the author's teacher, Sāriputta, namely (*Līna*)*Sāratthadīpanī* (Sp-ṭ I 2,3), and it is close to that of Sacc-ṭ, *Sāratthasālinī*.

10. *atthasāra* and *sārattha* both appear in texts, the first especially in explanations of *sārattha*; but in titles only °*sārattha*° is found: *Sārattha-dīpanī* (Sāriputta's *Vinaya* subcommentary), *Sārattha-ppakāsinī* (Buddhaghosa's commentary to the *Saṃyuttanikāya*), *Sārattha-mañjūsā* (Sāriputta's subcommentary to the *Aṅguttaranikāya*), *Sārattha-vilāsinī* (Saṅgharakkhita's commentary to the *Moggallānapañcikā*), *Sārattha-saṅgaha* (a manual by Siddhattha Thera), Sārattha-samuccaya (a *Parittaṭīkā*), *Sārattha-sālinī* (a commentary to the *Saccasaṅkhepa*), etc.

11. The introductory portion has been partly translated by Crosby 2004, 89f. (vv. 5–7); 90–93 (vv. 9–19), by Crosby and Skilton 1999–2000, 176 (v. 14), and fully by Cousins (unpublished). The translation on pp. 214–216 is mine, based on Cousins (unpublished) and taking into account the other translations.

12. For a similar statement, see Sp I 2,7–12:

saṃvaṇṇanā Sīhaḷadīpakena
vākyena esā pana saṅkhaṭattā,
na kiñci atthaṃ abhisambhuṇāti
dīpantare bhikkhujanassa yasmā, (v. 7)
tasmā imaṃ pāḷinayānurūpaṃ
saṃvaṇṇanaṃ dāni samārabhissaṃ.

'But on account of the fact that this exposition had been done in the language of the Island of Sīhaḷa, and because no benefit at all reaches the monks on the other island, therefore I shall now begin this exposition in conformity with the methods of the text (pāḷi, i.e. the *Vinaya*) ...' (Translation based on Jayawickrama 1986, 2).

13. This forest dweller Sumaṅgala, himself a pupil of Sāriputta, probably identical with the

Vin-vn-ṭ, ganthārambhakathā

	Text	*Translation*
1	ādiccavaṃsambarapātubhūtaṃ byāmappabhāmaṇḍaladevacāpaṃ dhammambunijjhāpitapāpaghammaṃ vandām' ahaṃ Buddhamahambuvantaṃ.	I pay homage to the Awakened One who resembles a great raincloud; who appeared in the firmament of the solar lineage like a rainbow with a halo extending a fathom; who has extinguished the heat of evil with the water of the Dhamma.
2	pasannagambhīrapadāḷisotaṃ nānānayānantataraṅgamālaṃ sīlādikhandhāmitamacchagumbaṃ vandām' ahaṃ Dhammamahāsavantiṃ.	I pay homage to the Dhamma which resembles a great stream; whose clear and deep line of words resembles a flow; whose various methods are like an infinite succession of waves; whose collections dealing with virtue, etc., are like innumerable shoals of fish.
3	sīloruvelaṃ dhutasaṅkhamālaṃ santosatoyaṃ samathūmicittaṃ padhānakiccaṃ adhicittasāraṃ vandām' ahaṃ Saṅghamahāsamuddaṃ.	I pay homage to the Community which resembles a great ocean; whose virtue is like its sandy shore; whose purification [practices] are like a garland of conch shells; whose joyfulness (*santosa*) is its water (*toya*), [and whose] calmness is the variety (*citta*) of waves (*ūmi*); whose striving is its activity, whose higher consciousness is his essence.
4	ye tantidhammaṃ munirājaputtā yāvajjakālaṃ paripālayantā saṃvaṇṇanaṃ nimmalam ānayiṃsu te pubbake cācariye namāmi.	And I bow down to the former teachers, the sons of the King of Sages (i.e. the Buddha) who, guarding the teaching in the scriptures until the present time, handed down the flawless exposition (*saṃvaṇṇanā*).
5	yo dhammasenāpatitulyanāmo tathūpamo sīhaḷadīpadīpo mamaṃ mahāsāmimahāyatindo pāpesi vuḍḍhiṃ jinasāsanamhi.	He who [bears] the same name as the 'General of the Dhamma' (Dhammasenāpati = Buddha's pupil, Sāriputta), who likewise was a light to the Sīhaḷa island, my great master (*mahāsāmī*), the great Lord of the monks (*mahāyatinda*), who brought about prosperity in the *sāsana* of the Conqueror;
6	ṭīkā katā aṭṭhakathāya yena Samantapāsādikanāmikāya Aṅguttarāyaṭṭhakathāya c' eva satthantarassāpi ca Jotisatthaṃ.	by whom a *ṭīkā* to the commentary named *Samantapāsādikā* was composed (the *Sāratthadīpanī*); and likewise to the commentary to the *Aṅguttara* (the *Sāratthamañjūsa*), and even, to another branch of learning, a treatise on the course of the heavenly bodies;

7	nikāyasāmaggividhāyakena raññā Parakkantibhujena sammā laṅkissarenāpi katopahāraṃ vande garuṃ gāravabhājanaṃ taṃ	to whom even the ruler of Laṅka, the king Parakkamabāhu, who established unity among the fraternities, payed due respect; I revere him, [my] teacher, worthy of respect.
8	namassamāno 'ham alattham evaṃ vatthuttayaṃ vanditavandaneyyaṃ yaṃ puññasandoham amandabhūtaṃ tassānubhāvena hatantarāyo.	Bowing down in this manner to the three things which have been and should be honoured (or: which should be honoured by the worshipper), the quantity of merit which I have obtained is extensive; by the power of this [merit], I have destroyed [all] obstacles.
9	yo Buddhaghosācariyāsabhena viññuppasatthena pi suppasattho so Buddhadattācariyābhidhāno mahākavī theriyavaṃsadīpo	The great poet, light of the lineage of elders (*theriyavaṃsa*), who bears the name Buddhadatta *ācāriya*, who was highly praised by Buddhaghosa, hero among teachers (*ācariya*), [and] also praised by the learned,
10	akāsi yaṃ Vinayavinicchaya-vhayaṃ sa-Uttaraṃ pakaraṇam uttamaṃ hitaṃ apekkhataṃ vinayanayesu pāṭavaṃ; purāsi yaṃ vivaraṇam assa sīhaḷaṃ	composed a treatise called 'Exegesis of the *Vinaya*' (*Vinayavinicchaya*), together with the '[Exegesis of the] Later [section]' (i.e. the *Uttaravinicchaya*) which is excellent and beneficial for those seeking skill in the methods of the *Vinaya*. The commentary (*vivaraṇa*) on it (i.e. on the *Vinayavinicchaya* plus *Uttaravinicchaya*?) which existed before was in Sinhalese;
11	yasmā na dīpantarikānam atthaṃ sādheti bhikkhūnam asesato taṃ; tasmā hi sabbattha yatīnam atthaṃ āsīsamānena dayālayena	because this [commentary] does not fully accomplish the goal for monks belonging to the other island (i.e. India), therefore indeed, I was asked with respect by him who wishes the benefit of the monks (*yati*) everywhere, by the excellent Elder Sumaṅgala, who is full of compassion, desires the morally good, who is a forest-dweller, who knows the [proper] methods, [and is] a mine of good qualities; because [of that]
12	Sumaṅgalattheravarena yasmā sakkacca kalyāṇamanorathena nayaññunāraññanivāsikena ajjhesito sādhuguṇākarena.	
13	ākaṅkhamānena cirappavattiṃ dhammassa dhammissaradesitassa Coḷappadīpena ca Buddhamitta- therena saddhādiguṇoditena.	and [because I was asked] by the Elder Buddhamitta, Lamp of the Coḷas, spoken of for qualities such as faith, desiring the long duration of the Dhamma taught by the Righteous Lord (or: Lord of the Dhamma, i.e. the Buddha);

14	tathā Mahākassapa-avhayena therena sikkhāsu sagāravena kudiṭṭhi-matte bha-vidārakena sīhena coḷāvanipūjitena	[and] likewise [because I was asked] by the Elder titled Mahākassapa, who reveres the rules of training, who tears up error in one enthralled by wrong views,[14] the 'Lion' worshipped on Coḷa soil;
15	yo Dhammakittī ti pasatthanāmo tenāpi saddhena upāsakena sīlādinānāguṇamaṇḍitena saddhammakāmen' idha paṇḍitena.	[and because] I was asked by both, him, the devout lay disciple whose praised name is Dhammakitti ('Renown of the Dhamma'), a scholar (*paṇḍita*) adorned with various qualities like virtue, etc., who loves the true Dhamma here (i.e. in this world);
16	saddhena paññāṇavatā vaḷattā- maṅgalyavaṃsena mahāyasena āyācito vāṇijaBhāṇunāpi varaññunā sādhuguṇodayena.	and by him, the Vāṇija ('merchant') Bhānu, who is devout, possessed of wisdom, renowned, of the auspicious lineage of Vaḷaṭṭā, of great fame, knows the excellent, and is a source of good qualities;
17	tasmā tam āropiya pāḷibhāsaṃ nissāya pubbācariyopadesaṃ hitvā nikāyantaraladdhidosaṃ katvātivitthāranayaṃ samāsaṃ	therefore, having translated this [commentary] into the language of the sacred texts (i.e. Pāli),[15] dependent upon the instruction of former teachers, avoiding the defect of the views of other monastic fraternities (*nikāya*), having made concise the extremely extensive style,
18	avuttam atthañ ca pakāsayanto pāṭhakkamañ cāpi avokkamanto saṃvaṇṇayissāmi tadatthasāraṃ ādāya ganthantarato pi sāraṃ.	elucidating meaning not made explicit, and not deviating from the order of the text, I shall explain the essence of the meaning of that [text], taking into account the essence also from other books.
19	ciraṭṭhitiṃ patthayatā janānaṃ hitāvahassāmalasāsanassa mayā samāsena vidhīyamānaṃ Saṃvaṇṇanaṃ sādhu suṇantu santo ti.	May good people listen well to [my] explanation (*saṃvaṇṇānā*) set out in brief by me, wishing for the stainless *sāsana*, that brings benefit to mankind to last long.

(vv. 11f.). The other four people were:

- an otherwise unknown Buddhamitta Thera, Lamp of the Coḷas (v. 13);
- Mahākassapa Thera, worshipped on Coḷa soil, identical with Coḷiya Mahākassapa, author of the *Vimativinodanīṭīkā* (Vmv) and *Mohavicchedanī* (see Skilton and Crosby 1999–2000, 177), and younger contemporary of Sāriputta whom he opposed in many instances (end of twelfth and/or beginning of thirteenth century CE; v. 14);
- a lay follower (*upāsaka*) named Dhammakitti *paṇḍita* (v. 15). An *upāsaka* Dhammakitti *paṇḍita* is mentioned together with a Vāgissara *ācariya* in Mhv 76.32. They were sent as envoys to Rāmaññadesa by Parakkamabāhu I in his twelfth regnal year (1164 CE) as stated in the Devanagala Inscription.[16] A Dhammakitti *paṇḍita* is further mentioned in the colophon of Sacc-ṭ, as the one who had supported the author and had asked him to complete Sacc-ṭ (see below, p. 228). Kitti is a frequent name in this period, as the mention of already three Kitti-s, all generals under Parakkamabāhu I, in the *Mahāvaṃsa* shows. As Cousins (unpublished) states, any layman with that name would be likely to become known as Dhammakitti. But the designation of the *upāsaka* Dhammakitti as learned (*paṇḍita*) which is found in all three instances at least makes it possible that it is the same person (see below, p. 232).
- as fifth, the author of Vin-vn-ṭ was asked by the otherwise unknown merchant Bhānu or Vāṇija Bhānu of the untraced Valaṭṭā lineage (v. 16). From the construction of the sentence it is evident that the author translated the Sinhalese commentary into Pāli (*yaṃ vivaraṇaṃ assa sīhaḷaṃ ... tam āropiya pāḷibhāsaṃ*, vv. 10, 17), took into account instructions from earlier teachers, avoided defects of other *nikāyas*, and so on (v. 17), and included the essence of other books[17] (*ganthantarato*; v. 18). The final verse expresses the author's wish that the good people may listen well to his commentary (v. 19).

---

author of the *Abhidhammāvatāranavaṭīkā* and the *Abhidhammatthasaṅgahaṭīkā* (von Hinüber 1996, §§ 343, 346), asked Saṅgharakkhita thera — also a pupil of Sāriputta — to write the *Khuddasikkhābhinavaṭīkā* (Khuddas-nṭ 237,11), and was head of an own branch and resident in Jambudoṇi (Daṁbadeṇiya; Pay C[e] 254,7). If he is identical with the Sumaṅgala Thera mentioned in the Pūjavaliya (Gunasekera 1895, 51) he is also called Sumaṅgala Mānetpāmula (Mahā-netra-prasāda), and is a brother of Mayūrapāda Thera, author of the *Pūjāvaliya* (1266 CE).

14. (opposite page) Crosby and Skilton 1999–2000, 177, suggest that *kudiṭṭhi* corresponds to *vimati*, *matta* to *vinodanī*, *bha* to *moha* and *vidāraka to vicchedanī*. 'Thus in praising Mahākassapa as one 'who tears up delusion in one enthralled by wrong views', *kudiṭṭhimatte bhavidārakena*, the author of the *Vinayatthasārasandīpanī* makes a clever allusion to all the elements of the titles of the two works attributed to Mahākassapa: *Vimativinodanī* and *Mohavicchedanī*.'

15. (opposite page) Crosby 2004, translates: 'On which the commentary was formerly in Sinhalese,' (p. 91) ... 'Therefore, having dressed that [commentary] in the language of the sacred texts (*pālibhāsā*/Pāli language).' (p. 92).

16. So already Cousins (unpublished).

17. Crosby 2004, n. 63 understands *ganthantara* to refer to the *Uttaravinicchaya*. But since the *Uttaravinicchaya* is commented upon separately, and since the author quotes from many sources, this is improbable.

From this it results that the Sinhalese commentary to Vin-vn was translated into Pāli by the author of Vin-vn-ṭ. Since he also quotes from other sources, his commentary is not a mere translation of the Sinhalese commentary, but the latter most probably forms the core of his *ṭīkā*. The only Sinhalese commentary to Vin-vn known to us is the now extinct *Vanavinisa* called *Nissandeha*, attributed to Parakkamabāhu II (reign 1236–1271), and written by him before his *Visuddhimaggasannaya*.[18] The author of Vin-vn-ṭ openly quotes from this *Nissandeha*, but also silently translates it (Kieffer-Pülz 2016, 11f.). Thus, the Sinhalese commentary mentioned in the introductory verses as having been translated into Pāli by the author most likely is the *Nissandeha*. But even if that were not the case, the *Nissandeha* represents the *terminus post quem* for the origination of Vin-vn-ṭ. The fact that no earlier insufficient commentary in Pāli is mentioned in addition, makes it likely that none existed.[19] Sources used in addition to canonical and *aṭṭhakathā* writings are Sinhalese and Pāli *Gaṇṭhipadas*, the *Khuddasikkhāpurāṇaṭīkā* (Khuddas-pṭ), *Vajirabuddhiṭīkā*, and *Sāratthadīpanī*.[20] Saṅgharakkhita's *Khuddasikkhā-abhinavaṭīkā* (Khuddas-nṭ) is not quoted. In the light of the fact that *Khuddasikkhā* (Khuddas) and Vin-vn have verses in common (Kieffer-Pülz 2013, I 195f., n. 473.), and that the author of Vin-vn-ṭ quotes from a *Khuddasikkhāgaṇṭhipada* and Khuddas-pṭ, the omission of his fellow-pupil's Khuddas-nṭ written some several years before 1266 (Kieffer-Pülz 2017, 32f., 47) could be understood as a sign that it did not yet exist,[21] an *argumentum* admittedly *e silentio*. Unclear is the case of Vmv. If Crosby and Skilton's interpretation of Vin-vn-ṭ v. 14 is correct, the author of Vin-vn-ṭ knew Coḷiya Kassapa and his texts (see Crosby and Skilton 1999, 176ff.). In his Vmv Kassapa discusses the rule concerning drinking of alcohol in a sense opposed to Sāriputta. Vin-vn-ṭ follows Kassapa's interpretation, but does not mention him or Vmv (Kieffer-Pülz 2005, 172ff.). This might well have been out of loyalty for his teacher, Sāriputta, who was heavily criticized by Kassapa concerning this question.

To sum up, the author of Vin-vn-ṭ was a Sinhalese, active after the reunion of the three *nikāyas* (1165 CE), after his teacher had become head of the Saṅgha (*mahāsāmi*) in Laṅka (between 1165 and 1186 CE), and after the *Nissandeha* attributed to Parakkamabāhu II (reign 1236–1271 CE) had been written. Parakkamabāhu is said to have written this and other texts towards the end of his reign.[22] But the fact

18. Godakumbura 1955, 6, 20. For the attribution of this text to Parakkamabāhu II, see also Wickremasinghe 1900, xvii; Buddhadatta 1928, xii; CPD 1948, 1.2.2,(4); Ñāṇatusita 2011, 1.2.2,3. The statement that Parakkamabāhu II wrote this text in the latter part of his life, goes back to a source of the sixteenth century, the reliability of which is questioned (see Kieffer-Pülz 2016, n. 9). Thus, the possibility that he wrote the *Nissandeha* in his early years, when he was educated by the Buddhist Saṅgha, and thus was made familiar with such texts as the *Vinayavinicchaya*, is not excluded.

19. If earlier Pāli commentaries existed the authors of the newer commentaries normally justify their writing a new commentary. See, for instance, Sp-ṭ I 2,5ff.; Khuddas-nṭ 237,8f.; Mūlas-anṭ 1,8; etc.

20. For further information, see Kieffer-Pülz 2013, I 30–34.

21. Already suggested by Crosby 2004, 93.

22. This made me formerly assume that Vin-vn-ṭ was written in the second half of the thirteenth

that Utt-vn-ṭ — which postdates Vin-vn-ṭ — was brought from Laṅka to what is now called Burma by Sīvali Thera some time before 1245 CE according to the secondarily added colophon (see below, p. 221), would render such a late date impossible. If this information is true, and if the attribution of the *Nissandeha* to Parakkamabāhu II is correct, then the *Nissandeha* must have been compiled before Parakkamabāhu's reign, that is before 1236. Parakkamabāhu II died in 1271 CE. If we assume a lifespan of approximately seventy to eighty years[23] then the years between 1190/1200 and 1271 CE are to be taken as his *floruit*. He would thus have been about 36 or 46 years old at the beginning of his reign. Assuming that he was at least twenty years old when he wrote the *Nissandeha*, the latter could not have originated before 1210/1220.[24] This would lead to a time window for the writing of Vin-vn-ṭ between 1210/1220 at the earliest and some time before approximately 1245 CE.

The Vin-vn-ṭ at our hand bears the title *Vinayasāratthasandīpanī* or, less likely, *Vinayatthasārasandīpanī*, which in the latter form corresponds to the title transmitted in Piṭ-sm of a commentary by an otherwise untraced Mahā-Upatissa. In Vin-vn-ṭ the author describes himself as a pupil of Sāriputta Thera. In the list of Theras who wrote religious works after Sāriputta as transmitted in Dharmakīrti's *Nikāyasaṅgraha* (fourteenth century CE), the following names are listed after Sāriputta: Saṅgharakṣita (Saṅgharakkhita), Sumaṅgala, Vāgīśvara (Vācissara), Dharmakīrti (Dhammakitti), Nāgasena, Ānanda, Vedeha, Buddhapriya (Buddhappiya), Anavamadarśīya (Anomadassi) (Fernando 1908, 24). An Upatissa is not among them, but rather a Vācissara. This could be understood in the sense that actually only one *ṭīkā* to Vin-vn existed, namely the *Vinayasāratthasandīpanī*, and that its author was Vācissara, not Mahā-Upatissa.

1.2 The *Uttaravinicchayaṭīkā* named *Līnatthappakāsanī*

Three commentaries on Utt-vn are mentioned in Pāli literary histories.[25]

1. an *Uttaravinicchayaṭīkā* by Vācissara (Gv 62,11),
2. an *Uttaravinicchayaṭīkā* by Mahā-Upatissa from Anurādhapura (Piṭ-sm 300), and
3. a commentary by Revata (Sās-dīp v. 1207)

century. Kieffer-Pülz 2013, I 30f.

23. This is an arbitrarily chosen lifespan taken as an approximation. No data are available for the average lifespan of monks at this or any other time to my knowledge.

24. According to Mhv 81.77 Vijayabāhu III gave his eldest son, the latter Parakkamabāhu II, to the *saṅgha* when he appointed Saṅgharakkhita Thera to the position of *mahāsāmi*, that is probably around 1232 (reign 1232–36), suggesting that Parakkamabāhu still was a child at that time. As stated by Paranavitana a similar description also exists for Parakkamabāhu II entrusting the government to his son, though the latter was already a mature person (Paranavitana 1960, 617, n. 21). Therefore, the statement that Parakkamabāhu II still was a child in 1232 has to be taken as a topos. It is to be assumed that Parakkamabāhu II's education by the monks began sometime before this event.

25. Saddhamma-s and Sās list none.

The third commentary, i.e. the one by Revata, listed in Sās-dīp v. 1207, can be dismissed. It is based on the secondary colophon (see below, p. 221), which mentions Revata solely as the one who transliterated the text or caused it to be transliterated (see already Kitsudo 2015, 11). Regarding the first two, the same two authors as in the case of Vin-vn-ṭ — Vācissara and Mahā-Upatissa — are mentioned in the same two sources originating from present day Burma, namely in Gv and Piṭ-sm. None of these sources gives a title. In Somadasa's catalogue of manuscripts in Sri Lankan temple libraries one manuscript is listed with the text title *Uttaralīnatthappakāsinī* and the generic description as *navaṭīkā* (Somadasa 1956, s.v.). Without reference the same text title, described as a *ṭīkā* (not as a *purāṇa-* or *navaṭīkā*), is combined with the author's name Vācissara by Buddhadatta (1928, xii). Probably from a combination of these statements Vācissara's commentary is identified as a *navaṭīkā*, and Mahā-Upatissa's commentary as a *purāṇaṭīkā* in CPD 1948 (1.3.4,1–2).

A printed *ṭīkā* on Utt-vn is at hand. The name of the author is not mentioned, but it is designated as a *saṃvaṇṇanā* to the *Uttara* (Vin-vn-ṭ II 399,9) in the introductory stanzas, as *Līnatthapakāsanī* on the *Uttara* in the twenty subheadings to the chapters,[26] as *Līnatthapakāsanī nāma Uttaravinicchayavaṇṇanā* at the end of the text (Vin-vn-ṭ II 529,24), and again as a *samvaṇṇanā* in the secondarily added colophon (Vin-vn-ṭ II 530,11). The various designations of the printed Utt-vn-ṭ do not indicate whether this is an old (*purāṇaṭīkā*) or a new *ṭīkā* (*navaṭīkā*). But as in the case of Vin-vn-ṭ the author does not mention an earlier Pāli commentary.

Only the introductory stanzas belong safely to the text. They simply contain a homage to the triple gem (v. 1), state that by the author's merit all calamities to the triple gem are cut off, and that he will comment on Buddhadatta's Utt-vn.

Utt-vn-ṭ, *ganthārambhakathāvaṇṇanā* (Vin-vn-ṭ II 399,4–9)

	Text	*Translation*
1	devātidevaṃ sugataṃ devabrahminda-vanditaṃ, dhammañ ca vaṭṭupacchedaṃ natvā vaṭṭātitaṃ gaṇaṃ.	Having bowed to the Well Gone, the god above the gods, honoured by the gods, Brahma and Indra, and [having bowed] to the Dhamma that cuts off the cycle [of transmigrations and having bowed] to the Community that has overcome the cyle [of transmigrations];
2	vandanāmayapuññena kammena ratanattaye chetvā upaddave sabbe ārabhissaṃ samāhito.	having cut off all calamities through the act [producing] merit proceeding from [my] paying homage to the triple gem, I, as one with a collected [mind], will begin according to [my] strength this clear exposition of the *Uttara* which was written in a condensed manner by the Elder Buddhadatta.
3	therena Buddhadattena racitassa samāsato Saṃvaṇṇanaṃ asaṃkiṇṇaṃ Uttarassa yathābalaṃ.	

Similar as in Vin-vn-ṭ (v. 8, above, p. 215) the author mentions that all obstacles

26. Vin-vn-ṭ II 410,3; 412,5; 415,17; etc.

are removed by his paying homage to the triple gem. Through an intertextual link to Vin-vn-ṭ for explanations of the homage to the triple gem, and so on,[27] subsequently to these introductory verses, common authorship of Vin-vn-ṭ and Utt-vn-ṭ is proved beyond doubt.

Utt-vn-ṭ has no colophon. However, in the edition a secondarily added colophon, consisting of five *śloka* verses (4cd metrically disturbed), is attached to the text. It is unclear who added it and when.

Utt-vn-ṭ, secondarily added colophon (Vin-vn-ṭ II 530,2–12)

	Text	*Translation*
	pacchā ṭhapitagāthāya[28]	Verses that have been added later:
1	therena thiracittena sāsanujjotanatthinā puññavā ñāṇavā sīlī suhajjo muduko tathā	By the Elder having a solid mind, [and] wishing to illuminate the *sāsana*, who possesses merit, insight, [and] virtue, is dear to one's heart, [and] likewise gentle,
2	yo sīhaḷārimaddesu candimā sūriyo viya pākaṭo Sīvalitthero mahātejo mahāyaso	who is famous in Sīhaḷa and Arimadda, like the sun and the moon; the elder Sīvalī, of great glory, of great fame;
3	tena nītā sīhaḷā yā idha pattā sudhīmatā esā saṃvaṇṇanā sīhaḷakkharena sulikkhitā.	by him, of excellent wisdom, this commentary well-written with Sinhalese letters, which has been obtained here (i.e. in Laṅka) was brought from Sīhaḷa [to Arimadda].
4	Revato iti nāmena therena thiracetasā Arimaddike rakkhantena parivattetvāna sādhukaṃ.	By the elder named Revata, having a solid mind, protecting [those] belonging to Arimadda, having had [it] thoroughly transliterated [into Burmese script],[29]
5	likhāpitā hitatthāya bhikkhūnaṃ arimaddike esā saṃvaṇṇanā suṭṭhu sanniṭṭhānam upāgatā tath' eva sabbasattānaṃ sabbattho ca samijjhatū ti	having caused [it] to be written for the benefit of the monks in Arimadd(ik)a, this exposition, having thoroughly arrived at [its] conclusion(?), shall likewise prosper everywhere for all beings.

27. Vin-vn-ṭ II 401,16–402,3: *pakaraṇārambhe ratanattayavandanāpayojanaṃ tattha tatthācariyehi bahudhā papañcitaṃ, amhehi ca Vinayavinicchayavaṇṇanāyaṃ samāsato dassitan ti na taṃ idha vaṇṇayissāma. pakaraṇābhidheyyakaraṇappakārapayojanāni pi tattha dassitanayānusārena idhāpi veditabbāni. sambandhādidassanamukhena anuttānapadavaṇṇanam ev' ettha karissāmi.*

'In the beginning of a treatise the teachers here and there have widely spread out the purpose of paying homage to the triple gem. By us too it has been briefly shown in the commentary to the *Vinayavinicchaya*. [Therefore] we will not explain it here. Even the treatise's subject matter, the mode of explanation, and [its] purpose are to be understood here too in conformity with the methods shown there. By way of showing the connection [of the words], etc., I will write here solely a commentary on obscure words.'

28. This remark was probably added by the editors. In the ms. of the U Pho Thi collection (ms. 528) these words are not contained.

29. It cannot be excluded that Revata also translated the text into Burmese. The word *parivatteti*

This colophon reports that Utt-vn-ṭ — or eventually Vin-vn-ṭ and Utt-vn-ṭ, if both were considered one single *saṃvaṇṇanā* — was brought from Lanka to Pagan (present day Burma) by Sīvali Thera, renowned in Laṅka and Pagan, and was caused to be transliterated from the Sinhalese to the Burmese script by a Revata Thera. This Sīvali Thera most probably is the one mentioned in the Kalyāṇī Inscription of King Dhammaceti (1476 CE), as one of three Sinhalese *bhikkhus* who accompanied Chapaṭa on his return to Pagan in 1190 CE. According to the Inscription the Elders Sīvali and Tāmalinda died before Ānanda, whose time of death is given with Sakkaraj 607, i.e. 1245 CE.[30] Sās hands down discrepant, and precise dates for the death of all three *theras*.[31] They are suspicious since Sās postdates this incident by approximately 600 years, and since already the Kalyāṇī Inscription, which only postdates it by approximately 230 years, gives an exact date solely for Ānanda. But since all three were *theras* (i.e. monks of at least ten years of seniority) when they left for Pagan with Chapata in 1190 CE, they were at least thirty years of age then, and taking seventy to eighty years as an average lifespan (see above, n. 23), 1245 CE should roughly be the last *terminus ante quem* for the transport of Utt-vn-ṭ to present day Burma.

Taking the information in Vin-vn-ṭ and Utt-vn-ṭ together the time window for the compilation of these two commentaries would be approximately twenty to thirty years between the writing of the *Nissandeha* (ca. 1210/20 at the earliest), and the death of Sīvalī Thera (sometime before 1245 CE).

The author of Utt-vn-ṭ is identified as Vācissara Thera in the *Bhikkhupātimokkhagaṇṭhi(dīpanī)* dating from 1492/1493 (BPāt-gd 14,24–15,12), and the slightly earlier *Samantapāsādikā-atthayojanā* (Sp-y I 289,1–12) of the grammarian Ñāṇakitti from the kingdom of Lan Na (present day Northern Thailand) (see also Kieffer-Pülz 2015, B.I.6.4). Several stanzas of the printed Utt-vn-ṭ are quoted there with the source mentioned as *Uttaravinicchayaṭīkā* written by Vācissara Thera.[32] Thus in fifteenth-century Lan Na the printed Utt-vn-ṭ, named *Uttara-Līnatthappakāsanī* in the subheadings, was considered the work of Vācissara. Whether it was a *purāṇa-* or a *navaṭīkā* or simply the only *ṭīkā* to Utt-vn remains unclear. In the light of this attribution the ascription of a Utt-vn-ṭ to Vācissara in Gv, can be understood as referring to the same commentary. There remains the nineteenth-century attribu-

according to Childers (s.v. *parivatteti*) is used for 'translate' too; see also Sās 27,31: *sīhaḷabhāsāya parivattitvā;* 28,8 *Māgadhabhāsāya parivattitvā*; etc. But since in the present case the text speaks about *sīhaḷakkhara* before, transliteration here seems the more probable.

30. Taw Sein Ko 1892, 154: *Ānandathērō pana catupaññāsavassāni Pugāmanagarē sāsanaṃ jotayitvā, muni-suñña-rasa-sakkarājē sampatte yathākammaṃ gato.* 'And Ānandathēra, after spending fifty-four rainy seasons in maintaining the Religion in splendour in Pugāma (Pagan), also passed away according to his deeds in the year 607, Sakkarāj.'

31. 591 Kāli yuga (= 1229 CE) for Sīvali Thera, 596 (= 1234 CE) for Ānanda Thera, and 598 (= 1236 CE) for Tāmalinda Thera (Sās 67,25–32).

32. *Uttaravinicchayaṭīkāyan tu "..." ti Vācissaranāmakācariyena vuttaṃ* (Bhpātgp 14,24–15,12; Sp-y I 289,1–12). 'But in the *Uttaravinicchayaṭīkā* it has been stated by the teacher named Vācissara: "..."'. Unlike von Hinüber (2000, 132f.) I assume that the reference goes to the text in which these stanzas are transmitted, not to the stanzas themselves. The main reason for this assumption is the fact that these stanzas are introduced by *honti c' ettha* (Kieffer-Pülz 2015) in both texts, and that the mention of the author is to be related to the *Uttaravinicchayaṭīkāyan*, not to the *honti c' ettha.*

tion to an otherwise not traced Mahā-Upatissa in Piṭ-sm. The situation is the same as in the case of Vin-vn-ṭ.

The *Saccasaṅkhepa* commentaries

According to Dhammakitti's Saddhamma-s (ca. 1400 CE) there exists a commentary (*vaṇṇanā*) to the *Saccasaṅkhepa* (Sacc) called *Nissayaṭṭhakathā* by the Elder Mahābodhi (Saddhamma-s 9.25).[33] The Saddhamma-s further mentions a commentary named *Sāratthasālinī* by a pupil of Sāriputta (Saddhamma-s 9.36). In Piṭ-sm 323 this commentary is listed with the name *Sāratthasālinī* qualified as a *navaṭīkā* by an unknown author from Sri Lanka.[34] Gv (62,16) also mentions two commentaries to Sacc: one without title by Vācissara (*Saccasaṅkhepassa ṭīkā*), written at the request of the Elder Sāriputta (Gv 71,35f. – it is mentioned in Piṭ-sm (322) without title as an old *ṭīkā* by Vācissara[35]), another one as *Saccasaṅkhepavivaraṇa* of an unknown author (Gv 75,19f.). Sās (34,7–9.12f.) mentions an old *ṭīkā* to Sacc by Vācissara, and a new one by a forest dweller. This is repeated by Vimalasāra in Sās-dip (vv. 1225, 1228).

From among the Pāli literary histories the *Gandhavaṃsa* states that the *Saccasaṅkhepaṭīkā* by Vācissara was written at the request of Sāriputta (Gv 71,35f.). Since it is not to be assumed that Sāriputta asked two different pupils to comment on the same *mūla*-text, Vācissara's *Saccasaṅkhepaṭīkā* of the *Gandhavaṃsa*, must be identical with the one mentioned otherwise as *Sāratthasālinī* but without an author's name, because in the *Sāratthasālinī* it is stated that its author, a pupil of Sāriputta, wrote the *Sāratthasālinī* at the request of Sāriputta (see below, p. 225, v. 3).[36] Thus in our earliest sources (Sacc-ṭ, and Saddhamma-s) a pupil of Sāriputta is given as the author of the *Sāratthasālinī*, who is identified as Vācissara in Gv. From then onwards Vācissara's *ṭīkā* is qualified as *porāṇa-* or *pubbaṭīkā* in the literary Pāli histories (Piṭ-sm, Sās, Sās-dīp). These same texts all list a *navaṭīkā*, which in Piṭ-sm is mentioned with the title *Sāratthasālinī*. Thus it is clear that the two commentaries mentioned in Piṭ-sm as *porāṇa-* and *navaṭīkā* are identical. Probably this also holds true for Sās and Sās-dīp, because they mention the author as forest-dweller. This again conforms to the statements in Sacc-ṭ, where in the extended colophon, it is stated that the author lived in the unidentified Tilaka park which is a residence for forest-dwellers.

In sum we have three commentaries to Sacc: (1) the otherwise untraced *Nissayatthakathā* by Mahābodhi; (2) the *Sāratthasālinī* by some pupil of Sāriputta, identified with Vācissara since the Gv or described as forest-dweller, who was asked to write it by Sāriputta, and (3) the anonymous *Saccasaṅkhepa-vivaraṇa* only mentioned in Gv 75,19.

---

33. This untraced text is qualified as an old *ṭīkā* (*porāṇaṭīkā*) in CPD 1948, 3.8.6,1, giving Saddhamma-s as well as a manuscript as a source.

34. See CPD 1948, 3.8.6,3.

35. See CPD 1948, 3.8.6,2.

36. Ñāṇatusita 2011, 3.8.6.3 explains that the *Sāratthasālinī* listed as CPD 3.8.6,3 is identical with the *ṭīkā* by Vācissara listed as CPD 3.8.6,2, though he mentions as author of the *Sāratthasālinī* Sumaṅgala Thera based on Malalasekera 1928, 200, 204; Jayawardhana 1994, 196, 199. No sources for this claim are given.

According to the Pāli literary histories, commentaries to Sacc are:

Source	*Text name*	*Author*
Saddhamma-s 9.25 (p. 63)	*Nissayatthakathā nāma Saccasaṅkhepavaṇṇanā*	Mahābodhī ti nāmena therena
Saddhamma-s 9.36 (p. 64)	*Sāratthasālinī nāma Saccasamkhepa-vaṇṇanā*	Sāriputtassa sissena therena[37]
Gv 62,16	*Saccasaṅkhepassa ṭīkā*	Vācissara
Gv 75,19	*Saccasaṅkhepa-vivaraṇā*	unknown
Sās 34,7–9	*Saccasaṅkhepa-porāṇaṭīkā*	Vācissara
Sās 34,12f.	*Saccasaṅkhepābhinavaṭīkā*	araññavāsī thera
Piṭ-sm 322	*Saccasaṃkhip-ṭīkā-hoṅ: (porāṇaṭīkā)*	Vācissara
Piṭ-sm 323	*Saccasaṃkhip-ṭīkā-sac (navaṭīkā)* named *Sāratthasālini*	unknown mahāthera from Anurādhapura, Sri Lanka
Sās-dīp1225	*Saccasaṅkhepaganthassa pubbaṭīkā*	Vācissara mahāsāmipāda
Sās-dīp 1228	*Saccasaṅkhepaganthassa anuttaṭīkā*	thera araññavāsi
Thūp 255,3	*Saccasaṅkhepe atthadīpanā* (Pāli or Sinhalese)	Vācissara

In Burmese manuscripts regularly two *ṭīkās* on Sacc are handed down, an 'old' and a 'young' one. The old one (*hoṅ:*) corresponds to the *Vivaraṇa* identified by Cousins (unpublished),[38] the new one (*sac*) is the *Sāratthasālinī*.[39] According to Cousins's examination, the chronological order of these two commentaries is exactly the other way round. The *Vivaraṇa* is the younger, the *Sāratthasālinī* the older commentary.

None of the commentaries to Sacc is edited. In addition to the *Vivaraṇa*, which is not considered here, the *Sāratthasālinī* is in our hands in manuscript form. It begins with three introductory verses:[40]

37. In v. 37 it is added that precisely this thera who is characterized as *sāsanujjotanatthinā*, wrote many small treatises as well *(anekā khuddakā ganthā racitā sāmanoramā)*. This line is literally identical with a line in the colophon of the *Sāratthasālinī* (Sacc-ṭ), and it, therefore, is highly likely that the author of the Saddhamma-s borrowed it from the colophon of this text.

38. Whether this *Vivaraṇa* is identical with the one listed in Gv, is unclear.

39. Cousins based himself on the manuscript in the British Library, IO Man/Pali 121, transliterated by Helmer Smith (B^{m1}). The two Sacc *ṭīkās* in the U Pho Thi collection confirm this observation.

40. The translation is mine, but based on Cousins (unpublished).

Sāratthasālinī, Ganthārambha

	Text	*Translation*
1	Buddhaṃ saddhammapajjotaṃ Dhammaṃ Buddhappaveditaṃ Saṅghañ ca sirasā vande sammāsambuddhasāvakaṃ. **d** °sādhakaṃ B^{m2}	I offer reverence with my head to the Buddha, light of the true Dhamma, to the Dhamma made known by the Buddha, and to the Community of the disciples of the Fully Awakened One.
2	kato yo Saccasaṅkhepo nipuṇatthavinicchayo Ānandatherapādena vicittanayamaṇḍito **d** °paṇḍito B^{m2}	I will comment on the *Sacca-saṅkhepa*, an Exegesis of subtle meanings, adorned with manifold methods, which was compiled by the eminent Elder Ānanda, having been requested by the wise forest-dweller, the Elder Sāriputta,[41] who loves the rules of training.
3	tam ahaṃ vaṇṇayissāmi sikkhākāmena dhīmatā therena Sāriputtena yācito 'raññavāsinā. **a** vaṇṇavaṇṇayissāmi B^{m2}	

The first verse contains the homage to the triple gem. The second mentions the *mūla*-text to be commented upon, and its author, Ānanda (see above, n. 4). Dhammakitti, when writing his Saddhamma-s, obviously had access to this commentary, since this second introductory verse appears verbatim in Saddhamma-s 9.16 (as already Cousins, unpublished). Finally, the third verse states that the author has been asked to comment on the *Saccasaṅkhepa* by the forest dweller Sāriputta Thera, who loves the rules of training, in other words the *Vinaya*.

What strikes immediately is that Sāriputta is mentioned here as a forest-dweller (he normally is considered a *gāmavāsin*[42]), and only with the title *thera*. There is no mention of him being a *mahāsāmi* (a position restricted to a single monk at a time, which he received between 1165 and 1186 CE, Rohanadeera 1985, 30). If our assumption that this Sāriputta is the author's teacher is correct, and if the mention as a *thera* is not due to metrical reasons, the writing of this commentary should have been begun before Sāriputta moved to the highest rank (i.e. *mahāsāmi*) of the *saṅgha* of the island (but see Conclusions, pp. 237ff.).

41. It is to be assumed that this Sāriputta is the famous Sāriputta of Poḷonnaruva, because he is also mentioned in the colophon as the author's teacher.

42. Liyanagamage (1968, 92) states that Sāriputta belonged to the *gāmavāsins*, but he also refers to the fact that in the *Saddharmaratnākaraya* (313, 33) his affiliation is given as *vanavāsī*. Liyanagamage considers this a fault. Given that in the above case a direct pupil of Sāriputta describes him as a forest dweller, this should be reconsidered. Liyanagamage (1968, 92, n. 4) also hints at the statement of Degammäda Sumanajoti Thera that such affiliations changed. This should in fact be considered, since we also have descriptions of monks as 'permanent forest dwellers' (*sadāraññavāsin*), as for instance Sumaṅgala, another pupil of Sāriputta, indicating that there may have been monks who constantly remained forest dwellers, while others switched between the two lifestyles. Since Sāriputta was a pupil of Mahākassapa who was a forest dweller living at Udumbaragiri, it should not be excluded that he was a forest-dweller in his early years, before he moved to the Jetavanavihāra built for him by King Parakkamabāhu I in Poḷonnaruva some time after 1165 CE.

The commentary ends with a colophon of nineteen verses, which seems to have been added in two rounds. First nine verses, appended by a pupil or, eventually the author (?), and then further ten verses, possibly supplemented by a pupil.[43]

Sacc-ṭ, Colophon

The first nine verses of the colophon form one unit which ends with the wish that the *Saccasaṅkhepavaṇṇanā* may last long. This unit contains information on the author's teacher, Sāriputta, and on the author himself. Though not formulated in the first person, similarities with the introductory verses of Vin-vn-ṭ suggest that these first nine verses could have been written by the author himself.[47]

The colophon begins with a description of Sāriputta *mahāsāmi*, the author's teacher (vv. 1–3), who is mentioned by referring to his resemblance with the Buddha's pupil, Sāriputta. This is reminiscent of Sāriputta's mention in Vin-vn-ṭ, which also is by an indirect reference to this pupil (v. 5; see p. 214). Regarding Sacc-ṭ itself there is a discrepance between the mention of Sāriputta *mahāsāmi* in the colophon, and Sāriputta *thera* in the introduction (v. 3; see p. 214). This could be explained if Sacc-ṭ was begun early and completed later. Exactly this is what Cousins suggests, based on the second part of the colophon and on his investigation of the text. According to that the author quotes from Sumaṅgala's *Abhidhammatthasaṅgahaṭīkā* and Sāriputta's *Abhidhammatthasaṅgahasannaya* only in the first three chapters, but not in the latter. And while he refers rarely to other post-Buddhaghosa sources in the first two chapters he begins to quote from a number of Abhidhamma manuals with the third chapter, suggesting that the author completed it with more books/manuscripts at his disposal.

Sāriputta is further described as being well versed in the canonical texts, and in grammar,[48] etc. (v. 2), and as having written a *ṭīkā* to the *Vinaya*, etc.,[49] and to another work[50] (v. 3). In Vin-vn-ṭ *ṭīkā*s to the *Vinaya* and the *Aṅguttaraṭṭhakathā* are mentioned (v.6; see p. 214).

43. Text and readings have been taken over from Cousins (unpublished). Cousins had access to two more manuscripts, not available to me. The translation is mine, but based on the one in Cousins (unpublished). Divergences from Cousins' translation are especially in vv. 5, 10, 16–17. Vv. 16f. are problematic, and my translation is tentative too.

44. (opposite page) Probably a reference to the Jotisattha mentioned in Vin-vn-ṭ v. 6.

45. (page 228) It seems that the learned lay follower Dhammakitti is the same as the famous person called Kūṭāpuravatī; at least the repetition of the word *paṇḍita* here gives this impression. Or are these two different persons, Kūṭāpuravatī who made the abode, and the learned (i.e. Dhammakitti) who supported him with requisites?

46. (page 228) The compound is unclear. There are several variants, but more manuscripts are needed. It could also stand for *āciṇṇa-citt'* (or *vitt'*)*-ociṇṇākhyo*, etc.

47. The verses are formulated, however, in the third person, not in the first. In addition the author is highly praised as 'a great sage reckoned supreme as Suneru is reckoned unshaken by wind' (v. 4), which gives reason to doubt that these verses were written by the author himself. On the other hand the first three verses are very similar to the introductory verses of Vin-vn-ṭ.

48. For his grammatical expertise, see Dimitrov 2010, 31ff.

49. The *ṭīkā* hinted at by 'etc.' refers to his *Aṅguttaraṭṭhakathāṭīkā*.

50. This, probably corresponds to the *jotisattha* of Vin-vn-ṭ (v. 6, p. 214).

Sacc-ṭ, Colophon

	Text	Translation
1	mahāsāmisamaññāya vissuto yati-puṅgavo Sāriputtamahātherakappo nāmaguṇehi yo **a** °sāmisaññāya B^{m3} **b** vissuto HS; visuto B$^{m1.2}$ vibhūto B^{m3}; °paṅkavo B^{m3}	A leader of monks, renowned for his title 'Great master' (*mahāsāmi*), in name and qualities resembling the great Elder (*mahāthera*) Sāriputta (i.e. the Buddha's pupil),
2	piṭakesu ca sabbattha saddasatthādikesu ca pārappatto mahāpañño jotento Jina-sāsanaṃ **b** satt° B$^{m2.3}$	one who had achieved mastery in every respect both in the 'baskets' (i.e. the canonical texts) and in grammatical and other textbooks,[44] one of great wisdom, who makes the Victor's *sāsana* shine,
3	Vinayaṭṭhakathādīnaṃ ṭīkaṃ satthantarassa ca akāsi, tassa yo sisso piṭakattayapāragū **a** °naya-aṭṭhakathādinaṃ B^{m3} **b** tikaṃ B^{m2}; tikā or ṭīkā B^{m3}; satta° B^{m3} **c** akāsi tatth' assa yo piṭaka- B^{m2}	composed a subcommentary (*ṭīkā*) both to the commentaries to the *Vinaya*, etc., and to a scientific treatise of a different kind. His pupil (i.e. the author of Sacc-ṭ), who had gained mastery of the three baskets,
4	vātādhutākhya-Sunerupara-mākhyamahāmuni mahato bhikkhusaṅghassa piṭakattaya-vaṇṇanaṃ **a** vātarutākhyadhuṇeru B^{m3} **b** hāramajjha° B^{m3}	a great sage reckoned supreme as Suneru is reckoned unshaken by wind, made an explanation (*vaṇṇanā*) to the three baskets for the great community of monks;
5	akāsi Tambapaṇṇimhi garubhāvañ ca rājunaṃ ṭīkā ca racitā yena Vinayassa vinicchaye **a** akāsi akāsi HS, Tampaṇṇimhi HS Tampapaṇṇi B^{m3} **b** Mss: rājūnaṃ **d** viyassa° B^{m3}	and he carried out the state of a teacher of kings in Tambapaṇṇi; and composed a commentary (*ṭīkā*) to the Exegesis of the *Vinaya* (*Vinaya-vinicchaya*),
6	Nāmarūpaparicchedavaṇṇanā ca samāsato Mahākaccāyanattheraracitassa samiddhiyā **c** Makaccā° B^{m3} **d** racittassa B^{m3}	and an explanation (*vaṇṇanā*) in brief of the *Nāmarūpapariccheda*; he successfully composed a *Padarūpa-vibhāvana* to the grammar composed by the Elder Mahākaccāyana, [and], desirous to illuminate the *sāsana*, composed many small books
7	racitaṃ saddasatthassa Padarūpa-vibhāvanaṃ aneke khuddakā ganthā sāsanujjotana-tthinā **a** °satta° B^{m3} **b** °vibhāvinaṃ B^{m3} **c** vandhā B^{m3}	
8	sāsanujjotanatthīnaṃ racitā buddhi-vuddhiyā, tenācariyapādena sucisīlanivutt<h>inā **b** Buddha- B$^{m1.2}$ **c** senācariyapādena caritassa nirutti B^{m3}	for the sake of increase in understanding for those desirous to illuminate the *sāsana*. That eminent teacher, [being] wise [and] dwelling with pure virtue, composed this explanation (*vaṇṇanā*) to the *Saccasaṅkhepa* too. May it last long in the world, accomplishing the benefit of mankind.
9	dhīmatā racitāyam pi Saccasaṅkhepa-vaṇṇanā. ciraṃ vattatu lokamhi sādhentī jana-tāhitaṃ. **c** tatthatu B^{m3} **d** °dhenti B^{m3}	

10	āraddhā Jambudoṇimhi kānane vasatā satā; vasatā tilakuyyāne nivāsena manorame **b** kānana° B^{m3} **c** thilaka° B^{m3} **d** nipāsena-manoramme B^{m3} panorammaṇe B^{m2}	[The *Saccasaṅkhepavaṇṇanā*] was begun by that good man when he was dwelling in a grove at Jambudoṇi (Daṁbadeṇiya); his pupil, while dwelling in the Tilaka Park which is delightful by means of [its] habitation(?), the learned (*paṇḍita*) lay follower, knowledgable as to methods, bearing the name that praises (*kittana*) the fame (*kitti*) produced by praising the Dhamma (i.e. Dhammakitti 'Fame of the Dhamma'), having requested him [to complete this commentary?], conducted him to the fine city of Salaḷī/Suḷali. In the very delightful Tilaka Park, the abode of forest dwellers,
11	Dhamma-kittanasañjāta-kitti-kittana-saññinā upāsakena sissena paṇḍitena nayaññunā **a** °sañcāta° B^{m3} **b** °saññītā B^{m3} **cd** ūpāsako ti *for pādas cd*	
12	ajjhesitvā samānīto Salaḷī-nagaraṃ varaṃ suramme tilakuyyāne nivāse 'raññavāsinaṃ **b** Suḷali° B^{m3} **c** tirākuyyāne B^{m3} **d** raññavāsinā B^{m3}	
13	yatinaṃ pīyasīlānaṃ dhutaṅgādi-guṇesinaṃ Kūṭāpuravatī nāma vissutena yasassinā **bc** omitted B^{m3}	of monks of pleasing conduct who seek such qualities as the *dhutaṅga*s, the famous one who is renowned under the name of Kūṭāpuravatī,
14	sāsanodayakāmena visālakulaketunā vassāvāsattham ajjhiṭṭho paccayehi upaṭṭhito **b** visālakutatetu° B^{m3} **c** vassāvāsa° $B^{m1.3}$, vāsāvāsa° HS, vasāvāsa° B^{m2} °ttaṃ B^{m3}	desirous of the rise of the *sāsana*, head of an extensive kin, requested him to stay in the rains residence [and] provided him with requisites.
15	ten' eva kārite ramme viharanto nivesane paṇḍitenāpi ten' eva yathābalam upaṭṭhito **a** so $B^{m1.3}$, rammaṇe B^{m2}, kamme HS **d** yathāphalaṃ B^{m3}	Dwelling in the delightful abode, which had been built by that same [Kūṭāpuravatī], he was supported also by that same learned (*paṇḍita*) [person] according to his ability[45]
16	sappāyapaccayoghena appamattena paccayaṃ samajjhiṭṭho samāpetuṃ yato saṃvaṇṇanaṃ imaṃ. **b** paccayo yena B^{m3} **c** samijjhisemijjhiṭṭho° B^{m3} **c** sapāsetuṃ or sahasetuṃ B^{m3}	with a small flood of suitable requisites; while relying [on it?] (*paccayaṃ*), he then (?) was thoroughly requested to complete this explanation (*saṃvaṇṇanā*).
17	ācinnacitto cinnākhyo aṅganāyaka-potthaki susamiddhāya saddhāya pasanno Buddhasāsane **a** °vitto $B^{m1.2}$, ādinacittodinakhyalyā B^{m3} **b** °potthakaṃ B^{m3} **c** saddhāya omitted in B^{m3} **d** pasannenā B^{m3}	The superintendent (*potthaki*) and head (*nāyaka*) of a subordinate division (? *aṅga*) with his habitually engaged mind (?) called the habitually engaged (? *ciṇṇa*),[46] because of [his] magnificent faith is one trusting (*pasanno*) in the *sāsana* of the Awakened One;
18	upaṭṭhahanto sakkaccaṃ paccayehi yathābalaṃ ajjhesanaṃ yato 'kāsi samāpetum atho imaṃ. **b** °phalaṃ $B^{m2.3}$ **d** samāsetum B^{m3}, ano B^{m2} ato B^{m3}	since, while providing [the author] with requisites in the proper way to his capacity, he made the request to then complete this [explanation],
19	tato 'yaṃ vaṇṇanā sammā Buddhasāsana-vuddhiyā catūhi ganthasahassehi sādhikehi samāpitā ti. **c** em. to catu; vandha° B^{m3} **d** sādhite B^{m3} samāpite B^{m2}, ti om. in B^{m3}	therefore this explanation (*vaṇṇanā*) was perfectly completed for the growth of the *sāsana* of the Awakened One with [the aid of] more than four thousand books.

The colophon then switches to Sāriputta's pupil, the author of Sacc-ṭ, who was a:

1. holder of the title *piṭakattayapāragū* (v. 3); The title *piṭakattayapāragū*, 'one who gained mastery of the three *Piṭakas*', is rare. Three other references are known: two in Vācissara's *Thūpavaṃsa*, as title of the person who asked Vācissara to write the *Thūpavaṃsa* and as Vācissara's[51] own title (Thūp 254f., vv. 153, 161); one in the *Mahāvaṃsa*, as a characterization of the monks fetched from present day Burma by Vijayabāhu I (1059–1114 CE) to bring a valid ordination lineage to Sri Lanka (Mhv 60.6).
2. author of commentaries (*vaṇṇanā*) to all three baskets of canonical writings (v. 4); The author's commentaries (*vaṇṇanā*) to all three baskets of canonical writings (*piṭakattayavaṇṇanaṃ*) are unknown.
3. teacher of kings in Tambapaṇṇi (v. 5) (Cousins 2013, 23ff.); This statement reminds one of the information in the colophon to Thūp that Vācissara was in charge of king Parakkamabāhu's preaching hall (*dhammāgāra*, Thūp 255, v. 161). A *dhammāgāra* is a place to which the king went to pay homage to the Buddha, listen to the Buddhist teaching, and so on.[52] Being responsible for a king's preaching hall could well be understood as holding the office of a king's teacher. Since in the present colophon the plural of 'king' is used, Cousins (unpublished) assumes that the author of Sacc-ṭ was the teacher of Vijayabāhu III as well as of Parakkamabāhu II.
4. author of a *ṭīkā* to the *Vinayavinicchaya* (v. 5); His authorship of a *tīkā* to Vin-vn, is to be related to the *Vinayasāratthasālinī*, since it is asserted in Vin-vn-ṭ and in Sacc-ṭ that the author was a pupil of Sāriputta. The probability that the pupil mentioned in Vin-vn-ṭ and the one mentioned in Sacc-ṭ as author of Vin-vn-ṭ, were two different pupils of Sāriputta writing *ṭīkās* to the same Vin-vn is remote. This mention further suggests that Vin-vn-ṭ was written before Sacc-ṭ. The comparison of a passage from the introduction of both commentaries makes one think otherwise (below, pp. 233ff.). But the problem is solved if we take into consideration that the introductory verses and the first three chapters of Sacc-ṭ were written early while the final chapters and the colophon were composed later. Vin-vn-ṭ then could have been written in between the two parts of Sacc-ṭ. This would fit in with the information from the extended colophon, from the character of Sacc-ṭ, and from the comparison of both commentaries.
5. author of a commentary (*vaṇṇanā*) to the *Nāmarūpapariccheda* (v. 6); No commentary to the *Nāmarūpapariccheda* is printed. In the Burmese manuscript catalogue of the U Pho Thi collection an old (*hoṅ:*) and a new (*sac*) *ṭīkā* to the *Nāmarūpapariccheda* are listed.[53] These two commentaries turn out to be one and the same. Further, this commentary contains neither

51. The name of the author of Thūp is proved to be Vācissara *therapāda* in the colophon of this text (Thūp v. 162).

52. See the detailed description of Parakkamabāhu I's *dhammāgāra* in Mhv 73.81; see also Kieffer-Pülz (forthcoming), n. 94.

53. U Pho Thi Ms. 526.4 (*hoṅ:*) and 528.4 (*sac*).

an introduction nor a colophon. In Gv (62,11–13) a *Nāmarūpaparicchedassa ṭīkā* or *vibhāgo* is listed as written by Vācissara on his own accord.[54] In Sās 34,7–9 and Piṭ-sm 313 this appears as *Nāmarūpaparicchedaporāṇaṭīkā* by Vācissara. Piṭ-sm 312, further, reports a new *ṭīkā* by some unknown *thera* from Anurādhapura. Sās-dīp (v.1213) lists an explanation (*vaṇṇanā*) of the *Nāmarūpapariccheda* by Vācissara *mahāsāmipāda*. Without an examination of the contents of the preserved *ṭīkā* nothing more can be said.

6. author of a *Pādarūpavibhāvanā* to Kaccāyana's grammar (vv. 6–7); The *Pādarūpavibhāvanā* to Kaccāyana's grammar is not at hand. In Gv a *Saddatthassa Pādarūpavibhānaṃ* or *Padarūpavibhāvanaṃ* is mentioned immediately after the *Nāmarūpaparicchedaṭīkā* written by Vācissara on his own accord (Gv 62,11ff.; 71,31ff.; see n. 54). This sequence of texts corresponds to the one in Sacc-ṭ. Probably the author of Gv had access to the colophon of Sacc-ṭ. In Saddhamma-s, Piṭ-sm, Sās and Sās-dīp this work is not listed. The identification of the *Padarūpavibhāvana* as a commentary to the *Nāmarūpapariccheda* by Malalasekera probably goes back to a misreading of Gv.[55]
7. author of the *Saccasaṅkhepavaṇṇanā* (v. 9). A number of commentaries to Sacc are listed (see above, p. 224). As authors are mentioned either Vācissara or a monk who was a forest dweller. The colophon of Vācissara's Thūp contains a list of works written by its author. It mentions among others an 'Illumination of the Meaning' (*atthadīpanā*) to Sacc. Vācissara states that he had written this text and the *Visuddhimaggasaṅkhepaṭīkā* in Sinhalese[56] or from Sinhalese, in other words based on a Sinhalese version,[57] which would mean he translated them into Pāli.[58] A *Visuddhimaggasaṅkhepaṭī*kā in Pāli is mentioned in Piṭ-sm (233), but admittedly without an author being named.

The mention of Vācissara as author of a commentary to Sacc in the Pāli literary histories, and of Vācissara's statement in Thūp that he wrote a commentary to Sacc

54. Gv E^e 62,11–13: *Nāmarūpaparicchedassa ṭīkā saddatthassa padarūpavibhānaṃ*; Gv E^e 71,31–34: *Nāmarūpaparicchedassa vibhāgo* (B^e; E^e *om.*; N^e *ṭīkā*), *padarūpavibhāvanaṃ ... attano matiyā Vācissarena katā.*

55. Probably the missing *ṭīkā* in Gv E^e led to this assumption (*DPPN* s.v. Padarūpavibhāvana).

56. Jayawickrama (Thūp 145) understands the text as 'compiled in the Sīhaḷa language'; Wickremasinghe (1900, 142) describes them as *sannayas*. Thus, both clearly grasp them as Sinhalese commentaries.

57. '[F]or him who, being possessed of the knowledge of the Dhamma, likewise carefully produced well the commentary on the (book) *Saccasaṅkhepa* from the Sinhalese language, for him who, for the benefit of the saints made the commentary on the *Visuddhimaggasaṅkhepa* from the Sinhalese language' (Thūp trans. Law, 97)

58. Thūp 255 (vv. 159f.): *atthadīpanā ... sukatā yena suṭṭhu Sīhaḷabhāsato* '[He], by whom was thoroughly well compiled the illuminator of the meaning in the Sīhaḷa language (or: from the Sīhaḷa language)'. It is well known that the ablative in *-to* can be used in a locative sense (von Hinüber 1968, § 194, only the ablative in *-to*). For an example of this usage, see *Rasavāhinī-porāṇaṭīkā* 1, 1,24: *hitāya parivattesi pajānaṃ Pālibhāsato*, 'translated this (original compilation of the ancient teachers) into the Pāli language for the benefit of the people' (Matsumura 1992, XXXV). See also the discussion in Matsumura 1992, li, n. 1.

requires a comparison of the data given for both authors. The similarity is conspicuous. They bear the same epithet (*piṭakattayagū*), both were teachers of kings, both wrote commentaries to Sacc, and in both texts the still uncommon title *therapāda* is used (Kieffer-Pülz forthcoming, § 4). In Thūp it is applied to Vācissara himself, in Sacc-ṭ to the author of Sacc. Eventually the introduction of the word °*pāda* as a last part of titles that comes into fashion in Sri Lanka with the beginning of the thirteenth century CE,[59] has to do with the fact that, starting with the restructuring of the hierarchy of the *saṅgha* connected to the Daṁbadeṇiya period, the title *mahāthera* was no longer freely available to designate eminent monks.[60] Because from then on the term *mahāthera* was restricted to the two heads of the *arañña-* and *gāmavāsin* respectively, who ranked next after the *mahāsāmi*, the head of the entire *saṅgha*. At least this would explain the sudden emergence of titles with °*pāda*. That Vācissara is termed *therapāda*, therefore, can be considered as another way to express his eminence. The fact that he was responsible for the king's preaching hall (*dhammāgāra*), and thus also had to teach the Buddhist doctrine to the king, and the fact that it is stated that among his *antevāsikabhikkhus* the *sāsana* was well established (Thūp 255, v. 162), leads to the assumption that he had major responsibilities, and was an already somewhat older and mature personality. If this Vācissara is identical with the author of Sacc-ṭ, then Thūp would postdate Sacc-ṭ.

Concerning the second part of the colophon of Sacc-ṭ (vv. 10 to 19) it deals largely with the author's lay supporter, and the latter's attempts to make the author complete this commentary. Sacc-ṭ was begun (*āraddhā*) in a forest at Jambudoṇi (Daṁbadeṇiya), the royal city built by Vijayabāhu III (1232–1236 CE). If this implied that Jambudoṇi was already built as a capital it would imply that Sacc-ṭ was begun after 1232 CE. This also would narrow down the time window for the compilation of Vin-vn-ṭ and Utt-vn-ṭ considerably (between some time after 1232 and some time before 1245 CE). The differentiation in Sāriputta *thera* in the beginning of Sacc-ṭ and Sāriputta *mahāsāmi* in the first part of the colophon of Sacc-ṭ, interpreted as a sign for an early beginning of Sacc-ṭ, and its completion at a later time after some break (see above, pp. 225ff.), would then be meaningless. The colophon proceeds to describe that the author of Sacc-ṭ was invited and conducted to the unknown town of Salalī or Suḷali by his pupil, the *upāsaka* Dhammakitti *paṇḍita*, who himself lived in the likewise unknown Tilaka Park (v. 10). The text states that the author was asked something by his pupil, but does not inform us what he was asked. In the light of the subsequent verses it was probably a request to complete Sacc-ṭ.

In the Tilaka Park, a residence of forest dwellers, an abode was built for the author by the famous person called Kūṭāpuravatī, who invited him to spend the rains there, and who supported him with requisites. This person, described as head of an extensive kin (*visālakulaketu*), is probably identical with the *upāsaka* Dhammakitti, since he is characterized as *paṇḍita* (v. 15) too, and requests the author to complete the

59. The earliest reference known to me is the one in Dhammakitti's *Dāṭhāvaṃsa* (151, v. 4) dated to 1211.

60. This structure is described in the *Daṁbadeṇi katikāvata*, but it cannot be excluded that its formation began earlier.

commentary to Sacc-ṭ (v. 16). In v. 17 the supporter is mentioned with the unknown title *aṅganāyakapotthaki*. *Potthaki* (connected with *potthaka*, 'book') often appears as a last member of titles, is understood as 'commander', and may denote members of the account office in the financial department according to Geiger (1986, 138). *Nāyaka* is another title appearing as a last member of various titles especially of officers in the army (Geiger 1986, 142f.). Finally, *aṅga* may describe some subordinate division (CPD s.v. [2]aṅga 2b). Eventually this *aṅganāyakapotthaki* had something to do with the provision of the author with the large number of books or manuscripts he is said to have had at his disposal in the Tilaka park, namely more than 4,000 (v. 19). In the reign of Parakkamabāhu I there were several Kitti-s as generals or ministers. One Kitti is exclusively designated as *ādipotthakī* (Mhv 72.27,160), *bhaṇḍārapotthakī* (Mhv 72.82) and *jīvitapotthakī* (Mhv 74.90; Geiger 1929, 321, n. 4). Geiger considered the possibility that he was a superintendent of the royal store rooms. The title *aṅganāyakapotthaki* of the Sacc-ṭ colophon is not found elsewhere. The *aṅganāyakapotthaki* is described as *ācinnacittocinna* (v.l. *ādinacittodinakhyalyā*). He is characterized as trusting in the Buddha's *sāsana* because of his magnificent faith. He supported the author with requisites to his capacity (v. 18) which is a repetition of what was said in v. 15 with respect to Kūṭāpuravatī. And here again it is stated that he asked the author to complete the commentary (v. 18) which repeats what was said in connection with the *upāsaka* Dhammakitti *paṇḍita* (v. 12), and with the famous Kūṭāpuravatī (v. 16). We thus can assume that vv. 10–19 deal with the lay supporter of the author, who as an *upāsaka* was called Dhammakitti; who as a head of his family was known as Kūṭāpuravatī, and who had the office of an *aṅganāyakapotthakī*, in connection with which he was called Ācinnacittocinna (?). If this interpretation is correct, the lay disciple Dhammakitti *paṇḍita* should be a mature personality that has reached the peak in his personal as well as professional life, and had at his disposal sufficient means to support the author of Sacc-ṭ even with the more than 4,000 books (*gantha*) mentioned in the final verse.

It can thus be taken as proven that the authors of Vin-vn-ṭ, Utt-vn-ṭ and Sacc-ṭ were one and the same, based on the information given in their introductory and concluding passages. It is evident that this author was a pupil of Sāriputta, and that the lay disciple Dhammakitti *paṇḍita* played a major role for the author. It is highly likely that he wrote Vin-vn-ṭ and Utt-vn-ṭ between 1210/1220 and 1245, and finished Sacc-ṭ after Vin-vnṭ.

Similarities between the author of Sacc-ṭ and the author of Thūp, which was written by a Vācissara Therapāda, suggest that Thūp may have been written by the same author too. If that is correct the author of all four works would be identified as Vācissara Thera. Such an identification is found for the author of Utt-vn-ṭ in a fifteenth-century source from present day Northern Thailand, and for all texts in Gv. If the *upāsaka* Dhammakitti *paṇḍita* mentioned in Vin-vn-ṭ and Sacc-ṭ were to be the same as the one mentioned together with a Vāgissara *ācariya* in the *Mahāvaṃsa*, we would even have proof of the thirteenth century for the name of the author. But this identification meets chronological problems (see below).

2. Comparison of *Vinayavinicchayaṭīkā* and *Saccasaṅkhepaṭīkā*

The information to be gained from the introductory and concluding portions of the three commentaries proves that Vin-vn-ṭ, Utt-vn-ṭ and Sacc-ṭ were written by the same author. In the following I am going to compare two passages in Vin-vn-ṭ and Sacc-ṭ which confirm this claim.

2.1 The introductory prose section

After the introductory verses Vin-vn-ṭ and Sacc-ṭ start with an introductory prose section which largely agrees except for quotations from the *mūla*-text. Utt-vn-ṭ does not share this section, but replaces it by the reference to Vin-vn-ṭ (above, n. 27).

Although many of the sub-commentaries from the twelfth century onwards start their commentaries with the explanation of the three jewels and the three reverential salutations (*paṇāma*) by body, speech and mind, none of the descriptions is identical with the one in Vin-vn-ṭ and Sacc-ṭ.[61] Therefore the agreement between the introduction of these two commentaries is conspicuous, especially because they comment on *mūla*-texts of different genres (Vinaya and Abhidhamma). In the following the text from Vin-vn-ṭ is reproduced. Portions identically transmitted in Sacc-ṭ are put in italics. Deviating readings of Sacc-ṭ are given in the notes. Underlined is a joint quotation from Sv. Bold indicates words quoted from the commented on text. It must be noticed that for Sacc-ṭ only one manuscipt was consulted for the present comparison.[62]

> Vin-vn-ṭ I 4,14–6,20 ≈ Sacc-ṭ B[m1] fols. ka v–ki r: *su*-vipulāmala-saddhā-paññādi-guṇa-samudayāvahaṃ sakala-janahitekahetu-jinasāsana-ṭṭhiti-mūla-bhūtaṃ vinayap*pakaraṇam*[63] *idam ārabhanto 'yam ācariyo* pakaraṇārambhe[64] *ratanattaya-ppaṇāma-pakaraṇābhidhānābhidheyya-karaṇa-ppakāra-payojana-nimitta*-kattu-parimāṇādīni[65] *dassetuṃ āha* **vanditvā**[66] *ti* (Vin-vn v. 1) *ādi. tattha ratanattayaṃ nāma.*
>
> [67-]"cittīkataṃ mahagghañ ca atulaṃ dullabha-dassanaṃ
> anomasatta-paribhogaṃ ratanaṃ tena vuccatī" ti (Sv II 443, 26f., etc.).
>
> niddiṭṭha-sabhāvaṃ
>
> "Buddho sabbaññutaññāṇaṃ dhammo lokuttaro nava
> Saṅgho maggaphalaṭṭho ca icc etaṃ ratanattayan" ti
>
> vibhāvita-ppabhedaṃ[-67] *sakala-bhava-dukkha-vinivāraṇaṃ tibhaven' ekapaṭisaraṇaṃ vatthuttayaṃ.*
>
> *tassa* **paṇāmo** *nāma paṇāma-kiriyā-nipphādikā cetanā. sā tividhā kāya-paṇāmo vacī-paṇāmo mano-paṇāmo ti.*
>
> *tattha* **kaya-paṇāmo** *nāma ratana-ttaya-guṇānussaraṇa-pubbikā añjali-kammādi-kāya-kiriyāvasa-ppavattikā kāya-viññatti-samuṭṭhāpikā cetanā.*

---

61. As-mūlaṭ 2f.; As-anuṭ,2f.; Mogg-p-ṭ 2,9ff.; Sp-ṭ I 2,21ff.; etc.

62. Since the text passage contains many long compounds I separate the words using hyphens for easier comparison of the similarities and dissimilarities of the two texts.

63. Sacc-ṭ *su*-nipuṇa-naya-vicittam acintiyānanta-sabbaññuta-ñāṇa-visayāsesa-ñeyya-dhammasaṅgāhakam *pakaraṇam*

64. Vin-vn-ṭ var. pakaraṇārabbhe; Sacc-ṭ paṭhaman tāva

65. Sacc-ṭ °-*nimittāni*

66. Sacc-ṭ **namassitvā** (Sacc v.1)

67. Sacc-ṭ rati-jananatthena citti-katādi-atthehi ca ratana-sammataṃ

vacī-paṇāmo *nāma tath' eva* pavattā *nānāvidha-guṇa-visesa-vibhāvana-*[68-]*sabhāva-thomanā-kiriyāvasa-ppavattikā*[-68] *vacī-viññatti-samuṭṭhāpikā cetanā.*

mano-paṇāmo *nāma ubhaya-viññattiyo asamuṭṭhāpetvā kevalaṃ guṇānussaraṇena citta-santānassa* tan-ninnata-ppoṇata-ppabbhāratāya *gārava-bahumānanavasa*[69]*-ppavatti-sādhikā cetanā.*

imassa tāva ratana-ttaya-paṇāmassa dassanaṃ yathādhippetattha-sādhanatthaṃ. guṇātisaya-yogena hi paṇāmārahe ratana-ttaye kato paṇāmo puñña-visesa[70]*-bhāvato icchitatthābhinipphatti-vibandhakena*[71] *upaghātakena, upapīḷakena*[72] *ca apuñña-kammena upanīyamānassa*[73] *upaddava-jālassa vinivāraṇena*[74] *yathāladdha-sampatti-nimittakassa*[75] *puñña-kammassa anubala-ppadānena ca tabbipākasantatiyā āyu-sukha-balādi-vaḍḍhanena* ca[76] *cira-kāla-ppavatti-hetuko ti yathādhippeta*[77]*-pakaraṇa-nipphatti-nibandhanako*[78] *hoti.*

*athā*pi[79] [80-]*sotūnañ* ca[-80] *vandanīya*[81]*-vandanā pubbakenārambhena anantarāyena uggahaṇa-dhāraṇādi-kkamena pakaraṇāvabodha-ppayojana-sādhanatthaṃ.*

api ca sotūnam eva viññāta-satthukānaṃ bhagavato yathābhūta[82]*-guṇa-visesānussavanena*[83] *samupajāta*[84]*-ppasādānaṃ pakaraṇe gāravuppādanatthaṃ, aviññāta-satthukānaṃ pana pakaraṇassa svākhyātatāya*[85] *tappabhave satthari gāravuppādanatthañ ca sotu-janānuggaham eva*[86] *padhānaṃ katvā ācariyehi ganthārambhe*[87] *thuti-*pp*aṇāma-paridīpakānaṃ*[88] gāthā-*vākyān*aṃ[89] [90-]*nikkh*epo vidhī*yati*[-90]. *itarathā vināpi tan nikkhepam kāya-mano-paṇāmen*āpi[91] *yathādhippeta-ppayojana-siddhito kim etena gantha-gārava-karenā*[92] *ti* (Sv-nṭ I 3) *ayam ettha saṅkhepo. vitthārato*[93] *pana* [94-]paṇāma-ppayojanaṃ

68. Sacc-ṭ °*sabhāvato thomana-kriyāvasa-ppavattā*
69. Sacc-ṭ °*bahumānavasa*°
70. Sacc-ṭ antarāyakarā-puñña-vighāta-kara-*puñña-visesa*°
71. Sacc-ṭ *vinibandhakena*
72. Sacc-ṭ *upapiḷikena*
73. Sacc-ṭ *upaniya*°
74. Sacc-ṭ *vinivārakena*
75. Sacc-ṭ °*nimittassa*
76. Sacc-ṭ om.
77. Sacc-ṭ *yathādhammeta-*°
78. Vin-vn-ṭ var. nibandhanako ti ettha nibandhanan ti mūlakāraṇaṃ; Sacc-ṭ *nibandhano*
79. Sacc-ṭ *atha* vā
80. Sacc-ṭ *sotūnaṃ*
81. Sacc-ṭ *vandaniya*°
82. Sacc-ṭ *yathābhucca-*°
83. Sacc-ṭ °-bh*avanena*
84. Sacc-ṭ *samūpa*°
85. Sacc-ṭ *svakkhāta*°
86. Sv-nṭ add *hi*
87. Sacc-ṭ *gandhā*°, Sv-nṭ saṃvaṇṇanārambhe
88. Sacc-ṭ Sv-nṭ °*-paridīpakāni*
89. Sacc-ṭ Sv-nṭ *vākyāni*
90. Sacc-ṭ Sv-nṭ *nikkhipiyanti*
91. Sv-nṭ °*paṇāmen' eva*
92. Sacc-ṭ *gandha-gārava-karaṇenā*
93. Sacc-ṭ *vitthāro*

Sāratthadīpaniyādīsu (Sp-ṭ I 2,21ff.) dassitanayen' eva ñātabbaṃ.[-94] ***abhidhāna**-kathanaṃ pana vohārasukhatthaṃ. **abhidheyyassa** samuditena pakaraṇena paṭipādetabbassa kathanaṃ pakaraṇassa*[95] *ārabhitabba*-sabh*āva*[96]*-dassanatthaṃ. viditāninditasātthaka-sukarānuṭṭhānābhidheyyam*[97] *eva hi pakaraṇaṃ* parikkhakajan*ā*[98] *ārabhitabbaṃ maññantī ti.* ***karaṇa-ppakāra**-sandassanaṃ sotu-jana-samussāhanatthaṃ.*[99] [100-]anākulam asaṃkiṇṇatādi-ppakārena hi *viracitaṃ*[-100] *pakaraṇaṃ "sotāro sotum ussahantī" ti.* ***payojana**-kathanaṃ pana pakaraṇajjhāyane sotu-jana-samuttejanatthaṃ. asati hi payojana-kathane aviññāta-ppayojanā ajjhāyane byāvaṭā na hontī ti.* ***nimitta**-kathanaṃ sarikkhaka-janānaṃ pakaraṇe gāravu-ppādanatthaṃ. pasattha*[101]*-kāraṇuppanne yeva* hi *pakaraṇe sarikkhakā*[102] *gāravaṃ janentī ti.*

2.2 Second parallel between Vin-vn-ṭ and Sacc-ṭ

The following parallel follows immediately after the preceding in Sacc-ṭ whereas in Vin-vn-ṭ there is a larger text portion in between. Vin-vn-ṭ is much more elaborate in this passage, but it can be easily recognized that the way of commenting follows the same structure in both commentaries. Identical passages are put in italics. Bold indicates words quoted from the commented on text.

Though this second parallel is less close than the first, it shows a similar structure used in writing these two commentaries, which is not traced in the same identity of structure and wording in other commentaries. Since the *mūla*-texts belong to different genres the author of Vin-vn-ṭ could not have borrowed the text simply from Sacc-ṭ (the early parts of which predate Vin-vn-ṭ), but he applied the same structure for Vin-vn-ṭ. This thus confirms that Vin-vn-ṭ and Sacc-ṭ are most probably written by the same author.

2.3 Unique expressions

In addition to the similar structure visible in the second specimen quoted above there appear in that passage two expressions which are not traced elsewhere in the Pāli texts as far as searchable to date.[103] These are the terms *bāhira*- and *abbhantaranimitta*, used to differentiate between an external and an internal motive for writing a treatise. In explaining Buddhadatta's introduction of Vin-vn the author of Vin-vn-ṭ states that in Buddhadatta's words 'as one well grounded I will explain

94. Sacc-ṭ gandhabhirūka-janānuggahena nodāhaṭo
95. Sacc-ṭ *pakarassaṇassa*
96. Sacc-ṭ *ā*rambhaniya*bhāva-°*
97. Sacc-ṭ su*viditāninditā*s*ukarānu*tt*ānābhidheyyam*
98. Vin-vn-ṭ var., Sacc-ṭ *sarikkhaka°*
99. Sacc-ṭ *°samussāha*-janan*atthaṃ*
100. Sacc-ṭ atthāvirodhi-pubbācariya-matānurūpa-saṅkhepa-kkama-*viracitaṃ* hi
101. Sacc-ṭ *pasaṭṭha-°*
102. Sacc-ṭ *sarikkhaka*janā
103. The usage in Pālim-nṭ I 7,4f., where the author explains the *yogāvacarabhikkhūnaṃ* (Pālim 1,6) as *bāhiranimitta*, belongs to seventeenth-century Burma. Incidentally, instead of *abbhantaranimitta*, Tipiṭakālaṅkāra uses *ajjhatikanimitta* (ibidem).

Second parallel

Vin-vn-ṭ I 7,4ff.	*Sacc-ṭ B^m1 fol. ki r*
tattha[103] *paṭhamagāthāyaṃ*[104-]tāva **vanditvā** ti (Vin-vn v. 1a) iminā tividho pi *paṇāmo*[-104]avisesato *dassito.* visesato pana **seṭṭhaṃ, appaṭipuggalaṃ, bhavābhāvakaraṃ, niraṅgaṇan ti** (Vin-vn v. 1b–d) imehi catūhi padehi vacīpaṇāmo, **sirasā** ti (Vin-vn v. 1a) iminā kāyappaṇāmo, **buddhaṃ, dhammaṃ, gaṇañ cā** ti (Vin-vn 1b–d) imehi pana tīhi padehi paṇāmakiriyāya kammabhūtaṃ ratanattayaṃ dassitan ti daṭṭhabbaṃ.	ettha ca *pathamagāthāya* ratanattaya*paṇāmo dassito* || dutiyagāthāya abhidhānādīni ||
Vinayassa vinicchayan *ti* (Vin-vn v. 2d) *iminā abhidhānaṃ dassitaṃ* aluttasamāsena vinayavinicchayanāmassa dassanato.	**Saccasaṃkhepen** *ti* hi *iminā abhidhānaṃ dassitaṃ* ||
*tassa anvattha*bhāvena saddappavattinimittabhūtaṃ sakalenānena *pakaraṇena paṭipādetabbam abhidheyyam* pi ten' eva *dassitaṃ.*	*tassa* pana *anvattha*tāya samuditena *pakaraṇena* saccānaṃ *paṭipādetabba*bhāvadassanato *ābhidheyyañ* ca *dassitaṃ*
samāsenā ti (Vin-vn v. 2c) ca **anākulam asaṃkiṇṇaṃ madhuratthapadakkaman ti** (Vin-vn v. 3ab) ca etehi *karaṇappakāro dassito.* **hitatthāyā** ti (Vin-vn v. 2b) ca **paṭubhāvakaraṃ vinayakkame** ti (Vin-vn v. 3cd) **ca apāraṃ otarantānan** ti (Vin-vn v. 4a) ādinā ca *payojanaṃ.*	**nissāya** || pa || **atthāvirodhinan** ti (Sacc v. 2ab) iminā saccānaṃ saṅkhipitvā kathanākaradīpakena abhidhānena ca *karaṇappakāro dassito* || **hitan** ti (Sacc v. 2d) iminā *payojanaṃ*
bhikkhūnaṃ bhikkhunīnan ti (Vin-vn v. 4c) *iminā bāhiranimittaṃ dassitaṃ. abbhantaranimittaṃ pana* bāhiranimittabhūtabhikkhubhikkhuni-visayā *karuṇā,* sā *ācariyassa pakaraṇā*rambh*en' eva viññāyatī ti visuṃ na* vuttā. **pavakkhāmī** ti (Vin-vn v. 2c) iminā samānādhikaraṇa-bhāvena labbhamāno "ahan" ti suddhakattā sāmaññena dassito. visesato pana pakaraṇāvasāne: ... [here follows a longer text passage (Vin-vn-ṭ 7,25–11,23) which is omitted here]. *ti ayam ettha samudāyattho. ayaṃ pana avayavattho:*	**kārakayoginan** ti (Sacc v. 2d) *iminā bāhiranimittaṃ dassitaṃ* || *abbhantaranimitta*bhūtā *pana ācariyassa karuṇā pakaraṇen' eva viññāyatī ti visuṃ na* dassitā *ti ayam ettha samudāyattho* || *ayam pana avayavattho:*
seṭṭhaṃ appaṭipuggalaṃ buddhañ c' eva bhavābhāvakaraṃ dhammañ c' eva niraṅgaṇaṃ gaṇañ c' eva sirasā vanditvā bhikkhūnaṃ bhikkhunīnañ ca hitatthāya samāsena samāhito Vinayassa Vinicchayaṃ vakkhāmī *ti* (Vin-vn vv. 1–2) *yojanā*[105]. *tattha* **seṭṭhan** ti (Vin-vn v. 1) sabbe ime pasatthā ayam etesaṃ atisayena pasattho ti seṭṭho.	**tilokaggaṃ dhammañ ca gaṇañ ca namassitvā pubbācariyamataṃ nissāya Saccasaṅkhepaṃ vakkhāmī** *ti* (Sacc vv. 1–2) sambandho || *tattha* **namassitvā** ti (Sacc v. 1a) pubbakālakriyānidassanaṃ.

for the benefit of monks and nuns' (*bhikkhūnaṃ bhikkhunīnañ ca hitatthāya samāhito, pavakkhāmi,* Vin-vn v. 2ac) the external motive for writing the treatise is expressed by the words *bhikkhūnaṃ* and *bhikkhunīnaṃ* (Vin I 7,18f.). The internal motive, however, is the teachers compassion (*karuṇā*) which has the monks and nuns, forming the external motive, as its object (*bāhiranimittabhūtabhikkhubhikkhunivisayā*). This internal motive is not expressed separately, because it is perceived by the introduction of the treatise (*viññāyatī ti visuṃ na vuttā,* Vin-vn-ṭ I 7,19ff.).[107] Though there are slight divergences in the word order, Sacc-ṭ contains a very similar statement, saying that in the introduction of Sacc in the words 'for the benefit of the monks who are acting [in a positive way]' (*hitaṃ kārakayogīnaṃ*) the compound *kārakayogīnan* expresses the external motive for the writing of the treatise (*iminā bāhiranimittaṃ dassitaṃ*). And, similarly to the Vin-vn-ṭ, the author here declares that the compassion of the teacher which is the internal motive (*abbhantaranimittabhūtā pana ācariyassa karuṇā*) becomes visible through the treatise itself (*pakaraṇen' eva*), and thus is not shown separately (*viññāyatī ti visuṃ na dassitā,* B^{m1} fol. ki r). Thus, we see in these two commentaries on Vinaya and Abhidhamma respectively an identical commentarial structure, and exactly the same way of expressing the same ideas. None of the other commentaries known to me contains such a section.

The wording *viññāyatī ti visuṃ na vuttā/vuttaṃ/dassitā* though found here and there in a similar manner, has no exact literal correspondent in any other text,[108] and it only appears in the three commentaries dealt with here: Vin-vn-ṭ (I 7,21), Utt-vn-ṭ (Vin-vn-ṭ II 477,21) and Sacc-ṭ (fol. ki r).[109] It is thus typical of this author's writing style.

Conclusions

From the three commentaries dealt with here, the two on monastic law are proven to stem from the same author's pen by an intertextual link. The third commentary, Sacc-ṭ, is demonstrated to have been written by the same author too, via the information given in the first part of the colophon to Sacc-ṭ. This is confirmed by the agreement of an identical passage, and a similar structure in the introduction

104. (opposite page) Sacc-ṭ *ettha ca* for *t.*

105. (opposite page) Sacc-ṭ ratanattayapanāmo

106. (opposite page) *yojanā and samb*andho are used in the same way to show how a verse text is to be given in a prose sequence.

107. The author of Vin-vn-ṭ uses the term *bāhiranimitta* a second time, namely at the end of his explanation of the treatise, when commenting on the name Buddhasīhaṃ, Buddhadatta's pupil who had asked him to write the Vin-vn. He says that the Vin-vn's statement, 'the Vin-vn was compiled in honour of Buddhasīhā my pupil' (*Vinayassa vinicchayo Buddhasīhaṃ samuddissa mama saddhivihārikaṃ, kato,* Vin-vn v. 3176–8) stands for the external motive (*iminā bāhiranimittaṃ dassitaṃ,* Vin-vn II 395,20).

108. Nevertheless, similar expressions appear, for instance, Vibh-mūlaṭ 115 = Vism-mhṭ II 317 (*vuttanayen' eva viññāyatī ti na vutto ti veditabbo*); Saṅgharakkhita's Khuddas-nṭ 241,13f. (*niddesavasen' eva viññāyatī ti na idha visuṃ dassayissāma*).

109. The two passages from Vin-vn-ṭ and Sacc-ṭ are found above; the one in Utt-vn-ṭ (Vin-vn-ṭ II 477,21f.) runs as follows: *upalakkhaṇato eten' eva viññāyatī ti visuṃ na vuttan ti gahetabbaṃ.*

of Vin-vn-ṭ and Sacc-ṭ which, considering the different genres to which the texts belong, seem to be more than simply reused text; and by the agreement in terminology and wording of Vin-vn-ṭ, Utt-vn-ṭ and Sacc-ṭ.

The chronological sequence in which these texts were written is clear. Sacc-ṭ was begun first, and then interrupted. Vin-vn-ṭ and Utt-vn-ṭ – in this sequence – followed and then Sacc-ṭ was completed. This explains the more elaborate introduction of Vin-vnṭ compared to Sacc-ṭ, despite the fact that Vin-vn-ṭ is mentioned in the colophon of Sacc-ṭ, and thus precedes the latter in its final stage.

From the chronological point of view Vin-vn-ṭ is written after Parakkamabāhu II's *Nissandeha* which was written at the earliest between 1210/1220 CE. This text is quoted in Vin-vn-ṭ, if Vin-vn-ṭ is not an extended translation of the *Nissandeha*. Utt-vn-ṭ was brought to Pagan by Sīvali Thera according to the secondarily added colophon. If this is based on historical facts, it leads roughly to an approximate *terminus ante quem* of 1245 CE for the transport of Utt-vn-ṭ to present day Burma. Vin-vn-ṭ predates Utt-vn-ṭ. These two commentaries were thus written roughly between some time after ca. 1210/20 and some time before ca. 1245 CE. From Sacc-ṭ we learn that its author began this commentary while living in a glade in Jambudoṇi. If this refers to the city as a capital of Laṅka, the earliest date implied would be 1232, since this is when Vijayabāhu III built the capital. This would further narrow down the time window for Vin-vn-ṭ and Utt-vn-ṭ to some time after 1232, and before ca. 1245 CE. If the reference to Jambudoṇi is not to be understood as presupposing the existence of Jambudoṇi as a capital Sacc-ṭ could have begun much earlier. Then the mention of the teacher Sāriputta as a simple *thera* in the introduction (not yet *mahāsāmi*) could be understood as evidence that Sacc-ṭ was begun before Sāriputta became *mahāsāmi* (between 1165 and 1186 CE), that is very early in the Thera's career.

In several points the author of Sacc-ṭ shows similarities with the author of Thūp, who is Vācissara *therapāda* according to the text: (1) they have the same rare title (*piṭakattayapāragū*), (2) they are a king's teacher, (3) they have written a commentary to Sacc, and (3) they both use the still rare title *therapāda*. If these similarities are not taken as sheer coincidence, they could indicate common authorship. The author of all four texts would then be Vācissara, and Thūp would postdate Sacc-ṭ, since a commentary to Sacc is mentioned in Thūp. This again would make clear that the responsibility of Vācissara for the king Parakkamanarinda's *dhammagāra* (Thūp v. 161) can only refer to Parakkamabāhu II (1236–1271). From the time-frame, the author of Thūp also could have been the author of the *Sīmālaṅkārasaṅgaha*, in which the author's name also is explicitly given as Vācissara (Kieffer-Pülz forthcoming, § 4). This text could be subsumed under the many smaller texts mentioned for the author in Saddhamma-s.

A common feature of nearly all the texts looked at here, is that they are translations and compilations of earlier texts. Vin-vn-ṭ is explicitly mentioned as a translation from a Sinhalese commentary. Whether or not this Sinhalese commentary also covered the *Parivāra* section of the *Vinaya*, and thus also served as a template for Utt-vn is unknown. If the author of Thūp and Sacc-ṭ are the same, the information in Thūp that Vācissara wrote a Sacc-ṭ from a Sinhalese source, would hint in the same direction as in the case of Vin-vn-ṭ. Concerning Thūp it is explicitly mentioned in the introduction that its author used an earlier Pāli and an earlier Sinhalese *Thūpavaṃsa* (Thūp vv. 3–4 of the introduction). Regarding the *Sīmālaṅkārasaṅgaha*, it is qualified in the text itself as a versified version of an earlier prose text (Kieffer-Pülz forthcoming, § 1). Thus, for all texts discussed here — except for Utt-vn-ṭ — it is ascertained that the author relied on earlier scriptures.

The identification of the author of the three commentaries with Vācissara, because of the resemblance with the author of Thūp, would be confirmed for Utt-vn-ṭ in a fifteenth-century source from what is now Northern Thailand. The earliest reference for the relation to Vācissara for all texts would be the mention of Vāgissara and the *upāsaka* Dhammakitti *paṇḍita* in the *Mahāvaṃsa* (thirteenth century CE). The fact that this lay follower is mentioned there as *upāsaka* Dhammakitti *paṇḍita* just as in Vin-vn-ṭ and Sacc-ṭ makes likely the assumption that it is the same person. But this leads to chronological problems. If we assume that Vācissara was about thirty when he was sent to Rāmaññadesa by Parakkamabāhu I in 1165 CE, he would have been 75 or 85 in 1210 and 1220 respectively (earliest date for the completion of the *Nissandeha*), and 97 or 107 at the time of the begin of the reign of Vijayabāhu III. It would imply that he wrote Vin-vn-ṭ, Utt-vn-ṭ and Sacc-ṭ at the earliest when he was around eighty years of age.

As is well known, in 1215 Māgha invaded Laṅka and reigned there till Vijayabāhu III (1232 CE) came into power. The Mhv reports that monks under the leadership of a Vācissara *mahāthera* fled to South India in 1215. If that were the same Vācissara as the one mentioned earlier he would have been around eighty when Vijayabāhu III recalled the monks in 1232. Vācissara is not mentioned among those honoured by the king for their help. This already led Jayawickrama to assume that Vācissara had died in the meantime. The information that Sacc-ṭ was begun in Jambudoṇi presupposes that there was a settlement there. According to the information available, Jambudoṇi only came into being with Vijayabāhu III. But if Vācissara was already dead, when Vijayabāhu III honoured the returners from South India, he cannot be the one who wrote Sacc-ṭ when he lived in a forest at Jambudoṇi. If we accept this latter information, and if we also accept that Jambudoṇi did not exist before Vijayabāhu III, then the Vācissara sent to Rāmaññadesa, and the author of Sacc-ṭ cannot be the same.

If the Vācissara who went to South India when Māgha invaded Laṅka was another monk, he must have been at least 40 (because of the title *mahāthera*) in 1215, and about 57 at the time of his return. This could be combined with the information that Sacc-ṭ was begun in Jambudoṇi, even if the latter refers to the capital. Thus, we had to assume that there existed two pairs of a Vācissara *ācariya* and an *upāsaka* Dhammakitti *paṇḍita* which, given the widespread use of the name Kitti and Dhammakitti, is not entirely impossible.

In sum, it is highly likely that the author of Vin-vn-ṭ, Utt-vn-ṭ, and Sacc-ṭ was Vācissara, the pupil of Sāriputta, who also wrote Thūp. He wrote these texts more or less in the second quarter of the thirteenth century CE. Since Thūp and

Sīmālaṅkārasaṅgaha were written in the same time period, he could also be the author of the *Sīmālaṅkārasaṅgaha*. This text could be subsumed under the many smaller texts mentioned for the author in Saddhamma-s. This author could further be identical with the monk Vācissara mentioned in the *Mahāvaṃsa* as the one who fled to South India in 1215 CE. It is, however, problematic to assume that he is identical with the *ācariya* who was sent to Rāmaññadesa in 1165 together with the *upāsaka* Dhammakitti *paṇḍita*.

In the Pāli literary histories the works of the *thera*s Saṅgharakkhita and Vācissara are mixed up. In order to be able to trace specific vocabulary, idioms, syntactic constructions, structural features or content-specific peculiarities used for scholarly Pāli to a specific author, and therewith to a specific region and time, it is necessary to find out which texts were written by which authors. The present investigation of three texts to be safely attributed to Vācissara Thera complements an earlier contribution of mine, in which I investigated texts which could be safely attributed to Saṅgharakkhita Thera (Kieffer-Pülz 2017). Through these contributions two text corpora could be established which are definitely linked to each of these *thera*s. These text corpora can serve as a basis for an investigation of the vocabulary and style typical for each of them. And this again might possibly allow us to find out which of the other texts ascribed to them probably was written by one of them. Furthermore, the knowledge about the oeuvre of an author allows us to see the spectrum of topics covered by him, the usage of Sinhalese or Sanskrit templates in creating a Pāli text, and therewith the manner in which a Buddhist monk scholar worked at a given time in a certain place.

Acknowledgements

This contribution is an outcome of my work on Wissenschaftliches Pāli (Scholastic Pāli) at the Academy of Sciences and Literature, Mainz, promoted by Deutsche Forschungsgemeinschaft (German Research Foundation). While working on this topic I was in constant contact with the late L. S. Cousins who at that time examined the relation of the old and the new *ṭīkā* to the *Saccasaṅkhepa*. The question of authorship forced us to examine the same commentaries and ascriptions. Lance's paper, not yet finished when he died, is at my disposal, and in writing this article I made constant use of it. It is, however, planned to publish his paper in a not too distant future in the *Journal of the Pali Text Society*. I thank the Academy of Sciences and Literature, Mainz (Germany), for financing the typing into the computer of Helmer Smith's transcript of Sacc-ṭ (manuscript B^{m1}), and Alexander Wrona (Vienna) for meticulously undertaking this laborious task. Thanks also go to William Pruitt for providing me with scans of the manuscripts in the U Pho Thi collection, and to Dhammadinnā Bhikkhunī for reading the final version of this paper and providing me with corrections and suggestions despite her own many projects. Last, but by no means least, I thank Naomi Appleton and Peter Harvey for accepting my contribution to this volume, for checking and correcting my English, and for their editorial tasks. It goes without saying that all faults are my own responsibility.

Abbreviations

As-mūlaṭ	Ānanda, *Atthasālinī-mūlaṭīkā* (CSCD)
As-anuṭ	Dhammapāla, *Atthasālinī-anuṭīkā* (CSCD).
Bhpātgp	*Bhikṣuprātimokṣaya saha Gaṇṭhidīpaniya* (*Bhikkhupātimokkha sameta Gaṇṭhidīpanī*), edited by Payiyāgala Vimalaraṃsi Tissa, Alutgama: Saddhammappakāsa Press 2471 (1927). [The text is printed after the *Bhikkhupātimokkha*. The pagination starts anew with p. 1].
Childers	Robert Caesar, Childers. *A Dictionary of the Pali Language*. 4th impression, London: Kegan Paul, etc., 1909.
CPD	*A Critical Pāli Dictionary*, begun by V. Trenckner, edited by D. Andersen, H. Smith, H. Hendriksen, Vols. 1–3, Copenhagen 1924ff.
CPD 1948	Helmer Smith, *A Critical Pāli Dictionary. Epilegomena to volume I.* Copenhagen: Eijnar Munksgaard, 1948.
CSCD	Chaṭṭhasaṅgāyana CD-ROM, Version 3.0 (Igatpuri: Vipassana Research Institute, 1999).
Dāṭh	*The Daṭhávansa; or, the History of the Tooth-Relic of Gotama Buddha*, by Mutu Coomára Swámy, London: Trübner, 1874.
DPPN	G. P. Malalasekera, *Dictionary of Pali Proper names*, 2 vols., London: Pali Text Society, 1974 (Original 1938).
Gv	[Nandapañña's] *Gandhavaṃsa* [Gv without any further specification refers to Gv E^{e}]
	B^{e} CSCD
	E^{e} *Gandha-Vaṃsa*, edited by by Professor [Ivan P.] Minayeff of St.Petersburg, *Journal of the Pali Text Society* 1886, 54–80.
	N^{e} *The Gandhavaṃsa* (A History of Pali Literature), ed. Bimalendra Kumar. Delhi: Eastern Book Linkers, 1992.
Khuddas-nṭ	[Saṅgharakkhita, *Sumaṅgalappasādanī nāma Khuddasikkhā-abhinavaṭīka*] *Khuddasikkhā-Mūlasikkhā, Khuddasikkhā-Purāṇa-Abhinava-Ṭīkā, Mūlasikkhā-Ṭīkā*, Rangoon: Chaṭṭhasaṅgāyana edition, 1962, 237–441.
Mhv	*The Mahāvaṃsa*, ed. Wilhelm Geiger, London: Pali Text Society, 1908, and *Cūlavaṃsa, being the more recent part of the Mahāvaṃsa*, 2 Vols., ed. Wilhelm Geiger, London 1980 [Original 1925, 1927] (PTS).
Mil-ṭ	*Milinda-ṭīkā*, ed. Padmanabh S. Jaini, Oxford Pali Text Society, 1997 (Original 1986). In *The Milindapañho with Milinda-ṭīkā*, Oxford: Pali Text Society, 1997.
Mogg-p-ṭ	*Moggallānapañcikā-ṭīkā, Sāratthavilāsinī* (CSCD).
Mūlas-anṭ	*Mulasikkhābhinavaṭīkā* (*Vinayavimaticchedanī*). In *Mūlasikkhā-aṭṭhakathā, Mūlasikkhā-purāṇaṭīkā, Mūlasikkhābhinavaṭīkā*, edited by Asabha Thera and Kheminda Thera, Mandalay, Burmese Era 1288 (= 1926 CE), 1–119.
Pāḷim-nṭ	Toṅ-phī-lā charā tō Munindaghosa [Tipiṭakālaṅkāra, *Pālimuttakavina-yavinicchayanavaṭīkā*] Vinayālaṅkāraṭīkā, 2 Vols., Rankun: Chaṭṭhasaṅgāyana, 1962.
Paṭis-gp	Be *Paṭisambhidāmaggaṭṭhakathāgaṇṭhipadaṃ*, (Rankun: Chaṭṭhasaṅgāyana) 1984.

Pay C^{e} — Medhaṅkara Vanaratana Mahāsthavira (Mahāthera), *Payogasiddhi. Mugalan viyaraṇa äsiri koṭa (A Pali Grammar based on the Moggallana System)*. Revised and edited with textual emendations by Kōdāgoḍa Siri Ñāṇāloka Mahāthera (Tripiṭakavāgīśvarācāryya). Koḷamba: Śrī Laṃkā saṃskṛtika maṇḍalaya, 2517/1974.

Piṭ-sm — Maṅ:-krī: Mahāsirijeya-sū, *Catalogue of the Piṭaka and other Texts in Pāḷi, Pāḷi-Burmese, and Burmese (Piṭakat-tō-sa-muiṅ:)*, summarized and annotated translation by Peter Nyunt. Bristol: Pali Text Society, 2012.

Sacc — 'Saccasaṅkhepa by Dhammapāla', ed. by P. Dhammārāma Bhikkhu, *Journal of the Pali Text Society* 1917–1919: 1–25.

Sacc-ṭ — *Saccasaṅkhepaṭīkā* named *Sāratthasālinī*. Manuscripts:

HS = handwritten transcript made by Helmer Smith from B^{m1} in 1947 (Original kept in Uppsala Universitet).

B^{m1} = British Library Ms I.O. Man/Pali 121 (formerly part of the Royal Library, Mandalay), dates from after 1857) [only the introductory portion was compared by me with the transcript of Helmer Smith]

B^{m2} = British Library Ms Or. 3001 [This ms. was consulted exclusively by L. S. Cousins. Readings of this ms. given above, are taken over from Cousins (unpublished) without check of the original.]

B^{m3} = Ms 524-G from the U Pho Thi Library (Saddhammajotikārāma Monastery in Thaton, Myanmar). [For more information, see http://www.palitext.com/subpages/thaton.htm; last accessed, 18.04.2017.]

Sadd — *Saddanīti. La Grammaire Palie d'Aggavaṃsa*, 3 Vols., texte établi par Helmer Smith, Oxford: Pali Text Society, 2001 (Original 1928–1954).

Saddhamma-s — Nedimāle Saddhānanda [Ed.], 'Dhammakitti, Saddhammasaṅgaha'. *Journal of the Pali Text Society* 1890: 21–90.

Sās — Paññasāmi, *Sāsanavaṃsa*, edited by Mabel Bode, London: Pali Text Society, 1897.

Sās-dīp — [Vimalasāra, *Sāsanavaṃsadīpa*] *The Sāsanavansa Dīpo or the History of the Buddhist Church in Pāli verse, compiled from Buddhist Holy Scriptures, Commentaries, Histories etc.*, Colombo: The Buddhist Press, 1929/2473.

Sp — *Samantapāsādikā, Vinayaṭṭhakathā*, 7 Vols., edited by J. Takakusu, M. Nagai (and K. Mizuno in Vols. 5 and 7), London 1924–1947 (PTS); Vol. 8: Indexes Hermann Kopp, London o.J. (PTS).

Sp-ṭ — Sāriputta [of Poḷonnaruva], *Sāratthadīpanī-ṭīkā*, 3 vols. Rangoon: Chaṭṭhasaṅgāyana Edition, 1960.

Sp-y — Ñāṇakitti, *Samantapāsādikā nāma Vinayaṭṭhakathā Atthayojanā*, 2 Vols., edited by Isiññāṇa Devasirindāvāsavāsin, (Bangkok), Vol. 1: 4th ed. 2522; Vol. 2: 3rd ed. 2503 (Mahāmakuṭarājavidyālaya).

Sv — Buddhaghosa, *Sumaṅgalavilāsinī, Dīghanikāyaṭṭhakathā*, 3 Vols., edited by T. W. Rhys Davids, J. E. Carpenter and W. Stede, London 1886–1932 (PTS).

Sv-nṭ — Ñāṇābhivaṃsa, *Sumaṅgalavilāsinī-abhinavaṭīkā, Sādhujanavilāsinī* (CSCD).

Thūp — see Bibliography, Jayawickrama 1999.

Thūp trans.	Law *The Legend of the Topes* (*Thūpavaṃsa*), trans. into English by Bimala Churn Law. 2nd ed., Calcutta: Manoharlal, 1986 (Original 1945).
Utt-vn	Buddhadatta, *Uttaravinicchaya*. In *Buddhadatta's Manuals*, pt. 2: *Vinayavinicchaya and Uttaravinicchaya, Summaries of the Vinaya Piṭaka*, edited by A. P. Buddhadatta, London: Pali Text Society, 1927, 231ff.
Utt-vn-ṭ	*Uttaravinicchayaṭīka*. In (*Vinayasāratthasandīpanī/Vinayatthasārasandīpanī*), 2 Vols., Rankun: Chaṭṭhasaṅgāyana edition, 1977, 401–430.
v(v).	verse(s)
Vibh-mūlaṭ	*Vibhaṅgamūlaṭīkā* (CSCD).
Vin-vn	Buddhadatta, *Vinayavinicchaya*, in: *Buddhadatta's Manuals*, pt. 2: *Vinayavinicchaya and Uttaravinicchaya, Summaries of the Vinaya Piṭaka*, edited by A. P. Buddhadatta, London: Pali Text Society, 1927, 1–230.
Vin-vn-ṭ	*Vinayavinicchayaṭīkā* (*Vinayasāratthasandīpanī/Vinayatthasārasandīpanī*), 2 Vols., Rangoon: Chaṭṭhasaṅgāyana edition, 1977.
Vism-mhṭ	Dhammapāla, *Visuddhimagga-mahāṭīkā* (CSCD).

Bibliography

Buddhadatta, A. P. 1928. *Buddhadatta's Manuals, Part II: Vinayavinicchaya and Uttaravinicchaya. Summaries of the Vinaya Piṭaka*. London: Pali Text Society.

———. 1962. *Pāḷisandesāvalī. Nānāvidha puraṇapāḷilipi saṃgrahayak* (*A Collection of Pali Documents and Letters with a brief Sinhalese Translation*), prathama bhāgaya (Part I). Koḷamba: Anula Press.

Cousins, L. S. 2013. 'Tambapaṇṇiya and Tāmraśāṭiya'. *Journal of Buddhist Studies* 11: 21–46.

———. (unpublished) = Cousins, L. S. 'The Sacca-saṅkhepa and its commentaries' (unpublished manuscript). [The posthumous publication is planned for the *Journal of the Pali Text Society*].

Crosby, Kate. 2004. 'The Origin of Pāli as a Language Name in Medieval Theravāda Literature'. *Journal of the Centre of Buddhist Studies, Sri Lanka* II: 70–116.

Crosby, Kate and Andrew Skilton. 1999. 'A note on the date of Mahākassapa, author of the Mohavicchedanī'. *Bulletin d'étude indienne* 17–18: 173–179.

Dimitrov, Dragomir. 2010. *The Bhaikṣukī Manuscript of the Candrālaṃkāra. Study, Script Tables, and Facsimile Edition*. Cambridge, Mass.: Harvard Oriental Series.

Fernando, C. M. 1908. *The Nikáya Saṇgrahawa, being A history of Buddhism in India and Ceylon*. Colombo: H.C. Cottle.

Geiger, Wilhelm. 1929. *Cūlavaṃsa being the more recent part of the Mahāvaṃsa*, Parts I and II, translated by W. Geiger (from Pāli into German), and from the German into English by C. Mabel Rickmers. Oxford: Pali Text Society.

Godakumbura, C. E. 1955. *Sinhalese literature*. Colombo: The Colombo Apothecaries' Co.

Guṇasekara, G. 1895. *A Contribution to the History of Ceylon. Translated from "Pujavaliya"*. Colombo: H. C. Cottle.

Gunawardana, R. A. L. H. 1979. *Robe and Plough. Monasticism and Economic Interest in Early Medieval Sri Lanka*. Monographs and Papers No. XXXV. Tucson, AZ: The Association for Asian Studies.

Hinüber, Oskar von. 1968. *Studien zur Kasussyntax des Pāli, besonders des Vinaya-Piṭaka*. München.

———. 1996. *A Handbook of Pāli literature*. Indian philology and South Asian studies, vol. 2. Berlin: Walter de Gruyter.

———. 2000. 'Lān² Nā as a centre of Pāli literature during the late 15th century'. *Journal of the Pali Text Society* 26: 119–137 [Reprinted in: von Hinüber. *Kleine Schriften*, I, 2009, 402–420].

———. 2009. *Kleine Schriften*, 2 Vols., edited by Harry Falk and Walter Slaje. Veröffentlichungen der Helmuth von Glasenapp-Stiftung, Bd. 47. Wiesbaden: Harrassowitz.

Jayawardhana, Somapala. 1994. *Handbook of Pali Literature*. Colombo: Karunaratne and Sons.

Jayawickrama, N. A. 1999. *The Chronicle of the Thūpa and the Thūpavaṃsa. Being a Translation and Edition of Vācissaratthera's Thūpavaṃsa.* Sacred Books of the Buddhists, Vol. XXVIII. Oxford: The Pali Text Society.

Kieffer-Pülz, Petra. 2005. 'Die Klassifizierung des Alkoholverbots in der buddhistischen Rechtsliteratur der Theravādin'. In *Im Dickicht der Gebote. Studien zur Dialektik von Norm und Praxis in der Buddhismusgeschichte Asiens,* ed. Peter Schalk *et al.*, 153–223. Acta Universitatis Upasaliensis, Historia Religionum, 26. Uppsala Universitet.

———. 2013. *Verlorene Gaṇṭhipadas zum buddhistischen Ordensrecht. Untersuchungen zu den in der Vajirabuddhiṭīkā zitierten Kommentaren Dhammasiris und Vajirabuddhis*, 3 Bände. Veröffentlichungen der Indologischen Kommission, 1. Wiesbaden: Harrassowitz Verlag.

———. 2015. '"And there is this stanza in this connection": The Usage of *hoti/honti/bhavanti c' ettha* in Pāli Commentarial Literature'. *Journal of the Pāli Text Society* 32: 15–162.

———. 2016. 'Reuse of text in Pāli legal commentaries'. *Buddhist Studies Review* 33(1–2): 9–45. https://doi.org/10.1558/bsrv.31640

———. 2017. 'Saṅgharakkhita Mahāsāmī's Oeuvre Based on Intertextual Links in his Texts'. *Annual Report of the International Research Institute for Advanced Buddhology at Soka University for the Academic Year 2016*, 20: 23–55.

———. (forthcoming). 'A Manual of the Adornment of the Monastic Boundary: Vācissara's *Sīmālaṅkārasaṅgaha*, Edition and Annotated Translation.' In *Sīmās: Foundations of Buddhist Religion*, edited by Jason A. Carbine and Erik Davis, 417–573. Honolulu: University of Hawai'i Press.

Kitsudo, Masahiro. 2015. *Pāli Texts Printed in Sri Lanka in Sinhalese Characters with Supplementary Information on Related Texts.* Bristol: Pali Text Society.

Malalasekera, G. P. 1928. *The Pāli literature of Ceylon*. Kandy: Buddhist Publication Society.

Matsumura, Junko. 1992. *The Rasavāhinī of Vedeha Thera. Vaggas V and VI: The Migapotaka-Vagga and the Uttaroḷiya-Vagga*. Osaka.

Ñāṇatusita, Bhikkhu. 2011. *A Reference Table of Pali Literature*, in: *An Analysis of the Pali Canon*, ed. Russell Webb, and *A Reference Table of Pali Literature*, compiled Bhikkhu Nyanatusita, 119–222. Kandy: Buddhist Publication Society.

Paranavitana, S. 1928–1933. 'No. 34. Devanagala Rock-Inscription of Parākramabāhu I'. *Epigraphia Zeylanica* III: 312–325.

———. 1960. 'The Dambadeni Dynasty'. In *History of Ceylon* I.1, edited by Nicholas Attygalle. Colombo: Ceylon University Press.

Rohanadeera, M. 1985. 'Mahāsāmi Saṅgha Rāja Institution in Sri Lanka: Its Origin, Development, Status, Duties and Functions'. *Vidyodaya Journal, Arts, Science and Letters* 13(1): 27–43.

Somadāsa, K. D. 1959 and 1964. *Laṅkāvē puskoḷa pot nāmāvaliya*, Vol. I. Koḷamba: Laṃkāṇḍuvē mudraṇālaya, 2503/1959; Vol. II. Koḷamba: Laṃkāṇḍuvē mudraṇālaya, 2508/1964.

Taw Sein Ko. 1892. *The Kalyāṇī Inscriptions Erected by King Dhammaceti at Pegu in 1476 A.D.: Text and Translation.* Rangoon: Superintendent, Government Printing, Burma.

Wickremasinghe, Don Martino de Zilva. 1900. *Catalogue of the Sinhalese manuscripts in the British Museum*. London: British Museum.

Petra Kieffer-Pülz is Senior Researcher at the Akademie der Wissenschaften und Literatur Mainz with the German Research Foundation project 'The dispute concerning the legal validity of the Buddhist monastic boundary (*sīmā*) of Balapiṭiya in Sri Lanka in the nineteenth century CE' (Der Streit um die Rechtsgültigkeit der buddhistischen Gemeindegrenze (*sīmā*) von Balapiṭiya in Sri Lanka im 19. Jh.). She is an internationally renowned expert in the study of Buddhist monastic law and Pāli literature, having published *Die Sīmā* (Reimer, 1992), *Sīmāvicāraṇa* (Fragile Palm Leaves Foundation, 2011), *Verlorene Gaṇṭhipadas* (Harrassowitz, 2013), and numerous articles relating to these areas, as well as co-editing ten books.

Schools and Scriptures

— 13 —

The Formation of Canons in the Early Indian *Nikāyas* or Schools in the Light of the New Gāndhārī Manuscript Finds

MARK ALLON

The new Gāndhārī manuscript finds from Afghanistan and Pakistan, which date from approximately the first century BCE to the third or fourth century CE, are the earliest manuscript witnesses to the literature of the Indian Buddhist *nikāyas* or schools. They preserve texts whose parallels are found in the various *Tripiṭakas*, or what remains of them, preserved in other languages and belonging to various *nikāyas*, including sections of *āgamas* such as the *Ekottarikāgama* and *Vana-saṃyutta* of the *Saṃyutta-nikāya*/*Saṃyuktāgama* and anthologies of such *sūtras*, besides many texts that are not generally classed as "canonical", such as commentaries. These very early collections of texts raise questions concerning canon-formation, such as whether the Gandhāran communities that produced these manuscripts had fixed *āgama* collections and closed canons or whether this material witnesses a stage in which collections and canons were still relatively fluid and open, and whether these manuscripts, which span several centuries, witness a shift towards fixity. This paper addresses these issues and re-examines our understanding of the formation of the canons of the early Indian *nikāyas* in light of the new Gāndhārī manuscript finds.

Overview of the new Buddhist manuscript finds

Recent decades have seen the appearance of several spectacular collections of extremely old Buddhist manuscripts from Afghanistan and northern Pakistan that preserve texts of a great diversity of genres and classifications, most of which are written either in the Gāndhārī language and Kharoṣṭhī script or Sanskrit written in various forms of Brāhmī script.[1] This includes classic early discourses, or *sūtras*, and verse collections whose parallels are found in the canonical collections belonging to early *nikāyas* or schools, of which only the Theravāda school survives to this day, commentaries on such texts, *avadānas*, biographies of the Buddha, works of *Abhidharma*, *Vinaya* texts, *stotras*, *dhāraṇīs*, texts that are generally classed as Mahāyāna, and texts that transcend *nikāya* and *yāna* labels, to name only a few.

1. There are a few instances of Sanskrit texts written in Kharoṣṭhī and several Bactrian documents written in Graeco-Bactrian script (see articles in Harrison and Hartmann 2014 mentioned below).

Keywords: formation of Buddhist canons, transmission of *āgama*/*nikāya* collections, Gāndhārī manuscripts, Gandhāran text culture

The Gāndhārī documents generally represent the earlier manuscripts, though there is some overlap between them and the Sanskrit documents. The earliest of the Gāndhārī manuscripts possibly date to the first century BCE if we are to accept recent radiocarbon dating of two of them, and the latest date to approximately the fourth century CE, while the Sanskrit manuscripts date from approximately the second to the eighth centuries CE.[2] These manuscripts thus span some 800 years of the Buddhist literary culture of the Northwest of the Indian subcontinent.

Although it will take many years of dedicated work to publish the individual texts in these collections, if not decades given that new Gāndhārī collections are appearing as I write, the identification of the individual texts and the general characteristics of these collections and their overall significance has been well documented. For this information and the most recent accounts of these collections, the reader is referred to the articles published in *From Birch Bark to Digital Data: Recent Advances in Buddhist Manuscript Research* edited by Paul Harrison and Jens-Uwe Hartmann (2014).[3]

In this article, which I offer in honour of Lance Cousins who was particularly interested in these new manuscript collections,[4] I would like to concentrate on the Gāndhārī texts that can loosely be referred to as "canonical" because they have parallels found in the surviving *Tripiṭaka*s, and particularly the *āgama* texts, that is, the *sūtra*s or discourses and verse collections, and discuss what these may tell us about the formation of *āgama*s and canons among the early schools. Here I use the term "canonical" without presupposing that the communities that produced these manuscripts had a "*Tripiṭaka*" as known in other sources,[5] though it is highly likely that they did and I follow Richard Salomon's definition of canon, that 'a canon in the stricter sense of the term ... is a comprehensive, organized, and standardized body of authoritative scriptures defined by a religious or secular authority' (2006, 365).

Relationship between the Gāndhārī texts and their parallels preserved in other languages

The relationship between the Gāndhārī "canonical" texts and their parallels in other languages, such as Pāli, Prakrit, Sanskrit, and Chinese, is complex, with the Gāndhārī version sometimes matching one parallel, at other times another, and sometimes differing from all versions (e.g. Allon 2001, 26–40; Salomon 2006, 358–

2. For the radiocarbon dating of Gāndhārī manuscripts, see Allon *et al.* 2006; Falk 2011, 19–20; Falk and Strauch 2014, 54; Salomon 2014, 9. For the dating of the Sanskrit manuscripts from Bamiyan, see Braarvig 2014.

3. This publication includes references to the main catalogues and studies of the collections and to the publication of individual texts. See also Allon 2008.

4. I first encountered Lance when he and John Smith, the two examiners of my Cambridge PhD thesis, questioned me for three hours in my Viva, or oral examination. I was particularly interested in Lance's comments because my thesis argued against the model he had proposed for the oral composition of early Buddhist discourses (Cousins 1983) and the subsequent publication of it was much improved by this encounter (Allon 1997b). In the following years until his death I very much valued the discussions we had, usually at conferences, on the formation of early Buddhist texts, Pali, and other related topics. He was very knowledgeable and a first class Pali scholar and thinker.

5. See footnote 12 below.

364). However, in the case of the Gāndhārī texts of the British Library and Senior collections, at least, wherever there is a parallel Dharmaguptaka version surviving in another language — which for the most part means a parallel in the Chinese *Dīrghāgama* or in their *Vinaya* also preserved in Chinese — the Gāndhārī version is closest to it, though rarely identical, showing that the *sūtras* and texts of these two collections clearly belong to the same or a closely related textual lineage as the Dharmaguptaka *Vinaya* and *Dīrghāgama* preserved in Chinese (Allon 2014, 23), which suggest that these two collections were produced by members of this community in ancient Gandhāra.[6] The *nikāya* association or textual lineage of the other Gāndhārī manuscript collections — the Bajaur and Split collections, the manuscripts discovered in the Bamiyan region — and individual manuscripts such as the University of Washington scroll, is for the most part yet to be determined.

Limitations in our ability to fully understand this material

A major problem with assessing and understanding these early Gāndhārī manuscripts is that we actually lack the means necessary to fully do so, since such a small proportion of the literature of the early Indian Buddhist communities survives and we have only a very rudimentary knowledge of these communities and their history and relations. We also do not know the context and reasons for the production of these manuscripts, for example, whether they were produced for ritual interment, for personal use by a monk, for teaching purposes, or as aid to memorizing the text, because the same text written for different purposes may not be identical (see Allon 2014, 30). As I have stated elsewhere (Allon 2014, 23), in order for us to fully understand these texts we would need at our disposal multiple examples of each text dating from different periods and originating from different geographical locations that had been transmitted by a diversity of *nikāyas*, and we would need to have a clear understanding of the context and reasons for their production.

What the new manuscripts tell us about canon formation, the development of stable *āgamas*, and fixity

With the above limitations in mind, an interesting question is what, if anything, do these new manuscripts tell us about the existence and makeup of *āgamas* in Gandhāra, and by extension India, at this period, that is, in the early centuries of the Christian era.

Evidence for the existence of *āgamas*

I would argue that, at minimum, these new Gāndhārī manuscript finds provide evidence for the existence of *āgamas* or collections of *sūtras* and verses arranged along the lines of the *āgamas*/*nikāyas* we know from Pāli, Prakrit, Sanskrit, and Chinese sources. The Gāndhārī texts and collections that concern us here most are the following:

(1) Three anthologies of Gāndhārī *sūtras*: (i) a manuscript in the British Library (BL 12 + 14) that preserves three *Ekottarikāgama*-type *sūtras* (all of which are con-

6. For the British Library manuscripts, see Salomon 1999, 166–178; for the Senior manuscripts, see Allon 2007, 5–6; 2014, 22–23.

nected with the number four, two of which have parallels in the Pāli *Aṅguttara-nikāya* and/or Chinese *Ekottarikāgama*), which could represent a section of an anthology of *Ekottarikāgama sūtras*, a section of an anthology of *sūtras* sourced from different *āgamas*, or represent a section of an *Ekottarikāgama*, namely, a 'Book of Fours' (Allon 2001, 22–24); (ii) the surviving *sūtras* of the Senior collection which have parallels in the *Saṃyutta-nikāya/Saṃyuktāgamas* and *Majjhima-nikāya/Madhyamāgamas*; and (iii) the list of fifty-five *sūtras* preserved on scrolls 7 and 8 of the Senior collection (RS 7 + 8).[7] As anthologies of *sūtras* these collections imply the existence of *āgamas* or larger collections from which these selections of *sūtras* were drawn.

(2) The *Saṃyuktāgama sūtras* of the Senior manuscript collection and the relationship between the structure of the *Saṃyuktāgama* from which they were selected, as implied by these Gāndhārī *Saṃyuktāgama sūtras*, and the structure of the Pāli *Saṃyutta-nikāya* and Chinese *Saṃyuktāgama*. As shown by Andrew Glass in his study of the *Saṃyuktāgama sūtras* of the Senior collection,

> it is evident that the sūtras with parallels in the Saṃyutta-nikāya/Saṃyuktāgama were selected from a Saṃyuktāgama (although it may not have been called that) whose sūtras were organized into saṃyuktas according to the same principles as those employed for the arrangement of suttas/sūtras in the Saṃyutta-nikāya and Saṃyuktāgamas that we know in Pali, Sanskrit, and Chinese.[8]

As stated by Glass (2007, 43),

> all five major divisions (Vagga) of the Pali Saṃyutta-nikāya are represented by one or more of the Gāndhārī sūtras, but only seven of the fifty-six saṃyuttas are. That is to say, the Gāndhārī sūtras cover the range of major divisions but, within each division, are concentrated on particular sets of sūtras.[9]

(3) The *Madhyamāgama sūtras* of the Senior collection, both the surviving *sūtras* and those listed in the text on scrolls 7 and 8 (RS 7 + 8), and the relationship between the structure of the *Madhyamāgama* from which they were selected, as implied by these Gāndhārī *Madhyamāgama sūtras*, and the structure of the Pāli *Majjhima-nikāya* and Chinese *Madhyamāgama*. As first noted by Blair Silverlock (2015, 52) and further articulated by Allon and Silverlock (2017, 43–47), the surviving *Madhyamāgama sūtras* in the Senior collection and those listed on scrolls 7 + 8 indicate that the *Madhyamāgama* of the community that produced this collection

> appears to have had a similar overall structure to the Pali *Majjhima-nikāya* with discourses grouped into groups of fifty *paṇṇāsa* and to a lesser extent with the Chinese *Madhyama-āgama* which groups discourses into recitations (*song* 誦). The Pali paral-

7. For the latter two, see Glass 2007, 49–50; Allon 2007, 21–23; 2014; Allon and Silverlock 2017.

8. As articulated by Allon 2007, 21. For Glass's discussion, see Glass 2007, 49–50, which is summarized in Salomon 2006, 365–368.

9. Cf. Salomon 2006, 365: 'Thus the Pāli parallels to the Senior *sūtras* that have been identified to date all occur in only three of the five *Vaggas* or major divisions of the Pāli *Saṃyutta-nikāya*, and, more strikingly, in only four of its fifty-six *saṃyuttas* or secondary divisions'. ... 'Equally striking is the clustering of the individual *sūtras* corresponding to the Senior *sūtras* in nearby positions in the Pāli and Chinese collections'.

lels to the entries on the first line of RS 7 + 8 are found in the First Fifty (*mūla-paṇṇāsa*) of the *Majjhima-nikāya*, the five entries on line 2 are found in the First and Middle Fifty (*majjhima-paṇṇāsa*), while the two entries on line 11 are found in the Final Fifty (*upari-paṇṇāsa*). (Allon and Silverlock 2017, 43)

(4) The *Vana-saṃyukta* of the Senior collection: The text on scroll 11 of the Senior collection (RS 11) preserves the same fourteen *sutta*s that constitute the *Vana-saṃyutta* of the Pāli *Saṃyutta-nikāya* and a similar division within the Chinese *Saṃyuktāgama*s, although the order of the *sūtra*s differs in each case (Allon 2007, 11, 21). This clearly shows that the Gāndhārī *Saṃyuktāgama* of the community that produced the Senior manuscripts contained a *Vana-saṃyukta*, though not necessarily called that, parallel to those we know from Pāli and Chinese sources.

(5) The five *sūtra*s listed on line 2 of the text on scrolls 7 and 8 of the Senior manuscripts (RS 7 + 8) that all appear to reference *sūtra*s that were found in the 'Division on Kings' of the *Madhyamāgama* of the community that produced this collection. As stated, the text on scrolls 7 and 8 of the Senior manuscript collection is a list of fifty-five *sūtra*s, which like the surviving texts of the Senior collection is an anthology, a selection of *sūtra*s drawn from larger collections. Many of the entries, or *sūtra* references, that constitute this list are like the entries we find for textual units such as *sūtra*s, *gāthā*s, and group of *sūtra*s/*varga*, in the *uddāna*s, or mnemonic verses, encountered in Pāli, Sanskrit, and Chinese collections, with the entries consisting of a key word or words found in the *sutta*/*sūtra* or textual unit being referenced (e.g. the name of a person or the location of the event or discourse, subject matter, etc.) that may or may not correspond to the text's title.[10] Most of the entries in this Gāndhārī list appear to reference *sūtra*s whose primary parallels are found in the surviving *Saṃyutta-nikāya*/*Saṃyuktāgama*s and *Majjhima-nikāya*/*Madhyamāgama*s.

The five entries on line two of this list, which represent entries 6–10 of the fifty-five entries, are:

6. *satarasoame* (Skt. *saptarathopama-*), '[*sūtra*] with the simile of the seven chariots';
7. *gaḍi̱kare* (Skt. *Ghaṭikāra-*), '[*sūtra*] concerning [the potter] Gaḍi̱kara';
8. *mahaḏeva* (Skt. *Mahādeva-*), '[*sūtra*] concerning [King] Mahaḏeva';
9. *bibis(*a)r(*a)*[11] (Skt. *Bimbisāra-*), '[*sūtra*] concerning [King] Bibisara';
10. *pas̱i(*ṇao)* or *pas̱e(*ṇao)* (Skt. *Prasenajit*), '[*sūtra*] concerning [King] Pas̱iṇao/Pas̱eṇao'.

For detailed analysis of these entries, their likely referents and their parallels in Pāli, Sanskrit and Chinese sources, the reader is referred to Allon and Silverlock 2017 (esp. pp. 12–14, 27–35). Here it is enough to say that the *sūtra*s these five entries are likely to reference all feature kings (Allon and Silverlock 2017, 42–43). In the case of entries 7 to 10, the Pāli *Majjhima-nikāya* and/or Chinese *Madhyamāgama* parallels are found in the 'Division on Kings' of the Pāli *Majjhima-nikāya* and/or Chinese

10. For more details on *uddāna*s and on the RS 7 + 8 list, see Allon and Silverlock 2017, particularly pp. 7–11.

11. Letters in parentheses preceded by an asterisk have been reconstructed.

Madhyamāgama, that is, the *Rāja-vagga* and *Wángxiāngyìng pǐn* 王相應品, respectively. Although no complete Sanskrit *Madhyamāgama* survives, according to statements in the Sanskrit *Bhaiṣajyavastu* of the Mūlasarvāstivāda *Vinayavastu* at least two of these four *sūtras* also formed a part of the corresponding 'Division on Kings', the *Rājasaṃyuktaka-nipāta*, of their *Madhyamāgama* (Allon and Silverlock 2017, 29–32). Further, although the Pāli and Chinese parallels to the *sūtra* referenced by entry no. 6 *satarasoame*, '[*sūtra*] with the simile of the seven chariots', are not found in the 'Division on Kings' of the *Majjhima-nikāya* and *Madhyamāgama*, the *sūtra* does deal with or reference a king. This raises the possibility that this *sūtra* was grouped together with the other four *sūtras* listed on line 2 of RS 7 + 8 in the *Madhyamāgama* of the community that produced the Senior manuscripts. Further, given that these Pāli, Sanskrit, and Chinese *Majjhima-nikāya*/*Madhyamāgamas* have (or had in the case of the Sanskrit) a 'Division on Kings' consisting of middle-length *sūtras* concerning kings, including the *sūtras* corresponding to entry nos. 7–10 discussed above, it is highly likely that the *Madhyamāgama* of the community that produced the Senior manuscripts similarly had such a division, though it may not have born such a title.

(6) The *Ekottarikāgama* fragments from Bamiyan: Among the hundreds of Gāndhārī/Kharoṣṭhī fragments from Bamiyan, Afghanistan, most of which now form a part of the Schøyen manuscript collection, are twenty-five (or possibly twenty-six) fragments of what the publishers of these fragments (Jantrasrisalai *et al.* 2016) consider must have been part of a complete manuscript of a Gāndhārī *Ekottarikāgama*, being the equivalent of the Pāli *Aṅguttara-nikāya*, which preserves the remnants of seventeen *sūtras* from the section of sixes, nines, tens, and elevens, and possibly also the sevens and eights. The manuscript is thought to date 'from between the latter half of the second century and the late third century A.D.' (Jantrasrisalai *et al.* 2016, 1).

Strictly speaking these new Gāndhārī manuscripts finds, or more accurately, the texts they contain, do not tell us whether the communities that produced them had a canon or *Tripiṭaka*, and if they did, whether it was open or closed. Nor do they tell us what the basic structure of their canon was, for example, how many *piṭakas* were involved, how many *āgamas* their *Sūtra-piṭaka* (if that is what it was called) contained, the ordering of the *āgamas* within their *Sūtra-piṭaka*, and so on.[12] But given that all of the early communities in India appear to have had such a corpus, it is highly likely that they did have a "*Tripiṭaka*" with divisions similar to those possessed by other schools. Besides, we do have at least three accounts of the basic structure of the *Tripiṭaka* of the Dharmagupatakas, the *nikāya* that were most likely responsible for the production of the British Library and Senior manuscripts, at least — the account found in their *Vinaya-piṭaka* (Taisho no. 1428, tr. 410–412 CE);[13] that in the preface to their *Dīrghāgama* preserved in Chinese (Taisho

12. As noted by Skilling (2009, 60), not all schools adopted the tripartite division.

13. See Lamotte 1988, 151 (I. *Sūtrapiṭaka: Dīrghāgama, Madhyamāgama, Saṃyuktāgama, Ekottarāgama, Kṣudrakapiṭaka*; II. *Vinayapiṭaka*; III. *Abhidharmapiṭaka*), 497 ('adding two new baskets to the traditional Tripiṭaka: those of the *dhāraṇī* and the *bodhisattva*'); Bareau 1955, 191.

no. 1, tr. 413 CE);[14] and that of Paramārtha (Bareau 1955, 190–192) — though we do not know how applicable each of these descriptions was at the time of their being written to Dharmaguptaka communities at large and especially to the community that produced these Gāndhārī documents some several centuries earlier. Further evidence for the Buddhist communities of Gandhāra during this early period having *Tripiṭaka*s is found in inscriptions from this region and period that refer to monastics who are learned in these corpora, *trepiḍaka-* 'who knows the *Tripiṭaka*',[15] parallel to those found in inscriptions from elsewhere in India from this and earlier periods.[16]

In my brief catalogue and overview of the Senior collection that appeared as the Introduction to Andrew Glass's 2007 publication of Senior scroll 5, I stated

> The Saṃyuktāgama *sūtras* in the [Senior] collection, and particularly the "Vanasaṃyutta" group on RS 11, indicate that a stable, if not fixed, Saṃyuktāgama was known to the Gandhāran community who produced these manuscripts in the first half of the second century A.D. But given that more than five centuries had passed since the death of the Buddha, this is not particularly surprising. Besides, this stability must predate our Gandhāran manuscripts by several centuries, going back into the centuries B.C. when the lines of transmission for the Gāndhārī and Pali nikāyas/āgamas separated. (Allon 2007, 21–22)

In his review of this publication, Gérard Fussman (2012, 196–199) argued against the idea of there being stable or fixed collections and fixed canons at this time in these communities. Referring to the Brussels Buddha inscription mentioned above that refers to a monk being learned in the *Tripiṭaka* (*trepiḍaka-*) attesting a division into three baskets or *piṭaka*s of the word of the Buddha in Gandhāra in the period of these Gāndhārī manuscripts, and also referring to references to *Tripiṭaka* and to the internal divisions going back at least to the second century BCE with terms such as *peṭakin* and *bhāṇaka* being found at Bhārhut and elsewhere (p. 196), he states that:[17]

> every monastery must have had manuscript collections slightly different from those of neighbouring monasteries, whether belonging to the same *nikāya* or not. As it was always the word of the Buddha (*buddha-vacana*), it hardly mattered, except for the Vinaya which maintained the differentiation between schools. (Fussman 2012, 198)[18]

---

14. Lamotte 1988, 151 with 'a *sūtrapiṭaka* in four Āgamas: *Ekottara, Madhyama, Saṃyukta*, and *Dīrgha*'; Bareau 1955, 191.

15. Brussels Buddha: *sa[ṃ] 4 1 phagunasa masasa di paṃcami budhanadasa trepiḍakasa danamukhe madapidarana adhvadidana puyaya bhavatu*, 'An 5, au cinquième jour du mois de Phalguna, don de Budhanada qui connaît le Tripiṭaka; que ce soit en l'honneur de son père et de sa mère décédés' (Fussman 1974, 54). The dating of this inscription varies: Fussman (1987, 72–77) 83 CE (78 + 5); Czuma (1985, 198) 182 CE; Errington and Cribb (1992, 16) 205 CE.

16. Dating from the 2nd century BCE onwards: *peṭakin* (Bhārhut), *trepiṭaka* and *trepiṭikā* (Sārnāth, Śrāvastī, Mathurā), *traipiṭikopādhyaya*. 'Master of three baskets' (Kānheri); see Lamotte 1988, 150; also Skilling 2009, 71–72.

17. I am indebted to Sonia Wilson, Lecturer in French Studies at the University of Sydney, for comments on my English translations of the following French passages.

18. '... chaque monastère devait avoir des collections de manuscrits très légèrement différentes de celles des monastères voisins, qu'ils appartiennent au même *nikāya* ou non. Comme il s'agissait

Fussman further states:

> It is possible that there were efforts to achieve a closed collection with a final or fixed internal arrangement and immutable wording. The legend of the Council of the Kashmir Sarvāstivādins held under the patronage of Kaniṣka reflects both this desire and a tradition indicating that there was no common canon for all Sarvastivādins before Kaniṣka. We have nothing like it for other *nikāyas* and it is not clear which religious and political authorities could have pressed for the realization of a closed and fixed collection of texts recognized only by the Dharmaguptakas.
>
> (Fussman 2012, 197)[19]

For according to him, strictly speaking for such a closed canon to develop 'it takes a threat against orthodoxy, a dominant central religious authority, a commentator, bibliographer or translator of great renown, and the support of political power', which he maintains is how the Pāli, Chinese and Tibetan canons were formed (p. 198).[20] And noting that the Theravādins of Sri Lanka had done the same as the Sarvāstivādins in fixing their canon (p. 199), he states that:

> For other *nikāyas*, there is no evidence to suggest they sought to build collections of stable and fixed texts which were their own. It is likely that the texts studied and transmitted within a school had many similarities (style, classification etc.), since the *sūtradharas* had the same line of ordination, but there is no evidence that there has been a systematic search for uniformity and even less that it was attained.
>
> (Fussman 2012, 198–199)[21]

Firstly, I was, in fact, not proposing that the Dharmaguptakas, or the communities that produced these manuscripts whoever they may have been, had fixed, closed canons, but rather that they had stable, if not fixed *āgamas* (*sūtra* and verse collections), or at least attempted to transmit them as such. And secondly, I believe the reason we do not have evidence that *nikāyas* other than the Sarvāstivādins and Theravādins 'sought to build collections of stable and fixed texts which were their

toujours de la parole du Buddha (*buddha-vacana*), cela n'avait guère d'importance, sauf pour le *vinaya* qui opérait la différenciation entre écoles'. Throughout this review Fussman seems to maintain that *Vinayas*, in contrast, were fixed.

19. 'Il est possible qu'il y ait eu des efforts pour aboutir à une collection close, à l'arrangement interne définitif et à la lettre immuable. La légende du concile *sarvāstivādin* du Cachemire tenu sous le patronage de Kaniṣka témoigne à la fois de cette volonté et d'une tradition indiquant qu'il n'y avait pas de canon commun à tous les *sarvāstivādin* avant Kaniṣka. On n'a rien de tel pour les autres *nikāya* et on ne voit pas quelles autorités religieuses et politiques auraient pu peser pour la réalisation d'un recueil clos et fixe des textes reconnus par les seuls *dharmaguptaka*'.

20. '... il faut pour constituer un canon *stricto sensu* une menace contre l'orthodoxie, un centre religieux dominant, un commentateur, bibliographe ou traducteur de grand renom, et l'appui du pouvoir politique. C'est ainsi que ce sont constitués les canons pāli, chinois et tibétains'.

21. 'Les *theravādin* de Śrī Laṅka auparavant en avaient fait de même, peut-être au départ parce que le pāli n'était pas la langue maternelle des moines cinghalais et tamouls, mais leur canon est resté longtemps ouvert. Pour les autres *nikāya*, aucun indice ne permet de penser qu'ils aient cherché à constituer des collections de textes stables et fixes qui leur fussent propres. Il est probable que les textes étudiés et transmis à l'intérieur d'une école aient eu entre eux de grandes similitudes (style, classement etc.) puisque les *sūtradhara* avaient la même lignée d'ordination, mais rien ne permet d'affirmer qu'il y ait eu recherche systématique d'uniformisation et moins encore qu'on y soit parvenu'.

own' (in the words of Fussman) is because we lack the material upon which we could make this judgement on account of so little of the literature of other *nikāyas* and the historical documents relevant to them surviving.

As is well known, Steven Collins (1990) similarly argued that the closed status of the Pāli canon, which was produced by the Mahāvihāra in Sri Lanka, came about because of the political and social circumstances in Sri Lanka in the early period, namely, the rivalry between the Mahāvihāra and Abhayagiri monasteries for royal patronage. He states, '[w]hen compared with other extant collections of scriptures in Buddhism, I think the Pali canon is unique in being an exclusive, closed list' (Collins 1990, 91). However, the extant collections he is comparing the Pāli canon with are the Chinese and Tibetan canons, which is not comparing like with like. The Chinese canon, for example, is not comparable to the Pāli canon, being rather an 'encyclopaedic' (Salomon 2011, 163) and 'archival canon' (Levering 1989, 95 n. 26),[22] containing material originating from many different sources, and its constituent texts do not tell us much about the makeup of the canons of the *nikāyas* to which the individual *āgamas* it contains belonged, nor whether the canons of those schools were open or closed. As just noted, we should rather be comparing the Pāli canon with those of the other early *nikāyas*, which we are unfortunately unable to do because they do not survive. But given that the rivalry between monasteries and *nikāyas* for limited resources and royal patronage, which Collins argues provided the impetus for the Mahāvihāra to close their version of the Pāli canon, was undoubtedly repeated innumerable times throughout the history of Buddhism, there must have been other instances of communities closing their canons on the basis of such a stimulus that have not been recorded. There is surely nothing special about the Mahāvihāra-Abhayagiri rivalry that sets it apart from any other instance of *nikāya* rivalry. The Pāli canon is unique only in that it is the only complete canon of the early schools (1) to have survived (2) in an Indic language, (3) that has been actively and uninterruptedly transmitted to the present day, (4) that is augmented by a large body of secondary literature that records how the communities that transmitted it understood and regarded the texts they transmitted, and (5) is the object of such statements by contemporary members of this *nikāya*. Were other *nikāyas* to have survived to the present day, or were even a substantial portion of their literature to have survived parallel to what we have in Pāli, our views would, I believe, be very different regarding the Pāli canon and canon formation.

In several of his recent articles on the new manuscripts finds, Richard Salomon has also argued that these manuscripts indicate that at the period of these manuscripts, *āgama* collections and canons had yet to be standardized (Salomon 2006, 375). For example, with reference to the complex relationships that are evident when you compare these Gāndhārī *sūtras* with their Pāli, Chinese and Sanskrit counterparts, he states

> All in all, one gets the impression that we are operating at a stage before Sūtra canons were definitively fixed and authoritatively edited, so that a considerable degree

22. Referenced by Salomon 2011, 163 n. 6.

of fluidity and flexibility still prevailed with regard to the structure and wording of particular sūtras, as well as to their inclusion and arrangement within corpora such as the *Ekottarikāgama/Aṅguttaranikāya* or *Saṃyuktāgama*. (Salomon 2014, 12)

In response to Fussman and Salomon's views, I now wish to modify my original statement quoted above (p. 255) (Allon 2007, 21–22). Just as these new manuscripts finds do not tell us whether or not these communities had open or closed canons, nor what the larger scale structure of their *Sūtra-piṭaka* was, and so on, so also one cannot definitively say on the basis of these manuscripts that these communities had 'stable, if not fixed' (my words) collections of *sūtra*s and *gāthā*s. However, it is also the case that they do not tell us that they had open collections, which each community and school regularly rearranged, that is, that individual *sūtra*s and *sūtra* collections were in a constant state of flux even within the same *nikāya* in a given region.

What the views of Fussman and Salomon are based on, as indeed are mine, is a very limited number of parallel versions of *sūtra*s and verse collections originating from different periods, locations, and mostly produced by different *nikāya*s, no doubt produced for a variety of purposes, which consistently exhibit diversity within similarity. As mentioned earlier, in order to determine whether the *sūtra* and verse collections were stable or fixed within a given *nikāya* and within a particular region or whether, as Fussman and Salomon would argue, parallel collections or *āgama*s differed from monastery to monastery even between those belonging to the same *nikāya* in the same region, we would need to have multiple examples of the same *sūtra* and collection of *sūtra*s (*āgama*) or section of it from monasteries of the same *nikāya* from both the same and differing regions spanning a generous period of time. And if they were in manuscript form, we would need to know the reason for their production. The ideal, of course, would be to have multiple manuscripts and multiple recordings of the oral performance of the same text or collection both by members of different monasteries belonging to the same *nikāya* and by different monasteries of different *nikāya*s from a diversity of regions spanning a substantial period of time.

Unfortunately, there are only two examples of more than one manuscript of the same text or section of a text among the Gāndhārī finds, new and old. This involves three Gāndhārī manuscripts that preserve sections of what are essentially two different *Dharmapada*s. They are the Khotan *Dharmapada* (Dhp-G^{K}) manuscript (Brough 1962), which preserves a large portion of a complete *Dharmapada*, the British Library or London *Dhammapada* (Dhp-G^{L}) fragment (Lenz 2003), which preserves thirteen verses of the *Bhikṣu-varga*, the Chapter on Monks, and an apparently complete manuscript in the Split collection (Dhp-G^{S}) that preserves a portion of a *Dharmapada* (Falk 2015). Whereas the Khotan *Dharmapada* manuscript has verses in common with the London *Dharmapada* and Split *Dharmapada*, the latter two do not have any verses in common.

The thirteen verses of the London *Dharmapada* are also found in the Khotan *Dharmapada*, with the main differences being a slightly difference in the order of the verses and the omission in the London *Dharmapada* of two verses found in the Khotan *Dharmapada* (verses 79 and 80), or at least in this section of the text. The two texts also exhibit what I would consider to be minor differences in spelling, word-inflexion, and word substitution.[23] The following table shows the order of verses in the two *Dharmapada* manuscripts.

Dhp-G^{L}	1	2	*3	4	5	6	7	8	9	10	11	12	13
Dhp-G^{K}	77	78	76	81	82	85	84	83	87	86	88	89	90

The very close similarities between these two Gāndhārī versions of the *Dharmapada*, indicates that they are essentially the same text, or at least are so in this section of the *Bhikṣu-varga*.[24] The problem here is that we cannot currently determine that these two manuscripts originate from the same region, were produced by members of the same *nikāya* and monastery, and are contemporary.[25] We also do not know whether they were written for the same purpose; for example, although the Khotan *Dharmapada* manuscripts clearly contained a complete *Dharmapada*, with the text carefully written and laid out on the manuscripts, suggesting that it may have been written for ceremonial reasons, or perhaps to transmit the text into Central Asia, it is unclear whether the London *Dharmapada* manuscript was part of a complete *Dharmapada* or contained just the *Bhikṣu-varga* written by the scribe for his private use, or other such possibilities.

In contrast to the Khotan and London *Dharmapada*s, the Khotan and Split *Dharmapada*s, despite sharing many verses in common, differ so greatly in the ordering of their verses that they are unlikely to have been produced by members of the same *nikāya*, representing two different *Dharmapada*s (Falk 2015).[26]

Although there are two other examples of different manuscripts of the same text amongst the new Gāndhārī manuscript finds, they do not preserve the same section of the text. The first are the two manuscripts of the *Anavatapta-gāthā*, one preserved in the British Library the other belonging to the Senior collections (Salomon 2008). The second example, though slightly different in nature, is the Gāndhārī commentary on a collection or anthology of verses in the British Library collection (Baums 2009), where the parallels to the root verses being commented on are mostly found in *Khuddaka/Kṣudraka* texts in the surviving canons (*Dhammapada*, *Udāna*, *Suttanipāta*, etc.). Of the thirty-nine or more root verses, five have parallels in the Khotan *Dharmapada*, which for the most part match in wording.

23. Lenz (2003, 21–24) attributes more significance to the differences in spelling, word-inflexion, and word substitution than I consider they warrant; cf. Norman's review of this publication (Norman 2004).

24. Lenz (2003, 18) attributes the differences in the ordering of the verses to the imperfect nature of oral transmission, though other explanations are possible.

25. Although they were found in very different regions, namely, Khotan and Gandhāra, it is quite possible that the Khotan manuscript was imported from Gandhāra, though we have no way of telling where in this relatively large region it was produced. However, Falk (2015, 24), in comparing the Split *Dharmapada* with the Khotan *Dharmapada*, notes that '[w]e are used to call [sic] the language of the Khotan Dhp "Gāndhārī", but when we now compare a version which really comes from Gandhara, we see that there are differences of a systematic kind, which may force us to re-christen the language of the Khotan Dhp "Central-Asian Gāndhārī"', that is, that the Khotan *Dharmapada* was produced in Central Asia.

26. See Falk 2015, 24–26 for the possible school affiliation of the Split *Dharmapada*.

Thus, we lack the material for assessing whether the collections or *āgamas* of a given *nikāya* in a given region (say, Dharmaguptaka in the case of the British Library and Senior manuscripts) were open to rearrangement or were stable, or fixed. However, I think that this evidence is provided by another factor, namely, the oral transmission itself.

Oral transmission and fixity

There is substantial evidence that early Buddhist communities memorized and recited texts individually and communally, and that *āgamas* were transmitted by communities of reciters, or *bhāṇakas*, well before the period of these Gāndhārī manuscripts.[27] Group recitation requires that the wording of the text and the arrangement of the textual units within a collection be fixed; otherwise you would have complete chaos.[28]

Sūtras and collections of such textual units were clearly designed with memorization, group recitation, and the faithful transmission of material in mind. This is indicted by two main factors. The first are the stylistic features of these texts — the use of formulas and repetition, the building up of strings of parallel word elements, the arrangement of such strings and of other textual units according to size from shorter to longer, words chosen to create sound repetitions, and so on (Allon 1997a, 1997b). The second is the arrangement of textual units such as *sūtras* and verses within major collections into *vargas*, *saṃyuktas*, *nipātas*, and the like, with *sūtras* or textual units being grouped within these divisions (at least for texts such as the *Saṃyutta-nikāya, Aṅguttara-nikāya, Dhammapada, Theragāthā, Therīgāthā*) according to genres, size, subject matter, a numerical feature, a connection based on key words, concepts, the manner of treating a topic, individuals involved, textual features (e.g. simile), and with *uddānas*, or mnemonic summaries, to ensure the correct arrangement of the textual units within the collection (inclusion and ordering).

The investment of time and labour that must have gone in to memorizing and transmitting *sūtra* and verse collections, as with any text, combined with the demands of communal recitation, would ensure that communities would have been slow to make changes to their collections since each change would involve considerable time and energy in relearning the material, besides the effort needed to arrive at a consensus to make the changes.

But here the seemingly strange question is, how fixed must a text be for it to be considered fixed? For example, are the British Library and Khotan *Dharmapadas* discussed above, which have, at least in this section of the *Bhikṣu-varga*, identical verses that differ only slightly in the arrangement of verses, the same, fixed text? I would argue that for our purposes a text — a *sūtra*, verse or textual unit or a collection of them — is fixed as long as it is memorized, repeated and communally recited without being intentionally changed, which of course allows for unintentional change.

27. See, for example, Allon 1997a, 1997b; Anālayo 2007, 2009; Collins 1992; Cousins 1983; Norman 2006, 53–74; Wynne 2004.

28. That is, unless we envisage a single lead reciter reciting a text, which was then repeated by the other reciters. However, there is no evidence that this was how the Buddhist oral tradition worked.

I would also argue that subsequent change to that text, either through the limitations of the medium of oral transmission or through intentional modification, does not nullify the previous status of that text being fixed; that is, because texts that were memorized and communally recited and transmitted unchanged for a given period of time did eventually change, either through passive or active agency, as we clearly see they did, does not mean that they were not transmitting as fixed texts by the community that transmitted them.

The Pāli canon itself, which is considered to be a closed canon containing texts of fixed wording, underwent many changes after becoming closed, and it may yet undergo further changes. A good example on the macro level, that is on the level of canon as list, is the addition over time of texts to the *Khuddaka-nikāya*.[29] As is well known, there was and is a tendency in the Burmese tradition to associate the paracanonical *Suttasaṅgaha*, *Milindapañha*, *Nettippakaraṇa*, and *Peṭakopadesa* with the *Khuddaka-nikāya*, leading some to maintain that the Burmese regard these texts to be part of the *Tipiṭaka* (e.g. Bode 1909, 4–5).[30] Despite Charles Duroiselle's criticism of this view, stating that 'No educated Burman, lay or monk, ever included these four works among the Piṭaka books of the Khuddakanikāya' (1911, 121), there is much evidence to the contrary.[31] These four texts are, for example, listed in the *Piṭakat-tō-sa-muiṅ:*, a list of texts completed in 1888 by the court librarian of King Mindon, immediately after the *Cariyāpiṭaka*, which is entry no. 37, as nos. 38–41 (Nyunt 2012, 48).[32] The last three of these four texts are included in the *Tipiṭaka* carved on 729 marble stelae at the Kuthodaw Pagoda in Mandalay at the command of King Mindon between 1860 and 1868.[33] Once again, they appear on the stelae that occur immediately after the *Cariyāpiṭaka*, the last of the fifteen books of the *Khuddaka-nikāya* according to other Theravāda traditions, which is carved on stelae nos. 691–692, in the following order: *Nettippakaraṇa* (stelae nos. 693–700), *Peṭakopadesa* (nos. 701–709), and *Milindapañha* (nos. 710–729). In the three Burmese language inscriptions at the site that give details about the founding of the Kuthodaw Pagoda and the texts carved there, 'there is a detailed list of the number of stelae per text and per *nikāya* (on the side labelled "6"). Here, the *Khuddaka-nikāya* is listed as having 169 stelae, which is correct only if you include the *Nettippakaraṇa*, *Peṭakopadesa*, and *Milindapañha*. So at least at this stage these three texts were considered to be part of the canon'.[34] These same three texts are included in the *Khuddaka-nikāya* of the Burmese *Chaṭṭhasaṅgīti* edition, which was published between 1950 and 1962 (Hamm 1973, 125), as the final

29. For disagreement among the *bhāṇakas* as to the number of texts in the *Khuddaka-nikāya* as well as the Burmese example discussed here, see Norman 1983, 9, 31–32; von Hinüber 1996, 42–43, 76.

30. Further references are given in Collins 1990, 108 n. 11.

31. Jackson (2006, 61–62) counters Duroiselle's statement with a significant contemporary Burmese example.

32. Though the statement after the *Cariyāpiṭaka* that the 'above Canonical texts (Pāḷi-tō) were thoroughly revised during the four Buddhist Councils' (Nyunt 2012, 48) suggesting that nos. 38–41 were not being treated as part of the *Khuddaka-nikāya*. See von Hinüber 1996, 3 for further references.

33. For the Kuthodaw Pagoda site and its inscriptions, see Allon *et al.* 2016.

34. Chris Clark, personal communication (27.5.17).

three volumes of the *Khuddaka-nikāya* in the same order as found at the Kuthodaw Pagoda.[35] In the printed volumes of the *Chaṭṭhasaṅgīti* edition, each of these three texts has -*pāḷi*, 'canonical text', e.g. *Milindapañhapāḷi*, as the final member of the title, as do all other books of the *Tipiṭaka*, with this title preceded by wording that clearly places the text in the *Khuddaka-nikāya*, e.g. *Chaṭṭhasaṅgītipiṭakaṃ Suttantapiṭake Khuddakanikāye Milindapañhapāḷi*, '*Chaṭṭhasaṅgītipiṭaka*. The *Milindapañha* in the *Khuddaka-nikāya* within the *Suttanta-piṭaka*'.[36] Thus a closed canon with a *Khuddaka-nikāya* containing fifteen books was expanded in Burma to form an equally closed canon with a *Khuddaka-nikāya* containing eighteen books. That change did not nullify the status of the former as a closed canon.

On a micro level, many changes to the reading of Pāli canonical texts were intentionally made after the canon became closed and the wording supposedly fixed. The Burmese Kuthodaw Pagoda recension discussed above provides a good example. As noted by Chris Clark, who compared the Kuthodaw Pagoda text of the *Apadāna* (stelae 665–687) alongside nineteen different manuscript versions as part of his doctoral research (Clark 2015).

> When closely compared to Burmese script manuscripts predating the 1860s, it became evident that the Kuthodaw Pagoda recension represents a rigorously edited and newly revised version with a number of key features. Firstly, it contains far fewer errors than most Burmese script manuscripts, though more than most modern printed editions. Secondly, hypermetric *pādas* within *śloka* verses have been avoided in favour of metrically standard eight syllable *pādas*. This usually involves an alteration of *sandhi*[37] or word choice.[38] ... Thirdly, grammar or word choice has occasionally been altered in order to make difficult passages more easily understood.[39] Fourthly, the text has been harmonised with parallels in other parts of the canon in order to improve textual consistency.[40] ... Lastly, there is evidence of occasional conflation, that is, the combination of two or more variant readings.[41]
>
> (Clark in Allon *et al.* 2016, 235–236; footnotes in this quote are original)

35. However, in both the printed and electronic versions of the *Chaṭṭhasaṅgīti* edition the order of the first sixteen books of the *Khuddaka-nikāya* (counting the *Mahā-* and *Culla-niddesa*s as two) differs from the traditional one in its latter part. While the order of the first nine books remain the same (*Khuddakapāṭha, Dhammapada, Udāna, Itivuttaka, Suttanipāta, Vimānavatthu, Petavatthu, Theragāthā, Therīgāthā*), the order of the remainder is *Apadāna, Buddhavaṃsa, Cariyāpiṭaka, Jātaka, Mahāniddesa, Cullaniddesa, Paṭisambhidāmagga* rather than the traditional *Jātaka, Mahāniddesa, Cullaniddesa, Paṭisambhidāmagga, Apadāna, Buddhavaṃsa, Cariyāpiṭaka*.

36. *Chaṭṭhasaṅgīti* edition, volume 28 (*Khuddhanikāya* vol. 11), title page.

37. For example, *catunavut' ito kappe* instead *of catunavute ito kappe* (*Apadāna* 55,19).

38. For example, *purāṇapuḷinaṃ hitvā* instead of *purāṇaṃ puḷinaṃ chaḍḍetvā* (*Apadāna* 79,3).

39. For example, *tiyojanāni sāmantā* instead of *tīṇiyojanasamantā* (*Apadāna* 73,32). As stated by Clark (2015, 201), 'While the cardinal three is most often *ti-* at the beginning of a compound, it may also be *tayo-* and *tīṇi-*'.

40. For example, *Apadāna* 59,1 (*ath' ettha satthā āgañchi*) has been harmonised with the reading found at *Theragātha* 559 (*bhagavā tattha āgacchi*).

41. Most notably, the Kuthodaw Pagoda recension of *Apadāna* 70–72 (verses 1–26) appears to have resulted from an editorial attempt to include the readings from two different versions of this passage. It consequently has four additional verses not found in the received text.

Clearly the Burmese, like many other Theravāda communities, have been willing to alter the wording of the fixed texts of their closed canon.

Summary reflections

The Gāndhārī literature that has come to light in recent decades is not dissimilar from what would result were we to take a random selection of a hundred or so manuscripts from different monasteries in Sri Lanka or from a similarly sized region in Southeast Asia, preferably in the pre-modern period, say, at the beginning of the eighteen century, before monastic libraries were disturbed, before printing and before the establishment of the Pali Text Society and the tradition of Western textual scholarship, and then randomly discard folios (plus let your dog play with them). The result would be a collection of folios and folio fragments of manuscripts containing a great diversity of texts. This may indeed include folios of complete *nikāya*s or sections of them, individual texts of the *Khuddaka-nikāya* or sections of them, books of the *Vinaya-* and *Abhidhamma-piṭaka*s or sections of them, and anthologies of *sutta*s or verses. But the majority of the texts would most likely be *jātaka*s, commentaries, works such as the *Visuddhimagga* and *Milindapañha*, *vaṃsa* texts, handbooks or manuals of *Vinaya* and *Abhidhamma*, works on grammar and poetics, and manuscripts containing texts of mixed genre, such as a selection of *sutta*s from different *nikāya*s combined with sections of non-*sutta* material, and so on. And this is to say nothing of bilingual texts that would undoubtedly be included, such as Pāli-Sinhala *sūtra sannaya*s and *pada-änuma*s in the case of the Sri Lankan material or *nissaya*s in the case of Myanmar.[42]

This random collection of texts alone would not enable us to determine the structure of the canon of the Theravāda monastic community or communities that produced these manuscripts, or even in fact whether they had a canon, or if they did have one, whether it was open or closed. Nor could we necessarily determine the degree to which the wording of a given text was fixed. The Theravādins, like other schools, preserve the same *sutta* or description of the same event in different sections of their canon, for example, in the *Saṃyutta-nikāya*, *Aṅguttara-nikāya* and *Vinaya-piṭaka*, that exhibit differences in wording, in the sequence of events, in the characters involved, in the identification of the person who delivered the discourse or spoke those verses, and so on.[43] If by chance samples of parallel versions of such a text that originated from different sections of the Pāli canon were amongst our random selection of texts, we might think that the community or school that produced these manuscripts, namely the Theravādins, had not fixed the wording of the texts it was transmitting. Similarly, Pāli manuscripts sometimes contain collections of texts, for example *sutta*s, that are incomplete and in an order that does not conform to the order of *sutta*s in the respective *nikāya*. An example is a nineteenth-

42. This list is not meant to be fully representative of the types of texts that would be encountered, being only suggestive of it. As an examination of catalogues of Pāli and other manuscripts and of monastic library handlists reveals, the Buddhist literature that has been transmitted in the Theravāda world is immensely diverse.

43. For some examples, see Norman 1983, 50; Allon 1997b, 39, 62, 163–166; Anālayo 2007, 9–13.

century Sinhalese manuscript in the British Library[44] I have discussed elsewhere (Allon 2001, 23) that contains six *Aṅguttara-nikāya suttas* or parts of *suttas*: *sutta* 156 and the first part of *sutta* 157 of the *Catukka-nipāta* (nos. 4.156 and 4.157.1); *sutta* 19 of the *Aṭṭhaka-nipāta* (no. 8.19); *sutta* 17 of the same *nipāta* (no. 8.17); *sutta* 42 of the *Tika-nipāta* (no. 3.42), minus the verse; and the second part of *sutta* 129 of the *Tika-nipāta* (no. 3.192.2). These six *suttas* are followed by an incomplete *anumodanā gāthā*, or verse text in praise of giving. Here *suttas* are not in traditional order (no. 8.17 follows no. 8.19) and in three instances the *sutta* is incomplete.[45] Were this manuscript and folios of the sections of a complete *Aṅguttara-nikāya* containing these *suttas* be amongst our random selection, we may well again conclude that the Theravādins had not fixed the wording of their texts.

Like this hypothetical random selection of Pāli manuscripts, these Gāndhārī manuscript finds only give us a small glimpse of what texts were being used, transmitted and composed by the Buddhist communities of Gandhāra from approximately the first century BCE to the third or fourth century CE. But in the case of these Gāndhārī texts, not only are we limited in our assessment of them by the relatively small number of texts that have survived, by the lack of *āgama* material of the early schools with which to compare them, by the lack of information on the purpose of the production and other such factors outlined above but, as significantly, these texts may not be fully representative of Gandhāran textual culture of this period. Manuscripts were certainly not the dominant medium for the transmission of texts at this time due to the expense involved in producing them, their cumbersome nature, and the traditional emphasis on memorization.[46] These manuscripts were undoubtedly produced for a variety of reasons, but it is unlikely that they were primary produced as a means of preserving and transmitting texts.

In short, I do not agree with Fussman and Salomon that neighbouring monasteries of the same *nikāya* transmitted different versions of the same *āgama* or collection of *sūtra* or verses. Rather, the Buddhist communities that produced these early manuscripts in Gandhāra of the first century BCE to the third or fourth century CE were transmitting 'stable, if not fixed' collections, as was the case well before this period throughout India. But the evidence for this does not come from the new manuscript finds themselves, but from the demands of oral transmission.

Note

This article is based on my paper 'The Formation of Canons in the Early Indian Nikāyas or Schools in the Light of the New Gāndhārī Manuscript Finds' presented at the XVIIth Congress of the International Association of Buddhist Studies, Vienna,

44. Or.6599(25) described in Somadasa 1987.
45. Further examples are described in the many published catalogues of Pāli manuscripts, including Somadasa 1987 mentioned here.
46. For trends in the writing of *āgama* collections in Gandhāra, see Salomon 2017 who observes that the earlier manuscripts tend to contain only individual *sūtras*, small anthologies of *sūtras*, or the initial sections of text collections, with complete *āgamas* only being written towards the end of Gāndhārī manuscript production.

August 18–23, 2014. I am indebted to Chiara Neri for her comments on an earlier draft of this article.

Bibliography

Allon, Mark. 1997a. 'The Oral Composition and Transmission of Early Buddhist Texts'. In *Indian Insights: Buddhism, Brahmanism and Bhakti: Papers from the Annual Spalding Symposium on Indian Religion*, edited by Peter Connolly and Sue Hamilton, 39–61. London: Luzac Oriental.

———. 1997b. *Style and Function: A Study of the Dominant Stylistic Features of the Prose Portions of Pāli Canonical Sutta Texts and their Mnemonic Function*. Tokyo: International Institute for Buddhist Studies.

———. 2001. (with contribution by Andrew Glass) *Three Gāndhārī Ekottarikāgama-Type Sūtras: British Library Kharoṣṭhī Fragments 12 and 14*. Gandhāran Buddhist Texts 2. Seattle: University of Washington Press.

———. 2007. 'Introduction: The Senior Manuscripts'. In Andrew Glass, *Four Gāndhārī Saṃyuktāgama Sūtras: Senior Kharoṣṭhī Fragment 5*. Gandhāran Buddhist Texts 4, 3–25. Seattle: University of Washington Press.

———. 2008. 'Recent Discoveries of Buddhist Manuscripts from Afghanistan and Pakistan and their Significance'. In *Art, Architecture and Religion Along the Silk Roads. Silk Road Studies 12. Proceedings from the Fifth Conference of the Australian Society for Inner Asian Studies (A.S.I.A.S.). Macquarie University, November 27th to 28th, 2004*, edited by Ken Parry, 153–178. Turnhout: Brepols.

———. 2014. 'The Senior Kharoṣṭhī Manuscripts'. In *From Birch Bark to Digital Data: Recent Advances in Buddhist Manuscript Research*, edited by Paul Harrison and Jens-Uwe Hartmann, 19–33. Vienna: Verlag der Österreichischen Akademie der Wissenschaften. https://doi.org/10.2307/j.ctt1vw0q4q.5

Allon, Mark, Wendy Reade, Chris Clark, Ian McCrabb, Tamara Ditrich, Royce Wiles and Bob Hudson. 2016. 'The Kuthodaw Pagoda Marble-stelae Inscriptions, Mandalay, Myanmar: Conservation, Photographing, and Study of a Neglected Recension of the Pali Buddhist Canon'. *Bulletin of the Chuo Academic Research Institute (Chuo Gakujutsu Kenkyūjo Kiyō)* 45: 222–249.

Allon, Mark, Richard Salomon, Geraldine Jacobsen and Ugo Zoppi. 2006. 'Radiocarbon Dating of Kharoṣṭhī Fragments from the Schøyen and Senior Manuscript Collections'. In *Buddhist Manuscripts, Volume III. Manuscripts in the Schøyen Collection*, edited by Jens Braarvig, 279–291. Oslo: Hermes Publishing.

Allon, Mark and Blair Silverlock. 2017. 'Sūtras in the Senior Kharoṣṭhī Manuscript Collection with Parallels in the *Majjhima-nikāya* and/or the *Madhyama-āgama*'. In *Research on the Madhyama-āgama*, edited by Dhammadinnā. Dharma Drum Institute of Liberal Arts Research Series 5, 1–54. Taipei: Dharma Drum Publishing Co.

Anālayo, Bhikkhu. 2007. 'Oral Dimensions of Pāli Discourses: Pericopes, other Mnemonic Techniques, and the Oral Performance Context'. *Canadian Journal of Buddhist Studies* 3: 5–33.

———. 2009. 'The Vicissitudes of Memory and Early Buddhist Oral Transmission'. *Canadian Journal of Buddhist Studies* 5: 5–19.

Bareau, André. 1955. *Les Sectes bouddhiques du Petit Véhicule*. Saigon: École française d'Extrême-Orient.

Baums, Stefan. 2009. *A Gāndhārī Commentary on Early Buddhist Verses: British Library Kharoṣṭhī Fragments 7, 9, 13 and 18*. Unpublished PhD thesis, University of Washington.

Bode, Mabel Haynes. 1909. *The Pali Literature of Burma*. London: Royal Asiatic Society.

Braarvig, Jens. 2014. 'The Schøyen Collection'. In *From Birch Bark to Digital Data: Recent Advances in Buddhist Manuscript Research*, edited by Paul Harrison and Jens-Uwe Hartmann, 157–164. Vienna: Verlag der Österreichischen Akademie der Wissenschaften. https://doi.org/10.2307/j.ctt1vw0q4q.10

Brough, John, ed. 1962. *The Gāndhārī Dharmapada*. London Oriental Series 7. Oxford: Oxford University Press.

Clark, Chris. 2015. *A Study of the Apadāna, including an Edition and Annotated Translation of the Second, Third and Fourth Chapters*. Unpublished PhD thesis, University of Sydney.

Collins, Steven. 1990. 'On the Very Idea of the Pali Canon'. *Journal of the Pali Text Society* 15: 89–126.

———. 1992. 'Notes on Some Oral Aspects of Pali Literature'. *Indo-Iranian Journal* 35: 121–135. https://doi.org/10.1163/000000092794742682

Cousins, L. S. 1983. 'Pali Oral Literature'. In *Buddhist Studies Ancient and Modern*, edited by by P. Denwood and A. Piatigorsky, 1–11. London: Curzon Press.

Czuma, Stanislaw J. 1985. *Kushan Sculpture: Images from Early India*. Cleveland, OH: Cleveland Museum of Art in Cooperation with Indiana University Press.

Duroiselle, Charles, 1911. Review of Bode 1909. *Journal of the Burma Research Society* 1: 119–122.

Errington, Elizabeth, Joe Cribb, with Maggie Claringbull, eds. 1992. *The Crossroads of Asia: Transformation in Image and Symbol in the Art of Ancient Afghanistan and Pakistan*. Cambridge: The Ancient India and Iran Trust.

Falk, Harry. 2011. 'The "Split" Collection of Kharoṣṭhī Texts'. *Annual Report of The International Research Institute for Advanced Buddhology at Soka University for the Academic Year 2010 (ARIRIAB)* 14: 13–23.

———. 2015. 'A New Gāndhārī *Dharmapada* (Texts from the Split Collection 3)'. *Annual Report of The International Research Institute for Advanced Buddhology at Soka University for the Academic Year 2015 (ARIRIAB)* 18: 23–62.

Falk, Harry and Ingo Strauch. 2014. 'The Bajaur and Split Collections of Kharoṣṭhī Manuscripts within the Context of Buddhist Gāndhārī Literature'. In *From Birch-Bark to Digital Data: Recent Advances in Buddhist Manuscript Research*, edited by Paul Harrison and Jens-Uwe Hartmann, 51–78. Vienna: Verlag der Österreichischen Akademie der Wissenschaften. https://doi.org/10.2307/j.ctt1vw0q4q.7

Fussman, Gérard. 1974. 'Documents épigraphiques kouchans'. *Bulletin de l'École française d'Extrême-Orient* 61: 1–66. https://doi.org/10.3406/befeo.1974.5193

———. 1987. 'Numismatic and Epigraphic Evidence for the Chronology of Early Gandharan Art'. In *Investigating Indian Art: Proceedings of a Symposium on the Development of Early Buddhist and Hindu Iconography Held at the Museum of Indian Art Berlin in May 1986*, edited by Marianne Yaldiz and Wibke Lobo. Veröffentlichungen des Museums für Indische Kunst, Volume 8, 67–88. Berlin: Museum für Indische Kunst.

———. 2012. Review of Glass 2007. *Indo-Iranian Journal* 55: 189–200. https://doi.org/10.1163/001972412X620295

Gethin, Rupert. 2007. 'What's in a Repetition? On Counting the Suttas in the Saṃyutta-nikāya'. *Journal of the Pali Text Society* 29: 365–387.

Glass, Andrew. 2007. *Four Gāndhārī Saṃyuktāgama Sūtras: Senior Kharoṣṭhī Fragment 5*. Gandhāran Buddhist Texts 4. Seattle: University of Washington Press.

Hamm, F. R. 1973. 'On Some Recent Editions of the Pāli Tipiṭaka'. In *German Scholars on India: Contributions to Indian Studies*, 123–135. Varanasi: Chowkhamba Sanskrit Series Office.

Harrison, Paul and Jens-Uwe Hartmann, eds. 2014. *From Birch Bark to Digital Data: Recent Advances in Buddhist Manuscript Research*. Vienna: Verlag der Österreichischen Akademie der Wissenschaften.

von Hinüber, Oskar. 1996. *A Handbook of Pāli Literature*. Indian Philology and South Asian Studies 2. Berlin: Walter de Gruyter.

Jackson, Peter. 2006. 'The Canonicity of the Netti and Other Works'. *Journal of the Pali Text Society* 28: 61–62.

Jantrasrisalai, Chanida, Timothy Lenz, Lin Qian and Richard Salomon. 2016. 'Fragments of an Ekottarikāgama Manuscript in Gāndhārī'. In *Buddhist Manuscripts, Volume IV. Manuscripts in the Schøyen Collection*, edited by Jens Braarvig, 1–122. Oslo: Hermes Publishing.

Lamotte, Étienne. 1988. *History of Indian Buddhism: From the Origins to the Śaka Era*. Translated by Sara Webb-Boin. Publications de l'Institut orientaliste de Louvain 36. Louvain: Peeters Press.

Lenz, Timothy. 2003. *A New Version of the Gāndhārī Dharmapada and a Collection of Previous-Birth Stories: British Library Kharoṣṭhī Fragments 16 + 25*. Gandhāran Buddhist Texts 3. Seattle: University of Washington Press.

Levering, Miriam. 1989. 'Scripture and Its Reception: A Buddhist Case'. In *Rethinking Scripture: Essays from a Comparative Perspective*, edited by Miriam Levering, 58–101. Albany: State University of New York.

Norman, K.R. 1983. *Pāli Literature, including the Canonical Literature in Prakrit and Sanskrit of all the Hīnayāna Schools of Buddhism*. A History of Indian Literature, vol. VII, fasc. 2. Wiesbaden: Otto Harrassowitz.

———. 2004. 'A New Version of the Gāndhārī Dharmapada?' *Acta Orientalia* 65: 113–133.

———. 2006. 2nd edn. *A Philological Approach to Buddhism. The Bukkyō Dendō Kyōkai Lectures 1994*. Lancaster: The Pali Text Society.

Nyunt, Peter, trans. 2012. *Catalogue of the Piṭaka and Other Texts in Pāḷi, Pāḷi-Burmese, and Burmese (Piṭakat-tō-sa-muiṅ:) by Maṅ:-krī: Mahāsirijeya-sū*. Bristol: Pali Text Society.

Salomon, Richard. 1999. *Ancient Buddhist Scrolls from Gandhāra: the British Library Kharoṣṭhī Fragments*. Seattle: University of Washington Press.

———. 2006. 'Recent Discoveries of Early Buddhist Manuscripts and their Implications for the History of Buddhist Texts and Canons'. In *Between the Empires: Society in India 300 BCE to 400 CE*, ed. Patrick Olivelle, 349–382. Oxford: Oxford University Press. https://doi.org/10.1093/acprof:oso/9780195305326.003.0014

———. 2008. (with a contribution by Andrew Glass) *Two Gāndhārī Manuscripts of the Songs of Lake Anavatapta (Anavatapta-gāthā): British Library Kharoṣṭhī Fragment 1 and Senior Scroll 14*. Gandhāran Buddhist Texts 5. Seattle: University of Washington Press.

———. 2011. 'An Unwieldy Canon: Observations on Some Distinctive Features of Canon Formation in Buddhism'. In *Kanonisierung und Kanonbildung in der asiatischen Religionsgeschichte*, edited by Max Deeg, Oliver Freiberger and Christoph Kleine, 161–207. Vienna: Verlag der Österreichischen Akademie der Wissenschaften.

———. 2014. 'Gāndhārī Manuscripts in the British Library, Schøyen and Other Collections'. In *From Birch-Bark to Digital Data: Recent Advances in Buddhist Manuscript Research*, ed. Paul Harrison and Jens-Uwe Hartmann, 1–17. Vienna: Verlag der Österreichischen Akademie der Wissenschaften. https://doi.org/10.2307/j.ctt1vw0q4q.4

———. 2017. 'On the Evolution of Written *Āgama* Collections in Northern Buddhist Traditions'. In *Research on the Madhyama-āgama*, edited by Dhammadinnā, 239–268. Dharma Drum Institute of Liberal Arts Research Series 5. Taipei: Dharma Drum Publishing Corporation.

Silverlock, Blair. 2015. *An Edition and Study of the Goṣiga-sutra, the Cow-Horn Discourse (Senior Collection scroll no. 12), An Account of the Harmonious Aṇarudha Monks*. Unpublished PhD thesis, University of Sydney.

Skilling, Peter. 2009. 'Redaction, Recitation, and Writing: Transmission of the Buddha's Teaching in India in the Early Period'. In *Buddhist Manuscript Cultures: Knowledge, Ritual, and Art*, edited by Stephen C. Berkwitz, Juliane Schober and Claudia Brown, 53–75. London: Routledge

Somadasa, K. D. 1987. *Catalogue of the Hugh Nevill Collection of Sinhalese Manuscripts in the British Library, Vol. 1*. London and Henley-on-Thames: British Library and Pali Text Society.

Wynne, Alexander. 2004. 'The Oral Transmission of Early Buddhist Literature'. *Journal of the International Association of Buddhist Studies* 27(1): 97–127.

Mark Allon is Senior Lecturer in South Asian Buddhist Studies at the University of Sydney. His primary research interests are the composition and transmission of early Buddhist literature, the ways in which texts have been used by Buddhist communities, and the Indic languages of early Buddhist texts (Pāli, Gāndhārī, Sanskrit). He is involved in two major research projects. The first concerns the study and publication of the recently discovered Gāndhārī Buddhist manuscripts from Afghanistan and Pakistan. The second involves the conservation, photographing, and study of the Kuthodaw Pagoda marble stelae recension of the Pāli canon in Mandalay, Myanmar. He is the author of *Style and Function: A Study of Dominant Stylistic Features of the Prose Portions of Pāli Canonical Sutta Texts and Their Mnemonic Function* (Tokyo, 1997), *Three Gāndhārī Ekottarikāgama-Type Sūtras: British Library Kharoṣṭhī Fragments 12 and 14* (Seattle, 2001), and numerous articles on early Buddhist literature.

— 14 —

Theriya Networks and the Circulation of the Pali Canon in South Asia: The Vibhajjavādins Reconsidered

ALEXANDER WYNNE

This article offers further support for Lance Cousins' thesis that the Pāli canon, written down in the first century BCE in Sri Lanka, was based largely on a Theriya manuscript tradition from South India. Attention is also given to some of Cousins' related arguments, in particular, that this textual transmission occurred within a Vibhajjavādin framework; that it occurred in a form of 'proto-Pāli' close to the Standard Epigraphical Prakrit of the first century BCE; and that that distinct Sinhalese *nikāyas* emerged perhaps as late as the third century CE.

Introduction

In more or less all the recent research on early Buddhism, and on Indian Buddhism more generally, very little has been said about the formation of the Pali canon, the only complete Tipiṭaka to have survived in an Indic language. The state of knowledge has hardly changed since K. R. Norman's *Pali Literature* was published over thirty years ago:

> The tradition recorded in the Sinhalese chronicles states that the Theravadin canon was written down during the first century B.C. as a result of threats to the *Saṅgha* from famine, war, and the growing power of the Abhayagiri *vihāra,* to which the king was more favourably disposed. There is no reason to reject this tradition, because there are indications that texts were already being written down before this date. It seems probable that the Sanskritisation of Pali was virtually fixed at the stage it had reached by the time of the commission to writing ... (Norman 1983, 5)

Apart from his comments on Sanskritisation, Norman here restates what is found in the Pali chronicles. But these works do not inspire much historical confidence. This is especially the case with the *Mahāvaṃsa*, which presents a simplistic account that can hardly be taken seriously: in a short series of verses (XXIII.80ff.), it tells of the foundation of the Abhayagiri-vihāra, its schism from the Mahāvihāra and the writing down of the Tipiṭaka and commentaries. This sixth century CE text is also remote from the events it describes, and differs from the *Dīpavaṃsa*, the simpler account of which probably dates to early fourth century CE.[1] But the *Dīpavaṃsa* is also a difficult work, whose verses on the writing down of the Tipiṭaka (XX.20–21)

1. According to von Hinüber (1996, 89, 91), the *Dīpavaṃsa* dates 'not long after 350 CE' and the

Keywords: Pāḷi, Tipiṭaka, *Aṭṭhakathā*, Vibhajjavāda, Theriya, Mahāvihāra, Nāgārjunakoṇḍa

tell us very little indeed. This means that Norman's assumptions are historically dubious at best; if so it would seem that no progress has been made in understanding a central problem in the study of Indian Buddhism.

It is most fortunate, therefore, that in a recent series of articles (2001, 2012, 2013), Lance Cousins formulated a more compelling account of the early Pali tradition. Cousins has argued that the Pali Tipiṭaka was written down in South India before being transmitted to Sri Lanka in the first century BCE; that Sanskritisation occurred gradually and slowly, in the centuries following the origin of a written canon; that the process of canonical formation occurred among the Vibhajjavādin Theriyas, an old monastic grouping dating to the Mauryan period; and that the schism between Mahāvihāra and Abhayagiri occurred in the third century CE, not the first century BCE.[2] These claims, even if only partially true, would transform the general understanding of early Theravādin history, and hence deserve a detailed examination.

1. The formation of a written Tipiṭaka

The notion that the Tipiṭaka was written down in the first century BCE is based on Dīp XX.20–21, verses associated with events that occurred in the period of Vattagāmani (late first century BCE):

> Monks previously handed down the text of the three baskets and its commentary by word of mouth (20). Upon seeing the decline in people, the monks held a gathering and had (it) written down in books, in order to preserve the Dhamma (21).[3]

These couplets were probably added to the old account of Sinhalese regnal history contained in Dīp XX. But this does not detract from their general historical value, given the patchwork nature of the *Dīpavaṃsa* (Cousins 2013, 108–109). Importantly, the claim that oral traditions were endangered by a 'decline in people' (*hāniṃ disvāna sattānaṃ*) is credible, for the Pali commentaries contain a number of passages on the 'danger' or 'terror' (*bhaya*) which afflicted the island at this time.[4] Cousins (2013, 110) has drawn attention to one such account in the *Manorathapūraṇī* (*Aṅguttaranikāya-aṭṭhakathā*), which seems to situate a nascent manuscript tradition within a redaction of Sinhalese and South Indian versions of the Tipiṭaka:

Mahāvaṃsa to 'the end of the fifth century CE'. Cousins (2012, 76) dates the *Dīpavaṃsa* to the early fourth century CE and the *Mahāvaṃsa* to 'two or three centuries later' (2012, 77).

2. I use the term Theravādin, Theriya and Thera(-vaṃsa) loosely and interchangeably; these terms occur variously in Pali commentaries and subcommentaries, and in Indian inscriptions, but have the same referent, i.e. monastic lineages belonging to the non-Mahāsaṃghika branch of Indian Buddhism. On these terms see Gethin 2012, 5ff.

3. Dīp XX.20–21: *piṭakattayapāliñ ca tassā aṭṭhakatham pi ca, mukhapāṭhena ānesuṃ pubbe bhikkhu mahāmati* (20). *hāniṃ disvā sattānaṃ tadā bhikkhu samāgatā, ciraṭṭhitatthaṃ dhammassa potthakesu likhāpayuṃ* (21).

4. On the terror, generally attributed to the Caṇḍāla or Brahmin Tissa, see Cousins 2013, 110, n.45.

Manorathapūraṇī I (*Ekakanipāta-aṭṭhakathā*, X.42): 91.22–93.25[5]

The disappearance of scriptural learning is the root cause of this fivefold disappearance.[6] For with the disappearance of scriptural learning, practice disappears, but when learning remains, (practice) endures. It is because of just this that on this island, during the great terror of Caṇḍāla Tissa, Sakka, king of the gods, had a great raft built and informed the monks: 'There will be a great terror, the rains will fail; lacking the requisites, *bhikkhus* will not be able to maintain scriptural learning. The Noble Ones must go to the yonder shore, to save their lives. Get on to this great raft and go, venerable sirs. For whom there is not enough room for sitting, they should rest their chests on pieces of wood and go; the terror will affect none of them.'

Then, upon reaching the ocean shore, sixty *bhikkhus* agreed: 'There is no need for us, now, to go; we will stay right here and preserve the Tipiṭaka.' Turning back from there they went to the Southern Malaya country, and kept themselves alive on tubers, roots and leaves. When able to keep their bodies going, they sat down and recited individually; when unable, they piled up sand all around, and keeping their heads in a single position, they mastered the scriptures. By this method they preserved the whole Tipiṭaka, along with the commentaries, perfectly, for twelve years.

When the terror had dissipated, seven hundred *bhikkhus*, who had not lost even a single character or phoneme of the Tipiṭaka and commentaries, in the place they had gone to, returned to this very island and took up residence in the Maṇḍalārāma monastery in Kallagāma country. Upon hearing the news that the Theras had returned, the sixty monks who had been left behind on the island decided to go and see them. When collating the Tipiṭaka with the Theras they did not find even a single character or phoneme in disagreement.

During that meeting a discussion arose among the Theras: 'Is scriptural learning or practice the root of the Dispensation?'. The Theras who wore rubbish rags said practice is the root, while the Dhamma-preachers said it is scriptural learning. But then the Theras said to them: 'We will not act on the mere word of you two groups: recite a Sutta spoken by the Jina.' Thinking it no difficulty to recite a Sutta, (the rubbish-rag wearers) recited these Suttas:

'And should these almsmen live correctly, Subhadda, the world would not be devoid of Arahants';[7] 'The dispensation of the teacher, great king, is rooted in practice, its essence is practice: it endures when practice is upheld'.[8]

Upon hearing this Sutta the Dhamma-preachers, in order to establish their own position, recited this Sutta:

'As long as the Suttantas endure, and as long as the Vinaya shines forth, so long will (people) see light, just like when the sun has risen.

If the Suttantas do not exist, and if the Vinaya is forgotten, there will be darkness in

---

5. See appendix for Pali.
6. For the fivefold disappearance see Mp I 87 3: *tattha pañca antaradhānāni nāma: adhigama-antaradhānaṃ paṭipatti-antaradhānaṃ, pariyatti-antaradhānaṃ liṅgantaradhāṇaṃ dhātu-antaradhānan ti.*
7. D II 151: *ime ca subhadda bhikkhū sammā vihareyyuṃ asuñño loko arantehi assa.*
8. Mil 133: *paṭipattimūlakaṃ mahārāja satthusāsanaṃ paṭipattisārakaṃ paṭipattiyā anantarahitāya tiṭṭhatī ti.* The citation from D II 151 (*Mahāparinibbāna Sutta*) is also found at Mil 133.

> the world, just like when the sun has set.
>
> When the Suttanta is protected, practice is protected; the wise man established in practice does not fail to reach the release from bondage.'
>
> When this Sutta had been recited, the rubbish-rag wearers fell silent, and the position of the Dhamma-preaching Theras alone predominated. Just as, when there is no milch-cow to protect the lineage within a herd of a hundred or a thousand cows, that lineage or tradition is not continued, even so when there are as many as a hundred or a thousand *bhikkhus* who have undertaken insight meditation, but without scriptural learning, they cannot penetrate the Noble Path. Just as, when characters are inscribed[9] on the surface of a stone, to identify a treasure trove, as long as the characters survive that treasure trove is not lost, even so if scriptural learning is upheld the dispensation does not disappear.

This account is the only attempt to explain in any detail the Sinhalese Saṅgha's response to the troubled period of Vattagāmani. The motive for leaving the island, and the account of what happened upon the monks' return, are both believable; the numbers involved are plausibly small (Cousins 2013, 111). The claim for complete agreement between the two groups ('they did not find even a single character or phoneme in disagreement') should not be taken at face value, for by using the language of collation ('purifying', *sodhentā*), the account suggests that redaction took place. As Cousins has pointed out, there must have been 'some kind of official acceptance of the new written texts, perhaps with a measure of reconciliation with any divergent local traditions' (2013, 111). The account thus implies that a Sinhalese 'proto-canon', consisting of texts transmitted in the Mauryan period, was harmonised with a Theriya canon that had developed on the Indian mainland subsequent to the Aśokan missions;[10] this took place at the Maṇḍalārāma monastery of Kallagāma, apparently a major centre of Sinhalese Buddhism in the first century BCE.[11]

The similes occurring at the end of the account suggest writing was involved in the redactional process. The first simile is not particularly convincing: the image of a 'milch-cow' maintaining a herd of cows suggests that persons – *bhikkhus* – are the best means of ensuring the transmission of Dhamma. But the simile of a stone inscription which records the identity of a treasure trove (*nidhikumbhiyā jānanatthāya pāsāṇapiṭṭhe akkharesu upanibaddhesu*) is more revealing: it suggests that the 'treasure' of the Dhamma can best be preserved through the written word.

9. *upanibandhesu* (Be *ṭhapitesu*); the Ee reading should be emended to *upanibaddhesu*, 'written, composed, arranged' (Monier Williams, *A Sanskrit-English Dictionary*, s.v.; this meaning is not noted in CPD, Cone or Rhys Davids & Stede).

10. Cousin's conclusion (2013, 113) is more cautious: 'the four *Nikāyas* ... were accepted at some kind of assembly of the Saṃgha in a district (*janapada*) whose Sinhaḷa name is Palicized as Kallagāma(ka) or Kālakagāma, but we do not know if any additions or amendments were made.'

11. On the Maṇḍalārāma, Malalasekera notes (1997, 429): 'A monastery in Ceylon, probably near the village of Bhokkanta. It was the residence of the Elder Mahā Tissa, reciter of the Dhammapada ... According to the Vibhanga Commentary the monastery was in the village of Kālakagāma, and, in the time of Vattagāmanī, it was the residence of many monks, at the head of whom was Tissabhūta.' On the tradition that the Pali canon was written down in the Alu-vihāra, see Norman 1983, 11.

The use of writing also makes sense if, as seems likely, the returning Sinhalese *bhikkhus* brought an expanded canon which required a transmission in manuscript form. Texts such as the *Milindapañha*, the *Nettippakaraṇa*, the *Peṭakopadesa*, the *Niddesa*, the *Apadāna* and even much of the canonical Abhidhamma were probably composed in post-Aśokan India.[12] In this connection, it is important to note that the citations offered in support of practice (*paṭipatti*), by the *paṃsukūlika* Theras, are both found in the opening, and probably original, section of the *Milindapañha*.[13] A canon of this extent would have required the redirection of resources towards the development of scribes and scholasticism. The *bhikkhus* who resisted this move perhaps feared the greater demands on monastic time and effort would come at the expense of practice. But after a lengthy period of disruption and danger, it is not surprising that the practical benefit of writing was recognized.

Cousins has commented at length on the extent of the canon at this time and its language, in particular the development of Pali in the new scribal tradition. He has argued that the language of the canon was 'Old Pali', a local version of the 'Common Epigraphical Prakrit' which resembles the older, more archaic, Aśokan dialect found at Girnār and Bombay-Sopārā, and which replaced Aśokan Prakrit in the post-Mauryan period (Cousins 2013, 120–122; Salomon 1998, 76–77). Standard Pali developed along the lines suggested by the epigraphic record, with an increasingly Sanskritised orthography reflecting the rise of Epigraphical Hybrid Sanskrit and then pure Sanskrit between the first century BCE and fourth century CE (Cousins 2013, 125–127; Salomon 1998, 81ff.). Salomon has pointed out that the influence of Sanskrit emerges in the early centuries CE:[14] Epigraphical Hybrid Sanskrit became predominant in this period, its influence probably emanating from Mathurā,[15] eventually culminating in 'the final triumph of classical Sanskrit in the Gupta era' (Salomon 1998, 84).[16]

2. A Vibhajjavādin canon?

Apart from the argument that the extant Pali canon was produced within a Theravādin network reaching from South India to Sri Lanka, Cousins also claimed that this network can be identified as the Vibhajjavādin wing of the Theriya/Sthavira Sangha. Apart from André Bareau's *Les Sectes Bouddhiques du Petit Véhicule* (1955), little attention has been paid to the Vibhajjavādins. Nothing is said of them in Erich Frauwallner's seminal *The Earliest Vinaya and the Beginnings of Buddhist Literature*

12. See Frauwallner (1995, 42), von Hinüber (1996, 61, 79–86), Norman (1983, 86–87, 91–92).

13. See n. 7–8, and von Hinüber's remarks on the composition of the *Milindapañha* (1996, 85).

14. Salomon (1998, 81): 'From about the first to the fourth century of the Christian era, a large number of inscriptions were written in a peculiar language which is neither fully Sanskrit nor fully Prakrit'.

15. Salomon (1998, 82): 'EHS ... was definitely the predominant language overall for the first three centuries of the Christian era ... the pattern of distribution of EHS inscriptions gives the impression that they radiate out from Mathurā toward the northeast and southwest'.

16. Norman's argument places Sanskritisation too early: he claims (1983, 5) that 'the progressive Sanskritization of the Mathurā inscriptions' begins 'around the end of Asoka's reign.'

(1956); Etienne Lamotte's monumental *Histoire du Boudhisme indien* (1958) largely ignores the group. Focusing on the reasons for the schism between Sthavira and Mahāsāṃghika, Lamotte bypasses most of the various denominations he lists. And since the Vibhajyavādins hardly feature in Lamotte's lists (1988, 534–36: 'List I of Bhavya', 'the Saṃmatīya List = List III of Bhavya', 'Mahāsāṃghika List'; p.545: 'Sarvāstivādin List by Vinītadeva'), Lamotte gives the impression that the group are yet another of the doxographic literature's 'pseudo-historical elucrubrations' (p.547).

Cousins has attempted to rebalance Lamotte's account by noting (2001, 146) that the latter tends 'to confuse by setting out many different accounts, as if they are all independent sources of evidence of equal value.' But five of the seven sources in Lamotte's section on lists with two subdivisions (1988, 529 ff.) are 'simply versions derived from the sixth — the treatise of Vasumitra' (Cousins 2001, 151). Cousins thus claims (2001, 155) that the only genuinely different account of the sects is to be found in 'List II of Bhavya' (Lamotte 1988, 536), which is 'probably earlier than the fifth century CE'. Cousins argues that Bhavya II was probably derived from a 'mainland Vibhajjavādin account', since it 'emphasizes the separateness of the Vibhajjavādins: they are treated as one of three roots with the Theriyas and Mahāsaṃghikas' (Cousins 2001, 158), which then separated into the Mahīśāsakas, Kāśyapīyas, Dharmaguptakas as well as the Sinhalese Theriyas (Tāmraśaṭīyas).

Cousins is surely correct to point out that Vasumitra's account of the sects has proliferated within the doxographic literature. Balancing this north-western, Sarvāstivādin/Mahāyānist account with List II of Bhavya instead suggests a different perspective, one in which the Vibhajjavādins had a more significant role in the sectarian development of Indian Buddhism. It is tempting, indeed, to hypothesise that the first century BCE transmission of Pali literature, from South India to Sri Lanka, took place within a general Vibhajjavādin framework. This is Cousins' conclusion (2013, 113): the 'written texts of the four *Nikāyas* at least' originated 'immediately from some Vibhajjavādin tradition located in the Karnataka-Andhra region ... in the first century B.C.' Direct evidence for this thesis is contained in a few *Dīpavaṃsa* verses (Cousins 2001, 135–136):

Dīpavaṃsa XVIII.1
'Nowadays there are also other senior, middling and young (*bhikkhus*), Vibhajjavādas who protect the tradition of the Vinaya (and) the Dispensation.'

idāni atthi aññe pi therā ca majjhimā navā, vibhajjavādā vinaye sāsane paveṇipālakā.

Dīpavaṃsa XVIII.41
'... and the acclaimed Samuddā, skilled in the lineage of the true teaching; [Samuddā and the *bhikkhunī* Dīpanayā,] they were both Vibhajjavādins, transmitters of the Vinaya, beautifications of the Sangha.'

abhiññātā ca samuddā saddhammavaṃsakovidā, vibhajjavādi vinayadharā ubho tā saṃghasobhaṇā.

Dīpavaṃsa XVIII.44
'Nowadays there are other senior, middling and young (*bhikkhuṇīs*), Vibhajjavādins, transmitters of the Vinaya, protectors of the tradition of the Dispensation, extremely

learned, endowed with virtue, illuminating this earth.'

idāni atthi aññāyo therikā majjhimā navā, vibhajjavādī vinayadharā sāsane paveṇipālakā, bahussutā sīlasampannā obhāsenti mahiṃ iman ti.

It is striking that the terms *vibhajjavādā, vibhajjavādi* and *vibhajjavādī* are followed by the terms *vinaye* and *vinayadharā*. This suggests a close connection between the Vibhajjavādin identity and Vinaya observance, one which could be strengthened by reading the terms as compounds; this would provide direct evidence for a Vibhajjavādin Vinaya, and hence a Vibhajjavādin Tipiṭaka. But this is not very likely. The term *vibhajjavādi* (v.41) should not be understood as a stem form within a compound, for the variation in vowel strength (*i/ī*) is common and insignificant in the Pali manuscript tradition. Furthermore, the expression *vinayadhara* hardly ever appears at the end of an extended compound in post-canonical Pali literature.[17]

The syntax of XVIII.1 is more open to interpretation. While the direct object of 'protecting' (*pālakā*) is clear (*paveṇi-pālakā*), it is odd that there are two indirect objects in the locative case (*vinaye sāsane*): 'protecting the tradition, with regard to the Vinaya, with regard to the Dispensation' is odd, and it might be preferable to read *vibhajjavāda* (rather than *vibhajjavādā*) and take the compound *vibhajjavāda-vinaye* as an adjective qualifying *sāsane*: 'with regard to the Dispensation, in the (tradition of) the Vibhajjavāda-Vinaya'. The reading of the Sinhalese edition is different: *vibhajjavādā vinaye sāsanavaṃsapālakā*, meaning either 'Vibhajjavādas, protectors of the lineage of the Dispensation rooted in the Vinaya' or 'Protecting the lineage of the Dispensation rooted in the Vibhajjavāda Vinaya'.[18]

None of this is conclusive. But it is important to note that Dīp XVIII is overwhelmingly concerned with Vinaya and the heritage of the Buddhist tradition in Sri Lanka, suggesting that early monastic and literary transmission in Sri Lanka occurred within a Vibhajjavādin tradition. Indeed, Cousins has noted (2001, 136) that since 'the specific context concerns nuns ordained on the island of Ceylon, the expression can only refer to an ancestor of the Pali Vinaya which I take to be the Vinaya as it was before the separation of the Ceylon school from some of its mainland counterparts.'

The use of the term *vibhajjavāda* in the *Kathāvatthu* commentary probably has a similar heritage to these *Dīpavaṃsa* verses. In its account of the third council of Pāṭaliputta, and in response to Asoka's question about what the Buddha taught (*kiṃvādī bhante sammāsambuddho*), Moggaliputtatissa states that the Buddha was a Vibhajjavādin (*vibhajjavādī mahārājā*).[19] Cousins has argued that this account 'can only have been composed at a time when the word was already known as the name

17. E.g. *tepiṭakābhidhammikavinayadharānaṃ* (Ja IV 219); *dhammadharavinayadharavibhāgato* (Spk-ṭ I.86, Be); *dhammavinayadharā* (Ps-ṭ II.241, Be).

18. Se *vibhajjavādī vinayaṃdharā sāsanapālakā* (v.44cd); The term *paveṇi* is also unusual in the *Dīpavaṃsa*, and if so the verse as printed in the Sinhalese edition might make better sense, even if the Sinhalese edition of the text is less reliable. Cousins has noted (2001, 135 n.11) that *vibhajjavādā* (Dīp XVIII.1) could simply mean 'followers of the Vibhajjavāda'.

19. Kv-a I.7: *ath' aññe bhikkhū pakkosāpetvā pucchi: kiṃvādī bhante sammāsambuddho ti? vibhajjavādī mahārājā ti. evaṃ vutte rājā theraṃ pucchi: vibhajjavādī bhante sammāsambuddho ti?* āma *mahārājā ti.*

of a school' (Cousins 2001, 138). At the least, the resonance of the term *vibhajjavādī* in this account would have been obvious in the commentarial period, for the old sections of the *Kathāvatthu* exemplify the *vibhajjavāda* approach to Buddhist teaching, that is to say, a metaphysically conservative approach which aims to hone insight without going beyond the bounds of Suttanta teaching (especially by falling into its *sabbatthivāda* and *puggalavāda* interpretations).[20] The combined evidence of the *Dīpavaṃsa* and *Kathāvatthu* commentary suggests that the Vibhajjavādins understood themselves to be a Vinaya-Abhidhamma school with roots in the Asokārāma of Pāṭaliputta.

If a Vibhajjavādin identity predominated during the formation of the written Tipiṭaka in the first century BCE, the formation of separate Mahāvihāra and Abhayagirivihāra Nikāyas would have been some way off. But the notion of an early schism has been accepted by some, based on the account in the *Mahāvaṃsa*. This brief account (Mhv XXXIII.80ff.) relates the schism to the expulsion of Tissa for 'the frequenting of lay-families' (v.95: *kulasaṃsaggadosena*).[21] There seems little to choose between this and the reasons given for schism in the *Dīpavaṃsa* (quarrels about the age of ordination and the use of ivory).[22] The traditions of both chronicles are equally plausible. But the account in the *Mahāvaṃsa* is condensed: it is possible, but hardly likely, that canonical formation, the establishment of the Abhayagirivihāra and then schism all happened in the troubled period of Vaṭṭagāmaṇi.[23] The *Dīpavaṃsa* places the schism significantly later, in its brief section on Mahāsena's rule in the third century CE. As such, it seems to cohere with the idea of a gradual emergence of local traditions starting from Vibhajjavādin origins in the first century BCE.

The picture of the Vibhajjavādins which emerges from Cousins' work is of a post-Mauryan Buddhist network, connected by monastic lineage as well as by the Abhidhamma perspective of the *Kathāvatthu*. Literature was shared throughout this network — texts such as the *Milindapañha* were received from Northern Vibhajjavādins — even if the Sinhalese canon was formed among the Vibhajjavādins of the South. This took place at the point when the Northern and Southern Vibhajjavādin lineages had started to separate into distinct schools, a process which soon led to the emergence of the Mahiṃsāsaka and Tambapaṇṇiya/Mahāvihāra traditions and so the gradual loss of Vibhajjavādin identity.

20. See Cousins' discussion (2005, 57–58) of the early sections of the *Kathāvatthu*, which is concerned especially with the *sabbatthivāda* and *puggalavāda*.

21. Mhv XXXIII.95: *theraṃ kulehi saṃsaṭṭhaṃ mahātisso ti vissutaṃ, kulasaṃsaggadosena saṃgho taṃ nīharī ito.*

22. Dīp XXII.72–74: *ubhosamaggabhāvissaṃ anuññātaṃ kumārakassape, akappiyan ti dīpesuṃ dussīlā mohapārutā* (72). *chabbaggiyānaṃ vatthusmiṃ ananuññātaṃ dantavattakaṃ, anuññātan ti dīpesuṃ alajjī dantagaṇikā* (73). *imañ c' aññaṃ bhikkhū atthaṃ aññe bahu akaraṇe, adhammo iti dīpesuṃ alajjī lābhahetukaṃ* (74). Oldenberg (1879, 112) has conjectured *upasampadaṃ gabbhavīsaṃ* for *ubhosamaggabhāvissaṃ* (72a) based on the *Mahāvaṃsa Ṭīkā*.

23. According to Cousins (2012, 80f), parts of the account (Mhv XXXIII.95ff.) are also corrupt and probably interpolated.

3. The demise of the Vibhajjavādins

The Vibhajjavādins are rarely mentioned in the Pali commentaries. The term is mostly avoided in the colophons (*nigamana-kathā*) to Buddhaghosa's commentarial works, the important parts of which focus on a different form of Theriya identity:

> This commentary on the Dīgha Nikāya, called 'Splendidly Unfolding the Most Auspicious' (*sumaṅgala-vilāsinī*), has been prepared by the Thera whose name is understood by revered teachers to be 'Buddhaghosa', who is adorned with supremely purified faith, intelligence and endeavour; who is endowed with a multitude of qualities, such as virtue, good conduct, quick-wittedness and gentility; who is capable of plunging the inner depths of his own and (other) traditions; who is endowed with a distinction of understanding in the dispensation of the teacher, with the divisions of scriptural learning contained in the Tipiṭaka along with its commentary; the might of whose knowledge is unobstructed; a great exegete; endowed with charming expressions, sweet and lofty, emanating from the bliss produced through his accomplishment in articulation; whose utterances are appropriate and devoid (of fault), the best of speakers, a great seer; whose intelligence is expansive and pure, (and) who is an adornment to the lineage of the Mahāvihāravāsin Theras, those illuminators of the Thera lineage whose understanding is well established in (that dispensation) which is encompassed by a profusion of discriminating knowledge, is adorned with the qualities found in such categories (of the Dhamma) as the six higher knowledges, and which transcends human phenomena.[24]

This standard 'conclusion' formula, found widely in the colophons of the commentaries attributed to Buddhaghosa, does not refer to the Vibhajjavādins, and nor do the colophons of the commentaries attributed to Dhammapāla or Mahānāma.[25] Since the colophons attributed to Buddhaghosa were probably not composed by Buddhaghosa himself, it would seem that the term *vibhajjavādin* was not an important form of identification in the post-Buddhaghosa era (Gethin 2012, 16). But a few occurrences within the commentaries and *Visuddhimagga* suggest that the term was still somewhat meaningful to Buddhaghosa himself. For example, toward the end of the *Visuddhimagga*, just before the standard conclusion formula, Buddhaghosa refers to the Mahāvihāravāsins as Vibhajjavādins:

> Accepting the request of venerable Saṅghapāla — a wise member of the lineage of

24. Sv III.250 (Be): *paramavisuddhasaddhābuddhivīriya-paṭimaṇḍitena sīlācārajjavamaddavādiguṇa-samudayasamuditena sakasamayasamayantaragahanajjhogāhaṇasamatthena paññāveyyattiya-samannāgatena tipiṭakapariyattippabhede sāṭṭhakathe satthusāsane appaṭihatañāṇappabhāvena mahāveyyākaraṇena karaṇasampattijanitasukhaviniggatamadhurodāravacanalāvaṇṇayuttena yuttamuttavādinā vādīvarena mahākavinā pabhinnapaṭisambhidāparivāre chaḷabhiññādippabh edaguṇapaṭimaṇḍite uttarimanussadhamme suppatiṭṭhita-buddhīnaṃ theravaṃsappadīpānaṃ therānaṃ mahāvihāravāsīnaṃ vaṃsālaṅkārabhūtena vipulavisuddhabuddhinā buddhaghoso ti garūhi gahitanāmadheyyena therena katā ayaṃ sumaṅgalavilāsinī nāma dīghanikāyaṭṭhakathā.*

    Buddhaghosa's commentarial introductions (*ganthārambha-kathā*) similarly refer to 'the tradition of Theras who dwell in the Mahāvihāra (and) illuminate the Thera lineage' (e.g. Sv-a I.1: *samayaṃ ... therānaṃ theravaṃsapadīpānaṃ .... mahāvihāre nivāsīnaṃ*; see Gethin 2012, 15–16).

25. Sp VII.1416, Ps V.110, Spk III.308, Mp V.99, Pj I.253, Dhp-a IV.235, Pj II.608, As 430, Vibh-a 523 and the *Paṭṭhānappakaraṇaṭṭhakathā* (Be 498). The work of Dhammapāla is identified with the Mahāvihāravāsins, and of Mahānāma with Theras and the Theravāda (Gethin 2012, 16–17).

> the Mahāvihāravāsins, illustrious Theriyas, the best of Vibhajjavādins, (who) practises purity and penance, is devoted to observing the moral discipline of the Vinaya, committed to practice, (and) whose mind is adorned with qualities such as forbearance, gentleness, and compassion — desiring the endurance of the true Dhamma, whatever heap of merit I have attained while making this (work), through its lustre may all creatures prosper in bliss.[26]

It is significant that Buddhaghosa's personal testimony refers to the Mahāvihāravāsins as the 'best of Vibhajjavādins', whereas the anonymous conclusions to the commentaries (and to the *Visuddhimagga*) do not. Might this imply that Buddhaghosa was aware of an ancient identity which the then incumbents of the Mahāvihāra had largely left behind? Perhaps this old identity was not important to the Mahāvihāravāsins of the fourth century CE,[27] who had by now ceased to refer to themselves as Vibhajjavādins, whereas Buddhaghosa, an incomer from South India, wished to draw attention to a former identity shared by the Mahāvihāravāsins and the Theriya Buddhists of South India. Another reference to the Vibhajjavādins, in the conclusion of the commentary on the *Paṭṭhāna*, lends support to this notion:

> The commentary, which I have undertaken out of faith — without deviating from the teaching of the (*Paṭṭhāna*'s) masters, pupils of the Vibhajjavādins — being without obstruction in the world, the obstructions of which are excessive and manifold, that (commentary) has today been made thus, in fourteen recitation sections, illuminating the meaning of the entire, choice, Paṭṭhāna. Just as (I have) reached the conclusion (of the commentary), thus, for the many, may every good intention quickly come to perfection.[28]

If the 'pupils' are taken as the present generation of Mahāvihāravāsins, it is tempting to understand their Vibhajjavādin predecessors as previous generations of Theriya masters, who maintained an old identity now largely surpassed with the rise of the scholarly tradition of the Mahāvihāra. A further passage from the commentary on the *Vibhaṅga*, found also in the *Visuddhimagga*, comments on the interpretation of Dependent Arising and lends further support to the idea of an older, shared, Vibhajjavādin identity:

> Now, directly related to that (analysis of the sense faculties) is the analysis of Dependent Arising. With regard to this, the one making the commentary on the meaning of the teaching (*tanti*) laid down in the method beginning 'from the cause of ignorance (arise) constructions', (he ought to proceed as follows): entering the circle of Vibhajjavādins, without criticising (its) masters or rejecting one's own tra-

26. *vibhajjavādiseṭṭhānaṃ theriyānaṃ yasassinaṃ, mahāvihāravāsīnaṃ vaṃsajassa vibhāvino. bhadantasaṅghapālassa sucisallekhavuttino, vinayācārayuttassa yuttassa paṭipattiyaṃ. khantisoracca mettādiguṇabhūsitacetaso, ajjhesanaṃ gahetvāna karontena imaṃ mayā. saddhammaṭṭhitikāmena yo patto puññasañcayo, tassa tejena sabbe pi sukham edhantu pāṇino.*

27. According to von Hinüber (1996, 102–03) Buddhaghosa dates to the late fourth/early fifth century CE.

28. *Paṭṭhānappakaraṇaṭṭhakathā* Be 497: *saddhāya samāraddhā yā aṭṭhakathā mayā, tassa ācariyānaṃ vādaṃ avihāya vibhajjavādi-sissānaṃ, atibahuvidhantarāye lokamhi anantarāyena, sā evaṃ ajja katā cuddasamattehi bhāṇavārehi atthaṃ pakāsayantī paṭṭhānavarassa sakalassa. sanniṭṭhānaṃ pattā yath' eva niṭṭhaṃ tathā bahujanassa, sampāpuṇantu sīghaṃ kalyāṇā sabbasaṅkappā.*

> dition, without pursuing (*anārūhantena*; Be: *anāyūhantena*) another tradition, without excluding Sutta [and] remaining in concord with Vinaya, considering (*olokentena*) the 'great authorities' (*mahāpadese*), illuminating the Dhamma, gathering together (*saṅgahantena*) the meaning, (and) repeatedly reverting to that very meaning (he should) give instruction even by means of other methods, since this is (how) a commentary on the meaning ought to be made.[29]

The doctrinal context suggests that the expression 'the circle of Vibhajjavādins' (*vibhajjavādi-maṇḍalaṃ*) refers to a tradition of exegesis, rather than a monastic lineage as such, and perhaps of a rather informal nature: the terms *maṇḍala* ('circle') and *samaya* ('concord', 'agreement', 'tradition') indicate vaguer forms of identity than 'lineage' (*vaṃsa*) or '(monastic) tradition' (*paveṇi*). If so, the passage gives no more than a general impression of a loose network of like-minded scholars, perhaps stretching across an extended area of South Asia.

These limited occurrences of the term *vibhajjavāda* in the commentaries indicate that an old and seemingly important identity had been largely surpassed by the fourth or fifth century CE. The gradual obsolescence of the Vibhajjavāda community through regional fragmentation is further suggested by the even less frequent use of the term in the sub-commentaries, on which Cousins (2001, 138) has commented as follows: 'It is clear that the original basis for the adoption of the name Vibhajjavādin ... becomes to a large extent forgotten, especially in later Pali sources.' This process would seem to have been well underway when Buddhaghosa prepared his commentarial works.

Conclusion: From Anurādhapura to Nāgārjunakoṇḍa and beyond

In many respects the history of Buddhism in the post-Mauryan period is more difficult to understand than the pre-Aśokan age. The Suttapiṭaka is a vast, sprawling, document which paints a realistic picture of Indian society and the place of Buddhism within it; rather surprisingly, for a document of such scale constructed from multiple oral sources, it contains vey few inconsistencies.[30] This lends credibility to its authenticity. Within a decentralised ascetic culture, and in an age of oral composition, it would have been difficult — perhaps almost impossible — to fabricate a coherent version of the Buddhist past. The significant disagreements to be expected of a multi-authored imagination of the past are more or less completely absent, a fact which rules against largle-scale invention.[31]

29. Vibh-a 130: *idāni tadanantare paṭiccasamuppādavibhaṅge yā ayaṃ avijjāpaccayā saṅkhārā ti ādinā nayena tanti nikkhittā, tassā atthasaṃvaṇṇanaṃ karontena, vibhajjavādīmaṇḍalaṃ otaritvā,* ācariye *anabbhācikkhantena sakasamayaṃ avokkamantena, parasamayaṃ anārūhantena, suttaṃ appaṭibāhantena vinayaṃ anulomentena mahāpadese olokentena, dhammaṃ dīpentena atthaṃ saṅgahantena, tam ev' atthaṃ puna* āvattetvā *aparehi pi pariyāyehi niddisantena ca, yasmā atthasaṃvaṇṇanā kātabbā hoti.* (Ñāṇamoli's translation (1991, 531) omits the problematic yasmā)

30. The most important inconsistency concerns the position of the so-called 'formless meditations', although this problem is not beyond historical reconstruction (see Wynne, 2007).

31. Sujato and Brahmali (2015, 25–26) have noted that the portrayal of 'political geography' in the early Buddhist world is consistent and pre-Aśokan. This observation can be generalised to the religious and social content of the Tipiṭaka.

Despite the serious challenges to understanding Indian Buddhism in the post-canonical period (Skilling 2012, xiv),[32] Lance Cousins' recent research has shown that significant progress can be made with a careful and judicious use of sources. References to the Vibhajjavādins are scarce in Pali commentaries and chronicles, and in the Indian doxographies; but they can be used to reconstruct a more plausible history. The writing down of the Pali canon can thus be attributed to the ongoing interactions within a post-Mauryan Theriya network, in South India and Sri Lanka, the old identity of which which gradually faded away.

If the dissolution of Vibhajjavādin identity was well advanced by the third or fourth century CE, we should expect Mahāvihāra and Abhayagiri identities to have emerged no later than the third century CE. There is direct evidence for this. A donative inscription in the Sinhalese monastery at Nāgārjunakoṇḍa, dating to the second half of the third century CE, contains important information on monastic identity and textual transmission in the period immediately prior to Buddhaghosa:[33]

> Success. The pair of feet of the Blessed one has been established for the benefit and happiness of all beings, in the monastery of the Theriya teachers, Vibhajjavādins, inspirers of faith in Kashmir, Gandhāra, Bactria, Vanavāsa and the island of Tambapaṇṇa, Mahāvihāravāsins, transmitters of the noble lineage and tradition, skilled in determining the meaning and letter of the nine-limbed dispensation of the Teacher.

The sequence *theriyānaṃ vibhajavādānaṃ ... mahāvihāra-vāsinaṃ* places the Mahāvihāra identity within two wider and overlapping notions of Buddhist identity: first within the Theriya/Theravādin branch of the the Sangha, and then within its Vibhajjavādin wing. The emergence of a purely Sinhalese *nikāya* within these broader frames of reference suggests that, even if the older Vibhajjavādin identity had not yet been lost, individual monastic identities had started to supplant it on the island. The inscription fits well with the evidence of the *Dīpavaṃsa*, both in its remarks on the Vibhajjavādin monastic lineage (Dīp XVIII) and in its brief account of schism (Dīp XXII).

Perhaps sectarian rivalry was one of the reasons that prompted Mahāvihāra missionary activity in the third century CE. Whatever the case, Nāgārjunakoṇḍa was a key centre of Theravāda interaction in South India. An inscription places the Mahiṃsāsakas there (Vogel 1929–1930, 24–25), and literary contact between the Mahiṃsāsakas and Mahāvihāravāsins is attested by the introduction to the *Jātaka* commentary;[34] the Mahāvihāravāsins perhaps also acquired their knowledge of the *Andhaṭṭhakathā* on the *Vinaya* here (see Cousins 2001, 142). This means that

32. 'We know very little about the history of these early communities, and much of it depends on Pali chronicles composed some centuries later in Lanka itself'.

33. Sircar and Lahiri (1959–1960, 250): 1. sidhaṃ [/] ācariyānaṃ theriyānaṃ vibhajavādānaṃ kasmira-gaṃdhāra-yavana-vanavāsa-taṃbapaṃnidipa-pasādakanaṃ 2. mahāvihāra-vāsinaṃ nava[ṃ]ga-sathu-sasana-atha-vyajana-vinichaya-visaradanaṃ ariya-va[ṃ]sa-paveni-dharanaṃ 3. vihāre bhagavato pāda-saṃghāḍā nipatiṭhapito sava-satānaṃ hita-sukhathanāya ti /

34. Ja I v.9: *mahiṃsāsakavaṃsaṃhi sambhūtena nayaññunā, buddhadevena ca tathā bhikkhunā suddhabuddhinā*. On this verse see Gethin 2012, 18.

Nāgārjunakoṇḍa was not just a major Mahāsāṃghika site: it was also an important centre of Theravāda Buddhism, at which monastic lineages derived from the Vibhajjavādins came together and shared literature. It was probably from here that the Mahāvihāravāsins subsequently spread elsewhere, to North India and South East Asia (see von Hinüber 1991, Falk 1997).

For clarifying these obscure events in the history of Buddhism in South Asia, and for much else besides, we are, indeed, greatly indebted to the work of Lance Cousins.

Appendix

Manorathapūraṇī, Ekakanipāta-aṭṭhakathā X (Ee I.91.22–93.25)

imassa pañca-vidhassa antaradhānassa pariyatti-antaradhānam eva mūlaṃ. pariyattiyā hi antarahitāya paṭipatti antaradhāyati, pariyattiyā ṭhitāya tiṭṭhati. ten' eva imasmiṃ dīpe caṇḍālatissa-mahābhaye sakko devarājā mahā-uḷumpaṃ māpetvā bhikkhūnaṃ ārocāpesi: mahantaṃ bhayaṃ bhavissati, na sammā devo vassissati, bhikkhū paccayehi kilamantā pariyattiṃ sandhāretuṃ na sakkhissanti. paratīraṃ gantvā ayyehi jīvitaṃ rakkhituṃ vaṭṭati, imaṃ mahā-uḷumpaṃ āruyha gacchatha bhante. yesaṃ ettha nisajjana-ṭṭhānaṃ na ppahoti, te kaṭṭha-kaṇḍe pi uraṃ ṭhapetvā gacchantu, sabbesam bhayaṃ na bhavissatī ti.

tadā samudda-tīraṃ patvā saṭṭhi bhikkhū katikaṃ katvā, amhākaṃ ettha gamana-kiccaṃ n' atthi, mayaṃ idh' eva hutvā tepiṭakaṃ rakkhissāmā ti. tato nivattitvā dakkhiṇa-malaya-janapadaṃ gantvā kanda-mūla-paṇṇehi jīvikaṃ kappentā vasiṃsu. kāye vahante nisīditvā sajjhāyaṃ karonti, avahante vālikaṃ ussāpetvā parivāretvā sīsāni eka-ṭṭhāne katvā pariyattiṃ sammasanti. iminā niyāmena dvādasa saṃvaccharāni sāṭṭhakathaṃ tepiṭakaṃ paripuṇṇaṃ katvā dhārayiṃsu.

bhaye vūpasante satta-satā bhikkhū attano gata-ṭṭhāne sāṭṭhakathe tepiṭake ekakkharam pi eka-vyañjanam pi anāsetvā, imam eva dīpam āgamma kallagāma-janapade maṇḍalārāma-vihāraṃ pavisiṃsu. therānaṃ āgata-pavattiṃ sutvā imasmiṃ dīpe ohīnā saṭṭhi bhikkhū, there passissāmā ti gantvā, therehi saddhiṃ tepiṭakaṃ sodhentā ekakkharam pi eka-vyañjanam pi asamentaṃ nāma na passiṃsu.

tasmiṃ ṭhāne therānaṃ ayaṃ kathā udapādi: pariyatti nu kho sāsanassa mūlaṃ udāhu paṭipattī ti. paṃsukūlika-ttherā paṭipatti mūlan ti āhaṃsu, dhamma-kathikā pariyattī ti. atha ne therā, tumhākaṃ dvinnam pi janānaṃ vacana-matten' eva na karoma, jina-bhāsitaṃ suttaṃ āharathā ti āhaṃsu. suttaṃ āharituṃ na bhāro ti, ime ca subhadda bhikkhū sammā vihareyyuṃ, asuñño loko arahantehi assā ti; paṭipatti-mūlakaṃ mahārāja satthu-sāsanaṃ paṭipatti-sārakaṃ, paṭipattiyaṃ dharantaṃ[35] *tiṭṭhatī ti suttaṃ āhariṃsu.*

imaṃ suttaṃ sutvā dhamma-kathikā attano vāda-ṭhapanatthāya imaṃ suttaṃ āhariṃsu: yāva tiṭṭhanti suttantā, vinayo yāva dippati; tāva dakkhinti ālokaṃ, suriye abbhuṭṭhite yathā. suttantesu asantesu, pammuṭṭhe vinayamhi ca; tamo bhavissati loke, suriye atthaṅgate yathā. suttante rakkhite sante, paṭipatti hoti rakkhitā. paṭipattiyaṃ ṭhito dhīro, yoga-kkhemā na dhaṃsatī ti.

imasmiṃ sutte āhaṭe paṃsukūlika-ttherā tuṇhī ahesuṃ, dhamma-kathika-therānaṃ yeva vacanaṃ purato ahosi. yathā hi gava-satassa vā gava-sahassassa vā antare paveṇi-pālikāya dhenuyā asati so vaṃso sā paveṇi na ghaṭīyati, evam eva āraddha-vipassakānaṃ bhikkhūnaṃ sate pi sahasse pi saṃvijjamāne pariyattiyā asati ariya-magga-paṭivedho nāma na hoti. yathā

35. Mil 133 (Ee) reads *paṭipattiyā anantarahitāya* instead of *paṭipattiyaṃ dharantaṃ*.

ca nidhi-kumbhiyā jānanatthāya pāsāṇa-piṭṭhe akkharesu upanibaddhesu[36] *yāva akkharā dharanti, tāva nidhi-kumbhi naṭṭhā nāma na hoti, evam eva pariyattiyā dharamānāya sāsanaṃ antarahitaṃ nāma na hotī ti.*

Abbreviations

As	*Atthasālinī*
D	*Dīgha-nikāya*
Dhp-a	*Dhammapada-aṭṭhakathā*
Dīp	*Dīpavaṃsa*
Ja	*The Jātaka together with its commentary*
Kv-a	*Kathāvutthu Commentary*
Mhv	*Mahāvaṃsa*
Mil	*Milindapañho*
Mp	*Manorathapūraṇī (Aṅguttara-nikāya-aṭṭhakathā)*
Pj I	*Paramatthajotikā I (Khuddaka-pāṭha-aṭṭhakathā)*
Pj II	*Paramatthajotikā II (Sutta-nipāta- aṭṭhakathā)*
Ps	*Papañcasūdanī (Majjhima-nikāya- aṭṭhakathā)*
Ps-ṭ	Ṭīkā on Ps
Sp	*Samantapāsādikā (Vinaya- aṭṭhakathā)*
Spk	*Sāratthappakāsinī (Saṃyutta-nikāya-aṭṭhakathā)*
Spk-ṭ	Ṭīkā on Spk
Sv	*Sumaṅgalavilāsinī (Dīgha-nikāya- aṭṭhakathā)*
Vibh-a	*Sammohavinodanī (Vibhaṅga- aṭṭhakathā)*

All Pali citations are from the editions published by the Pali Text Society.

Bibliography

Collins, Steven. 1990. 'On the Very Idea of the Pali Canon'. *Journal of the Pali Text Society* 15: 89–126.

Cousins, L. S. 2001. 'On the Vibhajjavādins. The Mahiṃsāsaka, Dhammaguttaka, Kassapīya and Tambapaṇṇiya branches of the ancient Theriyas'. *Buddhist Studies Review* 18(2): 131–182.

———. 2005. 'The "five points" and the origins of the Buddhist schools'. In *Buddhism, Critical Concepts in Religious Studies vol. II: The Early Buddhist School and Doctrinal History; Theravāda Doctrine*, edited by Paul Williams, 52–83. London: Routledge.

———. 2012. 'The Teachings of the Abhayagiri School'. In *How Theravāda is Theravāda? Exploring Buddhist Identities*, edited by Peter Skilling, Jason A. Carbine, Claudio Cicuzza, Santi Padeekham, 67–127. Chiang Mai: Silkworm Books.

———. 2013. 'The Early Development of Buddhist Literature and Language in India'. *Journal of the Oxford Centre of Buddhist Studies* 5: 89–135.

Falk, Harry. 1997. 'Die Goldblätter aus Sri Ksetra'. *Wiener Zeitschrift für die Kunde Südasiens und Archiv für Indische Philosophie* 41: 53–92.

36. Emended Ee: *upanibandhesu* (Be: *ṭhapitesu*)

Frauwallner, Erich. 1995. *Studies in the Abhidharma Literature and the Origins of Buddhist Philosophical Systems*, translated by Sophie Francis Kidd. Albany: State University of New York Press.

Gethin, Rupert. 2012. 'Was Buddhaghosa a Theravādin? Buddhist Identity in the Pali Commentaries and Chronicles'. In *How Theravāda is Theravāda? Exploring Buddhist Identities*, edited by Peter Skilling, Jason A. Carbine, Claudio Cicuzza, Santi Padeekham, 1–63. Chiang Mai: Silkworm Books.

von Hinüber, Oskar. 1991. *The Oldest Pāli Manuscript. Four Folios of the Vinaya-Piṭaka from the National Archives, Kathmandu*. Stuttgart: Franz Steiner.

———. 1996. *A Handbook of Pāli Literature*. Berlin: Walter de Gruyter. https://doi.org/10.1515/9783110814989

Lamotte, Étienne. 1988. *History of Indian Buddhism. From the Origins to the Śaka Era*, translated by Sara Webb-Boin. Universite Catholique de Louvain: Institut Orientaliste Louvain-la-neuve.

Malalasekera, G. P. 1997. *Dictionary of Pali Proper Names* vol. II. Oxford: Pali Text Society.

Ñāṇamoli, Bhikkhu. 1991. *The Path of Purification (Visuddhimagga) by Bhadantācariya Buddhaghosa*. Fifth edition. Kandy: Buddhist Publication Society.

Norman, K. R. 1983. *Pali Literature. Including the Canonical Literature in Prakrit and Sanskrit of all the Hīnayāna Schools of Buddhism; A History of Indian Literature Vol. VII Fasc. 2.* Wiesbaden: Otto Harrassowitz.

Oldenberg, Hermann. 1879. *The Dīpavaṃsa: An Ancient Buddhist Historical Record.* London: Williams and Norgate.

Rhys Davids, T. and Stede, W. 1921–1925. *The Pali Text Society's Pāli-English Dictionary*. Chipstead.

Salomon, Richard. 1988. *Indian Epigraphy: A Guide to the Study of Inscriptions in Sanskrit, Prakrit, and the other Indo-Aryan Languages*. Oxford: Oxford University Press.

Sircar, D.C. and Lahiri, A. N. 1959–60. 'Footprint Slab Inscription from Nagarjunikonda'. *Epigrahia Indica* 33: 247–250.

Sujato and Brahmali, Bhikkhus. 2015. *The Authenticity of the Early Buddhist Texts*. Supplement to *Journal of the Oxford Centre for Buddhist Studies* V.

Skilling, Peter. 2012. 'Introduction'. In *How Theravāda is Theravāda? Exploring Buddhist Identities*, edited by Peter Skilling, Jason A. Carbine, Claudio Cicuzza, Santi Padeekham, xiii–xxxii. Chiang Mai: Silkworm Books.

Vogel, J. Ph. 1929–30. 'Prakrit Inscriptions from a Buddhist Site at Nagarjunikonda'. *Epigraphia Indica* 20: 1–36.

Walleser, Max. 1973. *Manorathapūraṇī. Buddhaghosa's Commentary on the Aṅguttara-Nikāya, after the manuscript of Edmund Hardy. Vol. I: Eka-nipāta-vaṇṇanā*, second revised edition. London: The Pali Text Society.

Wynne, Alexander. 2007. *The Origin of Buddhist Meditation*. London: Routledge. https://doi.org/10.4324/9780203963005

Alexander Wynne is the Assistant Academic Director of the Oxford Centre for Buddhist Studies. His work focuses on the early history of Indian Buddhism and the Pāli tradition.

Literature

— 15 —

Yasodharā in *Jātakas*

Sarah Shaw

This paper discusses the role of the Buddha's wife, Yasodharā/Rāhulamātā, in Pāli *Jātakas*. Noting her continued popularity in South and Southeast Asian Buddhism, it considers her path to liberation seen as a composite whole, through many lifetimes, and considers some of the literary implications of this multiple depiction. The intention of this paper is to initiate more discussion about this figure as a sympathetic and central presence in Southern Buddhist text and practice.

Introduction

The Buddha's wife is a mysterious figure, mentioned only occasionally in the canon.[1] She is, however, an active presence in the Pāli *Jātakas*, where all kinds of psychological, dramatic and sometimes fantastic situations are explored for the Bodhisatta and his principal followers, impossible in their final lives, where they have specific, even typological, roles to fulfil (Shaw 2010). Yasodharā, or in *Jātakas*, 'Rāhulamātā', the mother of Rāhula, or Bimbā/Bimbādevī, features in many stories, always married to the Bodhisatta (TGBSB, 8). Here she seems to enact different approaches, or perhaps explorations, of marriage itself: one longstanding union is as if refracted through a glass, producing many narrative outcomes and multiple possibilities. We cannot assign a single authorial intent to the richly varied manifestations of this figure, but we can infer some animating principles, that colour and inform these different Yasodharās, configured for specific stations and types of lives as she accompanies the Bodhisatta on his path to an awakening, which, in the end, she finds too.

Her existences are diverse, though with parameters and scope that are not as wide as those of the Bodhisatta. Recent research and commentary on her identities in her Pāli past lives, particularly as Maddī in the *Vessantara-jātaka*, is starting to address past curious scholarly neglect of her role; a complex and highly eloquent companion to the Bodhisatta in his struggles is being revealed. John Strong argues that all the Bodhisatta's family undergo what he calls a 'family path', which in an ancient Indian context would not be considered inferior, but a collective journey, undertaken by all participants freely yet in conjunction with one another (Strong, 1997). Richard Gombrich gives some analysis of her in his introduction to the *Vessantara-jātaka* (Ja 547) (Cone and Gombrich 1977, xviii ff.). Steven Collins, discussing various 'felicities' described in early Buddhist texts that echo, anticipate

1. See Appendix to this paper.

Keywords: gender, interrelationship, marriage, narrative, number symbolism

or aid the path to *nibbāna*, demonstrates that heavenly existences of many kinds, enacted in the practices of single ascetics, forest-dwelling chaste marriages and conventional unions, are perceived as contributing and reflecting in different ways the nature of liberation itself (Collins 1998). As Jonathan Walters says, discussing her and other female presences in the *Apadāna*, 'marriage can even be a positive soteriological force' (Walters 2013, 191). So Yasodharā's earlier self, Maddī, performs an essential, active function in the fulfilment of the Bodhisatta's perfection of giving, not as a cipher, but as his main support, encourager and helper in their forest life. Justin Meiland's dissertation on renunciation in *Jātakas* shows complex play on motifs, symbolism and character revealing Maddī's centrality in enabling the Bodhisatta to achieve his goal (Meiland 2004). Comparing her portrayal to that of Sītā, he notes Maddī and her other rebirths in other *Jātakas*, show Yasodharā as an embodiment of the various possibilities of the female lay and ascetic life. As Maddī, she is seen as goddess-like in rural Thailand (Tiyavanich 2003). Naomi Appleton and Sarah Shaw consider her powerful presence in the various tales in the last ten *Jātakas*, in many of which she appears, significantly, as a key player (TGBSB, 18–21; Shaw 2006, 223–224, 160–161). Ranjini Obeyesekere, explaining Yasodharā's role in the life of the Buddha, has beautifully translated Sinhala laments and post-canonical literature (Obeyesekere 2009, 2014). I have found no study, however, that considers this woman's character and path as a whole, both as a wife and mother, and as a spiritual practitioner over many existences in the Pāli *Jātaka* literature. Defined as her life and lives are by her relationships with others, it seems interesting to investigate her as a single participant within this larger narrative. What role does she play in the larger Pāli Buddhist story?

Yasodharā's presence in thirty-two stories

Klaus Klostermeier notes regarding various Sanskrit treatments of the figure: 'The frequency with which Yaśodharā is mentioned, and the very positive role which she plays in the successive births of the Bodhisattva, indicates a loving relationship' (Klostermeier 1999, 26). But the few accounts of her occurrence in *Jātakas* have omissions; no study treats them all. So, this paper simply lists them in a table, and describes some features that, as far as I know, have not been noted or analysed elsewhere. *Jātakas* have a fourfold structure: the story from the present; the commentarial prose story in the past, which must contain earlier elements, as the verse parts, usually considered canonical, do not cohere on their own; largely canonical verses; and the *samodhana*, the final assignation of connections, usually prose. One story usually omitted from the list is the *Maha-ummaga/Mahosadha-jātaka* (546). This is crucial however, for, unusually, the assignments of characters in the present to their earlier counterparts are not in prose, but in verse, a rare *abhisambuddhagāthā* — an ancient verse made by Gotama 'in the present' (Geiger 1943, 31). Here the Buddha describes his earlier wife as a counterpart to Bimbāsundarī, using what appears to be an older name (Ja VI 478). This probably canonical verse, referring to the Bodhisatta's 'present' and a past-life wife, has been completely neglected in all

Table 1. Rāhulamātā/Yasodharā's thirty-two *Jātaka* lives + one.

	Jātaka	Rebirth	Name if given and other significant features
1	*Lakkhaṇa* (11)	Deer: RM mother, BS father of wise & foolish sons.	–
2	*Mahāsudassana* (95)	Human: chief queen of universal monarch	Subhaddā (Great Fortune)
3	*Maṇicora* (194)	Human	Sujātā (Well Born)
4	*Bandhanagara* (201)	Human	–
5	*Kurudhamma* (276)	Human: chief queen	–
6	*Abbhantara* (281)	Human: queen; BS an ascetic	Story from the present refers to RM as Bimbādevī
7	*Supatta* (292)	Crow: wife of crow	Suphassa (Softie). Story from the present refers to RM as Bimbādevī
8	*Anusociya* (328)	Deer: wife of deer	Samillabhāsinī
9	*Visayha* (340)	Human: merchant's wife	
10	*Sūci* (387)	Human: smith's wife	Canonical marriage proposal from the BS
11	*Kumbhakāra* (408)	Human: potter's wife	
12	*Susīma* (411)	Human: chief queen	Speaks canonical verse
13	*Kummāsapinda* (415)	Human: chief queen	–
14	*Gaṅgamāla* (421)	Human: chief queen	–
15	Āditta (424)	Human: queen	Samuddavijayā (Conqueror of the Ocean); 'wise and accomplished'
16	*Cakkavāka* (434)	Brahmani duck	
17	*Cullabodhi* (443)		
18	*Cakkavāka* (451)	Brahmani duck	
19	*Udaya* (458)	Human: princess	Udayabhaddā (Auspicious)
20	*Pānīya* (459)	Human: queen	
21	*Dasaratha* (461)	Human; queen	Sītā (Cool One)
22	*Candakinnara* (485)	Kinnara	Candā (Moon)
23	*Campeyya* (506)	Nāga: queen	Sumanā (Beautiful)
24	*Jayaddisa* (513)	Human: chief queen	
25	*Cullasutasoma* (525)	Human: queen	Candā (Moon)
26	*Kusa* (531)	Human: wife of prince/king	Pabhāvatī (Radiant)
27	*Mahājanaka* (539)	Human: queen consort	Sīvalī; 'wise and accomplished'
28	*Khaṇḍahāla* (542)	Human: queen consort	Candā (Moon)
29	*Bhūridatta* (543)	Nāga: queen consort	
30	*Vidhura* (545)	Human: queen	
31	*Mahosadha/Ummagga* (546)	Human: minister's wife	Amarā (Deathless). Canonical *Abhisammbuddhagāthā* sees her as past rebirth of Bimbāsundarī (Beautiful Bimbā).
32	*Vessantara* (547)	Human: wife of prince/king	Maddī (Crushed? Intoxicating?)
33	Buddha's final life (*Jātaka Nidāna*)	Human: wife of prince/king	Rāhulamātā/Yasodharā. She becomes a nun and attains awakening

Key: RM = Rāhulamātā; BS = Bodhisatta. In all cases, her husband/consort is BS.

discussions about Yasodharā/Rāhulamātā, and, incidentally, offers realistic support to the presence of a validated wife as a genuine historical figure.

Our heroine is reborn in many realms and species. She is usually strikingly beautiful, even as a goose, where her golden colour matches the Bodhisatta's handsome appearance (434, 451). She is often described as wise and accomplished (539, 424). She is occasionally tempestuous, when opposing asceticism (411, 525, 539), for instance, but in most lives is noble and respects the precepts. Unlike the Bodhisatta, she is never reborn in a 'low' rebirth such as a mouse or hare. Her attitude to renunciation varies. Where she does not renounce with him, she sometimes tries to seduce her husband away from asceticism (539, 459). Despite this, one does not find the elaborate descriptions of her as the classic abandoned wife that inform, for instance, the depiction of Sundarī in Aśvaghoṣa's *Saundarānanda* (Covill 2005). In practice the Bodhisatta rarely abandons her to renounce: only four stories see her not accompanying him when he pursues asceticism.[2] In the *Mahājanaka-jātaka* (539) she also becomes a solitary ascetic: this tale is distinguished by her attainment of *jhāna* on a *kasiṇa* after the Bodhisatta has left the palace. Although, in the *Cullabodhi-jātaka* (443), she has descended from a *brahmā* heaven, where beings are reborn through the practice of *jhāna*, no other story describes her attaining *jhāna*.[3] There are three tales where they live as ascetics together. In the *Kumbhakāra-jātaka* (408), she takes renunciation first. In this tale, the Bodhisatta, a potter, extols the superiority of the holy life. His wife rises, pretends to fetch water, but escapes out of the back door so she can become an ascetic first; he cares for the children until they are independent and he can become an ascetic (408). There are some stories where they co-habit chastely, usually in accordance with both their wishes. In twenty-four stories, however, they live as a 'married' couple, whether as brahmani ducks (434, 451), deer (328), *nāgas* (506) or in various human spheres, usually regal. In the *Mahāsudassana-jātaka* (95), at her husband's instigation, as his chief queen, she encourages him, before his death, to renounce his palaces and riches. In these environments she characteristically acts in accordance with her then species and station in life.

The still highly popular *Kusa-jātaka* (531) is curious as the Bodhisatta is, unusually, ugly. Yasodharā, as Pabhāvatī, deeply repulsed by his looks, runs away. Their marriage is from the outset characterized by a curious separation, at first engineered by him because of his ugliness, when he makes only night-time visits, and then by her, through her subsequent repulsion on seeing his physical unattractiveness. The kammic explanation of the curious circumstances of this oddly modern theme of relationship failure and its resolution, is important in this context, in part

2. *Jātakas* where they remain together, or we can assume they did in the absence of other evidence: 11, 95, 194, 276, 281, 292 (328 stay together as ascetics), 340, 381, 397, (in 408 she goes to be an ascetic before him), 415, 421, 424, 434, (in 443 both are married against their will and become ascetics), 451, 458 (but chaste), 461, 485, 506, 513, 531, 542, 545, 546 and 547. He leaves to become an ascetic without her: in 411, 459, 525, he goes off to be an ascetic and the rest of the village follow. In the *Mahājanaka* (539) she follows his ascetic path.

3. Pāli *Jātakas* impress the happiness and contentment of the couple, usually without meditation.

for their indication of the operation of will within the multi-life *Jātaka* narrative. The story says that in an earlier life his subsequent spouse had been married to a man who mistreated her. She, in the presence of the Bodhisatta, had vowed never to be reborn married to this man again; the Bodhisatta also made an aspiration to marry her, but did so after stealing a cake from a *paccekabuddha*, thus ensuring an ugly appearance in a later life, explained as a kammic consequence of tainted aspiration (Ja V 289). The theme is so compelling, and has ensured the story's continued appeal perhaps, because it suggests dynamics found in perennially popular tropes familiar in other traditions. It is reminiscent of the Eros/Psyche story of classical myth, the princess and the frog stories, and beauty and the beast, of Western folktale and, in the modern world, of the story of Cyrano de Bergerac, who hid his love through messages sent by an intermediary because of his great ugliness. In the *Kusa-jātaka* Pabhāvatī is not at first heroic, though she symbolically possesses a great radiance which threatens to reveal the Bodhisatta's face, even in deep darkness (Ja V 286). The trials of the couple appear like an alchemical journey, of great intensity and passion, as the Bodhisatta woos and works to transform his wife's perceptions of him through various tests and vicissitudes. For she does finally return to her husband, when the ugliness of the Bodhisatta's face casts terror around the king who wishes to put her to death (Ja V 306–07). At this point she undergoes a complete turnaround, and speaks in his favour for the first time in that narrative: she can state after her trials, at last truthfully, the virtues of her husband. She also, in her final recognition of her husband's calibre, starts to see beneath appearances and surface features to the goodness and strength she only then recognizes. It is perhaps one of the few *Jātaka*s where marriage and sexuality are explored extensively, symbolic of the need to separate 'appearance' and 'reality', 'beauty' and 'ugliness'. The trajectory of their marriage is seen through a passionate, if initially darkly troubled, meeting of minds, as well as a physical union based on her part, like a Jacobean tragic figure, on deep disgust, then completely transformed.[4] Here, truthfulness heals their union and produces heroism in him, as she finally acknowledges the truth of his nobility of character and status while he is working in disguise, as a lowly cook.

Imagery of gold accompanies their relationship; she is frequently decked in gold and jewels. In this story, as in two others, (328, 458), the Bodhisatta first finds her by having an image made of his perfect woman, crafted in gold, which is taken around the countryside to find its living counterpart. The statue that matches Rāhulamātā/Yasodharā, a Galateia more beautiful than the image, indicates too a perfect loveliness in the physical world, the sense-sphere. The Bodhisatta suffers many trials, before he can find an actively protective corresponding beauty beneath her outward form. The story works through this powerful metaphor to explore many levels of appearance and reality: finding 'truthfulness' is part of the way that the Bodhisatta has to find a path separating him from this worldly beauty, but which brings him

4. The theme is reversely comparable to Thomas Middleton's and William Rowley's, *The Changeling* (1622; Lake 1975), for instance, where Beatrice-Joanna's repulsion for the villainous De Flores changes to obsessive passion.

to it again. With the return of a wife who now recognizes him, and who amidst his, and her own, sufferings, he finds his courage too, and returns to his princely status.

Other tales also appear to draw upon a mythic and allegorical level in their depiction of the transformatory and sometimes redemptive power of love within marriage, and the relationship between male and female. As Sumanā, the *nāga*, an underwater creature, in the *Campeyya-jātaka*, true to all her species, Rāhulamātā acts with abandon and throws herself at the Bodhisatta in this underwater rebirth, so that he forgets, despite having the *nāga* ability to recollect past lives, all his time as a human before (506; Shaw 2006, 158–178). In accordance with her behaviour in every other tale, however, she is faithful, and exemplifies the heroic *sīla* her husband is developing in that lifetime. When her husband is captured in snake-form above ground, she transforms herself into a goddess and intercedes, in the manner of a Shakespearean heroine such as Portia, to argue with the snake-charmer who has enslaved him and made him dance in public. Such is her eloquence and dazzling beauty the *nāga* is freed, and both, after changing shape and standing for a moment together as humans, return reluctantly to the realm of their *nāga* rebirth, where skilfulness is less possible than as a human. Here, as in other tales, she employs all the resources available to her in a particular rebirth: in this case the ability to 'shape-shift' at will.

In other stations of life she also behaves appropriately to her role: in the *Visayha-jātaka* (340), as a merchant's wife, she shares her husband's generosity, practically hunting around the house to find presents for him to give.[5] In the *Āditta-jātaka* (424), she inspires the Bodhisatta to generosity: when he is dissatisfied with the unworthiness of the recipients for his gifts, she suggests he offers flowers and invites *paccekabuddha*s instead.

Eloquence and quickness of thought are recurrent features: she speaks in canonical verses in the *Susīma* (411), when she is the older queen of the young Bodhisatta, to try, unsuccessfully, to dissuade her husband from the renunciate life when he is alarmed by a grey hair — which she has just claimed is his, though it is really hers. When she sees the effect, she is alarmed:

> But it is mine, not yours, this grey, my lord!
> From the top of my head,
> For your good I did this, and spoke a lie.
> Please forgive this one fault, great king.
>
> You are young, and just so good-looking, O king!
> Like the first shoots of a sprouting plant,
> Govern your kingdom: look at me!
> Do not chase after now what is right for old age. (Ja III 394)

5. Āryaśura's version of the tale, *Jātakamāla* 5, does not include a spouse. The tales that include a wife, and her depiction in them, shows a figure that could be construed as less favourable: for instance, *Jātakamāla* 4, the equivalent to *Jātakatthavaṇṇanā* 40, includes a wife who is too scared to cross the threshold to give alms to a *paccekabuddha*, as Māra has created a hell realm just over the threshold. The events of this tale, interesting for its metaphoric depiction of the misgivings that can accompany generosity, are not associated with Rāhulamātā/Yasodharā in the Pāli *Jātakas*, where she is never fearful: in *Jātakatthavaṇṇanā* 40 a servant exhibits this timidity and there is no mention of a wife (Khoroche 1989; Meiland 2009, 2017).

She seems a female counterpart to her husbands' struggle, embodying qualities appropriate to the nature of the genre – one could say perfection in some instances – which the Bodhisatta is developing himself. Her regal births are frequent, and a certain hauteur and courage accompany this. As a princess she is majestic, sometimes imperiously disdainful to any threats to her position. As Sīvalī in the *Mahājanaka-jātaka* she inflicts terrible tests on all her suitors until the Bodhisatta outwits her (Ja VI 40–3); she also exhibits disgust for his eating of leftover food, a brahminic taboo (Ja VI 62–3). This tale is attributed by many traditions to show her vigour (*viriya*) (TGBSB, 5). Sīvalī's indefatigable and larger-than-life insistence first on following her husband, then making shrines to him, and then, finally, pursuing meditation, as he does, is magnificently heroic (Ja VI 67). As Amarā in the *Mahāummagga/ Mahosadha-jātaka* (546), she is marked by a brilliant intelligence and wit reflecting the Bodhisatta's own, aptly in this story always assigned to the perfection of wisdom (*paññā*) (Ja VI 329; TGBSB, 5). She forestalls a plot to overthrow the Bodhisatta as minister to the king by cleverly writing down dates and people who are giving 'presents' of stolen property; she also gives short shrift in her punishments to them (Ja VI 369–370). This means he is not implicated when his enemies claim he has taken the items from the palace. When he is a suitor, she speaks to him with enigmatic gestures and riddles that match the style and tempo of this endlessly investigative story, where riddles, spying, intrigue and conspiracy constantly test the central players to use skill in means, the *upāya-kosalla* (Ja VI 363–368; see TGBSB, 198–201).

So what do these multiple variations suggest? Certain features emerge amongst the tales' apparently random distribution. Many different environments are described, as the characters assume roles in many different species and modes of existence. Over the last few decades we have become fascinated by multiple narratives, of different, often fractured perspectives on one field or series of events: we enjoy literary works with manifold narrative viewpoints, like heartbeats, or endlessly multiplying possibilities in parallel universes, as demonstrated in the films 'Sliding Doors' (Intermedia Films, 1998), or 'Groundhog Day' (Columbia Pictures, 1993). The undifferentiated time of *atīte*, 'times past', the framing device that links these stories also permits these multiple perspectives, a variety of relative fields for the Bodhisatta and Yasodharā/Rahulamātā, in which different kinds of marital relationships and interactions can be explored, outside what the tradition comes to consider the typological requirements of their final life together.

Her fidelity embodies the virtue that ensures that the resources of the natural world work for her. Because she lives in trust and alignment with other beings that inhabit the physical environment around her, she can, at times of crisis, assume a pro-active, initiatory role. So truth-telling, a frequent device in early Buddhist narrative, is often the primary means by which she overcomes obstacles: her trust in the world around protects her when she invokes protective deities, or asks spirits identified with that locality to help her. In the *Candakinnara-jātaka* she saves the day by an act of truth (*sacca-kiriya*); King Sakka, stirred by her poetic evocation of the natural beauties of the environment, saves the Bodhisatta from 'death'. Sometimes she simply states her own virtue, and sometimes, as in this case, makes an appreciative declaration of the highly differentiated virtues within the immediate locality, such as the hills, mountains, lakes, skies, woods and streams.

> Oh, you are a bad man, you prince,
> Who has wounded my much-loved husband.
> You shot him, at the roots of a tree,
> And there he lies wounded, on the ground! (Ja IV 285)

She then invokes the beauties of the Himalayas — the flowers and hills, and the gold and white tips of the mountains — and finds her spouse revived, apparently because of her words. And the story finishes with her, characteristically, citing the environment around them as a background to what is suggested as an idyllic pastoral:

> Let's wander now to the mountain woodlands and rivers,
> Where streams flow, strewn with flowers,
> Dwelling places for all kinds of trees,
> And speeches of love to one another. (Ja IV 288)

According to the Abhidhamma, the beautiful (*sobhana*) or skilful (*kusala*) consciousness produces contact with beautiful forms (*kusala vipāka*) in the world around. So, the resonance within her to the auspicious properties of the physical world around seems to make their power available to her in times of need.

Her ability to invoke gods, natural reserves and local spirits within the endlessly rich *Jātaka* woodlands, marvellous landscapes, palaces and sometimes simple domestic spheres in which she is born, render her in some ways rather a modern figure: a kind of eco-heroine capable of survival and mobilization of the resources around her, skillfully deployed to support the Bodhisatta and other beings that share their environs. But it is not only deities she gets on her side; nor does her truthfulness necessarily involve citing virtues. In the *Khaṇḍahāla-jātaka* (542), as Candā, the princess wife, she has a genius for seizing the moment: rather than invoking supernatural aid, she realises that the king, about to fulfil his misconceived vow to kill his sons and daughters, will never respond to the arguments given by other members of the family, and herself. In what Appleton terms an 'impressive' way, she has even offered up her own children instead (TGBSB, 400). But she courageously and practically makes her formal declaration:

> By the truth 'foolish Khaṇḍahāla is doing an evil act' –
> By this spoken truth, may I have my lord. (Ja VI 155; TGBSB, 420)

She saves Canda, the prince/Bodhisatta, with one bluntly incontrovertible statement: that the king is being extremely stupid and cruel (Ja VI 154–155). This sensible measure ensures that the gods support her, for Sakka dispels the assembly and frightens the king with blazing iron, and, at the local level, the townsfolk rise up against the king and instate the Bodhisatta as their true sovereign. She has already used deft appeals to popular opinion in the *Mahājanaka-jātaka* (539). There, as queen, she stirs up her people through false claims of fire in what proves this time, however, an unsuccessful attempt to turn the Bodhisatta from his determination to renounce: the will of a Bodhisatta, unlike that of kings, cannot be deflected. But it is an indication that her true alignment, when in a royal house, is with her people and the inhabitants of the kingdom, whose aid she knows she can call upon when in times of need.

Her resourcefulness is tested to the limit in the *Vessantara-jātaka*. I will not consider it in detail: it has already been discussed elsewhere (Gombrich 1977; Collins 1998; Meiland 2004; TGBSB, 523–528). A recent important collection of essays highlights various aspects of its omnipresence in Southeast Asian ritual and cultural life (Collins 2016), as does the work on banner art and its association with Thai vernacular versions by Leedom Lefferts and Sandra Cate (2012). The story should be mentioned, however, as in this, as Maddī, Rāhulamātā/Yasodharā becomes one of the most popular heroines in Southeast Asia. As is well known, it describes Vessantara finding the greatest extent of generosity, by giving up his auspicious white elephant, the symbol of his kingdom, kingdom, horse, children and wife, before having them all returned in a chiasmic reversal. The theme of the story is obviously a very tricky one for westerners – but its shock value was probably always there for Asians too. It involves an extraordinary test of a spouse's virtue that is echoed in many other literary and religious contexts: in the Indian Harischandra legend, in Chaucer's tale of Gertrude, whose fidelity is put to gruelling tests by the king, her husband, and even in the English novel, Thomas Hardy's tale of *The Mayor of Casterbridge.*[6] In the *Vessantara*, by her acquiescence to being given away, to an ancient audience Maddī would be seen as finding the perfection of her auspiciousness too, a theme other events in the story support. Indeed, this applies to modern enactments: one Thai friend told me she saw Maddī as the embodiment of all women's struggle, a heroine on which all women can focus their losses, griefs and happiness. In modern festivals sometimes a strikingly beautiful actress takes the role, occupying centre stage while the monks in the background chant the story in its traditional form. Women present sometimes make offerings of flowers and fruits to the shrine so that in this one performance, at least, her sufferings can be alleviated and made less hard. For them the narrative is genuinely living: a drama going on whenever the story is chanted aloud. Maddī's behaviour throughout the story is perceived as an embodiment of what is possible for a woman in situations of terrible stress and misfortune. In the forest she is endlessly capable and practical, finding fruits, food and toys for the children wherever they go (Ja VI 520ff). Placing her trust in the forest when searching for food, she is not harmed by wild animals. She even continues willingly to live in the forest with her husband after he has given away their children. When Vessantara makes her his final gift, she acquiesces, with a simple statement of consent, so helping him in his struggle, in striking contrast

6. In the Indian Harischandra legend, the hero sells his wife and child to a brahmin to pay debts: when the son dies, the boy is subsequently revived because of the parents' virtue, and the family is restored to good fortune. In Thomas Hardy's *The Mayor of Casterbridge* (1886) Henchard 'sells' his wife.

to her sometimes stormy behaviour in other tales, such as the *Mahājanaka*, where she follows the Bodhisatta after he tries to renounce, attempting to trick him with lies and recriminations (539; Ja VI 54–57).

Jātaka stories are not arranged chronologically, but just as the last has been understood as the culmination of the spiritual path for Vessantara, so it seems to be intended to be for Yasodharā too. Unlike others in the story, she never breaks precepts, or puts her own wishes, however noble, before the needs and requirements that the beings in the immediate situation demand: she provides the true moral compass of the tale. It is interesting that the first gift of the Bodhisatta, in a scene that, as Gombrich points out, is considered one of the pivots of the tale, and one of the most popular in Southeast Asian depictions, is the auspicious rain-bringing elephant, involving a symbolic and profound relinquishment of the good fortune of his kingdom. The animal is called, curiously enough, *Paccaya*. This term, which means 'condition', is a technical description of each of the twenty-four *paṭṭhāna*, the links by which, in the Abhidhamma, all events that occur in any given moment of consciousness or situation are related to others, in manifold ways, both in space and time. Gombrich demonstrates that its use as a proper name is the result of a commentarial misreading.[7] It does, nonetheless, communicate the interconnectedness that unifies this story and which perhaps even historically influenced this reading. Maddī, like Vessantara, has to give up everything, but, unlike him, she never lets go of her sense of interconnectedness with other beings, whether her husband, her family, her environment, or, perhaps, her vow to accompany the Bodhisatta. She embraces interdependence, seeking at every juncture to act with mindful connectivity to others and the world around. In accordance with her invocation of the powers and beings of the natural environments of other *Jātaka*s, she addresses the wild animals of the forest as kindred beings. They, really divine beings, have been told by local spirits to obstruct her path so that she cannot meet danger by searching for her children. While it is getting dark, the trees do not give her fruits, and she is disorientated and lost: but her sense of kinship with other beings and the forest still persists, and she asks for their help not to block her path, and so lead her to her home (Ja VI 557).

She never ceases to know and acknowledge the causal relations that link her family and the beings around her. She is respectful of the forest, the means by which her livelihood and those around her are supported and come into being. Here she embodies a necessary counterweight to the Bodhisatta's overwhelmingly powerful generosity, which is aimed, albeit for altruistic motives, at attempting to separate himself, ironically through *dāna*, from those to whom he is most attached. The story is not really the 'sexist' fable modern readers might infer. Both figures, and perhaps the ideals of both sexes, are in some ways absurdly shocking. Vessantara in his determination to give despite the misgivings of his heart, is impossibly and endlessly generous, as Steve Collins notes, thus fulfilling the demands set for a Bodhisatta to become a Buddha in his final life: 'I am not indifferent to my chil-

7. Cone and Gombrich 1977, xxxiii-iv. See Ja VI 588–589; TGBSB, 518.

dren, nor to the princess Maddī. But Omniscience is precious to me, and for that I gave away even those people who were precious' (Collins 1998; Ja VI 570). Maddī, in her heroic acquiescence to this, by freely and nobly allowing herself to be given, is equally reckless, thus fulfilling in the tale the demands of an extreme counterpart of heroic womanhood. Through her support the Bodhisatta can make his gifts as the fulfillment of the last prerequisite in the attainment of the perfections. The events of the *Vessantara* would not be possible without her collusion, and her agreement to them involves her trusting the larger narrative of the Bodhisatta vow. This requires a *saṅgha*, as well as a teaching, and the participation of many family members as supporters and followers of the Bodhisatta. As Strong observes, in his discussion of the Sanskrit trajectory of her final life-story, as the spouse of the Buddha in the *Sanghabhedavastu*, their paths are interconnected:

> he leaves a wife, she loses her husband; he gives birth to Bodhi, she gives birth to a son; he emphasizes Dharma, she emphasizes rūpa. But in the final analysis, the broad themes of her questing remain the same, for she too, along with her son, is on a path that involves the realization of the truth of suffering and the consequent attainment of *nīrvāṇa*. (Strong 1997, 124)

This story presents us with a complex interplay of the renunciate and the lay life, issues of kingship, the relationship of the ruler to his people, and the choice of the ascetic path. It enacts throughout the essential interdependence of all the beings in the narrative, as it does the nettedness of so many other factors too. Maddī, by taking refuge in her virtue, cannot be relinquished by the Bodhisatta, despite his best efforts. Because of her unimpeachable virtue King Sakka descends from his heaven to request her, thus protecting her from coming to any harm from any other recipient. Amongst the many underlying themes of this story, this one strand demonstrates that however much any locus of consciousness seeks to free itself from the relationships which confine it to a particular place, status and people, freedom is found through acknowledging and accepting interdependence, yet not being bound or confined by it. In the world of *saṃsāra*, how can a king be extricated from the kingdom that defines him, subject separated from object, the denoter of male separated from that of female? One verse, uttered interestingly by Maddī, distils this understanding:

> The banner is the signifier of the chariot, smoke the signifier of fire;
> The king is the signifier of the kingdom; a husband is the signifier of a woman.
> (TGBSB, 564; Ja VI 508).[8]

Donald Swearer notes the popularity of these images in Thai vernacular verse (Swearer 1995). Featuring in an impassioned and universal speech on the miserable status of women alone, without husbands, the imagery subtly demonstrates something rather different: the great interdependence of male and female, just as

8. *Dhajo rathassa paññāṇaṃ, dhūmo paññāṇaṃ aggino / rājāraṭṭhassa paññāṇaṃ, bhattā paññāṇam ithiyā.* The word *paññāṇaṃ* is associated with the word for wisdom (*paññā*) and can be synonymous, but here its secondary meaning is taken, as a mark, sign or token (see PED 390 and Ja V 195).

the paired images demonstrate their dependence on each other too. Which element in these pairs is actually the more important? If form needs name, can name really be effective without substance? Can *nāma*, in the end, function without *rūpa*?

The Bodhisatta gives everything, and finds it all again, but from the perspective of a larger spiritual path, there is a great Buddhist irony: how can any character actually be 'his'? Given the operation of the laws of *kamma*, beyond life and death, can they be 'owned'? According to Buddhist principle, all the characters have their own *kamma*; all have their solitary as well as collective path. Even the children, in an implausible but necessary feature for volition (*cetanā*) to be demonstrated, each, singly, agrees to the gift of themselves. Maddī reminds her husband, that 'children are the greatest gift' (Ja VI 568). As I discuss in the introduction to my translation of this story, this is a deeply multivalent statement, resonant on many levels (TGBSB, 524–525). It encapsulates the manifold symbolism of the way the community of the Buddha's followers inform and support the whole narrative of his test of generosity: for children, in the *Jātaka* world-view, cannot *belong* to anyone, whatever the parameters of the outward relationship. They are, from the parents' point of view, a gift when they arrive, and each has his or her own *kamma* to fulfil — perhaps, if undertaken skillfully, their true gift to parents. The framing device of a number of interweaving paths to liberation that accompany that of the Bodhisatta, will in the final lives of these characters, offer resolution to all problems associated with interconnectivity and solitude, for these people, linked by vows to the Bodhisatta, aspire to be members of his final *saṅgha,* whatever their familial relationship. Maddī is a heroine equal to Vessantara as hero: she supports her husband, follows her own path, and trusts to the environment, her vow and the *kamma* with which her virtue has become aligned. She symbolically relinquishes her children, and her status, for the sake of Buddhahood. Her auspiciousness enables the Bodhisatta to make his gifts, ensures that they are returned, and permits their future life together to be realized, when he will return to teach her after attaining his — and their — goal. A separate being, she is presented as the female counterpart to, and hence natural consort of, Vessantara. As Sakka says, they are as alike in colour as milk and a conch-shell (Ja VI 572).

Rāhulamātā/Yasodharā operates in many different worlds and species, and her dramatic search is to find a way to accord with their rules and limitations. Perhaps like many other literary heroines, from Śakuntalā and Sītā, to Portia, Rosalind and Miranda, to Eliza Bennett, the ability to work creatively and resourcefully within the rules that govern a role and part of life is what has rendered them historically so adventurous and appealing. Her spiritual development is tracked through her free participation in so many differing worlds: her *bhāvanā* arises from *sīla, dāna* and, in the *Janaka*, meditation too. Within these, it seems, it is her very interrelatedness, even as it is enacted rather skillfully through her most common name, Rāhulamātā, which is her greatest strength.

A female microcosm: Number symbolism of 31/32/33

A further point should also be made about the number of stories in which she appears: thirty-two, with the final life as an extra element, thirty-three. In Pāli Buddhism, the number thirty-two denotes a whole organism or a complete world system. There are thirty-one parts of the body, which, with the thirty-second described by Buddhaghosa, the brain, makes thirty-two. There are thirty-one realms of existence, which, with *nibbāna*, also makes thirty-two. There are thirty-two miraculous marks (*lakkhaṇa*) which characterize the human whose destiny is to be a universal monarch or a Buddha. In all of these categories, another last element is in some way crucial, an encompassing or significant factor, denoting a self-sufficient system. In the Heaven of the Thirty-Three, King Sakka provides the final, thirty-third element of the realm associated in the Pāli canon with complex discussion, differentiation and a sense-sphere happiness, whose particular features also seem to be complexity, movement, and an underlying unification. The Great Man (*mahāpurisa*) is the thirty-third element in the thirty-two marks. The body as a whole includes its thirty-two different aspects. The cosmology of the entire Buddhist universe unifies all the different realms together. All of these lists describe entities with highly variegated features, movement and communication between the parts, unified by one, thirty-third, classificatory factor. These counterparts strongly suggest that the thirty-two links made to her in the *samodhanas* are the result of editorial deliberation. This possibility is supported by the fact that there are three stories where she is not mentioned in the tale itself, or her presence is quite unnecessary, except to provide this connection at the end (11, 411, 513). There are also one or two where she is clearly being *excluded* from the attribution, suggesting again some editorial doctoring to present her as an impeccable spouse for the aspirant Bodhisatta. Presumably her 'past lives', as well as her last, should be like that of Caesar's wife, beyond reproach. In the *Mataṅga-jātaka* (497), for instance, he falls in love with and marries a Brahmin woman. Even though the union is unconsummated, with offspring born after a visit to a heaven, this taint might reflect badly on Rāhulamātā, given the injunction of the *Dharmasūtras* and *Manu* that high-caste women should not marry beneath them (Olivelle 2009a; Olivelle 2009b,18; *Dharmasūtra* 1.9.1): so no mention is made of her in the *samodhana*.

In the *Ummadantī-jātaka* (527) the married femme fatale with whom the Bodhisatta falls helplessly in love is attributed to Uppalavaṇṇā, not Yasodharā, as in the Āryaśura version (*Jātakamālā* 13). Indeed Uppalavaṇṇā, often depicted in *Jātakas* as the daughter of the Bodhisatta and Yasodharā, provides a useful comparable, her dramatic and unusual 'past lives' supporting her presence as the nun pre-eminent in psychic powers. She is often a goddess, unlike Rāhulamātā, whose existences are usually earthbound, and, unlike Rāhulamātā, experiences more diverse rebirths, including a courtesan (276) and several that are divine, as the kindly goddesses in the *Mūgapakkha-jātaka* (538), *Mahājanaka-jātaka* (539) and *Sāma-jātaka* (540). She features as the Bodhisatta's daughter in the *Vessantara*, and, in her final life, becomes one of two of the Buddha's chief nuns.[9]

Such rebirths provide striking contrast to those of Rāhulamātā, for whom the editors clearly felt a regal, unimpeachable and 'humanly' respectable destiny should trace back aeons! The fact that there are thirty-two in which she is the Bodhisatta's spouse indicates that Rāhulamātā's path was perceived by the editors as a complex, highly elaborated and self-sufficient unity, completed by the thirty-third, her final life. The sense-sphere heaven of the Thirty-Three, where beings are reborn for *sīla*, generosity, faith, and investigation, offers a whole world of happiness. Her rebirths also appear to follow the pattern of other organisms or categories of complex interdependencies denoted by that number.

Her name

As these cosmological and bodily parallels indicate, Yasodharā/Rāhulamātā, the editors suggest, is being communicated as a heroine who lives through so many diverse and highly differentiated lives as part of a larger whole, her commitment to be the spouse of the Bodhisatta/Buddha. This paper has been preoccupied with her name (*nāma*), but it is through words associated with form (*rūpa*) that she is most described. Terms to do with appearance and form constantly surround her: her names mean glory (*yaso*); she is sometimes Kañcanā, golden (*kañcana*). Bimbā seems an ancient name for her: *bimba* can be a fruit; but in Sanskrit it is also an image, the disc of the sun or moon, a shape, a mirror, a representation such as a picture, or a round form (SED 731). This name is apt on several levels: the Bodhisatta's golden images of her; her 'mirroring' of his aspirations, and her counterpart path to him, enacting continued support to his long search. She adapts to different situations and different needs, even, as in the *Kusa* and the *Janaka*, where it is difficult and painful. But in each tale her destiny is treated as solitary as well as relational: her acquiescence to being made a gift by the Bodhisatta would be perceived as the final purification of many lives of their union together, in which she, like him, has chosen a particular path. Through the workings out of her individual and collective *kamma* over several lifetimes, and her willingness to participate in this larger narrative, she becomes a particularly Buddhist heroine.

Before death, she delivers canonical *Apadāna* verses describing her multi-life autobiographical history (Mellick 1993; Walters 2014), elaborated in a later Pāli text, the *Bimbābhikkhunī-nibbāna* (Skilling 2007). These give a first-person account of her initial vow, at the time of the Buddha Dipaṅkara, to become the spouse of the Bodhisatta-to-be. At that time, she says, the earlier Buddha Dipaṅkara has made two prophecies about her: that she will be beloved and she will attain enlightenment 'like a lion breaking out of a cage' (*Yasodharā-therī* Ap 588). The first prophecy has

9. As with Moggallāna, also of 'dark' appearance, this highly coloured excellence seems reflected in past lives of notable variety, passion and adventure. Uppalavaṇṇā, like Moggallāna, experiences some turbulent results from earlier existences: as an enlightened nun she is raped, an event which Gotama publicly notes was not associated with any present defilement in her mind.

certainly been fulfilled in her reputation in Southern Asia. The second is evoked by her final words, as Yasodharā:

> She then made herself into various forms: as an elephant, a horse, a mountain and an ocean, and then as the sun, the moon, Mount Meru and Sakka ...Then, having taken the form of a brahmā, she gave a teaching on emptiness. 'O great hero! I, Yasodharā, pay homage at your feet, the one with clear vision!' (Ap 578, 580)

Rāhulamātā, by her very name, is defined by interrelatedness, a principle that applies not just to her relationship with the Bodhisatta and her son but also to her embodiment of a connectivity that early Buddhists perceived as underlying all life, of every kind. This would not be underestimated. This doctrine permeates early Buddhist texts, from the teachingof dependent origination in the *Suttas*, to enjoinders concerning members of the *bhikkhusaṅgha*'s interdependence with one another and their relationship with the laity in the *Vinaya*, to the fully developed philosophical teachings of the connectedness of events on a momentary basis in the *Paṭṭhāna*. All beings are related to one another by manifold conditions; all beings are caught in the network of existence by thousands of factors, operating within their own bodies, in their relationships to one another and their interactions. By her alignment to so many other beings and environments in the tales she is constantly adaptive, fulfilling the needs of her station and environment. To the ancient Buddhists, it seems, it is this sympathetic engagement, fulfillment and occasional active transcending of her duty in life, her *svadharma*, which is her virtue, and constitutes the basis of her spiritual path in her preparation for final awakening. She appears 'lion-like': in one rebirth she is a lioness, and in the *Candakinnara-jātaka* (485) invokes the gods with a 'lion's roar', again roaring 'like a lion' when she defends the Bodhisatta for giving her away (Ja VI 570). Gotama's job might be to know all worlds; her awakening is figured by her capacity to embody and become them. By her assumption of the forms of natural features of the earth and sky, animals, the lord of a sense-sphere heaven, and a god of the meditative heavens of *jhāna*, she enacts both her command of the realms of behaviour (*sīla*) and meditation. She nonetheless demonstrates her ability to dissolve and let go of all identities, speaking, the verse says, from emptiness, produced by wisdom. She embodies, rather than describes, the Buddhist path.

This evidence of her arahatship shows that for early Buddhists, she is the true spouse of the Buddha, and finds freedom for herself, revealing in her final words her mastery of and freedom from all forms and all realms of existence. As it is hoped this paper demonstrates, her *Apadāna*, the canonical *Jātaka* verses referring to a spouse for the Bodhisatta, and her active and comprehensive engagement in *Jātaka* narrative, mean that her strength, purpose and highly coloured participation in the Bodhisatta vow should not be overlooked as we consider the Southern Buddhist treatment and discussion of women.

This short survey is intended as a beginning: more research on the history of local contexts, rituals, narratives, vernacular traditions, poetry and drama would help us to understand the special place this figure seems to have held, and continues to assume, in Southern Buddhist practice and culture.

Appendix: Some Pāli sources for Rāhulamātā/Yasodharā

Canon:

Vin I 82
Ap II 584ff
Bv I 98

Pāli Commentaries, apart from *Jātakas* listed above:

Ja I 54	Born same day as Gotama
Ja I 58	Married when sixteen and placed at head of forty thousand women
Ja I 62	Gotama leaves on the day of the birth of their son, Rāhula Gotama gives the *Candakinnara-jātaka* on his return
Mp I 198	She becomes a nun under Mahā Pajāpatī Gotamī
Mp I 376	Explanation of the name Bhaddakaccānā that her body was the colour of burnished gold; Buddhaghosa identifies her with Bhaddakaccānā, mentioned in A I 25, as chief amongst nuns in psychic powers and knowledges (*mahābhiññappattānam*). Bhaddakaccānā is mentioned as the daughter of the Sākyan Suppabuddha and his wife Amitā (Mp I 205).

Abbreviations

A	*Aṅguttaranikāya*
Ap	*Apadāna*
Bv	*Buddhavaṃsa*
DPPN	Malalasekera, G. P. 1974. *Dictionary of Pāli Proper Names.* 2 vols. London: Pali Text Society. First published in Indian Texts Series 1937.
Ja	*Jātakatthavaṇṇanā*
Mp	*Aṅguttaranikāya* commentary
PED	Rhys Davids, T. W. and William Stede. 1921–1925. *Pāli-English Dictionary.* London: Pali Text Society.
SED	Monier-Williams, Monier. 1899. *A Sanskrit-English Dictionary.* Oxford: Clarendon Press.
TGBSB	Appleton, Naomi and Shaw, Sarah. trans. 2015. *The Ten Great Birth Stories of the Buddha: The Mahānipāta of the Jātakakatthavaṇṇanā.* With a foreword by Peter Skilling. 2 vols. Chiang Mai: Silkworm Publications.
Vin	*Vinaya*

Pali Text Society editions used for Pāli texts.

Individual *jātakas* in the Pāli collection are denoted by their number in brackets, and references to the Pāli text by Ja and volume and page number.

Bibliography

Collins, Steven. 1998. *Nirvana and other Buddhist Felicities.* Cambridge: Cambridge University Press.

———. ed. 2016. *Readings of the Vessantara Jātaka.* Columbia: Columbia University Press.

Cone, Margaret and Gombrich, Richard F. 1977. *The Perfect Generosity of Prince Vessantara: A Buddhist Epic.* Oxford: Clarendon Press.

Covill, L. 2005. *Metaphors for Conversion in Asvaghosa's Saundarānanda.* Unpublished PhD thesis, Oxford University.

Geiger, W. 1943. *Pāli Literature and Language.* Translated by B. Ghosh. Calcutta: Calcutta University.

Hardy, Thomas. 1886. *The Mayor of Casterbridge: The Life and Death of a Man of Character.* London: Smith, Elder and Co.

Khoroche, Peter. 1989. *Once the Buddha was a Monkey: Ārya* Śūra's *Jātakamālā.* Chicago, IL: University of Chicago Press.

Klostermeier, Klaus K. 1999. *Buddhism: A Short Introduction.* Oxford: Oneworld Publications.

Lake, David J. 1975. *The Canon of Thomas Middleton's Plays.* Cambridge: Cambridge University Press.

Lefferts, Leedom and Cate, Sandra. 2012. *Buddhist Storytelling in Thailand and Laos: The Vessantara Jataka Scroll at the Asian Civilisation's Museum.* Singapore: Asian Civilisations Museum.

Meiland, Justin. 2004. *Buddhist Values in the Pāli Jātakas, with Particular Reference to the Theme of Renunciation.* DPhil dissertation: University of Oxford.

———. trans. 2009; 2017. *Garland of the Buddha's Past Lives by Aryashura.* 2 vols. Translation of Āryasūra's *Jātakamālā.* London: Clay Sanskrit Library.

Mellick, Sally. 1993. *A Critical Edition, with selected portions of the Pāli Apadāna.* Unpublished PhD thesis, Oxford University.

Obeyesekere, Ranjini. 2009. *Yasodharā, the Wife of the Bodhisattva: The Sinhala Yasodharāvata (The Story of Yasodharā) and the Sinhala Yasodharāpadānaya (The Sacred Biography of Yasodharā).* Albany: State University of New York.

———. 2014. 'Yasodharā in the Buddhist Imagination: Three Portraits Spanning the Centuries'. In *Family in Buddhism,* edited by Liz Wilson, 189–203. Albany: State University of New York Press.

Olivelle, Patrick. trans. 2009a. *The Law Code of Manu.* Oxford World Classics. Oxford: Oxford University Press.

———. trans. 2009b. *Dharmasūtras: The Law Codes of Ancient India.* Oxford World Classics. Oxford: Oxford University Press.

Shaw, Sarah. 2006. *The Jātakas: Birth Stories of the Bodhisatta.* Penguin Global Classics. New Delhi: Penguin.

———. 2010. 'And that was I: How the Buddha himself Creates a Path between Biography and Autobiography'. In *Lives Lived, Lives Imagined: Biographies of Awakening,* edited by L. Covill, U. Roesler and S. Shaw, 15–47. Boston, MA: Wisdom.

Strong, John S. 1997. 'A Family Quest: The Buddha, Yasodharā, and Rāhula in the *Mulasārvastivāda Vinaya*'. In *Sacred Biography in the Buddhist Traditions of South and South East Asia,* edited by Juliane Schobar, 113–128. Honolulu: University of Hawaii Press.

———. 2001. *The Buddha: a Short Biography.* Oxford: Oneworld Publications.

Swearer, Donald K. 1995. 'Bimbā's Lament'. In *Buddhism in Practice,* ed. Donald P. Lopez, 541–542. Princeton, NJ: Princeton University Press.

Tiyavanich, Kamala. 2003. *The Buddha in the Jungle.* Chiang Mai/Seattle: Silkworm Publications/ Washington University Press.

Walters, Jonathan. 2013. '*Apadāna: Therī-apadāna*; Wives of the Saints: Marriage and *Kamma* in the Path to Arahantship'. In *Women in Early Indian Buddhism*, edited by Alice Collett, 160–191. Oxford: Oxford University Press.

Sarah Shaw is the Khyentse Foundation Reader in Buddhist Studies, University of South Wales. She is a Member of the Faculty of Oriental Studies at the University of Oxford and Honorary Fellow of the Oxford Centre for Buddhist Studies. She has published a number of translations and studies relating to early Buddhist meditation and narrative, including *Buddhist Meditation: An Anthology and Texts from the Pāli Canon* (Routledge 2006), *The Jātakas* (Penguin 2006), *Introduction to Buddhist Meditation* (Routledge 2008), *The Spirit of Buddhist Meditation* (Yale University Press 2014) and *The Great Birth Stories of the Buddha* (with Naomi Appleton, 2 volumes, Silkworm 2015). She was fortunate in experiencing many years of Lance's teaching and friendship.

— 16 —

Jātaka Stories and *Paccekabuddhas* in Early Buddhism

NAOMI APPLETON

This article explores the role of *paccekabuddhas* in stories of the Buddha's past lives (*jātaka* tales) in early Buddhist narrative collections in Pāli and Sanskrit. In early Buddhism *paccekabuddhas* are liminal figures in two senses: they appear between Buddhist dispensations, and they are included as a category of awakening between *sammāsambuddha* and *arahat*. Because of their appearance in times of no Buddhism, *paccekabuddhas* feature regularly in *jātaka* literature, as exemplary renouncers, teachers, or recipients of gifts. This article asks what the liminal status of *paccekabuddhas* means for their interactions with the Buddha and his past lives as Bodhisatta.

Introduction

The last time I saw Lance Cousins was at the 2014 Spalding Symposium on Indian Religions in Manchester. At the time I was knee-deep in the complex story-network concerning kings called Janaka and Nimi and their renunciatory prowess.[1] I had headed off on a tangent exploring *paccekabuddhas*, since these apparently solitary renouncers feature large in such stories. I remember chatting with Lance over tea and a biscuit about the role of *paccekabuddhas* as a category and as a narrative device. I then had to set this area aside to complete work on my recent book, but I always wanted to come back to *paccekabuddhas*. Since this formed my last proper conversation with Lance, and since — like *paccekabuddhas* — he was both an accomplished meditator and a stimulating teacher,[2] it seemed an appropriate topic to address in this memorial collection.

The term *paccekabuddha* (or, in Sanskrit *pratyekabuddha*) is usually translated as 'solitary Buddha' or 'lone Buddha'.[3] Such figures are said to arise in times between Buddhist dispensations, achieve awakening without access to teachings, and pursue

1. Eventually published as chapter 6 of Appleton 2017.
2. I was lucky enough to benefit from Lance's Pāli teaching, both formally during my DPhil at the University of Oxford, and informally at his home, where Sarah Shaw and I spent many a happy afternoon reading *jātakas* with him. On *paccekabuddhas* as teachers see Appleton 2019.
3. Since I am primarily exploring Pāli sources I will tend to use Pāli terms except when explicitly referring to a Sanskrit text. I prefer to use *paccekabuddha* rather than the standard translation 'solitary Buddha', as in narrative occurrences *paccekabuddhas* are often *not* solitary. Leaving the term untranslated has the potential to mislead, however, since Norman (1983) has convincingly

Keywords: *Apadāna*, Bodhisatta, Buddha, *jātaka*, *paccekabuddha*, *Sutta-nipāta*

a life of solitary renunciation: they 'wander lonely as a rhinoceros', as the famous *Sutta-nipāta* verses put it.[4] They are liminal figures in more than one sense: Not only do they appear between full *buddhas* (*sammāsambuddhas*), but they are positioned between these and *arahats* in the enumeration of types of awakening, realising the truth themselves (like full *buddhas*) but not going on to found a Buddhist dispensation or monastic lineage. Because of their association with past times before the *Dhamma* was made available by the most recent Buddha, *paccekabuddhas* feature most prominently in *jātaka* and *apadāna* literature. In *jātaka* stories in particular their liminality comes to the fore, as they interact with the Bodhisatta in stories told by the Buddha. In such stories we find much more than silence and solitude: *paccekabuddhas* often gather in groups, sometimes bound by past-life friendship; they teach others, including the Bodhisatta, often through enigmatic verses, metaphors or images; and they offer a model of renunciation fit for the distant past, before the monasticism instituted by the Buddha.

In this paper I will explore the role of *paccekabuddhas* in *jātaka* literature, with a particular focus on the *Jātakatthavaṇṇanā*, but also making reference to *jātakas* in the *Apadāna*, *Avadānaśataka*, and *Mahāvastu*. I will also make some comparative comments about the non-*jātaka* occurrences of *paccekabuddhas* in the *Sutta-nipāta* commentary. The article will address the following question: What does the positioning of *paccekabuddhas* as interim figures, appearing as they do between the dispensations of full *buddhas*, mean for their relationship with the most recent Buddha or his past lives as Bodhisatta? I will start by considering stories in which *paccekabuddhas* appear as generic best renouncers or best recipients of gifts in the times between Buddhisms, as well as the karmic rewards of serving such figures. Next I will explore stories in which *paccekabuddhas* assist or teach the Bodhisatta, asking what this tells us about the various spiritual and social hierarchies exposed in *jātaka* literature. This will lead on to some concluding thoughts about how the *paccekabuddha* serves to both undermine and reinforce the status of Bodhisatta and Buddha in *jātaka* stories.

The *paccekabuddha* as interim figure

In a recent article in *Artibus Asiae*, Samerchai Poolsuwan (2016) explores the iconography of *paccekabuddhas* in a range of Pagan sites from around the twelfth to thirteenth centuries, and demonstrates that *paccekabuddha* images often represent the intermediate time between past and present — or present and future — *buddhas*. As such they are depicted in careful relation to, for example, the twenty-eight *buddhas* of the *Buddhavaṃsa*, or events in the life of the next *buddha*, Metteyya. Poolsuwan further argues that they may be iconographically intermediate too, being depicted with some of the iconography of full *buddhas* but not all, marking them out as some-

argued that the term may originally have been related to *pratyaya-buddha* and meant something like 'awakened by signs'. If pressed, I would translate as 'independent Buddha'.

4. Sn 35–75. On why the reference should be to a rhinoceros and not his horn see Jones 2014. For a translation and study of the verses and commentarial stories associated with *paccekabuddhas* see Kloppenborg 1974.

where between a *buddha* and an *arahat*.[5]

As Poolsuwan rightly notes, one of the main associations with *paccekabuddhas* is their position between *buddhas*, and between the *buddha* and his awakened disciples. As such, *paccekabuddhas* occupy a liminal space. This liminal role is particularly apparent in the narrative universe of *jātaka* stories, in which neither a full *buddha* nor any *arahats* can exist. As such, *paccekabuddhas* often feature as a substitute for these other forms of awakened being, either as a generic 'best field of merit' or as 'best renouncer'. We will therefore begin our examination of *paccekabuddhas* in the *jātakas* with these two functions of these independent renouncers.

In a famous story found in the *Jātakatthavaṇṇanā* (40) and the *Jātakamālā* (4), the Bodhisatta sees a *paccekabuddha* and decides to offer him a gift, but Māra creates a vision of a hell pit that he must traverse if he is to succeed in his intentions, and declares that gift-giving leads to hell. The virtuous donor, of course, sets out in any case to make his offering, and miraculous lotus-flowers appear beneath his feet as stepping-stones.[6] This is the only real occurrence of a *paccekabuddha* in the *Jātakamālā*, and his role is simply to demonstrate the Buddha-to-be's commitment to almsgiving. The importance of giving alms is also the focus of the *Dhajaviheṭha-jātaka* (Ja 391), though it is addressed through slightly different means: A false ascetic causes a king to stop supporting ascetics, and the god Sakka (the Bodhisatta) is forced to intervene to teach the king about the importance of venerating ascetics, using an old *paccekabuddha* as an example of a good recipient. In the *Āditta-jātaka* (Ja 424), *paccekabuddhas* themselves highlight the importance of gift giving, in a teaching given after they accept alms from King Bharata (the Bodhisatta) and his queen.

The idea that *paccekabuddhas* are the best available recipients is further highlighted in the *Dasabrāhmaṇa-jātaka* (Ja 495) in which King Yudhiṭṭhira consults his wise counsellor Vidhura (the Bodhisatta) about the qualities of brahmins. After a number of verses about those who are brahmins in name only, the king wishes to invite only 'true' brahmins to an almsgiving, and so they invite five hundred *paccekabuddhas*. Thus the story shows characters famous from the Brahmanical epic *Mahābhārata* acknowledging the Buddhist perspective on who makes the best recipient. In the very next story, the *Bhikkhāparampara-jātaka* (Ja 496), a king travels through his land with his brahmin chaplain in disguise, trying to find out if he is deficient in virtue. Upon receiving a gift of some food, he gives it to his brahmin chaplain, who gives it to an ascetic, who gives it to character identified in the verses as a *bhikkhu*. This term, which literally means 'one who lives by alms', usually refers to a monk, but is explained in the prose as here referring to a *paccekabuddha*. The discrepancy between verse and commentarial prose (which is itself reasonably common in the *Jātakatthavaṇṇanā*) serves to highlight the use of *paccekabuddhas* in this story as a simple substitute for a monk in a time when no Buddhist monasti-

5. It is noted that his arguments on this point are disputed by other scholars, and it is possible that the images he sees as *paccekabuddhas* are actually *arahats*.

6. A similar tale is found twice in the *Mahāvastu* (III, 41–7 and III, 250–254) though there the potential recipient is not named, and the tester is the god Śakra rather than Māra.

cism is in existence. Indeed, the appearance of a *paccekabuddha* is often described as similar to a monk, for example they wear orange robes, further blurring the lines. That a person with such an appearance is widely trusted is an important narrative device in two further *jātakas*, in which someone takes on a disguise as a *paccekabuddha* in order to catch and kill an elephant (Ja 221 and 514).

The worthiness of *paccekabuddhas* as recipients is reinforced by the karmic rewards of serving them, and this is another common theme in *jātaka* literature, as also in *apadāna/avadāna* literature. For example, in the *Kummāsapiṇḍa-jātaka* (Ja 415), a poor man (the Bodhisatta) gives four handfuls of food to four *paccekabuddhas*, and as a result is reborn as a king. In the *Mahāpanāda-jātaka* and *Suruci-jātaka* (Ja 264 and 489), a father and son build a shelter for a *paccekabuddha* and reap impressive karmic rewards including rebirth as a king. Karmic rewards can even fruit within a single lifetime: In the *Saṃkha-jātaka* (Ja 442) the brahmin Saṅkha (the Bodhisatta) is very generous and decides to go to sea to get more wealth to give away. A *paccekabuddha* sees that he will run into trouble and so appears before him to give him a merit-making opportunity. Saṅkha duly gives him his own sandals and a sunshade, as a result of which, when his ship is destroyed, he and his attendant survive and swim for seven days until the goddess Maṇimekhalā rescues them; she declares them worthy of rescue because of the gift Saṅkha made to the *paccekabuddha*.

Bad karmic interactions are also possible, as are mixed ones. In the *Mayhaka-jātaka* (Ja 390) we discover that the reason a rich merchant cannot enjoy his wealth is because in a past life he gave a gift to a *paccekabuddha* but was too miserly to rejoice in it. An episode of the *Kuṇāla-jātaka* (Ja 536) records that a woman's ugly face but soft skin is due to having given a gift to a *paccekabuddha* but in anger. In a little interlude of the *Kusa-jātaka* (Ja 531, with a parallel in *Mahāvastu* III, 27) we find the karmic cause of the ugliness of King Kusa (the Bodhisatta) and the reason he is despised by his wife: in a past life she had given away his portion of food to a *paccekabuddha* and he had become angry and taken it back (see Shaw article, p. 291).

As we can see, the Bodhisatta is far from exempt from these karmicly potent encounters with *paccekabuddhas*, and this is particularly true of Pāli literature.[7] Perhaps the most interesting examples appear in the *Pubbakammapiloti* chapter of the *Apadāna*, which, despite being about the Buddha, is tucked in with the verses of the *theras* (Ap 299–301). In this intriguing text we hear of past-life misdeeds that the Bodhisatta committed, and how these explain various minor sufferings in the Buddha's final life.[8] Several of these misdeeds involve *paccekabuddhas*: the Bodhisatta slanders a *paccekabuddha* (verse 4), throws a clod of earth at a *paccekabuddha* (verse 17), and attacks a *paccekabuddha* with an elephant (verse 19). All of these actions of

7. Sanskrit narrative literature also records plenty of stories of karmicly potent encounters with *pratyekabuddhas*, though the Buddha-to-be rarely features. In the *Mahāvastu*, for example, past-life service of *pratyekabuddhas* explains why Ājñāta Kauṇḍinya was first to understand the *Dharma*, and why Yaśoda mastered the powers so quickly. The only encounter between the Buddha-to-be and a *pratyekabuddha*, however, is in a past-life episode within the *Kuśa-jātaka*, discussed above. In the *Avadānaśataka* there are plenty of encounters with *pratyekabuddhas*, but none of them feature the Buddha-to-be.

8. For a helpful study of this text see Walters 1990.

course have bad karmic results, both in hell realms and in his final life, in which the Buddha was slandered and subject to attacks from Devadatta, including an attack with an elephant. Poetic justice abounds in the *Apadāna*.

Paccekabuddhas supporting or teaching the Bodhisatta

In addition to providing a powerful field of merit (or demerit) and serving as ideal recipient of gifts, *paccekabbuddhas* in the *jātakas* often function as teachers or exemplary renouncers, frequently encouraging the Bodhisatta to give up his worldly attachments.[9] Perhaps the most famous of such stories, and the one that initially prompted my interest in the whole category of *paccekabuddhas*, is the story of the four *paccekabuddha*-kings and the potter, found in the *Kumbhakāra-jātaka* (Ja 408). In this tale, the Bodhisatta is a potter, and he and his wife are visited by four *paccekabbuddhas* who used to be famous kings. The potter asks them how they came to be *paccekabuddhas* and they explain in a verse each. These verses speak of signs or experiences that led to renunciation, such as seeing a mango tree stripped bare, or hawks fighting over a piece of meat. The theme, of course, is the perils of worldly life and the benefits of renunciation. After hearing them, the potter decides to become a renouncer himself, but his wife – also inspired – beats him to it and leaves him to care for their children. Only once the children are old enough to fend for themselves is the Bodhisatta-potter able to fulfill his ambition.

This story is important for several reasons. First, it draws our attention to a key theme with which *paccekabuddhas* are often associated, namely seeing signs that lead to renunciation. Secondly, it shows how their means of learning – through direct experience or reflection on a powerful image – becomes their means of inspiring or teaching others, either through recounting their own encounters as here, or concocting new ones for their audiences, as in other narratives. Thirdly, it shows that this lesson about the benefits of renunciation is suitable for all audiences, not just royalty, and not just men. And one of the most common audiences for their teachings about renunciation in the *jātakas* is the Bodhisatta, in whatever form he happens to have taken birth.

Often the *paccekabuddhas* that teach the Bodhisatta turn out to be old friends. In the *Darīmukha-jātaka* (Ja 378), for example, while relaxing in a park the young brahmin Darīmukha realises that his friend – the Bodhisatta – is about to become king and that he himself is likely to be appointed as the commander of the army. Deciding that he prefers renunciation he hides himself at the key moment, when the people come to invite the Bodhisatta to be king. After the Bodhisatta has accepted their invitation and been taken off to the palace, Darīmukha emerges from the shadows, sits on the empty royal bench, and sees a withered leaf fall to the ground. At once he realises *paccekabodhi*, magically assumes the appearance of a renouncer, and flies off to the Himalayas. After forty years of being infatuated with the glories of kingship, the king recalls his former friend and conceives a desire to see him.

9. For a more extensive study of the content and methods of *paccekabuddha* teachers in Pāli literature see Appleton 2019.

Eventually the *paccekabuddha* Darīmukha decides it is time to visit, to encourage the king to renounce now that he is older and has many descendants to continue the line. The king, though pleased to see his former friend, takes some persuading before he is willing to detach himself from his worldly life, but he does eventually renounce. Of course, as he is the Bodhisatta he cannot achieve *paccekabodhi* like his friend, but he does achieve a heavenly rebirth as a result of his efforts.

A closely related story is the *Sonaka-jātaka* (Ja 529), in which the Bodhisatta, called Arindama, becomes king and his friend Sonaka becomes a renouncer.[10] As in the *Darīmukha-jātaka*, Sonaka achieves *paccekabodhi* as a result of seeing a withered leaf, that classic sign of impermanence, and immediately disappears off to the Himalayas. When the king much later wants to see him, Sonaka visits and offers some potent teachings, including outlining the eight blessings of being a renouncer (*samaṇa*), which are all benefits of non-attachment, such as remaining dispassionate even if one's city were to burn down. When the king remains unconvinced, Sonaka tells him the famous parable of a crow who is so greedy that he gets stuck inside an elephant carcass, busily eating away as the hide shrinks in the sun.

In these two stories the aim of the *paccekabuddha*'s teaching is to persuade the Bodhisatta-king of the need to renounce, but sometimes the teachings are about other related ideals, particularly the need for control of the senses and avoidance of various kinds of attachment. Thus, in the *Telapatta-jātaka* (Ja 96, see also Ja 132) the Bodhisatta-prince seeks a kingship across the other side of a wilderness, and some *paccekabuddhas* counsel him to be careful, as the wilderness is populated by demonesses who ensnare men's senses then eat them. The Bodhisatta sets off with five companions, each of whom falls foul of the demonesses' efforts, whether soft couches, beautiful music, sweet foods, enticing perfumes or seductive forms. Only the Bodhisatta has full control of all his senses, and his reward is to reach the other side in safety and gain a kingship. Having *paccekabuddhas* as your advisors turns out to be very beneficial.

It is fitting that kings should so often be the beneficiaries of the teachings of *paccekabuddhas*, since they are their polar opposites, being so dominated by worldly pleasures and attachments. Perhaps for the same reason, it is also very often kings that *become* such accomplished renouncers, though this is by no means always the case. In the *Pānīya-jātaka* (Ja 459), five householders each commit and then reflect upon a misdeed, and this leads to their renunciation and *paccekabodhi*. Later they recount their experiences to the Bodhisatta, who is a king. Their misdeeds are not severe: the first stole water from a friend, the second felt lust towards another man's wife, the third told a lie in order to save his own life, the fourth permitted slaughter of animals for sacrifice, and the fifth allowed the consumption of strong drink at a festival, which led to fights and injuries. Once again the Bodhisatta-as-king is able to benefit from the teachings of these *paccekabuddhas*, realising that unwholesome desires lead to bad behaviour and deciding to renounce as well. Although the verses

10. See also *Mahāvastu* III, 449–61 for a parallel story, though in this version the renouncer is not said to be a *pratyekabuddha*.

are recounted in a manner reminiscent of the four *paccekabuddha*-kings, the themes are rather different: these *paccekabuddhas* demonstrate that renunciation is a way to avoid bad deeds by cultivating non-attachment, whereas the *paccekabuddha*-kings reflect on the inevitable destruction of worldly wealth or the benefits of solitude. However, the end result is the same, with the Bodhisatta in both cases becoming a renouncer.

Even when he is already a renouncer, the Bodhisatta can benefit from the teachings of *paccekabuddhas*. In the *Pañcuposatha-jātaka* (Ja 490) the Bodhisatta is a brahmin sage who is afflicted with an excess of pride, which is, of course, a form of attachment. Four animals that live near him each wrestle with a different form of attachment: a pigeon vows to overcome his passion for his mate after she is eaten by a hawk, a snake vows to overcome the anger that led him to kill a bull, a jackal vows to overcome his greed after escaping an elephant carcass in which he has been trapped for a long time, and a bear vows to overcome greed that has led to him being attacked by villagers. All four decide to observe the holy day (*uposatha*). Meanwhile a *paccekabuddha* sees the Bodhisatta-sage's pride and deliberately comes to sit on his seat, making him angry. The *paccekabuddha* rebukes the sage for his pride, and – in a rather unusual passage for the *jātakas* – tells him that he will become a full *buddha*, and that such proud behaviour is unworthy of him. Despite this prediction and admonition, the sage remains silent, refusing even to pay respects to his visitor. Finally, the *paccekabuddha* shocks the sage by flying into the air, and all of a sudden the Bodhisatta realises what an opportunity he has missed as a result of his pride. He reflects on this and finally achieves the meditative attainments. He and the animals then exchange verses about their experiences, and we learn that pride, along with other forms of attachment such as greed, passion and anger, should be overcome.

In addition to showing how the Bodhisatta benefits from the teachings of a *paccekabuddha*, this story reminds us of the question of hierarchy. In relation to the proud brahmin sage, the *paccekabuddha* is superior, yet the proud brahmin sage is himself set to become a full *buddha*, clearly superior to a *paccekabuddha*. As a Bodhisatta, however, he cannot attain *paccekabodhi*, and so even after he has overcome his pride, all he achieves is a range of meditative attainments and a rebirth in the Brahmā realm. We might reasonably ask which of the two characters – the Bodhisatta-sage or the *paccekabuddha* – is the superior 'hero' of the story. This same question arises, though it is less directly addressed, in all the other stories in which the Bodhisatta is taught or encouraged to renounce by a *paccekabuddha*, for although he may follow their recommendations, he can never equal their attainments.

A Bodhisatta cannot be a *paccekabuddha*

The questions of spiritual hierarchy that arise in these stories are avoided in the many commentarial tales that accompany the rhinoceros horn verses of the *Sutta-nipāta* (Pj II 52–130). In this collection we find numerous stories in which kings are inspired by *paccekabuddhas* into renouncing and attaining *paccekabodhi* themselves, thereby equaling the attainment of their teachers, who are often said to have been their friends in past lives. The tricky thing for the *jātaka* genre, in contrast to the *Suttanipāta* commentary, is that a character has to be identified as the Bodhisatta, and the Bodhisatta cannot – by definition – achieve any form of awakening until his final life as a *buddha*. Evidence that the decision over which character ought to be identified as the Bodhisatta is not always straightforward is found in one of the most interesting stories that is associated with *paccekabuddhas*, the *Mahājanaka-jātaka* (Ja 539).

In the *Mahājanaka-jātaka*, the hero and namesake of the story is a prince and then king called Mahājanaka, or simply Janaka. As a boy, he grows up in a neighbouring city after his father, the king of Mithilā, is killed and ousted by his uncle. After an adventurous sea-voyage, the young Janaka ends up in the royal park of Mithilā just as the magical state chariot is set free to seek a new ruler, Janaka's uncle having died without a son. Unsurprisingly the magical chariot approaches Janaka and stops beside him. Having inspected the young man, the brahmins invite him to be ruler, and he is taken to the palace, where he further proves his worth by winning over the princess (his cousin Sīvalī) and solving riddles left by his uncle. It is in these riddles that we get our first indication that *paccekabuddhas* are important in this story. One part of the riddle says that treasure can be found at the sunrise and at the sunset. Janaka works out that this must mean the places where the previous king received and took leave of *paccekabuddhas*, since these glorious figures are like the sun, and indeed treasure is found buried in these places.

These worthy renouncers are referred to again later in the story, both explicitly and implicitly. After a happy time as ruler, supporting *paccekabuddhas*, married to Sīvalī and with a son and heir, Janaka one day decides to visit his pleasure park. On his way into the park he sees a mango tree bursting with ripe fruits, and he picks and eats a mango. Seeing this, all the members of his retinue follow suit, stripping the tree bare and breaking its branches. On his way home, the king sees this sorry looking tree, and next to it a fruitless tree that has remained lush and unharmed. Just as *paccekabuddhas* seem commonly to do, Janaka reflects that the kingship is like the fruiting tree, and wishes to become like the barren tree. When he returns to his palace, he hands over his state duties and lives on the roof terrace as a renouncer. This is not enough for him, however, and he reflects on those *paccekabuddhas* he has supported and wonders where he might find their good example and teachings now. Having got hold of a robe and bowl he shaves his head and descends the stairs in pursuit of proper renunciation. On the way down the stairs he meets his wife, and she mistakes him for a *paccekabuddha*.

There are no more explicit references to *paccekabuddhas* after this in the text, but what happens next continues to remind us of those characters. Not only does Janaka seek a particularly solitary form of renunciation, he declares that he has no teachers other than the mango trees, and speaks a famous verse about his detachment from his city, stating that even if Mithilā was on fire, nothing of his would be burning. Janaka also uses a variety of other images to try to persuade his wife to stop following him, images that are reminiscent of those often encountered by *paccekabuddhas*: a girl with two bracelets on one arm jangling annoyingly and a single bracelet on the other arm silent as a sage; a fletcher who shuts one eye in order to make his arrow straight; a plucked blade of grass unable to be rejoined to its plant.

What these various elements of the story suggest is that Janaka was once considered a *paccekabuddha*, yet in this story he is identified as the Bodhisatta. As such, all he achieves, after finally embarking on the solitary renunciation he so strongly insists upon, is a heavenly rebirth; his wife achieves the same, after a more modest form of renunciation in the royal gardens. That the identification of Janaka as the Bodhisatta and the concomitant restriction on his 'happy ending' was a change made to an existing story is supported by the wider story-cycle of kings of Mithilā famous for their renunciatory prowess. Such kings, who include those called Janaka, Nimi and Nami, are associated with awakening through signs, pursuing solitary renunciation, and expressing their detachment through a verse about their burning city. This verse is found associated with a King Janaka in the *Mahābhārata* (12.17.18, 12.171.56, and 12.268.4), and with a King Nami in the Jain *Uttarajjhāyā* (9.14). Elsewhere in the *Uttarajjhāyā* (18.45–47) King Nami is one of a group of four kings who renounce and achieve liberation after seeing a sign, in a parallel story to that of the four *paccekabuddha*-kings in the *Kumbhakāra-jātaka* examined above. In the *Nimi-jātaka* (Ja 541, see also Ja 9) the king of Mithilā may not be associated with *paccekabuddhas*, but he does renounce after seeing a sign — his first grey hair.[11]

What do we learn from this network of stories, and from the various references to and associations with *paccekabuddhas* in the *Mahājanaka-jātaka*? We learn that sometimes the generic conventions of the *jātaka* genre likely over-ruled previous associations with narrative characters, even when such characters were famous for their attainments. Indeed, it is precisely because Janaka was already a well-known royal renouncer that he had to be claimed as the Bodhisatta. The result, however, is that this famous renouncer can only renounce, and not achieve the liberation that his counterparts in Jain narrative and Hindu epic are said to achieve. We return once again to the question of the relative hierarchy of *paccekabuddha* and Bodhisatta.

A question of hierarchy: *paccekabuddha*, Bodhisatta and Buddha

Despite his heroic efforts and impressive achievements, as in all the other stories in which the Bodhisatta is inspired by *paccekabuddhas*, Janaka is inferior to these awakened beings. This sense of relative hierarchy is sometimes emphasized, for example in the *Gaṅgamāla-jātaka* (Ja 421), in which the Bodhisatta is King Udaya and his barber, Gaṅgamāla, renounces and becomes a *paccekabuddha*. When he returns to visit the king he uses a familiar form of address to greet him, and the king's mother and others are cross that he is not properly subservient. The Bodhisatta has to intervene and explain the merits of a *paccekabuddha* to his ignorant relations. Here, then, it is clear that a *paccekabuddha*-barber is superior to a Bodhisatta-king. However, the message is perhaps more to do with another important hierarchy: spiritual attainments trump social or caste rank.

11. For a full discussion of this network of stories see Appleton 2017, chapter 6.

A rather different answer to the question of hierarchy is found in the *Mahāmora-jātaka* (Ja 491), in which the Bodhisatta is a golden peacock who lives a holy life in the Himalayas. Nobody can catch him because of his holiness and protective chants. Eventually a hunter trains a peahen, and ensnares the peacock through lust. However, they then talk, and the peacock teaches the hunter such that he becomes a *paccekabuddha*. Despite this attainment he does not know how he can free all the birds he has left in bondage back at his home, and it takes the Bodhisatta — who is explicitly said in the commentary to be more knowledgeable than a *paccekabuddha* — to advise an Act of Truth. Thus the *paccekabuddha* declares the truth of his attainment, and through that all the creatures are freed. And while he too is freed, from the bondage of *saṃsāra*, he remains in at least one respect inferior to the Bodhisatta-peacock.

While there may be more than one perspective on whether *paccekabuddha* or Bodhisatta is superior, it is clear that the Buddha is definitely superior to *paccekabuddhas*, and in this certainty is found another solution to the question of hierarchy. In a series of verses in the *Apadāna* (I 7–14) the Buddha tells his disciple Ānanda how *paccekabuddhas* came to achieve awakening. He explains that they served former *buddhas* but did not achieve awakening in that time. This explanation neatly places the agency back in the hands of the Buddha again, making *paccekabuddhas* dependent on *buddhas* in a similar manner to *arahats*. Rather than being entirely independent and accomplished renouncers, *paccekabuddhas* are then said to achieve awakening without a teacher because they already had a teacher in a past life, and that teacher was a full *buddha*. However, this explanation appears only to have developed *after* the proliferation of stories about *paccekabuddhas*. I have not found any *jātaka* stories that tell of the past-lives of *paccekabuddhas*, who are instead associated with immediate and present awakening, in a manner that bypasses the teachings of a full *buddha*.

The *Apadāna*'s explanation of how *paccekabuddhas* sow the seeds of their achievements in past lives is, of course, broadly in line with *apadāna*/*avadāna* conceptions of awakening in general. In the same text, elder monks and nuns are said to have sowed the seeds of arahatship by serving past *buddhas* or, indeed, past *paccekabuddhas*. The Buddha himself is also said to have served past *buddhas* but not achieved awakening during that time. In the *Avadānaśataka* a chapter of ten stories (21–30) recounts how people become *pratyekabuddhas* after an act of service to — and prediction by — a *buddha*, though in most of these stories the *buddha* is the one of the present age, and the achievement will happen in a future time. We also find a similar theme in the *Sutta-nipāta* commentary, where the stories associated with eight of the verses tell of past lives of *paccekabuddhas* in the time of Buddha Kassapa, but here the focus is less on their prior achievements and more on their karmic bonds: their fellowship as a part of Kassapa's community leads to them coming together again once they have become *paccekabuddhas*, and helping any remaining member of their group to achieve that same end.[12]

12. Such multi-life group bonds appear in the stories associated with verses 38, 42, 47 and 58, while

These intricate networks of vows, predictions, service, achievements, and lateral karmic bonds are characteristic of the *apadāna/avadāna* genre, and, as we have seen, *paccekabuddhas* feature as recipients of karmicly significant acts of service as well as having past-life stories of their own. However, *jātaka* stories — in contrast to *apadānas/avadānas*, tend to emphasize the former of these two positions, portraying *paccekabuddhas* as figures that are solitary in the sense of being independent, awakened by and for themselves, in a time when the teachings of *buddhas* are not known. Theirs is a very direct form of awakening, based on personal experience, and not dependent on learning or formal monastic training. It is no wonder, then, that the question of their value relative to the Buddha became rather important.

These varying perspectives within Buddhist narrative sources are echoed by scholarly debates around the status of *paccekabuddhas*. Many scholars have argued that the character of the *paccekabuddha* allows for the inclusion of non-Buddhist (or pre-Buddhist) ascetics into the Buddhist fold.[13] Certainly in *jātaka* literature, as we have seen, *paccekabuddhas* often feature as generic renouncers in a time when no monks or *buddhas* can appear, and they offer a form of awakening that appears independent of learning or institutions. Indeed, Janaka and Nimi/Nami appear to be renouncer kings of particularly legendary status, and the fact that they — and the overall concept of a *paccekabuddha* — are shared with Jainism suggests a likely pre-Buddhist background. However, whatever its origins it is clear that the category entered Buddhism early, and took root in various different ways. For this reason, amongst others, it is important to consider the different understandings of *paccekabuddhas* across different genres and different schools, for the notion changed as Buddhist traditions developed and spread.

The distinction between the portrayal of *paccekabuddhas* in *jātaka* literature and their position in *apadāna/avadāna* literature, as discussed here, demonstrates the fruitfulness of such an approach. The differences between these genres' portrayal of *paccekabuddhas* suggest that efforts were made to subordinate these remarkably independent renouncers, by codifying their attainments in relation to past life encounters with *buddhas*. This careful positioning of *paccekabuddhas* as dependent on the Buddha should not, however, stop us from appreciating their unique position within stories of the Buddha's past lives, where they maintain much of their independence, and yet behave according to — and teach — an entirely Buddhist understanding of the world.

Conclusion

I began this paper with the following question: What does the positioning of *paccekabuddhas* as interim figures, appearing as they do between the dispensations of full

those associated with verses 36 and 39 simply imply that the *paccekabuddha* sowed the seeds in his past life, and the story that accompanies verses 45 and 46 explores how past-life affection can make it hard to achieve awakening.

13. For example this view is broadly shared, with some variation, by Gombrich 1979, Katz 1982, Kloppenborg 1974, Fujita 1985, Norman 1983, while Ray (1994) has suggested that they represent a form of early Buddhist 'saint', and Wiltshire (1990) argued that they are proto-*śramaṇas*.

buddhas, mean for their relationship with the most recent Buddha or his past lives as Bodhisatta? As we have seen, this interim positioning allows *paccekabuddhas* to fill a narrative gap in *jātaka* literature, which is almost always situated in a time between Buddhisms, by serving as 'best renouncers' or 'most powerful fields of (de-)merit'. In these roles *paccekabuddhas* are not particularly distinctive, and indeed they are often described as looking rather like Buddhist monks. More distinctive is their role in teaching the Bodhisatta about the benefits of renunciation or non-attachment. By recounting their own powerful experiences of confronting impermanence or the defiling power of desire, or by offering a parable or other illustration, *paccekabuddhas* provide a teaching and example for the Buddha-to-be to follow.

In these Bodhisatta-*paccekabuddha* encounters, the Bodhisatta often appears inferior, requesting and receiving teachings, struggling to overcome his worldly ties or social pride. The Bodhisatta often aspires to be like a *paccekabuddha*, following his example through renouncing the world. However, because of the restrictions of the *jātaka* genre, the Bodhisatta can never equal the attainments of his teacher, managing only to achieve successful renunciation, meditative attainments, and a heavenly rebirth. Alternatively, if the compilers felt the need to identify a truly heroic legendary king-become-*paccekabuddha* as the Bodhisatta, the association with *paccekabodhi* was necessarily pushed to the sidelines.

The superiority of these independent renouncers over the heroic Buddha-to-be is challenged by the development of the *apadāna*/*avadāna* notion of intricate karmic networks. We discover that *paccekabuddhas*, like *arahats* and full *buddhas*, all planted the seeds of this attainment through an act of service towards a *buddha* in the past. These vast networks of karmicly potent encounters between awakened beings of all types and stages allows the Buddha – and other full *buddhas* – to regain centre-stage, yet *paccekabuddhas* feature as fields of merit as well as as characters with a past-life encounter of their own. This closes the circle, bringing us back to those *jātaka* stories in which *paccekabuddhas* provide an opportunity for the Bodhisatta to make merit or demerit on his long path to buddhahood.

To conclude, *paccekabuddhas* seem always to be in the space in between two more established categories. Just as they are positioned between full *buddhas* and *arahats*, they also appear between Buddhist dispensations. They are powerful fields of merit, but their attainment ultimately came to be considered as dependent on encounters with even more powerful fields of merit. They teach but they cannot be seen to be teaching lest they threaten the authority of the Buddha and his dispensation. They help the Bodhisatta, and remain superior to him in most instances, yet their inferiority to the Buddha is clear to see. Contrary to their reputation, *paccekabuddhas* are neither solitary nor silent, but rather it is their possible independence from the Buddhist dispensation that makes them so interesting.

Abbreviations

Ap *Apadāna*
Ja *Jātakatthavaṇṇanā*
Sn *Sutta-nipāta*
Pj *Paramattha-jotikā* containing *Sutta-nipāta* commentary

Bibliography

Primary Sources

Apadāna: references to volume and page of Lilley:

Lilley, Mary E. ed. 1925–1927. *The Apadāna of the Khuddaka Nikāya*. 2 vols. London: The Pali Text Society.

Avadānaśataka: references to story number:

Speyer, J. S. ed. 1958. *Avadānaçataka: A century of edifying tales belonging to the Hīnayāna*. The Hague: Mouton.

Jātakamālā of Āryaśūra: references to story number:

Khoroche, Peter, trans. 1989. *When the Buddha Was a Monkey: Ārya Śūra's Jātakamālā*. Chicago, IL: University of Chicago Press.

Speyer, J. S. ed. 1895. *The Jātakamālā: Garland of Birth-Stories of Ārya-śūra*. Sacred Books of the Buddhists vol. 1. London: Henry Frowde.

Jātakatthavaṇṇanā: references to story number:

Appleton, Naomi and Sarah Shaw, trans. 2015. *The Ten Great Birth Stories of the Buddha: The Mahānipāta of the Jātakatthavaṇṇanā*. 2 vols. Chiang Mai: Silkworm.

Cowell, E. B. ed. (several translators). 1895–1907. *The Jātaka, or Stories of the Buddha's Former Births*. 6 vols. Cambridge: Cambridge University Press.

Fausbøll, V. ed. 1877–1896. *The Jātaka Together with its Commentary being Tales of the Anterior Births of Gotama Buddha*. 6 vols. London: Trübner.

Mahābhārata: references to book, chapter and verse of Critical Edition:

Sukthankar, Vishnu Sitaram, Sripad Krishna Belvalkar, Parashuram Laksman Vaidya *et al.*, eds. 1933–1966. *The Mahābhārata for the First Time Critically Edited*. Poona: Bhandarkar Oriental Research Institute.

Mahāvastu: references to volume and page of Senart:

Jones, J. J. trans. 1949–1956. *The Mahāvastu*. 3 vols. London: Luzac.

Senart, Émile, ed. 1882–1897. *Mahāvastu*. 3 vols. Paris: Imprimerie Nationale.

Paramattha-jotikā: references to volume and page of Smith:

Smith, Helmer. ed. 1916–1918. *Paramattha-jotikā*. 2 vols. London: The Pali Text Society.

Sutta-nipāta: references to page of Andersen and Smith:

Andersen, Dines and Helmer Smith. eds. 1913. *Sutta-Nipāta*. London: The Pali Text Society.

Uttarajjhāyā: references to chapter and verse as in Charpentier:

Charpentier, Jarl. ed. 1922. *Uttarādhyayanasūtra*. Uppsala: Appelbergs Boktryckeri Aktiebolag.

Jacobi, Hermann. trans. 1895. *Jaina Sūtras Part II*. The Sacred Books of the East volume 45. Oxford: The Clarendon Press.

Secondary Sources

Appleton, Naomi. 2017. *Shared Characters in Jain, Buddhist and Hindu Narrative: Gods, Heroes and Kings.* Abingdon: Routledge.

———. 2019. 'Dialogues with Solitary Buddhas'. In *In Dialogue with Classical Indian Traditions: Encounter, Transformation, and Interpretation,* edited by Brian Black and Chakravarthi Ram-Prasad, 37–50. Abingdon: Routledge.

Fujita, Kotatsu trans. Leon Hurvitz. 1985. 'One Vehicle or Three?' *Journal of Indian Philosophy* 3(1–2): 79–166.

Gombrich, Richard F. 1979. Review of Kloppenborg 1974, in *Orientalistische Literaturzeitung,* 74(1): 78–80

Jones, Dhivan Thomas. 2014. 'Like the Rhinoceros, or Like its Horn? The Problem of the *Khaggavisāṇa* Revisited'. *Buddhist Studies Review* 31(2): 165–178. https://doi.org/10.1558/bsrv.v31i2.165

Katz, Nathan. 1982. *Buddhist Images of Human Perfection: The Arahant of the Sutta Piṭaka Compared with the Bodhisattva and Mahāsiddha.* Delhi: Motilal Banarsidass.

Kloppenborg, Ria. 1974. *The Paccekabuddha: A Buddhist Ascetic.* Leiden: Brill.

Norman, K. R. 1983. 'The Pratyeka-Buddha in Buddhism and Jainism'. In *Buddhist Studies: Ancient and Modern,* edited by Philip Denwood and Alexander Piatigorsky, 92–106. London: Curzon.

Poolsuwan, Samerchai. 2016. 'Iconography and Symbolism of the Pacceka Buddhas in the Art of Pagan'. *Artibus Asiae* 76(1): 37–80.

Ray, Reginald A. 1994. *Buddhist Saints in India: A Study in Buddhist Values and Orientations.* Oxford: Oxford University Press.

Walters, Jonathan. 1990. 'The Buddha's Bad Karma: A Problem in the History of Theravāda Buddhism'. *Numen* 37(1): 70–95.

Wiltshire, Martin G. 1990. *Ascetic Figures Before and in Early Buddhism: The Emergence of Gautama as the Buddha.* Berlin: Mouton de Gruyter. https://doi.org/10.1515/9783110858563

Naomi Appleton is Senior Lecturer in Asian Religions at the University of Edinburgh. Trained in Buddhist Studies, her interests now span Buddhist, Jain and early Hindu narrative traditions. She has published extensively on Buddhist and early Indian narrative, including: *Jātaka Stories in Theravāda Buddhism* (Ashgate 2010), *Narrating Karma and Rebirth* (CUP 2014) and *Shared Characters in Jain, Buddhist and Hindu Narrative* (Routledge 2017). She was lucky enough to have Pāli reading classes with Lance Cousins during her time as a doctoral student in Oxford, and continued visiting him for reading groups after moving on in her career.

Index

Note that named Abhidhamma texts, *Jātakas*, *Saṃyuttas*, schools and *Suttas* are listed as sub-entries of these categories. All similes are also listed together. Numbers in bold indicate particularly significant entries.

A

Abhidhamma/Abhidharma, 5, 6, 8, 10, 11, 13, 15, 20, 21, 32, 37, 90, 114, 127, 154, 157–159, 162, 166–169, 172, 173, 175, 177–179, 183, 184, 186, 201, 202, 204, 212, 226, 233, 237, 249, 263, 273, 276, 294, 296
- *Dhammasaṅgaṇī*, 21, 184, 187, 190, 206
- *Dhātukathā*, 184, 187
- *Kathāvatthu*, 32, 36, 184, 187, 275, 276
- *Paṭṭhāna*, 11, 187, 190, 278, 296, 301
- *Puggalapaññatti*, 157–159, 166, 170–174, 177–179, 184, 187
- *Vibhaṅga*, 31, 184, 187, 278
- *Yamaka*, 6, 184, 186, 187

Āgamas, 6, 39, 131, 132, 145–152, 160, 161, 163–165, 181, 182, 209, 249, 250–258, 260, 264–268

aggregates. *See khandhas*

ancestors, 117–119, 121–124, 126–129, 275

animitta (signless meditative state), 104, 105

Annihilationism, 131, 137, 141, 142

Apadāna, 262, 273, 288, 300, 301, 306, 308, 309, 314–317

apophaticism, 99, 107

Appleton, Naomi, 1, 4, 5, 288, 294, 303, 305, 318

Arahat/Arahant/Arhat, 47, 49, 50, 55, 66, 77, 90, 127, 157, 158, 160–179, 301, 305–307, 314, 316

arūpa (formless, immaterial) states, 28, 30, 33–35, 37, 40, 41, 48, 55–57, 74, 83–90, 96, 97, 104, 108, 148, 167–169, 175, 176, 279

āsava (taint/canker/corruption/influx/outflow), 48, 55–57, 68, 74, 90, 91, 96, 158, 166, 169, 173, 174, 177, 178, 193, 197

Ātman, 101

Aṭṭhakavagga, 131, 134–136

atthapada, 51–53

Avadāna, 249, 308, 314, 315, 316

avyākata (unexplained issues, undetermined questions), 89, 140, 141

B

bhāṇaka (reciter), 50, 255, 260, 261

bhāvanā (meditative cultivation), 13, 46, 50, 55–57, 192, 196, 204, 298

bhavaṅga (background resting state of consciousness), 37

Bimbā/Bimbādevī, 287, 289, 300, 303

Bodhisatta, 287–301, 306–314, 316

bojjhaṅga (awakening factor), 22, 73, 77

Boonman Poonyathiro, 7

Brahmā, 28, 29, 220, 290, 301, 311

Brahman, 100, 101, 122

brahma-vihāras, 29, 74, 108

Brahminism, 51, 85, 117, 118, 120, 123, 125, 293, 307

Buddhadatta, 212, 213, 215, 220, 235, 237, 243

Buddhaghosa, **13**, 45–48, 51, 53, 59, 84, 98, 99, 102, 106, 108, 113, 158, 159, 161, 162, 165, 170, **172–174**, 178, 213, 215, 226, **277–280**, 283, 299

C

canons, formation of, 151, 250, 251, 257, 269, 270, 276
cessation of perception and feeling, 33, 34, 40, 56, 88–90
chanda (desire-to-do), 20, 63, 64, **76**, 77
Channa, 161–164, 167, 179, 181, 182
Christianity, 14, 83–85, 95–100, 102–104, 107, 109, 111, 112, 127, 137
Cloud of Unknowing, 99, 100, 104, 106, 107, 109, 110
Confucianism, 118, 129, 130
constructivist, 99–103
contemplation, 41, 66, 86, 92, 99, 104, 107–111, 148, 160
contentment, 63, 64, 70, 72–75, 88, 290
Cousins, Lance, 3–16, 19, 20, 21, 32, 35, 38–40, 45, 46–49, 51–55, 58–60, 84, 87, 96, 99, 100, 102, 103, 106, 110, 118, 131, 132, 145, 146, 169, 179, 183, 212, 217, 224, 226, 229, 240, 242, 250, 269, 270, 272–276, 279–281, 305, 318
craving (*taṅhā*), 41, 63, 70, 71, 75, 76, 79, 83, 91, 96, 134, 137–139, 147, 148, 176
  for metaphysics, 131, 133

D

dark night of the soul, 83, 91
death, 34, 117–124, 126, 128, 137, 139–142, 149, 290, 298
  Arahantship at, 157–162, 165–167, 170, 177–179
  of an Arahant, 171, 172, 174
deathless, 41, 51, 56–58, 67, 129, 169, 289
  doors to, 41, 70
dependent origination, 49, 301
desire — always to be avoided?, 70–72
  See chanda (desire-to-do), and craving
desire for sense-pleasures *(kāmacchanda)*, 35, 36, 76, 88, 106, 109, 175
devas. *See* gods
dhammakathika (*Dhamma*-preacher), 46–48, 50, 59
dhammānusārin (*Dhamma*-follower), 54
dhammayoga (one devoted to *Dhamma)*, 45–49, 51–58
Dīpavaṃsa, 269, 270, 274–276, 280
dogmatism, 135–138
domanassa (unhappiness), 26, 29–33
dukkha, 20, 23, 24, 26, 29–33, 57, 66, 70, 71, 74, 91, 128, 138, 139, 141, 149, 160, 164, 176, 186, 187, 192, 233, 297

E

early Buddhism, 117, 127, 131, 136, 137, 269, 305
effort, 33, 57, 63, 65, 78, 79, 93, 94, 273, 313
  right, 64, 74, **75**, 76, 78
  wrong, 65, 67–70, 72
emptiness, 13, 92–94, 104, 105, 108, 301
energy/vigour (*viriya*), 20, 22, 63–65, 69, 73, 76–78, 90, 176, 293
equanimity, 9, 20, 23, 24, 26–29, 31, 73, 77, 87, 89, 90, 91, 96
Eternalism, 131, 137, 138, 140, 141

F

faith (*saddhā*), 20, 48, 78, 129, 149, 150, 151, 176, 177, 215, 228, 232, 277, 278, 280, 300
feeling (*vedanā*), **23–24**, 25–27, **29–33**, 34, 40, 43, 56, 79, 90, 137, 161, 173
formless states. *See arūpa* states

G

Gandhāra, 249, 251, 255, 259, 264, 280
gender, 118, 121, 147, 153, 287–304
Gethin, Rupert, 5, 7, 28, 31, 32, 88, 89, 99, 114, 168, 177, 179, 266, 270, 277, 280, 283
gladness (*pāmujja)*, 19, 20, 28, 88, 175

goal-directedness, 64, 65, 69, 71, 74, 75
God, 83, 85, 86, 91, 93, 94, 95, 100, 101, 104, 107, 109–112, 137
goddess, 288, 292, 299, 308
Godhika, 161, 162, 165–167, 179
gods (*devas*), 7, 25, 28, **29**, 51, 79, 120–122, 124, 127, 128, 149, 150, 220, 271, 294, 301, 307
grace, 83, 110–112

H

Harvey, Peter, 3, 4, 19, 43, 49, 51, 55–58, 61, 91, 127, 160, 176, 181
hearing, 36, 37, 38, 49, 54, 89
heavens, 28, 29, 118, 120, 124, 127, 128, 149–151, 168, 288, 290, 297, 299–301, 310, 313, 316
hell, 91, 118, 120, 121, 124, 127, 128, 129, 148, 292, 307, 309
hindrances, five, 19, 20, 22, 24, 28, 29, 35, 67, 69, 70, 72, 74, 88, 90, 91, 95, 106, 109, 110, 139, 175, 176
Hinduism, 117, 118, 120–129, 313, 318

I

iddhi-pādas (roads to success), 63, 64, 77
immaterial states. *See arūpa* states
impermanence, 33, 41, 57, 74, 79, 89, 96, 106, 138, 141, 145, **147–149**, 159, 160, 200, 310, 316
Indian and Chinese Buddhist traditions, 11, 118, 130
insight (and see *vipassanā*), 20, 40, 49, 50, 54–60, 68, 74, 87, 89–91, 96, 139, 142, 148, 162, 164, 169, 170, 172, 173, 176, 221, 272
interrelatedness, 298, 301

J

Jainism, 120, 313, 315, 318
jātakas, 1, 205, 262, 263, 280, 287–302, 305–318
  Kusa, 290, 291, 308
  Mahājanaka, 290, 293, 294, 299, 312, 313
  Mahāummagga/Mahosadha, 288, 293
  Vessantara, 287, 289, 295, 297, 300
jhāna, 12, **19–43**, 56–58, 59, 69, 83–85, 87, **88–91**, 97, 108, 109, 168, 169, 175, 176, 186, 192, 195, 290, 301
  first, 20–24, 28, 29, 31–33, 35–37, 39
  fourth, 26–28, **29–31**, **33–35**, 37, 38, 56, 96, 108, 109
  hearing in, **35–38**
  insight in, **40–41**, 49, 74
  second, **24–25**, 28, 29, 31–33, 39, 95, 96
  third, **25–26**, 28, 29–31, 96
jhāyin (meditator), 45–49, 51, 52, 54, 56–58
John of the Cross, 83–87, 91–98, 100, 109
Jotipāla, 11, 212
joy/rapture (*pīti*), **19**–20, **21–25**, 28–33, 41, 73, 77, 88–93, 95, 96, 102, 110

K

karma, 89, 118–121, 123–125, 127, 130, 168, 186, 298, 300, 304, 308, 318
kāya (body), 20, 21–24, 26, **30**, 32, 33, 56, 105, 161, 186, 233
kāya-sakkhi (body-witness), 56, 58
khandhas (aggregates/groups), 30, 41, 55, 96, 137, 140, 148, 169, 172, 174, 175, 179, 186, 187

L

learning (*pariyatti*), 45, 46, 49, 50, 59, 271, 272, 277, 315
Līnatthappakāsanī, 211, 212, 219, 222

M

Maddī, 287–289, 295–298
Mahācunda, 46, 51–54, 56, 162
Mahānāma, 176–178, 277
Mahāvaṃsa, 217, 229, 232, 239, 240, 269, 276
Mahāyāna, 6, 10, 125, 127, 147, 152, 153, 154, 249
Māra, 66, 89, 90, 95, 161, 292, 307

marriage, 287, 288, 290–292, 304
masteries, 35, 38, 39, 40, 41
meditation, 1, 4–9, 12, 15, 19, 42, 47, 48, 50, 51, 54, 55, 58, 59, 61, 63–80, 86–88, 93, 97–99, 104, 106–108, 110, 111, 113, 129, 161, 164, 170, 204, 272, 283, 290, 293, 298, 301, 304, *See bhāvanā, jhāna, samatha, vipassanā*
merit (*puñña*), 125–130, 200, 213, 215, 220, 221, 278, 308, 313, 316
  field of, 307, 309, 316
  transfer of, 125, 126, 129
middle path, 84
middle teachings, 131, 137, 141
Milindapañha, 261–263, 273, 276
mindfulness (*sati*), 19, 20, 24, 26–29, 31, 41, 43, 55, 63, 65, 75, **77**, 78, 89, 90, 91, 98, 161, 176, 201
  of breathing (*ānāpānasati*), 7, 12, 26, 33, 34, 41, 67, 170, 171, 172
mortuary rituals, 121–126, 129
mysticism, comparative, 4, 13, 14, 84, 99–101, 103, 104, 109, 112, 113

N

Nāgārjunakoṇḍa, 51, 279, 280, 281
narrative, 87, 147, 287, 291, 293, 295, 297, 298, 300, 301, 304, 305, 307, 308, 313, 315, 316, 318
Nettippakaraṇa, 157, 261, 267, 273
Nibbāna/Nirvāṇa, 11, 13, 32, 41, 45, 46, 49, 50, 54–58, 60, 64, 67, 79, 80, 85, 87, 97, 100, 101, 104, 128, 136, 138, 141, 143, 148, 149, 161, 162, 166, 169, 171, 172, 174, 177, 179, 181, 288, 299, 300
nimitta (impression of a focus of meditative concentration), 20, 21, 29, 34, 37, 38, 110
Non-returner, 29, 41, 57, 149, 160, 166, 168
not-self (*anattā*), 74, 85, 96, 111, 160
number symbolism, 299

P

paccayas, twnety-four, 186, 187, 195
paccekabuddha, 292, 305–318
  and full *buddhas*, 306–309, 315
Pali canon/*Tipiṭaka*, 46, 257, 261, 269, 271–273, 276, 280, 282
Pali heart formulas, 183, 199, 201
Pali inscriptions, 184, 189, 203–206
paññā (wisdom/insight), 49, 50, 53–58, 60, 72–75, 78, 79, 90, 96, 97, 135, 142, 149, 159, 168, 216, 221, 227, 293, 297, 301
paññā-vimutta (liberated by wisdom), 54–58, 160, 166, 182
Parakkamabāhu I, 213, 215, 225, 229, 232, 239
Parakkamabāhu II, 218, 219, 229, 238
passivity, 63, 72
Path of Purification. See Visuddhimagga
Paṭisambhidāmagga, 39, 157, 173, 175–179, 262
perennialist, 99, 100–102
Peṭakopadesa, 21, 157, 261, 273
Petavatthu, 124, 126, 127
practice (*paṭipatti*), 45–48, 50, 59, 63, 74, 76, 271, 273, 281
Prajñāpāramitā literature, 132
preta/peta (departed one, ghost), 122–129
Pure Abodes, 145, 149–151
Pure Land, 145, 150, 151, 154

R

Rāhulamātā, 287–302
rapture (*pīti*). *See* joy/rapture (*pīti*)
rebirth, 28, 117–121, 124, 126, 129, 145, 149, 150, 151, 154, 171, 177, 289, 290, 292, 299–301, 308, 310, 311, 316, 318

S

Saccasaṅkhepaṭīkā, 211, 212, 223, 233, 242
saddhānusārin (follower of faith), 48

Sakka, 271, 293, 294, 297–299, 301, 307
Salomon, Richard, 250, 252, 257, 258, 264, 273
samāsin (equal-headed), 157–182
samatha (calm, tranquillity), 7, 12, 13, 55–59, 87
Samatha Trust, 6, 7
Saṃyuttas
  Avyākata, 140
  Saḷāyatana, 91
  Vana, 249, 253, 255
Sāriputta
  commentator, 213, 217–219, 223–226, 229, 231, 232, 238, 239, 242
  leading disciple, 59, 73, 90, 136, 162, 163, 166, 214, 227
schools and their followers
  Abhayagiri, 10, 257, 269, 270, 276, 280
  Dharmaguptaka/Dhammaguttaka, 10, 132, 145, 157–160, 169, 178, 251, 255, 256, 260, 274
  Haimavata, 145
  Kassapiya/Kāśyapīya, 10, 132, 274
  Mahāsāṃghika, 10, 132, 145, 147, 153, 159, 160, 274, 281
  Mahāvihāra, 257, 269, 270, 276–278, 280
  Mahāvihāravāsins, 11, 277, 278, 280, 281
  Mahīśāsaka, 10, 132, 145, 274, 276
  Sarvāstivāda, 10, 31, 104, 129, 132, 145–147, 157, 160, 162–164, 166–169, 178, 179, 254, 256, 274
  Sthavira, 159, 160, 273, 274
  Tambapaṇṇiya, 10, 169, 276
  Theravāda, 7, 10, 13, 47, 104, 130, 132, 134, 145, 146, 151, 157, 159, 160, 165, 166, 169, 178, 206, 249, 261, 263, 277, 280, 281
  Theriya, 10, 269–283
  Vibhajjavāda, 10, 169, 269, 270, 273–281
sense-pleasure (*kāma*), 20, 28, 32, 35, 36, 89–91, 95, *See* desire for sense-pleasure
Shaw, Charles, 6
Shaw, Sarah, 1, 5, 6, 7, 42, 86–88, 287, 303, 304
Sīmālaṅkārasaṅgaha, 238, 239, 240, 244
similes
  deer and trapper, 89
  extinct fire, 139
  for abandoning hindrances, 88
  for *jhānas*, 22, 25–28, 89, 110
  for joy, 22
  raft, 132, 133, 137
  seven chariots, 253, 254
  snake, 132, 133
  stone inscription, 272
  tuning strings of a *vīṇā*, 66
  wearing down a handle gradually, 68
somanassa (happiness), 24, 26, 29, 30–32
speculative reason, 134, 136
speculative views, 137
Stream-enterer (*sotāpanna*), 55, 61, 73
striving. *See* effort
suffering. *See dukkha*
suicide, 157, 161–167, 179, 181, 182
sukha (physical pleasure and/or happiness), 19–21, **23–26, 29–32**, 192, 196, *See* and see *somanassa*
Sukhodaya/Sukhothai, 183–185, 187, 188, 190, 191, 199, 202–206
Suttanipāta, 131, 134, 135, 201, 259, 306, 311, 312, 314
Suttas
  Aggi, 73, 77
  Aggivacchagotta, 139
  Ākaṅkheyya, 129
  Alagaddūpama, 131–133, 137, 138, 140–142
  Alagaddūpama 150, 152
  Anattālakkhaṇa, 74
  Anupada, 83, 84, 90
  Assalāyana, 85

Aṭṭhakanagara, 74
Bahuvedanīya, 57
Brahmajāla, 134
Cetokhila, 64
Channa, 162
Channovāda, 162
Cūḷasuññata, 99, 104–106, 108
Cūḷataṇhāsankhaya, 79
Cūḷaviyūha, 135
Cunda, 46, 58
Dhammacakkappavattana, 70
Duṭṭhaṭṭhaka, 134
Godhika, 161, 174
Jīvaka, 146, 151
Karaṇiyametta, 199
Katthī, 46, 58
Kīṭāgiri, 55, 56, 57, 78
Kosambī, 56
Kūṭadanta, 85
Māgandiya, 136
Mahācunda, 45, 46, 48, 49, 51, 54, 58
Mahādukkhakkhandha, 91
Mahāparinibbāna, 271
Mahāsakuludāyi, 89
Nivāpa, 83, 84, 89, 90, 91, 96
Sāmaññaphala, 19, 83, 84, 88–90, 96
Saṅkhārupapatti, 149, 150
Uppaṭipāṭika, 29
Vakkali, 163
Vitakkasaṇṭhāna, 106, 109

T

Tambapaṇṇi (Ceylon), 227, 229
taṅhā. *See* craving
Teresa of Ávila, 84–86, 97, 99, 100, 102, 109
Thūpavaṃsa, 229, 239, 243, 244
transmission of *āgama/nikāya* collections, 104, 146, 206, 249, 255, 269, 272–275, 280
transmission, oral, 145, 151, 259–261, 264, 265, 268

U

ubhātobhāgavimutta (liberated in both ways), 56–58, 154, 182
Upaniṣads, 120, 122, 137
Uttaravinicchayaṭīkā, 211, 212, 219, 222

V

Vācissara, 211, 212, 219, 220, 222–224, 229, 230–232, 238, 239, 240, 244
Vakkali, 161, 163–165, 167, 179, 181
Vedas/Vedic, 117, 119, 121, 122
Vessantara, 295, 296, 298
Vimānavatthu, 124, 127
Vimuttimagga, 22, 27, 37, 43
Vinaya, 46–48, 50, 61, 65, 132, 145, 157, 163, 201, 203, 212, 215, 225–227, 233, 237, 238, 242, 243, 249, 251, 254, 255, 263, 271, 273–276, 278–280, 283, 301, 303
Vinayasāratthasandīpanī, 211–213, 219
Vinayavinicchayaṭīkā, 211, 212
vipassanā (insight), 12, 13, 48, 56, 58, 59, 87, 168, 170, 173, 174
vision-attainer (*diṭṭhippatta*), 54, 55
Visuddhimagga, 22, 32, 34, 37, 78, 84, 99, 102, 108, 170–172, 218, 230, 263, 277, 278
vitakka and *vicāra* (mental application and examination), 12, 21, 24, 25, 28, 29, 32, 33, 36, 108, 192, 196

W

wisdom, 57, *See paññā* (wisdom/insight)

Y

Yama, 121
Yasodharā, 287–304

CPSIA information can be obtained
at www.ICGtesting.com
Printed in the USA
JSHW010911301119
2705JS00001B/2

9 781781 798928